Also by Richard Hack

Madness in the Morning

When Money Is King

Jackson Family Values

Memories of Madison County

Next to Hughes

Richard Hack's Complete Home Video Companion for Parents

Hughes

Hughes

The Private Diaries, Memos and Letters

The Definitive Biography of the First American Billionaire

By RICHARD HACK

NEW MILLENNIUM PRESS

BEVERLY HILLS

Library of Congress Cataloging-in-Publication Data Available

ISBN 1-893224-35-X

Printed in the United States of America

New Millennium Press
A division of NM WorldMedia, Inc.
301 N. Cañon Drive, Suite 214
Beverly Hills, California 90212

www.newmillenniumpress.com

10 9 8 7 6 5 4 3 2 1

In memory of

Truman Capote

who encouraged me to write

for all those years

CONTENTS

A Man Called Hughes

Bob, Please read the attached article. It refers to me as a millionaire, *while others have called me a billionaire. I'm very concerned about this change in perception and the effect it will have on our businesses.*

Las Vegas, Nevada
September 4, 1966
Memo to executive Robert Maheu.

HOWARD HUGHES WAS AN AMERICAN ORIGINAL. IN A country known for creating its share of unique and colorful individuals, Hughes stands apart for his level of eccentricity, lack of compassion, and thirst for control.

He was a film director, a producer, a test pilot, inventor, investor, and entrepreneur. And for most of his life, he was considered to be the richest man in America. At a time when being a millionaire was rare, Hughes had several *billion* dollars. That alone would have made him intriguing. But Hughes' allure was about far more than money.

He was the ultimate playboy with matinee-idol looks, a daredevil streak, and a lust for passion. He had a penchant for privacy so extreme that it would eventually consume his entire life, but not before he influenced heads of state and captains of industry as the consummate power broker who held himself above the law and its scrutiny.

For the last twenty years of his life, he was cared for by a team of male aides, a cook, a barber, and several on-staff doctors. He lived in a single room, windows blocked from the sun, a blacked-out asylum from which there would be no escape. Yet, it was a world of his own making, totally under his control and direction. If it was insanity, it was *his* insanity, cultivated by more wealth than many third-world countries, and a work ethic that drove him to toil round-the-clock, often without sleep or food.

To unravel his story required the help of hundreds of journalists, lawyers, doctors, investigators, archivists, librarians, acquaintances and lovers, each contributing pieces of the grand puzzle Hughes. In addition to interviews, court transcripts and depositions, Hughes' own original papers were examined. While he never kept a private diary as such, he wrote over 8,000 pages of memos, notes, letters and instructions that chronicled his loves, hates, fears and frustrations. Recently declassified FBI and CIA files were also analyzed—2,500 pages of detailed surveillance reports. Likewise, over 100,000 pages of sealed legal briefs, corporate records, and inventories were uncovered and read in an effort to gain entrance into the mind and life of this ultimate outsider.

The result of years of research, this book tears away the facade that Hughes worked his entire life to create, and reveals a man so complex that during his life he remained an illusion even to the few who knew him best. It is a story that only he could tell, of a life so extraordinary that it can be found recounted nowhere else, but in *Hughes*.

—Richard Hack
July 1, 2001

Hughes

Death by Neglect

I do not want to be bothered. Unless I call you,
I do not want to be disturbed for any reason.

Acapulco, Mexico
March 28, 1976
The last words written by Howard Hughes.

IT WAS EARLY EVENING AT THE ACAPULCO PRINCESS
Hotel, a time when the sun had lost its heat and pushed
shadows of palm trees and hibiscus across the manicured
lawns of the most expensive resort in Mexico. At the El
Grotto pool bar, a trio of tanned women in brightly-colored
bikinis ordered Margaritas, acutely aware that they were
being ogled by a nearby group of fat, aging businessmen
who were in the coastal city to attend a convention of sporting goods manufacturers. They were the kind of women
that would have appealed to Howard Robard Hughes, on
another day, in another time. Not now, however. At age 70,
weak and tired, he did not want to be bothered.

Hughes tore the yellow page from the legal-size pad,
folded it in thirds with thin, feeble fingers, creased it with
inch-long nails, and handed the note to his aide George
Francom, who was standing by his bedside. Francom, in
turn, read the note, folded it once again, and left the room
without speaking. It was the fourth memo he had received
that day from his employer instructing him to leave him
alone, and the aide gave it little thought. He had no way of
knowing that his billionaire employer lay dying in the next
room.

Inside the master bedroom of the Penthouse Suite,
Hughes lay naked on a hospital bed, his frail body covered
by a single cotton sheet and propped up in an inclining position. The large windows of the room on the twentieth floor

were sealed from within using sheets of plywood and heavy black cloth, their edges taped flat preventing even a whisper of light from entering the space. There was a fetid smell of decay about the place, as much from the lack of fresh air as from the aging billionaire.

Silence. Hughes appreciated the silence that had become his most valued friend as he weakly attempted to shift his position off the untreated sores that covered his back. Unable to get comfortable, he reached over to the night stand next to his bed, and moved his hand across its surface until he felt the metal top of the box that contained what Hughes liked to call his "medication." He pushed past empty syringes, past pill bottles containing codeine, Empirin #4 with codeine, and capsules of Librium and Seconal until he found a jar filled with 10-milligram Valium, nick-named Blue Bombers by his aides. He removed six of the tiny pills, placed them in his mouth one at a time, and swallowed.

The single reading lamp attached to his bed cast sharp shadows about the room. A long dresser and two chairs were barely distinguishable amid the black womb of solitary confinement that was Hughes' home. He stared into the void as he took a mental inventory of his holdings. His Las Vegas casinos, hotels and television station, his helicopter plant, his air-line, his medical institute, and thousands of acres of undeveloped land in four states, most of which he had never seen. The one-time record-breaking aviator even thought of flying again; piloting the Sikorsky S-43 amphibian, the single-engine Northrop Gamma, the wooden *Hercules* with its massive 320-foot wings, the XF-II with its blue and white Air Force insignia. And with that, he fell into a restless sleep.

In the outer room, Francom made note of the memo in a log kept methodically by Hughes' six aides, one of whom was never far from his bedside. These six men plus two assistants and a doctor on duty were the billionaire's only human contact. This eclectic mix of employees, who dubbed their boss the Old Man, held what outsiders would later call "the keys to the kingdom," for they were the only individuals allowed access to the elusive billionaire.

Access was not control, however. There was no controlling the Old Man. In the past, Hughes had gone through periods of severe illness, and had proven to be a stubborn, ornery, and self-destructive patient, and that did not seem about to change. He refused to see his doctors or be given a thorough physical exam, self-medicated himself with amply available narcotics, and told all who questioned his methods to mind their own business.

For the past week, the reclusive eccentric had stopped eating, refusing even his favorite ice cream and strawberry tarts. He repeatedly demanded and received glasses of refrigerated Poland water, and then left them untouched to warm by his bedside, only to call for more. Increasingly listless, Hughes had spent the majority of his time sleeping, particularly odd for a man who was known to work days at a stretch without stopping to rest.

When he wasn't sleeping, Hughes was hallucinating, launching into rambling monologs about needing to buy life insurance, and his plan to build a multimillion-dollar mansion in the city of Houston, the place of his birth in a state he had not visited in nearly forty years.

By Saturday, April 3, Hughes slipped into a "trance-like state" according to the aides' logs, again on Francom's watch. When the man waved his right hand in front of Hughes' staring eyes and found no reaction, Francom rushed to call Dr. Lawrence Chaffin, an 83-year-old Los Angeles surgeon, who was one of three physicians[1] on Hughes' medical team. Concerned that Hughes was plunging into an inexorable coma, Chaffin called the hotel doctor, 45-year-old Victor Manuel Montemayor, to arrange for Acapulco's *Laboratorio Central de Analasis* to run blood tests on his failing patient. The lab technician who came to the hotel brought a malfunctioning vacuum tube, forcing Chaffin to withdraw Hughes' blood using an empty syringe.

Complicating matters further: the technician spoke no English. Since none of the Hughes staff in Acapulco spoke Spanish, it was impossible for Chaffin to communicate the blood tests he needed to be run immediately. Rather than involve hotel staff in the now critical situation, a three-way call was placed between the nurse, the doctor, and aide Chuck Waldron's brother-in-law, a Hughes employee in Las Vegas. *He* spoke Spanish and carefully translated instructions and questions between the two. By the time the test results were finally returned to the Acapulco Princess, it was after midnight on Sunday, April 4.

When Chaffin saw the results, one set of numbers alerted him to a serious problem. While Hughes' glucose result was reported at a nearly normal level of 122 (average glucose readings range from 80 to 120), and an average level of uric acid and creatinine, his urea level was extraordinary, 104.5 milligrams. A normal level was in the 20-38 mg. range. Compounding Chaffin's confusion was his lack of knowledge of the amount of medication that Hughes had consumed during his stay in Acapulco.

Eager to get an additional opinion, Chaffin placed a call to Hughes' lead physician, 50-year-old Dr. Wilbur Thain, only to discover that Thain was in the Bahamas attending a charity ball benefitting a center for retarded children, and was unreachable. At nearly the same moment,

---

1. A fourth physician, Utah pathologist Dr. Homer Clark, was on a regularly scheduled two-week leave at the time.

however, Hughes began to show signs of alertness, stemming some of Chaffin's fears.

Late in the afternoon on April 4, aides George Francom and Gordon Margulis entered Hughes' room and discovered the Old Man attempting to give himself an injection of liquid codeine in his left arm. Already drugged and weakened to the point of exhaustion, Hughes dropped the syringe on the floor, begging Francom to retrieve it. Although Francom recovered the syringe, he was too frightened to help the exhausted Hughes inject himself with the potent prescription. Margulis also rejected Hughes' pleas.

Alarmed at what he saw and uncertain of the outcome, Francom frantically summoned yet another doctor, Norman Crane, a 71-year-old Los Angeles internist and Hughes' other physician in residence. Seemingly unfazed by the unfolding drama, Crane injected Hughes with the drug, and returned to his own room without comment. He was calm, though not unconcerned. After conferring with Dr. Chaffin, Crane agreed the situation warranted Dr. Thain's immediate notification. With the help of Thain's secretary, the doctor was eventually tracked down in Miami.

"I changed my plans and booked the first flight the next morning from Acapulco," Thain later stated in an interview in the *American Medical News*. Sometime after midnight, Thain reported that he was told "that Hughes had suddenly become very critical and it looked as if he was going to die. It was a shock and a surprise. I had been called to see Hughes in mid-March because he was not eating and drinking, but he put me off and put me off and, finally, fell to sleep without seeing me. But he ate and drank more the day I was there than he had in the previous two days, and I looked in on him as he slept and although he had lost a little weight, he didn't look a lot worse than before. . . . "

This time, Hughes was not as fortunate. When aide Chuck Waldron came on duty just before midnight, April 4, Hughes was passive, immobile, and staring blankly toward the ceiling. He had fallen into a deep coma and needed immediate emergency care. Both Drs. Crane and Chaffin would later testify that they were aware their patient was dying. In an effort to counteract Hughes' severe dehydration, Chaffin began an intravenous glucose drip and instructed Waldron to charter a plane to fly Dr. Thain to Mexico immediately.

Graf Jet, an air ambulance service in Fort Lauderdale, Florida, was hired to transport Thain and some extra intravenous glucose to Acapulco. The flight left Florida at 3:30 a.m. Pilot Roger Sutton and co-pilot Jeff Abrams were not informed of the name of the patient they would be flying from Mexico, nor were they told where the patient was going. There was far more to the mystery than mere secrecy. In reality, the decision of a destination had yet to be made.

If there was ever any doubt that Howard Hughes was in control of his own destiny, all such skepticism disappeared during the early morning hours of April 5. Amid the plush surroundings of the Penthouse Suite, bedlam reigned. Waldron and Margulis were continuously on the telephone attempting to get direction from Hughes' executives in Los Angeles. They contacted their immediate superior, Kay Glenn, a long-time Hughes employee, who in turn reached executive vice president Bill Gay. Their boss needed immediate hospitalization if there were to be any hope of saving his life; yet, no one could agree on an appropriate strategy. No contingency plan was in place for such a situation. Hughes had never considered the prospect of his own death, and his employees were ill-prepared for its eventuality.

As it became more apparent that Hughes would have to be moved, Waldron and Margulis were told by Glenn to "make the Old Man look presentable." It was a harder assignment than the simplicity of the statement would suggest. The last time Hughes had a haircut was in March, 1973. Shoulder length, thinning and gray, Hughes' hair was also matted and dirty. He wore a Van Dyke beard, gray and unkempt.

While Waldron trimmed five inches of hair from Hughes' head and trimmed his beard, Margulis tackled a far worse assignment: trimming the Old Man's fingernails and toenails. While not seven inches in length as some rumors had sized them, his nails where well over an inch long, thick, curling and yellowed from onychomycosis, a fungal condition from which Hughes had suffered for fifty-five years. Margulis softened the nails in warm water and cut them to a normal length, placing the nail ends with the shorn hair in a plastic bag for shipment back to Hughes' offices in California.

Just before 5:30 a.m., Hughes began to experience convulsions—first on his left side and then on his right. Concerned that the intravenous needle would infiltrate Hughes' tissue, Dr. Chaffin stopped the lifesaving drip. With no options, even less time, and Dr. Thain still in flight, Chaffin placed another emergency call to Dr. Montemayor, requesting that he immediately come to the Penthouse Suite.

Montemayor arrived within fifteen minutes and was met in the empty hotel lobby by Eric Bundy, the Hughes aide in charge of telephone communications. "He was nervous and obviously upset," Montemayor later remembered, "and kept saying we needed to hurry. I thought that since I had been told this was an emergency, the need for speed would have been obvious. Apparently not."

Using a private key to open the elevator doors on the hotel's twentieth floor, Bundy escorted the doctor past the security guard on duty, Rudolfo Castro Maganda, and introduced him to Drs. Chaffin and Crane. "I saw two very tired men," said Montemayor. "And Dr. Crane's eyes were swollen, as if he had been crying. Although no one had yet to mention the name Howard Hughes, I knew from the importance of the situation that he had to be the patient."

Given his preconceived impression of Hughes' wealth and reputation, Montemayor was stunned by what he witnessed when he entered Hughes' room. "I saw a naked man covered by a sheet who looked extremely emaciated. He was approximately 70 years of age, 75 centimeters in height, white, very long grayish hair, baldish, with a rather long beard and pale. His right eye was opened and his left eye was only partly opened. His breathing was short and slow, and the man was unconscious," Montemayor testified to Mexican Federal Judge Antonio Uribe Garcia. "I told the doctors that their patient should be in a hospital. They explained to me that the man was very stubborn and refused medical treatment. So I said, 'The man is unconscious. Unconscious men do not put up a fight.'"

For the next two hours, Montemayor examined Hughes and found him to be extremely dehydrated. His back was covered with numerous untreated bedsores, needle marks pocked both arms and his groin. There was an open wound bleeding from the left side of his scalp, and his blood pressure was nearly undetectable. When Montemayor subjected Hughes' eyes to direct light, there was no response from his pupils. "The pupils were paralyzed," Montemayor later stated. "It meant that his brain was off."

He immediately ordered the aides to lower Hughes' inclined hospital bed so that more blood would reach the dying man's brain. He recommended that a glucose I.V. be started immediately and that the patient be transferred to a hospital for care. When he learned from Bundy that a private jet was en route to take Hughes to a medical facility, Montemayor telephoned the Manzanaris Funeral Parlor to request an ambulance to transport the patient to the plane.

When Dr. Montemayor left the hotel at 8:30 a.m., the ambulance had arrived but Dr. Thain had not. The Graf Jet had landed at the Acapulco airport a half-hour earlier, but Thain was still maneuvering through airport traffic. When he finally arrived at the hotel minutes later, Hughes' condition remained unchanged, primarily because no intravenous had been restarted.

What happened next is the subject of much speculation. Thain insists that when he arrived in the Penthouse Suite, he walked immediately to Hughes' room and spent the next three hours with his patient. Other witnesses suggest that Thain began to shred paperwork, allegedly related to Hughes' enormous drug intake. Regardless of who was operating the shredder, this much was clear: it was working overtime in the morning hours of April 5, as documents, logs, memos, and receipts were fed into the machine to remove all evidence of Hughes' occupancy.

Upon seeing Hughes, Thain thought his boss had suffered a stroke, and administered two intravenous shots of Solu-Cortef, a hydrocortisone anti-inflammatory, to the Old Man. He suspected that pressure on the brain was causing his bodily functions to shut down, and hoped that the drug would reduce any cerebral edema.

By 9 a.m., the decision was made by Bill Gay in California to fly Hughes to the Methodist Hospital in Houston, Texas. Methodist had received funds in the past from Hughes' medical foundation, and Gay anticipated that he might have some control over the Old Man's treatment at the facility as well as the inherent publicity that would surely follow Hughes' admittance. Additionally, Houston could be reached in three hours, and, as such, was as close as any major American city.

That Houston's Methodist Hospital was not as close as nearby Acapulco's *Hospital Magallanes* was unimportant. Admitting Hughes to a Mexican hospital placed him under the control of a foreign government. And *controlling* the situation was foremost in Bill Gay's mind. If Howard Hughes was going to die, it could not be on Mexican soil, opening the opportunity for a government autopsy and unforeseeable financial implications.

Yet, despite the fact that a final decision had been made, Howard Hughes remained unmoved and untreated for the next two hours, a life-threatening delay. Thain would later state that the holdup was caused by efforts to find a non-leaking oxygen tent and a new aircraft capable of transporting Hughes on a stretcher. Unexplained was the reality that the Graf Jet had both the capacity and the oxygen to accommodate the patient, as was later proved when Hughes finally was carried onto the plane at 10:30 a.m.

His aides had lifted the Old Man onto a stretcher and had taken him down in the hotel's service elevator, past astonished maids who attempted to enter the car during several unscheduled stops. Covered in a yellow blanket, Hughes breathed haltingly through an oxygen mask.

Ambulance driver C. Jaime Quevedo would later tell reporters that he saw the patient on the stretcher as it was loaded onto the plane. He was "unconscious, not moving," Quevedo said, unable to confirm that Hughes was still alive. Drs. Thain and Chaffin, aboard the plane with Hughes and aide John Holmes, insisted that he was, and began administering a glucose I.V. to the billionaire as the plane taxied for takeoff at 11 a.m. As the jet climbed above the *Sierra Madre del Sur* mountains and headed toward Houston, the air turned choppy. "It was bad, bumpy stuff," the pilot later commented, otherwise the flight was "very routine." Below, a thin cloud cover obscured the land as mountains turned to arid plains and the dust that transformed the Rio Grande into the muddy brown of a café latte.

At the Methodist Hospital in Houston, elaborate preparations were being made to receive Texas' favorite son. Dr. Henry D. McIntosh, professor and chairman of the Department of Medicine at Baylor College of Medicine, as well as the Chief of Medical Service at Methodist Hospital, received a telephone call from Kenneth Wright, CEO of the Howard Hughes Medical Institute in Miami, at 8:15 a.m., on April 5. The subject of Mr. Wright's call was to be held in the utmost secrecy, Dr. McIntosh was advised.

According to files maintained by McIntosh, he was advised that Howard Hughes was critically ill and that the "working diagnosis was thought to be a diabetic coma." Wright inquired as to the ability of the critical care unit of Methodist Hospital to provide "top security without compromising medical therapy." McIntosh indicated that not only was Methodist Hospital capable of such service, he would personally see that the hospital would do "everything possible to maintain the lifestyle of the prospective patient that was consistent with quality care" while at the same time not disrupting the medical management of other patients.

The wheels that Dr. McIntosh set in motion in the next half-hour indicated just how far Methodist Hospital was willing to go to accommodate the eccentric billionaire. It was an exercise in efficiency, organization, and accommodation that suggested a military deployment. In concert with Ted Bowen, president of the hospital, it was decided to place Hughes in the Fondren Recovery Room, the main surgical recovery area of the hospital. The room was made available for the exclusive use of Hughes by transferring the existing patients to the Fondren Intensive Care Unit.

Bowen assigned Hughes the alias John T. Conover in an effort to cloak his identity, while McIntosh assembled a team of physicians to provide for his care. Hand-selected for the assignment: Dr. Wadi Suki, professor of medicine and chief of Methodist's nephrology[2] section; Dr. Alan Garber, assistant professor of medicine and an expert in diabetes; Dr. Paul Stevens, professor of medicine and chief of pulmonary service; Dr. Kinsman (Ted) Wright, assistant professor of medicine and an expert cardiologist; Dr. Ben Cooper, a clinical neurologist; Dr. Robert Berglund,

---

2. Nephrology is the study of the kidneys.

the chief resident in medicine at the time; and Dr. Jack Titus, professor of pathology and chairman of the department of laboratory studies. McIntosh selected his staff based on their expertise and their ability to be "readily available around the clock."

Dr. McIntosh next pulled a Methodist Hospital ambulance out of service, and had it equipped with necessary resuscitation equipment including a Code Blue cart, an oxygen tank, a defibrillator, 200-foot extension cord, a suction machine and any additional equipment suggested by Dr. Berglund, who was assigned alternating 12-hour shifts in the Fondren Recovery Room with Dr. Rodney Richie, a pulmonary disease specialist. Administrative assistant Jim Henderson was instructed to prepare two cars to accompany the ambulance on its trip to the airport to transport Drs. McIntosh, Garber, Wright and Berglund, plus ICU nurses Patricia Temple and Sherry Jones.

At 10 a.m., Dr. McIntosh received a second telephone call from Kenneth Wright, who advised him to expect to hear from Kay Glenn, described as a "Hughes executive, reachable at area code 213-990-6000." Glenn was said to be providing additional details and requirements relating to Hughes' care. It was an added distraction that McIntosh did not need at a time when each element of the medical emergency was being delegated and examined. It became all the more irritating when the phone call was not forthcoming. Eager to eliminate any unknown variables, McIntosh asked Bowen to telephone Glenn at his office in Los Angeles. Glenn refused to accept the call, leaving Bowen, McIntosh and the administrative staff at Methodist chafed and uncertain.

Now worried that perhaps he was a victim of some practical joke, McIntosh called Kenneth Wright in Miami. He needed immediate reassurance of the authenticity of the situation. Wright attempted to calm McIntosh by explaining that crank calls constantly came into Hughes' headquarters, and repeating his advice to wait for Glenn's call. As the minutes ticked, McIntosh paced. He had now committed eight physicians, two nurses, an ambulance, and a recovery room to the sole service of a reclusive billionaire whose condition was uncertain and illness unknown.

When Glenn's call finally did arrive 30 minutes later, it related not to Hughes' medical care, but the choice of arrival airport and method of customs clearance. Upset at now being turned into a travel administrator, McIntosh referred the decision to Bowen, who relayed what he thought was rather obvious information even to the relatively uninformed. Houston had only one international airport, located at Houston Intercontinental. At the time, the William P. Hobby Airport had been converted to a regional facility. In an effort to accommodate Hughes, however, Bowen offered to place calls to the Department of Immigration and Naturalization Service to expedite the clearance of the critically-ill patient. Bowen was told that the identification number on the side of the blue-striped, white Lear jet was N-855W. What he was not told, however, was that the airplane had yet to even leave the ground in Acapulco.

By the time the jet finally left Mexico at 11 a.m. with two pilots, two doctors, one aide and Hughes on board, Bowen already had sent his administrative assistant Edward McLellan to Houston Intercontinental to alert customs officials there of Hughes' pending arrival. As was typical of the magic that the mere mention of the name Howard Hughes evoked, the customs officials agreed to arrange to meet the plane on the runway, a breach of accepted procedure, in an effort to expedite the patient's transfer to the Methodist ambulance.

For over two hours, McIntosh's team was assembled and waiting. For what seemed like an interminable length of time, and in medical terms it was, much of Houston's Methodist Hospital was placed on hold. Despite Bowen's efforts to maintain secrecy, the rumor that a "famous patient" was about to be admitted soon began to make the rounds of the various floors. From obstetrics to cardiology, guesses ranged from Elizabeth Taylor to President Gerald R. Ford. As testament to Bowen's clampdown, no one thought of Howard R. Hughes.

Just before 1 p.m., the Methodist Hospital doctors, administrators, and nurses drove to the airport in two cars and one ambulance, keeping in contact using a CB radio and walkie-talkies. Conversation during the 30-minute ride centered on anything but the elusive billionaire, until just before the trio of vehicles pulled up to an airport security car waiting at a side entrance. Only then was Hughes' name brought up, and only to discuss personnel assignments one final time. Drs. McIntosh and Berglund were to enter the plane to examine the patient, while the remaining doctors and nurses were to stay on the runway awaiting further instructions.

Edward McLellan had cleared the medics' approach through airport supervisor Paul Porter, and had done his job well. The coterie of manpower and equipment was waved onto the runway and appeared prepared for any development—except perhaps the one that eventually materialized.

At 2 p.m., the Lear jet carrying Howard Hughes descended into the smog-filled skies of Houston Intercontinental Airport and was directed onto a side gateway where the doctors and ambulance were waiting with customs officer Marie Denton. For Dr. McIntosh, this was a moment of prideful exhilaration. His plan was working flawlessly; and as he approached the jet's opening door, he tightened his grip on his medical bag and silently prayed.

McIntosh was met at the door by Dr. Wilbur Thain who matter-of-factly announced, "I lost the beat just a few minutes ago. He's gone." McIntosh was astounded. In the course of the morning, he had gone from beginning a typical day at the hospital, to arranging for medical care for a comatose billionaire, to now suddenly dealing with a corpse. Not willing to believe the inevitable, he offered to try resuscitation. All the equipment, after all, was in place. "It's no use," Thain countered, repeating, "he's gone, he's gone."

When the gurney carrying Hughes' body was removed from the jet, customs officer Marie Denton commented that Hughes appeared to be "like an old emaciated man. Well, really, I couldn't even tell that it was a man from the side view. I only saw a profile, and went by his birth certificate."

What struck ambulance driver Jay Dixon as strange was the mood of those now standing around as the body of the late billionaire was covered and loaded for transport to the hospital. "There was some laughter at one point. It seemed out of place," he said. The customs official agreed, adding that no one, including Hughes' doctors or his aide, seemed unduly upset or distraught.

Perhaps the most stunned was pilot Roger Sutton. He was not even told that Hughes had died until the plane had landed. "I was shocked and saddened," he said. "I've never had a passenger die before."

Fifty minutes after Howard Hughes' jet had landed in Houston, his body arrived at the morgue dock of Methodist Hospital. The clouds that had obscured much of the sky had parted only minutes before. Dr. Jack Titus felt the sun on his arms as he waited for ambulance attendants Jay Dixon and Len Stom to unload the stretcher on which Hughes lay, still shrouded in the bright yellow blanket. It fell to pathologist Titus to make the initial external examination of the body as soon as it was delivered to the morgue.

"I found an elderly white male," Titus reported, "with gray hair, somewhat thinned, and a gray beard. The body appeared remarkable, emaciated and dehydrated. The estimated length of the body was about 6' 2". A plastic intravenous catheter was present in the left antecubital fossa[3] and the left arm was taped to a towel-covered board. The eyes were open and the pupils dilated and fixed. Although there were contractures of moderate degree of the knees, it should be noted that there was not evidence of rigor mortis in any of the skeletal muscles of the body. Based upon the information that the body came from the cabin of an airplane at appropriate environmental temperatures, was transported immediate-

---

3. The area of the arm in front of the elbow, typically used to draw blood.

ly by an ambulance, and this examination done essentially immediately upon arrival of the body at The Methodist Hospital morgue, it is my firm opinion that death occurred less than three hours prior to the time of my examination," Titus concluded, thus confirming Thain's timing of Hughes' death just prior to landing.

After the initial examination, Hughes' body was placed in a body cooler within the morgue, and autopsy technician Ray Henderson and a hospital security guard were left to maintain the integrity of the corpse. With the body secured, hospital president Ted Bowen faced an entirely different set of crises: containing the media circus that would inevitably follow any announcement of Hughes' death, and determining exactly why and how Hughes had died. Both challenges came with their own set of legal restrictions, and a new and very powerful variable: the next of kin.

Annette Gano Lummis, the 85-year-old sister of Hughes' mother, was the recluse's closest known living relative. Equally as important, she was intensely private and avoided any hint of spectacle during her long and distinguished life in Houston. When she was notified of Hughes' death by the hospital, she asked her son William to make the funeral arrangements. Her only instruction: that there be no autopsy of the body of her nephew. It was a request that put her in direct conflict with Houston's medical examiner, Dr. Joseph Jachimczyk, who was about to be brought into the unfolding drama.

After clearing customs, Drs. Thain and Chaffin plus John Holmes were brought to Methodist Hospital where they assembled in Bowen's office with Drs. McIntosh and Berglund to recount the events leading up to their arrival in Houston. During that meeting, Thain announced that Hughes died at 1:27 p.m. According to Chaffin, the plane had just passed over Brownsville, the Texas border town across the Rio Grande from Matamoros, Mexico. "He died in Texas," Chaffin repeated, in case any seated in Bowen's office had missed the point. Of more concern at the moment to Bowen was the fact that neither Chaffin nor Thain were licensed to practice medicine in Texas, necessitating a call to the coroner's office and the formal involvement of Joseph Jachimczyk.

While Dr. Titus took responsibility for notifying Jachimczyk, Bowen grappled with his other growing problem. The media had begun receiving bits and pieces of the story, and a half-dozen journalists had appeared at the hospital and an equal number of photographers were attempting to gain entry to the morgue. CBS had already assembled a news team on the scene, anchored by Terry Drinkwater. CBS interrupted its regular feed to broadcast the news of Hughes' death. They were unable, however, to confirm the cause.

In an effort to keep the news media at bay, Bowen decided to issue an official press release worded to relate what was now common knowledge while avoiding what all were eagerly seeking to learn: what had killed the mysterious Mr. Hughes and what did he look like when he died?

At 5:30 p.m., administrative assistant Larry Mathis read the following press release:

> At 9:00 a.m. today, The Methodist Hospital was notified that Mr. Howard R. Hughes was to be flown to Houston from Acapulco for medical treatment at The Methodist Hospital. At approximately 2:00 pm today, a Lear jet arrived at Houston Intercontinental Airport carrying the body of Howard Hughes. Mr. Hughes was accompanied by two physicians and one administrative aide. A physician who accompanied Mr. Hughes informed The Methodist Hospital that Mr. Hughes had expired about 1:27 p.m. en route from Acapulco to Houston. The body was brought to The Methodist Hospital. Further questions will be answered by Mr. Arelo Sederberg[4] in Los Angeles.

In making the announcement and accepting no questions, Mathis managed to elude more than he revealed, and only heightened the efforts of the media to uncover relevant data. Drs. Thain and Chaffin were followed back to their rooms at the Warwick Hotel, where Hughes executive Bill Gay had also registered. The home of Annette Lummis was photographed, and attempts were made to interview the elderly woman, who was horrified at the prospect of publicity. Additional guards were placed outside the morgue in addition to the continual surveillance adjacent to the cooler holding Hughes' body. And the Houston medical examiner called a meeting of those involved, including William Lummis, for 8 p.m. that evening.

Dr. Joseph Jachimczyk had a comfortable working relationship with Drs. McIntosh and Titus, and wanted to cooperate with the hospital to minimize discomfort for the family while at the same time satisfying Texas law. Legally, he could have demanded control of the case and the body, performed a complete autopsy, and arrived at his own educated conclusions as to the cause of death. Instead, he agreed to allow the hospital to take charge of Hughes' autopsy, that Lummis was convinced was required, particularly in light of the fact that Hughes' nephew insisted that the billionaire had wanted to be cremated.

Positive identification of the body was proving to be another stumbling block, both legally and with Aunt Annette. The Hughes next-of-kin was against any fingerprinting or photographs of any kind. Given the condition of the deceased eccentric, it stood to reason that the Hughes organization and his medical team were opposed to it as well. Dr.

---

4. Arelo Sederburg worked for the public relations firm of Carl Byoir & Associates who had represented Hughes for nearly 50 years.

Jachimczyk, however, was not to be so easily outmaneuvered, and for that matter, neither was the FBI, who wanted some definitive proof that the body that had now been in the cooler of the hospital morgue for over four hours was indeed that of Howard Robard Hughes. Drs. Thain and Chaffin were ready to swear that it was, and had already signed documents to attest to that fact So too did long-time Hughes aide John Holmes.

By the following morning, when the group met for a second time in the office of Ted Bowen, the issue was still undecided. Helping to push for privacy, Annette Lummis had decided that cremation was no longer necessary, despite Hughes' previously revealed wishes. Predictably, it was Drs. Thain and Chaffin who seemed most concerned about the potential leak of any autopsy photos to the press.

"My immediate thought," Chaffin said, "is that (columnist) Jack Anderson would go to any lengths to get photographs of the body of Howard Hughes."

"That's why we are using security," countered Titus.

"They'd go to any means–pay any amount of money to get those photographs," repeated Chaffin.

"Unless it is absolutely necessary, positively mandatory, let's don't take the photographs," emphasized Thain. "Safes are not safe at all with these people. We've been through this with people like Anderson and Greenspun.[5]" After all, he reasoned, the Lummises were no longer pressing for cremation, which was the initial reason that photographs were mentioned.

"There are hazards to having him buried," Chaffin thought out loud. "Someone could dig him up."

"The *National Enquirer* would pay $100,000 to get pictures," Thain said. "They may pay up to $250,000!" he added for drama.

The desperation in Thain's voice hid a motive that had little to do with money. Thain and Chaffin were both concerned about their reputations should details of Hughes' actual condition at the time of death be elaborated in the press. Accompanying photographs would be ultimate proof to reinforce what Dr. Montemayor was then stating publicly in Mexico.

As Hughes' doctors were meeting in Houston, Dr. Montemayor was testifying in Acapulco, explaining his theory that Howard Hughes died an unnecessary death. "In my opinion, he died of a disease called neglect," Montemayor stated after describing how he came to treat Hughes the previous Saturday. "The man needed to be in a hospital . . . weeks ago," he later told attorneys. "Dr. Chaffin and Dr. Thain told me that

---

5. Hank Greenspun, publisher of the *Las Vegas Sun* newspaper.

their patient rejected medical help. When a patient becomes unconscious, you put him in a hospital."

At Methodist Hospital, the media coverage continued to expand.
News trucks were parked along the edge of the visitor parking lot in
spaces that had been assigned by the administrative offices. Coffee,
donuts, and orange juice were made available to journalists who had been
given a working-press area in the hospital's north conference room. By
1:00 p.m., however, they had all made their way to the basement morgue
where Hughes' autopsy was starting.

Dr. Malcolm McGavran, pathology's chief prosector,[6] began the
autopsy by fingerprinting the corpse now known as N-76-92, while
administrative assistants, Mike Williamson and Gary Cottongim, kept a
running account of events as required by law. Dr. McGavran was assisted
by Dr. Titus, senior pathologist Dr. Roberto Bayardo, and autopsy technician Ray Henderson. Medical examiner Jachimczyk and his assistant,
Dr. Ethel Erickson, were occupied at the time in an animated discussion
with Drs. Thain and Chaffin, who were still concerned about photographs being taken of the body. They had been informed that Mathis
Pittman, Methodist Hospital's pathology photographer, was waiting to
enter the autopsy room under police guard.

Pittman, in fact, was upstairs at that moment in the administration
offices, having camouflaged his photographic equipment under sheets on
a stretcher. It was the autopsy room itself that was under police protection at this point, with Houston Police Officer E.C. Tyler on duty in the
autopsy anteroom with Len Stom. Chief Martin of the Houston Fire
Department ambulance division arrived at the anteroom in time to hold
the door for David Workman and Buster Fontenot, Methodist Hospital
x-ray technicians, who entered the now-crowded autopsy room with Dr.
Henry McIntosh, Ted Bowen and hospital vice-president Ted Gilbreath.

The strong halogen lamp bathed the room in harsh white light that
only added to the surrealistic theater taking place. Howard Hughes, who
had spent his life trying to escape medical examination of any sort, was
now being scrutinized by eight doctors, two hospital administrators, two
assistants, and three technicians. To this mix was added yet another player:
Dr. Oscar Maldonado, an oral surgeon, who had been called to examine
the deceased's teeth.

While Jachimczyk ultimately came to the decision to prohibit photographs of the body, he also rejected the initial set of fingerprints that
were taken as being insufficient for the purpose of identification, and
called his fingerprint expert, Horace Tucker, into the mounting drama.
With Tucker's help, water was injected under the skin of Hughes' shriv-

---

6. A prosector is a physician or biologist skilled in dissection.

eled fingers in order to plump them up enough to produce a valid set of prints.

With the pressure off of Drs. Thain and Chaffin regarding potentially damaging photographs, their mood lightened to the point that Chaffin asked for help in changing some Mexican pesos into American dollars (a runner was eventually sent to the bank across the street from the hospital), and Thain joked about the lushness of Acapulco and the poor timing of Hughes' death. Thain, it seemed, had enjoyed his few months on the Mexican Riviera.

As McGavran, Titus and Bayardo removed the various body parts, they were weighed with the resulting figures then posted on a blackboard: heart 340, liver 1180, right lung 300, left lung 390, spleen 170, right kidney 90, left kidney 110. All weights were listed in grams.[7]

The routine business of identifying the cause of death took on more subtle tones as McGavran and Jachimczyk huddled, comparing written notes and repeatedly looking at the kidneys. "Chronic malnephritis," "renal failure," "renal death" were suggested as contributing factors before Titus joined the discussion and a formal decision was made.

At 4:00 p.m., the undertakers from the George H. Lewis & Son Funeral Home removed the body from the morgue and placed it in their hearse parked at the morgue dock. At the same moment, reporters and photographers were listening as Larry Mathis introduced Ted Bowen, who waited before approaching the microphone until he was certain that the body was well on its way. "The preliminary autopsy findings demonstrated that Mr. Hughes died of chronic renal disease." He offered no further elaboration. It was left to McIntosh to explain. "Renal means kidney, two of them. Chronic means a long time. And failure means that they don't work so well."

In answering questions from the gathered newsmen, Joseph Jachimczyk said that there was nothing unusual about the death of the reclusive billionaire. "As far as I am concerned, it's an ordinary death. It's an extraordinary individual involved, perhaps, but the death is like any other death."

What Jachimczyk, McIntosh and Bowen failed to mention was that Hughes' weight had fallen to ninety-three pounds. His parchment-like skin, that had been denied sunlight for over thirty-five years, hung from his bones which were clearly visible without any protective layer of fat. X-rays indicated that five hypodermic needles were broken off in his upper arms. His forearms, biceps and groin area were filled with track marks from continued injections of drugs. His body oozed fluid from

7. Normal weights for such organs are heart 112 grams, liver 1456, right lung 400, left lung 406, spleen 180, right kidney 112, and left kidney 112.

open bed sores, his left temple had a severed, bloodied tumor, and his left shoulder was dislocated. The level of codeine in Hughes' body was five times a lethal dose. And his teeth were so loose that merely examining them caused them to fall out of his gums and into his throat.

This strangest of executives who died a "normal death" was buried the next day at Glenwood Cemetery next to his father and mother. For all his efforts at privacy during his life, no effort was made to keep the press away from the funeral. In fact, Annette Lummis seemed to be surprised to find thirty reporters at the gravesite. She was joined for the short eight-minute service by her family, plus Thain, Chaffin and Holmes, none of whom she had ever met.

The Very Rev. Robert T. Gibson, dean of Houston's Christ Cathedral where Lummis was a member, performed the service, reading from the Episcopal Book of Common Prayer. "We brought nothing into this world, and it is certain we can carry nothing out. The Lord gave, and the Lord hath taken away."

As the family sat on gray folding chairs under a faded red awning protecting the gravesite, there were no tears for their famous relative. They showed no emotion, for indeed he was a stranger to them. At 8:05 a.m., fifteen minutes after they had arrived, the family silently retreated to their cars and drove away into the early morning traffic.

Cemetery workers lowered Hughes' 1000-pound coffin into a stainless steel vault, and the bier mechanism strained and creaked under the unusual load. As they locked the vault lid and proceeded to fill the grave with dirt, only a handful of reporters remained. In another five minutes, the gravesite was deserted. Five tall, narrow and empty trumpet urns stood as silent sentries, bordered by bamboo shrubs and a chain-link fence along the Buffalo Bayou. Finally, Howard Hughes had found the peace that had evaded him for much of his existence, back in the very town where he was born. But not even in death would the mystery that swirled around his life abate. If anything, as executors attempted to settle his estate by examining his life, his saga took on a new and even stranger reality.

Unto Us a Son Is Given

Howard Robard Hughes Jr.
Born: September 24, 1905
Baptized: October 7, 1906
Parents: Howard R. and Allene Hughes
Witnesses: Mrs. W. B. Sharp and Rev. R. C.
McIlwain

Keokuk, Iowa
October 7, 1906
Entry on page 120 and 121 in the baptismal
record Saint John's Episcopal Church.

HOWARD HUGHES WAS BORN ON DECEMBER 24, 1905—OR
so his tombstone says. Like everything else about the man,
nothing is as obvious as it first appears. On the evening that
Hughes claimed to have been born, he was actually three
months old. His parents, Howard Robard Hughes Sr. and
Allene Gano Hughes, were celebrating Christmas Eve dinner at Houston's Rice Hotel.

It was a gala event, attended by twenty-four of the city's
up-and-coming elite, including the hotel proprietor James
Lawlor, along with Allene's younger sisters and brother,
Annette, Martha and Chilton Gano, visiting from Dallas on
Christmas vacation. The Hugheses dined on Lamb Chops
Farole, Patties of Fowl with Truffles, Roast Christmas
Turkey with Chestnut Dressing, Roast Beef with Juice
Gravy, and Prairie Owl, Larded and Stuffed. The buffet also
included Santa Claus Potatoes, Candied Jersey Sweets,
Apple Sauce, Asparagus with Cream, and St. Francis Salad,
followed by dessert of Macaroons, Hot Mince Pie, Fruit
Cake, and Vienna Charlotte Russe.

Although Howard's Aunt Annette would testify after his
death that she first saw him during that Christmas "when he

was two or three months old," she did not explain why she signed her name to a notarized replacement birth certificate in 1941, swearing that he was born on December 24. Apparently she had forgotten about both her Christmas vacation and the Prairie Owl, for based on her signature, Hughes' erroneous birth date was later literally carved in stone on his grave.

For Howard and Allene Hughes, the birth of their son was a blessing and a relief. It was a difficult delivery for Allene, and one that her doctor, Oscar L. Norsworthy,[1] thought neither she nor the baby would survive. She hemorrhaged severely, and after four blood transfusions, he advised her against having any other children. Such was the miracle of the birth, in fact, that upon seeing his son for the first time, Big Howard, as he would thereafter be called, promised to settle down and live a proper family life. It was no small challenge.

Howard Robard Hughes Sr. was born on a farm near Lancaster, Missouri, in 1869, the son of Felix T. Hughes and Jean Amelia Summerlin. His father was a rather practical man who taught himself law and became superintendent of the local schools, before eventually moving his family to Keokuk, Iowa, where he was elected mayor and the town's judge. Irascible and cantankerous, Felix would bang his silver-tipped walking stick on the bench to demand silence from his court.

Jean Hughes, who everyone called Mimi, was a dreamer who spent her childhood fantasizing chapters in the endless romance she intended to live. While her life may not have turned out to be quite as quixotic as she had hoped, she managed to convey her aspirations and dreams onto her children who she spoiled excessively. Her only daughter, Greta, born in 1867, had a lovely voice and eventually studied opera in Chicago, New York and Paris. Her youngest son, Felix Jr., born in 1874, also studied music, traveling to Paris as well, at a time when it was the center for voice. Her middle son, Rupert, who was born in 1872, could not sing a note, but had a gift for writing that he carried through his studies at Cleveland's Adelbert College and his graduation from Yale. Upon moving to New York, he became both famous and wealthy writing short stories and novels about glamorous life. And then there was Howard.

The oldest son in the family had no musical talent, no interest in writing, and, according to Rupert, "barely made it out of high school with a full set of teeth," so inclined was he to get into fistfights with the local bullies. Bowing to pressure from his father, Howard enrolled at

---

1. In a touch of coincidence, Dr. Norsworthy, who had moved to Houston in 1895 and built his own hospital in 1908, donated it to the Texas Methodist Conference in 1923. It was enlarged and became The Methodist Hospital, eventually growing to 1,527 beds–the largest non-prof-it hospital in the United States. It was to The Methodist Hospital that Howard Hughes was taken after his death.

Harvard College to study law, but dropped out after his first year. Returning to Iowa, the restless youth made another attempt at college by attending Iowa State University, but only briefly.

Howard was not a student. Howard was mechanical. While he had no patience to sit at a desk and learn, he could spend hours at a workbench tinkering with clocks and motors. When Felix attempted to put his oldest son to work in his Keokuk law office, Hughes rebelled after only a few months and set out on what he would later call his "adventure in the frontier of opportunity." The year was 1895, and for a rugged, tall, 26-year-old, America was a land of discovery.

For the next eight years, Hughes traveled across the Midwest, roaming through Colorado and Oklahoma, looking for his fortune in zinc and silver mines, and on gambling boats full of wanton women and desperate men. It was an erratic existence that found Hughes riding the ebbs and tides of riches and poverty. When he found himself with pockets of cash, he spent it on the finest clothes, most expensive hotels, and courting incredibly beautiful women, who in turn thought his brand of charm and roguish good looks to be an exciting and sophisticated change from the roughness around them.

With the dawn of a new century, Hughes traveled to Joplin, Missouri, where he worked as an engineer in the local lead mines, and lived in a room in the Elks Building. It was in Joplin that he met and proposed to Frances Geddes, the 16-year-old daughter of an investment broker and the girl he called the "woman of his dreams." When Frances attempted to elope with the 31-year-old Hughes, she was literally plucked from the hands of lechery by her father. Three months later, on January 10, 1901, an oil well produced a major gusher in Spindletop,[2] adjacent to Beaumont, Texas. Hughes left the infatuated Frances and never looked back in his rush to join the rough riggers trying to cash in on the find.

"I heard the roar in Joplin," he later wrote in a Harvard reunion review, "and made for the seat of the disturbance. Beaumont in those days was no place for a divinity student . . . I turned greaser and sank into the thick of it. Rough neck, owner, disowner, promoter, capitalist and 'mark'—with each I can claim kin, for I stood in the steps of each."

Hughes blindly speculated on oil leases from a makeshift office he established at the Crosby House, a saloon hotel, and tried drilling for oil himself with rented equipment. While his schemes failed to generate continuing income, they did bring him in contact with another wildcatter named Walter Bedford Sharp, and a partnership that would lead both to riches.

2. The Spindletop well was owned by William Lucas who went on to form Guffey Petroleum Company that later became Gulf Oil Corporation.

Sharp was tall, rangy, and a tireless worker who was one of several founders of the Texas Company (Texaco). In the scabrous days of oil strikes and broken dreams, he joined with Hughes and his partner, oilman Ed Prather, to form the Moonshine Oil Company, which had patented a process that pumped air into blocked wells to restore their flow. The price for their service: half of all the oil produced. Pushing the Moonshine process and hoping for a strike of his own, Hughes moved from boom town to boom town, learning about drilling from hands-on experience.

Arriving in Dallas in the spring of 1902, he was flush with funds from the sale of land leases, had three Brooks Bros. suits in his valise, a bowler hat, a diamond stick-pin, a pair of spats, a pair of boots, and a pair of gray suede gloves which he carried, not wore. He was 32 years old and walked with a confident gait that set him apart from the Texas dandies around him.

As he entered the ballroom of Gaiety Hall for the 1902 Christmas Cotillion, heads turned in his direction. Among those noticing his entrance was Allene Stone Gano. At nineteen, she was as elegant and refined as she was charming and intelligent. The daughter of a Harvard-educated Texas judge, Allene Gano was tall and thin, and moved with quiet sophistication, a quality that Hughes found irresistible. He proposed under a full moon in late March, and the couple were married at the home of her parents on Masten Street in downtown Dallas on May 24, 1903.

Hughes' parents took the train from Keokuk, along with the Rev. R.C. McIlwain of Saint John's Episcopal Church, to attend the wedding. Howard's brother Felix and sister Greta (then married to Henry Witherspoon, a basso with the Metropolitan Opera) took the train from Manhattan. His other brother Rupert, at the time also living in New York and already a literary celebrity, was in the throes of a nasty divorce proceeding with his wife Agnes Wheeler Hedge Hughes—so nasty, in fact, that it repeatedly made front-page news in the *New York Times*. Rupert had publicly accused his wife of having a half-dozen lovers during their six-year marriage. And she accused him of having the same. Apparently, the Ganos thought better than to bring that issue to the wedding, which was featured in the local Dallas papers as a "society celebration."

White roses were intertwined with pink and white ribbons made into arches through which the bride and groom entered. The bride wore a white gown of Bruges lace and *mousseline de soie*, and the groom newly purchased white tie and gray tails. Greta Hughes Witherspoon performed several operatic selections as well as the popular "Memories," while Felix Hughes played the piano.

Using $10,000 in cash grubstaked by both sets of parents as a wedding gift, the newlyweds traveled first to St. Louis and New York, and then on to a six-month tour of Europe with stops in London, Paris, Berlin, Florence and Athens. As money became scarce, the pair returned to America and settled in the Rice Hotel in downtown Houston. Houston at the time was just beginning to emerge as a thriving city. It had a large, twin-towered City Hall, an enormous train station that welcomed passenger traffic and cargo cars, and newly installed electric lamps that cast their amber tones across street corners at night. There were social clubs for women, gambling clubs for men, the newly built Houston Carnegie Library, and summer band concerts at various city parks.

The city of over 80,000 was conveniently close to the oil industry, in which Hughes still intended to make his fortune. Unfortunately, he did not make it quickly enough for the management of the Rice, who threw both husband and wife out on the street over the issue of unpaid bills. Moving next to a two-story Victorian home at 1404 Crawford Street in a less-than-affluent part of town, the Hugheses were hardly the average neighborhood couple. He found relief from his lack of success in the gambling clubs on Main Street, while she found terror in the local outbreak of yellow fever that had swept the south, killing many in its path.

At the time, Houston roads were mainly unpaved, Crawford Street among them. A ditch with standing water in front of the house was a breeding place for mosquitoes and crawfish. The neighboring Buffalo Bayou that flowed into the Gulf of Mexico was brown with the decaying carcasses of cattle from the stockyards, and traveled by noisy steamers carrying freight and steerage passengers. And the area was overrun with cats of which Allene was deathly afraid. When she discovered she was pregnant in the spring of 1905, she convinced her husband to move to the neighboring town of Humble—the countryside compared with Houston. And it was in that Houston suburb that Howard Hughes was born.

Settling into a house at 14 Park Street, Allene finally felt at home. She had a small garden and a giant magnolia tree under which she sat and rocked her child to sleep. "Sonny," as baby Howard was called, was thin even as an infant, and a fussy eater. Constantly worried about his health, his mother sat for hours in an effort to get him to take spoonfuls of applesauce and milk, but to little avail. As she changed his diapers, Allene scrutinized his bowel movements for any sign of tapeworms from which she feared he suffered.

The first week of October, 1906, Big Howard and Allene traveled with their baby boy and Walter Sharp's wife Estelle to Keokuk. They stayed with his parents in their large frame house at 312 North Fifth Street. On October 7, Howard Robard Hughes Jr. was officially baptized into the Episcopal faith, with the Rev. R. C. McIlwain officiating.

Early in 1907, the Hugheses moved again, this time to Shreveport, Louisiana, following the scent of oil and the promise of easy money. He moved his family into the Caddo Hotel, which overlooked the Red River, a major artery thick with potter's clay the color of terra cotta. Steamboats traveled down the river from Arkansas, carrying gamblers, prostitutes and "musical entertainment to suit all tastes," according to the hotel directory. It was in Shreveport with its stench of sulfur and unceasing din of drills and hootenanny that Hughes formed the Caddo Co. as an oil exploration firm and developed an alliance with local riggers that would prove invaluable in the years ahead.

After six months of effort and several dry wells, Hughes moved his family yet again, this time twenty-five miles northwest to Oil City on the border between Louisiana and Texas. He was made deputy sheriff and postmaster of the town of 600, mainly because he was taller and heavier that any of the other men and "didn't take sass from the locals," according to an article in the *Shreveport Times*. While Hughes was pushing his weight around town, his unfortunate wife was suffering in silence at home. Their rented two-bedroom house had a well-pump for water and an out-house for comfort, with the tracks of the Santa Fe Railroad as neighbors. In Oil City, even the moon rose thin and tired as Allene gazed for solitary hours at its hollow glow.

For a woman of culture and Southern charm, Allene found Oil City the wild frontier. Unable to appreciate the local saloon mentality, Allene devoted her life to doting over her growing son. She sang to him, read to him, played with him and slept with him—Big Howard being ostracized to the smaller bedroom. And when Hughes chased oil strikes in Pierce Junction, Goose Creek, and Harper, Texas, Allene stayed behind, unwilling to continue to live the life of a wildcatter's wife.

By the start of 1908, Howard Hughes Sr. felt like a failure. He had lost the attention of his wife, rarely saw his son, and found his friends from his days at Spindletop now enjoying the finery and riches of fruitful careers as oil tycoons. Striking it rich was no longer the fanciful dream of a young vagabond; it was now a necessity for the 38-year-old braggart. Ironically, the key to his fortune was to be found in his failure.

Throughout his years as a wildcatter, Hughes was repeatedly frustrated by his lack of success in striking oil. The problem, he claimed, was not with the location of his wells, but rather with his inability to drill deep enough to tap into the oil reserves he was certain remained undiscovered beneath bedrock. Faced with the reality that no known drill bit could dig through the impenetrable rock, he became obsessed with the challenge to design such a bit, and worked for months in a futile effort to achieve positive results.

It took a chance meeting in a Shreveport bar called The Oyster Pub to motivate Hughes toward his future. It was there that he happened upon a millwright named Granny Humasson, who was attempting to interest the riggers in a drill bit he had conceived that resembled two engaging pine cones. His concept called for the cones to rotate in opposite directions, meshing like a coffee grinder. While the other riggers laughed at the design, Hughes took it seriously enough to pay $150 for two sewing-thread spools that Humasson had carved to illustrate his invention.

Hughes took the spools and his excitement at what they represented and ran two blocks to the Phoenix Hotel where his partner Walter Sharp was headquartered. A half-hour later and $1,500 poorer, Sharp was half-owner of an incomplete concept for a make-believe drill bit. Leaving his wife with a third of the cash, Hughes took the next train to his parents' home in Keokuk, Iowa, where he labored for weeks on a detailed drawing of a working model—one that eventually had 166 cutting edges on three sharp, ribbed cones that meshed against each other as they moved.

St. Louis patent attorney Paul Bakewell was hired by Felix Hughes to go to Washington, D.C., and file for a patent on the device that was labeled a "new and useful improvement in drills." While Bakewell struggled to convince the patent office of the merits of Hughes' bit, Big Howard engaged a machine shop to fabricate a prototype of the drill for experimental use. Still uncertain that his concept would actually work, Hughes took the finished prototype, mounted it on a rod in a press, and attempted to drill through a six-inch thick piece of granite. Legend has it that the bit drilled through the granite, drilled through the work bench, and was chewing through the concrete floor of the workshop before the machinery could be stopped. Washington was equally convinced of the unique merit of the invention, granting Hughes U.S. patent numbers 930,758 and 930,759 on August 10, 1909, as sole inventor of the "rock bit."

With patents in hand, Big Howard, Allene and Sonny made a triumphant return to Houston, arriving in a Buick Model C roadster, and staying at the Rice Hotel once again, until a more suitable home could be found. Automobiles were so rare at the time that the Rice kept Hughes' Buick parked in front of the hotel to attract customers.

Despite her earlier disdain for the smells and contamination of the Texas boom town, Allene thought Houston to be paradise compared to the filth and squalor of Oil City and Shreveport, and settled into a comfortable life of formal city living. There were lunches in the hotel restaurant, afternoon teas on the sun porch, walks along ever-expanding promenades, and, of course, her continuing devotion to her only child.

While Big Howard was expending all his energy with Walter Sharp building the newly-formed Sharp-Hughes Tool Company in one corner of the Houston Car Wheel & Machine shop, his wife was dressing their son in frilly white shirts and knickers, white socks and black MaryJane shoes for outings on his wooden and brass tricycle—a gift from his Aunt Greta, who was then living in Paris.

Though the Hugheses were still far from wealthy, Big Howard spent money as if they were, ordering clothing and furniture from New York and Europe, and lavishly entertaining on credit provided by the Rice Hotel. His was a world in which illusion cast a long shadow, and pride in accomplishment sparked many boastful conversations over after-dinner cigars and brandy. To project the proper image, the couple joined Christ Church Cathedral and its upper-class Episcopal congregation; and, in 1910, when Sonny turned five, he was sent to his first school in the parish house of the church.

Miss Eichler's University was hardly your average school. Run by the German-bred Jenny M. Eichler from Oyster Bay, New York, the school was split into three age groups. In the youngest class, Sonny was joined by Dudley Sharp, son of Hughes' partner, Walter; and Ella Rice, daughter of David Rice, whose Uncle William had funded Rice Institute (later Rice University). Miss Eichler was a strict disciplinarian who ran her classes with an iron will, demanding and getting absolute attention and promptness—from all except Howard R. Hughes Jr.

It was not Sonny's fault, of course, that he arrived late to school most days. His mother had begun an elaborate pre-school ritual with the child that included a thorough washing with lye soap, inspection of his feet, ears, throat and teeth, and the constant examination of any toilet waste, still in search of tapeworms. She then dressed him, brushed his hair, and delivered him to the front door of the church. She was standing there again when school was dismissed.

It was not until Sonny, at the age of eight, entered the Prosso School that he was able to escape his mother's suffocating grip. Prosso was an elite private school run by James Richardson and his wife, both of whom held Ph.D. degrees. The Richardsons, with their faculty of eight, taught thirty students in their house on Main and Rosalie Streets, with an emphasis on individuality. Pressed by Mr. Richardson, Sonny began to slowly emerge from his cocoon of maternal protectiveness. Each day, the students would give a one-on-one recitation in each of their subjects, earning a daily grade. Under Richardson's strict learning structure, Sonny had little choice but to break from his shell, and, as he did, the first sign of a budding mechanical genius became evident.

Although withdrawn and shy around most of the students, he developed a close bond with Dudley Sharp. Together, they built a workshop behind Sharp's home at the corner of Main and Eagle Streets.[3] It was an expansive house on a property peppered with oak trees and a lovely rose garden, beyond which the boys set up shop. Together, the friends built a radio transmitter and broadcast their own radio show around a fifteen-block radius to surprised neighbors.

It was also at Prosso that Sonny began to borrow his mother's diamond jewelry to show off at school. Allene learned about her son's new habit only when the mother of Margaret Cullinan, a classmate, returned several diamond earrings that Sonny had given her 8-year-old daughter. Rather than punish her son for stealing, Allene merely instructed him to give away only the smallest stones. It was the beginning of Hughes' lifelong fascination with diamonds—and females—that would continue all his life.

On November 28, 1912, Walter Sharp died at the age of 42, leaving his share of Sharp-Hughes Tool Co. to his widow Estelle, Allene Hughes' best friend, and Dudley Sharp's mother. Initially, Estelle attempted to help make decisions concerning the direction of the growing company. In early 1913, the company was incorporated, $300,000 worth of stock was issued and equally divided between the two owners. New manufacturing facilities were constructed and production on the rock drill increased ten-fold. With the oil business in a boom phase, there seemed to be an unlimited thirst within the industry for the essential Hughes bit.

In what was considered to be an astute business decision, Hughes refused to sell his bit outright to any oil company, wildcatter or rigger. Instead, he leased the bit on a monthly basis, providing free sharpening and maintenance as the device required. In this manner, each bit paid for itself within a few months, and, with each successive month, was generating nearly all profit.

To a normal businessman, such a set-up would have provided an endless pot of gold from which to dip. Big Howard, however, was no ordinary businessman. Still devoted to a lifestyle of lavish spending, Hughes traveled around the country in a private railroad car, with a separate car added to transport his growing wardrobe. He entertained oil men in the south and west with extravagant dinners and expensive presents. Hughes was popular with everyone—except perhaps Mrs. Walter Sharp, who saw her profits dwindling.

In a deal that indicated her own lack of business savvy, Estelle Sharp sold her share in Sharp-Hughes Tool to Ed Prather, Hughes' partner in the Moonshine Company. Her selling price: $65,000. When Prather

---

3. At the time, the property was on the outskirts of town. As Houston expanded, the estate was later torn down and turned into a Sears store.

attempted to cap Hughes' spending, he found himself personally funding Big Howard's excesses instead. On February 3, 1915, the name of the company was officially changed to Hughes Tool, leaving little doubt as to who was in charge.

The same year, Sonny Hughes was officially welcomed as royalty. While his mother had always treated him like a prince, she made certain that the entire town saw his regal side when she lobbied to have her son named King of the May at Christ Church Cathedral's annual May Day celebration. "Howard is both tall and polite," Allene wrote to the church rector, "and would make an excellent King of the May Fête. I feel the enclosed check for $250 might be used to ensure a successful day." The added incentive apparently inspired the church to see her point. On May 1, Sonny was attired in a custom-made costume with white puffed, gathered sleeves and gold piping to stand tolerantly atop the front steps of the church, to be crowned. His court was a resplendent group of forty-two youngsters, also in white and appropriately indulgent.

On Christmas that year, Sonny asked for a black horse which he planned to name Coon. So certain was the 10-year-old that his wish would be granted that when he sat on the lap of Santa Claus while visiting the Majestic Theater in downtown Houston, he asked for a saddle to ride a horse he had not yet been given. Both horse and saddle arrived on Christmas morning.

February 21, 1916. Sonny was in geography class when he received word that his Aunt Greta Hughes Witherspoon had died in New York of tuberculosis peritonitis.[4] He was immediately taken to the hospital to be tested for the disease. His uncle Rupert, upon hearing the news, fainted and was carried to his bed where he remained until his parents arrived three days later. Felix Hughes attended the funeral with his wife, and sang several hymns. Big Howard, who was in New York at the time on business, sent a wagon of flowers pulled by a white horse. Greta, who had been abandoned by her husband, was interred in a plot owned by Rupert at the Kensico Cemetery in Valhalla, New York. Sonny stayed at home with his mother and received instructions on tuberculosis and its symptoms. Although the child was fond of his aunt, Sonny was not as affected by her death as the rest of the family members. His mind was occupied with other things, in particular thoughts of adventure.

He had seen advertisements for a Pennsylvania camp called Teedyuskung in *Boy's Life* magazine. For ten years, he had spent every single day and night with his mother. Now he wanted to demand freedom, and it would take all the cunning he could muster. Assembling several dif-

---

4. Tuberculosis of the abdominal lining.

ferent advertisements for the camp, run by Daniel Carter Beard[5] as part
of an outdoor school, he first approached his mother about the idea in
late April. He also enlisted the help of Lewis Thompson, the son of a
wealthy logger and a former classmate at Miss Eichler's University. The
previous summer, Lewis had been allowed to become a Woodcrafter, as
Dan Beard's campers were called, and came home to Houston full of stories of canoe rides, hunting trips, and campfires. Lewis had his father
contact Dan Beard who in turn mailed his propaganda to Allene.

"My dear Mrs. Hughes," Beard wrote on May 29, 1916, "Mr. J.
Lewis Thompson has been kind enough to let me know through his son
that you have a boy suitable for our summer school. Lewis Thompson
was a pupil of mine last year and you may, if you desire, inquire of Lewis
or his parents regarding the sort of camp I run. . . During the years which
I have been running boys' camps, I have learned to follow certain rules
which summer after summer produce exceptional results. I had one hundred and forty boys in camp with me July and August 1915. At the end of
the eight weeks, I turned over to parents one hundred and forty-one [sic]
of the finest boys you ever saw. Everyone of them was hard as nails, everyone of them was bright-eyed, everyone of them was stronger morally,
mentally, and physically than when they entered camp and not one of
them on the sick list."

Seeing Camp Teedyuskung as a way to physically condition her frail
son, Allene wrote back the day after receiving Beard's note stating that
"Mr. Hughes and I feel that the life at your camp and your personal influence will be of great benefit to Howard . . ." She enclosed an entrance
application, while querying Beard if he took boys "as young as Howard"
and if so, "how many boys near his age will (he) probably have in camp?"
She added, "This will be Howard's first experience away from his family
and we think it desirable to place him in a rather small camp for this
year."

Her son was elated by his mother's eagerness to allow him an opportunity to spend the summer living within a stockade, as the troops of
campers were called. He could study nature, hike through the wooded
Pocono Mountains, live in a tent, and become independent at last. What
Allene saw as conditioning, Sonny saw as liberating, and on June 22,
1916, they boarded a train together to meet up with Big Howard in New
York, and travel on to Camp Teedyuskung by chauffeured car.

Sonny's summer adventure was the happiest of his young life. He had
an opportunity to explore himself while learning practical skills for the
very first time. He attempted to fit in with the other Woodcrafters, devel-

5. Dan Beard ran the Dan Beard Outdoor School until the late 30s, and was one of the co-founders
of the Boy Scouts of America.

oped a friendship with his stockade leader, 13-year-old Victor Aures of Baltimore, Maryland, found whittling tree branches to his liking, and even developed a taste for flapjacks cooked over an open fire.

He did not make it through the summer without his mother's intervention, however. Staying in New York at the Vanderbilt Hotel while Sonny played at Camp Teedyuskung, Allene read several articles about the spread of infantile paralysis in the *New York Times*. She clipped out the news pieces, gave them to her husband, and attempted to convince him to bring their son home. Refusing to indulge Allene's germ phobias, Hughes nevertheless sent the articles along to Dan Beard with a note that said that he thought "these clippings might be of interest as the clippings show how easily the violent germs are carried even by a well person."

Beard's overnight response was not what the Hugheses were expecting to hear. "Your boy seems to be holding his own here in camp," he wrote. "He is an interesting little chap, full of fun and well liked. Please tell his Mother that the last time I saw him he did not look a bit like he was going to cry. His mouth was open and he was yelling, but he was yelling to the rest of his stockade to hurry up, and get a move on. In fact, he has shown no signs of homesickness at all, and seems very happy. Hastily and cordially yours, Chief."

Allene Hughes was more than skeptical that her son was adjusting without her influence. She begged her husband to allow her to go back to Pennsylvania and retrieve the child. If Big Howard did nothing else for his son, he succeeded that day in giving him six weeks of freedom. He took his wife to Newport, Rhode Island, where they were the guests of Theresa and Hermann Oelrichs[6] at their estate, Rosecliff, and mingled with New York and Philadelphia society. It did not stop Allene from worrying, but at least it provided a temporary distraction that sufficed until early August, when she again attempted to remove her son from his summer playground.

As he promised, Beard had written to inform the Hugheses about Sonny's progress. On his health, Beard wrote: "Physical condition, bowels, feet, O.K. General appearance, better than when he first entered camp. Heart, much better now." On his performance, Beard noted that Sonny had difficulty sticking "to one thing very long, but he is doing fairly well in scoutcraft and never gives us any trouble."

Allene answered Beard by announcing her intention to visit her son "for a few minutes" and determine his condition herself. "His letters are

6. Hughes was a friend of Theresa's father, James Fair, a partner in Nevada's Comstock Silver Lode. Theresa and Hermann's daughter, Marjorie, married pianist Eddie Duchin and was portrayed by Kim Novak in the film, *The Eddie Duchin Story* (1956). Rosecliff was used as the location for Robert Redford's 1974 film, *The Great Gatsby*.

so short and unsatisfactory that I feel I must talk to him if it is possible . . . ,"
she wrote. When Allene eventually arrived in the Pocono Mountains, she
stayed temporarily at the Buckwood Inn at Shawnee-on-Delaware,
Pennsylvania. From there she retrieved her boy, arriving in the camp
with a car, driver, maid, and four trunks of baggage. With much drama
and apologies to Beard, she removed a humiliated Sonny from his stockade and took him to stay with Howard's brother Felix in Cleveland,
where he was then living and teaching voice with his wife Adella.

Sonny carried a health certificate that read: "This is to certify that the
bearer Howard Hughes, of Houston, Texas, has been at the Dan Beard
Outdoor School, at Lake Teedyuskung, Pike County, Pa. between June
28th, 1916 to August 26th, 1916 and has not left the camp within that
time. All measure to prevent exposure to any disease has been taken. The
camp has been isolated and visitors prohibited from entering the camp-
ing grounds. The camp doctor's examination finds him in excellent
health."

When the Hugheses finally returned to Houston, Sonny was placed
in yet another school. Montrose School was near the fashionable
Beaconsfield Apartments where the Hugheses had rented Suite 2-A. The
large three-bedroom, second-floor unit on the southwest corner of the
building featured a marble fireplace, hardwood floors, and a formal dining room. It was from Beaconsfield that Sonny wrote to "Chief" Dan
Beard on December 29, 1916, in response to a note from the camp leader
that suggested that former President Theodore Roosevelt might visit
Camp Teedyuskung the following season.

"Dear Chief, I was glad to get your letter, and I hope that I can come
to your camp next year, and bring my friend Dudley Sharp. I have joined
the Y.M.C.A. and like it very much. Enclosed please find my Buckskin
Badge. I have returned it on account of eating some candy. With love
from Howard. P.S. I hope that you and Mrs. Beard and Bartlett and
Barbara have a Happy New Year."

When the time came the following year for the 11-year-old boy to
strike off on his own once more, his mother decided that it was not a wise
idea, writing to Beard that she wanted the family to stay "close at home."
Sonny explained in a separate letter to the Chief, "I don't think that I will
be able to come up to camp this summer allthough [sic] I would like it
very much. We have just bought a boat and I think that we will stay here
all summer except about one or two months."

The "boat" was a sixty-foot yacht with mahogany floors, brass railings,
gold fixtures in the head, and a crew of six. Christened the *Rollerbit*, it was
initially docked in Galveston. Hughes took his son for several cruises in
the Gulf of Mexico, only to hear continuously about Camp Teedyuskung.

Big Howard was caught between a wife frantic over contagious diseases and a son who wanted to sleep in a tepee in Pennsylvania. The choice was clear. He told his son, he could not, would not risk the boy's health. For Sonny, the discussion was an epiphany. It was as if some door had opened and he saw that clutched within the fear of illness was the path to Teedyuskung.

When Allene came into her son's room to kiss him goodnight, she found him shaking with chills. He stopped eating for the next four days, and succeeded in staying out of school for the remainder of the month. Allene arranged daily house calls by the doctor, who was unable to find anything causing her son's illness. It was only when she decided that the mountain air of Camp Teedyuskung might be a healing influence that Sonny suddenly recovered. Allene called it a miracle; her son, good planning. It was but the first of feigned illnesses that Hughes would use to his advantage. He soon learned, however, that his victory came with a price.

Howard was sent by train to Pennsylvania, accompanied by Dudley Sharp and a Black driver named Johnson, who worked for Hughes Tool. When the trio arrived, Sonny again suffered the humiliation of his mother's interference. As directed, the driver unpacked Sonny's bag in his tepee tent, as his fellow Woodcrafters looked on in amusement. The following day, the Chief received a letter from Allene dated July 16, 1917, begging him to take special care of her son.

"I hope the doctor will keep an eye on him, watching his feet and teeth, and see that he takes his Russian oil[7] every night—I put a large bottle of it in his suitcase but I am sure he was tempted to throw it out of the car window and he may have done it. We think that neither he nor Dudley should go on very long hikes or eat the precious flap-jacks [sic]."

Sonny found the camp changed from his previous year. Many of the familiar counselors were no longer there, having enlisted in the army at the start of World War I. He felt bullied by some of the other youngsters and wrote to his mother, complaining of "having bad dreams, not sleeping well, and feeling tired all the time." Now certain that she had made a mistake in allowing her son to return, Allene Hughes called Camp Teedyuskung and begged Chief Beard to have a doctor examine young Howard and "check his digestion and elimination." She also asked that her son be excused from any more classes in arithmetic, since she was certain it was causing him headaches.

In addition Allene wrote to Sonny's stockade leader, Lieutenant Aures, noting her concern. "I am trying hard to overcome too much anxiety over my one chick, but don't seem to make much headway. As I wrote the Chief, he has not been at all well this spring and ever since he left

7. Mrs. Rokamov's Russian Oil was the trademark name of a brand of castor oil.

camp last year has been having trouble with the arches of his feet. Please if you notice any of his shoes getting run over, throw them away." She also alerted Aures to what she labeled her son's "supersensitiveness," adding, "I think you understand him well enough to help him over the many times he gets his feelings hurt."

Aures' subsequent conversation with the Chief prompted a return letter to the distressed mother, reassuring her that her son was "doing splendidly." Furthermore, Beard added: "In regard to your request concerning his shoes, wish to say that I shall gladly keep posted as to condition of same and have him throw them away should they become run over. I have, so far, noticed no signs of nervousness from him and feel sure that he will be as much benefited [sic] in this respect as he was last summer. I am glad to say that I have noticed very few of his faults to which you have called my attention. However, I shall make every effort to rid him of his sensitiveness as much as possible."

Beard's evaluation of Sonny's progress signaled some interesting traits. While informing Allene that her son was "very attentive" in scout-craft and bird study, his mathematics instructor found Sonny's work lacked "reasoning power." And as for constantly being tired, Beard added: "Not being hardened to the strenuous routine of camp life, it is not at all strange that he should feel tired the first few days. Both boys are doing fine and enjoying themselves immensely."

The summer passed without further letters from Mrs. Hughes, but only because she was having problems of her own. With their son in camp, Allene and Big Howard traveled to New York and registered in their now-familiar suite at the Vanderbilt Hotel. As they arrived at the Vanderbilt, Hughes was introduced to an 18-year-old model for Eastman Kodak named Eleanor Boardman.

While Eleanor was with her mother, and Hughes with his wife, Hughes set his eyes on the teenager and everyone else faded away. The girl said she had ambitions to be an actress, to the obvious chagrin of her mother. Mrs. Boardman was openly irritated when Hughes offered to arrange for her daughter to meet his brother Rupert, who was then writing stories for films, including the enormously successful *Gloria's Romance*, a 1916 silent movie which he had authored with his second wife, Adelaide Manola.

Handing Eleanor his card, Big Howard allowed his hand to linger too long for casual politeness, his eyes never leaving their mark. Allene wisely took his arm and asked to be taken back up to their suite. Following the dictates of her Southern upbringing, she did not challenge her husband about his behavior. Instead she attempted to re-energize their romance by devoting herself to his every whim. Thus occupied, she had less time for her son upon his return in mid-August from Camp Teedyuskung.

While Allene still managed to maintain her diligence where his daily health and toilet checks were concerned, she relaxed her restrictions on her son to that point where he became suspicious of the change in her mood. She was so impressed by his well-fed and healthy appearance that she wrote to Beard with words that glowed with praise and pride. "He is in better condition, I think, than he has ever been," she wrote. "His cheeks are round and fat and rosy and he is full of 'pep.'"

Further perplexing to her young son, she encouraged him to spend several nights at Dudley Sharp's house, something Allene had never allowed before. Just days after he arrived home, the younger Hughes was at the Sharps when tragedy struck the city of Houston, igniting a chain of events that ultimately would change Sonny's life forever.

T W O

From Boy to Man

*I can summerize my attitude about employing
more negroes very simply—I think it is a
wonderful idea for somebody else, somewhere else.
I know this is not a very praise-worthy point of
view, but I feel the negroes have already made
enough progress to last 100 years, and there is
such a thing as overdoing it.*

Las Vegas, Nevada
April 4, 1968
Written after hearing that Martin Luther
King had been assassinated.

ON THE AFTERNOON OF AUGUST 23, 1917, 11-YEAR-OLD
Sonny Hughes rode his bicycle across town to Main and
Eagle to visit his best friend, Dudley Sharp. It was one of
those vibrantly hot, humid days made for mint juleps and
ceiling fans, when even the mosquitoes seem to move a little
slower to save energy. Sonny was wearing his uniform from
Camp Teedyuskung, a dark green shirt, knickers, and
peaked cap, and found Dudley dressed the same, waiting for
him in the front yard of his home.

Three-and-a-half miles away, the 3rd Battalion, 24th
Infantry, was patrolling the grounds of Camp Logan, then
under construction by the War Department as an army base.
The 24th Infantry was an all-Black outfit that had come to
Houston from San Francisco where they were lauded for
their fine service. What passed for law in San Francisco was
not the canon of the South, however. In Houston as in all
Southern states, they lived under Jim Crow law, an arbitrary
set of rules and regulations that decreed segregation in
transportation, schools, churches, cemeteries, theaters, and
restaurants.

At Camp Logan, there were drinking fountains for the white construction workers, and others marked "Guard" for the Black soldiers. The infantry was harassed by the police, who routinely called them *niggers*, and expected the "colored visitors," as they were labeled, to mind their manners while in Texas. There were pushing and shoving matches that did little to cool tempers, and the heat of bigotry built to an explosive level under the helmets of the 3rd Battalion.

Nearby the Camp, two small boys were caught playing craps by a police officer named Lee Sparks, who chased the children into a house where a Black woman was ironing her clothes. When she claimed she had not seen the boys, Sparks slapped the woman, outraging an MP from the 24th Infantry who witnessed the abuse. Coming to the aid of the woman, the Black man was shot by Sparks and pistol whipped, before being taken into custody.

When word of the altercation spread back to the infantry, the rumor mill had twisted the news to wrongly state that the MP had been murdered. Suddenly, the pent-up rage of the soldiers found direction. Grabbing rifles and ammunition, and led by Sgt. Vida Henry, hundreds of soldiers marched in columns as night fell on an unsuspecting city. As they headed toward the San Felipe district and through the section of town known as Brunner looking for Officer Sparks, they shot at white men, women and children randomly, killing them as they walked on the sidewalk, rode in their cars, and sat in their homes. When Illinois National Guard Capt. J. W. Mattes stood his ground in an open car and ordered the troops to halt, he was shot and killed along with his two companions.

For two hours, the Black riot shattered the Southern town before the soldiers returned to their base, but not before Sgt. Henry had shot himself in the head. As Houston whites heard the news, they looted local stores for guns and ammunition to protect their families. Joining them on the streets, Allene Hughes hysterically rushed to safeguard her son who she took home and hid in the closet of her bedroom.

Martial law was declared by Texas Gov. Jim Ferguson as Houston's most prominent citizens tried to control the vigilantes. A special train from Galveston brought in army reinforcements while another from Austin arrived, loaded with a backup battalion of infantry. Though the military was legally responsible for its mutineers, an *ad hoc* posse of 300 Houston leaders was assembled to patrol the streets to ensure peace. In all, that night, twenty-six whites were left dead along with four Blacks. After a month-long trial, thirteen Black infantrymen were found guilty and hanged for the killings.

Allene Hughes kept her son secluded in her closet in the Beaconsfield

Apartments for four hours. When Sonny finally was allowed to go to his room, the curtains were drawn and no lights allowed. For the impressionable youngster, the experience left an indelible imprint, one that labeled Blacks as murderers and misfits. It turned him into a bigot, so outspoken in his views that he could have succored Harriet Beecher Stowe. His mother was so infuriated that her husband was out of town on business during the riot, leaving her unprotected, that she demanded and received his assurance that he would build her a home able to pass the highest security standards.

Hughes purchased a corner lot in the fashionable Montrose section of the city on Yoakum Street, one block from the three-story mansion of developer John Wiley Link, who brought in seven trainloads of palm trees to line Montrose Boulevard. Hughes hired William Ward Watkin, the first chairman of Rice Institute's architecture department, to design his home, a brick Georgian residence with marble floors, five bedrooms and a separate, two-car garage. The Hugheses moved into their new home at 3921 Yoakum Street[1] in the summer of 1918, upsetting plans for Howard's return to Camp Teedyuskung. The Chief had been in contact with the Hugheses for months, promising that Sonny would wear "three stripes on his sleeve" and be addressed as "sir" by the tenderfoot newcomers. Although Allene had initially made plans for her son's return, in the end the lure of a new house and, in little Howard's case, a new room complete with a radio transmitter and electronic gear, were too big an attraction. They remained in Houston for the summer of 1918, except for a single short trip to Keokuk, Iowa, to visit Sonny's grandparents.

At this point in their lives, Felix and Mimi Hughes were constantly bickering—two strong-willed individuals each set in their ways and stubborn as tar on a beach blanket. Felix was so deaf, he spoke in loud barks that were largely ignored by his fastidious wife. When Big Howard witnessed the depth of their aggression toward one another, he offered to build the couple a second home in Keokuk to give them what he labeled "breathing room."

Once again he called upon William Ward Watkin to design the house located at 925 Grand Avenue on a bluff above the Mississippi River. Though situated only ten blocks from their Fifth Street residence, the new house was called the "summer home," while their other was called the "winter." Due to Mimi Hughes' fear of bugs, the new house was built without any closets which Sonny's grandmother thought harbored the creatures. Instead, she used walnut armoires that could be carried outside and purified in the sun.

---

1. The home was purchased in 1953 by the University of St. Thomas, Houston, and renumbered 3901 Yoakum. It is currently in use by the Modern and Classical Language Department of the school.

The quarreling that was rampant with the grandparents seemed to young Sonny to have passed to his parents. With Big Howard's continuing travel to expand the reach of Hughes Tool, Allene stayed at home with Sonny and brooded over her husband's absence. She had not forgotten the overt attention he had bestowed on Eleanor Boardman and was outraged to learn that her husband had made a side-trip to Philadelphia, where the young model lived.

It was while his father was on one such business trip in May, 1919, that 13-year-old Sonny overheard his mother having a heated telephone conversation. Allene was begging her husband to return home to Houston, citing her continuing frustration at his long and, what she termed, "mysterious" absences. Whether psychological or deliberate, the effect on Sonny was immediate and dramatic.

The following morning when Sonny awoke, he screamed for his mother to come to his room. Rushing to her son's bedside, Allene found Sonny unable to move, his legs paralyzed and his mind panicked. Allene immediately placed a long-distance call to her husband in New York and hysterically blurted out that their son had contracted infantile paralysis.

Disregarding the fact that infantile paralysis does not strike overnight, Big Howard made immediate plans to return to Houston, but not before calling Dr. Simon Flexner, a pioneer in researching the disease and the first director of the Rockefeller Institute for Medical Research (now Rockefeller University). According to the Rockefeller Archives, Hughes offered Flexner "any amount of money" to travel to Houston to examine his son. While Flexner had his own schedule to keep, he agreed to send his associate Dr. H.T. Chickering to Houston in exchange for a donation to the Rockefeller Institute of $10,000 plus Chickering's expenses.

When Dr. Chickering examined Sonny, he was able to find nothing clinically wrong with the child, who was confined to bed or a wheelchair. For six weeks, Chickering hovered over the boy, running blood, muscle fatigue and breathing tests to no avail. He even traveled with Allene, her sister Annette, and Sonny to Michigan's Mackinac Island where they lodged at the Grand Hotel in three large suites. Each day, young Howard would be wheeled in his chair unto the hotel's 660-foot veranda and watch the horse-drawn carriages arrive with new guests.[2] At the end of the summer, no sooner had Dr. Chickering departed, than Sonny's mystery illness disappeared. His father would later write that he just "picked up," apparently satisfied that his ploy to reunite his parents and gain their attention had worked flawlessly. The Hugheses were so excited to have

---

2. The Grand Hotel is still in existence and was featured in the 1979 film, *Somewhere in Time* starring Jane Seymour and Christopher Reeve. Even today, no cars are allowed on the island and all guests arrive via horse and carriage.

their fully functioning son back again, they finished the summer with a trip to Coronado Island, California, where they yachted until it was time for Sonny to return to school.

Not willing to allow him to be sent away so soon after an illness Allene considered life-threatening, she enrolled him in Houston's South End Junior High, a public school near their Montrose home. While the choice managed to keep her son under her watchful eye, it did little to expand his mind. The South End teachers repeatedly sent notes home with Sonny alerting his parents to his "disinterest in all things academic." His Aunt Annette, who had moved into the Yoakum Street house, tutored him nightly to little avail. She would later call his mind "a wondering body that had no thought for books." His report card from the school gave him barely passing grades in reading, English, Bible, French, and science. In the first ninety days of classes, he had twenty-eight absences, all approved by his mother.

The following year, Big Howard decided that his son's sporadic education was in dramatic need of a jump start. In an effort to motivate the spoiled fourteen year old, he enrolled him at the prestigious Fessenden School in West Newton, Massachusetts, just outside Boston. In a letter to the founder, Frederick James Fessenden, Hughes wrote from the Touraine Hotel in Boston, "Herewith my cheque for $1000.00 on account. I want Howard to have the best of everything open to the pupils regardless of the expense. When you require further funds, please advise me. Please let Howard purchase anything which he may require and which is not against the school regulations. I wish him to fully uphold the subscription for anything which would serve to increase the prestige of the Fessenden School, so you may feel free to charge my account liberally for such and should some one or two boys not be in funds or need my assistance, I would be more than pleased to help them through the year. If consistent and you have the time, I should be glad to hear of Howard's progress and especially to have angles or sidelights on his progress and development."

Fessenden found the time to keep Hughes informed regularly, noting that "it is not easy for a boy who has never attended boarding school and has been indulged at home to get adjusted to so many new conditions. I think he has done well under the circumstances, and I believe he is going to show general improvement as the year advances. He has ability, we think, but he finds it somewhat hard to keep down to the business day after day." Fessenden also made mention of the fact that Sonny tended to "make mountains out of mole hills."

When his father visited in the late fall, he found Sonny on the school's nine-hole golf course perfecting his swing. Defying the rules forbidding students to leave the forty-one-acre campus, he spirited Sonny off to the Yale-Harvard crew races held annually on the Thames River in New London, Connecticut. With the bravado with which Hughes typically spoiled his son, he promised to buy him whatever he wanted if Harvard should prove victorious on the water. When his old alma mater managed to clip Yale by fourteen seconds on the clock, Hughes was beaming with pride. His son, in turn, was delirious with anticipation, for he already knew what he wanted from his father to celebrate the victory. He put out his hand and requested a five dollar bill.

"$5.00—that's it?" his father questioned.

Shaking his head in excitement, Sonny took the five dollars as he pointed to the Curtiss seaplane anchored in the New London harbor, and the sign overhead, "$5 a ride."

The plane was part of the Piper-Hudson Seaplane Service, a local sightseeing and tourist attraction. Although Big Howard had never himself been in an airplane, and had little faith in their safety, he joined his son in the seaplane with Capt. Horace Hudson piloting the craft. The ten-minute flight was agreeably short for the elder Hughes, who felt sick from the ride. As for his son, he was exhilarated and inspired by the sensation of flying, and knew he had found his calling in life.

When the school year ended, and Sonny brought his report card home, he had scored an 88 in Algebra, 74 in Bible, 75 in English, 62 in Spelling, 86 in Geography, and 77 in Latin. Hardly stellar marks, but given his history, a great improvement. His father was pleased with his progress; his mother delighted to have him back safely at home.

During the nine months away from Houston, "little" Sonny had grown to be six feet in height. He was now towering over Dudley Sharp and his other local friends, yet remained shy and withdrawn in their company. He spent most days alone up in his bedroom or in his garage workshop where he fashioned a motor and starter onto his bike, turning it into a primitive motorcycle. Word spread quickly that there was a new addition to the neighborhood, turning Sonny into a entrepreneur when he began charging five cents a ride.

While the Chief was busy lobbying to have "Buckskin" Hughes return for yet another year at Camp Teedyuskung, Sonny had turned his camp cap into a windsock on the roof of the Yoakum house to measure the wind direction and velocity in Houston. He had begun to read about a pair of British fliers, Captain John Alcock and Lieutenant Arthur Whitten Brown, who had won a 10,000-pound challenge from London's *Daily Mail* as the first pilots to fly across the Atlantic. They had accomplished the remarkable feat a year earlier. To Sonny, it was more than an adventurous exploit; it was fascination, exploration, and fantasy in an arena that had yet to be tapped. It became his arena, his dream.

When he spoke to his father about his desire to be a pilot, Big

Howard dismissed it as a child's fancy. "After Harvard," his father said. "First comes school." and ended the conversation. Sonny had forgotten that only two months before, he had told his father he wanted to be the world's most famous golfer. Apparently, his father had forgotten as well.

Sonny knew better than to tell his mother. She became nervous when he leaned out of his second-story bedroom window. The concept of heights, like most things, frightened her. His plan, therefore, remained a secret, except to himself to whom he talked incessantly in the privacy of his bedroom.

In the fall, when his father decided to send him to Thacher, a boarding school in Ojai, California, Sonny did not object. In fact, he hardly even listened. This school, that school, it was relatively unimportant, considering he had made up his mind about flying. Algebra and spelling did not fit into that picture. In September, he packed his windsock in his suitcase, an even larger bottle of Russian oil, kissed his mother goodbye, and headed West, accompanied by his father. He had not expected the reception at the train station—a car, a driver, and the personal welcome of the headmaster, Sherman Day Thacher, all business in his three-piece suit and wire-rim glasses. But then, he was not privy to the fact that Big Howard had promised to finance a school gymnasium in exchange for his son's admission to Thacher.

It was not an easy sell. Sonny's poor grades and erratic classroom attendance were not the marks of a Thacher boy. Sherman Thacher knew nothing of Big Howard or his ways, of course. "My own life has been a constant uphill fight and I never like to give up once I start to accomplish any definite thing," Hughes wrote to Thacher, who remained unmoved, or at least until the word *gymnasium* entered the negotiations.

The school itself was set on 200 acres of canyons, orchards, and pastures, with an administration building and three-story dormitory built in the Mission style, an infirmary, museum, laboratory, barns and shops. Though outwardly lacking the sophistication of Fessenden, the regimentation of Thacher was equally as rigid. Neckties for the boys were mandatory, as was singing the Banquet Song, including the Thacher theme of "honor and fairness and kindness and truth." Unfortunately, those four qualities did not impress Sonny as vital prerequisites for conquering the skies, and were all-too-soon forgotten in his rush to adventure.

His father arranged for his horse, Coon, to be transported by box-car to the Ojai school, even though there were nearly as many horses as students on the property already. It was to his horse that Sonny directed most of his free time, riding the open pasture land and dreaming of future exploits.

Despite Big Howard's reassurance to Thacher that little Howard would be free of parental interference, the first letter of concern from

Allene arrived on the headmaster's desk just six weeks into his enroll-
ment. "I think it is awfully hard for an only child to adjust himself well in
school and make friends as he should, and I am very interested to hear
from you about him," she wrote in a letter dated October 19, 1921.

As typical a letter as that was from Allene, it hardly reflected the
drama that was surrounding her in Houston. Her otherwise poetically
phobic existence was shattered by a conversation she had had with her
mother-in-law Mimi, who, while innocently bragging about her son
Rupert's growing achievements in Hollywood, happened to mention his
next motion picture. It was titled *Souls for Sale*, which Mimi described as
a "tale about a girl struggling to make it in Hollywood." The star was to
be a beautiful, unknown actress named Eleanor Boardman, "a friend of
Howard's," according to Mimi who was thrilled at the cooperation
between her sons.

Allene Hughes was on the next train to Los Angeles to join her
husband who was then ensconced at the Ambassador Hotel, set among
tropical gardens and home to the Cocoanut Grove nightclub. If her
unexpected appearance upset her husband, he certainly did not show it as
he accommodated her excesses and need for attention with a gallant attitude. He went so far as to appear pleased when she arranged a dinner
party a week after her arrival to include Rupert, his wife Adelaide,
Adelaide's two adult children from a previous marriage—Rush and Avis—
Avis' fiancé, writer John Monk Saunders, and the "beautiful unknown
actress" Eleanor Boardman. Should Eleanor have had any doubt that Big
Howard was still in love with his wife, it was erased that evening as Allene
cooed and clutched her husband like a star-struck schoolgirl, as he relished her flirtations.

With renewed anticipation, she romanced her husband and reminded
him of the debutante he first met in Dallas nearly two decades before.
She escorted him on business trips to New York and Chicago, traveling
with him in his private train coach, and sharing his excitement over his
expanding manufacturing base. They made plans for a trans-Atlantic
cruise to London and Paris, joyful in the prospect of revisiting sites from
their honeymoon. Big Howard would later write, "We were so very
happy that I could not stop smiling, and even stopped giving argument to
my associates."

Hughes' euphoria collapsed with his world, when on March 28,
1922, while on a shopping trip with her sister Annette, Allene experienced abdominal pains. Before she could be driven home, she was
hemorrhaging. Hughes rushed Allene to her physician, Dr. Gavin
Hamilton, who ordered her to Baptist Hospital for a *curettage*, a scraping
of the uterus. The next afternoon, she kissed her husband on the lips

before she was rolled into surgery. At 2:27 p.m., Allene Hughes died, at the age of thirty-nine, having never awakened from the anesthesia nor hearing the news that she was two months pregnant with her second child.

Hughes was devastated by his wife's death, finding little comfort in the prayers and tears of his sister-in law. He moved as if by instinct to send telegrams to his brother Rupert and Sonny. Years later, Rupert Hughes wrote in *American Magazine* about hearing the news. "I received one night a heartbroken telegram from my brother, saying that Allene, his wife, had died suddenly. He had telegraphed young Howard at Ojai, telling him merely that his mother was ill and he had better come home. My brother asked me to meet the boy when he came down from Ojai and put him on the first train for Texas. Young Howard, then just sixteen, arrived in great anxiety and suspense. I hesitated a long while over telling him the bitter truth."

Before putting Sonny on the train bound for Houston, Rupert told him that his mother had died. Unable to weep, the boy merely shook his head, and looked down in thoughtful silence. Rupert had asked his wife to accompany the teenager back home. At the moment, Rupert Hughes could not leave town. He was too busy directing a film.

Allene Gano Hughes was placed on view in the living room of the Yoakum Street house where a funeral service was held at 2 o'clock on Saturday afternoon. She was buried later that day at Glenwood Cemetery in a family plot her husband had purchased three months earlier. Her coffin of carved rosewood was carried by cotton factor W. D. Cleveland; oilmen W. S. Farish and Ed Prather; Dudley's brother, Bedford Sharp; and Christ church members F. C. Proctor and Roy G. Watson.

The day after the funeral, Sonny was visited by a casual friend, Elliot Cage, who was forced to pay his condolences by his mother. Cage remembered that afternoon with unexpected excitement. "We were alone in this big house, and spent the entire time in Sonny's room, playing with his radio transmitter. I remember saying that I was sorry to hear about his mother, and he replied, 'By turning this knob, we can hear Cleveland.'"

Big Howard accompanied his son back to Ojai three days later. He was distant on the trip, ignoring his boy's mindless chatter until it finally slowed to a silence. When they reached Thacher School, Sonny shook his father's hand, and never mentioned his mother's name again.

As if incapable of acknowledging his loss, Hughes checked into the Ambassador Hotel and began a round of parties and drinking that alarmed the management with its mania. Finally, Hughes' brother Rupert was called, and he invited Big Howard to stay at his home on Western Avenue in the Los Feliz section of Hollywood. The rambling showplace offered little distraction for the mourning businessman, who left within the week, bound for business meetings in New York.

When he finally returned to Houston ten days later, Howard Hughes checked into the Rice Hotel, unable to face the empty rooms of the Yoakum Street house, where every corner furnished a new memory of his old life. Convinced that he was incapable of handling single parenthood, he begged his sister-in-law Annette to help him raise his son.

"He was frantic, emotional and possessed," Annette later remembered. "So I told him I would give him one year and live with Sonny. Then I was going to get married." Her fiancé, Dr. Frederick Rice Lummis, was amazingly nonplused and went along with the plan that put his own carefully structured life on hold.

The only thing missing in this rewritten version of a normal family life was Sonny. Now back at Thacher and surprisingly free from grief, he was renewing his studies and having a particularly close kinship with his physics professor, Owen McBride, all the while innocent of the tug-of-war going on in the school's office of administration.

Hughes had reached the decision that he needed his son by his side. Sherman Thacher wrote to Hughes pleading with him to reconsider. "Your son needs more than most boys the contact with other fellows such as he gets in school; and I think your desire and tendency to indulge him in every way would probably be hard for him to resist and probably not at all good for him. I feel sure that the fact is it is not the best thing for a boy to be held in constant sympathetic association with those of an older generation, even his own father. . . "

Given Hughes' history of leniency toward this son, Thacher's words were wise counsel. Had they come at any other time, their sagacity would have been accepted without argument. But for Hughes, these were not normal times, but rather one of total self-pity and absorption, ripe with the kind of indulgence that only grief can engender. Hughes exposed his despair and loneliness to Thacher, in an atypical shedding of macho veneer. He told Thacher of "the emptiness that has become my life." And again he was told about the danger of overindulging his vulnerable son.

"I think he needs to be treated like any other boy," Thacher told Hughes, "and to learn more about how to carry himself among other fellows. I think he himself really feels conscious of this. . . "

An emotional Hughes sent for Annette Lummis to travel to Pasadena, California, where he had booked a bungalow at the luxurious resort Vista del Arroyo. She came across country joined by Sonny's favorite cousin, Kitty Callaway from Dallas, and had no sooner set foot onto the manicured lawns of the elite hotel than Hughes summoned his son to Pasadena for a visit. He never returned to Thacher. His clothes were transferred by limousine, and his horse Coon was donated to the Thacher stables.

With all the elements now in place to resume somewhat of a typical home life, Hughes disrupted the plan he had carefully laid and took to the road, escaping the domesticity of Pasadena for a trip to Europe and a cruise through the Panama Canal. He left strict instructions with Sonny's Aunt Annette to see "to his needs and comfort." Although Annette would later testify that each day young Howard would take classes at California Institute of Technology, there is no official record of his registration there. There is, however, an entry of membership in the Los Angeles Country Club for Howard R. Hughes Jr., with a daily tee-time from September through November, 1922, of 11 a.m.

Annette, Kitty and Howard sat on their veranda, watched the setting sun put reflections of the pool on the ceiling, and ate dinner together every night. They ordered from room service, occasionally with accompanying musicians. "He was perfectly beautiful, and he was a charming young boy," Annette said, "and that year I was with him in California, he couldn't have been more thoughtful." Or apparently more spoiled.

Other than indulging his growing talent in golf, the teenager was chauffeured to the movie studio by his Uncle Rupert, then in the throes of filming *Souls for Sale*. Roaming freely on the set, Sonny was the immediate inquisitor, asking questions of grips, electricians, make-up artists and set designers. He met Charlie Chaplin, who had a cameo in the film, and Eleanor Boardman, unaware of his father's fondness for the star. The 16-year-old Hughes was also introduced to a young actor named William Haines, appearing in his first picture, and allowed Haines to introduce him to Hollywood nightclubs, then thick with flappers and the redolence of excitement for the wide-eyed innocent.

March 31, 1923. Annette and company returned as pledged to Houston. While Kitty Callaway continued on to Dallas, Sonny and his aunt moved back into the Yoakum Street house to prepare for Annette's wedding. Big Howard, still full of wanderlust, promised to return to Houston to escort her down the aisle, but found a cruise around the Bahamas took a sudden precedence leaving her stranded and scrambling for a substitute.

"He disappointed me greatly. . . considering," Annette recounted in 1977. "I suppose I shouldn't have been surprised." But she was, as was Sonny, who was looking forward to his father's return.

Now seventeen and having reached his full 6' 3" in height, Sonny had grown into a handsome, lanky, brooding and sullen teen whose direction in life was as camouflaged as his personality. Through family connections, he had enrolled at Rice Institute, but was taking classes intermittently. Dr. Fred Lummis' mother was a Rice, and helped Sonny gain entry into the esteemed college, despite his lack of not only a high school diploma, but a high school education. "Money changed hands," is how Annette Gano Lummis remembered the day Howard matriculated. Apparently, a *lot* of money, given the number of rules broken and requirements bent.

It would take months before Big Howard regained his emotional footing. With the success of the automobile, the oil industry was outpacing growth projections, and carrying Hughes Tool on its back like the Barbary Macaques monkey in the jungles of Algeria. In September, 1923, Hughes returned to Houston and the Rice Hotel, and began to reestablish contact with his son, whom he saw as blithe and uncentered. While ostensibly a student, Sonny spent the majority of his time on the golf course of the Houston Country Club or driving his new yellow Duesenberg, a gift from his father. With few friends and even less direction, young Howard showed no indication that he intended to join his father's business. When they spoke, it was only of social events and planned vacations.

His one request—that he be able to take flying lessons—was dismissed categorically. At the merest hint of danger, the overly protective Hughes became obstinate and unbending. Commercial flying was still in its infancy and the news full of reports of crashes and death. Unused to being refused anything, Sonny retaliated by withdrawing further into his private world, helped along with a raise in his allowance to $5,000 a month, at a time when $5,000 represented the median annual income for the average family of four.

Ten days before Christmas, 1923, young Howard was told that his Aunt Adelaine, his Uncle Rupert's second wife and the woman who had provided him solace aboard the train on his way to his mother's funeral, had committed suicide on a cruise ship in Haiphong harbor, in French Indochina. She was on the trip, accompanied only by her nurse. Her husband was at home, having an affair with a struggling actress and would-be writer named Elizabeth Patterson Dial, who had a small role in Rupert's *Souls for Sale*.

The news impacted Sonny in a bizarre way. When told that his aunt had hanged herself with a belt strung from a ceiling fan, the teenager launched into a study of the dynamics of strangulation with such enthusiasm that Big Howard asked Annette to remove all his belts, lest he experiment on himself.

The Hugheses celebrated Christmas at the Rice Hotel, and brought in the New Year with a champagne party at the home of the Sharps. Dudley regaled Sonny with tales of his new life at Princeton, a world that seemed full and exciting compared with the monotonous solitude of his best friend's existence. It was an existence, however, that was about to be shattered forever.

On January 14, 1924, Big Howard attended a luncheon of oil tycoons on whose business he relied for his own wealth. At fifty-four, he was in an enviable position—secure, affluent, respected, and loved. As he ate prime rib and a baked potato laden with sour cream and broccoli shards, he spoke of new versions of his roller bit that were designed to be self-lubricating. There was talk of his continually expanding offices in Southern California, where oil exploration was increasing.

When he returned to his offices on the fifth floor of the Humble Building, he launched into intense discussions with S. T. Brown, his company's sales manager, inspired by the positive input he received over lunch. Midway through the meeting, as he paced back and forth emphasizing a point, Big Howard suddenly grabbed at his desk, convulsed, and fell to the floor.

Brown placed an emergency call to Hughes' doctor, C. M. Aves, who arrived minutes later to find his patient dead. Big Howard had died of a massive heart attack caused by an embolism. Sonny heard about his father's death from his Aunt Annette, who located him on the seventh tee of the Houston Country Club. She later said that the news came as a "horrible blow."

This time there would be no long train ride, or distant relatives to hold his hand. With the death of his father, Sonny Hughes made the transition from boy to man with the instinct of a survivor and the sorrow of an orphan. His world went from a life where days slid beyond themselves into weeks without distinction, to minutes that lasted for hours with an ache that saw no joy.

The man who was his hero, the man he only wanted to please, died without a warning or an opportunity to say goodbye. News of the tragedy appeared on page one of the *Houston Post* under the banner headline, "Called by Death: Howard R. Hughes, Noted Business Leader, Dies While at Work in Office." The story that followed referred to Hughes as having graduated from Harvard in the class of 1897, which was not the case, and placed his marriage to his wife two years later than it actually occurred. It quoted oil men who thought that Hughes deserved credit, "more than any other man in America, for revolutionizing the oil producing industry." His wealth spoke to the truth of that statement.

While Big Howard's body was taken to the Settegast-Kopf Company funeral home, Annette Lummis made arrangements for his burial next to her sister Allene in the family plot in Glenwood Cemetery. In the year and a half that had passed since Allene's death, the bamboo shrubs that had been planted along a bordering chain-link fence had grown and were in need of trimming. Groundsmen were brought out to sweep the concrete surface of the memorial site holding Allene's granite tombstone as calls were placed to Hughes' parents, and his brothers Rupert and Felix, none of whom attended the funeral.

The house on Yoakum Street became a focal point of newspaper reporters, friends, business associates and employees, who sent bouquets of flowers, funeral wreaths, notes of condolence, and offers of assistance. Sonny neither needed nor wanted flowers or help. The only request he made of his aunt was to be left alone in his room, where he once again turned to his radio transmitter and sent out his call letters 5CY in search of a return signal.

On the day of the funeral, the dean of Christ Church Cathedral, Dr. Peter Gray Sears, officiated at the service attended by Houston's most prominent citizens and benefactors. Among the pallbearers: oilmen Hugo V. Neuhaus, Lee R. Blaffer, Harry Weiss, Ed Prather and Steve Farish; Hughes Tool executives Robert Kuldell and C. S. Johnson; plus Dudley Sharp's brother, Bedford. Of the group, Neuhaus, Blaffer and Weiss were strangers to Sonny. He knew Ed Prather as his father's one-time partner (Hughes had bought out Prather several years earlier). Kuldell and Johnson were employees, not friends. And Bedford Sharp had last seen the teenager when he helped to bury his mother.

Sonny sat restrained and unmoving through the service, but never actually visited his father's grave. Though his aunt later said she thought his response was "unusual," she thought most things about her nephew were unusual, including his habit of throwing a rock through the glass of the French doors on the front of the house every time he forgot his key. "There were things about Howard that I never could explain," she said. One of them was his insistence on an immediate reading of his father's will by his attorney Frank Andrews.

Big Howard had drawn up his legal will some 11 years prior to his death. In it, he left his wife Allene one-half of his estate and his son one-quarter. The remaining one-quarter was to be split equally between his parents, Mimi and Felix Hughes Sr., and his brother, Felix Hughes Jr.[3] Since Allene was dead, her share went to Sonny, giving him 75 percent of his father's estate. Rupert Hughes was not mentioned.

The estate was valued for tax purposes at a conservative $861,518.00 with $750,000.00 of that amount estimated as the value of Big Howard's stock in Hughes Tool. Col. R. C. Kuldell, the general manager of

---

3. Hughes' will as originally written gave his sister Greta Hughes Witherspoon the share eventually inherited by his brother Felix. After Greta's death in 1916, a codicil was added changing his will to include Felix, who had been excluded in the first version.

Hughes' company, was named executor of the will, and began the process of dividing the estate and paying Hughes' debts which, as it developed, were not insignificant. Big Howard had borrowed $200,000.00 from his company at 6% interest just two weeks before his death. In addition, he owed various bills to local businesses—$2,248.06 to Brooks Brothers for custom-made suits, $3,252.00 to Cartier Jewelers in New York for cuff links and a wristwatch, and $207.00 to Carroll Florists for a standing order of flowers for his wife's grave.

In prophetic fashion, Hughes had also left specific instructions in his will for the care of his son in the event he was still a minor at the time of his death. "I desire and request that my son Howard be given as good an education as possible to fit him for such business or profession as he may desire to enter, and particularly request that if possible, a part of such education be given him in the University of the State in which he may expect to make his home." Hughes also made mention of appointing the Houston Land & Trust Company as the guardian of his son's estate until he turned 21 years of age.

As the *de facto* guardian of the 18-year-old, Annette Lummis and her husband were prepared for Sonny to complete his education at Rice Institute. Sonny, it seemed, had another plan for his life—one that did not include school. While he did not drop out of Rice officially, he simply stopped attending any classes, which effectively produced the same result. Instead, he spent the months following his father's death in California, where he moved in with his Uncle Rupert and Rupert's young girlfriend, Elizabeth Dial.

At the same time, his grandmother was also living with Rupert, dressed in the mourning color of black and dramatically feeling the pain of her oldest son's death. In a letter to her friend Mary Hollingsworth, Mimi wrote, "Life is so dark and cold. That precious Howard was my idol, more to me than all the world. But why try to tell you. For you must realize that all my heart was given to that precious child. My life is finished. Nothing left." Rupert, who for months was so upset over the death of his sister, shared none of his mother's sorrow for his fallen brother.

Rather, he set about organizing a plan to have himself appointed guardian of his nephew. Howard, who announced he would no longer answer to the name of Sonny, was told of Rupert's decision one evening as the sodium light on the adobe stucco turned walls to ashen misery. They were not unlike Howard's expression upon hearing the news. If Rupert's intent was to maneuver himself into a position to have access to his nephew's considerable wealth, he could not have picked a less diplomatic way. Having previously shown no particular interest in the welfare of his nephew, his timing now was seen as grossly inappropriate.

Howard wasted few precious moments in packing his golf clubs and returning to the sanctity of his Yoakum Street home. His reappearance was greeted by his Aunt Annette as a reconsideration of his need for school. Such was not the case. Rather, Howard began a detailed and organized effort to take control of both his life and his money. With a heretofore-unrecognized brilliance, he began his blitz by announcing his intention to pay his relatives for their shares of Hughes Tool Company.

In one way, his timing could not have been better. His grandmother, distraught and clutching her remaining family close to her bosom, had decided to leave Iowa and move permanently to Los Angeles. She had located a large home on Rossmore Avenue in Hollywood and convinced her son Felix to join her and her husband to calmly live out their days. Felix, who was undergoing a divorce, agreed. They accepted Howard's offer of cash in exchange for a company they had no chance of running in any case. The documents were drawn up, notarized, and on May 28, 1924, Hughes Tool Company became Howard's, in its totality.

That feat accomplished at no small expense,[4] Howard turned his attention to the clipped greens of the Houston Country Club and became obsessed with perfecting his golf game. He played regular matches with prominent members of Houston's gentry including weekly outings with a circuit judge named Walter Montieth. To the world of Houston society, it appeared as if the teenager had returned to the playful idleness of his recent past. They were unaware that away from the course, Howard was studying the inheritance laws of Texas. In particular, he was fascinated by a statute that allowed a 19-year-old resident of the state to be declared by the court an adult in the eyes of the law.

Upon reaching the age of nineteen, Howard petitioned the court on his own behalf to have the disabilities of his youth removed. The judge hearing the case was Walter Montieth. "Walter Montieth said he couldn't ask him any question that Howard didn't know the answer," according to his Aunt Annette. Additionally, the teenager blatantly lied as he solemnly promised to return to school, indicating his desire to join his friend Dudley Sharp at Princeton. Judge Montieth needed only two days to consider the appeal, and on December 26, 1924, declared 19-year-old Howard Robard Hughes Jr. to be free "of the disabilities of minority and of full age."

Howard returned to the house his father built with a confidence that few teenagers can muster. He was tall, handsome, rich, and inspired. He

---

4. Howard's grandparents were disgusted with his negotiations for the company so soon after the death of their son, and agreed to sell their interest in Hughes Tool in exchange for $10. Felix Hughes was not as accommodating. He held out for the inflated sum of $250,000 and received it all in a cash transfer.

moved through the stately mansion on Yoakum Street, master of his domain, his heels clicking on the marble floors, his teeth visible through a smile. Emerging into the backyard, he walked amid the statues and sculpted hedges; the azaleas and eugenia planted by his mother. Looking up, he saw his destiny. There on the edge of space, it was written in the sky.

Freedom

Things I want to be,
1. The best golfer in the world.
2. The best ~~flyer~~ pilot.
3. The most famous producer
*   of moving pictures.*

Houston, Texas
January 5, 1925
Hughes' goals as written on the back of a
receipt from Foley's men's store.

SOME MOMENTS ARE ETCHED IN MEMORY FOREVER, translucent yet indelible. For Howard Hughes, such a moment occurred on the fourth of January, 1925. He was alone as usual—not bored, just existing—without a job or necessary purpose in life. It was early afternoon. He was walking along the edge of Rice Institute and found himself passing the section of Houston known as Shadyside. Ahead was the home of Joseph Cullinan, a magnanimous oil man and friend of his father's, who had built an estate on Remington Lane and its surrounding thirty-seven acres. He called his house Shadyside, which had then given its name to the entire development of large, stately homes being built on his subdivided land. Most were incomplete and empty. Dried leaves lay matted and unswept in the gutter, the branches of the great oaks naked against the harsh winter breeze.

Howard stopped and allowed his eyes to roam across the houses, each representing an outward display of amassed wealth and successful careers. It was then, at that moment, he realized that any one of these homes could be his. At nineteen years of age, he had entered that rarified niche of humanity known as endless fortune. With no hall monitor or crossing guard to guide his way or correct his behavior, he was the foremost explorer of either unlimited opportunity or unbridled excess—take your pick. As he stared out at the mansions rising before him, he knew the choice was his to make. It was the ultimate scary thought—that most coveted of dreams that those without money long to possess, yet when faced with its actual delivery would be no more prepared to leap into the quagmire of excess privilege than he was. This would take some concentration, he knew, and he immediately began to consider his options.

The initial reflections that came to mind were of those things he did not want to do. Run his father's business, for instance. He had little desire to sit in an office in Houston, Texas, and sell drill bits. In fact, he had little desire to be in Houston at all. He had Col. Robert Kuldell to run Hughes Tool, the man hand-picked by his father.

On the back of a receipt from Foley Bros., a clothing store, he wrote the words *HUGHES TOOL*, and then promptly crossed it out. Thinking again, he topped the small piece of paper with *Things I want to be*, carefully contemplating his response. Finally, certain of his answer, he wrote, "1. The best golfer in the world." Satisfied with that, he began to place the receipt down when he stopped and added, "2. The best flyer." He wanted to fly. No, more than that, he thought, he wanted to be a *pilot*, crossed out the word "flyer" and wrote "pilot" next to it instead. Now certain he had his life planned, Howard put the paper on his dresser next to his sterling silver comb-and-brush set, and began to live his future. It would be several more days before he added a third line to the list. "3. The most famous producer of moving pictures."

He showed the list to only one person—Ella Rice, his classmate from Miss Eichler's University and the girl he intended to marry. At twenty-two, dark-haired, thin, elegant, and the epitome of breeding and refinement, Ella was not, and never had been, impressed by Howard Hughes. Although she had always ignored Miss Eichler's rule never to speak to "that Hughes boy" when he arrived late to school (Ella and her best friend Margaret were the first to befriend the thin, shy student), such courtesies did not extend to marriage. When Howard first brought up the subject on one of their early dates in 1925, she laughed off the suggestion with a wave of a hankie. When he showed her his list and asked her again, she told him of her love for James Winston, "the dearest boy in all the world," to whom she was informally engaged.

Unfazed by her rejection, Howard took his plea to a higher power: his Aunt Annette. He told his aunt that he was moving to California and wanted Ella for his wife. "Howard came to me and asked me to go and convince Aunt Mattie[1] to let Ella marry him, and I was against it. I didn't think he ought to. I thought he ought to go to Rice," Annette later recalled. "But I went and asked her. Somehow I convinced Aunt Mattie she ought to let Ella marry Howard. I said, 'I can't send him with all that money to California with all those vampire movie people.' And Aunt Mattie agreed with me."

While Annette Lummis' plea held influence, it was hardly enough to sway Ella Rice. This was Houston in the deep South, where arranged marriages were commonplace, to insure a young girl's position and future. Love was not an integral ingredient in the recipe, so it did not factor into the conversation that Mrs. David Rice had with her daughter. While Mattie talked of money, Ella talked of James. While mother spoke of security, daughter spoke of romance. In the end, security won out. James Winston was a young, promising financier with no capital but lots of potential. Howard Hughes was a sure thing. And so it was that Ella Rice said yes to a boy she hardly knew, and turned her back on one she loved with all her heart.

Howard Hughes was not in love. He saw in Ella Rice a functional prop who could provide him with the necessary illusion of maturity as he began his journey into adulthood and the three items on his to-be list—a list that he now had pinned to the wall next to his bedroom dresser. He duplicated his goals in a notebook he had purchased at the F.W. Woolworth store on Fannin Street. It was small enough to fit into his shirt pocket, for ready access; and it soon began to fill with notes on Texas inheritance laws.

While Ella and her sister Libbie planned her wedding, Howard was busy planning his estate. He wanted to protect his newly inherited fortune, and set about writing a will that preserved its bulk while providing for his future wife. After several meetings with attorney Frank Andrews, and seeming endless corrections and updates, Howard signed his first, and perhaps only, will. It was executed on May 30, 1925, two days before his marriage.

He bequeathed $10,000 to his friend Dudley Sharp; $15,000 to his late mother's brother Chilton; $25,000 to his mother's sister Martha; and $100,000 plus the Yoakum Street house to his dear Aunt Annette. To Ella Rice, he left $500,000 in "first-class, high grade securities to be delivered to her by my Executors as soon after my death as can conveniently be arranged." In addition, he bequeathed Ella an annuity of $50,000 a year for life. Additionally, he set up a lifelong pension of $20 per week for Lily Adams and John Farrel, who he identified as "my colored household servants." There was also an arrangement for small dividends to be paid

---

1. Mattie Rice was Ella's mother, and related to Annette's husband, Fred.

from the profits of Hughes Tool Company to several of the firm's executives.

The bulk of the estate was transferred to a corporation named the Howard R. Hughes Medical Research Laboratories to be based in Houston. The purpose of the business was to be "the prosecution of scientific research for the discovery and development of antitoxins for the prevention, and specific remedies for the cure, of the most important and dangerous diseases to which this section of the country may be subjected." Howard specifically cautioned that this corporation was not to be a school for doctors, but rather a "laboratory devoted to discovery and development." Heady stuff for a teenager to consider, and an attestation of things to come.

"THE WEDDING OF Miss Ella Rice, daughter of Mr. and Mrs. David Rice, and Howard Robard Hughes took place Monday evening, at 7 o'clock at the home of the bride's brother and sister," the *Houston Post-Dispatch* announced in its "Society" column on June 2, 1925. The bride made a "beautiful picture" according to the *Houston Chronicle* as she walked down the aisle through her sister's rose garden at her just-finished home at 10 Remington Lane. "She wore an exquisite wedding costume of soft white chiffon and rare old rosepoint lace, with a court train of tulle and silver ribbon, over which fell the filmy folds of her sweeping tulle veil held in place with a cap of the rosepoint lace adjusted with orange blossoms and gardenias," the *Chronicle*'s society columnist wrote.

The local Berge Orchestra played *Lohengrin* as she swept in on the arm of her father. Hughes' Aunt Annette and Ella's sister Libbie were the matrons-of-honor, dressed in matching apricot chiffon gowns, as was Laura Rice, Ella's cousin and her maid-of-honor. Dudley Sharp was Hughes' best man and his only friend at the ceremony. Other than his Aunt Annette, no other member of Hughes' family attended his wedding, for no other members were invited. The ceremony that the *Houston Chronicle* called "a notable event of the year on the social calendar," was also its most hastily arranged. After eating a meal of pheasant stuffed with grapes, carrots glazed with syrup and broiled new potatoes, the bride and groom left her sister's home to begin their three-month honeymoon in New York and Long Island—a time of sightseeing, shopping, and sailing.

Whatever sexual curiosity occurred between the two virgins apparently took place in their compartment aboard the train to the east coast, for when the couple arrived at the Vanderbilt Hotel, they were booked, not in the honeymoon suite with its canopied double bed, wood-burning fireplace and romantic claw-foot bathtub for two, but in the Cornelius Suite with two separate bedrooms, each housing a single bed, divided by a large living room with a grand piano from Germany, two carved sofas from France, a Chinese armoire, and Tiffany lamps. Multi-cultural, to be sure, but hardly conducive to romance.

By October, the pair had returned to Houston just long enough to pack their winter clothes and head to Hollywood, where the Hugheses took up residence in the Ambassador Hotel, just as Big Howard had done several years earlier. They had two Rolls Royce Silver Cloud automobiles shipped from New York, established two separate bank accounts at the Bank of America on Wilshire Boulevard, opened two separate house charges at the hotel, and set about living two separate lives. As Ella was being introduced to the society matrons like the Dohenys and the Chandlers, Howard began advertising for an "executive assistant," as he maneuvered his way into a career in show business.

A 36-year-old one-time fistfighter turned certified public accountant working at the reputable firm of Haskins and Sells heard about the job search from an associate and showed up one morning in early November at the Hugheses suite in the Ambassador Hotel. Hughes had just returned from a round of golf and was attired in knickers, argyle socks, a white, short-sleeve shirt, and a knit beret. The accountant, five-foot seven, thick shouldered, and wearing a three-piece suit took one look at the tall, thin, 19-year-old and stifled a laugh. "Dietrich?" Hughes asked. "I'm Hughes." First Sonny, then Howard, now Hughes; his names were falling like apples from the tree of youth. With a handshake that Noah Dietrich remembered as firm and long, Hughes invited the accountant inside, and sat him down in a living room of heavy furniture and thick brocades.

As Dietrich handed Hughes his résumé, he launched into a recitation of his job history, from bank teller to auditor to CPA. He never mentioned that he was the son of a Wisconsin minister or once worked for the Doheny Oil Company. Hughes listened unsmiling, and then excused himself. He had forgotten to tally his golf game, and handed the accountant his score card. Without being asked, Dietrich totaled the numbers for the 18 holes in his head, and handing the card back to Hughes, said, "78," before continuing to reflect on his qualifications without missing a beat.

It was the kind of response that only a boy-man like Howard Hughes would find a deal-clincher. He told Dietrich about Hughes Tool Company, his father's untimely death, and his desire to enter the film business as a producer. He asked him how a battleship found its target, about the workings of an internal combustion engine, and got tangled in an argument about the virtues of the offset crankshaft. When the last came to a draw, Dietrich was dismissed and went back to being an accountant without a clue as to how the interview had gone.

He found out that he had been hired when Hughes sent for him again, on Thanksgiving Day, and offered $10,000 a year for his services—an offer Dietrich accepted. Pulled away from his family, Dietrich had no idea that Hughes failed to realize it was a holiday. Despite a history of joyful holiday celebrations spent with his family, the new Hughes, the adult Hughes, celebrated none ever again. It took Dietrich only until Christmas to fully comprehend that fact when he was called again on Christmas to travel to Houston with his boss.

It was not a visit Hughes wanted to make, but he had little choice. There was only one person who could still give him orders and expect him to listen, and that person—his Aunt Annette—had spoken. The telegram she sent was short and to the point: "You have a wife in Houston who needs you. Return home immediately."

Ella Hughes had traveled back to her parents' home in Texas shortly after Thanksgiving at her husband's request. Under the pretense of preparing their Yoakum Street home for Christmas, Howard shipped her to Houston with $12,000 and orders to wait for his arrival. In the four weeks he had spent with his wife in California, he found her clutching and a petty annoyance. It was a problem he had not anticipated. Faced with having to actually spend time being a real husband, he manipulated her sense of duty and turned it into a tool to rid himself of her interference.

Once back in Houston, she waited for her husband's return, certain that he would keep his word to join her in a few days. What she failed to realize: California without Ella became Hughes' giant playground. He went to the hotel's Cocoanut Grove and met struggling Hollywood starlets only too eager to be spoiled by the handsome Hughes, with his deep pockets and Rolls Royce. While Ella was pining for her husband and attempting to explain his absence, Hughes was discovering how to be a playboy. It did not matter that he had little experience, Hollywood was full of women who were anxious to teach him what he did not know.

When Hughes neither arrived in Houston nor telephoned, Ella sent telegrams—several dozen of them, each one more desperate than the last—attempting to understand how their honeymoon had dissolved into first separate bedrooms and then separate states. As Christmas approached, she became frantic. When he refused to accept her telephone calls, she wired, "Cannot understand why I have not heard from you. Am counting on you leaving Los Angeles tomorrow." By Christmas Eve, she was beyond worry. "Did you attend to my bank account? If not please do so as I want to give the servants their Christmas money immediately. Be sure and tell me you are leaving tomorrow." As usual, Hughes ignored her pleas, and at that point, Annette Lummis stepped in.

Not wanting to face his loveless marriage and a wife he saw as nothing more than a business accessory, he instructed Noah Dietrich that they would be traveling on Christmas Day to Houston. This was not to be a short visit, but rather a lengthy stay to allow Hughes to wrap up all his business in Texas, pay his taxes, and establish a permanent base in California. While Hughes moved back into the Yoakum Street house, Dietrich brought his wife and two girls to stay in a large suite at the Rice Hotel, then splendid in its Christmas decorations. The three months Hughes spent in Texas would be his last, except for infrequent day trips to his hometown. Texas and its oil belonged to his father. Howard Hughes Jr. was walking his own path.

Returning to California in April, 1926, Texas now a memory and his wife still in Houston, Hughes became increasingly focused on achieving his three life goals. In an effort to improve his golf game, he joined the Wilshire Country Club and scheduled a daily game with either George Von Elm, then the U.S. National Amateur Champion, or Ozzie Carlton, a state champ from Texas. Both men were paid to coach Hughes on his game, and managed to improve it to the extent that he lowered his handicap to two.

While golf was a learned skill, the art of movie-making was a talent that required far more than instruction. The fledgling film business was fast becoming Hollywood's mainstay, but entering the industry from the top was more of a challenge than young Hughes had imagined. It was risky business, and Hughes was not spared from learning his lesson the hard way.

Ralph Graves[2] was a striking 6' 2" actor with over three dozen films and comedy shorts to his credit when Hughes first met him on the links at the Wilshire Country Club. The personable, handsome performer regaled the young millionaire with stories of glamorous parties and life on the set. It was an off-limit world that Hughes intended to conquer, and to the now 20-year-old rich kid from Texas, Ralph Graves looked like his ticket to cinema central.

Graves happened to mention to Hughes that he had written a film. It took little coaxing before the natural-born ham was acting out each scene and playing all roles, including the dog. Like many actors at the time, Graves was attempting to move behind the camera and gain experience as a director. He had arrived in Hollywood as a fresh-faced 17-year-old and by 1926 had already worked with silent-film luminaries D.W. Griffith, Mack Sennett, Gloria Swanson, Lillian Gish, and Frank Capra.

2. Ralph Graves' real name was Ralph Horsburgh. He was born in Cleveland, Ohio, in 1900, came to Hollywood in 1917, and continued acting until 1949. He died in Santa Barbara, California in 1977.

As each man moved to seize the opportunity before him, it took but a handshake to open a new chapter in show business history. When Graves told Hughes that he needed $40,000 for the film's budget, the gullible Texan never flinched as he took out his checkbook and gave the actor the entire amount.

As Graves began the picture, Hughes haunted the set, just as he had done several years earlier with his uncle. Taking copious notes in his Woolworth book, Hughes dogged the actors and cameramen, questioning everything they were doing. When he returned to the Ambassador exhausted at night, there were always several telegrams from his wife, first asking, then pleading to be allowed to return to California.

"I shall stay here as long as you think best in spite of the fact that it is against my judgment and desire," she wrote in early May. "Can't imagine why I haven't heard from you," she lamented mid-month. "Have you forgotten about the fun we had in New York?" she asked in late May. "Please, please, write and tell me when I may return." Finally, unable to hold her at bay any longer, Hughes relented and Ella finally boarded a train to Los Angeles during the first week of June.

By that point, Ralph Graves had spent the $40,000 and would ask for another $40,000 more before he had finished Hughes' first film, titled *Swell Hogan*. When Hughes screened the finished picture, he discovered that however wonderful an actor Graves may have been, he had little talent as a director. *Swell Hogan* was said to have been such an embarrassment that Hughes ordered the projectionist to burn the only print, and to never mention its contents to anyone. Hughes was $80,000 poorer, but a whole lot wiser. He would not make the same mistake on film number two.

Three weeks after the official burning of *Swell Hogan*, it was one of those harsh, bright days in Los Angeles when even the crows hide from the sun. Hughes had not allowed the heat to keep him off the greens at the Wilshire Country Club, but by the time he had played nine holes of golf, his lungs were burning from the smell of dried grass. Wiping off his woods, he stumbled across an old friend of his uncle's in the clubhouse. Marshall Ambrose Neilan had been a director in Hollywood for over a dozen years, and had known Hughes' Uncle Rupert for much of that time. He had even made a cameo appearance playing himself in *Souls for Sale*.

Neilan, like everyone else in Hollywood, had an idea for a new picture. His was plotted around five bachelors and a baby. He filled his pitch with plenty of yuk and pathos, slapping Hughes on the back like a long-lost friend. It took only moments for him to realize that Hughes was no longer as interested in the money-hungry movie business. He had learned his lesson, and might not have ever made another film if it had not been for a call from drunken Uncle Rupert, lashing out at his nephew for his naivete in funding *Swell Hogan*. It took only his uncle's arrogant advice to quit the business to persuade Hughes that he had to prove him wrong.

He hired Marshall Neilan the following day and paid him $20,000 to direct *Everybody's Acting*. The film, budgeted at $150,000, made Hughes over $75,000 in profit for the newly formed Caddo Productions, a sub-sidiary of Hughes' Caddo Company. It was enough to convince him to continue in production in early 1927 when Dietrich passed along another story idea, this one from writer Donald McGibney titled *Two Arabian Nights*. Hughes was driven to make another film quickly, for less than three weeks earlier, he had placed his first director under contract, and guaranteed the man a three-picture deal with Caddo Productions. Working or not, the Russian-born Lewis Milestone was being paid. Recently dumped by Warner Bros. studios after a bitter contract dispute, Milestone was hired by Hughes at a time when no other studio would take a risk on the temperamental talent.

Two Arabian Nights starred William Boyd (who would later reach fame as Hopalong Cassidy on television), Louis Wolheim, Mary Astor, and Boris Karloff in a comedy set during World War I. Hughes arrived each day on the set, eager to be inspired and instructed. Astor nicknamed the young producer "Faunt," a veiled reference to Frances Hodgson Burnett's *Little Lord Fauntleroy*. "There was Howard Hughes scribbling in a tiny notebook, sitting in a corner," Astor wrote in her notes for her autobiography, *My Story*. "Every day, he was dressed in some new outfit that looked as if it had just been taken out of the box. There we were run-ning around being crazy, and Howard just seemed afraid to smile."

If Mary Astor did not see Hughes smile, it was only because she was not around when he was told by Dietrich that the film made $614,000 profit. It subsequently won a Best Director of a Comedy Oscar for Milestone in the first Academy Awards presentation held in the Blossom Room of the Hollywood Roosevelt Hotel. More than just smiling, Hughes was crowing, particularly when he thought of his smug Uncle Rupert, who had neither an Oscar to his credit, nor the $614,000 in his pocket.

On May 21, 1927, Charles A. Lindbergh successfully piloted the first non-stop solo transatlantic flight in his single-engine plane, the *Spirit of St. Louis*.[3] It was a flight that captivated an envious Hughes who eagerly

---

3. Lindbergh won a $25,000 prize for his flight. Businessman Raymond Orteig sponsored the contest to generate interest in his Hotel Lafayette at University Place and East 9th Street in New York. Orteig was a one-time maitre d', and attracted a large celebrity clientele to his hotel based on good service and French food. The hotel was demolished in 1953 to make way for the six-story Lafayette Apartments.

sought details of the journey, and forced him to squarely face his last goal. He was eager to return to the sky, and hired a pilot to teach him to fly.

Each day on the golf course, Hughes would see a barnstormer tip his wings in salute as he flew his bi-plane back to Clover Field in nearby Santa Monica. He copied the plane's I.D. number off its wing and tracked down the flyer to a small shack on the far end of the field where his Waco-6 stunt plane was hangared. Hughes offered the man $100 a day to teach him to fly. J. B. Alexander later said he would have taken the job for a quarter of the price.

Howard Hughes was a natural when it came to flying, according to Alexander, who rated his talent with any in the sky. Each day when the pair would take to the air, Hughes found his shyness disappearing as the air thinned and the clouds turned to wisps of white dew on the windshield. If there was a God, Hughes found Him there, for at 12,000 feet he was in heaven.

It was then, in mid-1927, that Howard Hughes, at twenty-one years old, knew he was living his dream. While it was true he had not won any amateur golf tournaments, he won nearly all the games that he played, and, for Hughes, that was a more personal triumph. True, he had not gotten his pilot's license, but he was flying every day, his hands on the throttle. And Caddo Productions had signed a distribution deal with United Artists Pictures to screen his films in theaters across the country. Things even seemed to be settling down with his marriage, if only because his beautiful wife was beginning to get used to being sent home to her mother.

As his reputation began to slowly grow around Hollywood, Hughes decided he wanted to move into what he labeled "a suitable house." He assigned Dietrich the task of locating the place, but not before listing his requirements. He wanted a home not "directly adjacent to street traffic, with an entrance suitable for multiple automobiles." Additionally, he wanted a house that had "windows that opened on all floors, with metal screens permanently attached to prevent insects from nesting inside" and one that had a "stone or marble floor in any area used for the preparation of food."

After much searching and some intense negotiation, Dietrich settled on a house located at 211 South Muirfield Road in the Hancock Park section of Los Angeles. The seven-bedroom house was owned by a widow named Eva K. J. Fudger, who had never heard about the wealthy heir to the Hughes Tool fortune. She stalled for over a month, before she could decide whether a "child without obvious gainful employment" could be counted on to pay the $1,000 a month she expected for her home.

Eventually, Mrs. Fudger decided Hughes was responsible enough to occupy the house her husband had built and she had carefully furnished with "appropriate antiques and *objets d'art*." Hughes had to pay her $6,000 in advance–not as a security deposit (there was no clause for security in the rental agreement), but rather for the first six months' rent in advance. The remaining rent was due on the first of each month and payable to the "A.P. Johnson Company in the C.T. Johnson Building, at the northeast corner of Fourth and Broadway in said city of Los Angeles."

The house was a rather ominous-looking, Spanish-style mansion with a slate roof and thick, exposed brown beams. Casement windows bordered the entire second floor of the home, flooding the rooms with light in the morning. The entrance hall was reached through a heavy, solid oak door with a wrought-iron knocker. Beyond the entrance, down a hall, was the living room with stone fireplace. A study, dining room, butler's pantry, kitchen, kitchen pantry, maid's sitting room, laundry, bath and grand staircase completed the first floor.

The living room was baronial in size, and large enough to hold ten stuffed chairs, an overstuffed settee, an overstuffed couch, a four-foot long oak bench, nine antique end tables, a walnut chest, a Venetian lacquered secretary, eleven original works of art, twelve vases, a sterling silver bud vase, an ebony Steinway grand piano, and an antique Italian violin "beautiful enough to be the work of Stradivarius or one of his pupils." Across one entire wall was a built-in bookcase containing the entire works of Honore de Balzac; the *Encyclopedia Americana*; the works of James Fenimore Cooper; *The Life of Walter Pater* by Thomas Wright, and, appropriately, France Hodgson Burnett's *Little Lord Fauntleroy*.

Hughes' favorite room was the study. It faced the back yard, with its forsythia, bamboo and sycamore trees, that could be reached through French doors. The room contained an olive-wood, pedestal key-hole desk with a "carved vine and leaf design, and a top with Marquetry ribbon border," a Holtzclaw overstuffed davenport, two overstuffed easy chairs, four occasional chairs, six end tables, a bamboo footstool, a world globe on a mahogany stand, a Tabriz rug in rose, blue, and gold, plus a large fireplace on whose mantelpiece sat a French bronze 400-day clock that "was not to be over-wound for any reason."

The large dining room featured a round antique oak table seating eight, sterling silver flatware complete with oyster forks and a lemon spear, an oak sideboard filled with service pieces and coffee set, plus a complete set of Wedgewood china for twelve. The kitchen featured a six-burner Reliable gas stove with two ovens and a broiler, and, unusual for the time, a Frigidaire electric "cooling system" for fresh meats and dairy.

On the second floor were a master suite and four guest bedrooms, each with its own dressing room and bath, plus two maid's rooms, a sewing room, plus broom and linen closets. While Hughes officially occupied the master suite with its carved French maple single bed with a feather mattress and duvet cover, Ella was assigned the room down the hall in the corner, and slept in a brass single bed with "portable foot warmer." The only double bed in the entire house was located in a room called the "Southwest Chamber," and was reserved for visitors, of which there were none—at least officially.

In Ella's absence, Hughes began to flagrantly violate their marriage troth, inviting starlets to the home where Robert G. Quantrill, the gardener who lived over the two-car garage, would observe his employer and various women "making whoopee" on the living room davenport. Quantrill, who had been paid $25 per week by Mrs. Fudger, found his salary increased to $50 by virtue of his uncanny ability to ignore what he saw while trimming the hedges and tending the flower beds.

As Hughes was occupied building his reputation as the newest playboy in town, his wife was taking a summer holiday with her sister at Pecketts-on-Sugar Hill in Franconia, New Hampshire. Amid the thick maple trees and bucolic country lanes of the picturesque New England village, Ella attempted to forget what she saw as her husband's deliberate effort to humiliate her in front of her friends, family and all of Hollywood. There was little evidence that she succeeded, however, for while she was quite willing to forgive her husband's dalliances, she could not forgive his immaturity that caused them. He had simply failed to grow mentally into his physical body that, at this point, was craved by women as much for its appearance as any fringe benefits his wealth might offer.

Not about to give up on her marriage, Ella hoped to entice Hughes away from Hollywood and his "vices"—under that category, she included movies, golf, and flying. And she had the ultimate carrot to hang on the stick. Ella mentioned that Charles Lindbergh was coming to Manchester, New Hampshire, just ninety miles south of Franconia. It was part of his celebrated victory tour that followed his record-setting flight. While not taking the bait, Hughes nevertheless was still curious.

"Were you able to see Lindberg [sic]?" Hughes asked in a telegram he sent Ella on July 26, 1927. "And did he live up to your fair expectation? And how was the sweet little *Spirit of St. Louis?*" Totally oblivious to the fact that his wife was enduring painful emotional turmoil, his self-absorption was obvious. "Am going to try to qualify in the Brentwood Invitational Tournament this afternoon. Talked to Ozzie the other day and he says he will be able to come out for the Del Monte Tournament, so I'm trying to get my work cleaned up before the tournament. I really have no business going, on account of the picture, and I have been playing very badly lately. Although maybe I will pep up when I get a chance to play a little more often. I have only played about three times in the last two weeks. Am having a lot of trouble getting the picture started."

Hughes was referring to the film *Hell's Angels*. He had been given the story for the picture by Marshall Neilan, and it was a film that Hughes felt he had to make. More than just a film about flyers, it was a film about flying. The story followed two brothers in the British Royal Flying Corp., and both in love with the same dissolute woman. It was World War I, the Germans were acting up, and it was up to the brothers to save the day and each other, or die trying. While the melodramatic script was being written by Harry Behn and Howard Estabrook, Hughes began to work with director Neilan on designing the most realistic aerial war sequences ever filmed.

The excitement of this moment seemed to crystallize all of Hughes hopes, fears, and ambitions and wrapped them in the illusion of reality. The world of Howard Hughes was of his own creation. Every person, every costume, every scrap of scene decoration—all became his personal domain, and with an eye to detail that frustrated as it impressed, he began to take control.

The first casualty of his obsession was Ella. While she was used to being ignored, now she was no longer even tolerated. Hughes had zero time for whining, zero tolerance for romance, and absolutely no interest in those who did. And at the top of that list was Ella Rice Hughes. She came back to Los Angeles to find herself in a new home with an old problem—lots of time and no husband. When he was at home on Muirfield, he locked himself in the downstairs study, a room that had been transformed into an office, bedroom, and sanctuary that Ella was forbidden to enter.

On the set, Hughes was micro-managing each and every aspect of *Hell's Angels* to the point that Neilan could no longer even concentrate, let alone plan his direction. In late August, 1927, he walked out of the *Hell's Angels* offices at Metropolitan Studios, slamming the door behind him. The next day, Hughes replaced him with Luther Reed, the former aviation editor of the *Herald Tribune*, and a director under contract to Paramount. Hughes suggested, Hughes needled, Hughes overruled to the point that on September 30, Reed threw up his hands and shouted the immortal words: "If you know so much about it, why don't you direct the damn thing yourself." That was all Howard Hughes needed to hear. He accepted the challenge and when interior shooting began for the film on Halloween Day in 1927, it was Hughes sitting in the director's chair. With a cast of 34, a crew of 116, and over 1000 extras, *Hell's Angels* was set to enter the record books as the most expensive film in the short history of motion pictures.

Pulling over a million dollars from the growing coffers of the Hughes Tool Company, Hughes hired stunt pilot Frank Tomick to scour the country for British and German planes. There were precious few to be found, so work began on transforming Curtiss Jennies into replicas of British Avros, and Sikorskys into German Gotha bombers. Noah Dietrich found a pasture in Van Nuys, California, that Hughes named Caddo Field and began assembling the planes among the startled cows.

Stunt pilots were handpicked by Armstrong who was given the title Chief of Aeronautics. Names like Roscoe Turner, Al Wilson, Ira Reed, Hank Coffin, Garland Lincoln, Ross Cooke, Leo Nomis, and Maurice and Stewart Murphy would be uncredited despite risking their lives performing daredevil feats that had never before been tried, much less filmed.

Stars Ben Lyon and James Hall were contracted to play the lead actors with Norwegian actress Greta Nissen hired as their tart. Young blond John Darrow was cast to co-star as German Zeppelin crew member Karl Armstedt, with pilots Frank Clarke and Roy Wilson paged to play flyers in the film. Hughes' rapport with Lyon was groomed by the actor's reputation as a ladies' man, urged on by Lyon's messy and highly publicized breakup with Marilyn Miller, a major musical star on Broadway who had just divorced Mary Pickford's brother, Jack, an MGM sound engineer. Hughes found far less in common with the prudish Hall, who had a tan so dark it was nearly audible. Around Greta Nissen, Hughes found himself nervous, a reaction to her heavy Scandinavian accent and dominating personality. He looked upon her as something begat by Frigga, Norse goddess of the sky.

Despite the pressure of sixteen-hour days on the film set, Hughes managed to spare some extra moments to maintain his current status as Hollywood's most notorious playboy. He bummed rides on stunt planes to Palm Springs, Del Mar, and San Diego, California, using the excursions as unsubtle excuses to meet and bed struggling starlets. Lyon encouraged Hughes' outrages on these trips, at times having two or three of these unaware actresses bedded in different rooms of the same hotel.

It was the Roaring Twenties, a time when nightclubbing and flappers mixed with gangsters and easy money. Prohibition and speakeasies flourished, and with them a sense that amoral behavior was not only acceptable, but encouraged. And nowhere was it encouraged more than in Hollywood. Hughes seemed to take the nation's heartbeat as permission to slip ever deeper into a lifestyle that was not only physically damaging, but morally corrupt.

With the dawn of 1928, *Hell's Angels* interior scenes were complete, leaving only the aerial combat sequences to be filmed. To coincide with the start of aerial photography, Hughes was granted his first pilot's license on January 7. No longer dependent on others for his spur-of-the-moment flights of fancy, Hughes bought his own Waco plane, and kept it fueled and ready at Mines Field[4] in Inglewood. He bought acres of land surrounding the airfield to serve as a base of production, and built a replica of the British Royal Flying Corps. there.

He mounted cameras inside planes, a technique that had never been attempted before, and began to film dogfights between the ersatz Germans and British. With seventy-eight planes in his film's inventory, Hughes owned more planes than anyone in the world, outside of the air forces of several countries. It was inevitable that as dozens of planes flew overhead, he would feel the need to participate. That time came in late January when the scene being shot was a dangerous one.

Against the advice of his crew, he leaped into a small Thomas Morse scout plane and took off to join his stunt pilots in the air. As the cameras rolled, Hughes' plane went into a sudden tailspin and shot toward the ground. Hughes was only beginning to bring the plane up from its free fall, when it slammed into the ground, its propeller digging into the macadam runway, landing gear splintering, and wings ripped from the fuselage.

The following day, newspaper reports of the crash suggested that Hughes walked away from the accident, "waving a lucky Stetson hat and wiping off soot and grime." In fact, the playboy was lucky to be alive. Trapped inside the cockpit, he was pulled to safety by his crew and rushed via ambulance to Inglewood Hospital where he was in a coma with a crushed cheekbone and numerous lacerations. In the days that followed the accident, Hughes had plastic surgery on his face. Subsequent photos show a subtle difference. Gone was the cleft in his chin.

At the time of the crash, Ella Hughes was in Houston with her sister. When notified of the accident by Noah Dietrich, she immediately returned to Los Angeles, only to be berated by her husband for over-reacting to the situation. She pleaded with him to cut his work schedule and hire another director for *Hell's Angels*. It was a suggestion that impacted their marriage in the most fundamental way. Hughes considered *Hell's Angels* to be his baby, spools of celluloid to be sure, but if possible to be wrapped in flesh, it would have been no less meaningful than a first-born son. To suggest abandoning the project was a huge misjudgment on Ella's part. The couple moved to opposite corners of the ring of marriage, and prepared for a fight.

---

4. Mines Field was later enlarged and renamed Los Angeles International Airport.

Hughes threw the first punch by announcing to Ella that not only was he not curtailing his work schedule, he had added two new pictures onto his slate. *The Mating Call* was based on a novel by Rex Beach[5] and written by Herman Mankiewicz, who would later go on to share an Oscar award with Orson Welles for their script of *Citizen Kane*.[6] The drama about a marriage of convenience starred Thomas Meighan and Evelyn Brent, and barely recouped its $400,000 budget. *The Racket* based on a play by Bartlett Cormack also starred Meighan as well as Louis Wolheim from *Two Arabian Nights*. It was gangster drama directed by Lewis Milestone, and based on the life of Al Capone. If *Hell's Angels* was his baby, *Mating Call* and *Racket* were Hughes' step-children. Their addition into his already full work schedule eliminated any hope that Ella may have harbored for a normal married life.

Being a woman of the South, she was raised to expect adversity, and initially responded to Hughes' declaration of intent in typical Southern style. She decided to throw a dinner party to which were invited many of her husband's Hollywood co-workers in addition to her society friends. Happy that Ella was involved in a project, Hughes encouraged her activity, fully aware of its date and size. A few days before the Saturday gala the last week of September, 1928, Ella began to pin notes to the door of her husband's study. As the notes would disappear, she would leave another in its place.

On the night of the dinner, Rolls Royces, Deusenbergs, and Packards lined the Muirfield house driveway. Society matrons dripping in jewels and their husbands armed with cigars and success, began to arrive at the appointed hour and were served martinis from Hughes' special supply of bootlegged gin. The show biz contingent were not quite as prompt but began to trickle in, donned in sports clothes and flashy dresses that spoke to attention and the fashion of the moment. Since members of the one group did not know members of the other, the two cabals of Hollywood staked out their own section of the living room and uneasily stalked it as if waiting for prey.

Ella Hughes, floating in a gossamer gown of peach organdy and desperate over the fact that her husband was not there to greet their guests, smiled bravely as she sprinted between the divergent groups with the anxiety of a prep-school freshman on Parents' Day.

The two groups had moved into the dining room and were seated eating when Hughes finally arrived. He was wearing a soiled white shirt with cuffs rolled to the elbows, tan corduroy slacks, and dirty tennis shoes

---

5. Rex Beach wrote a number of novels that were turned into films, most famously *The Spoilers*, which was filmed five times over the years.
6. Mankiewicz appeared uncredited in the film as a newspaperman.

without socks. According to Noah Dietrich, he sat down at the table without greeting a soul, announced that he had worked late at the studio, and said, "I'm hungry." Diving into his meal, he mixed vegetables, meat, and salad together, washed it down with a glass of chilled water, pushed back his chair, and with a simple, "Excuse me," left the room and locked himself in his study.

For Ella, that evening sealed the fate of the marriage and her life in Los Angeles. She finished her meal calmly chatting with her guests, walked with them as they left the house, closed the front door, turned out the lights, and went upstairs to pack her bags. She never saw her husband to say goodbye.

A Star Named Billie
A Mistress Named Angel

I know I promised, but I hope you understand
why I can not be with you again today.
It is crucial that I deal with Warners
regarding your contract. I am only
thinking of you in this regard.
Love,
—Howard

Los Angeles, California
August 1, 1930
Hughes' note to actress Billie Dove
enclosed with a pair of diamond earrings.

HOWARD HUGHES FIRST MET SILENT FILM STAR BILLIE
Dove at the Starlight Ballroom inside the Biltmore Hotel in
downtown Los Angeles. The place was crowded with the
glamorous people who seemed to move from party to party
with the diligence of bees gathering pollen. Against the polished dance floor and muted rhythms of a swing band, they
pulsed with the studied movement of choreographed beauties,
all trying to capture their own share of a scattered spotlight.
All except Billie Dove.[1]

Dubbed the "American Beauty," Billie was physical perfection. Rather than move to the center of the stage, she
demanded the spotlight come to her. Her flawless creamy
complexion, large hazel eyes, and pouting lips meshed with
an exciting, electric personality that snared men with such
ease that they were eager to be trapped by her elixir of illu-

---

1. Billie Dove's real name was Lillian Bohny. She was born on May 14, 1903
and nicknamed Billie as a child.

sion. When Hughes walked past the beauty, surrounded by an adoring throng, he was mesmerized by an attraction he could not define. Marion Davies could. The mistress of publishing magnate William Randolph Hearst, Marion played matchmaker in her own direct fashion.

"Don't just pant in lust, Mr. Hughes," she said, wrapping her arm through his. "Come, I'll introduce you," pulling him through the crowd and toward the electric force at its core.

"Billie," she said. "This is Howard Hughes. He's been wanting to meet you."

Flushing in embarrassment, Hughes hung his head in characteristic shyness, and extended a hand as he looked out from underneath the brown bangs covering his eyes. "He just looked at me, not saying a word," Billie later said. "I thought that this couldn't be the man everyone was raving about. This millionaire."

Backing away bashfully, Hughes left Billie to wonder about the handsome stranger as he followed Marion across the crowded room. Yet, he was nothing if not persistent. The following night, at the Montmartre Café, Hughes appeared again. White suit, white tie, wing-tipped shoes, he was dashing but no less tongue-tied. This time, however, as Hughes extended his hand, Billie wrapped her own in his, and proceeded to pull him away from the crowd, leaving a group of disappointed admirers in their wake. "I've heard about you, Mr. Hughes. Is it all true?" she asked. Hughes tried to speak, but the words mixed in a ball that refused to budge beyond his mind. Taking his silence as verification, Billie added, "That's what I thought. I'm impressed."

During the first half of 1929, Billie would become more impressed with each passing day. She adored Hughes' need to be mothered and protected, loved the way he was able to take command over an entire organization yet fall helpless in her arms at night. His love-making was that of a child, uncertain, tentative. She liked that too, though she did not know why. It would have been an ideal pairing if it were not for the fact that he was still married. . . as was she.

Ella's hasty departure had cleared the Muirfield mansion for a love nest, and Hughes was not reluctant to bring the box-office champion into his home. His housekeeper, Beatrice Dowler, gave him looks of disapproval that he chose to ignore, right along with those of Noah Dietrich. What was harder to disregard was the wrath of Billie's husband, director Irwin Willat. He was a jealous and tyrannical man whose fits of rage were legend on the set and off. While Billie expressed no great love for her husband, and in fact had separated from him months before meeting Hughes, Willat was not about to allow her to flaunt their marriage break-up in public.

Hiring a private detective to follow his wife, Willat received weekly reports of her activities. He could have saved himself the trouble. Although he was clearly smitten, Hughes was also a realist. Any documented evidence of infidelity on his part might provide his wife with ammunition to sue for half his estate under Texas' community property divorce law. Love was one thing; his fortune another. While he allowed the affair to simmer in the background, his work load on *Hell's Angels* only increased.

After the production was nearly finished, Hollywood discovered sound. Talkies had finally come of age and suddenly *Hell's Angels* was looking terribly silent and dated to a producer who thought of himself on the cutting edge. At this point in production, Hughes had already invested $2 million of his own money in a film he was now certain would fail. Unwilling to allow that to happen, he decided to scrap all the dramatic scenes and reshoot the movie in sound. When Noah Dietrich heard the news, he had but one question: "How much?"

Hughes' latest impulse was budgeted at an additional million dollars. By the time shooting was completed, that number had jumped to $1.8 million. Yet, at this point, money was not Hughes' biggest problem. That honor fell at the feet of Greta Nissen. The star of his picture had such a thick Norwegian accent she was barely understandable and had to be replaced. Two years into production, Hughes was starting again: a new star had to be found, a new script written, new sets and wardrobe had to be created. As if that were not enough, he also had the challenge of teaching British and German accents to American stars.

To solve the latter problem, Hughes hired James Whale,[2] a British director who would later reach fame with his productions of *Frankenstein* and *Bride of Frankenstein*. Replacing Greta was not as simple. Unwilling to pay an established star to jump into the role, Hughes began to look at unknowns, hoping to strike gold while paying for pyrite. And he did just that when his production manager, Joseph W. Engel,[3] introduced him to a newcomer named Jean Harlow, being pushed on the movie by her agent, Arthur Landau. When she arrived for her screen test, Jean had "albino blonde hair" (unheard of at the time), a "puffy somewhat sulky little face," a dress that was so tight around the hips that writer Joseph Moncure March said she had "the shape of a dustpan," and a Missouri accent so strong she sounded like a "bar maid screaming for a fresh keg." Hughes took one look at her and left the room.

---

2. James Whale was the subject of the Oscar-winning film *Gods and Monsters*.
3. Joe Engel was an early Hollywood producer and at one time was president of Metro Pictures. He lost control of the studio when it merged with Louis B. Mayer Pictures to form Metro-Goldwyn-Mayer, and was reduced to being a studio guard before given work by Howard Hughes on *Hell's Angels*.

Jean rehearsed the six-minute screen test with Whale for over an hour. The scene called for her to seduce Ben Lyon, who patiently sat as the actress tried and failed to project sex appeal. Finally in frustration, she lashed out at Whale with impatience, "Just tell me, tell me how you want me to do it."

"I can tell you how to be an actress, but I can not tell you how to be a woman," the unflappably droll Whale was said to respond. Had it not been that she agreed to do the role for $1,500, the lowest fee allowed by the Screen Actors Guild, Harlow would never have gotten the part.

By the time Howard Hughes redesigned her image, however, she gave new meaning to *femme fatale*. On film, Jean Harlow was transformed. She wore a satin, bias-cut gown that displayed her ample figure, and the lighting dramatically highlighted her hair. Hughes later coined the phrase "Platinum Blonde" to describe its color, and the nickname "Baby" to describe Harlow.

With Whale bringing a British flavor to the set, and March writing new dialogue for the performers, Hughes was filming pages as soon as they left the typewriter in a breakneck schedule that was devouring the budget at the rate of $25,000 every twenty-four hours. After the day's shooting would wrap, Hughes continued working into the night, editing his spectacular flight sequences and adding necessary sound effects. It was a pace that no one, not even Howard Hughes, could maintain.

In the pre-dawn hours of May 31, 1929, Hughes arrived back at the Muirfield home, sweating profusely and stumbling as he walked into the kitchen. He poured himself a glass of water and began to head toward his study. It was there he was found the next morning by his housekeeper, lying on the Tabriz rug, unconscious and barely breathing, the broken water glass by his side. Suspecting that he was drunk, she called Noah Dietrich who arrived at the house within minutes. By that time, Hughes had begun to convulse.

Lifting his boss onto the sofa, Dietrich called Verne Mason, the doctor who had treated Hughes at Inglewood Hospital after his plane crash. When Dr. Mason arrived, he ordered Hughes carried to his bed and diagnosed him with bacterial meningitis, almost always fatal in the era before penicillin. For the next two days, Dietrich maintained a death watch over his boss, with round-the-clock nurses applying moist cool towels as the only available treatment.

On the third day, when Hughes failed to respond and continued in a coma-like state, Mason suggested that Dietrich alert Ella that her husband was dying. Given the hysteria with which Ella Hughes had left the Muirfield house, Dietrich hesitated, uncertain of the correct course of action. Finally, he telegraphed Ella, who was then in New York with her sister and about to board the cruise ship *Normandie* on their way to France.

"Howard dying. Stop. Dr. Mason advises return to Los Angeles. Stop." His telegram was to the point; written to convey the urgency he felt.

When Ella Hughes first received the message, she saw it as another ploy by her husband to exact sympathy. He had certainly used feigned illness in the past to get what he wanted. Yet, it suddenly appeared that, in this case, what he wanted was her. Thrilled to think that Hughes had finally realized the error of his ways, Ella made reservations to leave New York for Los Angeles on the next train. Her mind was churning imaginative scenarios of a husband longing to have her home, but unable to find the words to apologize.

Her sister Libbie remained unconvinced and considered Hughes to be a philanderer and prevaricator. She refused to allow Ella to make the long trip on her own and cancelled her own plans for the cruise, joining her sister on the Sante Fe Limited.

"Tell the doctor I am coming. Stop. Let him use his own judgment about informing Howard should Howard regain consciousness. Stop. Thanks for the message. Stop. Best wishes, Ella."

Hughes' fever broke later that afternoon and when he awoke, he found himself surrounded by a doctor, a nurse, his housekeeper, and his executive assistant. He had a three-day growth of beard, was damp with sweat, and incredibly hungry. Immediately upon discovering that his wife was on a train hurrying back to Los Angeles, however, he replaced appetite with anger. Dietrich defended sending the telegram based on the doctor's diagnosis—a diagnosis that ultimately proved wrong. He had not had meningitis after all, but rather severe influenza, Mason later determined.

Hughes wanted Ella stopped and turned back—at any price. Telegrams were sent to the Chicago Western Union office to be handcarried onto the train. Hughes personally reassured his wife of his recovery. "My temperature is down to 100 today. It is ridiculous for you to spend three days on the train so please go back to New York and call me from there. By all means, don't come."

According to Western Union, Ella received the telegram just as she left the dining car at 7:45 p.m. She read it, or more precisely misread it, interpreting the message as Hughes' way of showing he cared whether he was causing her inconvenience. Now more than ever, she was convinced of his restored interest in both her and their marriage. As the Sante Fe Limited streaked toward Pasadena, Hughes ordered his doctor, the nurse, and Dietrich out of his house. In their place, a concerned Billie

Dove arrived dressed in a lavender pelisse with matching feather boa.

Billie was still in the house when Ella arrived at the train station, met and driven to Muirfield by Noah Dietrich. It was only by luck and split-second timing that the two women did not collide in the entrance hall—Ella arriving through the front as Billie made a hasty exit through the rear. Unfortunately, when Ella entered her husband's room, he told her to leave. She did, but not before seeing a lavender boa draped across an arm chair.

Dietrich was stunned, Ella was furious, and Libbie was vindicated. Before her sister burst into tears, Libbie had Ella safely in Dietrich's car on the way back to the Pasadena train station. They had been in Hughes' Los Angeles house all of three minutes. They would never return again.

Ella Hughes went home to Houston where she filed for divorce from her husband of four years, citing "excesses and cruel treatment." The uncontested divorce was granted on December 9, 1929. In her divorce settlement, Ella Rice received $1.25 million payable in five $250,000 installments. At the time, Hughes' estimated worth was just over $30 million. He considered the settlement a bargain.

The stock market had crashed, the Great Depression had started, and Hughes was still not finished with *Hell's Angels*. The movie had now gone on for so long that it became the brunt of popular jokes. According to Jerome Beatty, writing in *American Magazine*, the wisecrackers would not let up. "A man was discovered who was celebrating his 105th birthday, and it was said that he was the only living person who could remember when *Hell's Angels* was started. It was predicted that airplanes would be as out-of-date as ox carts before the picture was released. They told of young men who went to work on *Hell's Angels* when it started, who were now giving up their jobs to their great-great-grandchildren." And on and on. Hughes heard them and ignored them all.

What he could not ignore was Irwin Willat. The coarse director was refusing to divorce his wife, and threatening to expose details of their love life to the reigning gossip queen, Louella Parsons. Hughes had no doubt that he would make good on his threat, and offered to buy Billie the divorce she so desperately wanted. Hughes had learned from his father that every man has his price. Irwin Willat's was half a million dollars.

When Hughes and Willat met in person to discuss what amounted to divorce blackmail, both men realized that the game they were playing could become dirty very fast. One leak to the press, and the wholesome image of Billie Dove would be grist in an ugly court battle. In 1929, she was commanding $100,000 a picture, and earning more than any other star in Hollywood. Her studio, First National-Warner Bros. had spent a small fortune in building her image, and had just added to its investment by signing her to a five-picture contract.

Willat, whose head was as thick as his neck, refused to back down from his money demand, until Hughes began to walk out of the negotiations. Fearing he would lose both the money and his wife, Willat settled on a "compromise figure"—$350,000, but would only accept the money if it was hand-delivered in a leather briefcase and all in $1,000 bills. Hughes quickly agreed to the terms, and then called Dietrich to work out the details.

For Dietrich, getting the cash was easy. Getting it in thousand dollar bills proved more difficult. It took a trip to the Federal Reserve Bank to get the money which Dietrich then nervously hustled across Los Angeles. "Any holdup man would have enjoyed a bonanza if he had knocked me over," Dietrich later wrote. With Willat paid, Billie was free to file for divorce from the husband she hated. Not yet content, Hughes could not resist devising a larger-than-life plan to accomplish a simple feat.

According to Billie, Hughes was in such a rush to marry her himself that he insisted she establish residency in Nevada where quick divorces required only a six-week stay. They took a train from Union Station in downtown Los Angeles to a remote Nevada farm community. There, they were picked up by Floyd and Arlene Struck, who owned a 140-acre spread on the outskirts of the town. Hughes had primed his pump of subterfuge by telling the Strucks that his name was George Johnson and that Billie was his sister, Marion. The brother and sister had come to town to learn how to farm, or so Hughes' story went.

The elaborate hoax that Hughes had arranged included his promise to work in the fields with Floyd, while Billie, or rather, Marion, helped Arlene with canning vegetables. It was typical Hughes when it came to intrigue; a complex plan where simplicity would have better served the purpose. George and Marion lived in what Billie later described as a "shed with a dirt floor." They slept on two twin beds, side by side, and saw each other only after the sun went down. They were two weeks into Hughes' elaborate hoax when he learned that their "shed" did not qualify as a residence under Nevada divorce laws. They remained in Nevada for another two days, two days that Billie remembered as the most romantic of her life, before heading back to the reality awaiting them in California.

For Hughes, it meant round-the-clock editing sessions, pruning 2.3 million feet of *Hell's Angels* footage down to a 15,000 foot, two hour movie. For every foot of film used, Hughes discarded 166. The task would take over six months, with twelve editors working around-the-clock shifts.

For Billie, it meant doing publicity for her latest film *Her Private Life*,[5] and preparing to divorce her husband of six years. On January 2, 1930, First National Studios leaked word through its publicity department that Billie had separated from Willat, even though the pair had not been living as husband and wife for well over six months. According to the studio, "Rumors of their separation arose in Hollywood film circles after she failed to join him for the Christmas holidays." There was no mention that she had spent December in the Muirfield home of Howard Hughes, who barely made it back from work only to return to the editing room and his real mistress, *Hell's Angels*. Recently discovered appointment books testify to the fact. For every hour he spent with Billie, Hughes was devoting 36 to his film.

When the 127-minute film was at long last ready for its premiere, Hughes leased Grauman's Chinese Theater and spent another $40,000 to make certain it was an event that Hollywood would not soon forget. After weeks of meetings with theater owner Sid Grauman, who came out of retirement for the premiere, Hughes had assured himself that every detail had been handled. His print of the film was being hand-tinted. All 15,000 feet of it. The sound in the theater was reconfigured with attention to the sub-woofers, all-important to re-create the sound of aerial combat. A replica of a Sopwith Camel was painted on the theater curtain in shimmering silver, and an actual Fokker fighter was positioned in the theater's entrance court.

June 7, 1930. Howard Hughes paced like a caged jaguar in his Muirfield bedroom. After three years and four million dollars, he was ready for what would be his opening night in Hollywood. Dressed in black tie and tails, patent leather slippers, and wearing his mother's wedding ring on his pinky finger for luck, he sucked in a deep breathe and bounded down the stairs to his waiting limousine. Billie Dove had arrived fifteen minutes early, to make certain the perennially-tardy Hughes was not late for his own premiere. She was dressed in pale blue, and held a nosegay of pale violet orchids and cascading ivy.

On Hollywood Boulevard, police estimated the crowd at 15,000 people, pushing behind barricades to catch a glimpse of their favorite stars. Lionel Barrymore, Gloria Swanson, Dolores del Rio, Maurice Chevalier and Cecil B. DeMille were there, speaking into microphones hooked to live radio broadcasts. Charlie Chaplin called the spectacle the "greatest night in show business," when he addressed the crowd. Leslie Howard, Irving Berlin, Jerome Kern, and Florenz Ziegfeld had flown in from New York for an advance look at the film that would not debut in Manhattan for another two months.

A radio broadcaster, swept up in the hysteria of the moment, said, "There are at least 45,000 cars out here, making the greatest traffic jam

---

5. *Her Private Life* was based on the play *Declassée* written by Zoe Akins, who would later write the play *How to Marry a Millionaire*.

ever known in the west. Five hundred thousand people are prowling the streets to get a glimpse of the stars and celebrities."

As Hughes' limo led the sleek string of Duesenbergs carrying Ben Lyon, James Hall, Jean Harlow, and John Darrow, the crowds shoved and screamed to get into better viewing position. As the entourage of cars turned onto Hollywood Boulevard, the police on horseback nervously watched the excited fans. Overhead, a squadron of fighter planes in formation emitted trails of colored smoke—red, white and blue. The planes were banking and twisting in syncopated rhythm as they staged a mock showdown for the spectators below.

Klieg lights scanned the heavens, sweeping across the Hollywood skyline. A full mile of Hollywood Boulevard was lit with arc-lights every few yards, sending beams of white Corinthian columns into the perfect spring night. Models of planes in action were suspended above the street at each intersection. Floods of color lit up the Chinese Theater, boasting *HELL'S ANGELS* in vivid red neon. A cardboard cut-out of Jean Harlow, alluring in a strapless red gown, seemed to rise out of flames as she caressed Ben Lyon's cheek on the theater's marquee.

One thousand and twenty-four guests, most paying the unheard-of price of $11 per ticket, were each escorted to reserved seats by an army of uniformed ushers, as a 46-piece orchestra played music from the film's soundtrack, including Tchaikovsky's *Symphony No. 6 (Pathétique)*. Every guest was given a leather-bound souvenir program of the night that not only detailed the long history of the film, but also attacked the rumors of its enormous cost head-on.

$225,475	for negative and development of the film
$562,000	for planes, purchased and reconditioned
$754,000	for salaries of pilots
$389,000	for rental of planes and locations
$408,000	for salaries of mechanics, technicians, and airborne cameramen
$520,000	for sets
$328,000	for salaries of actors
$220,000	for salaries of directors, cameramen, and editors
$460,000	for Zeppelin sequence

As LARGE as it was, the listed total of $3,866,475 did not include marketing, theater rental, or the cost of prints.

Although the invitations stated an 8:30 p.m. showtime, Hughes and his entourage did not even arrive at the theater until shortly after 9, and finally took their seats in the packed house at 9:45. Master of ceremonies,

Frank Fay,[6] began the program at exactly 10 p.m. with the introduction of pilot Roscoe Turner and his mascot, a lion cub named Gilmore. Turner had flown from New York and set a transcontinental speed record of eighteen hours, Fay announced, before introducing an "elaborate vaudeville diversion" consisting of the Abbott Dancers, the Albertina Rasch Dance Company, and a selection of singers and comics, plus Mrs. Alice Vernon's Dancing Poodles.

Finally, at 11 p.m., after many of the audience had already been seated for three hours, the film began. Hughes clutched Billie's hand, and "squeezed the life out of me and the orchids," the actress privately recalled. "He was understandably nervous." He had little reason to be. Despite scattered laughs and amusement at the over-staged dramatic scenes between Lyon, Hall, and Harlow, the audience was spellbound by the aerial photography and stunt work, giving the film and Hughes a twenty-minute standing ovation at its conclusion.

The following day reviews of the film spoke glowingly of Hughes and his spectacular aviation footage, while mocking the stilted dialogue and performances of its leads. Edwin Schallert, of the *Los Angeles Times*, wrote, "Hughes' 'folly' is a magnificent picture." Mordaunt Hall, writing in the *New York Times*, added "thrilling flashes of airplane fighting in the clouds and magnificent scenes of a Zeppelin supposed to be bombing London during the war counteract silly episodes" which featured Harlow, an actress Hall labeled a "flaxen-haired creature." Viewers had a different take on the star, finding Harlow's hair and cleavage as intriguing as the war footage, if not more so.

The evening and the film were a triumph for Hughes, and he would later remember it as the best night of his life. At 24, he had completed the most expensive film ever made in Hollywood without any help from a studio, he had orchestrated a premiere event that would never again be equaled in its complexity or effect, and he had captured the love of a woman who was a major star in Hollywood—and done it all on his own terms. His image was that of a rich, handsome daredevil and lover of women, who had his life, and all those in it, under control. It was an image that he not only created with careful design, but enjoyed playing to the world-at-large. Unfortunately, it was an illusion so perfect that no one, most certainly not Howard Hughes, was capable of actually maintaining it for long.

The first crack in his armor was his hearing. Billie Dove noticed that Hughes had trouble understanding normal conversation soon after they first met. She made a point of not calling attention to the problem, always speaking deliberately to his face, and allowing him to subconsciously read

6. Frank Fay was the husband of film star Barbara Stanwyck.

her lips. She had no way of knowing that it was an inherited disease called otosclerosis, a gradual thickening of a bone in the inner ear, leading to deafness if left untreated. Hughes' Uncle Rupert suffered from the illness, and like his nephew, refused to have it examined.

His second, and to Billie, far more immediate delusion was that he was a ladies' man. She encouraged that image, finding it strengthened his self-confidence. As in most things Hollywood, the truth was not close to perception. While not totally impotent, for a young man, Hughes had a diminished sex drive that dramatically ran counter to his public persona. Rather than examine the situation as a problem to be corrected, Hughes chose to camouflage his lack of sexual prowess through multiple con-quests of women. And not just *any* women. Only the most glamorous, sexually-alluring females would do, beginning with Billie Dove.

On the eve of Billie's divorce, she felt confident of her position. Hughes had proposed to her multiple times over the past several months, the last being on a weekend trip to Del Monte Lodge in Del Monte, California. To her, they were all but married. She only needed to set the date.

Billie officially filed for divorce from Willat on June 12, charging that he "frequently displayed an ungovernable temper and struck her." The news came as no secret to many in Hollywood and most of America who were fans of Louella Parsons' column that had revealed the previous January: "Instead of the dove of peace, the menace of a beating constantly hovered over the home of Billie Dove. Irvin Willat, in fact, walked right up to his wife at a party and knocked her down flat. I was there to see it." On Tuesday, July 1, 1930, Hughes' golfing buddy Judge Henry R. Archbald officially declared Billie's marriage to Willat[7] ended. It was uncontested, with no children, no community property, and no alimony to consider. The judge, who professed to have seen every Billie Dove film and requested her autograph, took less than an hour to free her from her "demeaning and violent husband" so that she could marry the man she called her "one true love."

It was a cause to celebrate, and Hughes, free from work for the first time in several years, allowed himself to relax. He wanted to escape the intensity of his image and the challenges of his work, and decided that the open sea provided the perfect setting for the purpose. As it turned out, Billie loved the ocean, and leapt to second the suggestion as something akin to divine revelation. Parting the Red Sea may have, in fact, been easier since Hughes did not own a yacht, or even a row boat, for that matter, and assigned Dietrich

---

7. Irwin Willat would do only one more picture, ironically titled *Damaged Love*, before his career came crashing to a halt in 1931. He briefly reemerged in 1937 to film three westerns before retiring from show business. He died in Santa Monica, California, in 1976 at the age of 85.

the task of locating "something appropriate, not too showy."

The 170-foot *Hilda* was both appropriate *and* showy. Owned by the widow of steel magnate Charles Boldt, the yacht had a crew of eighteen. When Hughes took the craft on a test cruise for a weekend to Catalina Island off the coast of Los Angeles, the widow Hilda was ecstatic. She had been trying to unload the yacht for months, with no takers. When Hughes "tested" it again for the following two weekends, the wealthy woman began to sense that perhaps she was a bit hasty in her enthusiastic welcome of the young producer. But it was not until Hughes asked to take the yacht on a cruise to Mexico that she finally drew the line in the surf. Mrs. Boldt's asking price was $450,000; Hughes ended up paying $350,000 in the form of a cashier's check drawn on Houston National Bank, with the Hughes Tool Company as the registered owner.

In August, Captain Hughes pulled himself away from the sea to prepare for the double premiere of *Hell's Angels* in Manhattan. Originally, Hughes planned to showcase the film at New York's George M. Cohan Theater, but later decided to launch the film at two different theaters to increase seating capacity. In typical Hughes style, it was decided at the last possible moment, necessitating changes in invitations, police protection, and street closures—all vital elements that Hughes had not considered in his change of venue.

As it happened, the premieres almost had to be cancelled entirely. On the day Hughes was due to take the two sets of prints to New York, he procrastinated leaving his Muirfield Road home until he had virtually only minutes left to catch his train. Too nervous to drive, he asked Noah Dietrich to get behind the wheel, promising him Hughes' brand new Pontiac if he did not miss the train's departure. In later years, Dietrich delighted in relating the story of his harrowing high-speed trip to Union Station in downtown Los Angeles. Although with each telling, the trip got more dangerous and the roads more stifled with traffic, the punch line of the story was always the same. Hughes made the train; Dietrich got the car.

Billie Dove was also on the same train, having boarded in San Diego with six trunks of clothing, two boxes of jewelry, two maids, three dogs, and four bottles of bootlegged gin. The dogs were being transported for a friend, the gin was a gift to her agent, and jewelry and clothes were for the vacation that Hughes had promised her after the *Hell's Angels* premiere, and the maids—well, Billie always traveled with her maids. True to his word, Hughes and Billie plus entourage boarded the *Europa* and cruised to England and the south of France the day after the New York premiere–at that point an anti-climactic affair.

The pair toured London, stopped in Paris, visited Vienna, and on

Billie's insistence took a side trip to Prague. Under the guise of touring the Ball House of the Royal Garden in Prague Castle at Praha, she took him to see renowned hearing specialist Karl Bruner at his clinic. There, Hughes underwent tests to determine his degree of hearing loss. Dr. Bruner determined that Hughes was incapable of hearing 40 percent of voice sounds, particularly those in the lower ranges. In addition, Hughes was diagnosed with tinnitus, a constant ringing in the ears, in addition to otosclerosis. Bruner's suggestion of a hearing aid was not only refused by Hughes, he labeled the doctor's methods as quackery, and was asked to leave the property.

"Rumored here Howard Hughes buying Universal, Paramount, United Artists, Fox, Warner Brothers, First National, Metro-Goldwyn-Mayer and other studios in order to have original cast for *Queer People*. Can you confirm?" The recently discovered telegram had been sent in September, 1930, by Caddo Company's publicity man, Lincoln Quarberg, to H. Wayne Pierson, the head of Hughes' office in New York. Pierson had heard the same rumors, but had no answer; and the man who did, Howard Hughes, was holding hands with Billie Dove aboard a gondola in Venice, Italy. And Hughes was not talking.

He had bought the rights to *Queer People*, a novel by Carroll and Garrett Graham, in early August, creating a outpouring of outrage among other Hollywood producers. The brothers Graham scandalized the movie community with their tale of sudden wealth and wanton behavior within the movie industry. It was blatantly anti-Semitic and included a caricature of MGM's Louis B. Mayer among others. Hughes signed Ben Hecht to write the script for the film, and actor William Haines to star in the lead role of a reporter named Whitey through whose eyes the story unfolds. Eventually the enormity of Hollywood's ire over the project caused it to be shelved, with blame being cast on "opinion in Hollywood" of the novel labeled as "bitter satire."

Tales of Hughes' plans to buy every other studio in town were actually based on fact. He had made inquiries into the availability of Warner Bros. and Universal, and had entered into negotiations with Joseph M. Schenck, president of United Artists. In October, upon his return from Europe, Hughes decided against the purchase. "I was prepared to take over Art Cinema Finance Corporation at a reasonable figure, but the price asked was beyond all reason in view of the unsettled and none too prosperous condition of the motion-picture industry at this time," Hughes stated in a wire to Schenck.

Eventually, Hughes and Schenck worked out a distribution pact through which Hughes received office space at United Artists in exchange for UA's exclusive rights to Hughes' forthcoming films. And there were many. Incorporating outtakes from aerial footage of *Hell's Angels*, Hughes rushed into production on *Sky Devils*, a comedy starring Spencer Tracy and William Boyd and written by Robert Benchley, and Carroll and Garrett Graham.

In addition, as Hughes worked to get Billie released from her contract at First National-Warner Bros. To take control of her career, he bought the rights to the Ben Hecht/Charles MacArthur celebrated Broadway play *The Front Page*. Louis Wolheim, who was still under contract to Hughes' Caddo Company, had signed to star in the picture with Pat O'Brien. During the first week of filming, however, Wolheim collapsed and died on the set. Production was halted for only two days with Hughes' inking Adolph Menjou in Wolheim's role. With Lewis Milestone back in the director's chair, the film was completed in a record 30 days, and made its debut in March, 1931.[8]

In addition, Hughes entered negotiations to purchase Multicolor Films, Inc., a color processing firm, for half a million dollars. He also maneuvered Caddo Company into the theater business by forming Hughes-Franklin Theaters Company with Harold B. Franklin, a theater operator. Hughes' initial investment was $5 million that bought him 65 theaters in Texas, Oklahoma and California.

To keep Billie Dove working, he bought the script of *The Age of Love*, in which Billie played a woman torn between a career and a husband who expected her to keep house. The miscast beauty looked as uncomfortable in the role as the plot suggests. Her anger over the role was hardly helped when Hughes immediately cast her in a second film for Caddo. Titled *Cock of the Air*, it was a comedy starring Chester Morris as an aviator who falls in love with Billie's Lilli de Rosseau, a French damsel.

Hughes was working at a pace unmatched by even the major studios. At one point in early 1931, he had four films in various stages of production, and insisted on producing each one himself. Driven by his need to become "the most famous producer of moving pictures," he was unwilling to delegate responsibility, thus ensuring that the shotgun of glory not miss its mark.

At a time when much of America was standing in bread lines and selling apples, Hughes was spending at a rate of $250,000 a week. He bought the Muirfield Road home from Mrs. Fudger for her asking price of $135,000 including furniture. He then spent an additional $50,000 on new carpets, draperies and furniture, hand selected by Billie Dove. He bought two new cars, a new Rolls Royce Silver Cloud and a Duesenberg coupe. He turned down a request for $10,000 to help fund the Los

---

8. *The Front Page* went on to be nominated for three Academy Awards, including Best Actor for Menjou, Best Director for Milestone, and Best Picture.

Angeles Public Library, but spent $20,000 on jewelry for Billie, each gift sent with a hand-written note explaining his absence due to "the pressure of business."

Finally, despite an increasingly vigilant censorship movement from Washington which was attempting to rid films of violence and sex, he optioned the rights to *Scarface*, loosely based on the life of gangster Al Capone. After securing the property, Hughes was determined to hire the young director Howard Hawks to helm the picture. It was not a simple negotiation. At the time, Hughes was suing Hawks over the director's World War I drama, *The Dawn Patrol*, a film Hughes insisted contained footage from *Hell's Angels*.

In the end, it was the *Scarface* subject matter that won over Hawks, just as it had Howard Hughes. The director took on the project only on the basis that Hughes gave him a free hand to fill the screen with blood and machine-gun fury. To cast the title role, Hughes selected Jewish stage actor Paul Muni. To Muni fell the task of portraying Tony Camonte, a twisted and ambitious gangster climbing the ladder of mob success over the carcasses of his weaker competitors; a man full of sick energy who lusts after his own sister.

Will H. Hays, a former U.S. Postmaster General who had been hired by the studio heads to counter government charges of film immorality, was incensed. Hays had created the Motion Picture Production Code to maintain a certain standard of civility in films, and Howard Hughes had seemingly gone out of his way to flaunt his disregard for the Hays Code. Hays rejected the film and refused to give it his seal of approval, essential to theaters. He demanded that extensive changes be made throughout the movie, including a totally different ending. Howard Hawks refused to make a single change, and left the picture. Hughes, with $600,000 tied up in the film, initially wavered, and began to make the required cuts. Muni was asked and refused to do a new ending, in which the gangster is hanged for his crimes. In an effort to appease Hays, a stand-in was hired and the scene shot in silhouette. Unfortunately, that was not enough to satisfy the prudish Hays. He wanted more modifications and the title changed to *Scarface: The Shame of the Nation*.

Even more upsetting for Hughes, Al Capone, who had recently been jailed for income tax evasion, sent word that he was not very pleased either. Hughes was threatened with death unless he agreed to soften Muni's character to show compassion. Moreover, the Mafia insisted that all artwork connected with the film have the scar of Muni's face retouched to look less like Al Capone.

For three months, Hughes changed and rechanged *Scarface*, capitulating to censorship and Hays' dictates. It was as out of character as it was humiliating for the producer-playboy who had built his reputation on independence and making his own rules. On January 12, 1932, with all the changes made, Hughes and Billie boarded the *Hilda* to sail to West Palm Beach, Florida. While Hawks was furious and the Mafia still threatening, Hughes at least thought it had satisfied the Hays office. He was aboard the *Hilda* when he received word from Will Hays that the film still would not pass the censorship boards in New York, Pennsylvania and Ohio. It had taken awhile, but finally Hughes had had enough.

He wired his team in California to restore the film to its original version. His production staff were dumbfounded and desperately attempted to reach Hughes who at that point was cruising between Florida and Cuba. When he resurfaced in Havana, Hughes was energized and sent a telegram informing the Hays office that the original and unedited *Scarface* would be premiered in New Orleans using its original title, and in a state without a censorship board.

Picking up the beat of Hughes' anti-censorship campaign, newspapers across the country began to write editorials in his support. Concurrently, Hughes began to file suits against each state that refused to allow his film to be distributed. Dropping Billie off in Florida, Hughes continued to campaign in various states for the film. There was a groundswell of succor from organizations in favor of free speech, the most telling being an endorsement from Wilton A. Barrett, the executive secretary of the National Board of Review, an *ad hoc* citizens' group, who telegraphed Hughes with three words: We Endorse Scarface.

After standing ovations followed screenings in New Orleans and Los Angeles, and successes in courts in New York and Pennsylvania, *Scarface* won its Seal of Approval from the Hays Office, in a stunning victory for Howard Hughes. As he was being championed across the country, however, he was failing miserably at home. Upon returning to his Muirfield house, he discovered that Billie had left him. The closets that once held her gowns and furs were bare; dressers and book shelves empty. In the face of his most dramatic victory, Hughes had experienced his most crushing defeat.

Billie never discussed the reason for her dissolution with the man she had planned to marry, and Hughes, himself, never uncovered why. In 1933, she married wealthy rancher Robert Kenaston, retired from the screen, and had a son and adopted a daughter, who thought the answer was obvious. "She wanted a home and a family; with Hughes she got diamonds and a room down the hall."

The departure of Billie Dove left Hughes visibly shaken. Riding the crest of popularity, he found himself suddenly alone. The *Hilda* remained unused, moored in Malibu; the house on Muirfield empty, its guest rooms continuing reminders of opportunities lost. Yet, for all his desolation, Hughes ended 1932 facing an even bigger devastation. The millionaire playboy, the high-flying adventurer, the producer and director of Hollywood features, was out of money—totally broke. Moreover, he was deeply in debt.

FIVE

Up From the Ashes
Into the Air

All I did was sit there.
The engine did all the work.

Newark, New Jersey
January 14, 1936
Upon hearing that he had broken the
record for the fastest trans-continental
flight.

BY 1932, THANKS TO THE GREAT DEPRESSION, THE U.S.
economy had hit rock bottom and banks were folding up
like concertinas. Hughes Tool Company had failed to generate a profit for the first time in its history, and had been
forced to lay off employees. Having never paid any attention
to business, Howard Hughes knew nothing of the declining
oil market or bankruptcies in Texas. It did get his attention,
however, when Noah Dietrich arrived at the Muirfield
house, sat him down in the kitchen, and told him the money
cupboard was bare.

Since Hughes never carried cash, and charged everything he bought to Hughes Tool, at first he did not realize
the impact this news would have on his life. While the rest
of America was having trouble placing food on the table,
Hughes felt the effect only when he decided to buy a new
plane, and was told that he needed to pay for his purchase
with cash. It was a foreign concept; one that took some getting
used to.

When Dietrich delivered the news that Hughes was
attempting to spend money he no longer had, he reacted in
typical fashion. Rather than acknowledge the situation and
make an effort to economize, Hughes sent Dietrich to live

in Houston to "find out why those fellas are running my company into the God damn ground." He took the opportunity to back away from the declining film business, close his Caddo Company offices, dismiss Lincoln Quarberg and H. Wayne Pierson, sever his contracts with stars and directors, and refuse to comment to the press.

This financial calamity also brought him back into contact with his ex-wife Ella, for he could not afford to pay her the now-overdue 1932 installment of their alimony agreement. For a man whose entire persona was linked to his unbelievable wealth, it was a humiliating circumstance. So too was dealing with Ella's brother-in-law, William Stamps Farish, who represented Ella in the negotiations. Operating from a lofty position of power, Farish made no attempt to spare Hughes embarrassment, alerting Aunt Annette of the overdue payment of $250,000, and placing Hughes on notice that any alteration of the alimony agreement would be exacted at a very high price.

With Dietrich representing Hughes, the deal that was ultimately struck called for a extension of Ella's alimony payments until 1939. Because Farish distrusted what he termed "Hughes' financial responsibility," Ella was awarded temporary ownership of 1700 shares in Hughes Tool—slightly more than 25 percent. Additionally, the agreement called for Hughes to refrain from making any further motion pictures until 1939. He also lost the right to make any purchases in excess of $100,000 without written permission from Ella. For his part, while Dietrich won the concession that the terms of the arrangement would be kept private, the reality of Houston society meant that everyone who cared to know did.

Now officially no longer in show business, Hughes devoted his time to his other love—flying. Out of touch from human demands and domestic worries, for Hughes the sky represented freedom. With every liftoff, he felt the same release of worry and frustration. And at the start of 1933, more than any other time in his life, flying provided a needed escape.

Just three months earlier, he had shocked pilots and passengers alike when it was discovered he was working as a co-pilot with American Airlines at the wage of $250 per month.[1] Had the airline not mishandled the processing of his paperwork, he claimed he would have kept the job. As it was, for three weeks, American was pleased with his performance. He actually piloted one flight from Los Angeles to New York in a Fokker F-10, helped passengers with their luggage, and happily collected boarding passes. When the airline discovered that it had a millionaire for a pilot, American fired Hughes, not because he was a bad flyer, but rather because he had falsified his identity and credentials, using the name Charles W. Howard.

1. His employment with American Airlines was the sole time in Hughes' life when he earned a salaried income.

Selling off a half-dozen of his arsenal of fighter planes left over from *Hell's Angels*, Hughes ordered a $59,000, 8-passenger Sikorsky amphibian that was specially outfitted with a leather divan along one side of the cabin, and took delivery of the plane on January 4, 1933. It marked the first official aircraft sold to the newly organized Hughes Aircraft Corporation, headquartered in a leased hangar at the Grand Central Airport in Glendale, California. The plane kept company with a leftover Boeing pursuit plane that Hughes had bought the previous year. It was made for the United States Army Air Corps and not for civilian owner-ship. Hughes said he acquired the plane through a "special arrangement" with the Department of Commerce, which later claimed it knew nothing about a sale.

Hughes hired Glenn Odekirk, a pilot that had worked on *Hell's Angels*, as a mechanic to overhaul the Boeing plane. His instructions were speed-specific: "Turn this sweet ass prop into the fastest plane in the world." While Odekirk ripped the engine apart, and worked for months improving its original 580-horsepower, Hughes began to fly his Sikorsky amphibian across the country, usually with a budding starlet on his leather divan. Marian Marsh, who had appeared in a bit role in *Hell's Angels* under the stage name Marilyn Morgan, and went on to gain fame as Madame Svengali in the John Barrymore movie *Svengali*, warmed the divan for months before being replaced by Ida Lupino, Lillian Bond, and Mary Rogers, teenage actresses all.

It was during this period that Hughes would meet the man who would become his most enduring friend. Dudley Sharp, who had previously worn that compliment, gladly gave it back in 1928, when he had written to his oldest friend to ask him to be the best man in his wedding. Sharp had, after all, been Hughes' best man at his wedding to Ella. Unmoved by sentiment, Hughes turned Sharp down, citing problems on the film *Hell's Angels*, but suggested he spend his honeymoon in California—not with Hughes, but rather at the Del Monte Hotel.

This had actually been the second time Hughes had disappointed Sharp. A long-hidden letter written October 17, 1925, and revealed here for the first time, conveys a plea from Sharp for help. Still at Princeton, Sharp states that his mother is low on cash and therefore cannot keep up his previous allowance. According to the letter, Sharp had made an arrangement with the Alloy Steel Corp. in Dayton, Ohio, to pay him a kick-back of $12,000 if Hughes Tool would begin ordering its metal from Alloy Steel. At the time, Hughes' estate was worth over $8,000,000, based solely on money generated by a company started by Dudley Sharp's father. Hughes refused to consider his friend's plea, marked the letter "File–Sharp," and went to play golf at the Wilshire Country Club.

The man who would replace Sharp in Hughes' adult life was actor Cary Grant. Grant first walked into Hughes' home on Muirfield Road on the arm of actor Randolph Scott. The two struggling performers were roommates at a beach house they named Bachelor Hall for the constant turnover of women who crossed its threshold. Scott had preceded Grant to Hollywood by three years, having come from Orange County, Virginia, to be a star. In his pocket, he brought a letter of introduction to Hughes, whose father had known Scott's father in his oil-rigging days. Hughes sent the strapping 6' 4" Southerner over to Fox studios, where he did some extra work and bit parts, before making his name in Westerns. But it was Grant, not Scott, that meshed with Hughes' unusual personality, for indeed, he often said, they were cut from a similar cloth.

They were both perceived as playboys—Grant, debonair with his British suits and charming accent; Hughes, the adventurer with his planes and fast cars. Underneath the facade of raffish allure were two shy sullen boys who had been overindulged by their mothers and then ripped from their protection too early in life. They bonded firmly at the hip and remained friends throughout the remainder of their lives.

As for Dudley Sharp, Hughes would see his old friend one last time in January, 1934. Odekirk had completed work on Hughes' Boeing pursuit plane, and announced it was ready to test. Hughes decided that the proper stage for the plane's debut would be at the All-American Air Meet in Miami, an annual race that Hughes entered in the Sportsman Pilot Free-for-All category.

On the way to Miami, Hughes flew into Houston to visit his Aunt Annette, and inspect the new library he had built at the Yoakum Street house. It was a peace offering of sorts. Annette and Fred Lummis wanted to move from the Hughes mansion into something they could call their own. Rather than allow this to happen, Hughes had offered to give his aunt the family home, sweetening the deal by suggesting he could add a swimming pool in the back yard. His aunt laughed off the concept of a pool, with the revelation that a "proper Southern lady does not flaunt her fair skin in full spectacle of neighbors." Annette did, however, have need of a library, she told her nephew, who set about having the addition built onto the home. When finished, it was the "loveliest room in the house," according to Annette, when she reflected on the residence years later.

Upon seeing Dudley and his wife Tina, Hughes made no mention of his previous affronts, but rather raced upstairs, taking the steps two at a time, and gifted Tina with a childhood photograph of her husband, a personal keepsake, as a belated wedding present. During the same visit, Hughes met his aunt's children for the first time—his cousins Allene, Annette, Fred and Willie, the latter he thought an "adorable" 4-year-old carbon-copy of himself as a youth.

In Miami, Hughes would discover the thrill of victory as he took to the skies in his open-cockpit racer, a blue and silver streak compared to the competition that he handily beat, averaging a speed of 185.7 miles per hour. In flight goggles and a brown leather jacket, Hughes bounded onto the winners' platform to accept the victor's trophy from General Rafael Trujillo, the former head of the Dominican Republic's National Guard who had risen to become the country's brutal dictator.

The taste of success was a narcotic that the young Texan inhaled and savored. The isolated victory in a locally-sponsored race was the stimulus that unlocked an obsession in the flyer to be the best in the air. Not just the fastest but the most renowned for innovation, daring, and determination as well. His will was to conquer the skies.

A buoyant Hughes returned to California, inspired to revolutionize the fledgling aeronautical industry. Shedding more of his armada of planes from *Hell's Angels*, he generated capital with which to hire Richard W. Palmer, a recent graduate of the California Institute of Technology, and a friend of Odekirk. Extremely bright and intuitive, Palmer was far more radical than his learned, outward appearance would suggest. His designs for airplanes caused him more grief than glory at Cal Tech, so innovative and *avant-garde* that he was constantly upsetting his professors who failed to be inspired by his genius. Hughes, on the other hand, found Palmer to be the prophet of the future in aeronautical design and was bright enough to subsidize his talent and stand out of the way.

For months, Palmer and Odekirk worked on a revolutionary plane whose sole purpose was to move faster than any man-made vehicle had ever done before. As the plane began to take shape, Hughes hired workers to help assemble it—eventually employing eighteen men under the Hughes Aircraft umbrella. As word of the project leaked out to the press, it was dubbed Hughes' "Mystery Ship" and was said to feature retractable landing gear, a rivetless fuselage, with a propeller muscled by a 1,000 horsepower engine.

While his men labored in Glendale, Hughes himself was flying from Los Angeles to New York; back and forth, and then again, experimenting with various altitudes and wind patterns, interrupting his adventure only long enough to entertain a lucky starlet who happened to cross his path. While on Cape Cod, in Edgartown, Massachusetts, on July 29, his love of speed attracted the attention of a patrolman named Henry Porter, who stopped the car Hughes was driving, claiming it had reached a speed "in excess of 80 miles an hour." The fact that Hughes had neither a car registration nor a driver's license landed him in the local lock-up until early the next morning, when Judge Abner Brayley found him guilty and placed him on 30 days probation, with a sternly-worded warning not to venture near Martha's Vineyard again.

Contenting himself with joining the crew in Glendale nearing the completion of the Mystery Ship, now called the H-1, Hughes finished out the year by awarding each of his Hughes Aircraft employees with two weeks paid vacation, an extra bonus that did not sit well with the unheralded workers at Hughes Tool. Dietrich had managed to turn business around at the Houston plant, but through slightly unconventional means.

With the end of Prohibition in 1933, Col. Kuldell had opened the Gulf Brewing Company inside part of the Tool Company complex, in an effort to offset the business fall-off from the Depression. With Dietrich's arrival in Texas, the struggling brewery took on new life, his taste buds leading the way to a celebrated beer called Grand Prize—although it had not won any. With the success of his beer and a turnaround underway in the oil business, Hughes Tool returned to profitability. For a while, the only one who did not know it was Howard Hughes. Dietrich deliberately kept him in the dark about profits in an effort to curb his extravagance. For once in his life, Hughes actually listened to advice, and concentrated both his attention and spending to the H-1.

On the very day in June, 1935, that the H-1 was having her wings attached with Palmer's revolutionary smooth-rivet process, Hughes received a call from Cary Grant, on location shooting *Sylvia Scarlett*. He begged his friend to fly up the coast to Trancas Beach above Malibu and join him for lunch. That Hughes should say yes to a lunch invitation was unusual enough. To agree to be pulled away from the H-1 during her wing installation was testament to his abiding friendship with Grant. The cameras were still rolling when Hughes buzzed overhead in his Sikorsky amphibian, landing just feet from director George Cukor, who was not amused. The same thing could not be said for Grant's co-star Katharine Hepburn, who remembered Hughes' entrance as "nervy and rather romantic, in a bravado sort of way."

Unfortunately for Hughes, the lunch itself was not as successful. As Katharine, Grant and Cukor sat at a long picnic table eating fried chicken, biscuits, and fruit, followed by heaping scoops of vanilla ice cream, they made inside conversation about the Hollywood all three hated with a passion. All the while, Hughes sat silently watching ants crawl across the table's redwood planks. However uncomfortable he may have been, he was certainly not put off. He was hardly the type to stop when he saw something he wanted, and he wanted Katharine Hepburn. He would wait more than a year before making his next move.

While Katharine Hepburn played *Sylvia Scarlett*, Howard Hughes played flyer. On August 18, 1935, he took his first test flight in the H-1, the small size of the plane out of proportion to the gangly pilot. The H-1 was a squatty 25-feet long, with a wingspan of equal length, giving it a cartoonish character. In the air, however, it was anything but funny. The plane took off from Grand Central Airport and circled Los Angeles at a ripping 300 miles per hour. At the time, the world speed record of 314 mph was held by a Frenchman, Raymond Delmotte. On September 12, 1935, Hughes was prepared to take his crown.

Under the auspices of the National Aeronautic Association, a three-kilometer test course had been set up at Martin Field in Santa Ana, equipped with a chronograph to snap photos at the beginning and end of each run. Hughes was required to make four consecutive passes in the H-1, in front of a trio of airborne observers. In the first plane were stunt pilot Paul Manta, who Hughes knew from his work on *Hell's Angels*, and NAA official Lawrence Therkelson. The second plane was piloted by Amelia Earhart, the top female flyer in the world.

As the afternoon sun turned the warm summer air into plumed gold, Hughes settled into the cockpit wearing a black suit and tie, a leather helmet and oversized goggles, a rather extraordinary look against the brilliant silver of the H-1. As the three planes launched themselves into the air, Hughes was in his element. He knew he had victory in the bag, as he made his first pass, then a second. On his third pass, the sun began to dip over the Pacific Ocean, cooling the air and turning the bean fields below a rather unearthly shade of blue. By his fourth pass, the darkness of long shadows had crossed the course, preventing his final lap from being photographed. He was told he would have to try again the following day, Friday, the 13th.

Not being a suspicious fellow, Hughes considered the omen a lucky break, allowing him another opportunity to fly the H-1, and once more impress the visiting judges. The next day, dressed in the same suit, tie, helmet and goggles, he once again brought the H-1 airborne and once again pulled down on the throttle, freeing the engine to propel him to fame. He made seven passes that day, all easily faster than Delmotte's speed. He could have stopped at four runs across the course, but Hughes was a child playing with a toy, unwilling to share, unable to stop.

On his final pass across the chronograph, he had just banked west when his engine stopped, the mighty motor unforgiving without fuel. Plummeting to earth at slightly over 180 miles per hour, Hughes skimmed a fence and slid to a rather bumpy stop in a beet field. Hughes hoisted himself out of the cockpit, and leaned against his damaged plane waiting for his rescuers. Only then did he learn that he had beaten the old record with an average speed of 352 miles per hour. His only comment: "It'll go faster."

While he renamed the H-1, the *Flying Bullet*, Hughes had begun to look beyond speed. He wanted speed and *distance*. He set his sights on the transcontinental record then held by Roscoe Turner and his mascot Gilmore. While the *Flying Bullet* could easily beat Turner's time, it did not have the fuel capacity to fly across country. Hughes needed another plane, and had no intention of waiting while his team developed and built one.

He found what he considered the perfect airplane at Mines Field in Los Angeles—a single-engine, high-powered Gamma from Northrop Aviation. For weeks, he watched as its pilot ran it through speed tests. It was an incredible sight and almost as beautiful as its pilot, Jacqueline Cochran.[2] The 26-year-old blonde left home at fourteen and headed to New York to be a beautician before drinking the elixir that was flight, and forever changing the remainder of her life. After what seemed to Hughes to be an eternity, but was actually only three weeks, he managed to convince the cash-poor Jacqueline to lease him the plane, knowing full well he had no intention of ever returning it.

For the next three months, his team of mechanics did not so much fine-tune the plane as reconstruct it, with a new engine (another special arrangement with the military), new seats, and new instruments in the cockpit. Had Jacqueline been privy to the changes, she most certainly would have been upset, but once Hughes flew the plane from Mines Field to his base in the San Fernando Valley, she was not allowed visitation rights. Armed security guards were posted around the hangar 24 hours a day as if guarding the cure for yellow fever, and remained in place until at last on January 13, 1936, Hughes was ready to make a run at the title.

He was eating lunch in Los Angeles when he received word that the weather conditions were perfect across the entire United States to attempt a run at the transcontinental record. Pushing back from the table, Hughes rushed across Laurel Canyon Boulevard to the San Fernando valley where the Gamma had been sitting ready and fueled with 700 gallons of gas. Dressed in a light Palm Beach suit, Hughes grabbed a flight jacket, goggles, oxygen mask and leather helmet, and settled into the open cockpit.

Taking off from Union Air Terminal in Burbank just after noon, Hughes and the Gamma powered into the sky, heavily weighted down with the fuel. Not two minutes into the flight, Hughes realized that his radio was not working, a casualty of an antenna snapped off on take-off. Rather than turning back, he decided to fly the entire way without ground contact, a risky strategy at best. Reaching his cruising altitude of 15,000 feet, Hughes encountered clouds as thick as smoke from a fat-ren-

---

2. By the time of her death in 1980, Jacqueline Cochran would hold more speed, altitude and
   distance records than any other pilot–male or female–in aviation history.

dering vat. He would not see the ground for the next two hours. When finally breaking into clear weather, a shift in wind caused him to hit numerous air pockets, and the resulting bumpy ride knocked the needle from his compass. For the remaining 1200 miles of his trip, he was forced to rely on visual contact with the ground to determine his location. For Hughes, these developments were not set-backs, but rather part of the intrinsic thrill of flying. While he could never be part of the sky, like the clouds and the stars, he could amaze at their glory and share in it.

When he landed safely in Newark nine hours, twenty-seven minutes, and ten seconds after taking off from California, he had set a new transcontinental record. The only one who realized it, however, was the sole timer who greeted him in Newark, and authenticated his claim to fame. His victory was but a glimpse at the future. Later that night Hughes told interviewers, "I wanted to go to New York, so I tried to see how fast I could do it in."

Hughes considered his triumph a shallow win, his time too slow to be meaningful in the record books. He had cut only 36 minutes off the previous mark, and Turner had stopped to refuel. Obsessed with flying faster, Hughes piloted Jackie's plane back to California, offered to buy the Gamma outright, and then five months later, decided to sell it back to her for less than he paid. His indecision, although confusing to Jacqueline Cochran, was typical Hughes. What seemed viable one minute looked absurd the next, and if Jackie thought it strange, she would have gotten no argument from Howard Hughes himself.

Rather than attempt to improve upon the Northrop design, he decided instead to reformat the *Flying Bullet* to equip it to fly across the country. New and longer wings were designed, an increased capacity fuel installed, a transparent cockpit enclosure fabricated, and new instrumentation developed. The process would take the better part of a year. But not before Hughes added two more trophies to his collection. On April 21, 1936, he flew the Gamma from Miami to New York in a record time of four hours, twenty-one minutes and thirty-two seconds. On May 15, while having lunch in Chicago, a man bet him $50 that he could not fly back to Los Angeles in time to have dinner. Leaving Chicago at 1:05 p.m., Hughes landed in L.A. at 7:15 in the evening. He had a steak, some peas, mashed potatoes and ice cream, and wired the man in Chicago for his money. His record time: eight hours, ten minutes, and 25 seconds. He later told the news media, "I have learned more in the last eight hours than in the last ten years."

While his workmen catered to his vacillating whims, Hughes fell back on his conquests of women to supplement his need for validation. During much of 1936, he favored debutantes to actresses as his seduction of choice, for as he told Cary Grant, "They're better in bed and they buy their own flowers."

To provide a proper setting for his peccadillos, Hughes traded in the *Hilda* on a larger yacht. At 320 feet, the *Rover* was the fifth-largest yacht in the world. Hughes thought it perfect for his floating Shangri-La, purchased the ship with funds from Hughes Tool European branch, rechristened it the *Southern Cross*, hired a captain named Carl Flynn and a crew of thirty-two, and had it sailed to Newport Beach, California, where it was outfitted in Egyptian linens, English china, Austrian crystal, and American debutantes.

While cruising in Santa Barbara, Hughes met a local socialite named Nancy Belle Bayly at the Montecito Country Club, where he plucked her off the dance floor and carried her onto his yacht. As impressed as Nancy was with Hughes' floating estate, she found the man himself even more amazing. Rather than the playboy Casanova he was rumored to be, he come across "like a little boy who needed to be cared for." Nancy, only twenty herself, was hardly in a position to care for anyone, but continued the romance until the evening of her twenty-first birthday. Hughes promised her a night she would always remember, and more than delivered on his pledge.

July 11, 1936. They began the evening at Trader Vic's, a Polynesian restaurant where they toasted with a rum drink called a Volcano and Hughes bought her a gardenia lei. Then followed dinner and dancing at the Cocoanut Grove nightclub, with its *papier-mache* palm trees and mindless clucking. The couple was joined by agent Pat Di Cicco, who smoked a cigar, adding to the blue hue of the room, before they left to drive to Santa Monica to ride the merry-go-round on the pier. The night was perfect California weather, with the heat of the day lingering on the air, scented by Nancy's gardenia lei. Hughes' yellow Duesenberg moved down Third Street, the trolley tracks underneath the tires making the car wobble, much to the annoyance of its driver. As they passed Lorraine Street, Hughes rounded the bend and then gave the wheel a sudden twist, sending Nancy hard against the tan leather of the passenger door. Bright headlights shone in through the windshield as the car skidded to an abrupt halt.

Getting out, Hughes raced behind the car towards the curb and saw a man lying dead in the street, his straw hat rolling down Lorraine having been caught by the wind. As Nancy reached Hughes, he pushed her back, away from the man. Cars had stopped in both directions, and spectators began to rubberneck at the scene. As a streetcar drew up to the intersection, Hughes moved quickly. Taking off Nancy's gardenia lei, he shoved her onto the trolley, telling her to get off at the Muirfield house and wait there for him. The startled debutante tried to protest, just as the streetcar shut its doors, lurched forward, and continued on its way.

Officer C. P. Wallace, the first patrolman on the scene, questioned Hughes about the accident, only to be told that he would not speak without his attorney present. An United Parcel Service driver named Walter Scott, and an unemployed housewife, Florence Smuckler, gave Wallace their names as eyewitnesses, stating that the man was killed while standing in a pedestrian safety zone.

On the basis of the eyewitness accounts, Hughes was taken first to the Hollywood Receiving Hospital where he was checked for injuries and given a sobriety test, which he passed. Still unwilling to cooperate with the police, Hughes was then driven to Central Jail in downtown Los Angeles, and booked on suspicion of negligent homicide. While he gave the police his name, he identified himself only as a "manufacturer" who lived at 3921 Yoakum Street, Houston, Texas. After his attorney Neil McCarthy arrived, Hughes spent two hours being questioned by Detective Lieutenant Ralph N. Davis. Hughes repeatedly denied having seen the man that was hit before he heard what he described as a "thump" and stopped to investigate.

"I have driven automobiles since I was 12-year-old," Hughes said. "My father had the first automobile in the state of Texas,[3] and I have driven automobiles for 18 years. I never even had any sort of accident. Never hit a dog or a cat. This car I have had six-and-a-half years and never scratched the paint," Hughes proclaimed, his voice high and nasal.

Released on a writ of habeas corpus obtained by McCarthy, Hughes went back to Muirfield and the waiting Nancy Bayly, who was packed off to Santa Barbara in the backseat of a car driven by a hired private detective. It was not until the next morning, when the press reported the story, that Hughes learned the identity of the dead man. Gabe S. Meyer was 59 years old, single, and worked in the furnishings department of the May Company department store. He walked by the corner of Third and Lorraine every night on his way home from work. His body had been taken to the W.M. Strother Inc. mortuary; Hughes' 1929 Duesenberg to the Pacific Auto Body & Parts impound.

On July 15, 1936, a coroner's inquest was held in downtown Los Angeles. Although Hughes never provided her name, the local police were able to locate Nancy Bayly through information given to them by Pat Di Cicco. She arrived at the inquest outfitted in a black Chanel dress with white fresh-water pearls, clutching a lizard-skin bag and wearing matching shoes. She looked nervously at her diamond wristwatch, wishing

---

3. At the time Howard Hughes Sr. returned to Houston with his wife in 1904, there were seventeen automobiles registered in that city alone. Hughes did not own a car before that time.

she were anywhere but there. She thought Hughes looked disheveled in a wrinkled lightweight suit, a white shirt and thin black tie. He smiled at her, and then dropped his eyes, embarrassed by having gotten her involved.

Coroner Frank A. Nance interrogated Hughes, Bayly, Wallace, Davis, Scott, and Smuckler at the inquest, but was unable to develop a clear picture of how Gabe S. Meyer ended up in front of the fender of Hughes' Duesenberg. Each witness said that the area was poorly lit, the safety zone weakly marked, and Hughes' car was traveling at a safe speed. Even the previously undaunted UPS driver changed his story and had no explanation of how the accident took place. By the end of the inquest, Hughes was found not guilty, and made a statement to the press that he had "never been drunk in [his] life."

The relatives of Gabe Meyer, his brother Mendel and sisters Laura Loewenthal, Viola Davis, Stella M. Carlisle and Rose M. Schiff were understandably outraged by the verdict, but were later comforted by a donation of $10,000 that Hughes made to the family "in their time of need." Hughes never drove the Duesenberg again, nor saw Nancy Belle Bayly.

The following month, Hughes was back in the air, this time behind the controls of a Douglas DC-1 that he called his *Flying Laboratory*. What the press was labeling a dress rehearsal for a round-the-world flight attempt, Hughes called a routine flight, despite having applied for and been granted a special radio wave-length by the federal government. Only later would it be learned that Hughes was testing the first automatic pilot, designed by the Sperry Company using a gyro system.

October, 1936, was Indian Summer in Los Angeles. The Santa Ana winds were blowing their basking breeze, and it seemed much of the city stayed outdoors to be saturated in summer before winter's cold curtain of rain. Katharine Hepburn was taking a golf lesson at the Bel Air Country Club and had just reached the seventh tee when overhead she heard the familiar sound of a low-flying plane. Despite her pleas to the golf pro to pay no attention, the fury of sound and wind that erupted on the green was typhonic.

Howard Hughes landed his amphibian plane between two trees, pulled his clubs from the cockpit, and asked if they needed a third in their party. Kate thought it was outrageous behavior, and told Hughes exactly that, before allowing him to join them through the ninth hole and then asking him if he needed a lift home.

As Kate would later write in her autobiography *Me*, "Howard and I were indeed a strange pair. He was sort of the top of the available men—

---

4. To get the plane off the golf course, it needed to have its wings dismantled and then be trucked back to Burbank.

and I of the women. We each had a wild desire to be famous. I think that this was a dominant character failing. People who want to be famous are really loners. Or they should be."

Strange or not, Hughes was besot, and followed Kate to New York where she was in rehearsals for the play *Jane Eyre*. One afternoon while she was working, Hughes took the opportunity to test ride an amphibian plane at New York's North Beach Airport. As he was landing, a tail wind caught the back of the plane and flipped it on its right wing, causing considerable damage. The owner, Dean Franklyn of Jackson Heights, Queens, was paid in full on the spot.

When Kate opened as *Jane Eyre* in New Haven, Connecticut, on December 26, 1936, Hughes was not in the audience. He thought his presence might jinx her performance. But as soon as the production moved to Boston, he was front and center to see the woman he said he was ready to marry. While the reviews for Hepburn were not sterling ("One wonders if it is not easier to see Katharine Hepburn in *Jane Eyre* than *Jane Eyre* in Katharine Hepburn"), she was playing to standing-room-only audiences in every city, with the extra publicity of a Hepburn-Hughes romance helping the box office.

In January, Hughes kissed his sweetheart goodbye and whispered that he had a plane to catch. The $125,000 *Flying Bullet* had been gassed and blocked on the tarmac of the Union Air Terminal in Burbank, and at 2:14 a.m. on January 19, 1937, Hughes taxied down the runway. The newly repainted blue and silver monoplane gained speed, staggered briefly, and then accelerated in lift-off to the cheers of his crew. Heading west out over the ocean, Hughes banked right and turned toward the San Bernardino Pass, as he climbed up to his cruising altitude—20,000 feet, a record of its own. He had chosen it specifically to test his theory that his speed would increase while using less fuel in the thinness of the air.

Ninety minutes into the flawless flight, while passing across Winslow, Arizona, he began to feel the dizzying effect of hypoxia. The very air which was allowing him to fly faster than any man had done before was robbing him of his ability to breath. Gasping for air through his oxygen mask, Hughes could no longer feel his right hand on the throttle, his brain beginning to swell and throb. Hurtling through the black abyss of endless night at over 350 miles per hour, he was helpless to drop his altitude and gain needed oxygen. His breathing rapid, his blood pressure dropping, Hughes pulled on his oxygen line hoping to start the flow into his mask. Nothing. He screamed the cry of desperation to no one, his mouth a crocodile yawn. Another scream, this time from frustration before he bit through the rubber lines and sucked the lifesaving oxygen straight from the tubes.

For the next five hours, Hughes flew toward his destiny, unsure if his oxygen would last until he reached the East coast. Finally, as he flew through the Ohio Valley, the clouds below him broke, and he saw land. The ground was wet from melting snow, his *Flying Bullet* reflecting in the puddles collected on muddy fields. Crossing the army base at Middletown, Pennsylvania, he nosed down the plane and began a long glide into Newark, New Jersey, at speeds in excess of 380 miles per hour. The ground crew at Newark Airport had just cleared a United Airlines flight to depart when the racer appeared overhead and was clocked in by William Zint of the Longines Watch Company at 12:42 and 25 seconds p.m.

Seeing the United flight on the runway, and unable to reach the control tower through his malfunctioning radio, Hughes pulled up into a sweeping *chandelle* maneuver that he had learned filming *Hell's Angels*. He continued circling the airport for another eighteen minutes waiting for the United flight to clear his airspace, and then executed a perfect three-point landing. Local press coverage said Hughes approach "made the buildings tremble from the sound vibration."

Emerging from the cockpit, his face oil-slicked and ashen, a weary Hughes told the ground crew, "I heard somebody else was going to try to break my record, so I decided to beat him to it." That *someone*, it was later learned, was pilot Frank Hawks who had his own racer, *Time Flies*, ready to set out on a cross-country run. Hawks cancelled his flight based on Hughes' performance.

Once on the ground, Hughes sent a telegraph to Katharine in Chicago. "Safe and down in Newark. Love, Howard." He had no way of knowing that the actress was frantic, having read the headlines of the *Chicago Tribune* that screamed,

AVIATION HERO LOST!

WHILE THE New York press was busy reporting the flight and making note that "Hughes will be in New York for some time," they had not counted on the flyer's need to join Katharine, for after a scrub and a change of clothes he was off for Chicago and his lady fair.

If, as the actress said, both of them wanted fame, the reception of the pair in Chicago left no doubt that they had achieved their wish. Reporters and fans mobbed the lobby of the Ambassador Hotel, where the manager called police to "return a sense of decorum to the property." With Hughes in one suite and Katharine in another, the couple found themselves captives of their own popularity. While the Cook Country clerk, Michael J. Flynn, held his own press conference to say that he was expecting the arrival "any moment" of the pair to obtain a marriage license, and that he had bought a new suit for the occasion, Flynn, like the rest of Chicago, was left waiting. Finally, at 5 p.m. on the afternoon following Hughes' record-breaking flight, the *concierge* at the Ambassador issued a statement: "Miss Hepburn will not marry Mr. Hughes in Chicago today." He could have added, "or any other day," for that matter, but did not.

Like the love-sick boy that essentially he was, Hughes continued to dog Katharine's performances nightly in Pittsburgh, Washington, D.C., and Baltimore, and was with her there when the play closed on April 3, 1937. His Uncle Rupert, who he had seen all of four times since he arrived in Los Angeles thirteen years earlier, had written a two-part article for *Liberty* magazine, titled "Howard Hughes—Record Breaker: The story of an exciting life." Hughes considered it an invasion of his privacy, and rife with inaccuracy, and informed his uncle that he would "commence litigation should a single additional word be printed from (his) pen concerning Howard Robard Hughes Jr." Arched with melodrama, Rupert's article forever divided the two men. As much as he detested the piece, Hughes nevertheless clipped its final paragraph and placed it among his personal papers.

> Born without wings, man has made them for himself. He out-climbs the eagle, leaves the hawk behind, outplays the swallow in the air.

HUGHES KNEW the words better than most men. He was awarded the Harmon International Trophy as Outstanding Aviator of 1936 in a ceremony held in the Oval Office at the White House, where President Franklin Roosevelt presented Hughes with the 30-inch high bronze trophy. Designed by G. de Vreese of Belgium, and named for pioneer aviator Clifford B. Harmon, the award was given annually by the Ligue Internationale de Aviateurs. The only other Americans to win the award were Charles Lindbergh and Wiley Post.

Returning to Los Angeles, Hughes asked Katharine to move into the Muirfield house, and was delighted when she readily accepted. He was somewhat less thrilled when she arrived with her cook and chauffeur, Ranghild and Louis Prysing, and her personal maid, Johanna Madsen, plus three dogs, a gray cocker named Mica, a black one named Peter, and a scruffy French poodle who answered infrequently to the name of Button. The gardener, Mr. Quantrill, was still living over the garage, Mrs. Dowler was still the housekeeper, and Hughes' personal valet and *major-domo*, Richard Dreher, brought the household staff to six.

Katharine occupied the former suite that previously Ella Hughes had called home, while Hughes himself continued to prefer his study over the master bedroom. A normal home routine was established to the extent that anything was normal within the sphere of the Hepburn-Hughes world, with informality the definite hallmark of everyday life and entertaining.

During the month of September 1937, Hughes accompanied his love back to visit her parents in Connecticut. It was the first time that Hughes had agreed to meet Dr. and Mrs. Norval Thomas Hepburn. They flew together in Hughes' new Sikorsky S-43 amphibian, a twin-engine luxury craft that once again was redesigned as a playboy's hideaway. Despite his fame, or perhaps because of it, Hughes' arrival at the Hepburn's summer home in Old Saybrook was anticipated with a certain apprehension, the sort typically reserved for occasions like visits to the dentist or tax auditor. Hughes' reputation as a ladies' man did not place him high on the Hepburns' list of proper suitors for the daughter they called Red; and for what it was worth, Hughes had little tolerance for the Hepburn's liberal thinking and indulgent lifestyle.

The house called Fenwick after the strip of land on which it stood was a chaotic hodgepodge of uninvited guests, spur-of-the-moment meals, and individual dress. Its very informality and acceptance caught Hughes by surprise, and his typical discomfort around crowds grew even more evident around the Hepburns.

Katharine's former husband, Ludlow Ogden Smith, known as Luddy, was there—guesting as he frequently did and referred to as "our dear sweet ex." His love of photography also riled Hughes, who hated having his picture taken unless he was standing in front of a plane. Katharine loved to tell the story of the day the family was on the golf course, Hughes included, with Luddy trying to capture the moment on film.

When Hughes complained, Dr. Hepburn spoke up. "Howard, Luddy has been taking pictures of all of us for many years before you joined us and he will be taking them long after you've left. He is part of this family. Go ahead. Drive. You need a seven iron." Hughes did, and sunk the shot in two. As Katharine would say, "Cool in a pinch."

He proved that point often during the two-and-a-half years that the pair were together, but never more so than late in 1937, when the Independent Theatre Owners Association (ITOA) published a list of performers they labeled "Box Office Poison." Leading the list was Katharine Hepburn, followed closely by Greta Garbo and Marlene Dietrich.[5] Katharine had just finished filming the comedy *Bringing Up Baby* with Cary Grant for RKO. Despite the fact that the studio already had invested

---

5. The list's favorites were Shirley Temple, Deanna Durbin and Ginger Rogers.

a million dollars in the movie, the ITOA list frightened them into shelving the production after the completion of principal photography. Coming to the aid of his friends, Hughes bought the picture from the studio and released it through the Loew's chain of theaters. For that moment in time, Hughes was Katharine's private hero. She had no way of knowing that within a few months she would be forced to share him with the entire world.

SIX

An American Hero

Well, all I can say is that this crowd
has frightened me more than anything
in the last three days.

Brooklyn, New York
July 14, 1938
Upon facing the crowd at Floyd Bennett
Field after completing his record-breaking
around-the-world flight.

KATHARINE HEPBURN WAS THAT RAREST OF BREEDS IN THE
late Thirties—an independent woman who had her own
concepts about life and expressed them freely and continuously. She was an effervescent gush of ideology and fascination
that ran in counterpoint to the stoic Hughes whose mind
worked silently and methodically in the background. In
November, 1937, they celebrated her birthday, despite the
fact that she was born in May[1]; and in December, they celebrated his, unaware that he was born in September. They
spent Christmas day flying in the amphibian, and prepared
for what they anticipated would be a fabulous new year.

Katharine had been unsuccessful in shaking off her
"box-office poison" label. Even with Hughes' bail-out,
Bringing Up Baby lost nearly $365,000 for RKO studios
which offered her a variety of insignificant films that they
knew she would refuse, including *Mother Carey's Chickens*[2].
While actress Anne Shirley eventually starred in the film,
Katharine recoiled at the prospect and bought out the
remainder of her contract from the studio for $220,000.

---

1. Hepburn's oldest brother Tom committed suicide by hanging himself at the
   age of fifteen while on a visit to his aunt in New York. Katharine discovered
   the body. From that point, she adopted his birthday of November 8
   as her own. She was actually born May 12, 1907.
2. *Mother Carey's Chickens* was based on a play by Kate Douglas Wiggin who
   wrote the novel *Rebecca of Sunnybrook Farm*, later turned into a classic
   Shirley Temple film.

Saved from unemployment by an offer from her friend, director George Cukor, to star with Cary Grant in the film *Holiday* at Columbia Pictures, Katharine appeared to have risen above the fray of innuendo swirling around her, and landed once more on steady career footing. Her life at home with Hughes also gave the illusion of normalcy, with occasional dinner parties setting the tone. Such was not the case.

Living in comfortable co-existence with Katharine Hepburn brought Hughes a sense of family he had not known as an adult, and a contentment that had long eluded him. Despite her resistance to marriage, he found her rather like a pair of worn slippers—comfortable, accessible and warm. Hughes devoted himself to his live-in lover as he pleased, alternating between showering her with attention and impromptu adventures aboard the amphibian, to disappearing for weeks at a time. He told her he was planning to fly around-the-world; that much was true. That he was playing with an assortment of debutantes and starlets while he was at it did not enter the conversation.

Katharine discovered that while she loved the excitement of being with Hughes, she did not love him. Moreover, he had a way of influencing her choices that bothered her, for she suddenly realized that for the first time in her life she was losing track of where her own desires ended and his began. Like a rare eagle in captivity, she sat in her cage and glared. She was confused; she was lonely. What she needed, she instinctively felt, was family, and departed Muirfield. She left her help, took her dogs, and headed home by train to Connecticut.

It was then, in the quiet of his isolation from Katharine, that Hughes began the actual work of detailing his attempt to set the world record for circumnavigating the globe. His decision to make the trip was taken with the same amount of trepidation that the rest of us might give to parallel parking. While it took advance planning, he thought of it neither as risky nor foolish. He had reached a point in his life where impulse had given way to evaluation, a trait he did not share with the impetuous Miss Hepburn. For weeks, he plotted and intricately projected his flight plan, supplies, equipment, and crew. Equally as important, he also decided to rewrite his will.

Working with attorney Neil McCarthy, Hughes restructured his will of May 30, 1925, to remove his ex-wife, the previously mentioned Hughes Tool employees, and John Farrel, who was no longer employed at the Yoakum Street house. He left untouched his bequeaths to his aunts and uncle, who by that time between them had sired thirteen children of their own. The majority of his estate was still left to the Howard R. Hughes Medical Research Laboratories. The will was signed and witnessed on March 3, 1938, and in an elaborately conceived plan worthy of Hughes at his best it was placed in a safe deposit box in Houston, Texas.

Because Hughes was in Los Angeles at the time, a letter with a signed signature card was addressed to Houston's First National Bank. It stated that there were two envelopes enclosed, the first containing instructions and the second containing his will. Neither envelope was to be opened, but rather both were to be placed in a safety-deposit box, with the two keys to be sent back to Hughes in care of his attorney. One key was to be kept in the attorney's safe and the other key given to Hughes himself. According to sources within the attorney's office, the instructions given to the bank stated that should Hughes disappear and his body not be found, the will should not be probated for a period of three years. During that time, "every reasonable effort should be made to determine if Howard R. Hughes Jr. is alive or dead."

The First National Bank, used to dealing with the idiosyncracies of the Hughes account, assigned him box number 3102, forwarded the keys to McCarthy, who kept his in a manilla envelope locked in his safe, and gave the second key to Hughes. Now satisfied that his estate was handled, Hughes turned his full attention to making history.

Originally planning to fly his Sikorsky amphibian, he was denied approval to use the plane by the federal government after another Sikorsky had mysteriously crashed. In its place, Hughes selected the brand new Lockheed 14, a 12-passenger plane that could be adapted for the flight. Lockheed gave him free use of the plane in exchange for the inherent publicity, and authorized the changes that Hughes meticulously dictated. From their base in Burbank, Glenn Odekirk and his crew worked for two months on the Lockheed, fitting it with new engines (donated from the Curtiss-Wright Corporation), increasing its fuel capacity, and dramatically altering its instrument panel to allow for the latest in electronic equipment to be aboard the flight. Given his previous problems with malfunctions, Hughes also had three separate radio systems installed, and a self-contained oxygen supply facility.

On July 4, 1938, Hughes took off with his crew, bound for New York. On board was radioman Richard Stoddart, a 37-year-old employee of NBC; navigator Lt. Thomas L. Thurlow, 33, and a member of the Army Air Corps; co-pilot Harry P.M. Connor, a 37-year-old employee of the United States Department of Commerce, and flight engineer Edward Lund, a 32-year-old pilot from Montana. A fifth member of the crew was W.C. Rockefeller, a meteorologist who would remain on the ground in New York constantly monitoring weather conditions to be relayed to the plane.

Hughes struck a deal with the World's Fair of 1939 to name the plane after the international exposition and call his flight a goodwill mission for the fair. When he landed in New York, at the Floyd Bennett Field[3] in Brooklyn, Hughes was met by Grover Whalen, the popular head of the fair, and thousands of spectators that had come to wish him well. Unfortunately, mechanical problems with the engine caused the trip to be delayed.

While other books on the subject suggest that Hughes spent the time going over weather maps and flight plans, his actual activities were far more Hughesque in scope. He spent days comparing the nutritional values of fourteen different breads, and having decided on the brand most vitamin enriched, he set about making snacks for the flight. Reporters and photographers were busy hunting for him at his New York hotel and had set up observation posts outside Katharine's house in Connecticut, at a time when the pair was actually in clandestine joy at the apartment of American Express heiress Laura Harding, a dear friend of Hepburn's. Under Hughes' supervision, the pair assembled roast beef and Swiss cheese sandwiches for the entire crew, wrapped them in butcher paper, and boxed them to be carried aboard the Lockheed.

July 10, 1938. It was one of those sticky, humid New York days made for open fire hydrants and children. In late afternoon, Hughes changed into a pair of gray worsted trousers, an unironed, white Brooks Bros. shirt, black tie, double-breasted jacket, topped off with his lucky fedora that had accompanied him on his record-breaking transcontinental flight. He packed the sandwiches and Katharine into her Lincoln limousine, and was chauffeured to the field by her driver, Charles Newhill.

Playing in the back seat like two children on summer vacation, Katharine and Hughes were at their most relaxed, having won their continual game of outfoxing the press. Hughes promised to contact Katharine from each stop on his route, pretended to forget her phone number at Fenwick, then rewrote it on a slip of butcher paper, and stuck it in the band of his hat. He had no sooner accomplished the task than the siren of a police car sounded behind them.

Rolling down the interior window of the limousine, Katharine cautioned the temper-prone Newhill, "Charles, don't lose your cool. Take the ticket. Take anything! Just don't let them find out that H.H. is with us."

Newhill, playing his part beautifully, announced his shock when the

---

3. At the time, Floyd Bennett Field was the only airport in New York. LaGuardia and Kennedy had yet to be built. It was named for a Brooklyn aviator that accompanied Admiral Richard E. Byrd on his expedition to the Arctic. The Byrd party made history by being the first men to fly over the North Pole. The airport was later turned into a Naval Air Station that was ultimately decommissioned in 1971. Today, it is used by the New York City Police Aviation Unit for helicopter flights. Abandoned hangars still stand, including No. 7, the one that housed Hughes' New York World's Fair 1939.

officer told him he was speeding, graciously accepted the ticket in his thick, freckled fingers, and even managed a smile for the cop. Hughes was slinking his long legs into a puddle on the back floor and enjoying every minute of the charade. He would later remember it as the most enjoyable part of the entire day—a day filled with exciting firsts.

Hughes was dropped off at hangar seven, surrounded by hundreds of press and thousands of spectators. For a man who always claimed to hate attention, Hughes waved to the crowd, flashed a broad grin and sent the group into a frenzy. Grover Whalen, standing at a microphone, called Hughes and his four-member crew up to acknowledge the crowd. A newspaper reporter at the scene described the flyers as "looking like they were shoving off for a trip to the beach instead of a flight across the ocean."

Whalen dramatically christened the plane *New York World's Fair 1939*, and turned the microphone over to Hughes. The millionaire-flyer-director-producer-ladies' man blushed at his introduction, and shuffled to the microphone for what was to be his first speech. He had scribbled it on a sheet of paper that he removed from his pocket and read to the assembled crowd.

> We hope that our flight may prove a contribution to the cause of friendship between nations and that through their outstanding fliers, for whom the common bond of aviation transcends national boundaries, this cause may be furthered.

Turning to join his crew, Hughes added a little apology to the reporters if he had seemed "rude and impolite" during the repair of the plane. "I had received favorable weather reports and had only the thought of those hopping on my mind." And with that, he boarded the plane, took his place in the captain's chair, and fastened his seat belt, just as he had done hundreds of times before, and waved farewell.

But this was to be no regular flight. The Lockheed-14 had been loaded with 1,500 gallons of fuel and 150 gallons of oil, making his take-off extremely dangerous. Hughes knew it, the crew knew it, and every man on the plane said a prayer before the *New York World's Fair 1939* began to taxi down to the far end of the northwest runway. At thirteen seconds after 7:19 p.m., Hughes pulled on the throttles, and began to lumber down the tarmac. The Lockheed strained at its excessive weight, appearing to groan at its Herculean effort. The crowd drew a collective breath as the plane increased speed, neared the end of the runway, yet failed to lift off.

Still gaining speed, it left the asphalt and rolled onto the muddy grass field beyond, bumping its way amid the stifled cries of those watching. Finally, the plane's tires left the ground, surrounded by clouds of dirt and cheers from the running crowd. Hats were thrown into the air. Howard Hughes was on his way. Before turning east, Hughes aimed his plane north, following the twinkling lights of the New York coastline. As he flew over Old Saybrook, he tipped his wings to Katharine. That done, he banked to the east, and headed into the darkness of the night.

The flight across the Atlantic was longer than Hughes expected. The weather reports suggested smooth air and a helpful tailwind, but just three hours into the flight, the Lockheed encountered severe turbulence and 100-mile-an-hour headwinds that slowed its speed. The mood of the crew was still jovial, however, as Hughes exchanged messages with cruise ships making the Atlantic crossing. When the headwinds did not wither, Hughes became obviously concerned and messaged Rockefeller back in New York: "I hope we get to Paris before we run out of gas, but I am not so sure. All I can do is hope we get there."

It took seven more hours before the weather cleared. Finally, the promised tailwind appeared and greeted their arrival into Ireland. With heavy cloud cover, the plane radioed the *Ile de France*, asking for a bearing. The ship radioed the Le Bourget Airfield in Paris, alerting them of the plane's approach. And by the time the ship determined the plane's position, it had already made a 242-mile-per-hour dive into Paris and a perfect landing at Le Bourget, the same airfield where, eleven years earlier, Charles Lindbergh had landed his *Spirit of St. Louis.*

Hughes had taken 16 hours and 38 minutes to reach French soil, and had cut Lindbergh's time in half. The French were astonished, as was Hughes himself. He had initially estimated a 20-hour flight. His jubilation fell silent, however, when he discovered that a rear strut on the plane had been seriously damaged during his take-off and needed to be repaired before he could continue his flight. It would take eight hours and a miracle to accomplish the feat, but at midnight, the Lockheed was back on the tarmac, refueled and ready for take-off once more.

The next leg of the journey took Hughes and crew over Germany, where Adolf Hitler had made it clear the plane was not welcome. The Nazi government was concerned about the potential for spying, and with a legitimate reason. The country had annexed Austria and part of Czechoslovakia, and was arming itself for war. A compromise was reached when Hughes agreed to fly at 12,000 feet, well above the range that any spying could effectively be carried out. Nevertheless, the Lockheed was tracked as it crossed the country by Luftwaffe escorts. A lightning storm lit up the sky, sending arcs of electricity in a modern dance of energy. Having had no sleep, Hughes seemed to be recharged by the storm, so that by the time he landed in Moscow, the following morning at 11:15, he seemed remarkably alert and excited to have made it half-way around the world.

The Russians greeted the Americans with bowls of corn flakes and milk, a treat eagerly accepted by the five while the Soviet technicians resupplied the crew with food and water, including a can of caviar from General Secretary Josef Stalin. Anxious to keep pushing on his trip, Hughes checked his fuel and returned to the air at 1: 31 p.m. A short time after, the British Broadcasting Corp. informed American listeners that "the Russians fell in love with the American millionaire who had a patch on the seat of his pants." One hour later, they cautioned that the "famed aviator from the United States is currently heading to the desolation of Siberia." And much of America held its breath.

Although it was very early in Old Saybrook, Katharine Hepburn was up and pacing in the large kitchen of Fenwick. She had slept in fits and starts throughout the flight, but now it seemed she was unable to concentrate on anything, particularly sleep. She scanned the radio for every update, and woke the entire family with her screams of joy when she heard that Hughes had landed in Omsk. She was aware that high winds and a fierce rain had drenched the runway, causing the plane to slide in thick mud that splayed itself under the wings. And it made taking off again even more dangerous.

Over forty-eight hours into their journey, the crew of *New York World's Fair 1939* was fading. Each of the crew had taken small cat naps, but none had slept for any extended period. Hughes refused to relinquish control of the plane to his co-pilot for any extended period of time, more out of ego than uncertainty. Harry Conner was clearly worried and questioned Hughes repeatedly with a series of tests to judge his alertness.

Their flight plan took them next over some of the most desolate geography in the world—the furthest reaches of northern Siberia. Approaching the port city of Yakutsk with its grand meandering Lena River carving its way through granite mountains was a magnificent sight to the adventuring five. Of all the regions the Lockheed explored, this city on the edge of the world impressed the team by its noble splendor.

For all its glory, Yakutsk was without an interpreter, leaving Hughes to draw diagrams to request fuel. A local schoolteacher was able to supply a rough translation for *gasoline*, but despite repeated attempts at communicating, the concept of *aviation octane* remained foreign. Fortunately, among the supplies packed on the trip was high-powered ethyl to mix with regular fuel. As he taxied away from Yakutsk, Hughes was in awe as Ed Lund pointed to the sun and moon hanging over the craggy Siberian mountains. Their amazement quicky turned to panic when Tom

Thurlow screamed in alarm. The maps Hughes was using to navigate the area were limited but the best available from the United States Hydrographic Survey. The Siberian mountain range was charted at a height of 6,500 feet; Hughes was flying at an altitude of 7,000. Yet, straight ahead lay a wall of granite directly in their path.[4]

As Hughes pulled in a steep ascent, the Lockheed slowly responded. Its 1600 gallons of regular fuel fought the engines' pleas for power. As they passed the ninety-seven-hundred-foot crest of the mountain, Richard Stoddart could count the pebbles on the surface, less than twenty feet below. Had they not been delayed in Paris for eight hours and followed their original flight plan, they would have been flying over the Siberian mountains at night—on a direct course to disaster.

The near-miss outside of Yakutsk pumped enough adrenaline into the crew to keep them up for the twelve hours it took to reach Fairbanks, Alaska. As they landed at 3:01 p.m. on July 13, on the runway of the airport stood the widow of Wiley Post,[5] whose husband held the record for an around-the-world flight, completed in 1933. Hughes considered it a special honor when Mae Post squeezed his hand and kissed his cheek, whispering, "Godspeed—and success," tears running down her face.

With only one more stop in Winnipeg, Canada, Hughes assumed he would have no trouble fulfilling her prayer. He had not counted on a freak storm that blanketed much of Manitoba and kept him from landing. Thurlow quickly rerouted them into Minneapolis where a lone radio reporter had the scoop of the decade literally drop into his lap as the *New York World's Fair 1939* arrived unannounced. With no welcoming party to delay their departure, they were refueled and back in the air within thirty-four minutes.

As radio reports across America heralded the success of the flight and the imminent arrival of its crew, thousands of people in the New York area decided to turn the occasion into a party and head to Floyd Bennett Field. The roadways became choked with traffic as cars poured into Brooklyn. Grover Whalen, who thought he had the logistics of the arrival ceremony under control, was overwhelmed by the response. The area was cordoned off with barricades, and 1000 policemen were strategically placed. A welcoming stand with microphone was erected near the spot where Wiley Post had ended his 1933 flight. Diminutive Mayor Fiorello H. LaGuardia waited patiently, his prepared welcoming speech in hand. And a message was sent to Hughes' Lockheed: "You are in no danger of being mobbed."

---

4. Upon landing, it was learned that the maps were written in meters, not feet. They correctly indicated the height of the mountain range.
5. Wiley Post died in a plane crash with humorist Will Rogers in Point Barrow, Alaska, on August 15, 1935.

Katharine Hepburn heard the radio reports as well, and comman-deered her Lincoln to drive to New York. Bypassing Brooklyn, she headed to her Manhattan townhouse which, as it turned out, was the other site chosen for a spectator party. When she arrived, her house was surrounded by press, revelers, and complaining neighbors. Dressed in shorts, a sport top, and her hair wrapped in a bright red scarf, the indefatigable star sprinted through the crowd, up the front steps, and into the house, where she became part of the event by turning on her radio and blasting cover-age of her boyfriend's landing out the window to the collected crowd.

By this time, Hughes had crossed into Pennsylvania and was beginning a power dive across the state into New York and triumph. His mind was on achieving the fastest time possible for the final few miles of his journey. Pulling wide the throttle in heady victory, he pushed the Lockheed that had served him flawlessly over 14,000 miles. As he neared Floyd Bennett Field, Hughes and his crew were astounded by the spec-tacle below them. Where there previously was a runway, now ran over 20,000 human ants, moving in groups, pointing in unison at the first sight of the aircraft. He saw the cordoned-off area, the presentation stand, the memorial wreath of lilies to Wiley Post, LaGuardia, Whalen, and several other guests of honor. He heard the directions of the air-traffic controller on the ground, indicating his runway clearance. And he decided to ignore them all.

Rather than landing in the designated area, preplanned and protected, Hughes overshot the runway and elected to touch down at the other end of the airport. His thought was to avoid the crowds and spectacle. What he achieved instead was pandemonium. Seeing the Lockheed land across the field, the throngs broke through the barricades and ran in its direction. The police were helpless to stop them, so joined in the stam-pede. Whalen and LaGuardia were deserted on the stand, and were left following the crowd and the press toward the five heroes who had set a new around-the-world record of three days, 19 hours, 8 minutes and 10 seconds.[6]

The mass circled the front of the plane as it inched foot-by-foot down the runway; Hughes hesitant to move for fear of hitting someone with the plane's propellers. Sirens screamed their welcome amid the horns, whistles, and cheers of the fans, who pressed forwarded in a wave of hysteria. It was all too much for Ed Lund's secretary, nineteen-year-old Miss Elinore Hoaglund, who collapsed and had to be carried off the field on a stretcher.

---

6. Initially, Hughes' time was reported as three days, nineteen hours, seventeen minutes, which reflected the moment his plane's wheels hit the tarmac. The record time was later shortened based on when his plane passed over the administration building at Floyd Bennett Field.

Hughes was the last of the crew to alight from the plane to a tumultuous round of applause. A lanky man in his most nourished moments, he appeared to be weak, gaunt, and in need of rest. But the crowd was not in a tolerant mood. They had waited for a hero, and demanded he take the mantle they offered. "Microphones were pushed in his face, flash bulbs blinded him throughout the episode and the crowd became a mob," reported the *New York Times*. Attempting to collect his thoughts, Hughes sputtered isolated words that said little. He was exhausted, impatient, and wanted nothing more than a hot bath and long rest. Finally, Whalen made it through the crowd to rescue the pilot and his crew, taking them in waiting limousines into the city.

The group had rooms reserved for them at the Hampshire House on Central Park. Before being taken to their hotels, however, the crew rested at Whalen's home on Washington Mews. As the various members were interviewed, Hughes excused himself, to wash and change his shirt. When he failed to return, Whalen discovered that the aviator had disappeared without a trace. At that moment, Hughes was in a Yellow Cab heading to a rendezvous with his lover, only to be stymied by the traffic surrounding Katharine's house. Detouring down 48th Street, Hughes ended up at the Drake Hotel, where he presented himself and requested a suite. That he neither had cash nor identification was not a problem. The manager of the Drake said that he "had heard" that Hughes was back in town, paid the cab driver, and placed a do-not-disturb sign on the outside of the Honeymoon Suite. Hughes did not reappear for sixteen hours.

The following day, all of New York gave a hero's welcome to the aviator who had "the face of a poet and the shyness of a schoolboy," according to the *New York Times*. As he sat in an open car waving to a crowd estimated at 1,500,000, the streets rained confetti as the traditional ticker-tape parade headed from City Hall to Battery Park. Schools were closed and business halted so that no one would miss what the world had labeled "the most spectacular feat in aviation history."

Hughes had refused to take part in the parade unless cars were provided for not only each of his crew members, but also the nineteen men who assisted the effort on the ground, including Glenn Odekirk and W.C. Rockefeller. Smiling from his perch inside the Pontiac convertible, Hughes was idolized for his courage, his talent and his accomplishment. He was no longer Howard Hughes; he was America's hero. It was his zenith; it would become his bane.

In the days that followed Hughes' triumph, he disappeared from New York and was reported "in seclusion." In reality, he was being pampered and loved at Laura Harding's apartment by Katharine, who had rigged a series of elaborate costumes to keep them camouflaged from discovery during solitary walks around town. After a day of parades in Chicago, and another in Houston where he stayed overnight with his Aunt Annette, Hughes made his way back to Los Angeles where the city welcomed him with its own version of a ticker-tape parade through downtown.

While Katharine remained at Fenwick, Hughes took to the seas in the *Southern Cross*, accompanied by a selection of rotating starlets. For over a month, he vanished from sight. His business continued to operate under the capable hands of Noah Dietrich, who heard only sporadically from his boss during this period. Newspaper articles claimed that he had fled to Europe, where he was "spotted in Italy and Austria." All the while he remained less than fifty miles off the coast of California.

His calls were now being taken at a switchboard installed at 7000 Romaine Street, the former home of Multicolor Ltd. The bankrupt company had left the space years before, leaving Hughes free to rent the building to the Koch Brewing Company, which had planned on producing 1,000 barrels of beer from its plant on the site. When that business failed as well, Hughes absorbed the loss and set up the Los Angeles office of Hughes Tool in the stucco building that resembled a fortress.

In August, Katharine read that Hughes had joined Bette Davis at a fund-raiser for Davis' pet charity, the Tailwagger's Club. At the time, Bette was considered an Oscar favorite for her portrayal of Julie Marsden in *Jezebel*,[7] and as such, attracted Hughes' attention. He walked up to the actress who was dramatically costumed in a pink lace ball gown and carried a white basket of raffle tickets, and purchased her entire supply. He also asked her out on a date. A flutter of Bette Davis eyes and a "yes" were all it took to alert Katharine Hepburn that her love affair with Hughes was over.

If she needed any further evidence, it came on September 21, when a surprise hurricane battered the coast of New England and a twenty-foot-high wall of sea water battered Fenwick. The gale-force winds destroyed the old house, with Katharine, her mother, and brother Dick barely escaping with their lives, and taking temporary refuge at the Riversea Inn. When Hughes learned of the disaster, he sent his plane filled with emergency rations of water. "I knew that Howard and I had become friends and not lovers," Hepburn remembered. "Love had turned to water. Pure water. But water," she wrote in her autobiography.

Bette Davis, on the other hand, thought Hughes' advances were the preamble to a long and ardent relationship. After their first date, she

---

7. Bette Davis went on to win her second Academy Award for *Jezebel* (1938). Her first Best Actress Oscar was for her performance in *Dangerous* (1935).

immediately took Hughes to meet her mother, and began picking a china pattern. Hughes, in the flush of his aviation triumph, was just beginning to feel revived sexually and fancied himself a Lothario with his pick of any woman in the world. For the most part, he was right. However, Bette would later relate that he had a limp sexual libido that needed her special coaxing to excite, which only proved that Hughes' fame had impressed himself as much as anyone.

When after three dates he stopped calling, Bette covered her embarrassment with an elaborate tale of a night of lovemaking on a bed covered in gardenias during which her estranged husband Harmon (Ham) Oscar Nelson Jr. was supposed to have crashed his way into the room and demand $70,000 for his silence. While many books repeat the story as truth, although occasionally the flowers of choice are orchids, it happens that during the time the incident was supposed to have occurred, Hughes had already moved on and taken up courting the most famous debutantes in the world on the opposite side of the country.

On November 14, 1938, Brenda Diana Duff Frazier was on the cover of *Life* magazine. She had made her debut in New York City several months before, was heir to a $5,000,000 fortune, received fan mail with just her photograph on the envelope to guide the post office, and was said to be the envy of every teenage girl in America. Brenda was all of seventeen herself. She smoked, went to the Stork Club and El Morocco, and on a winter trip with her mother to Nassau in 1938, attracted the attention of Howard Hughes.

Socialite-columnist Elsa Maxwell, a short, stout cross between a jeroboam of champagne and a little brown jug, was from Keokuk, Iowa, and played matchmaker for Hughes as she brought him across the dance floor and up to Frazier's table. "Brenda, dear, this is the famous Mr. Hughes, as if you didn't already know." Brenda extended her hand to Hughes, dressed in dinner jacket and bow tie, as he bowed slightly from the waist. Sometime during the awkward silence that followed, Elsa, always the catalyst, said, "Well, for heaven sakes, ask her to dance, Howard." He did, and the dance that followed turned into a three-month flirtation that moved from Nassau to California.

He romanced her aboard the *Southern Cross*, offered her caviar and champagne for breakfast, flew her to Hollywood where he promised to make her a star, and proposed to her over candlelight while docked off the coast of Newport Beach. Forty-two years later, after multi-marriages, alcoholism, several suicide attempts, and inoperable bone cancer, Brenda told her nurses that she turned down Hughes "because he was a faggot."

Her frustration over Hughes' sexuality was a by-product of his lack of libido and need to toss ever-increasing fuel on the pyre of his reputation.

In his nights of indiscriminate nightclubbing, often in the company of Cary Grant, he took to frequenting a place called BBB's Cellar in Hollywood. It was a favorite homosexual hangout of Marlene Dietrich and Tallulah Bankhead, as well as the first openly gay actor, Billy Haines, who frequently showed up holding hands with his lover Jimmie Shields.[8] Known for its bawdy drag shows, BBB's Cellar and its clientele were the grist for gossip columns in the trade paper *The Hollywood Reporter.* And frequent mention of Howard Hughes could not help but get tongues wagging.

To say Hughes was a homosexual was incorrect in the sense that he was not interested in having sex with another man. He did, however, feel far more comfortable in the company of men than with women, who he only saw as items to be conquered and ultimately abandoned. He found his reputation as a ladies' man a double-edged sword. It gained him access to the most famous females of the day, who only too soon discovered that the sheep in wolf's clothing was actually, well, a sheep.

Newly separated or divorced actresses were his favorite target, referring to them as "wet decks." He looked upon them as vulnerable and susceptible to his good looks, free spending, and lush lifestyle. While his lines worked on most, they were not effective on all, as was the case when he tried and failed to date Joan Crawford, who in early 1940 had just divorced actor Franchot Tone. For Hughes, she was the ultimate catch, and one known for her love of sex. "I need sex for a clear complexion," she once said, "but I'd rather do it for love."

Joan was one of those in Hollywood who had heard the rumor of Hughes' love of men, and told biographer Jane Ellen Wayne, "Bette went to bed with Howard Hughes. She said he couldn't 'get it up' with anyone else, but that's because he couldn't decide which he liked better—men or women. This is common in Hollywood, and I would say just about everyone tried it once. Maybe you'd label it bisexual, but I would not. Howard Hughes called me many times. I turned him down many times."

Despite his appearance weekly in one column or another, with the dawn of 1940, Hughes was concentrating on far more than just his love life. With the outbreak of World War II in Europe, Hughes' business fortunes improved enormously. There was a drastic need for oil to fuel tanks and planes, and with it an expansion in production at Hughes Tool in Houston, which still controlled a virtual monopoly on drilling bits. Profits from the business had grown dramatically from the shock of the Depression, and reached $20 million by the turn of the decade. Hughes Tool had over 200 versions and sizes of the bit in its catalog. Under

8. By this time, Haines had abandoned his acting career and, through the influence of his friend Joan Crawford, had become Hollywood's most in-demand interior decorator

Dietrich's watchful eye, the plant expanded into research and development, and continued to grow with an eye on the future.

Hughes, as ever, was more interested in aviation than oil bits, and became determined to own his own airline. He found what he thought was the perfect company in the fledgling Transcontinental and Western Air Inc., a one-time mail carrier that had recently expanded into passenger travel. Hughes initially purchased twenty percent of the stock in TWA at $5 a share in the late 30s, and eventually added another ten percent in March, 1940, with the support and encouragement of company president, Jack Frye. With Hughes' financial input, the company was able to purchase the latest Boeing Stratoliners, then the ultimate in passenger comfort.

While no longer seeing Katharine Hepburn romantically, Hughes remained in constant touch with the actress, intent on helping her surmount her "box office poison" label that had virtually eliminated attractive film roles. It was for that reason that when playwright Philip Barry approached Katharine and offered to write a Broadway play just for her, Hughes entered the negotiation process and backed it up with cash.

The Philadelphia Story was to be set in a rich family on the eve of the second marriage of their eldest daughter. It was that role, Tracy Lord, that Barry envisioned for Hepburn. To his credit, Hughes insisted that if Hepburn wanted to do the play, she should pre-buy the film rights to the production, thereby ensuring her own casting in the role should it ever be turned into a motion picture. It was not something that was typically done, but then, neither Hughes nor Hepburn were typical.

When Hepburn was successful in getting the unwritten play half funded by the Theater Guild, Hughes offered to join her in paying for the remaining half, but only if Kate fell in love with the written page— none of which she had yet seen. By the time the play went into production, Kate owned one-quarter of a play she optimistically called *The Answer to a Maiden's Prayer.* Hughes had pledged to put up $30,000 to buy the film rights for Hepburn, and eventually paid the money to Barry, who in turn reinvested it in the production.

By 1940, *The Philadelphia Story* had opened on the East Coast and played to packed houses. Katharine received universally positive reviews for her role, and temporarily halted the tour of the production to travel to Hollywood to pitch the film to Louis B. Mayer at M-G-M, a man most of the film industry considered a messiah and groveled at his feet to indicate their unworthiness. It was to be Katharine Hepburn's golden moment in Hollywood, bringing the All-Highest Mayer to his knees in a negotiation that she not only controlled but won. That she owed her victory to Hughes was not lost on the actress, who made every effort to credit her former lover with her success.[9]

In his typical manner, Hughes rebuffed the praise but did not hesitate to take his share of the profits from the production, which eventually totaled a half-million dollars. By this point, Hughes had restored his own position as a Hollywood producer by reopening the Caddo Company offices at Romaine Street and beginning work on a new film of his own.

He had been infatuated with the story of Billy the Kid, the old West gunslinger, William H. Bonney. He envisioned a film that would combine the story of the rogue outlaw with a fictional tale of his sexual conquest of a buxom female whose brother he had killed. To Hughes, the film had all the makings of a Hollywood blockbuster; to the censors, it meant pornography. As Hughes announced a talent search to find two unknowns to play his leads, Hollywood braced itself for what could only be a collision course with Washington. But not even the most ardent filmgoer could have predicted the impact that Hughes' film, *The Outlaw*, would have on America, a country that was about to be plunged headlong into the war to end all wars.

---

9. *The Philadelphia Story* went on to win Academy Awards for its screenplay, by Donald Ogden Stewart, and for James Stewart as Best Actor. Katharine Hepburn was nominated for Best Actress for her role as Tracy Lord. Additional nominations went to director George Cukor, Best Supporting Actress Ruth Hussey, and executive producer Joseph L. Mankiewicz for Best Film.

A Plane Made of Wood And a Bra Made of Steel

Howard—
I know that you are making every effort to
showcase Miss Russell's breasts, but I am
just saying that they seem artificial or padded,
which I know they are not. I want to see the
tops of her breasts move as she moves, not be
held in place as if they were supported by
concrete. This is an engineering problem,
and I will handle it personally. HRH

Los Angeles, California
November 18, 1940
Note to director Howard Hawks
concerning Jane Russell's bra.

THE BASEMENT OF HUGHES' ROMAINE STREET OFFICES had been transformed into a barnyard. Hay was stacked in one corner. There was a pitchfork, some old timber, even dirt scattered across the faded green and white linoleum floor. The most amazing thing about the set was that it did not seem out of place. The Romaine Street offices had history, and, like most things that have lingered beyond their vital bloom, had collected its share of wrinkles and unwanted baggage. There were remnants of its past to be found throughout the building, so to turn a corner and find a haystack seemed as appropriate as discovering a closet full of unused beer bottles.

In 1940, Jane Russell[1] was earning $10 a week working

---

1. Jane Russell was born Ernestine Jane Geraldine Russell in Bemidji, Minnesota, on June 21, 1921.

as a receptionist for a chiropodist in Hollywood when she saw the ad running in *Variety* announcing the search for an unknown to play the lead in Howard Hughes' next film. If there was one thing that 19-year-old Jane Russell was, it was totally unknown. That she mailed a picture of herself, posing in a tight-fitting sweater stretched over her ample breasts, showed she had some awareness of her assets. Her lips were pouting, as if someone had just told her that she had taken one too many lumps of sugar for her coffee. When Howard Hughes first discovered her photograph in a stack of several hundred, he was not looking at her lips. As he called Noah Dietrich to say that he had found his star for *The Outlaw*, he only remembered "the most beautiful pair of knockers I've ever seen in my life."

Jack Buetel[2] was a part-time insurance salesman living in a one-room apartment he shared with three other guys just steps from Hollywood and Vine. Agent Zeppo Marx, the only non-performer of the Marx brothers, had Buetel as a client and submitted his photo to Hughes. Buetel was twenty-five, slim, muscular, with a cocky attitude that a life on the streets had accentuated.

Hughes paired Buetel's stance and Jane's breasts with art director and costumer Perry Ferguson. It fell to Ferguson to create a Western set and a wardrobe that Hughes labeled "authentic, but with more skin and less dust." Jules Furthman,[3] who wrote the script, was hired not based on his Oscar-nominated effort in *Mutiny on the Bounty*, but rather on his ability to tell off-color jokes. He was also a favorite of Howard Hawks, who Hughes had once again called upon to direct.

Filming began in November, 1940, in the backwater town of Tuba City, Arizona. On the edge of the Navajo nation, Tuba City had few buildings and even fewer accommodations to house the Hollywood newcomers, but when the sky opened to the gold and rose palette of the Old West, cinematographer Gregg Toland captured panoramic vistas and sagebrush plains. Viewing the first few days of rushes shipped via train into Hollywood, Hughes was happy with his actors, but irritated by the lack of clouds. Hughes had waited months for the correct cloud formations during the shooting of *Hell's Angels*, and he informed Hawks that he was willing to wait for them to surface over Arizona.

Hawks, who was never known for his patience, refused to allow Hughes to hold up *The Outlaw* in much the same way he had disrupted *Hell's Angels*. In an effort to keep production on schedule, he began to

---

2. Jack Buetel was born Warren Higgins on September 5, 1915, in Dallas, Texas. He starred in the 1956 TV series *Judge Roy Bean* and died in 1989.

3. Jules Furthman went on to write the scripts for the films *To Have and Have Not*, *The Big Sleep*, *Nightmare Alley* and *Rio Bravo*, among others, and was the pen behind Lauren Bacall's famous line: "You know how to whistle, don't you Steve? You just put your lips together. . . and blow."

shoot closeups with his male leads, freeing Jane Russell for publicity shots. Having never worked before in film, the fledgling actress presumed that all productions crawled at a Hughes pace, and eagerly offered herself to publicity chief Russell Birdwell for exploitation. If America had never heard of Jane Russell before 1940, they had no doubt of who she was by 1941. Her face and barely-covered bosom were featured on billboards from New Mexico to Maine, with a particular concentration in California. "Two good reasons to see *The Outlaw*" the billboards screamed, with Jane's out-thrust chest center stage. The film, of course, was still in production and for two good reasons of its own. One named "Howard." The other named "Hughes." The producer was constantly arguing with the director over the budget—not because Hawks was spending too much, but because he was spending too little. Hughes had given Hawks a percentage of the profits on the picture, and had convinced himself for no apparent reason that the director was cutting corners to improve his own bottom line, a spurious notion, at best.

Around daily shouting matches with Howard Hawks, Hughes occupied his time courting Ginger Rogers, then at the height of her fame, and just divorced from her second husband, Lew Ayres.[4] Learning his lesson from his Hepburn experience, Hughes did not invite Ginger to move into Muirfield. At the time, she was living with her mother, Lela, and Hughes found courting the mother to get to her daughter far more efficient and cost effective.

Lela was flattered by the daily calls from her daughter's famous suitor, and gladly committed Ginger to all of Hughes' plans, regardless of how outrageous or inconvenient. With Lela as a go-between, and Hawks handling the detail work in Arizona, Hughes found himself with enough free time to take on several other projects. The first was designing a new plane; the second, the discovery of a love-child.

With the entrance of Europe into World War II, Hughes became obsessed with designing a high-speed bomber that could help the Allies overpower the Nazis. With steel at a premium, Hughes decided to construct his bomber out of wood, using the recently patented process called Duramold. The D-2, as he labeled the plane, was the brunt of jokes throughout the military, whose generals were well aware of the susceptibility of wood to cracking under stress and breaking under fire. Typically stubborn to outside influence, Hughes not only persevered in his plans, but moved the entire Hughes Aircraft operation to 1,200 newly-purchased acres on the Pacific coast in El Segundo, California, near what is now the Los Angeles International Airport, where he built the longest private runway in the world.

---

4. At the time of his divorce from Ginger Rogers, Lew Ayres was busy at MGM in a popular series of films playing Dr. Kildare, a role later played on television by Richard Chamberlain.

To staff his newly-enlarged facility, he hired 200 engineers and installed them in a 60,000-square-foot, air-conditioned plant along with construction crew, draftsmen, and scientists. And to keep his D-2 under wraps, he hired security to patrol the building and the surrounding acres. The design for the plane was so secret, in fact, that not even President Roosevelt's War Department was made privy to its plans. While it served to protect what Hughes saw as his biggest triumph, it also meant that he could expect no orders for the plane.

Fortunately, Hughes was making money from his Tool division faster than any other single business in the United States. While the war meant tragedy to many, its by-product produced a manufacturing boom for America, and with it, increased fortunes for Hughes. The timing could not have been better. With Hughes Aircraft in expansion mode, Hughes was spending a million dollars every six weeks, with no prospect of any government business, even in the distant future. When Noah Dietrich explained the ramifications of continuing to do business in such an unstructured way, he was rewarded by having his future calls referred to Hughes' new executive secretary, a woman named Nadine Henley. Henley had been a secretary in the Hughes Aircraft offices, and was promoted by Hughes to his Romaine Street headquarters to become his personal foil. Everyone, including Dietrich, was now required to deal with Henley before they could speak with Howard Hughes. Everyone, that is, except a teenager named Faith Domergue.

Faith Domergue was a new starlet on the Warner Bros. lot when she wandered into Hughes' life in the summer of 1940 as a guest at one of many yacht parties arranged by agent Pat Di Cicco and a Warner publicity flack named Johnny Meyer. The dashing Di Cicco and the short, pudgy but personable Meyer selected the guests with a discerning eye toward Hughes' preference for beautiful, young naive girls who might be impressed by his wealth and reputation. Fifteen years old and a studio newcomer, Faith was qualified on all counts. She had dark hair and large green eyes, set off by a smooth white complexion and a thin, lithe body just beginning to bloom.

When she first met Hughes aboard the rented yacht *Sea Queen*[5] on Memorial Day, 1940, she thought he was shy and awkward around the girls half his age. She had no way of knowing that much of what she observed was a performance aimed at enticing nubile flesh into a well-planned web. On that particular day, of all the girls Hughes had paraded before him by Di Cicco and Meyer, Faith was the youngest and as such

---

5. Hughes rented the *Sea Queen* to keep his own yacht *Southern Cross* out of sight in San Diego. At the time, the War Department was appropriating large ships like the *Southern Cross* for military use. His effort was a failure. The *Southern Cross* was forced into military service by the government in 1942.

the most susceptible to his routine. Hughes sat her next to him at lunch, invited her to go sailing, and personally drove her home late that night, leaving her girlfriend Susan Peters[6] to explain her absence to Faith's parents.

Using a now-accustomed route, Hughes appealed to Faith's mother Adabelle to be allowed to date her daughter, and with the predictable outcome. When faced with the potential of Hughes' wealth and connections, the innocence of Faith Domergue came in a distant third. There were moonlight sails, private screenings, parties at a rented house in Palm Springs, and in October, a six-carat, emerald-cut diamond ring from Tiffany. Hughes proposed marriage, and Faith accepted. She had just turned sixteen.

October, 1940, had a great harvest moon that hung red and gold in the sky for many, many evenings, casting a spell on much of Los Angeles. Whatever magic it possessed apparently worked on Hughes, who also proposed to Ginger Rogers that same month. Her ring was a five-carat, square-cut emerald from Cartier. Rogers, too, accepted his promise of marriage, but took the proposal one step further when she engaged designer Edith Head to create a special wedding gown for the occasion. Ginger, of course, did not know about Faith who, in turn, knew nothing about Ginger. And neither female realized that Hughes was also courting sixteen-year-old heiress Gloria Vanderbilt, whom he had arranged to date through a series of calls to her mother as well.

Hughes installed separate telephone lines in the Muirfield house and gave a unique number to each woman. Nadine Henley kept Hughes' date book, separating the various liaisons by miles and days, and for a few months, Hughes' Lothario routine was successful. Gloria Vanderbilt fell out of the running when she fell madly in love with another man—in this case, the equally lecherous Pat Di Cicco.[7] Ginger Rogers, never one to be throttled by a man, began to chafe under Hughes' need to exercise control over his fiancée's every move. Looking for a way to disentangle herself from an ever-tightening noose, Ginger was given her exit cue by a friend, writer Alden Nash. The playwright, who had multiple script rejections from the Caddo Company, was only too happy to even the score. His voice was light and full of gossip, his tongue a wooden spoon in the stock pot of scandal, as he exposed Hughes' many visits to Faith's

---

6. Susan Peters was another Warner starlet who went on to enjoy some fame at MGM before being shot by her then-husband actor Richard Quine in a hunting accident in 1945, leaving her a quadriplegic . She died in 1952 of complications from the shooting. Quine had divorced her in 1947, went on to a career in directing, and eventually took his own life, with the same shotgun, in 1989.

7. Gloria Vanderbilt eventually married Pat Di Cicco, who physically and emotionally abused her. She divorced Di Cicco in 1945 and went on to three other marriages and successful careers as a designer and author.

home, conveniently located across the street for Nash's in a section of Hollywood tightly compacted with bungalows.

The sound that came from Ginger's room rocked the Rogers house to the point that Lela ran shrieking through the door, certain her daughter was being attacked. Scarfs, bras and panties flew as Ginger rummaged through her drawers removing any item that Hughes had ever given her. Dumping them all in a brown bag, including several necklaces, a ruby bracelet, and the emerald engagement ring, Ginger busied herself writing a farewell note, just as the telephone rang once more.

"Miss Rogers," came the clear, pinched voice. "This is Nadine Henley, Howard Hughes' secretary. He's asked me to call to tell you he's been injured in an automobile accident and wishes you to visit him in the hospital."

Half an hour later, Ginger Rogers stunned the nurses, patients and visitors of the Hollywood Presbyterian Hospital when she strolled unescorted into the lobby, took the elevator to the fourth floor, walked past the nurses' station without saying a word, and entered room 418. The curtains were drawn against the day, a slit of light escaping to cut its way through the darkness and cast its shadow upon Hughes, lying in the bed, his head stitched and bandaged.

Walking directly to the bed, Ginger slammed the bag into this chest, and announced, "Faith Domergue needs these more than I do." Before Hughes could answer, the actress spun around on her strapped pumps, moved to the door, and with a dramatic toss of her head, slammed it behind her as she left.

The following morning, Ginger discovered that the station wagon that Hughes had given her early in their relationship was missing from her garage. She reported it as stolen to the police, only to later learn that the car had been repossessed by its owner, the Hughes Tool Company of Houston, Texas. She never saw Howard Hughes again.

For the actors toiling on *The Outlaw*, the news that their director had quit the production (out of frustration) and was being replaced by the producer (out of necessity) came in mid-December, 1940. The train that had brought them to Arizona was ordered back to Los Angeles, along with the wardrobe, sets, makeup and stars. Between Christmas and New Year's, the entire production was relocated onto the lot of California Studios, where Hughes took possession of the director's chair and began, once again, to methodically analyze each movement, word, look and piece of fabric that crossed the camera's lens.

His chief obsession continued to be optimizing exposure for Jane's breasts, having designed a special metal bra to lift and hold them cantilevered like a flying buttress. The resulting apparatus proved as uncomfortable as a mediaeval instrument of torture, and Jane disposed of the appliance under her bed, and in its place substituted her own bra padded with tissues. Much of the shooting took place at night, since Hughes continued to spend his days overseeing development of the D-2 bomber. Filming on *The Outlaw* wrapped in February, 1941, with Hughes having shot 450,000 feet of film. He then began the arduous process of editing to a final length of 10,000 feet.

At the same time, Katharine Hepburn was continuing to tour in *The Philadelphia Story*, and among her engagements was the city of Houston, Texas. She was out of Hughes' heart but not far from his mind, as witnessed by the only surviving letter he wrote to his Aunt Annette.

> Dear Annette,
>
> Kate Hepburn arrives in town Jan. 10. She is an exceptionally good friend of mine, and one of the nicest people in the world—next to you, of course.
>
> Will you please invite her out to see the house one afternoon? Please don't invite anyone else, as she is shy and it gets her upset to meet strangers. She is very tired at the end of a long road tour.
>
> She would love to see the house and you and the children—no one else—not even Martha or Fred.
>
> If she asks to see the plant, please drive her out but not in the gate. I have specific reasons for this and you can find some excuse—Fletcher, or Noah, the only ones you know, are out of town, etc. You had better tell Noah about that so he won't do it himself—by any chance.
>
> Please see that she gets back to the hotel by four-thirty for her nap before the show. This is most important, as she won't take care of herself and is headed for complete exhaustion and a break-down.
>
> Tell her I said I was writing you on the specific condition that she promise to get her nap and go to bed immediately after the show both nights, and that if you did anything to interfere with it, I would be terribly disappointed. And I mean this.
>
> Well, Annette, I'm afraid I am imposing a great deal. Please forgive me—and I do thank you ever ever so much.
>
> My love to you,
> Son.
> I want to tell you also how much I appreciate your phoning.

ANNETTE FOLLOWED her nephew's instructions precisely and invited Katharine to see the Yoakum Street house on January 12. She told her husband Fred he was not allowed to be home, and specifically forbid her sister Martha from dropping by. In a letter to Hughes describing the visit, Annette was dripping with accolades for Katharine, but seemed rather startled to find her wearing yellow slacks. "I have never seen a woman in pants before," she wrote, in genteel surprise.

As Katharine was visiting Texas, Hughes was meddling as well in the life of Faith Domergue. In an effort to tighten his control over the fledgling actress, Hughes bought her contract from Warner Bros., and placed her under an exclusive arrangement with Howard Hughes Productions Inc., a newly-formed corporation and heir to the Caddo Company rights and royalties. He arranged for Faith to have classes in drama and speech at the Romaine offices, under the tutelage of Katherine Braden, an experienced private teacher from the 20th Century-Fox lot. He gifted her father with a palomino pony and installed him in a job at Hughes Aircraft; and give her mother the sterling silver tea set from the Muirfield house.

In April, 1941, Hughes developed a rash on the palms of his hands, and visited Dr. Verne Mason at his home. As always, Hughes presumed he understood his condition and blamed it on a response to the chemicals used in developing the film of *The Outlaw*. Dr. Mason knew immediately that Hughes' was not suffering an allergic reaction.

"Syphilis," Mason said. "It's my third case this week."

Hughes face reddened in a mix of embarrassment and outrage, and when he tried to speak, rather than words, spurts of sound came from his lips like a flooded engine attempting to start. Fortunately, Mason had only recently received a supply of penicillin, a revolutionary new antibiotic rushed into manufacture for war wounds. He gave Hughes an injection, advised his patient that he was extremely contagious, and to avoid all sexual contact for six weeks. Furthermore, Mason alerted Hughes that the tiny blisters on his hands could also spread the disease.

"Don't shake any hands until this thing clears up," Mason recommended, imbedding in his patient's mind an indelible phobia that would remain a lifetime.

Never one to settle for simplicity where prodigality was possible, Hughes demanded that Mason also administer colloidal silver and arsphenamine, the accepted treatment for the disease since the turn of the century. It was a dangerous therapy that was based on killing the bacteria that caused the disease with an arsenic derivative. For Hughes, it meant periods of intense fever and stomach cramps, leaving him disoriented and weak.

Certain that he had contaminated his clothing and sheets, Hughes returned to Muirfield and began a systematic cleansing of the entire house. While Mrs. Dowler was told to scrub the floors with lye soap and cover all the furniture in the living room and study with freshly purchased white sheets, Hughes began to pack away his extensive wardrobe in canvas laundry bags that he subsequently padlocked and placed on his front lawn. Gone were his Brooks Bros. suits, his alligator shoes, his double-breasted tuxedo, and several white dinner jackets. Every bed linen, pillow, blanket, spread, and duvet was bagged as well, even in those rooms where Hughes never ventured. Noah Dietrich was summoned from Houston and told to "burn the locked bags and bury anything that remains." Finding the bags contained expensive clothes, Dietrich later revealed he did not follow instructions and dropped all the items at the downtown Salvation Army headquarters.

In his obsession to purify, Hughes also disposed of his collection of cars, including the Duesenberg, his Rolls Royce, and his Packard convertible. In their place, he bought a used 1938 Chevrolet with a cracked mirror and chipped windshield, and a new Pontiac that was immediately sent to Houston where the Hughes Tools engineers were told to install "an air purifying system with washable cloth filters."

In his closet, he left one black suit, one black tie, one black belt, and two pairs of chino slacks—purchased new from Sears, Roebuck & Co., plus one pair of shoes, a stained brown terry-cloth robe that Mrs. Dowler was told to "hang in the sunlight to sanitize," five new white cotton dress shirts, and his lucky fedora. The remainder of his entire wardrobe fit into a single dresser drawer in his bedroom, and consisted of freshly washed socks, underwear and several handkerchiefs monogrammed HRH.

Besides Dietrich and his doctor, only Cary Grant was informed of his illness. Though there was no symptoms to suggest that Grant had contracted the disease, he too covered his furniture and underwent treatment with penicillin. And when Faith Domergue asked about the transformation, she was only told that "old clothes are more friendly," and believed what she heard.

In the aftermath of his bout with the venereal disease, Hughes dedicated himself to proving the D-2 was the plane of the future. He worked tirelessly, refining lines and its aerodynamics before taking the plane for several test flights over a dry lake bed near Palm Springs, only to rework the engines' thrust and flaps. Each night he returned back to Muirfield merely long enough to have his evening meal with Faith, before sending her home to her parents, and then heading to the studio to attempt to edit *The Outlaw*.

It was a schedule that left little time for socializing, and for most of 1941, Hughes stepped outside the spotlight of eccentricity while tumbling further into its depths. At times caught up in the editing process, he would work forty-eight hours straight without sleeping or eating, leaving the darkened basement of Romaine Street, his eyes squinting at the harsh reality that was squalid Hollywood. With the news that Japan had bombed Pearl Harbor, and America was at war, his workday lengthened, if that was possible for someone already working twenty-four hours a day.

He redirected his energy to creating a flexible ammunition line for fighter planes whose guns came equipped with inadequately small boxes to hold bullets. He formed an armament division of Hughes Tool, placed it under the direction of a manager named Claude S. Slate, who hired 500 employees to manufacture more than a million feet a year of the flexible chute, the basics of which are still in use today.

With the nation at war, Hughes was also obliged to provide his birth certificate to the military in anticipation of service. At thirty-six, with poor hearing, he seemed an unlikely candidate for the draft. However, pilots of all types were being enlisted, and in 1941, Howard Hughes remained one of the most famous pilots in America. Since no birth certificate for Hughes existed, his Aunt Annette appeared before notary public Feodora K. Harlan, together with her friend Estelle Sharp. She swore that the facts were "true and correct to the best of her knowledge and belief" that Howard Robard Hughes Jr. was born legitimate on December 24, 1905. A copy of the birth certificate was filed with the state, and delivered to Hughes Tool on June 24, 1942. By this time, Hughes was considered a "military supplier" and was exempted from active duty.

Photographs of Hughes from 1942 show the toll his work schedule and lack of sleep was taking on the once-handsome playboy. His face became lined, with circles of gray beneath dull eyes, his shoulders drooped in a permanent slouch. As Hughes aged, so too did Faith, as her body developed into the chic figure of a model. She remained devoted to her fiancé despite the fact that no official announcement had been made of their engagement or any plans made for their wedding.

While waiting for Hughes to arrive at Muirfield in the spring of 1942, the teenager found his bedroom unlocked and, seizing the opportunity to snoop, discovered dozens of letters tied in stacks in the bottom drawer of Hughes' bedroom dresser. Among the letters were notes from his first wife, Ella; some written by his mother while he was attending Fessenden School; and a note written from C.M. to C.M. tucked in with some carved wood figures. Carefully refolding the letters and placing them back into their original envelopes, Faith closed the bureau drawer, and went downstairs. When Hughes arrived home that evening, Faith was waiting for him as always, reading her schoolwork in his study.

Beatrice Dowler had made sirloin steak, mashed potatoes, petit peas, and a green salad, Hughes' standard evening meal. Coming in through the kitchen, Hughes bolted up the back stairs to his bedroom to change his shirt and wash his hands. Even in the dim light of dusk, he noticed that the bottom drawer to his dresser was not completely closed. He reached down to pull on the brass knobs fronting the drawer just as Beatrice was placing the food on the table.

When Hughes was under stress, he reacted with silence. No rants, no raves, no flailing of hands. At the dinner table, Hughes ate quietly, not even raising his eyes to look at Faith. She was stunned; the kind of nervous anxiety that comes from knowing something is wrong and not certain if it is proper to laugh or cry. Pushing himself away from the table, Hughes left the room and waited for Faith at the door. Finally, she risked speaking. "I don't know what I've done," she said, wondering if he could see the trembling she felt.

"You've been pussy-footing around, playing the Pinkerton detective," Hughes answered. "You've been in my upstairs drawers and you found the card with the little fairies on it. You even rumpled the paper covering when you put them back in the envelope."

Her mind ran to the card "C.M. from C.M." That must have been what he meant. She felt herself slumping, like a potted geranium left in the sun without enough water.

"Look, little baby. Those little figures were given to me by Katharine Hepburn. They were for good luck when I made the flight around the world. C.M. stands for country mouse, and city mouse. Just friendly, funny names she and I used to call each other many years ago. If you ask me, I will open any drawer or any room in his house you want, but ask me. Don't pry."

Humiliated, embarrassed and caught red-handed, Faith flew into a rage, left the house, and threatened never to cross its threshold again. Had Hughes the wisdom to allow that to happen, his might have been a different story. Certainly his shock at her behavior foretells his lack of emotional maturity; so too his highly dramatic reaction that found him spending the next several weeks ignoring his businesses in an effort to gain the teenager's forgiveness.

Perhaps such is the dues that is payable on demand when dealing with the excesses of spoiled children. To placate the situation, Hughes invented a resolution as if writing a scene from a melodrama. He rented an estate in Bel Air, a sixteen-room furnished house at 619 Sarbonne Road, staffed it with the former crew of the *Southern Cross*, and showcased it as a gesture of love to Faith and her family. What he neglected to tell them was that the Internal Revenue Service had attempted to tax him as a California resident, basing its claim on his ownership of the Muirfield property. Hughes sold the mansion at a loss and never personally owned another home again.

As World War II deepened, and America's fighting force became casualties to the German and Japanese, there was an ever-increasing demand for military ships and planes to reinforce the dwindling U.S. supply. Henry J. Kaiser, a one-time builder of roads and dams,[8] revolutionized the shipbuilding industry with an assembly line that was capable of building an entire military vessel in four-and-a-half days. Upon learning that his ships were sitting targets for enemy submarines, he concocted a concept of a "flying cargo ship" that would be able to transport men and supplies across the Atlantic in the sky where "no submarines could shoot them down." Had someone else suggested such a concept, it is doubtful that anyone would have listened. Coming from the mouth of Kaiser, however, made it sound totally feasible.

With a groundswell of popular support, Kaiser presented his proposal to Donald Nelson, the head of the War Production Board, into whose lap fell the decision for such an enormous undertaking. Kaiser had already performed impossible feats for the U.S. government, and, despite his reservations, Nelson decided to bet that Kaiser had one more additional miracle within his grasp. It did not hurt that the industrialist was full of hyperbole, stating outright that "our engineers have plans on their drawing boards for gigantic flying ships beyond anything Jules Verne could ever have imagined." Apparently no one asked for proof, or questioned who these engineers were, since Kaiser had never built a single plane in his entire life.

Returning to his home in Oakland, Kaiser, a man who coined the quotation "Trouble is only an opportunity in work clothes," put his organization into seeking the most concentrated source of aeronautical engineering manpower. While companies like Lockheed, Boeing and Douglas had the experience, they were operating at peak capacity for the war effort. Hughes Aircraft, on the other hand, had excess engineers, all devoted to developing the D-2. While Kaiser had never met Hughes personally, he was well aware of his aviation accomplishments and placed a call to his aircraft division, his tool company, and his Romaine Street headquarters in an effort to speak to him directly.

When days evaporated into weeks, and Hughes failed to return his calls, Kaiser became outraged with both Dietrich and Henley, stressing it was their patriotic duty to locate a man they claimed checked in with his office infrequently at best. While Kaiser was putting the pressure on the Hughes organization to produce its boss, the man himself was cloistered in San Francisco battling pneumonia. He had gone to the Bay area to fin-

8. Henry Kaiser organized construction companies to build the Hoover, Grand Coulee, and Bonneville Dams as well as the San Francisco-Oakland Bridge. During World War II, he ran seven shipyards that used assembly-line production to build 1,490 ships for the U.S. By his death in 1967, he had founded over 100 companies including Kaiser Aluminum, Kaiser Gypsum, Kaiser-Frazer Automobiles, Kaiser-Permanente Hospitals, and the Hawaiian Village Resort, which he sold in 1961 to the Hilton Corp. for $21,000,000.

ish work on the final edit of *The Outlaw.* After eighteen months of work, he had only reduced the film down to four hours and sixteen minutes, still double its presentation length. The long hours and infrequent eating schedule had left his body depleted and ripe for the infection that finally put him in a San Francisco hospital where he registered under the name George Hoyt. He was still using that name at the Fairmont Hotel, at the time Kaiser located him and made an appointment to meet the aviation legend.

When the sixty-year-old Kaiser strolled briskly into Hughes' suite at the Fairmont, the millionaire was dressed in his only suit, and was lying on the living room sofa groaning. Seeing the ailing Hughes did not deflate his spirit, as Kaiser lifted both hands and boomed, "Get up man. We've got a war to win."

For once, Hughes was not so easy to convince, telling Kaiser, who had promised the government delivery of the first "flying boat" in ten months, that he was "crazy." Or at the very least, overly optimistic. After all, Hughes had spent three years developing the D-2, and was still not in production with the plane. Either Kaiser's enthusiasm was contagious, or Hughes was too sick to resist. Whatever, the headlines of newspapers across the country on August 24, 1942 screamed the news that Kaiser and Hughes had formed an alliance to build 500 of the giant airplanes in what was labeled "the most ambitious aviation program the world has ever known."

On November 16, 1942, the contract for the initial three planes was signed by Kaiser and Hughes with the War Department. The pair was authorized to spend $18,000,000 on the three planes, and receive "no fee or profit from their service." Hughes was granted complete autonomy on the design of the plane called the HK-1 or Hercules, which Kaiser promised to assemble.

With predictable enthusiasm, Hughes summoned his engineers and laid out the situation, breaking them into groups of ten, and dividing the work load by sections of the plane. While Hughes handed out the assignments as if picking positions for a softball team in gym class, the task at hand was incredibly complicated. No one in the world had ever designed a plane weighing 200 tons, the estimated finished weight of the *Hercules*; no engines had ever lifted such weight; and no building was large enough to hold the plane. Faced with the ultimate challenge and an impossible deadline, Hughes' engineers launched into the project without a clear vision or even a leader. Hughes himself was seldom around and feeling pressured to finish *The Outlaw.* Glenn Odekirk was basically a mechanic, without the degree of management skill to coordinate a project of this size. To complicate matters further, Hughes had named his attorney, Neil

McCarthy, as Hercules Project Chief, despite the fact that McCarthy had absolutely no design experience and was terrified of flying.

With the situation at Hughes Aircraft in a state of chaos, Hughes locked himself away in the basement of Romaine to finish the final edits on *The Outlaw* and work on its soundtrack. He authorized publicist Russell Birdwell to plan a premiere of the film in San Francisco, despite the fact that the national film censors had not viewed the finished film or given permission for its exhibition.

On February 5, 1943, the Geary Theater[9] became the first theater in the world to screen the long-ballyhooed movie. Billboards throughout San Francisco proclaimed *The Outlaw* as "the picture that couldn't be stopped." Fans lined up along Geary Street around the block to Mason Street, many holding some of the 43,000 photos of Russell that had been distributed in Birdwell's publicity blitz.

Jane Russell and Jack Buetel were dressed in skin-tight Western wardrobe and placed on stage to perform a scene from the film before its screening. Hughes and Birdwell had flown in forty-eight reporters, columnists and writers for pulp fan magazines for the event. Police held back protesters from the Catholic League who claimed the film was created by Satan himself. At eight o'clock, as the lights dimmed in the theater, Hughes paced backstage like an expectant father. It had been over a decade since he had released a movie, and his tension was written in every movement.

Unfortunately, as the curtain rose, the mechanism jammed causing the heavy fabric to catch suspended two feet off the stage. The only view the audience had was of Jane Russell's ankles and Buetel's buckskin chaps. Those seated out front found the situation comical, like a slapstick burlesque without the striptease. By the time the curtain calamity was finally resolved, Hughes and his two stars had fled the theater, unable to face the judgment of the public.

There was no way they could escape the press, however, who were neither kind nor complimentary in reviewing the film. The local critic for the *San Francisco Chronicle* declared "nothing happens" as if he expected a live sex performance. Far more damaging was the national publicity released on February 22 in *Time* magazine which labeled the picture "a strong candidate for the flopperoo of all time." Not content with lambasting the stars, the reviewer criticized Hughes personally. "An incredible perfectionist, solemnly eccentric Director Hughes exasperated his actors, once made veterans Thomas Mitchell and Walter Huston go through the same scene 26 times, after which Mitchell took off his hat, jumped on it

---

9. Located at 415 Geary Street, the Geary Theater is a San Francisco showplace that now houses the American Conservatory Theater.

and stalked away." The review said that Hughes was gone all day to "design planes for Henry J. Kaiser" and that he would call his assistants at all hours of the night. That the critic was right only made the criticism more painful. And while he thought the film might make money, "since many a bad picture has been profitable," the *Time* reviewer let everyone in America know that Red, the horse, "stole all the honors."

Hughes went into a depression after reading the reviews—alternating between fits of rage and gloom. He telephoned Neil McCarthy and threatened to sue *Time* for its attack. Well aware that the magazine had done nothing but allow its critic to write his opinion, McCarthy advised against it, suggesting in its place that a letter to the editor might be more appropriate. In the end, Hughes did nothing—at least in regard to *Time* magazine. To alleviate his depression, Hughes turned once more to romance, this time with the rising MGM contract player Ava Gardner.

When Hughes met the sultry Southerner in 1943, he had lost much of his notoriety as a world-class flyer, but still ranked as one of the most eligible and envied bachelors in America. The fact that he had taken to driving beat-up cars and wearing one wrinkled suit only added to the millionaire's charisma. While no longer the baby-faced boy with the doe-eyes and moppish hair, he had developed into a slightly weathered icon that could still turn heads and generate whispers. Simply by entering a room, he became that catalyst that turned amity into fervor. Hughes, the lodestar of mystery.

Ava was exactly Hughes' type. Exquisitely beautiful, glamorous, and on the rebound. She had married puckish film star Mickey Rooney at the height of his career and the start of hers, only to discover ten months later that he lost something in the translation from big screen to real life. It was then that Hughes attempted to sweep her off her feet. She would later state that Hughes was "not her type" and her feet stayed firmly on the ground, but not before the deluded playboy flew her across the country and plied her with jewels.

Of all the stars that Hughes dated during his life, Ava was the most unimpressed by her celebrity, and indifferent to its benefits. The daughter of a North Carolina tobacco farmer, she had no acting training and even less interest in the stardom that her beauty had foisted upon her. Her generally phlegmatic personality was quick to fuse, however, when she felt abused. "When I lose my temper, honey, you can't find it anyplace," Ava said from experience. It was something Hughes had to learn, and as usual the hard way.

After inviting Ava on several dates, Hughes decided that it was an appropriate time to move the relationship forward. Sitting at a table in Player's Restaurant, owned by producer Preston Sturges, Hughes slipped a black velvet box across the table. Ava looked perplexed, opened the box, and looked perplexed again.

"It's an engagement ring," Hughes smiled, without adding the words, "that I once gave to Ginger Rogers, who gave it back and now it's yours." The five-carat, square-cut emerald sparkled in the glow of candlelight, until it was sealed in darkness as Ava snapped the lid shut and pushed it back toward Hughes. "What's the matter?" he asked. "I'm asking you to marry me."

"Howard," Ava answered, taking her time. "We are not getting engaged."

"And give me one good reason why not," he said.

"First, because I'm still married. And second, I don't love you. And I will never love you."

Hughes was used to being turned down, and was unfazed by the rejection. He did not, however, expect Ava's blunt response when he pushed the issue and asked, "Why?"

"Because you smell, Howard. Your collar is dirty and you stink. Like a Goddamn canary died under your shirt and it felt so good you left it there."

Ava stood up and asked to be taken home. It was not, as is said, a good evening. It was, however, about to get worse. As Hughes drove the belligerent starlet toward her apartment where she lived with her sister Bappie, they drove down Sunset Boulevard, turned south on Fairfax, and were heading toward Wilshire, when Hughes caught sight of Faith Domergue driving her convertible in the opposite direction. She had no sooner passed his car, than she made a swift U-turn and began speeding back in their direction. Pulling quickly into the empty parking lot of a shopping complex called the Farmer's Market, Hughes stopped his car, and gave Ava a startled look that she returned.

Without warning, the headlights of Faith's car aimed their high-beams directly on Ava's face. She shielded her eyes before a scream rushed from her throat as Faith drove her roadster directly at Hughes' car, smashing in the passenger door. Backing up, she reloaded her fury, and smashed into the car again. Hughes was stunned into stillness, the crisp night air cut by the cries of hysteria as Ava attempted to push open her door. Only the unexpected arrival of airline magnate Sherman Fairchild[10] stopped Faith's jealous rage. Fairchild helped Ava from the car and offered to take her home, while Hughes dealt with the outraged teenager.

That evening Faith turned her back on Howard Hughes, returned to

10. One of the founders of Pan American Airlines and American Airlines, Sherman Fairchild also invented an aerial camera that pioneered the way for aerial reconnaissance and mapping.

her parents, and swore that she had learned her lesson. Hughes was now alone again, thinking he had lost Faith, knowing he had lost Ava. Yet, as Faith would later write in her secret diary of their affair: "There is a strange quirk in Howard, stranger than all of his other peculiarities. Once he has become involved with a project or a person, he can not let them get away from his control. Once owning something, he has to own it for always, and this is so strong in him, I believe it is unconscious. It is so much a part of his presence that it is like his brown-black eyes, his high-pitched voice, it is him. And it is the most self-destroying element of his character."

Hughes had reached a crossroad. His film career was being mocked, his romantic self-image was shattered, his aviation reputation was being challenged, and his mind was slipping further away from anything resembling control. His life was the avalanche that dares not sleep long enough for the mountain to recover. And soon the entire world was likely to learn his truth.

Crash and Burn

*A dash, or two, shall be used to denote words
preceding, or following a quotation. Two dashes
shall be used to denote the deletion of words when
a group of words are quoted and one dash shall
suffice when only one word is quoted. In either
case, there shall be a space between the quotation
mark, the dash, or dashes, and the quoted word,
or vice-versa: i.e. " — and will best assure — "*

Bel Air, California
April 3, 1944
Hughes' instructions to his secretary on the
correct form to use in typing his will.

MAY 16, 1943. THE MOON STILL HUNG IN THE WESTERN
sky as the sun rose in the east, giving one a sense of omen or
perhaps just a gift for being alive at that point in time.
Howard Hughes had risen early from a restless sleep in his
suite at the Desert Inn Hotel in Las Vegas. His mind was full
of countless bits of information, all waiting to be placed in
their proper file. Countless bits of information that fought
each other for attention, only to ultimately be forgotten
after having been noted on a growing number of yellow
legal pads stacked neatly next to the bed.

He had come to Las Vegas with Ava Gardner and her
sister Bappie—a forgiving Ava having left no doubt that
there was to be no more talk of romance. Hughes had flown
them in his Sikorsky amphibian. It with the larger of his two
Sikorskys, the S-43; the one that he had allowed Katharine
Hepburn to fly from under the Fifty-ninth Street bridge in
New York City, and dive naked off its wings into the Long
Island Sound. Now he was to sell it, forced by the military

who needed it for their Army Corps of Engineers in Reykjavik, Iceland.

Before relinquishing the plane, however, Hughes wanted to take it for one final flight, ostensibly to test its newly upgraded engines. He knew, of course, it was really a sentimental farewell flight to say goodbye. He was dressed in his usual white shirt and khaki slacks, once-white tennis shoes stained the color of spilt cappuccino, and his lucky fedora that he adjusted on his head as he looked in the gold-and-white framed mirror above the dresser. He noticed a hair sticking out of his nose, and pulled on it ineffectively with his fingers. They were the long fingers of a flautist with the dirt encrusted nails of a mechanic. "Damn," he said as the stubborn hair refused to budge.

Before leaving his room, he made a note on the third yellow pad from the top: "Remove hair, right nostral." That he misspelled nostril did not matter. He knew what he meant, and underlined it twice as if to signify its importance. The note came right after another reminder, this one not underlined, concerning the forty planes Hughes had ordered from Lockheed Aircraft for TWA. "Check status of Constellation delivery," it read. It was an order worth $18 million, paid for by Hughes Tool Company.

The Sikorsky was docked on Lake Mead, the largest man-made body of water in the U.S., created by the building of Hoover Dam with the help of his partner Henry Kaiser. As Hughes took his place in the pilot's seat, Charles W. Von Rosenberg, a Civil Aeronautics Administration executive, slid in next to him in the co-pilot's position. Behind them, a CAA inspector named William M. "Ceco" Cline sat with Hughes' mechanic Richard Felt, and further back, Gene Blandford, Hughes' flight engineer. Glenn Odekirk from Hughes Aviation was manning a camera on the ground, taking pictures of the plane's hull as it moved through the water to be used as research in the design of the *Hercules*.

As the Sikorsky took off, the translucent blue of Lake Mead barely stirred as the plane lifted over the surrounding russet cliffs and blanched Nevada desert. There was nothing extraordinary about the flight, other than it would be Hughes' last with his beloved Sikorsky. After circling Hoover Dam three times, Von Rosenberg instructed Hughes to land the plane in a section of the massive man-made lake known as Vegas Wash. It was a simple landing on a placid lake, witnessed only by Odekirk, a few sea birds looking for lunch, and a sole fisherman in a motorboat. As the Sikorsky hit the water, Hughes skimmed its surface before the plane suddenly bucked and pitched right, its wing slamming into the water. The right engine's propellor cracked in two on impact and sliced its way through the cockpit, hacking a hole in the fuselage which began to flood.

Hughes was stunned in his seat as the frigid mountain water hit his legs and chest. Von Rosenberg felt a flash of pain and then a numbing sensation cleansed his body as he screamed to Hughes to open his escape hatch. The rush of water broke the Sikorsky in two and then discarded it like a peanut shell on a barroom floor. Pushing Hughes through the small window by the pilot's seat, Von Rosenberg hoisted himself through the open roof hatch and out onto the plane's broken fuselage.

"Cline. . . . Cline," Von Rosenberg shouted as he slid down the side of the plane into the water. Blandford was gripping the edge of the Sikorsky with his left hand, his right arm supporting Felt. Part of the mechanic's head had been severed off by the propeller blade. Blood pulsed from the gaping wound, and began to flow unabated into the lake, red swirling into crystal blue like a pop-art painting at a county fair. Von Rosenberg saw Hughes waving toward the motorboat being steered at the wreckage. Ceco Cline had disappeared with his seat and an entire section of fuselage into the depths of the lake.

In the hospital later that afternoon, the four remaining crew members were separated. Von Rosenberg had suffered a broken back and spent the next three months in a full body cast. Blandford and Hughes had only suffered cuts and scrapes and were released later that same afternoon. Felt died within two hours of massive brain damage and blood loss. Cline's body was never recovered.

Before returning to the Desert Inn, Hughes had Odekirk drive him to the J.C. Penney store in nearby Boulder City, Nevada. There he removed his blood-drenched khakis and replaced them with a new pair using money borrowed from Odekirk. Ava Gardner remembered that the pants were six inches above his ankles, but he continued to wear them for the next several years. Hughes paid everyone's medical bills, and the funeral service for Richard Felt. He gave Felt's widow $48,000, representing four years' salary for her late husband. He spent $120,000 for Navy divers to bring up the wrecked Sikorsky, and an additional $220,000 to have the plane rebuilt in Culver City, where it was put back in service, complete with its leather divan.

When Hughes returned to Bel Air following the deadly accident, he was a changed man. Reminded again of his own mortality, he was a reptile shedding its skin, stripping away memories of the past, or at least material possessions attached to them. One evening in the living room of the house on Sarbonne Road, Hughes opened a packing box containing all the letters that Faith had discovered at Muirfield, and began destroying them in the fireplace. As she watched, he examined each letter one last time, and tossed the paper into the flames.

Letters from Billie Dove disappeared, those from Dudley Sharp and Ella Rice, the fairy note from Katharine Hepburn, the good luck carvings, a photograph of Katharine laughing aboard the *Southern Cross*—all destroyed in a ceremonial pyre of release. Faith attempted to convince Hughes to save at least one letter from his father and mother, but to no avail. Those letters in particular he made certain were burned completely, lest she try to rescue them after he had left the room. It was a rite of passage that suggested he had crossed an invisible line—one that separated boy from man, weak from strong, naive from jaded. In her diary, Faith remembered the night for its sadness. "There was nothing left from his past. Not even memories."

Noah Dietrich would later testify that Hughes was showing the first signs of enormous strain. He began to haunt the empty hangars at Hughes Aircraft long after his employees had punched out for the evening. Night watchmen clocked his activities as he roamed the various research divisions, using a flashlight to illuminate blueprints for plane designs and development. He would often spend hours simply staring at the D-2, a plane that had been overshadowed by the rush to construct the *Hercules*. Hughes would talk to himself as he rubbed his fingers over the Duramold skin of the high-speed bomber. And it was the D-2 that he unveiled for Elliott Roosevelt when the President's son came to make an official visit to Hughes Aircraft on August 8, 1943.

It was a stagnant period in America's war effort. The Japanese and Germans were battering both Allied ships and planes. Franklin Roosevelt appointed his second-oldest son, an Air Corps Colonel, to head a five-man team to survey the nation's aircraft plants to find a plane capable of handling aerial reconnaissance, and Roosevelt, the younger, fell into the hands of Howard Hughes—or more precisely, Hughes' press flunky, Johnny Meyer.

Meyer, of course, knew nothing about reconnaissance planes, nor anything else about the war for that matter, having been deferred from the draft six consecutive times because of his employment by Hughes Aircraft. What Meyer *did* know about was women—especially beautiful women. Hughes was aware that Roosevelt was unmarried and available, and while all the other aircraft plants were attempting to impress the President's son with their expertise by extensive tours of facilities and lunches with scientists and engineers, Hughes told Meyer to wait until Roosevelt returned to his hotel and pay a visit with what he labeled "a boob buffet"—one redhead, one blonde, and one brunette. If Roosevelt was embarrassed by Hughes' approach, he covered himself nicely by cancelling appointments during the day to make himself available for Meyer.

While the other members of his committee handled Lockheed, Boeing, and Douglas, Roosevelt concentrated on Hughes Aircraft. Instead of planes, what he saw was the inside of MGM, RKO, Paramount and Warner Bros. studios. Each day, Meyer made certain that there was always a "boob buffet" waiting for Roosevelt's arrival. Meyer hit pay dirt when he moved Roosevelt through the executive dining room at Warner Bros. and introduced him to Cary Grant, who was then shooting *Destination Tokyo*[1] at the studio. They joined Grant and actress Faye Emerson for lunch, with Faye recommending the day's special, Mulligan Stew. As it turned out, Roosevelt was far more interested in Faye than the stew, and began to monopolize the conversation with the actress.

Faye Emerson was not one of the "boob buffet," although Hughes would later take credit for the introduction. Clearly smitten, Roosevelt asked Faye to join him for dinner at the Beverly Hills Hotel, and she accepted, fawning over the President's son and allowing her hands to linger on his shoulders as she rose to return to work. The following day, Hughes gave Roosevelt a personal tour of his plant, after hearing about Faye Emerson's charms, and he personally flew all five members of the Air Corps team to Lake Helen to inspect the secret D-2, still unfinished after four years of development. Visually, the plane appeared to be something out of science fiction with a sleek and smooth body that made other fighters look more like machinery. The D-2 clearly was art. Commander D.W. Stevenson, with the British Royal Air Corps declared it "magnificent."

After Roosevelt left Los Angeles, he traveled to Manhattan, and although he was on Air Corps business, Johnny Meyer accompanied him on the trip. The next day, Faye Emerson joined the men in New York for a week of dinner and dancing at the Copacabana and the Stork Club, compliments of Hughes Aircraft. Roosevelt stayed in Hughes' suite at the Waldorf-Astoria Hotel, with Faye Emerson in an adjoining room. Faye was the perfect complement for the educated Air Corps colonel: she was socially prominent, elegant, impeccably attired, and quietly attentive as she listened to his endless tales of life at Hyde Park with the President and First Lady.

When Roosevelt returned to Washington, D.C., he wrote to the head of the Air Corps, General H. H. "Hap" Arnold, recommending that the Hughes D-2 be immediately ordered as the newest U.S. photo-reconnaissance plane. Roosevelt noted that Hughes had agreed to convert the plane from wood to metal, and Arnold, despite his own reservations, accepted Roosevelt's suggestion. Hughes received an order from the government for one hundred planes, renamed the XF-11 by the military. Many in Washington were astounded by the move. While no one in the Capitol had seen the D-2, everyone was acquainted with it if for

---

1. *Destination Tokyo* was a World War II propaganda film with Grant portraying a submarine captain who makes an espionage run into Tokyo bay. John Garfield co-starred with Alan Hale. Faye Emerson had a bit part as "the girl back home."

no other reason than its lack of airworthiness. For the Air Corps to order one hundred planes without ever seeing one leave the ground was so unorthodox that Major General Charles E. Bradshaw wrote to Arnold calling the Hughes plane "undeveloped and unstable." Arnold, however, was not to be budged, and appropriated $48 million in funds to Hughes Aircraft for the contracted planes.

At Hughes Aircraft, aeronautical designers were struggling to furnish what Hughes had promised to deliver. The *Hercules* was too heavy a plane to fly completely empty, let alone filled to capacity with hundreds of service men and assorted tanks, guns, and machinery. The XF-11 was beautifully designed, but utilized an engine that no one had built. Compounding the problem even further, there was no one operating in a supervisory capacity at Hughes Aircraft—except Hughes himself.

For the first time since its formation, Hughes Aircraft had the honor of ongoing visits from its namesake. Nearly every afternoon, Howard Hughes arrived at the aircraft plant to oversee production of the *Hercules*. Workers who spent all morning playing cards and reading newspapers suddenly became active when they were notified that Hughes' old Chevy was entering the parking lot. Always the perfectionist, Hughes spent hours evaluating every element of a plane that was the width of a football field. He worked with the intensity that old maids give to picking locks, gauging the adhesive quality of wood glue, the tensile strength of bolts, the appropriate size of gauges, door openings, seat widths. All without training; all on instinct.

Weeks melted into months as minutiae obsessed the millionaire who nightly found himself working alone in the cavernous hangar housing various parts of the unassembled plane. It was there under the stark lights of his own plant that Hughes noticed the scars on his hands; tiny white dots that remained where the syphilis blisters once bubbled and burst. He rubbed at them, feeling the hard scar tissue that hid in silence beneath the surface of his skin. At the Sarbonne Road house, he would scrub his hands with the deliberate intention to make them bleed as if the flow of blood would free him of the reminder of the disease.

During the first month of 1944, Faith Domergue made notations in her diary that, in an apparent reaction to his increased pressure, Hughes had begun eating his dinner in his room, spending hours alone in his twin bed. "We no longer ate formally in the dining room, or even used the beautiful living room and library. And of all the bedrooms, he had picked the simplest, the most austere for himself, and had installed special phone amplifying equipment so he could hear. There he slept and there he worked, and there we finally had dinner every night."

The pattern came to an arresting halt when Hughes received word in

February, 1944, that the War Department was set to cancel the Hercules contract. As if transformed by the threat to his reputation, Hughes flew to Washington, and settled into a lavish suite at the Carlton Hotel from which he lobbied to keep his flying boat on target and "from being turned into kindling." Now convinced that there was a "plot of enormous magnitude" against him personally, he pleaded with Jesse H. Jones, an old family friend, to intercede on his behalf. Jones was the chairman of the President's Reconstruction Finance Corporation, and had known Hughes since he was a small boy. It was Jones who introduced Hughes at New York's City Hall after his around-the-world flight, and it was now Jones on whom Hughes was depending to keep Washington from scraping the *Hercules*.

It was through Jones that Hughes was introduced to Major General Bennett E. Meyers, a cigar-chomping pilot who had risen through the military to the number two position in the Materiel Command, the purchasing and logistics arm of the military. The balding career soldier had the appearance of an over-stuffed couch, his body poured into his uniform, the buttons straining against their fabric. That Meyers liked to eat was obvious. Hughes discovered he had a passion for filet mignons, lobster tail, and rack of lamb as well as an assortment of other delicacies his salary could not afford, and made certain that Meyers' refrigerator was well supplied. In return, the general enlightened Hughes on the power brokers in Washington, and where his enemies lay. As Meyers got fatter, Hughes got wiser, and soon realized that only the President himself had the power to keep the *Hercules* alive.

It was Jesse Jones that eventually spoke to Roosevelt on Hughes' behest after a cabinet meeting in mid-February. The President, who was fighting poor health and the increased presence of American military in a drawn-out war, had a full plate without the intrigue caused by any project associated with Howard Hughes. Yet Roosevelt remained attracted, not by the plane itself, but rather by the engineering required to lift such a massive weight. For that reason alone, he wondered aloud if there was at least knowledge to be gained from continuing the project. That single thought was enough for Jones, who passed along the President's reflection to Donald Nelson, who in turn gave the *Hercules* a temporary reprieve.

The grace did not come without a price, however. Hughes had made a seeming friend of Meyers, who did not want to let the Hughes fortune escape his grasp without more to show for it than some digested beef steak. He wanted nothing less than to run Hughes Aircraft upon his retirement from active duty. Hughes' profuse praise of the general over glasses of port and Honduran-made Sancho Panzas had gone to his head and he made it clear that he expected an executive position at the company. Fortunately, Hughes had just hired the highly-regarded aviation executive Charles W. Perelle away from Consolidated-Vultee Aircraft to bring some much-needed organization to his aviation division, promising Perelle "full autonomy" plus shares in TWA as an incentive.

Fearing a backlash from Meyers, however, Hughes sent Neil McCarthy to gently dissuade the general from aspirations of an executive career. While the strong arm of Noah Dietrich would have seemed a more likely choice for the assignment, McCarthy nevertheless accepted the job and flew to Washington to break the news to Meyers, who received the disappointment unabashed. Perhaps, Meyers suggested, Hughes would be willing to lend him $200,000, interest free, to be used to secure War Bonds as an investment in his future. McCarthy was appalled at Meyers' arrogance, and promptly broke off the discussion.

When Hughes heard about Meyers' suggestion, he was in a meeting with writer/director Preston Sturges. The Oscar-winner had entered into an agreement with Hughes to form Sturges-Hughes Inc., with its sole mandate to turn Faith Domergue into a star. Hughes left the flabbergasted Sturges mid-sentence, screamed at McCarthy for his incompetence, labeled Meyers' proposition "nothing short of blackmail" and refused the loan outright. That did not, however, mean it left his mind. Like most things Hughes, the kernel of even the smallest concept rolled around in his brain like birdshot on a counter. He badgered McCarthy relentlessly for his opinion, waking him in the early morning hours for absolution on his decision. After weeks of dodging calls and insults, McCarthy had had enough, and resigned the Hughes account. He had witnessed the growth of a boy into a man, and a man into a legend, and had decided that the end result was a sad mix of excess and denial at odds with reality, or at least McCarthy's reality. For Hughes, it was a rancorous loss and tore at an emotional make-up so fragile in its balance that it threatened to forever damage its core. His mind was like the unfallen leaves of winter, unable to escape even though to remain meant certain death.

The meticulous perfectionist began to repeat himself, giving an instruction three, four, five times in the course of the same minute. His employees were reluctant to criticize their boss and allowed his unusual behavior to continue. Only Noah Dietrich felt confident enough to challenge Hughes; more than challenge, he urged him to seek immediate medical help.

"I think you ought to see a doctor," Dietrich recommended. "I made a tally on a pad. You've repeated the same sentence thirty-three times. You've been repeating yourself a great deal lately."

When Dr. Verne Mason took Hughes' call, he instantly recognized the symptoms of a nervous breakdown. His advice took the form of an edict. "Stop work and take a vacation, or your body will do it without you."

Howard Hughes was petrified when he returned the telephone receiver to its cradle. His hands trembled. He slipped them between his knees and allowed his head to drop. Still his hands trembled, joined now by a flood of tears. His mind raced with details: plane specifications, soundtrack scores, movie deals, the gardenia perfume of Ava Gardner, the mist green eyes of Faith Domergue, his unfinished will, 3800 employees, faces, names, figures, details, details, details.

When Hughes opened his eyes, he discovered that he had fallen asleep. Hours had passed. His shirt was damp with nervous perspiration. He was cold, yet felt like he had a fever. He wanted to hide but had no where to run. He only knew he had to try. Telephoning Noah Dietrich, he confirmed his assistant's suspicions and informed him that he was taking some time off. "I don't want you trying to find me, either," Hughes warned. And with that, Howard Hughes disappeared into the night.

For the next eleven months, Hughes never contacted his office, had no interaction with his aviation company, was out of touch with Ava Gardner, Faith Domergue, and Cary Grant, and became a nomad—albeit a rich one with his pockets full of cash. Only a single Hughes employee—Joseph Petrali—knew about all of his activities, and he did not speak of those months until after his own death in a posthumously-published article in *True* magazine in 1975.

Petrali was Hughes' chief of services and flight at Hughes Aircraft, and, as such, was in charge of restoring the damaged Sikorsky to flying condition. After the plane was repaired, Petrali began to receive calls from Hughes saying that he was heading to his Culver City plant to give the plane a test run. After each call, Petrali rolled the plane onto the runway, warming the engines for the expected flight. For months, the exercise began the same—and ended the same. The Sikorsky was rolled back into its hangar when Hughes failed to make an appearance. In October, 1944, with Petrali nearing the end of his patience, Hughes telephoned once again. This time Petrali was sworn to secrecy, and told to prepare for a trip "of a couple of weeks." Hughes had made a similar call to a mechanic named Richard Beatie, a specialist on the amphibian. The men were still attempting to hurriedly pack when Hughes arrived at Culver City and announced he was ready to depart.

It was to be a short trip. Looking haggard and worn, Hughes piloted the Sikorsky over the San Gabriel Mountains, its lush pine elegance giving way to the parched earth of the dry Coyote Lake in the Mojave Desert. Skimming the Joshua trees and creosote brush of the Toiyabe National

Forest, Hughes landed the plane on the outskirts of Las Vegas, deliberately avoiding the city's airport with its inherent publicity, and selected
instead an isolated rural strip with a dirt runway twenty miles outside of
town. Heavy crosswinds caught the plane's right wing, and pushed the
Sikorsky off the runway into the mesquite, shattering shrub pods in a
flurry of dry splinters. By the time Hughes had managed to stop the aircraft, he had torn off its rear wheel supporting the tail and buckled the
fuselage across the wings. After over a quarter of a million dollars in
repair, the Sikorsky had flown less than an hour before being severely
damaged yet again.

It would take several weeks to fix the plane, with Petrali flying in
parts and mechanics from Culver City. Hughes had been driven to the El
Rancho Hotel, the first hotel on what was to become the Las Vegas Strip.
At the time, the El Rancho consisted of sixty-three individual cabins in
rugged southwest motif, with extra long beds that appealed to Hughes,
who asked that his room be darkened against the Las Vegas sun by hanging
bedspreads across windows that looked out onto the small front porch.

Hughes remained in darkened seclusion for the next two months,
with only sporadic side trips to Reno and Palm Springs breaking up the
monotony of his solitary confinement. He was happiest when he was
alone, illuminated by a single light bulb, and allowing his mind to wander
to its farthest fantasies. Time had no meaning and reason no purpose.

By the time Christmas had turned Las Vegas into a landscape of artificial snow and metallic trees, Petrali and Beatie were bored by the sheer
idleness of their work and desperately missed their families. When
Hughes refused to give them time off to return home, they slipped a note
under the door to his rustic bungalow and flew back to California, advising
Hughes they would return in two days. When they reappeared at the El
Rancho on the day after Christmas, Hughes' bungalow had been vacated;
their boss had vanished.

After three weeks passed, and Hughes failed to return to Las Vegas,
Beatie became paranoid that perhaps the pair had been fired, did not realize
it, and instead of playing solitaire on a card table in the lobby of their
hotel, he should be out looking for work. Beatie returned alone to Los
Angeles, only to discover that his job was waiting—his work piling up in
his absence. It was midday, on February 2, 1945, when Hughes showed
up again at Petrali's hotel, without offering an explanation of where he
had been, nor mentioning his employee's holiday disappearance.

Hughes arrived by cab and had in his possession a box the size of a
small coffin, the type that might be used to bury a baby. Petrali was
instructed to wrap the box with butcher paper and secure it with string,
without the aid of any "stickum." The box was then loaded onto the

Sikorsky which Hughes flew to Shreveport, Louisiana. Petrali was in the co-pilot's seat, yet he and Hughes never spoke for the entire eight-hour flight. Upon landing in Shreveport, the pair went to the Jefferson Hotel[2] on Louisiana Street, where Hughes went promptly to sleep.

It was a wet night in a strange town. Unable to settle himself, Petrali walked several blocks in the rain to see the film *Dick Tracy*, playing at the Rialto. Although he was gone less than two hours, it was ample time for Hughes to disappear yet again. When Petrali returned to the Jefferson, a rotund clerk at the front desk was waving his arms as if he meant to fly to the ceiling. He was babbling about the police and Howard Hughes and the word "vagrant" keep creeping into the hysteria in a way that made Petrali very nervous.

By the time Petrali ran the half-block to the station house, Hughes was walking out the door in the care of a man named Elias Long who was a local salesman for Hughes Tool Company. The way Long told the story, the police had picked up Hughes standing in the dark in a gas station, eating a bag of chocolate cupcakes. When Hughes refused to give his name, he was searched and found to have $1,200 in cash in his pockets.

According to Long, Hughes continued to refuse to speak until he heard the sound of the cell door locking. Only then did he declare that his name was Howard Hughes. The detective in charge, a man named Davis, was said to have answered, "Yeah, and I'm Shirley Temple." It was only after the laughter died down that Hughes convinced the police to try to call Petrali at the hotel. When that failed, the local office of Hughes Tool was telephoned and Long was summoned to the station. While he had to admit he had never met Howard Hughes, Long knew that it was better to release a vagrant with $1,200 in his pocket than chance having his boss spend the night in jail. He received a bonus of $500 for his trouble.

The vagabond life of Hughes moved next to Miami and on to New York City, where he checked into the Plaza Hotel. With Petrali sent back to Los Angeles with the mysterious coffin-sized box in tow,[3] Hughes had tailors from Brooks Bros. sent up to his room. He was measured for a new dinner jacket, a new pair of black slacks, and bought seven white cotton oxford-weave shirts. He began to appear at nightclubs in the company of show girls from the *Ziegfeld Follies*, and made a point of speaking to *New York Post* columnist Earl Wilson who later wrote, "Howard Hughes wears tennis shoes around New York proving something

---

2. The Jefferson was built in 1922 as a railroad hotel and was placed on the National Register of Historic Buildings in 1980.
3. The box was placed in storage and was later found to contain old newspaper comics from the *Houston Chronicle*, a baseball bat, and several douche bags.

fascinating about men's fashions: If you're Howard Hughes, it doesn't matter."

While in Manhattan, Hughes attended a screening of *Salome, Where She Danced* featuring Yvonne DeCarlo[4] in her first starring role. Billed by Universal Studios as "The Most Beautiful Girl in the World," Yvonne had long dark hair that she would whip across her face in a way that enticed Hughes—from New York across the country and into Canada, where the star was appearing in person in a hometown "Yvonne DeCarlo Week." With Meyer in tow to arrange an introduction, Hughes took particular pleasure in romancing DeCarlo, as much to announce his return to his role as America's Lothario as to entertain the rising star. He made no secret of his pursuit, as DeCarlo spent the next two weeks with Hughes in Canada, then Reno, Las Vegas, and then Los Angeles, where he checked into the Town House hotel on Wilshire Boulevard under the name J.B. Alexander, rather than return to Faith Domergue who was still eating her dinners at his Sarbonne Road mansion as she had been instructed to do.

It was the third week of September, 1945, when Hughes felt the landing gear of his plane touch the tarmac of his Culver City runway. He had been gone for eleven months, and much had happened during his absence. Harry Truman was the new President, FDR having died in Warm Springs, Georgia, on April 12. His son, Elliott, had married Faye Emerson, who was given away by Johnny Meyer. Rupert Hughes' third wife, Patterson Dial, had died from an overdose of barbiturates. The Allied forces had won World War II, prompting the government to cancel its order for the XF-11 reconnaissance plane, and authorize delivery of the two planes Hughes Aircraft had managed to manufacture. Even more impressive, with Hughes away and Charles W. Perelle in charge, the *Hercules* had been finished, with only final assembly of the engines to the wings, and the wings to the fuselage yet to take place.

With his mental problems seemingly under control and his businesses on their best footing in years, Hughes should have been pleased. Outwardly, he was magnanimous. It appeared that he had released his demons and confronted his insecurities to the extent that he was accepting social invitations and making definitive business judgments. Among those was a renewed enthusiasm for a national release of *The Outlaw*, which had still only played several weeks in a single theater in San Francisco.

In what could be seen as a sterling example of patience over bureaucracy, Hughes had outlasted the Hays Office, which at one point had

---

4. Yvonne DeCarlo was born Margaret Yvonne Middleton in Vancouver, Canada. After a twenty-year career in films, Yvonne starred in the TV series *The Munsters*.

demanded over one hundred different edits in the film. They eventually reduced their objections to Jane Russell's breasts down to twenty-eight scenes; and later cut that amount down to ten. Finally, the censors advised Hughes that if he would simply remove one sequence in which Jane bent over a dresser drawer as her bosom cascaded into the frame, the Hays Office would give its stamp of approval. Even that compromise was too much for Hughes, who had locked the film away in a lead-lined vault in the basement of the building on Romaine Street.

Dusting off the negatives, Hughes appropriated a million dollars for an advertising campaign to launch the movie whose star continued to be featured on the covers of fan magazines four years after shooting had been completed. In his enthusiasm, he pulled two engineers off the line at Hughes Aircraft to work on a blimp that would advertise *The Outlaw*. "A giant breast floating down Hollywood Boulevard," Hughes wrote in his notes for the event.

What Hughes considered inspiration, Charles Perelle saw as interference in his control over Hughes Aircraft. He rushed off a letter to Hughes in which he took the millionaire to task for what he labeled "this interruption to organization." After reminding Hughes that he had been promised autonomy in the direction of the aircraft division, Perelle wrote, "Continuance of such breakdown of organization will necessitate my setting up rules and regulations which will undoubtedly be very embarrassing to you and others involved. I trust that you will not make this necessary." Within eight hours of sending the memo, Perelle was fired from his $75,000 a year job.

While it was true that Hughes Aircraft was again without a leader, at least it had some nearly-finished product and an owner who occasionally came to work. While still micromanaging his companies, Hughes did pay $16,970 for the Star House Moving Company to transport the *Hercules* to the Long Beach Naval Base in what itself turned out to be a major news event. The wooden plane was so large that at certain points along the 26-mile route from Hughes Aircraft, telephone lines had to be cut and reinstalled. The police departments of ten towns along the way had to direct traffic and plan detours as the mammoth flying machine inched its way slowly to its destination at Terminal Island with nearly 100,000 people watching in awe at the spectacle. Overhead, a blimp advertised *The Outlaw* to the gaping throng. In the end, the transfer of the *Hercules* went flawlessly. To the public, Hughes Aircraft was both organized and efficient. Out of the glare of the media, however, chaos and disarray permeated the organization.

In the weeks leading up to the test flight of the XF-11, Howard Hughes showed little sign of concern. He debuted *The Outlaw* around the country to a healthy box-office despite dismissive reviews. Hughes was on a whirlwind party circuit, coordinated and directed by Johnny Meyer.

The Federal Bureau of Investigation had been following Johnny Meyer for ten months, tracking his activities and bugging his telephone at the request of the War Department, which had received information alleging payoffs from the Hughes organization in exchange for government contracts. Inside word suggested that Elliott Roosevelt was on the take to the tune of $75,000, and a list of other highly-placed officers were not far behind. While the FBI reports during the end of 1945 through mid-1946 failed to support such a charge, they did reflect Hughes increased social life and varied love interests.

When Hughes first piloted the new breed of TWA Lockheed Constellation from Los Angeles to New York on February 15, 1946, the FBI was onboard. So too were Cary Grant (sitting in the co-pilot's seat); Virginia Mayo; Walter Pidgeon; William Powell; Veronica Lake and her husband, director Andre De Toth; Jack Carson; Linda Darnell; Edward G. Robinson; Tyrone Power; Janet Blair; Paulette Goddard; Gene Tierney; Myrna Loy; and Randolph Scott, among others. When the party moved from the plane to suites at the Sherry-Netherland Hotel, the FBI went along. Agents bugged phones, intercepted telegrams, bribed bellmen, and hired informants. Gleaning from the confidential reports sent to FBI Director J. Edgar Hoover, about all they learned was that sixteen cases of champagne had been consumed during the flight, and the everyone seemed "extremely happy."

When Hughes arranged to be introduced to actress Lana Turner by Johnny Meyer, the FBI was listening behind a banana palm. They followed the pair to New York in April, where an agent reported that Hughes was taking no calls "except from Lana Turner." While both Hughes and Turner stayed at the Sherry-Netherland, the FBI reported they were in separate rooms "not nearby each other." When Hughes took Meyer to the Kentucky Derby to see the horse race, Lana Turner stayed in New York, the FBI went to Louisville. When Hughes filed a $5 million suit against the Motion Picture Association of America (MPAA) for undue censorship of *The Outlaw*, the FBI knew about it the same time as Hughes' attorney. Unfortunately for Hoover, the more the FBI looked, the less they found, even though by July 1946 over two dozen operatives were assigned to the case in Los Angeles, New York and Washington.

On Independence Day, the sun burned through the Los Angeles haze early in the day and the temperature rose to a dry, hot 86 degrees. At Newport Beach, producer Bill Cagney was placing the second plate of hamburgers on his barbecue grill when he noticed the tall, lanky Howard

Howard Robard Hughes Sr. invented the "roller bit" and, with it, the family fortune.

Big Howard tests an early drill bit outside the Hughes Tool Company factory.

UGHES TOOL COMPANY.

9-29-17

The 1921 graduating class of Fessenden School, West Newton, Massachusetts. Hughes, at fifteen, is in the top row, center.

Hughes was only twelve when he designed a way to motorize his bicycle and began charging a nickel a ride to neighborhood children.

As a youth, Hughes dreamed of being the most famous golfer in the world. In his twenties and thirties, he successfully competed in regional championships.

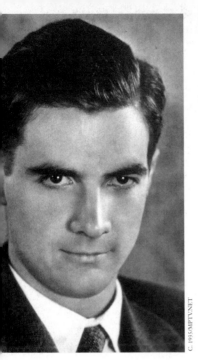

age of twenty-eight, Howard Hughes was ered the most eligible bachelor in America.

Hughes set a transcontinental speed record flying from Los Angeles to New York in nine hours, thirty-seven minutes, ten seconds in 1936.

ghes set the world land speed record flying in the H-1 in 1935. The first plane he helped design, the , is now on display in the Smithsonian Institute.

Though they were actually never lovers, Jean Harlow and Howard Hughes were rumored to be romantically linked for several years.

Noah Dietrich was at Hughes' side when he received a hero's welcome in Houston following his round-the-world flight.

The Outlaw 1943/Photo by George Hurrell/AMPTVNET

Photo by George Hurrell/C. 1935/AMPTVNET

When Hughes discovered Jane Russell, she was working as a $10-a-week receptionist. Hughes showcased her breasts around the world in his film *The Outlaw*.

Jean Harlow went on to stardom at MGM after Hughes discovered her for his film *Hell's Angels*.

Photo by George Hurrell/C. 1940/AMPTVNET

The Killers 1946/Universal Photo by Ray Jones/™M.B/AMPTVNET

ria Vanderbilt was only 17-years-old when began an affair with Howard Hughes.

Ava Gardner maintained a love-hate relationship with Hughes for over a decade.

In the late thirties, 17-year-old Brenda Frazier was known as the "Debutante of the Century" and spent two months on Hughes' yacht, the *Southern Cross*.

When she became engaged to Howard Hughes, Academy Award-winner Ginger Rogers earned more than any other actress in Hollywood.

Linda Darnell was willing to leave her husband, cameraman Peverell Marley, when she fell in love with Hughes in 1944.

Lana Turner was at the peak of her stardom when she had her sheets embroidered *HH* in anticipation of marrying Hughes.

a 15-year-old, Faith Domergue was romanced by
ghes, with the full permission of her parents.

Actress Billie Dove was known as the "American
Beauty" for her stunning looks, and was said to
be the true love of Hughes' life.

spite his nickname for her of "Country Mouse," Katharine Hepburn was elegant, sophisticated, and
ghes' live-in love for nearly three years in the late thirties.

Ella Rice was twenty when she married 19-year-old Howard Hughes.

Actress Jean Peters had dated Hughes for over a decade before they officially wed in 1957.

Terry Moore claimed to have been married to Hughes aboard a yacht sailing in Mexican waters in the late forties. She later married four other men.

demy Award-winning actress Bette Davis
egarded her marriage vows to spend a
mer in Malibu with Hughes. By September,
affair was history.

Her dark hair and stunning figure attracted
Hughes to Yvonne DeCarlo. During their two-
year affair, she was constantly under surveillance
by the FBI.

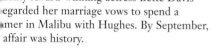

a Hayworth met secretly with Hughes in the Santa Monica beach house of actress Marion Davies.
was married at the time to Orson Welles.

Photo by George Hurrell/1941/MPTV.NET

Hughes once called Cary Grant
his only friend. The actor and
the billionaire remained close
for thirty years.

The handsome Hollywood attorney, Greg
Bautzer, helped Hughes avoid process servers
and jilted lovers.

Robert Maheu was known as his alter ego
when he was head of Hughes Nevada
Operations.

Hughes was looking far older than his forty-two years when he worked round-the-clock editing his film *Jet Pilot*.

The largest ticker-tape parade to hit New York City followed Hughes' successful round-the-world flight in 1938. He is seated between 1939 World's Fair chief Grover Whalen and Al Lodwick, a Hughes press agent.

© Bettmann/

The largest plane ever built, the *Hercules*, was popularly called the *Spruce Goose* and flew only once, in 19

The last known photograph of Howard Hughes (1952).

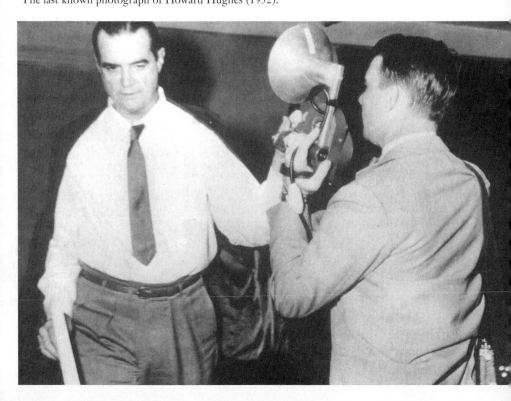

Hughes, dressed in white slacks, an argyle sweater, and tennis shoes, enter his back yard through the open French doors. His brother, actor James Cagney and his wife Bill, rose briefly to say hello. As usual, Hughes was attended by Johnny Meyer who immediately went to work, collecting young starlets from around the pool and motioning to Hughes leaning against the doorway.

When actress Jean Peters saw the shy man standing all alone, she was touched by what she described as "the most lost soul in the world." At the time, she was a newcomer to Hollywood, and had been brought to the Cagney party by Audie Murphy, the most highly decorated soldier in World War II, who himself had just arrived in town. As she walked in Hughes' direction, he flashed a quick smile, then looked away. "It was like he walked off a farm," she later said, "and into a stranger's backyard."

By the time Peters reached Hughes and extended her hand in intro-duction, Meyer had pushed to his side and was attempting to move his boss over to the pool as they had prearranged. There never was any ques-tion in Hughes' mind when in looked into the eyes of Miss Ohio State 1946 that she was special. So special, in fact, that he moved Jean away from Meyer and the French doors to sit inside the library and talk.

Jean knew about Howard Hughes from the newspapers. His around-the-world flight and his movies, mostly. And then there was his love of big-breasted women. She had heard about that too, and subconsciously clutched her arms across her chest as if to hide a presumed inadequacy. Her smooth voice had a lilting quality that Hughes leaned into, feeling her breath against his ear. She was aware he had "this problem with hearing" so she kept her voice elevated, and soon found herself laughing at how much she was revealing to a total stranger not saying a word.

"There was a fascination about him," she said, when he had left the room. "That's the word—I was *fascinated*." Hughes was fascinated too.

By the time Jean returned to her date, her thoughts were no longer on Audie Murphy. She was thrilled when Hughes invited guests from the party to fly on his plane to Catalina Island for the rest of the holiday weekend; even more excited when Hughes invited the Cagneys, Murphy and her to see his test flight of the experimental XF-11 on Sunday afternoon.

Hughes rose early on July 7, joining his engineers at his Culver City plant. He was dressed in his standard white shirt and khaki slacks, his lucky fedora cocked back on his head. Before the pre-flight inspections were completed, Hughes ate a large slice of banana cream pie with a scoop of vanilla ice cream, and then paced tensely as his mechanics and engineers made the final checks on the airplane. Per Hughes' order, the XF-11 was filled with twelve hundred gallons of fuel, despite federal regulations mandating a six hundred gallon limit for test flights. The engineers were confident of the XF-11 and its ability to easily handle the extra weight the gasoline added to the plane.

Hughes spent the morning on taxi runs, testing the plane in take-offs and landings. Afternoon shadows were beginning to pull across the tarmac as Jean Peters arrived with Audie Murphy and Bill Cagney at the Hughes plant. Seeing the trio, Hughes walked over to Glenn Odekirk, who would be following the XF-11 in a tracking plane. "Odie, take those two bums with you," Hughes told his friend, indicating Murphy and Cagney. "I want Johnny Meyers to look after Jean and set things up for me." Hughes flashed a little boy grin, pushed his fedora back on his head, and climbed up the plane's ladder as if he had not a care in the world.

For the next hour and a half, he was right. The XF-11 performed flawlessly as Hughes circled the Culver City field. A red signal lamp that earlier had warned of a stuck landing gear had gone out, and all looked routine. Still, Hughes needed to confirm that his landing gear was down, and unable to reach the tracking plane on his radio, he called the tower at the Los Angeles Airport. Flight controller Dick Fischer responded to Hughes' message. Identifying himself as Army 47155, he asked for help reaching Odekirk on another radio frequency.

"Roger, Army 47155," came Fischer's response.

As Hughes turned to make another run past Culver City, he felt a sudden drag on the right side of the plane, "as if someone had tied a barn door broadside onto the right wing." Hughes scanned his gauges, and all read normal. The XF-11 began to pull to the right, as Hughes fought to turn the plane to the left. Odekirk, seeing the maneuver, thought Hughes was making his approach for Culver City, and dropped back to return to Hughes Aircraft as well.

Suddenly Hughes was all alone, and in trouble. He unclasped his seat belt, pushing to the right side of the cockpit to see if he could identify the problem, but saw nothing. He reduced power to the right engine, with no effect. He flexed his spoilers and held full left rudder, desperate to control altitude. Still he lost lift. Now too low to bail out, Hughes found himself flying at 1,000 feet, over some of the most expensive real estate in the world—Beverly Hills.

The manicured lawns and pristine flower beds held no space for a plane the size of the Army reconnaissance. He could do little more than brace himself by propping his feet high up on the instrument panel. He knew what was next. Hughes was going to crash. The only unanswered question: Was he going to die?

Citizen Hughes

*I am a little tired of being pushed around and
intimidated by Senators Brewster and Ferguson
just because they have some very strong powers
which are granted to all Senators but which were
not intended to be misused for the promotion
of a three-ring publicity circus.*

> Los Angeles, California
> July 31, 1947
> Written in an open letter to the American
> people before the start of a special Senate
> investigation into Hughes Aircraft's
> government contracts.

THE XF-11 WAS TRAVELING AT 155 MILES PER HOUR WHEN
it smashed into the shake roof of the home of dentist Jules
Zimmerman at 803 North Linden Drive in Beverly Hills,
shearing off the top half onto the lawn. Seconds later, the
plane's right wing sliced through the upstairs bedroom of
actress Rosemary DeCamp[1] who was in the room with her
husband John. The plane continued its rampage through
the DeCamp garage, plowed through a row of poplar trees
lining their neighbor's yard at 808 Whittier Drive, before
finally exploding through the rear wall of the home of Lt.
Col. Charles A. Meyer, and bursting into flames. The
impact of the explosion was so great that it sent one of the
plane's two engines flying sixty feet into the air, ripping off
the corner of the home owned by Gosta B. Guston, the
Swedish industrialist, before landing in his front yard.

It was a dramatic intrusion of real life into the posh,
quiet neighborhood where on a typical day the only expected
noise might have come from the gardeners' lawn mowers or

---

1. Despite years of film work, Rosemary DeCamp was perhaps best remembered as Marlo Thomas' mother, Helen, on TV's *That Girl*.

pool boys' skimmers. The normal illusion of Sunday vacancy was shattered as flames shot one hundred feet in the air, fed by ruptured gas lines and the plane's own high-octane fuel. Marine Sergeant William Lloyd Durkin, who was visiting the Guston's son James, raced to the edge of the burning XF-11 just as Hughes pushed his way out of the cockpit, stumbled onto the wing and fell to the ground. Durkin rolled Hughes away from the intense heat and flames, and then dragged the pilot out of danger. It would take three hours to contain the flames and reopen the streets to traffic, and another four days for the remains of the plane to be moved.

"I'm Howard Hughes," the multimillionaire said as he was pushed on a gurney through the entrance of Beverly Hills Emergency Hospital. They were the only words he uttered before going into shock. By the time Hughes regained consciousness, he had been transferred to Good Samaritan Hospital on Wilshire Boulevard in downtown Los Angeles with a lung punctured in six places, eight broken ribs, a broken left shoulder, third-degree burns of the left hand, a severe gash to the left side of his head, and a broken nose. Despite his injuries, the following morning, he was reported to be "resting and talking rationally."

The headlines of newspapers across the country painted a grim prognosis. "Multimillionaire Flyer Given 50-50 Chance," wagered the *Los Angeles Times*. "Howard Hughes Gravely Injured in Crash," read the *New York Times*. For weeks after the accident, news coverage of a crumpled Hughes continued to dominate the front pages as daily accounts detailed his life-or-death struggle, as well as the number of visitors attempting to see the fallen pilot. What even the most conscientious follower of the reports never learned was that Hughes Aircraft's general manager, Glenn Odekirk, had been installed in the room adjoining his boss, had outside phones lines wired in place, and began to conduct business with an efficiency that far exceeded typical Hughes operations.

While the news media correctly reported that 3,400 ccs of fluid had been drained from Hughes' chest cavity, and that he had been given a number of blood transfusions, they neglected to mention that Hughes had Marian Miller, a secretary from his Romaine offices, placed in a small room in the hospital to receive visitors and keep track of gifts, flowers, and get-well notes. Hughes ordered that photos of the plane's engines be taken before its removal from Lt. Col. Meyer's lawn, and that Walter Reynolds of Hughes Productions return to the crash site to assess damage and arrange for estimates on repairing the property.

Previously published accounts of Hughes' injuries stating that he was burned over 78 percent of his body and had periods of excruciating suffering in which he cried out in pain are inaccurate. According to hospital records, Hughes received skin grafts on his left hand only. Burns on his left side, buttocks and feet healed with standard treatment, and morphine injections were administered at the first sign of discomfort. Typically, Hughes was dictating instructions to his attending physicians, Dr. Verne Mason and Dr. Lawrence Chaffin,[2] and restricting the amount of pain-killer prescribed, according to Odekirk who seldom left his side.

As if blessed by St. Jude, patron saint of hopeless cases, Hughes' survival from such a dramatic crash was miraculous, and not lost on the multimillionaire himself, who saw in his struggle an opportunity to embellish his already considerable legend. "He *loved* publicity," Odekirk said when interviewed years later, "but tried to act as if he didn't." According to Odekirk, Hughes himself carefully orchestrated the visitors who sat waiting patiently for an audience with the recovering pilot— Lana Turner, Linda Darnell, Jane Russell and Ava Gardner among them. After he was certain that the press had ample opportunity to seize their interviews, Hughes would send Odekirk to announce to the faithful that Hughes remained critical and too broken to receive visitors.

Relatives did not fare any better. When his Aunt Annette and her husband Fred entrained from Houston, they were intercepted and told to return home. "I'm sure Howard didn't even know I was there," Annette railed at the reporters. "It's a disgrace, coming all this way." When Hughes heard about his Aunt's reaction, he chortled, "Keep up the good work, boys," and went on with business.

The more days that passed, the more intense the press scrutiny became, feeding upon the exquisite buffet of purposeful delusion. The hospital continued to prepare Hughes' authorized press releases about his critical condition, elaborating on the intense fight to keep him alive. That his doctors were fighting was true—though what they were fighting for was to keep Hughes contained in bed and away from the phone and his obsessive concern about his money. They were only marginally successful. Each day, their patient would read the newspapers delivered to his room by nurses, and rebut those reports he found that cast dubious light on his reputation.

The first to generate a Hughes spin was hero Sgt. William Lloyd Durkin. When a photograph appeared of a grinning Durkin accepting praise from Beverly Hills Fire Chief Lloyd B. Canfield in the *Los Angeles Examiner* two days following the crash, Hughes instructed Johnny Meyer to issue a statement that Hughes had climbed from the cockpit under his own power, and had in fact leaped to the ground where he was met by Durkin who guided him out of the crash site. On July 11, the *Hollywood*

---

2. Dr. Chaffin was a surgeon from the Santa Fe Railroad's hospital in Los Angeles.

Citizen-News ran a feature on Hughes' "flying fedora." His felt hat had been recovered from the crash site "amid mud and debris in the forward end of the wrecked ship." It was described as a slouch-brim felt, gray-brown, size $7^1/2$. When it deemed to label the hat his "good-luck piece," Hughes responded by saying he was not superstitious but just "hated to get a haircut."

Dr. Mason held a press conference, called Hughes "the man of steel" with a "terrific determination to live," and announced that his patient had eaten his first solid food to cheers from the reporters, who had been given their own selection of sandwiches catered from the cafeteria of Hughes Aircraft. As the nation listened to every word, Hearst syndicated gossip columnist Louella Parsons in her radio broadcast called Hughes "America's aviation hero who went down with his ship rather than risk unnecessary loss of life." She had no way of knowing that Hughes was more concerned with his $8 million investment in a plane he hoped to salvage.

On July 12, Mason announced that Hughes had "taken a turn for the worse. Hughes is breathing pure oxygen twenty-four hours a day. His left lung has failed to respond and is still functioning poorly. He is surviving through the restricted use of his right lung to the extent permitted by his crushed chest." As instructed, Mason then told the assembled press that Hughes had weakly asked him, "Am I going to live?" When Mason was not able to guarantee it, Hughes asked Mason to deliver a message to the Army, and then proceeded to dictate a four page letter that analyzed the problem with the experimental aircraft, laying the blame for the crash with the propellers. "Tell the Army to look in the wreckage, find the rear half of the right propeller and find out what went wrong with it. I don't want this to happen to somebody else." In reporting the situation, the press were caught in the uncomfortable position of attempting to explain how a dying man could generate such a detailed report. "Flyer Rallies to Dictate Report on Crash Cause," was how the *Los Angeles Times* chose to interpret the situation; "Hughes Worse, Tells How Plane Crashed" was the *New York Times* take, before adding "with his last bit of energy."

By Saturday, July 13, over 6,000 letters had been received at Good Samaritan, including a telegram from President Harry S. Truman stating, "I am watching eagerly all the reports concerning you. I feel sure that you will win this fight." Certain as well was New York Mayor William O'Dwyer who told Hughes to "give 'em hell." At that point, the multi-millionaire needed little encouragement, having bolted from his oxygen tent on two separate occasions, much to the distress of his round-the-clock nurses and two doctors.

Hughes had ordered his aviation engineers to devise a mattress that could be adjusted mechanically with his body's movement as he continued the healing process. Working through the night, the factory created foam bedding that was divided into thirty-two sections, each controlled by a pneumatic piston and its own motor. When the mattress was rolled into Hughes' room, he took one look at the complicated controls and sent it into storage, while leaking news of its invention and taking credit for its creation.[3]

Eventually, the coverage slowed to casual mentions every third or fourth day in the news, with generalized reports of Hughes' overall improvement. Ironically, after weeks of effort and hundreds of man-hours, when Hughes actually admitted his first guest, no one from the press was around to witness the rarity. The privilege went to Jean Peters, who had waited for an invitation before traveling to Good Samaritan.

It was an unusually hot day, the first week in August, and Hughes had been allowed to get out of bed and sit in a chair for the first time. When he was notified that Jean Peters had entered the hospital and was on her way up, Hughes deliberately returned to bed, hoping to appeal to her "mothering instinct," Odekirk later said. "She touched his face when she walked in, as a child would hold a wounded bird. I can't explain it other than to say he looked a whole lot better when she left."

When Hughes checked himself out of Good Samaritan on August 12, 1946, it was against the advice of his doctors. He had spent a quiet night with Odekirk, who fell asleep on a chair in his room, leaving Hughes to write his thoughts on his ever-near yellow legal pads. That night he wrote, *Remember Jean's birthday surprise.* Jean Peters would be turning twenty on October 15. The "surprise" he had in store was a square-cut, emerald engagement ring, the fourth such ring he had ordered from Cartier, the day before his crash, and two days after first meeting her.

Early in the morning of August 12, as he was preparing to leave the hospital, Hughes had Odekirk telephone Cary Grant to ask him for a lift. Grant rallied to the call and arrived to pick up his friend less than an hour later. Hughes was placed in a wheelchair and transported down the service elevator to the hospital's loading dock, where he was transferred into Grant's car along with six wooden crates of Valencia oranges[4] that were stacked in the back seat.

Hughes spent the next four weeks with Grant in his home, refusing to listen to the advice of his doctors regarding dressing his burned left

---

3. The mattress was discovered, unused, in a storage locker at Hughes Aircraft in 1976.
4. Hughes had credited his quick recovery to drinking fresh-squeezed orange juice. He insisted on seeing the juice prepared in the room, believing that its nutrition escaped into the air within ten minutes of leaving the orange.

hand and breathing exercises for his lungs. According to Grant, the pair spent the month "vegetating and eating oatmeal cookies." Hughes also managed to make $2,860 worth of long-distance calls, most of which were to New York City to his attorneys handling his suit against the MPAA.

The Outlaw had run into renewed opposition from the MPAA because of Hughes' advertising campaign for the film which, of course, concentrated on Jane Russell's breasts. When the censorship organization pointed to its membership rules regarding permissible advertising graphics and slogans, Hughes simply resigned from the association. When the organization yanked its approval from the film yet again, Hughes hauled the association into court, and announced he intended to keep them there. It was a lawsuit that the MPAA could ill-afford to lose— or fight.

Tuesday, September 10, 1946. Sporting a new moustache to cover scars on his upper lip, Howard Hughes stepped into the cockpit of a converted B-23 bomber with a brown paper bag containing a carton of milk, some crackers, and a turkey sandwich. The gauze bandage that was wrapped around his left hand was the only visible sign of the crash that had nearly taken his life. As Hughes lowered himself into the pilot's seat, he placed his right hand on the throttle and felt the cool metal grip. He smiled like a soldier returning from war—a war he had won.

Behind him, Lt. John Sleeter boarded the B-23 along with mechanic Earl Martyn. Sleeter helped care for Hughes in Good Samaritan and was bumming a ride to Kansas City, while Martyn had assisted in the conversion of the bomber and was keeping the flight log. They buckled themselves in their seats silently. This was not a time for idle chatter. Hughes was running through his pre-flight checklist, and no one aboard wanted any problems—especially Howard Hughes.

When he arrived in Kansas City, Hughes looked gaunt and drawn as he waved away photographers and announced he wanted to sleep. The door to his suite at the Hotel Muehlbach was posted with a "Do Not Disturb" sign, while a guard outside the door lent an air of authority. There would be no visit from Johnny Meyer, no collection of young women, no buckets of champagne. This was a different Howard Hughes than had stayed in this same hotel over the years during stop-offs from various flights to New York. This man was sadder, the eyes duller; a spark of rebellion lost in a memory of naivete, where youth knew no fear and paid no caution.

Since leaving the hospital, he had been weaned off the morphine onto a steady diet of codeine pills that had constipated Hughes so badly that he told Dr. Mason he preferred the pounding pain in his head to the side-effects of the drug, and stopped taking the medication. His decision came with a price, of course. All of his decisions did, Hughes knew. This time it was his sleep that suffered with the constant drumming in his ears keeping the steady rhythm of unrelenting agony. Even when he managed to fall asleep, he dreamed that he was awake, so by the time he actually rose from bed, he wore the gray and ghostly pallor of those near death.

His arrival in New York was greeted by a phalanx of photographers, their flashbulbs capturing the exhausted pilot on his rushed entrance to his waiting limousine. His usual suite at the Sherry-Netherland had been prepared for his arrival. The staff, in their typically efficient manner, pretended not to notice as he walked through the lobby. No check-in was necessary; he paid by the year. Between glances at ledgers and guest registers, the hotel's employees sneaked furtive glances at the lanky, bowed man, unable to accept what first glimpse suggested. Surely, no one could have aged that dramatically in just three months.

Hughes noticed it, too. With each labored stare into the mirror above the chifforobe, he pulled at his skin as if to determine its authenticity. The face that looked back was that of a stranger, old, tired, with eyes of garnet and a frightened expression. At first, he attempted to ignore his reflection as he passed. But, after two days, he asked that all the mirrors in his suite be removed. He had to admit that he hated the way he looked, almost as much as he hated the fact that he cared.

When he returned to Los Angeles, he saw Ava Gardner and her sister Bappie for dinner several times in the privacy of their apartment. He also spent time with Lana Turner, who attempted unsuccessfully to cook, expressed her dislike for his moustache, and announced one evening that she had had her sheets and towels monogrammed *HH*, to which Hughes replied that if she were that set on marriage, perhaps she should consider Huntington Hartford.[5]

Through the efforts of Johnny Meyer, Hughes also met and bedded Rita Hayworth, then separated from her husband, actor/director Orson Welles. That the compulsively shy Rita should find the compulsively shy Hughes attractive was not surprising, and for a while both seemed content to use the other for what they brought to a relationship that was long on sex and short on romance during brief, late-night rendezvous at Rita's home in Brentwood, California, or clandestine meetings at actress Marion Davies' sumptuous beach house in Santa Monica.

And then there was Jean. Since Jean Peters had entered his life, Hughes had come to the realization that he had never learned how to love. He had learned desire, certainly, and lust for sure, but love was as

5. Huntington Hartford, heir to the A & P grocery-chain fortune, was also a wealthy patron of the arts, building a theater on Vine Street in Hollywood, and naming it for himself.

alien to him as a jelly doughnut to a Slovakian rebel. Yes, he had heard of it; he even directed it on film; but felt it? No, Hughes realized. He had never learned love.

With Jean Peters, he felt protective. She had a certain unsullied freshness he wanted to safeguard and even cultivate. She had told him she was a virgin that first day on the sofa in Bill Cagney's den, and he believed her. She had no obvious pretensions, admitted to sewing her own clothing, enjoyed the feel of the earth between her fingers as she gardened, and seemed to be genuinely happy. That last part, the happiness, was actually the most intriguing quality. For all his money, Hughes had not found it, yet here Jean Peters was, pre-packaged with it in abundance.

Lana Turner never had it. She was always quite willing to hop into bed. *Hell*, Hughes thought, *she didn't need a bed*, remembering the time they had sex on the floor of the Sikorsky while it flew at 12,000 feet on autopilot. Lana was good at it, although, like Bette Davis, not quite so good after he made it clear that he was not interested in marriage. Then came the telephone call in which Lana revealed she had syphilis, a disease she alleged she had caught from Austrian actor Turhan Bey.[6] With flashes of déjà vu, Hughes did not wait to be tested for the disease. He immediately began to bag his clothes, then called Noah Dietrich in Houston to fly into Los Angeles "for an emergency of an extremely confidential nature." When Dietrich arrived in town that evening, he discovered that Hughes had been moved to a new suite at the Town House hotel. Upon seeing the bagged clothes, he did not need an explanation. He confirmed that a very disgruntled Dr. Mason had been called, medication delivered, and arranged for another delivery to the Salvation Army of suits, pants, tuxedos and dinner jackets.

Although Hughes never again saw Lana Turner, he delighted in disparaging her name, and despite any proof of his involvement, that of Turhan Bey as well. MGM singing star Kathryn Grayson later stated that Hughes related the story to her on several occasions.

Dietrich's arrival in Los Angeles turned out to be timely, and for a reason unconnected with Hughes' health. The newly-elected Republican majority in Congress had begun to look at military orders placed during the Roosevelt administration. The legislators found no more obvious target than the beleaguered Mr. Hughes and his aviation company. They had been awarded $40,000,000 from the government over a five-year period and had yet to deliver a single airplane. Officially known as the

---

6. Turhan Bey was born Turhan Gilbert Selahattin Sahultavy on March 30, 1920. His exotic good looks helped make him a star in the 1940s. He had a second career as a photographer in his hometown of Vienna in the 60s. He returned to acting in the 90s and played the Centauri Emperor in TV's *Babylon 5*.

Special Senate Committee Investigating the National Defense Program, it might have better been called the Hate Hughes Club. The new breed of Republican had little use for a man they saw as a cocky, infantile, thrill-seeker who merited his position in life through a mere accident of birth.

Behind the investigation was a barely-hidden agenda that had more to do with TWA than it did with its major shareholder. The previous year, TWA had been awarded international routes to Paris and the Middle East by the Civil Aeronautics Board. For the first time in its history, Pan American Airways, the dominant international carrier from the Unites States, had competition. No sooner had TWA begun to fly to Paris and beyond than a bill was introduced into Congress called Chosen Instrument. The purpose of the bill was to establish an international airline to exclusively service off-shore routes from the U.S. The president of Pan Am, Juan Trippe, held close Republican ties and was pressing for its passage, since, as the largest U.S. international airline, Pan Am would control the consolidated corporation.

While the Chosen Instrument Bill was defeated in Congress, it was quickly followed by a similar piece of legislation titled the Community Airline Bill that Hughes was quoted in the *New York Journal-American* as calling the "same baby in a different set of diapers." It did not make Congress happy. Neither did Hughes' refusal to allow the senators to audit Hughes Aircraft's books. For months, Hughes took joy in tossing obstacles in their path in a duel that had dangerous ramifications.

By the end of 1946, Hughes' personal fortune had risen to $520,000,000. At a time in America when only 381 people held mere millionaire status, Hughes was rocketing toward the *billionaire* mark. He found toying with the United State Senate to be an amusing diversion from his continuing migraines, his left hand partially crippled by ugly red and yellow bands of scar tissue, and his constant concern over catching another dreaded disease. In his rush to trivialize the government's ability to control him, however, he failed to see the steamroller heading directly toward his back. And at the controls was a bombastic Republican senator from Maine named Ralph Owen Brewster.

Brewster was a Harvard-educated lawyer and one-time governor of Maine who, during his second term in the U.S. Senate, became the chairman of the Special Senate Committee on National Defense. As such, he was pitted in a showdown with Howard Hughes that would leave only one man standing when all eventually was said.

Noah Dietrich walked into that maelstrom in late 1946 prepared to do battle. His first opponent was Francis D. Flanagan, the Senate Committee's chief assistant counsel, who came to Los Angeles carrying subpoenas for Hughes Aircraft's books. That anyone could purport to have the right to examine what Hughes viewed as personal property did not sit well with the multimillionaire. He dodged and feigned, using Dietrich as a shield, before disappearing altogether on an extended trip to Mexico to see Jean Peters.

Jean had gone on location outside Guadalajara to film her first motion picture, *Captain from Castile* starring Tyrone Power. The lavish costume drama set during the Spanish conquest of Mexico cast her in the role of Catana Perez, a servant girl, with Power playing her caballero lover. Hughes timed his visit to coincide with Jean's love scenes with Power, and watched pensively, though silently, on the fringes of the set.

Back in Hollywood, Dietrich was further occupied following Hughes' instructions to sever his partnership with director Preston Sturges. At that point, Sturges was just beginning production on *Vendetta*, a film starring Faith Domergue, who was then married to Teddy Stauffer. She had eloped with the playboy-heir to the Stauffer restaurant and frozen food fortune several months earlier.[7]

With Hughes in Guadalajara, Dietrich took advantaged of the vacuum created in his absence to seize additional power within the organization, consolidating his control of both the Tool and Aircraft divisions, which now reported directly to Dietrich. Hughes was happy with that arrangement, if only to give him more time to spend in Guadalajara, where he had taken three suites at the Reforma Hotel under the name Arthur Procieri. The city was a sun-ripened spectacle of color, as musical mariachis wandered the streets, stopping below Hughes' window to receive the coins Jean tossed to them for their serenades.

Hughes stayed in Mexico until late December, when he was summoned to Manhattan for an emergency board of directors meeting of TWA. By the end of 1946, Hughes owned 46 percent of the airline's 985,929 shares. Never on solid ground financially, TWA was severely hurt by a 25-day pilots' strike as well as the cost of its overseas expansion, and needed a hasty influx of cash. Jack Frye, the airline's president, proposed floating another two million shares of stock to raise $100 million. Such a move would have reduced Hughes to a minority position, and he raged at the concept of giving away even a small percentage of control.

Although the purpose of his trip to Manhattan was the TWA board meeting, Hughes failed to attend. Without his presence, the board lacked a quorum, placing the company's entire future in question. With its bank accounts nearly empty and the company unable to pay for fuel, Frye had little choice but to reach a truce with a man who refused to compromise.

---

7. The marriage would last less time than it took to complete *Vendetta*. The film would go through four more directors over another three years, before being released in 1950 to a dismal box-office.

After a six-hour meeting most notable for the Swiss cheese and turkey sandwiches Hughes made at the table, Hughes finally offered to loan TWA $10 million on the condition that he could convert the loan to stock at any time, thus ensuring his controlling position, even if additional stock should be proffered. He also demanded, and got, the resignation of Frye. What looked like a victory for Hughes eventually would have a startling effect on his future. At that moment, however, his thoughts were of romance, and his senorita south of the border.

Hughes left immediately to fly back to Guadalajara in the company of buddy Cary Grant, who had just returned from England where he was shooting a film. With Hughes at the controls of a personalized Douglas DC-3 and Grant mixing drinks in its wet bar, the plane known as the *Flying Penthouse* took off on January 9, 1947, for a refueling stop in Amarillo, Texas. Intense storms across much of the Midwest made communication difficult, with rain, wind and lightning grounding planes in six states. A control tower in Indianapolis reported receiving a partial message and then a dropped signal from the Hughes plane, which failed to reach Amarillo.

Across America, newspapers headlined the news that the famed aviator and handsome actor were missing and believed dead. Obituaries were rushed into type as executives of Hughes Tool met in an emergency session to determine the legal implications of heirless ownership. Noah Dietrich operated a command center at Hughes' Romaine Street offices, attempting to cap the growing speculation in the media. Air Force scout planes were assigned to look for wreckage as they flew over Hoosier, Shawnee and Mark Twain National Forests in Indiana, Illinois and Missouri.

As the tumult gained strength like an Oklahoma dust storm, Hughes and Grant sat eating leftover turkey sandwiches and drinking chilled milk on a remote runway in El Paso, Texas. Having flown south of Amarillo to avoid the storms, Hughes arrived at the border ahead of schedule before his Mexican customs' clearance was expedited. While their death knell tolled its dirge, the two playboys of the Western world toasted each other, blissfully unaware of the furor caused by their premature demise.

They remained oblivious to the expanding search for the wreckage of the D-3 and the charred remains of their own bones as they arrived in Guadalajara, went to Hughes' suites at the Reforma Hotel, took warm showers and needed naps, and scared a Mexican *criada* named Consuela Marijan when she entered the rooms to find two naked men who were thought to be dead. Her screams not only woke Hughes and Grant, but alerted the hotel's *seguridad* who took no uncertain pleasure announcing to the local press their discovery of the *presumidos muertos* (presumed dead).

Hughes' amusement at the fuss over his "detour," as he would later call his stop in El Paso, was fleeting when he was met by an hysterically-relieved Jean Peters in the hallway of the hotel. Having heard about his safe arrival in Mexico, she had rushed to his side from her make-up chair, swallowing tears that spontaneously erupted out of relief. Seeing the concern mapped in the lines on her forehead, he was surprised at how touched he was by her genuine sentiment. She made no effort to hide her emotions; she was incapable of lying like that. It was one of the reasons he felt so strongly about this woman, and might have married her right there in Guadalajara that day or the next if she had only said yes.

The thought of it frightened him, as no test flight in an experimental plane ever could. His yellow legal pads were beginning to fill with pre-emptive notes to her—the words "Dear Jean" begun and then crossed out, as indecision flowed like a frothy wave that soaked the sand and then dried in the sun. His business kept beckoning for attention as if the fit of a jealous lover. He had little choice but to pay attention, for the buzz of a Senate investigation continued to sound like swarming bees. And its potential to sting was just as certain.

Hughes was not intimidated by an investigation; he was challenged by it. He loved the sport, the flexing of foils in a duel where strategy held more power than thrust. Had the timing of the Senate investigation been any other than at the start of his new relationship, Hughes would have had no problem in concentrating his full and exacting energy on it. In the end, he did, leaving Mexico to return to California, his body and mind girded for a fight, his heart left in Guadalajara.

As Noah Dietrich would later write, "Howard could teach a few lessons to the master of manipulation, Machiavelli himself." If such were the case, his first chapter began with Republican Senator Owen Brewster. In an effort to better know his enemy, Hughes flew to Washington in an attempt to schedule a meeting with the chairman of the Senate Special Committee. As it happened, Brewster was out of town, giving a series of speeches in different cities. Unwilling to wait the several days for Brewster's return, Hughes offered to fly him via TWA to the capital and back to his various engagements as necessary, under the guise that he was eager to meet with the senator to expedite a potential merger between Pan Am and TWA. Brewster, a longtime advocate of Pan Am's air supremacy, jumped at the bait and into a web of his own making.

By privately meeting with Hughes, Brewster gave the impression that he was willing to deal with the very man he was supposed to be impartially investigating. And thanks to Hughes' propitious offer of transportation, he had accepted free travel on TWA. Two skeletons in a closet that as it turned out already had several, and each one primed and ready to be pumped by Hughes as he played an artful adversary.

Returning to Los Angeles, Hughes next extended an olive branch to the president of Pan American Airways, Juan Trippe. He invited the head of TWA's chief competitor to come to California. Hughes wanted to meet Trippe, ostensibly to discuss the possibility of merging TWA with Pan Am, and creating an American flagship carrier.

Eager to reinforce Pan Am's position of superiority in the world aviation market, Trippe did not hesitate to board his private plane armed with concepts of a megacarrier. He had no way to know that the furnished house Hughes rented in Palm Springs for the meetings was a bear trap disguised as tranquil hospitality. For several days, the two men exchanged pleasantries, talked about equity, shared routes, and personnel. When they concluded their meetings, they shook on an agreement to exchange balance sheets and continue negotiations to merge the two airlines. While Trippe returned to the airport flushed with expectation, Hughes spent the next hour washing his hands.

When it became obvious to both Brewster and Trippe that Hughes was not serious about moving TWA into partnership with Pan Am, the pressure from Capitol Hill sent the committee's counsel Flanagan back to Hughes Aircraft, and this time he did not bother to ask permission before entering the Culver City plant and removing pertinent files associated with Hughes' government contracts. Among the documents subpoenaed and received were all of Johnny Meyer's expense records, many featuring the name of Elliott Roosevelt.

As the court of public opinion began to receive the first flurry of rumors concerning Hughes' flagrant efforts to buy favor within the federal government, Hughes countered the impact by taking to the skies in a dramatically-staged second test flight of the XF-11, a virtual twin of the one that nearly took his life less than a year earlier. Noticeably absent from the XF-11 was the counter-rotating propeller blades that Hughes had pinpointed as the cause of the accident. In their place were standard, four-blade props which Hughes commented to reporters "worked well enough for a safe landing" upon his return to the runway.

Whatever positive press was generated by the successful test flight was soon dissipated through a relentless campaign by Senator Brewster to position himself as a public crusader for a corruption-free White House. Republicans were heard to have floated his name in connection with the vice-presidential nomination in the next election, to a favorable reaction. Buoyed by his own self-importance, the second-term senator monopolized the front-page headlines as he subpoenaed records from the estate of the late President Roosevelt, to the consternation of many Democrats outraged by his tactics.

In an effort to appear amused by Brewster's grandiosity, Hughes looked unconcerned as he was photographed at the Mocambo nightclub in Hollywood, usually entertaining a military highroller, or arranging flights on TWA for high-profile stars who vociferously endorsed his position. When the word began to spread, however, that Brewster was considering issuing subpoenas for the entertainers to appear before Congress, the previously loyal stars seemed to vanish—on vacations to Europe, South America, or undisclosed hinterlands—Lana Turner, Faith Domergue, Ava Gardner, and Linda Darnell among them.

Rita Hayworth was in Europe as well, having traveled via TWA to New York, and then aboard the *Ile de France*. Although Hughes had helped expedite her travel, and arranged for representatives to meet her at various ports of call, he was unaware that Rita was pregnant with his baby, and arranged for a secret abortion soon after she completed filming *The Loves of Carmen*. Upon arrival at the Hotel Lancaster in Paris, Rita began to hemorrhage, and was discreetly checked into the American Hospital in Neuilly, outside the city. She underwent a dilation and curettage, the same procedure that had resulted in the death of Allene Hughes. Fortunately, Rita suffered no complications from the curettage, and was about to be released from the hospital, when reporters discovered her in Neuilly and attempted to interview her from her hospital bed. While American and foreign newspapers headlined "Rita Hayworth Found Ill in Hospital near Paris," they mistakenly attributed her problem to anemia. Hughes was never told the real reason for her hospitalization, and never saw Rita again.

In Washington, Owen Brewster found the departure of the film stars from American soil confirmation of a massive cover-up, one that he intended to expose. During the last ten days of July, 1947, Hughes' name became associated with Johnny Meyer's arranged wild parties and paid women as Brewster subpoenaed Judy Cook, described as a "free-lance actress and former Aquacade girl," and Martha Goldthwaite, a 26-year-old "free-lance model."

Columnist Cholly Knickerbocker[8] laughed that "Capitol Hill will look like the *Ziegfeld Follies* the first week of August" with Brewster planning on placing Hughes' guests and girlfriends on the stand for what was being labeled as "the most sensational investigations in the nation's history." Brewster slapped subpoenas on Elliott Roosevelt, his wife Faye Emerson, as well as Secretary of the Interior Julius A. Krug, all placed at Hughes' late-night soirees. Never far from the hot-seat by choice,

---

8. Cholly Knickerbocker was the trademark pen name owned by W.R. Hearst's *New York Journal-American* as the paper's society columnist. It was used by a number of writers, including Igor Cassini, brother of fashion designer Oleg Cassini, in the Forties and Fifties.

Johnny Meyer was also among the missing, and was said to be "traveling on business in Europe," chased by a federal marshal as well.

On July 25, Hughes responded to the allegations by claiming that parties he organized followed the awarding of government contracts, not preceding them. "I feel I must deny emphatically right now the charge that my company has spent $40 million of government funds without completing or delivering an airplane," he said. "This statement is absolutely untrue.

"The Army formally accepted delivery of the completed Hughes flying boat, the largest airplane in the world, in February 1947, five months ago. The obligation specified in the contract was completely fulfilled on that date and all work done since has been done because I voluntarily elected to do so," Hughes added, without mentioning that the plane still had not been finally assembled or left the ground in flight.

"I have invested, at this date, $7 million of my company's money in this flying boat and intend to expend considerably more before testing of the airplane is completed," Hughes said. "I have put this money into the airplane because I believe in it and because it will advance the art of aviation in this country considerably further than the same amount of money invested in other popular forms of aeronautical research."

While the War Department argued semantics over what constituted "delivery," denying they had officially received any planes from Hughes Aircraft other than the scraps of metal from his crash and the shell of a prototype XF-11, it became obvious to Hughes that the investigation would go forward, and his attempts to stay above the fray had failed. When a federal marshal arrived at his Culver City plant and attempted to subpoena him to appear before the Senate committee, Hughes happened to be on an afternoon sail with Jean Peters. But the news of the attempted service sent him into hiding, moving from house to house in a cat-and-mouse game to escape a tightening dragnet. The experience, while exciting on the surface, would leave a deep psychological impact that would affect his behavior for the remainder of his life.

As the public Senate hearings began in Washington on Monday, July 28, 1947, Hughes was listening to the events unfold over a radio in a bedroom in the San Fernando Valley home of Frank Angell, the head of security for Hughes Aircraft. He sputtered in indignation as he heard subcommittee chairman Homer Ferguson, the Republican senator from Michigan, question Grover Loening,[9] an aeronautical engineer and consultant to the War Production Board, about pressure Hughes was alleged to have placed on the White House. It mattered little that Loening

9. Loening is credited as the engineering genius behind the autogyro, forerunner of the helicopter.

denied the charges. Hughes was outraged to even hear them suggested.

Hughes vented anger at the cynical way Ferguson labeled Meyer as "the master of expense accounts" while promising that he would produce the missing Hughes employee within the week. Additionally, Ferguson went on to guarantee the appearance of Hughes himself, asserting that the expertise of the "group of experienced agents currently working to subpoena Mr. Hughes" would be successful. Jean Peters described Hughes' reaction to Ferguson's announcement as "something close to a Highland jig," as the aviator began to dance around the room chanting, "You gotta catch me first, shit-ass," shit-ass being his newly-acquired curse phrase. "You gotta catch me first."

The government had sent a team of marshals to Los Angeles for exactly that purpose, and held a press conference to introduce them, as if to put Hughes on notice that his days of flaunting his power against theirs were ending. Among the men was an agent named George Rossinni, who identified himself as "the man who brought in Al Capone." There was no mention of Eliot Ness.

Now openly defying the Senate committee, Hughes pleaded his case before the American public through a bylined article in William Randolph Hearst's chain of newspapers. Hughes referred to the "known relationship between Brewster and Pan American Airways" as well as Brewster's efforts to have the Community Airline Bill passed. "Then, (Pan American Airway's president) Juan Trippe, who already has the biggest airline in the world, would wind up with a complete monopoly, automatically and quite legally putting all the smaller airlines out of business and taking over their routes and airplanes."

In Washington, Owen Brewster found *himself* on trial as news of his denials of collusion and conflict of interest did little to quell calls for a justice department investigation into his conduct. Facing humiliation by his peers, Brewster attempted vainly to refocus the spotlight of scrutiny back where he insisted it belonged.

On August 4, Hughes flew with Jean Peters to Las Vegas and ate a leisurely dinner in the restaurant at the Frontier Hotel, but had conveniently disappeared by the time federal agents were alerted and arrived with a subpoena. At 2:32 p.m. the following day, Hughes ducked aboard his B-23 airplane, took his seat beside his flight engineer Earl Martyn, waved to two security guards seated in the back of the plane, and took off for Washington, D.C.

When he walked into the second-floor caucus room of the Senate Office Building, Hughes looked the part of a multimillionaire. He was perfectly groomed, wore a gray wool, custom-made double-breasted suit, black brogans, a freshly-ironed white Oxford-cloth shirt, and a navy blue tie with small white polka dots. That he looked remarkably rested belied the fact that he had spent the night flying through a treacherous thunderstorm peppered by air pockets and turbulence that tested his skill as a pilot and navigator. The standing-room-only crowd of over 1,500 people gave him an ovation that caused Senator Homer Ferguson, who sat in the front behind a forest of microphones and underbrush of wires, to begin banging his desk with a glass ashtray for order. Hughes was forty-five minutes late.

For the next five days, Hughes testified before the committee, infuriating them as much as intimidating them in what *Newsweek* magazine called "the biggest circus that had pitched its tent in Washington in years." They said it had acrobats (the photographers climbing on tables and ladders, exploding 600 flashbulbs per day), clowns (Johnny Meyer mugging for the camera, screaming, "Get that light out of my eyes. Every time I see a bright light I raise my hand and begin to testify"), and romance (with women spectators that sighed over Hughes "as though he were Frank Sinatra, and the sound was like small winds murmuring in the spring").

Ferguson's purpose was presumably to discover what the government had bought with its $42 million in cash. By the time he got his answer, the question had been left twisting in the wind so long that it no longer resembled an investigation of Hughes, but rather an investigation of the Senate itself. "Senator Brewster told me in so many words that if I would agree to merge TWA with Pan American and go along with his scheme for a community American airline, there would be no further hearings in this matter," Hughes alleged as he took the stand. In his first forty-seven minutes in front of the committee, he had the crowd inflamed into applause, laughter, and contempt as Ferguson vainly moved to restore order, ashtray in hand.

Brewster, taking the stand in his own defense, attempted to defuse the situation. His voice cracking, his answers uncertain, he spent an hour and thirty-seven minutes digging a hole for himself, a hole that Hughes had mapped and outlined. After hearing Brewster's version of his meetings with Hughes, Ferguson made the mistake of asking Hughes if he had any questions for the senator. "Yes," Hughes answered, "about two hundred to five hundred." The audience applauded, Ferguson banged his ashtray, and Hughes stretched his long legs out under the table as if he were lounging by a neighbor's pool with no place to go.

As the days toiled on, Hughes maintained the pressure on a Senate committee that was constantly outflanked, second-guessed, and understaffed. Hughes' publicity campaign including sending out press releases, photographs, and specification sheets to the media. He provided recordings of the meetings with Brewster, and transcripts of the recordings. In addition to the millions of listeners that heard the proceedings over live radio broadcasts, it was also the first Senate committee investigation to be seen live over a new invention called television.

What Americans heard, they cheered. They liked the outspoken spunk of a man who, when asked by Ferguson to once again produce Meyer for questioning, answered, "I don't think I will." A manufacturer who was so impassioned by the *Hercules* that he said, "I have put the sweat of my life into this thing. My reputation is wrapped up in it. I have stated that if it fails, I will leave the country. And I mean it." A citizen who said, "Nobody kicks around in this country without acquiring a reputation, good or bad. I'm supposed to be capricious, a playboy, eccentric, but I don't believe I have the reputation of a liar. For twenty-three years, nobody has questioned my word. I think my reputation in that respect meets what most Texans consider important." Cheers were heard from the Chesapeake to the San Francisco Bay.

And after five days of the sideshow to end all sideshows, the Special Senate Committee had learned little more than the maximum number of spectators it could fit into its caucus chambers. Like the walking wounded, Ferguson and his committee showed up on day six and unexpectedly announced to Hughes and the gathered spectators that the investigation was recessed until November 17. Washington needed a break.

Hughes had fought the federal government in a public forum and won. David (albeit a incredibly rich David) had felled Goliath, and the country flocked to follow his lead. Immediately there were calls for Hughes to run for President. When Hughes heard about the grass-roots effort as he boarded his plane for home, he said, "I think I've seen just about enough of Washington," and was not about to return.

In the weeks following the Senate investigation, Hughes Aircraft was ablaze with activity. The crews worked round-the-clock shifts in a race against a timetable that a regenerated leader had set for the completion of both the *Hercules* and the XF-11 photo plane. On November 1, 1947, the XF-11 was officially turned over to the Army. At the same time, over a hundred reporters and news crews were assembled in the Los Angeles Biltmore Hotel where Hughes personally handed each member of the press a solid-gold lighter and matching cigarette case, along with hand-out sheets publicizing the photo reconnaissance plane and the wooden *Hercules*.

On the morning of November 2, the entire group was bussed to Pier E in Long Beach, and shown to press tents, where typewriters, telephones, and hand-held radio receivers and microphones had been installed. Famed Beverly Hills restaurateur Dave Chasen had catered the food and drinks, including hot bowls of Chasen's chili to ward off the cold from a brisk autumn morning.

Thick cumulus clouds the color of whipped cream bunched together like huge cotton balls, casting picture shadows of rabbits and tigers and church steeples across the murky water of the Long Beach harbor. They were the kind of clouds Hughes had wanted but could never find for *Hell's Angels*. Now, they blew unnoticed as he steered the *Hercules*[10] carefully through the crowded water for what were billed as taxi tests of the largest airplane in the world. Hughes had used boats to bring thirty of the press on board the *Hercules*, and his flight crew took their seats.[11]

The harbor was full of sightseers in pleasure craft and yachts, including one that held Jean Peters, Nadine Henley and Cary Grant. Overhead, the sky was pock-marked with planes, their pilots and passengers waiting to catch a glimpse of the famous flying boat. For the next few minutes, Hughes opened the throttles unleashing the eight powerful engines and taxied the plane down the harbor, amid the air horns and cheers from thousands of spectators lining the pier.

The waters were choppy and the reporters, feeling the effects of the sea, made a mass exit when Hughes returned to the dock—racing to file their stories of the successful test run. Although other published accounts of this day have stated that only a single reporter was left on board for the third and final run, in fact there were a half-dozen journalists left on the *Hercules*, mainly those from weekly and monthly magazines with less time-sensitive deadlines, plus broadcast pool radio newsman James C. McNamara from Los Angeles station KLAC.

As the *Hercules* moved away from the pier and down the harbor, McNamara broadcast the moment, as his engineer Harold Huntzman monitored the recorder.

> This is James McNamara speaking to you from aboard the Howard Hughes two hundred-ton flying boat, the world's largest aircraft. At this moment as we speak to you from the spacious flight deck, this mighty monster of the skies is slowly cruising along a northwest course in the outer Los Angeles Harbor.

---

10. The *Hercules* would be later nicknamed the *Spruce Goose* by the press, but the name was found nowhere in the press reports of the period.
11. Hydraulic engineer Dave Grant sat in the co-pilot seat, even though he was not a pilot. Behind Hughes and Grant were crew chief Chuck Jucker, chief engineer Rae Hopper, program manager Bill Berry, flight engineers Joe Petrali and Don Smith, radio operator Merle Coffee, electrical engineers Jim Dallas and Chris Reising, power plant mechanics Al Geverink, Mel Glaser, John Glenn, Harry Kaiser and Don Shirley, systems mechanics Phil Thibodeau and David Van Storm, electrical mechanics Jack Jacobsen and Ben Jiminez, hydraulic mechanics Tom Dugdale, Vic Leonard and Bill Noggle, radio and electrical engineer Dave Evans, CAA representative George W. Haldeman, assistant chief engineer Warren Reed, and power plant engineer Dave Roe.

HANDING THE MICROPHONE TO HUGHES, McNamara asked the pilot to offer a running commentary. In his high-pitched, nasal voice, Hughes calmly told the radio audience that he was taxiing very slowly to the entrance to the harbor to make what he labeled, "a high-speed run."

McNamara counted off the airspeed into the microphone, "It's fifty. It's fifty over a choppy sea. It's fifty-five; it's fifty-five. More throttle. It's sixty. It's about sixty-five. It's seventy."

To the audience across America, what followed next was silence. They could not hear Hughes push the throttles forward or the *Hercules* leave the water. It was up to engineer Harry Kaiser to yell, "It's off!" followed by the excited applause and chatter of those aboard. The *Hercules* flew for less than a minute, for less than a mile, at an altitude of only seventy feet. After bringing the plane down to a flawless landing, Hughes broke into a sly grin, and just nodded his head in satisfaction.

"At one time," McNamara told his radio audience, "Howard said that if this ship did not fly that he would leave the country. Well, it certainly looks at this moment that Howard Hughes will be around the United States for quite some time to come."

TEN

Hooray for Hollywood

*It is extremely important to me that nobody ever
goes into any room, closet, cabinet, bathroom, or
any other area used to store any of the things
which are for me—either food, equipment,
magazines, paper supplies, Kleenex–no matter
what. It is equally important to me that nobody
ever opens any door or opening to any room,
cabinet or closet or anything used to store any
of my things, even for one-thousandth of an
inch, for one-thousandth of a second.*

Beverly Hills, California
December 1, 1950
Memo to all staff.

THE HOLLYWOOD TO WHICH HOWARD HUGHES RETURNED
in the winter of 1947 was no longer the Hollywood that had
inspired him as a youth. The star system at the studios was
breathing its last bit of rancid air, having been eaten alive by
the stars themselves: over-indulged, ego-gorged optical
illusions that had all but disappeared in the reality of a hap-
pier America and a new device called television. This was a
time of Clarence Birdseye and his frozen dinners, William
Levitt and his suburban Levittowns, Reynolds Wrap,
Tupperware, and a Castro convertible sofa that could be
turned into a bed. It was a Camelot where returning soldiers
believed they had a shot at the American dream. It was a
place that Hughes did not recognize, and did not particularly
enjoy. Unlike others who were forced into accepting the
world they were delivered, Hughes stubbornly determined
to live in one of his own creation.

With World War II ended and military orders evaporating, Hughes was uncertain about the money-making potential of the aircraft industry, and all but ignored that division of his enterprise, hiring a trio of men to run the business with a free hand. Hughes' employment of retired Air Corps Lieutenant Generals Ira C. Eaker and Harold L. George, plus Charles B. Thornton, a former executive with Ford Motors, was inspired. They were capable executives with proven ability and who, despite Hughes' opinion of the marketplace, would transform Hughes Aircraft into a profitable enterprise of major importance to national defense. With George and Thornton one and two in command at the plant, and Eaker running interference between the Aircraft and Tool divisions, Hughes' only obligation was to stay out of the way and allow the trio to work magic.

That Hughes *did* keep himself out of their business was more an emotional necessity than a deliberate business decision. While Hughes considered himself an aviator in his soul, his experience in Washington had soured him on actively fronting his own aviation company. The personal contact, the politics, and the intense scrutiny were folded into an enormous part of Hughes' life that he so disliked that he elected to shut it out and determined never to endure again. Let Noah Dietrich and Ira Eaker tolerate such exposure and vulnerability in the name of enterprise. The less Hughes knew about *that* part of his business he felt, the more private he could, and would, remain.

It was with that conceit firmly in mind that Hughes reorganized his Romaine Street offices. During preparation for the Senate hearings and his time on Capitol Hill, Hughes recognized that his staff at Romaine were quite adept at operating a business office, but knew little about handling him personally. What Hughes needed, he decided, was a personal assistant whose responsibility would be solely the care and handling of Howard R. Hughes. To fill the opening, he turned to Nadine Henley, who in turn suggested a Mormon student she had hired to help prepare files for the Senate hearings. His name was Frank William Gay. Like Hughes, he was lanky; unlike Hughes, he was organized. At twenty-seven, he had a wife and four years' worth of credits at Brigham Young University. And according to Nadine, he was meticulous.

Meticulous was a word Howard Hughes understood. He was, after all, the most meticulous person he had ever encountered. "Meticulous attitude is good," he wrote to Nadine, who set up an appointment for Gay to meet Hughes on Thanksgiving morning, 1947. As usual, Hughes had picked the day to determine how hungry Gay was for the opportunity. Gay was hungry, plus smart and wise—or at least smart and wise enough to recognize a ground-floor opportunity when it stood up and refused to shake his hand. He got the job.

His first assignment was to set up a twenty-four-hour switchboard service within the Romaine Street facility, as well as hire a team of drivers for sporadic duty around-the-clock. He selected a group of young, non-drinking, non-smoking Mormon friends who would owe their employment and thus their loyalty to the meticulous former student. That loyalty business is a funny thing. It just hangs there in the background, unnoticed, despite its value. Unnoticed, that is, until it is needed. Right now, it was enough for Gay to know that these men were his responsibility.

On November 5, the Senate reconvened its special investigation into Hughes Aircraft, though with the delivery of the XF-11[1] and the flight of the *Hercules*, much of the urgency of the hearings seemed to be lost. Certainly the press had moved on to other, bigger issues, leaving the maneuvering in the Senate caucus chamber to play out on the inside pages of Washington papers and to be ignored entirely by others.

Hughes created a modicum of excitement when he revealed that General Benny Meyers had attempted to get Hughes to loan him $200,000 in the War Bond scheme. After some dodging and prancing, Meyers had to admit that Hughes was telling the truth, and suddenly the hearings took on a witch-hunt of a different theme, this time with the gold stars and bars of the military in question. Like a balloon leaking air, the hearings seem to sputter under their own lack of direction, and on November 22, 1947, were adjourned without reaching an indictment or even a consensus.

Hughes returned to Los Angeles without the fanfare accorded his previous departure from Washington. He had decided against returning to the Town House hotel, and instead took up residence at Cary Grant's home in Beverly Hills. Grant was away making the film *I Was a Male War Bride*, so Hughes moved into the empty house with twenty-four white shirts, two pairs of pants, two suits, and one pair of shoes—all that remained of his Senate ordeal besides a distaste for all things Washington.

With Gay on phones, Nadine on keyboard, Dietrich on Tools, and George on Aircraft, Hughes found himself with nothing to do for the first time in his twenty-three years in California except count his money, which was then reproducing itself at the rate of $42,000 a day at a time when the average salary in the U.S. was $8,000 a year.

Considering his total lifetime experience had been limited to aviation, motion pictures, the manufacturing of a single motorized bicycle, and collecting berries and merit badges at Camp Teedyuskung, Hughes

---

1. The XF-11 was placed into service in Florida at Eglin Air Force Base where it was used for training. After less than two years, it was phased out of service and dismantled for scrap metal.

decided to once again explore his options in Hollywood. Specifically, he wanted to buy RKO.[2] At the time, the studio was ranked third among the Hollywood giants, just behind M-G-M and Warner Bros. In 1947 alone, RKO released 37 films, including the Oscar-nominated *The Bishop's Wife* starring Cary Grant, Loretta Young and David Niven, Eugene O'Neill's *Mourning Becomes Electra* with Rosalind Russell, *The Fugitive* starring Henry Fonda and directed by John Ford, *Tycoon* with John Wayne, plus Danny Kaye in *The Secret Life of Walter Mitty*; and in the past had scored with hits like *Citizen Kane*, *King Kong*, and the Fred Astaire-Ginger Rogers musicals.

The lot's principal owner was Floyd B. Odlum, a New Yorker whose Atlas Investment Corporation held 929,020 shares of the studio. For several months, Hughes negotiated with Odlum at his estate outside Palm Springs, and used the opportunity to reconnect with Odlum's wife, Jacqueline Cochran,[3] the flyer in whose plane Hughes set his cross-country record. Both men were reclusive multimillionaires with an eccentric reputation. Odlum conducted his business while floating on an innertube in his heated pool, while Hughes sweated in wool slacks and a well-worn long-sleeve shirt, watching dates fall from the palm trees.

While the two men jostled in a world that tossed millions of dollars onto the playing field with an apparent nonchalance mastered by only the very rich, Hughes found himself being drawn into another federal investigation. This time, however, it would not be played out in a public forum. On April 23, 1948, a United States grand jury in Honolulu, Hawaii, found that there was enough evidence to implicate Hughes Tool Company in a scheme to defraud the government through the acquisition of six C-47 cargo planes at a discounted rate. The planes, worth $100,000 each, were purchased by two employees of Hughes Tool for $17,500 using their status as veterans to receive a discount. The planes were resold at a profit, and Hughes' reputation was on the line as a result.

Hughes knew nothing about this transaction, as he knew nothing

---

2. RKO (Radio-Keith-Orpheum) was one of the film industry's Big Five thanks primarily to its distribution deals with, at various times, Walt Disney, David O. Selznick, and Samuel Goldwyn, along with its own output since 1921.

3. The late Sydney Guilaroff, MGM's long-time head of hair and make-up, claimed to have known Jacqueline Cochran when she was a manicurist at Antoine's Beauty Salon located in Saks Fifth Avenue at the same time Guilaroff worked there as a stylist. According to Guilaroff, Cochran overheard Floyd Odlum's wife saying how overworked her rich husband was and that she had insisted they take an ocean cruise to work out some rough spots in their marriage. Cochran is said to have booked herself aboard the same cruise and before it was over, she seduced him and extracted a promise of marriage from Odlum. Claire Booth Luce used the story as the basis for her Broadway hit play *The Women*, that was later made into a film starring Joan Crawford in the Jackie Cochran-based role of Crystal.

about most Hughes Tool transactions, but was reluctant to be flung head-long back into a court proceeding, this time with criminal implications. Despite Noah Dietrich's impassioned pleas to Tom C. Clark, the Attorney General of the United States, the local chief prosecutor was out to establish his own name by hitchhiking on that of Hughes. Fortunately, he was also eager to be elected a state senator.

From Hughes' simplified perspective, all things problematic could be settled with money. "Every man has his price," Hughes said. "If they didn't, people like me couldn't exist." In this case, the price was $100,000. Dietrich placed a call to the head of the Democratic National Committee promising a donation of $100,000 to candidates of the DNC's choice, courtesy of Howard Hughes. And while the donation came without covenants, Dietrich let it be known that Hughes would be "very pleased" to have his company removed from the litigation. Several telephone calls later, and twenty individual $5,000 checks, Hughes Tool was dropped from the formal charges, and the two employees pleaded *nolo contendere* to a lesser offense. Hughes ended up paying their $20,000 fine, and had the men immediately fired.

The experience impacted Hughes in a major way. It was the first major test of his ability to conduct business from his darkened suite in Beverly Hills. His first use of a political contribution to influence the government. As far as Hughes was concerned, it was the triumph of leveraged coercion, and he delighted in the power. When he heard from Dietrich that his effort had been successful, he was lying naked on his bed in a room lit only by the ear-to-ear grin on his face.

In May, 1948, Hughes agreed to pay a full dollar over the market share, and got control of RKO for $8,825,690, which he borrowed from Mellon Bank in Pittsburgh to keep the purchase separate from Hughes Tool. For that price, Hughes got twenty-four percent ownership in the studio's twenty-six sound stages on Melrose Avenue in Hollywood plus some in Culver City, a ranch in the San Fernando Valley used to shoot Westerns, and a chain of one hundred and twenty-four movie theaters in twelve states.

When word reached the studio executives that Howard Hughes had become their boss, the reaction was one of mass panic. His reputation as a fanatic perfectionist with an indecisive streak sent shockwaves through every department with the energy of an earthquake on the San Andreas fault. Studio president Peter Rathvon attempted to keep the calm by issuing a written statement to his employees reassuring them that their jobs were safe and that Hughes had "no hungry army of relatives looking for jobs or substitutes waiting to step into the RKO management." And indeed that was very true.

Production chief Dore Schary, who was out of town attending his mother's funeral at the time of the takeover, returned to Hollywood wearing a black armband of mourning, certain that he would be out of a job. As much out of curiosity as a courtesy to Rathvon, he agreed to meet with Hughes at Rathvon's home to discuss his future at the studio. Schary remembered Hughes as looking like "the capable quick gun one saw in westerns, so often played by Gary Cooper." He did not comment when Hughes touched his hand instead of shaking it, told him he had heard he wanted to quit, and asked him to reconsider, saying he thought he was doing a great job.

He remembered Hughes leaning in to hear his reply, looking sideways through a mop of hair that hung across his face. "I know you've made films and I know that since you've bought this studio, you'll want to run it. I understand that. You won't need me at my price to deliver your orders," Schary said. Hughes continued to look at the ground as he announced to both Rathvon and Schary that he was not interested in running a studio, that he wanted things to continue as they had been. Only after Schary agreed to stay at his job did Hughes look up. When he left, he did not shake their hands, but instead waved a polite "Thank you" and nodded slightly, like the Japanese do in acknowledgment.

As he left Rathvon's house, Hughes noticed a decaying bee being surrounded by a nest of ants and a large water bug that dared to intrude into their space in the hope of stealing dinner. He saw an empty tin can being blown by the wind across the lawn, as if driven to escape the heat of an early summer. He felt his shoes crush the loose gravel under his feet, as he reached the curb and the street beyond. Once inside his old brown Chevrolet, Hughes took a yellow legal pad and wrote the words *Ants*, *Can*, *Wind*, and *Shoes* before starting the car and driving away.

Schary thought the meeting strange and told Rathvon as much as he was walked to his car. The way Hughes looked at the floor made Schary wonder if Hughes had even heard what he said. "He's in his own world," Rathvon said, slamming the car door and waiting until Schary disappeared down the street before turning and walking back up the path and into his house, never noticing the ants who had managed to drag the bee several feet. He failed to see the water bug that had reached the shade of a flat rock and paused to hide in its shadow, and the tin can that by this time had blown into the corner of his yard, and rolled under a hedge where it would remain undiscovered for the rest of the year.

Schary returned to RKO where he had two World War II films in pre-production, an action-adventure titled *Battleground* and the melodrama *Malaya*. The only film then shooting at the studio was called *Caught* starring Robert Ryan and Barbara Bel Geddes. It took only two weeks before Hughes broke his word, and telephoned Schary late one night during an editing session. He did not feel that war pictures had very much left to say and wanted both *Battleground* and *Malaya* scrapped. He disliked Barbara Bel Geddes[4] and wanted her fired. Schary refused, and only would agree to meet Hughes the following day to tender his resignation in person.

When Schary arrived at the appointed hour of 1 p.m. at Cary Grant's house, he saw a woman in a back bedroom hooking her bra as Hughes opened the door. "There wasn't a paper, a cigarette, a flower, a match, a picture, a magazine—there was nothing except two chairs and a sofa. It had the look of a place someone had just moved out of or was moving into," Schary later recalled.

As he told Hughes he could no longer work for RKO because of his interference, he directed his comments once again to Hughes' bowed head and dangling hair. After a moment of silence, Hughes finally spoke. "Where did you get those shoes?" he asked. Schary smiled despite his irritation, and told Hughes he thought they were Johnston & Murphy shoes that he had purchased for around $35. "Comfortable?" Hughes asked. Schary said they were, after which Hughes nodded his head and accepted the production chief's resignation.

Dore Schary left RKO Pictures on July 31, 1948. The following month, he was hired to replace Louis B. Mayer at M-G-M Studios. During his first year, Schary brought sixty-eight films to M-G-M. Among them were *Battleground* starring Van Johnson, Ricardo Montalban, and James Whitmore; *Malaya* starring Spencer Tracy, James Stewart, and Lionel Barrymore; and *Caught* starring Robert Ryan and Barbara Bel Geddes. All three films made money for M-G-M. *Battleground* returned the studio $5.1 million in profit, earned an Oscar Award for Best Black and White Cinematography, and was nominated for an additional four Oscars including Best Picture.

After Schary's departure from RKO, Peter Rathvon likewise resigned, sending the studio department heads scurrying to find new jobs like roaches caught in a spotlight. Rather than make an effort to stop the talent hemorrhage, Hughes gave instructions to trim the employee pool by an additional 700 persons, equal to a cut of between fifty and seventy-five percent in most departments. At the same time, Hughes sold RKO the three films he had produced—*The Outlaw* from Caddo Productions, plus *Mad Wednesday* and *Vandetta* from Preston-Hughes. In addition, he paid himself $100,000 for the rights to use Jane Russell in RKO films, and he did it all without once ever having stepped foot on the lot.

---

4. Barbara Bel Geddes went on to have a moderate film career, but found her true metier in the theater where she created the part of Maggie in Tennessee Williams' *Cat on a Hot Tin Roof.* She won an Emmy for her portrayal of Miss Ellie on TV's *Dallas.*

According to Hollywood legend, the closest he ever came to the studio was the one time he flew over it in his new DC-4, thought it looked tattered, and left instructions with Noah Dietrich, who he had appointed to the board of directors, to have the place painted. It was. When he received a bill for $88,000 for one set on the film *It's Only Money*, he ordered it dismantled and shipped to an office he kept at Goldwyn Studio on Santa Monica Boulevard for his approval. He changed the color of the walls, the location of the doors and a fireplace, sent the entire set back and had it rebuilt, at a cost of an additional $62,000 and five days of lost production.

At the time of Hughes' takeover, one of the biggest stars at RKO was Robert Mitchum. A man's man and a Hughes favorite, Mitchum walked around with sleepy eyes with lids like awnings, and a voice that resonated with a rumble like boulders loosened in an avalanche. He had just completed work on a film titled *Rachel and the Stranger* (Loretta Young played Rachel, Mitchum the stranger) when Hughes received a late night call that his male star had been arrested and was cooling his heels in the L.A. County jail.

It was September 1, 1948, and the next day's headlines shouted the charges of marijuana possession and use, a serious crime at the time. Had Floyd Oldlum still owned the studio, Mitchum's career would have been finished. With Hughes at the helm, the criminal case was just another way to promote *Stranger*, that was rushed into release to packed movie theaters. Hughes paid for Mitchum's defense and objected loudly and publicly when his star was found guilty and sentenced to a year in prison.

Still capitalizing on his star's misfortune, Hughes sent photographers into the prison farm in Castaic, California, to shoot Mitchum's muscled body swabbing floors with a rag mop, and working out in the prison's gym. Hughes also arranged to advance his star $50,000 at five percent interest, to be taken out of his contracted salary of $3,500 per week, which Hughes continued to pay even though Mitchum was not working. Despite all the hype for Mitchum, RKO still managed to lose $5.6 million for the year.

Noah Dietrich, who was officially in charge of watching the purse strings, regarded the loss philosophically. "It was a cheap way to keep Hughes occupied while the rest of his businesses made money," Dietrich said in 1976. Hughes Tool Company sales reached $100 million in 1948 for the first time in its history. Hughes Aircraft, under the direction of Harold George, had hired two scientists, Dr. Simon Ramo and Dr. Dean E. Wooldridge, who together moved the company away from airplane design into military electronics, a field so new that Hughes Aircraft had a monopoly on its technology. Based on the work by Ramo and Wooldridge, the Aircraft Division was awarded an $8 million contract to place its all-weather interceptors in Lockheed's F-94 fighters–all 200 of them.

At the time of the remarkable turnaround, Howard Hughes was busying himself pursuing a teenager he had first seen in a film titled *The Return of October.* Her name was Helen Koford, but to the world she would soon be known as Terry Moore. At nineteen, Terry had been involved in show business for nearly half her life. The quintessential fresh-faced, wholesome, bubbling slice of energy, she had attracted Hollywood's excitement, and that of Hughes, because of her naive, unsophisticated take on the world. To see life through Terry's eyes was to see a milieu brimming with endless excitement and potential.

Where Jean Peters represented calm serenity, Terry Moore was raw enthusiasm. The untouched plain; the virgin forest; the next unscaled mountain to conquer for the explorer Hughes. The prerequisite ice-breaking introduction occurred through the paid services of Johnny Machio, a Hollywood agent and flesh peddler who arranged to bring Terry and her date, actor Jerome Courtland, to the Beverly Wilshire Hotel where Hughes was conveniently lurking in the shadows.

When Hughes appeared at their table, Terry found him "repulsive," while Courtland was immediately drawn into his discussion of flying, airplanes and the great blue yonder, and accepted an invitation for them both to join Hughes the following day in a night flight over Los Angeles. In remembering that first flight with the legendary pilot, Terry recalled less about the trip than about Hughes' lack of style. In her memoir, she said he wore a white shirt with a "frayed collar, brown orthopedic-looking shoes, smooth beige wool slacks, and carried a blue sports jacket with a rumpled tie in the pocket."

When Terry later left town to go on a six-week publicity tour for *The Return of October,* she thought Howard Hughes was out of her life. The film cast the teenager as the naive niece of a dying man who promised to come back in his next life as a horse—the October of the title. That the actress should call the part "the choicest girl's role of the decade" suggests more about her mind-set than the quality of the film, particularly given that Elizabeth Taylor, three years younger than Terry, had already completed ten films, including *National Velvet,* and was about to begin work on her eleventh, Louisa May Alcott's *Little Women.*

Hughes appeared unannounced, uninvited, and unwanted at various stops along the tour, standing and watching like a voyeur in his element. Hoping to convince Hughes of the hopelessness of his infatuation, the young actress decided to invite him to join her family for dinner, urged

on by her mother who thought the idea of entertaining a multimillionaire in her Glendale home would make her life complete. And that is how
on a rather crisp spring night in 1948, Howard Hughes happened to find
himself sitting at the dining room table in the Koford house, eating
Mama Blue's famous Swiss steak smothered in onions and tomatoes.

He was met at the front door by a large German Shepherd, more
greeter than watchdog, that leaped up on his hind legs, placed his front
paws on Hughes' blue sport coat, and left a thick layer of dog saliva as he
lapped at Hughes' face the way a child attacks a lollipop.

"Mom, Dad! Come quick. Stormy's got his front paws on Mr.
Hughes' shoulders," Terry screamed her welcome, according to her
memoir, and so the night began.

By the time it was over, Hughes had learned that Terry was a
Mormon, her mother picked out all her clothes, her father sold insurance, she had a brother named Wally, and lived in a house that reeked of
suburbia and the slight smell of disinfectant masking dog odor. He was
taken by how genuine their emotions seemed, fully surfaced and without
a hidden agenda. And as he walked back to the car, with an extra piece of
apple crumble Mama Blue had put in a brown paper bag, he caught himself smiling for no reason at all.

Preferring to call Terry "Helen" as her parents did, Hughes began an
elaborate courting dance that included candlelight dinners and plane trips
to nowhere. Though he was four years older than her mother, he was
determined to get Helen into his bed, and her ample breasts into his hands.
Helen, who was as protected growing up as a rare wine in a connoisseur's
cellar, found the attention flattering, and seemed fully prepared for his proposal of marriage when he dropped to a knee one night atop Mulholland
Drive in Los Angeles, and slipped a diamond, ruby and sapphire engagement ring in the shape of an owl on the third finger of her left hand. Helen
squealed an excited *yes*, only to calm down substantially when told by her
suitor that they were now married "in the sight of God under the stars and
moon," and should head immediately to his newly rented bungalow at
the Beverly Hills Hotel to consummate the relationship.

The maneuver did not work any better on the unsophisticated Terry
Moore than it had earlier in 1948 with Jean Peters or budding starlet
Vera Ralston. While Jean laughed at the proposal and went off to film
Deep Waters in Vinalhaven, Maine, with Dana Andrews and Cesar
Romero, Vera said no because she had fallen in love with one of Hughes'
Mormon drivers, Robert Miles. The pair got married later in the year
and as Vera Miles, she became a major star.[5]

---

5. Vera Miles played Henry Fonda's beleaguered wife in Alfred Hitchcock's *The Wrong Man*, as well
as Janet Leigh's sister in *Psycho*.

The truth about Mulholland Drive was that Howard Hughes made a habit of bringing dates to a certain spot halfway between Laurel Canyon and Benedict Cañon. It was nothing more than a dirt pull-off that hugged the crest of the Santa Monica Mountains with an opulent view of the San Fernando Valley where a million lights twinkled their sorcery in a sky so black that it had no end. There, in that magic of moonlight and star bright, Hughes tried to weave a spell, hoping that the setting would make up for his lack of real emotion. Hughes was faced with what he told Cary Grant was "libido shock." Since his near-fatal crash, his ability to become aroused was "eager but lazy," he said, and hindered further by his return to medicating himself for his continuing headaches with codeine supplied by Dr. Mason. America's most eligible bachelor was not impotent, merely less potent. And his reputation as a playboy increased his stress to perform.

As a result, Hughes spent a great deal of time alone, cloistered in Bungalow Nineteen of the Beverly Hills Hotel. He selected that particular bungalow for easy and private access to the street, as well as its limited windows which he had sealed and covered in black-out drapes to block light, sound and germs. After his extended stay in Good Samaritan Hospital and his subsequent exposure to syphilis, Hughes' fear of contamination was heightened to the point that he ordered his first carton of Kleenex to use as *insolation*—his term for a perceived level of increased protection. He did not use the tissues himself at first, but required it of all of his aides, waiters, and housekeepers. He wrote his first set of instructions and sent them to Nadine Henley, who typed them in a general book of employee guidelines that would continue to grow over the next two decades.

> First use six or eight thicknesses of Kleenex pulled one at a time from the slot in the box. . . then fit them over the door knob and open the bathroom. Please leave the bathroom door open so there will be no need to touch anything when leaving. This same sheaf of Kleenex may be employed to turn the spigots so as to obtain a good force of water for cleaning.

HUGHES ALSO SHOWED a renewed interest in writing another will, with numerous notes and dictates written, still on yellow legal pads, hand-carried by a driver to Nadine at his Romaine Street offices. In an effort to set a value on Hughes Tool for his estate, Hughes engaged in a flurry of negotiations in which he purported to be posturing to sell the business. For months, he listened to offers from Dillon, Read & Company Inc., an investment banking firm, that was ready to pay $170 million in cash for

45 percent of Hughes Tool, thus placing the total value of the company at nearly $380 million.

As soon as Dillon, Read had placed a figure on the sale, Hughes announced that there were "certain legal and technical obstacles to the completion of this deal." He offered no specifics, not even to Dillon, Read. Noah Dietrich would later claim that he never had any intention of selling any percentage of the company.

In early 1949 as well, he established the Howard Hughes Fellowships in Creative Aeronautics at California Institute of Technology as a way to encourage interest in airplane design. In addition to scholarship funding, he guaranteed employment to selected students at Hughes Aircraft in its research and development department, with the stipulation that any inventions or discoveries became the sole property of his company.

His continual meddling in the affairs of RKO Pictures increased by increments during the year, culminating in his announcement that he had assumed the title of Managing Director-Production, a role he was essentially filling in any case, albeit without any previous official status. Now, as the managing director, he assumed responsibility for the selection of films to be produced at the studio. His first announcement proved to be extraordinary to both the studio and the talent involved. In February 1949, Hughes signed a distribution deal for a film in pre-production from Italian director Roberto Rossellini to star Ingrid Bergman. At the time, the title of the film was *Terra di Dio* (*Earth of God*) and was to be shot in Italy on the desolate island of Stromboli. It had no script, but rather extensive notes provided by Rossellini who preferred to work from impulse, and for which he would receive $150,000. Hughes agreed to pay Ingrid her usual salary of $175,000. The film's overall budget was $1 million, a large sum for an Italian picture—for that fee RKO received the distribution rights in America as well as ten percent of the foreign profits.

Stromboli was a dreary place, an island without tropical breezes or swaying palms, dominated by a volcano that had been in constant eruption for 15,000 years, and which would play a major role in the movie. When word reached America in May that the film's star and director had fallen in love, despite the fact that both were already married with families, Hughes leapt into the scandal by supporting his talent, ignoring the outrage of the pious, and announcing that he was far more interested in finding a new title for the picture than interrupting true love.

For Hughes, the Bergman-Rossellini tryst was a bigger publicity event than he could have created with his own staff, who danced around in a delicate balance of inflaming the notoriety while casting the illusion of astonishment. That Hughes had his own romantic intrigue unfolding was another story entirely, and one he worked hard to see remained private. He had begun spending his evenings having sex with Jean Peters at her rented home on Veteran Avenue in Westwood when he was not sleeping on the sofa in the Koford's living room as a gesture of loyalty to Terry Moore. During the same period, he had Bill Gay at Romaine Street involved in an intricate choreography of logistics that found him courting dancer Cyd Charisse in the afternoons, even though she preferred the company of singer Tony Martin.

In between his attempts at courtship, Hughes found an increasing need to take showers, wash his hands and hair, trim his nails, and instruct his staff on the correct handling of what he labeled "live items"—those papers, clothes, and toiletries that he handled every day. Much as it had during his mental breakdown of 1944, the pressure of business and his social life manifested itself on the surface in lengthy memos that took their form in instructions on procedure, each intricately described and impossible to follow. While many of his memos concerned the correct technique for removing Kleenex tissues from their box, oftentimes contradicting one another as to exact procedure, it was with his personal clothing that he made the greatest effort to ensure that they were adequately "insulated" from outside contamination. To Hughes, dirt itself was fine; germs were the enemy and a separate entity altogether.

Writing in the third person, and typically referring to himself as HRH, Hughes gave the following instructions to Gay to be distributed to his staff. "He wants all coats that need to be cleaned to be cleaned and hung together some place. He wants the same thing done with the trousers and hung together away from the coats at least five feet. This may be in the same closet, but only if large enough to accommodate the insulation provided by the indicated space. He wants all shirts and everything else laundered and put in a container of some kind. A white cardboard box is preferable to wood. It is not good to leave these in laundry boxes however because there are other items in there too."

Old memos were not to be kept, but rather "memorized and then placed in a Kraft paper sack. They should then be lit with a wooden match and burned to a white ash." This technique was only to be done after dark, and only by a selected team of "trusted men."

Hughes also believed that his telephones were tapped, based largely on his experience in Washington, D.C., when his phone lines actually were bugged by the FBI. Files from that period indicate that although the Bureau was not actively involved in wiretapping Hughes' phones in 1949, there were men assigned to follow his movements, which they felt were "unexplained and erratic." What the FBI failed to ever realize was that Hughes' most elusive behavior at the time was manifested in an effort to outwit them.

According to Nadine Henley, Hughes arranged for Terry Moore and her mother, Luella, to be picked up by a company car, and taken to the Beverly Hills Hotel. Though the exact date is not known, Terry testified in 1979 that it must have been in November, 1949. "Everything in my life happens in November," she said while being deposed. "Every marriage, divorce—everything. All my beginnings and endings seem to happen in November in my life."

Nadine had made arrangement for food and champagne to be sent to a rented yacht docked in the San Diego harbor. The evening was designed, she said "to be a romantic night under the stars." According to Terry, it turned out to much more. Hughes had finally decided, he said, to make good on his proposal and solemnize their marriage. This time, of course, more than God would be a witness.

With flight engineer Earl Martyn in the co-pilot's seat, Hughes flew mother and daughter to San Diego where they were met by the former captain of the *Southern Cross*, Carl Flynn, who was still on salary, along with his first mate, Frank Cordell. Weighing anchor, the crew piloted Hughes and the Kofords into a sun that seemed to be setting quicker than usual out of embarrassment. As mother and daughter took to their cabins in various stages of primary seasickness, the portly captain and his rather unwell looking mate decked the ship with candles encased in brandy snifters and gardenias flown in from Mexico.

When Terry and her mother regained consciousness after nausea-induced naps and returned to the deck, they found that the yacht was now miles out to sea, an insignificant fleck on a vast expanse of saltwater and a moonless sky. With all the flourish of a circus ringmaster, Hughes produced a meal of hot dogs, buns and French fries, flown on TWA from Coney Island for the occasion, followed by a document which Moore later swore was a marriage license, despite the fact that she had neither applied for one nor signed it.

As the boat drifted toward Baja California, Captain Flynn read from the Episcopal Book of Common Prayer, the same liturgy that was used at Hughes' first marriage, though Flynn was considerably less familiar with the words than Dr. Peter Gray Sears of Houston's Christ Church Cathedral. He slurred through the part about "wilt thou love her, comfort her, honor and keep her in sickness and in health; and forsaking all others, keep thee only unto her" as if he already knew the answer, and by the time Flynn got to "you may kiss the bride," Hughes already had Terry in his arms, his tongue probing her throat and tasting the last remains of a frankfurter.

As Mama Blue led the group in a toast to her daughter and new son-in-law, Terry burst into tears of happiness, and later wrote that marrying Howard Hughes was a "dream come true" and she felt like pinching herself "to make sure it was real." Her trepidation was understandable, but must have come from some part of her female intuition that fought unsuccessfully to surface, for when the yacht returned to port and deposited her mother, the captain and first mate on shore, Terry was only too willing to set up housekeeping in the master stateroom and prepare to lose her virginity to her new husband.

Hughes had taken great care to ensure that the yacht had traveled into international waters where the captain had no legal authority to perform marriages, if indeed he ever did. After over a year of intense pursuit, Hughes achieved his goal, and bedded the 20-year-old Terry in a night she would liken to "a majestic symphony" in her memoir. The honeymoon lasted all of eight hours, by which time Hughes flew Terry back to Los Angeles, and returned to his bungalow at the Beverly Hills Hotel, conveniently urging her not to mention their marriage to anyone "for the sake of their careers."

Ten days later, Bruno, the room service waiter, had just brought Hughes' dinner of New York steak (medium rare) and hearts of lettuce salad with Roquefort cheese dressing, when the telephone rang in Bungalow Nineteen. Joseph H. Steele was on the line. Joe Steele was Ingrid Bergman's publicist and her first real friend in America. That he would call Hughes on this night was out of a sense of loyalty to them both. He felt obligated to reach out to help Ingrid, who in December, 1949, was still married to her husband, Dr. Petter Lindstrom, but living in Italy with Roberto Rossellini.

They were desperate for cash, Steele informed Hughes, and wanted his guarantee that Hughes would help by rushing the release of their film, now titled *Stromboli*. Hughes responded by slicing into his steak and moving to get off the telephone. Steele could not afford to allow Hughes to hang up without giving his word. With great difficulty, he betrayed a trust and revealed that Ingrid was six months pregnant with Rossellini's baby. Somehow, he argued, *Stromboli* had to be released before the baby was born; before the boycotts and the uproar; before the zealots could have their say.

It took Howard Hughes less than twenty seconds to pledge to Steele that he would keep the news a secret and push *Stromboli* through the post-production pipeline. Steele was elated, and hung up the telephone feeling triumphant in his decision. He had less than twelve hours to celebrate.

No other decision in Hughes' entire life said as much about his priorities than the one he made next. Suddenly, his New York steak could wait. He immediately placed a call to gossip columnist Louella Parsons and revealed the news he had just promised to keep sacred: Ingrid

Bergman was having an illegitimate baby. Louella was beside herself with excitement. This was "stop the presses" news, and she did just that.

Hughes thought nothing of the impact his betrayal might have on his star, her lover, her publicist, or their lives. And even if he had given it some thought, he would not have cared in any case. His only concern was for *Stromboli* and the effect the news would have on its business. He saw the controversy as a publicity boom, and was still smiling as he hung up the phone and then calmly ordered another steak from room service to replace the one that had gotten cold. The two-inch headlines that topped the next morning's edition of the *Los Angeles Examiner* read:

INGRID BERGMAN BABY DUE IN THREE MONTHS AT ROME

AS FOR INGRID, Hughes only mentioned her once, and that was to Noah Dietrich who thought the indiscretion despicable. "Does that broad know how to promote a movie!" Hughes said, laughing as he contemplated the profits.

Unfortunately, America found the film to be dull and slow, the island stark, and the plot, about a prisoner from a detention camp who marries a fisherman, to be as absurd as Hughes' advertisements that featured an erupting volcano which the MPAA said looked like "an ejaculating penis" with the accompanying slogan, "Flaming Volcano! Flaming Emotions!" Hughes was forced to admit he had made a mistake, and after asking the opinion of an astonished Dore Schary, ordered the ads discontinued.

Hughes wore his disappointment well, like the felt fedora that he occasionally still angled across his head in the privacy of his bungalow. He felt suddenly out of touch; he had lost the heartbeat of a country that had moved in a direction that he found altogether unpleasant.

While he loved planes, he hated the bombs they were now designed to carry. He loved movies but could not understand why anyone would go to see a musical. Frank Sinatra. Now *there* was a mystery even Dietrich could not explain. Hughes did not understand television, and was certain that the glass tube emitted radiation. He did not like the concept of women truck drivers, or men who washed dishes. He had forgotten what his mother looked like; forgotten her perfume. But most of all, he had lost track of himself.

Hughes expressed his concern to Dr. Mason in a two-page memo he read over the phone, and when told his paranoia was caused by stress insisted that his work helped him to relax. Mason offered more pills, but Hughes refused, afraid how they would affect his mind that was already running a marathon that never stopped at red lights. Initially defensive, Hughes began to instruct his doctor at length on the signs of nervous disorders. He explained that he was not out of control, just watching his life change without his permission. The subtlety of the difference was not lost on Mason, who began to keep extensive notes in his medical files of his observations of a mind he felt on the verge of another breakdown—or worse, a plunge into an abyss of darkness from which there would be no return.

ELEVEN

Communists, Lovers, and Other Strangers

*Do you think if they asked a man if he was a
Democrat or a Republican that he would refuse
to answer on the grounds that his answer might
incriminate him? The very fact that this man
pleaded his constitutional privilege—that is
admission that he is not talking about politics.
He is talking about crime. If you believe that the
Communist Party is in the same category as the
Democratic Party or the Republican Party,
then I think I can answer you in this way:
We are not fighting Democrats or
Republicans in Korea.*

> Los Angeles, California
> April 1, 1952
> Speaking to the American Legion about
> alleged Communist Party member writer
> Paul Jarrico.

AT FORTY-FIVE, HOWARD HUGHES WAS ALREADY OLD.
When other men were entering middle age by going to the
high-school graduations of their sons and daughters, worrying
about crab grass that returned with a determined stance
each spring, and paying for college tuition, Hughes was living
a legend in which each day was a calculation of what had to
be bettered the next.

It was a new decade and time to reflect. He had set
world records, produced famous films, made banner headlines, bedded the world's most desirable women, been the
subject of extraordinary rumors (some of which he even

started), and was clearly one of the richest men in the United States, and perhaps the world. He had more money than he could ever spend, if, in fact, he could think of anything he wanted to spend it on. He couldn't.

He now had a fleet of eighteen used Chevrolets in black, brown, and green, six private planes (the largest of which held fifty-five), one yacht which he did not use, a closet with adequate clothes, six number two pencils, two Parker pens, twelve fresh legal pads, and a torchiere lamp that he had taken from the Muirfield house and rather fancied for its stable base. He needed nothing else, except perhaps some peace of mind. But there, he realized was the problem.

His body ached with a constant pulse like the vanes on a turbine that had been left in the elements far too long. His back was bent in a perpetual slouch and burned with the onset of rheumatism, especially when the weather turned damp. It hurt to get out of bed to face his life, so most days he never bothered, except for extended visits to the toilet where he strained to eliminate hardened excrement the size of tennis balls. His skin had taken on the pallor of campfire ash and sagged as if deflated by some invisible valve that had been left open by mistake. His head hurt from a spot hidden deep within his skull, the pain eased but not erased by codeine.

Yes, at forty-five, Howard Hughes' body felt old and looked even older; his mind, however, was not informed of the fact. It stayed awake for unreasonable hours, forcing the body into service it could no longer easily provide as if it thought it was still a teenager climbing the great oak in Dudley Sharp's backyard to install a radio antenna wire. It raced with concepts for new designs that somehow were not really new at all. It begged to be shown the same old films, finding comfort in the repetition of the scenes, each prized like a favorite Christmas ornament brought down from the attic and revisited with regularity. At the moment, its favorite was Agatha Christie's *And Then There Were None*, starring Barry Fitzgerald, Walter Huston, and Louis Hayward, and any of those old Charlie Chan mysteries. His mind liked those especially.

Even from the darkened sanctuary of his Beverly Hills Hotel bungalow, Hughes could hear the familiar sound of airplane engines as they flew on their assigned flight path to the Los Angeles Airport. Although he was flying considerably less, his love of aviation remained unabashed, and translated itself into another airplane picture that he envisioned as a jet-aged *Hell's Angels*. The advent of jet engines was beginning to transform the airline industry, with Hughes poised to capitalize on the movement on film. He purchased the rights to a story called *Jet Pilot*, and hired the swaggering arch-conservative John Wayne to play the title role, with MGM ingenue Janet Leigh cast improbably as a Soviet pilot with whom he falls in love.

Hughes brought German director Josef von Sternberg out of retirement to helm the picture for no discernable reason other than charity, and then characteristically decided that he could do a better job, unceremoniously fired von Sternberg, and took over the director's chair himself. By January, 1951, Hughes had shot 150,000 feet of film, enough for a twenty-four hour movie and over ten times more than the finished picture required. As could be expected, there were stunning aerial photography sequences, which stunt pilot Paul Mantz[1] shot over a period of months. Unfortunately, by the time the film was finally edited and released, it would be 1957, and most of the aerial footage would be useless because of the technical advances in jet propulsion made since the original filming. John Wayne and Janet Leigh looked as if they had been stalled in time capsules, their youth standing in odd playback compared to their current films running in the theaters at the same time.

During the several years that *Jet Pilot* was in production, Hughes continued to attempt to recapture his youth through Terry Moore, whose perky effervescence and incredibly naive wonderment brought the man she considered to be her husband a great deal of honest pleasure. Had he not been living a lie with a girl too unworldly to appreciate the extent of his deception, his hoax would have been merely cruel. As it was, he was poised to misdirect the career of a starlet who thought the most important thing in life was the key light on a movie set.

Six weeks after their yacht charade, Hughes had arranged to borrow Terry from Columbia Pictures to star her in an RKO film called *Gambling House* as a young social worker who reforms gangster Victor Mature. It was a role which needed the depth that a mature star like Barbara Stanwyck or Loretta Young could bring to the role. Instead Hughes forced executive producer Sid Rogell to use Terry, and ended up with *Gidget Goes to the Big House*. The experience should have left the actress too humiliated to stay in the country. Fortunately, she continued to judge her acting depth by the number of fan magazine covers her publicists generated, and took to reading the in-depth articles about her career as if they were the latest canto from Ezra Pound.

Following *Gambling House*, Terry flew off to the wilds of Silver Springs and Naples, Florida with ex-flame Jerome Courtland to star with Robert Cummings in *The Barefoot Mailman*. It was during the filming of this movie that Terry learned how to imitate the mating call of an alligator—a sound she shared with Hughes. From that point forward for the

---

1. Paul Mantz was Amelia Earhart's technical advisor on her ill-fated around-the-world flight. A stunt pilot for over thirty years, he came out of retirement in 1965 to perform aerial stunts for the film *The Flight of the Phoenix* starring James Stewart, and was killed simulating a take-off in a C-82 Boom aircraft.

next several years, it became a intricate part of their own mating ritual, even long distance on the telephone.

As if destined to spend the remainder of her career perpetually miscast, the budding star was then rushed directly into a musical in which her character had romantic illusions over a jazz great played by Frankie Laine, sixteen years her senior. Shot at Columbia Studios, *The Sunny Side of the Street* had just completed production when Terry accidentally discovered that Hughes was seeing a long-legged chorus girl in Las Vegas by the name of Gloria Alton, the revelation of which sent the youngster into a tantrum far more dramatic than anything she had yet played on the screen.

In 1978, she would reflect on the fact that her temper and disappointment in Hughes drove her into the arms of West Point grad Glenn Davis,[2] the 1946 Heisman Trophy winner and Associated Press Athlete of the Year who came out of the Army to play with the Los Angeles Rams in 1950. In her own bit of cruelty, she began dating the star athlete, hoping to make Hughes jealous, and continued the charade right down the aisle dressed in a wedding gown.

The fact that she expected Hughes to rush into the Mormon church and carry her away on a white horse or some other form of immediate transportation indicated her lack of understanding of the true basis for their relationship. It was not that Hughes had been particularly subtle in his approach. Upon seeing the engagement announced in the newspapers, Hughes called Terry to his bungalow and presented her with a present: a white bag full of various sizes of contraceptive diaphragms for her honeymoon.

"You can have your fling, Helen, but you mustn't get pregnant," she said in her memoir that he told her. "If you do, your nipples will get all brown instead of pretty pink and you'll get stretch marks, and then I could never take you back." On February 9, 1951, Terry Moore became Mrs. Glenn Davis, and according to her, a bigamist.

At the very time the about-to-be Mrs. Davis expected to be rescued, her white knight was cloistered in his bungalow reviewing the script for RKO's *The Las Vegas Story*,[3] a film championed by Hughes because of his fondness for the city. He frequently spent evenings in Las Vegas in the company of Hollywood agent Walter Kane. Billionaire oilman Marvin Davis, who at one-time owned 20th Century-Fox Studios, remembers that Hughes would sit in the back of packed showrooms to watch feath-

---

2. Davis' fascination with pretty, young movie actresses had previously included a fling with Elizabeth Taylor, 16-years-old at the time.
3. *The Las Vegas Story* was a murder mystery that was shot on location, and starred Jane Russell as a one-time lounge singer married to a gambler, played by Vincent Price.

ered dancers prance half-naked amid the pink and blue spotlights aimed to give the ultimate definition to long legs and ample bosoms—among them presumably those of Gloria Alton. Kane billed these evenings of flesh ogling under the heading: "talent search" on his expense account.

Most who looked at Las Vegas saw gaud; Hughes saw untold riches and made plans to transplant his entire aircraft research division to the desert floor in the shade of the gambling casinos and prostitutes. That the 7,500 acres he selected as his site was owned by the federal government might have intimidated a more cautious man. For Hughes, it simplified the transaction.

He hired attorney Clark M. Clifford, the one-time aide to President Harry S. Truman, and paid him $100,000 to handle the deal. It was that easy. Political problem? Pay to influence the outcome. In this case, what Hughes was proposing was a land swap: 73,000 acres he already owned in northern Nevada in exchange for what Hughes labeled "a stretch of sand that's near an airport." That it was adjacent to the fledgling Las Vegas Strip was not mentioned. Hughes was planning laboratories, not casinos after all, and, anyway, the government surely knew where its own land was located. Hughes caught himself smiling again, the grin he always felt on his lips when he knew that bureaucracy was designed for the rich to exploit. He got his land, just as he knew he would, all 7,500 acres of it, and proceeded to announce his intentions.

To Drs. Ramo and Wooldridge, the suggestion of transplanting their operation to Nevada was akin to moving an asthmatic to a coal mine. They were incredulous, stomped their feet like the prima dons they rightly were, and refused to budge. They cited the heat, the dust, and the reluctance of skilled scientists to move to the desert. But mostly, they stood their ground. So powerful was their position within the organization that Hughes was forced, albeit begrudgingly, to enlarge his Culver City facility to accommodate his growing staff that then numbered fifteen *thousand*.

In Houston, the Hughes Tool Company found itself outperformed by its legal subsidiary in a disquieting turn of profits. Characteristically, the tool division plodded along, with the strength of a Clydesdale pulling a beer wagon. Its steady growth remained predictable and consistent under Dietrich's firm hand. With the meteoric rise in both business and profits at Hughes Aircraft, however, the tool company took on the complexion of an ugly stepmother—stern, crude and unglamourous when positioned against the sleekness of its high-tech electronics stepchild.

That Dietrich had approval of the subsidiary's budget created additional strife and a demand from the aircraft division's leadership for a meeting with their elusive boss. Now comfortable within the cocoon of his darkened bungalow, Hughes found such requests both annoying and perplexing, and he refused to respond unless proper procedure was followed. As he wrote in a memo in 1951, "I cannot understand the need for what you refer to as a 'personal audience.' Any question you have for me should be addressed to me in writing or via telephone at operations through Bill (Gay) and his staff. Your continuing refusal to follow my instructions is only delaying a response even further. I do not expect you to understand my priorities, but I would appreciate it if you would realize they exist."

One such priority remained Terry Moore Davis. Married for nearly two months, three weeks of which was a Mexican honeymoon, Terry was now living in a one-room apartment in Lubbock, Texas, with a Murphy bed and a Pullman kitchen, and finding life with an off-season football star "mundane."

She spent her days baking bread in a portable oven that had been a wedding present. For an over-indulged girl used to pointing her toes for photographers, the let-down of living in the cottonseed capital of the world was predictable. It took only a telephone call from Hollywood regarding an RKO picture titled *High Heels* to have her on a plane, leaving her husband on his easy chair in his underwear listening to basketball games on the radio.

Called to see Hughes in his Goldwyn office for a wardrobe check, Terry appeared on the lot in a Hughes' designed gown of thin black jersey that she later wrote felt like "a veil of water after a skinny dip." It took Hughes all of two minutes before he had her undressed, *en flagrante delicto*, as the office staff took bets on how long Terry's marriage would last. According to the news reports, Davis received a call the very next morning asking for a divorce.

Davis' response was predictable and was played out in the living room of the Koford's Glendale home where he arrived and demanded "to take his woman back to Texas." In Lubbock, they would have used a six-shooter; in the foothills of Pasadena, it was bare fists at high noon, with Hughes on the receiving end of a knockout punch. Terry's mother threw herself bodily over the flattened multimillionaire, who it turned out needed the protection. Terry went into hiding in the Hughes-provided Holmby Hills mansion in which Judy Garland had once slit her throat. She filed for divorce with the help of Hughes' attorneys, and sat around practicing her alligator calls.

She did not seemed bothered by the fact that *High Heels* turned out to be another Hughes ploy, particularly after she found herself borrowed by Paramount Pictures to star in *Come Back, Little Sheba*. Based on the

William Inge play, Sheba would be Terry's most challenging role.[4] Under the direction of Daniel Mann, she immersed herself in the role of college student Marie Buckholder who rents a room in the home of Doc and Lola Delaney (Burt Lancaster and Shirley Booth), and innocently unleashes his pent-up desire.

Hughes was forbidden on the Paramount lot during the production of the film by its director, who wanted Terry's full concentration. Hughes had little time to worry about the slight, having been drawn into another drama that became an instant *cause célèbre* that rekindled his legend as well as his popularity.

Hughes hated Communists with the enthusiasm he otherwise reserved for Blacks and watched in horror the emergence of Russia as a super power, worrying incessantly about their continued threat. This was a time of bomb shelters and fall-out drills where Red was no longer just a color in a Crayola box, but now implied something very anti-American. Hollywood was being pulled into the controversy through Washington's House Un-American Activities Committee, whose chairman, J. Parnell Thomas, had conducted hearings to ferret out Communist sympathizers among show business luminaries.

The committee had been in business for four years and had ruined the careers of dozens of writers by the time it reached the name Paul Jarrico in April, 1951. When asked if he was a member of the Communist Party, Jarrico refused to answer. Jarrico was hardly the only writer unwilling to enter the growing fracas created in the late 1940s by HUAC and taken up in the 1950s by the Republican senator from Wisconsin, Joseph McCarthy. He was just the only one employed by Howard Hughes.

Jarrico had been the original writer on *The Las Vegas Story*, and was promptly fired by Hughes who declared his intention to "never hire Communist sympathizers." Jarrico was replaced on the picture by Earl Felton and Harry Essex, who had no Communist agenda. They were, however, union members, and when they learned that Jarrico's name was being removed from the final credits on the film, reported the fact to the Writers Guild of America, who championed the cause of their members and insisted that Jarrico's credit be preserved.

The TWA flight that transported fifty-eight members of the press as well as the stars from Los Angeles to Las Vegas for the premiere of the film on February 12, 1952, was labeled the "booze boat" for all the liquor consumed on the forty-five-minute flight. Hughes' publicity director Perry Lieber gave each journalist fifty silver dollars to spend in the casinos, and brought in young soldiers from the Desert Rock Training

---

4. Terry Moore was nominated for an Academy Award for her performance in the film as Best Supporting Actress. Shirley Booth won an Oscar that year as Best Actress for her role in the film.

Center to hold back the crowd, estimated at several thousand. When the lights dimmed and the movie unspooled, the name Paul Jarrico was not to be seen.

The WGA was outraged and threatened a strike. Hughes immediately retaliated and filed suit in Los Angeles Superior Court asking for a declaratory judgment that would free RKO from any damages Jarrico might claim. Jarrico, Hughes alleged, had violated the morals clause in his contract when he refused to reveal his status within the Communist party. Standing on his principle, Hughes stated that placing a credit for Jarrico on the screen would have cost him nothing, except his integrity. "As long as I am an officer or director of RKO Pictures Corporation, this company will never temporize, conciliate with, or yield to Paul Jarrico or anyone guilty of similar conduct," he said.

Hughes wrote to the Writers Guild and demanded to know if it intended to announce a strike against RKO. As he waited for a response, he paced within his bungalow at the Beverly Hills Hotel. His mind festered over his situation, rethinking, condemning, rethinking again. On March 27, he stunned most in Hollywood by saying he would not be bound by any arbitration of the Writers Guild, the union's first weapon in such a disagreement, because, said Hughes, "my conscience cannot be changed by a committee of arbitrators."

The following day, Paul Jarrico answered back with a $350,000 damage suit in L.A.'s Superior Court claiming that Hughes and RKO had denied him film credit and damaged his reputation. In a hastily-called news conference, Hughes welcomed the challenge and said that he would "personally meet Mr. Jarrico's charges and confront the reality of his deceit."

On April 6, Hughes announced that he was curtailing all production at RKO until he could get the "Communism problem resolved." With the announcement, one hundred and eight employees were laid-off, with Hughes labeling them as "innocent victims of Hollywood's Communist problem."

His mind seething with a mixture of ideology and the irritation of the knowledge that "a Goddamn Commie" was working on his payroll, he launched negotiations to sell the studio rather than continue to manage its intricacies. On September 22, 1952, his entertainment attorney, Gregson Bautzer, announced that papers had been signed and the sale concluded with a five-man syndicate of investors headed by Ralph E. Stolkin, described as "president of Empire Industries, a Chicago mail-order house, and vice president of National Video Corp., manufacturers of television tubes." RKO was sold for $7.00 a share, $1.50 less than Hughes had originally paid. What appeared on the surface to be a loss, and was continuously reported as such in the press, was actually an enor-' mous profit for Hughes since the sale excluded the RKO theater chain which Hughes had spun off into a separate company.

The tall, dark, and handsome Stolkin was only thirty-four, the son of a butcher. He was an errand boy before the war, then borrowed $15,000 to set up a mail-order business that he sold at a profit of $1 million two years later. He subsequently traveled to Texas "where the money was," linked up with a pair of wildcatters and promptly struck oil. If Hughes felt any simpatico with the RKO buyers, he certainly kept it to himself, arriving an hour late to the meeting in the Beverly Hills Hotel where they handed him a certified check for $1,250,000. Life was good.

Over the next few months, Hughes continued his fight against Communism in Hollywood, and seemed kindled with renewed energy, making appearances in nightclubs and restaurants dressed in his one coat and tie, and pledging his support of the America ideal to those who stopped at his table and extended their hand in agreement. In the evening, he transformed from fighter to lover, spending hours on the phone with Terry Moore, who had flown to Munich, Germany, to star with Fredric March in the psychological thriller, *Man on a Tightrope*, for director Elia Kazan.

Terry played a performer in a Czech circus whose members were trying to escape from behind the Iron Curtain. Her part required her to perform a number of stunts, including riding horses and elephants, which she tackled with her usual unabated enthusiasm. When she recalled the filming during testimony in 1978, Terry swore that she had no idea that she was pregnant with Hughes' baby until her water broke and she went into what she termed "endless labor." Mama Blue, who had accompanied her daughter to Germany, apparently missed the signs as well, chalking up her daughter's ten-pound weight gain to eating too much *Wiener schnitzel*. She was able, however, to reach Hughes with the news that he was about to be a proud papa.

Hughes reply has been lost in history, but since he had previously shown no desire for children, upon receiving such news, his response might well have been as Terry later testified. She swore in deposition that Hughes sent Dr. Verne Mason to Germany, where the doctor supervised the birth of what she said was a baby girl, too premature to survive.[5] According to her testimony, she never asked to see the child, nor went to its funeral. "Dr. Mason took care of all that because I was too sick and too

---

5. According to Terry Moore, Verne Mason later told his wife and children that the baby had lived for twelve hours and died of septicemia. In 1978, Mason's son, Dr. Verne Mason Jr. testified that he remembered his father flying to Germany to treat Moore for a horrible infection from which she nearly died.

depressed to do anything," she said. Nor did she know what she had named the child. During her deposition about the events of the birth, she offered only a blank stare, before adding, "Let me tell you later. I just can't think of it right now. I've gone blank."[6]

Hughes never traveled to Germany, but continued to bathe in the adoration of an appreciative citizenry who saw him as the epitome of truth, justice and the American way. Richard M. Nixon, then the junior senator from California, went so far as to insert in the *Congressional Record* that Hughes had taken a stance "to establish the principle that no industry need support those whose loyalty to this country is questionable, and by public statement he has rallied the support of right thinking people across the land behind his campaign to get the Reds out of the motion picture industry."

As America's flag-bearer of democracy, Hughes gave a speech before the Hollywood Post 43 of the American Legion after receiving a com- mendation and said, "In spite of all the movement to whitewash the industry, to say that there was no Red influence in Hollywood; to sweep this matter under the carpet and hide it and pretend it doesn't exist, in spite of that, there are a substantial number of people in the motion pic- ture industry who follow the party line."

Hughes was lauded by the Los Angeles City Council for his "intes- tinal fortitude" in a "ceaseless battle against Communist infiltration in business and government." He was praised by the Veterans of Foreign War's commander-in-chief Frank C. Hilton, who wrote, "I am sure the majority of American people, and most certainly the 1,200,000 members of the Veterans of Foreign Wars of the United States, have about reached the limit of patience in temporizing with and conciliating men and women of subversive tendencies and particularly those who have been associated with Communist front organizations."

Hughes' Aunt Annette read the articles appearing almost daily in the *Houston Chronicle* and attempted several times to contact her nephew via the switchboard at Romaine Street. "It's just not right that I had to leave messages with that woman," she told lawyers in the late Seventies. "How was I to know whether he even got my calls? He never called me back, so I just stopped trying." Well, almost.

On September 5, 1952, Palmer Bradley, of Hughes' Houston legal firm of Andrews, Kurth, Campbell & Bradley took up the torch and wrote to Noah Dietrich in Los Angeles, informing him that Annette's daughter Allene Lummis, Hughes' own goddaughter, was being married at the end of the month and Annette's fondest wish was for him to attend

---

6. Terry later suddenly recalled that the girl's name was Maria or Marie, she did not remember which.

the ceremony. "Please, please keep my name out of it," Bradley wrote, "because I have no interest in it one way or the other except to accommodate Annette Lummis, whose son married my daughter and with whom I have a sincere friendship."

Four days later, Dietrich hand delivered the wedding invitation to Hughes at his bungalow at the Beverly Hills Hotel. He confirmed the delivery the next day in a note to Bradley, bittersweet in its mordancy.

> Dear Palmer:
> Yesterday evening I personally delivered Annette's note to Howard. I also reminded him that you and he are kinfolks. It is unfortunate that the poor boy has become so cynical and displays no affection for his relatives or anyone else for that matter. Best wishes and kind regards,
> Noah.

WHEN I SHOWED HOWARD the note," Dietrich said, "he read it over and then handed it back to me. I waited, expecting him to say something. He kept looking down at his note pad and writing something, so finally I said, 'Howard, so what should I tell her?' He looked up from his writing and without so much as a blink said, 'What she wants is some fancy wedding present. Now damn it, Noah, if I buy a present for her, I would have to buy one for all my nieces and nephews. I don't even know how many there are. You care so much about it, you buy her a Goddamn present.' And then he continued writing."

Hughes went on to win every legal battle against Paul Jarrico[7] although *The Las Vegas Story* ultimately lost money at the box office.

If he had not been so successful, he might well have been better served. As it was, with the victory over Jarrico behind him, Hughes lost his renewed vigor, his sense of purpose—the spark that one needs to make life more than a calculated chore of rising, eating, working, sleeping—and once again faded back into the shadows of a very private world. A photograph taken of him leaving the courthouse after his triumph over Jarrico by a United Press International photographer would be the last time a camera would ever point in his direction. A check-up by his dentist, Dr. George Hollenbeck, would be the final time he sat in a dentist's chair and offered up his opened mouth for inspection. And a trip to Dr. Verne Mason's office for treatment of onychomycosis, a nail fungus, the last time he would venture outside his room to seek medical help.

---

7. In 1997, the Writers Guild of America honored Paul Jarrico in a ceremony saluting screen writers blacklisted during the Fifties. Tragically, on the way home from the observance, Jarrico was involved in an automobile accident and fatally injured. In 1998, the WGA voted to reinstate his name on the credits for *The Las Vegas Story* and three other films he co-wrote during the blacklist era under an assumed name.

After December, 1952, Hughes' movements became restricted to the Goldwyn Studios where he continued to maintain an office he now seldom used and kept a screening room with his own projectionist. He made isolated flights to Catalina Island, San Diego, San Francisco, and Las Vegas, though found his time increasingly taken up with litigation and made a game of outwitting process servers.

Chief among the litigants attempting to pull him back into the courtroom was a trio of RKO stockholders who filed a million-dollar lawsuit in mid-December for "reckless abandon" in his management of the studio. The complaint cited Hughes' $100,000 payment to Hughes Tool for the services of Jane Russell, "whose acting liability and talent are of a minor nature and value" as an example of his "waste of corporate funds." During the same week, Hughes had been elected chairman of the board of the corporation running the studio on a lot he still had not visited.

Actress Jean Simmons, who Hughes had imported from England and placed under contract, also wanted to see her boss in front of a judge, claiming that he had failed to live up to his terms of her contract and was now keeping her from working with other studios. At one point, her husband Stewart Granger[8] had gotten so angry at Hughes' obstinance that he formulated a plan to murder him and make it appear an accidental death.

According to an interview he gave to the BBC, Jean was going to lure Hughes out onto the terrace of her home, perched along the rugged beach cliffs. At a certain point, she was to begin screaming that Hughes was trying to rape her, an unlikely reality but nonetheless the plan. Upon hearing the screams, Granger, every bit as tall as Hughes though younger and more muscled, was to rush to her defense and with a great heave push Hughes to his death on the rocks below. As with many a plan conceived in anger, this one seemed less sound the following day after a cup of strong coffee and a fresh *brioche*.

Hughes loved the ruckus; he thrived on the melodrama, felt suckled by its energy as if drawing strength from the controversy itself. It was only when all the pieces fell into place and efficiency droned predictably that he felt cheated. The fact that his cash flow improved in such a circumstance did not enter into his thinking. It was the narcotic of turmoil he craved more than anything, for only in chaos could his manipulation have its ultimate effect. As it happened, turmoil triumphed.

At RKO, the Stolkin investment team had stumbled and could not make its second payment as due. In mid-February, 1953, Hughes took

---

8. Stewart Granger was born in London and originally named James Stewart. He appeared in more than sixty films as well as the TV series *The Virginian*, and portrayed Prince Philip in *The Royal Romance of Charles and Diana*.

back RKO, keeping the $1.25 million down-payment for his trouble. Feeling obligated to place something in production, Hughes looked over a pile of scripts that had been previously been rejected and selected a screenplay *Second Chance*. He cast his one-time flame Linda Darnell as a woman who falls for prizefighter Robert Mitchum while on the run from her gambling boyfriend in Cuernavaca, Morelos, Mexico. *Second Chance* was filmed in 3-D, a process Hughes thought was the cutting edge of technology.

He also selected the 3-D process for Jane Russell's next film, *The French Line*, and saddled it with a publicity campaign that promised "Jane Russell in 3-D. It'll knock *both* your eyes out." Jane played a Texas heiress who takes a cruise to Europe to find true love. The ship is merely an excuse for the actress to wear Hughes-designed bikinis that offered such revealing looks at Jane's breasts that the film board once again refused to give its seal of approval to a Hughes movie.

In characteristic defiance, Hughes premiered the film without an MPAA seal in St. Louis during Christmas, 1953. The chosen theater held five-thousand seats, and everyone of them was sold four hours before showtime. The St. Louis police morals squad was called by the Roman Catholic Archdiocese that had labeled the unscreened film as "a mortal sin" and demanded that it be seized. After opening night, the film critic of the *St. Louis Post-Dispatch* trenchantly observed, "The only crime. . . was a dramatic one. The police would not investigate the fraud being committed—that of continuing to exploit Miss Russell as an actress."

Howard Hughes spent the entire evening on the telephone receiving a detailed narrative of the event, living vicariously through the recounting by publicist Perry Lieber. He found the cheers of the crowd as they waited in line an elixir nearly as potent as the cutting words of *Newsweek* which said the film was "more to be pitied than censored." The negative thrilled him as much as the positive; it was the dispute that served to amuse and preoccupy.

Had Hughes nothing better to do with his time, such enthrallment with the ongoing ecclesiastical and critical arguments might have been understood from a position of sheer boredom, if for no other reason. But at end of 1953, Hughes was at the center of a potential debacle that far exceeded any damage that Jane's bosom brouhaha might convoke. It had begun several months earlier in August, when Hughes Aircraft paid the ultimate price for its owner's unavailability with the surprise resignation of Simon Ramo and Dean Wooldridge, who left their positions with the company to form Ramo-Wooldridge Corporation,[9] a firm created to

---

9. Ramo-Wooldridge Corp. was funded by Thompson Products Inc., a Cleveland-based company. After years of research and manufacturing, the company became TRW, which not only had a space division but also expanded in the area of credit reporting.

develop anti-ballistic missiles for the Air Force, setting themselves up in direct competition to Hughes' aircraft division. With Ramo and Wooldridge gone, their entire scientific team was in danger of revolt, and Hughes, with his inconsistencies and skewed priorities, was ill-prepared to prevent it. General Harold George resigned next, followed quickly by Charles Thornton The word *chaos* comes to mind.

The Secretary of the Air Force, Harold E. Talbott, was new in the job, and not a man to be underestimated. He looked upon Hughes Aircraft as a critical supplier to America's national defense, and any unrest within the company translated into nothing short of a military emergency. Unable to reach Hughes directly on the telephone, and irritated at the excuses he received from Deitrich, who had now moved his office to Culver City, Talbott called for a plane and flew to Los Angeles, where he demanded to see Hughes.

At the time he arrived at the Beverly Hills Hotel, Talbott was prepared to cancel every contract currently awarded to Hughes Aircraft if he did not come away from the meeting totally satisfied with Hughes' reliability. The multimillionaire was unaware that the FBI had been investigating his emotional stability, and Talbott carried with him several confidential reports in which Hughes was described by an informant as an "unscrupulous individual who at times acted like a 'screwball paranoiac,' to the extent that he might be capable of murder." This informant stated that Hughes was "of a highly unstable nature, was ruthless and, accordingly, would be capable of almost anything."[10] As Talbott read the report on the plane flying to California, his preconceived notion was not of a man who, at that very moment, was totally obsessed with making Jane Russell's breasts look bigger in 3-D.

After being kept waiting for an hour and twenty minutes, Talbott did not waste time on pleasantries or question the lack of a handshake.

Hughes had dressed in a suit for the occasion, after some dogged persuasion from Noah Dietrich, who stayed by his side as Talbott launched into an attack that Hughes absorbed without comment. "You personally have wrecked a great industrial establishment with gross mismanagement," Talbott said, standing in front of Hughes, who remained seated during the entire confrontation. "I don't give a damn what happens to you, but I am concerned for this country. The United States is wholly dependent on Hughes Aircraft for vital defense systems. It would take at least a year to set up alternative sources of supply. I am, however, prepared to do that, though it could lead to national tragedy. It was a terrible mistake entrusting the nation's security to an eccentric like you!"

---

10. FBI file number 62-78335-220, 221, May 7, 1952.

Hughes' eyes were malachite. Either out of astonishment or trepidation, he made a vague reply that pointed to "the unfortunate departure of a few executives," only to be interrupted by Talbott, whose normally ashen skin had reddened until his entire face glowed crimson, aided in no small part by the dilated blood vessels bulging on his neck.

"Don't patronize me, Mr. Hughes," the Air Force secretary said. "You have a choice. Either sell Hughes Aircraft or accept a new management team that I, myself, will designate." Hughes noticed that the veins in Talbott's neck had changed to a pale shade of purple. Dietrich noticed it too. "Take your choice, Mr. Hughes. I give you seventy-two hours to decide. If you don't do one or the other, I'll see to it that all of your contracts are canceled and you'll get no more business from the government."

Hughes was silent, the air between the men as thin as the tissues that laid unexplained on the bungalow's end tables. The moment was frozen; no one spoke or moved, as if a spell by some wicked witch had been invoked by the sound of the words themselves. Finally, Dietrich stood up and asked Talbott to step into the next room. Well, perhaps Dietrich stepped; Talbott *stalked*, his anger apparent even in his stride, a man attempting to contain a fury that threatened to consume his flesh. Dietrich shut the door, leaving the Assistant Secretary of the Air Force, Roger Lewis, to stand guard over Hughes, who was then concentrating on the floor with such discipline that he appeared to be counting the fibers in the carpet. Only there, in the privacy of the bungalow's second bedroom, did calmer minds prevail. A truce was struck; a deal worked out. It gave Hughes ninety days to rectify the management problems at his aircraft division, "or else," as Talbott threatened.

Talbott left the room and then the bungalow without speaking further, leaving Lewis to say goodbye. When Hughes and Dietrich were finally alone, Hughes railed in annoyance, a circuit breaker reset. It was a dramatic performance meant to save face, yet did little more than prove Hughes' own underestimation of the problem, as he insisted that no one was going to tell *him* how to run his own business. It was left to Dietrich to explain that someone just did, and that unless he was very cautious, Hughes Aircraft would be *out* of business.

Over the next three months, Hughes accepted the Talbott nominated William Jordan, one-time president of Curtiss-Wright Aircraft, to become the temporary head of his aircraft division, while he had his attorneys work on attacking the problem from another perspective altogether. Still smarting from Talbott's personal attack, Hughes moved to protect himself from government intervention, not with a skilled executive as Talbott had hoped, but with a barrier, a firewall as it were. In this case, the Howard Hughes Medical Institute.

On December 17, 1953, which by no small coincidence was exactly ninety days after Talbott had delivered his ultimatum, Tom Slack of Houston's Andrews, Kurth, Campbell & Bradley traveled to Delaware to author the necessary paperwork for two new Delaware corporations. One, the Hughes Aircraft Corp., now no longer a division of Hughes Tool; and two, the Howard Hughes Medical Institute Corp., a charity whose stated purpose was to promote "human knowledge within the field of the basic sciences and its effective application for the benefit of mankind." Hughes, as the sole trustee, would be the first of mankind's fraternity to so benefit.

He placed all the stock of the new Hughes Aircraft Corp. in the name of the Medical Institute, and sold the Institute all the inventory of the former Hughes Tool aircraft division for $74,618,038. Since Hughes Medical was not funded, the charity assumed $56,574,738 in Hughes Tool liabilities from the old aircraft division, and signed an $18,043,300 promissory note to Hughes Tool for the remainder. The Tool Company leased the buildings and land to the Medical Institute, which in turn leased them back to Hughes Aircraft, self-generating $2 million dollars in annual working capital for the Institute.

It took less than two weeks for the man who the FBI thought a screwball paranoiac to create a charity not only without cash, but over $18 million in debt that would pay Hughes millions of dollars in interest per year. The $2 million in self-generating income would allow Hughes to maintain the foundation without ever investing capital into it. Hughes Tool received a tax write-off for its lease payments to the Institute, while Hughes Aircraft Corp. lease money came right from the government. And while the brilliantly-conceived accounting setup was designed to heap millions of dollars into Hughes' bank accounts, the real benefit from Hughes' perspective was that he could no longer be labeled as the owner of Hughes Aircraft. Let Talbott deal with the Medical Institute in the future.

The resulting publicity from the announcement of the medical foundation was immediate and predictable. Hughes was nominated for sainthood by the research community, who saw the Howard Hughes Medical Institute as a money machine. President Dwight D. Eisenhower said that Hughes had "created a high water mark for American philanthropy." At the moment, it looked as if the legal equivalent of a Fred and Ginger quickstep was succeeding in its smoke-and-mirrors illusion. Only Hughes knew that he had no intention of actually funding medical research. To do so would actually take money out of his pocket. And that was definitely *not* part of the plan, and the thought made him smile.

From the shadows of his darkened room, he actually laughed. What fools people were, he thought, and wrote on a legal pad, "Eisenhower." He rethought his approach, crossed out the word and wrote "Nixon," followed by the words, "how much?"

He thought of the Howard Hughes Medical Institute, the joy that America was taking in exploiting its potential for their own hopeless dreams, and laughed again. This time, however, the high-pitch of the sound was more cackle than chuckle. It surprised him, and he instinctively pulled it back inside. Sucked his laughter into hiding. No one must hear him laugh like that.

He had already heard the rumors that his behavior was not just that of an eccentric, but of something far less colorful and dangerous. Uncontrollable. Of someone who laughed in cackles and needed treatment. Only there in the blackness of his bedroom, in air so still that even layers of dust found no current, did he dare to wonder if it could be true.

TWELVE

From Darkness to Shadows

Before opening the door to the room, the third
man is to stand with a folded newspaper in his
right hand and rapidly wave it for at least one
minute to eliminate the possibility that flies will
enter the room. Using eight Kleenex placed in the
left hand, the man who is rapidly waving the
newspaper will knock on the door. When HRH
responds, the man will open the door, using the
hand with the Kleenex. The door is never to be
opened further than twelve inches nor longer than
ten seconds at a time. This will allow a second
man enough time to enter the room.

February 27, 1955
Beverly Hills
Instructions for entering Howard Hughes'
bungalow at the Beverly Hills Hotel.

WHEN HOWARD HUGHES THOUGHT ABOUT GOING MAD,
he remembered Miss Eugenia Holster Grant of Montrose,
Iowa. As a small child, Hughes had seen Miss Genia, as she
was known, walking down the center of Fifth Street past his
grandparents' house, singing as she led a mule by a rope tied
around its neck. Though she did not appear to be old, her
hair was gray and stood out from her head as if it might be
harboring a nest of hornets.

Little Sonny found the sight of the singing woman with
the mule and the hornet hair so frightening that, upon seeing
her, he would run and clutch the long, cotton skirt of his
grandmother, trying to hide his fear in the folds of fabric.

"It's only Miss Genia, Sonny. I told you before, child,"
Mimi Hughes said. "She won't hurt you. Miss Genia," Mimi

called out. "Stop that singing; you're scaring Sonny again," at which point Eugenia Holster Grant would let out a cackle, lift her skirt, shake it in his direction and then go running down the street, pulling her old mule behind her. Sonny heard his mother say that she was crazy. "Should be put away," she said. And apparently she was, for one day Miss Eugenia Holster Grant disappeared right along with her mule.

AFTER HUGHES' CONFRONTATION with Air Force Secretary Talbott, he took temporary leave from the Beverly Hills Hotel and moved to Las Vegas, where he had leased a five-room house from the Sun Villa Motel on Desert Inn Road. Called the Green House by Romaine Street, it was a wooden box whose only distinguishable characteristic was its chipped paint the color of dogwood leaves. It sat on a slit of sand, open and unprotected, shielded solely by its blandness against curiosity seekers. For the next year, off and on, Hughes would call the Green House home, shut off from the world with his black-out drapes and taped windows, a chrome-legged kitchen table his makeshift desk, and eight amplified telephones his lifelines.

His staff converted one bedroom into a screening room in which Hughes placed his upholstered Barcalounger, an ottoman, and a folding metal table that wobbled under the weight of two telephones, a stack of legal pads, a reading lamp, and a jelly glass that held assorted number two pencils and a few Parker pens. There were two noisy black 35-mm projectors used to fill the portable movie screen on the opposite side of the room, spilling onto the walls and ceiling with images that distorted in plaintive regret at the screen's inadequacies.

It was from the Green House that Hughes placed the call in early 1954 to alert Noah Dietrich that he wanted to silence the suing stockholders of RKO by purchasing all outstanding stock in the studio. Hughes offered to pay $6.00 a share, more than twice the current value of the stock. "He just didn't want to be bothered by stockholders' complaints, he didn't want to show up in court, and he didn't want to have to answer to anyone else," Dietrich said in 1978. "So he bought the joint." And in doing so became the first individual ever to own a major studio.

Hughes eventually wrote a check for $23.5 million to pay for the stock purchase that did not clear its last legal hurdle until April 11, 1954. In doing so, Hughes now owned outright a studio with no major stars under contract, twelve completed pictures that had not been released (including his own *Jet Pilot*), and losses of $10 million for the previous year.

While the *Wall Street Journal* labeled the buy "of questionable strategy," the financial newspaper neglected to consider Hughes' growing stable of unknowns, a plethora of attractive young women of undetermined talent that he began to collect with the enthusiasm of a child chasing fireflies on a hot summer night. Whether they could act was unimportant for, even though they were each promised the opportunity of a movie career from the man who now owned RKO, they became little more than specimens to be trained and caged like the curiosities he considered them to be.

That Hughes kept these women, well, girls really, in various apartments and hotel rooms throughout Beverly Hills, Brentwood, Westwood and Hollywood, has been well documented. Less well known but equally amazing are the detailed notes that he maintained on each girl, not only specifying her name, age, height, bra size, dress size, and shoe size, but any personal likes and dislikes as well as those of her mother, Hughes being a man never to underestimate the value of parental influence.

> Julie Altmon   JULIE
> Mother: Norma Louise Trevor   LOU
> CR 6-1491
> Brunette   35D   size 6   shoe 6M   5'3"
> Perrino's Tuesday
> White roses, no ice cream, no chocolate, bad skin

DURING THE DECADE of the Fifties, Hughes had as many as three dozen of these Hollywood hopefuls under contract at any one time, the exact number rising and falling depending on the patience and motivation of the individual involved. They were given contracts and an income, typically $175.00 a week, taken to drama classes, voice lessons, and movie screenings—not, of course, by Hughes, who typically never met the girls in person. His drivers, under the control of Bill Gay and Gay's assistant at Operations, Kay Glenn, would handle transportation and serve as escorts during weekly dinners at restaurants like Perrino's on Wilshire Boulevard and the Crystal Room at the Beverly Hills Hotel.

These girls were not allowed outside dates or casual contact, unless approved by Hughes, and became virtual prisoners for as long as they were willing to tolerate the conditions. When they realized that there were not to be any movies, records, or television shows in their future, they eventually packed up their clothes and headed back home, dreams shattered but lives intact.

Dietrich compared Hughes' collection of hopefuls to bonsai plants. "They were all gorgeous to look at, and had been trained and manipulated to meet Howard's version of perfection," he said. "Howard liked to look at them and appreciate their beauty. In one way, he was the ultimate collector. Where others had stamps, Howard had girls."

His main source of these woman in the mid-Fifties was talent agent

Walter Kane, who at one point worked exclusively for Hughes Productions finding beautiful teenagers, all with large breasts and brunette hair. Kane lived in an apartment at 8484 Sunset Boulevard in West Hollywood, above the photo studio of Paul A. Hesse, a Hollywood pioneer in color portrait photography. Through a two-way mirror, Hughes would often watch silently as Hesse or his various assistants would photograph the hopefuls, always in tight sweaters and from a profile to accentuate their breasts, with a select few later introduced to Hughes in Kane's apartment and served dinner by chef Robert Poussin.[1]

An even smaller percentage would be lured into having a relationship with the multimillionaire, though actual sexual relations were typically short-lived. Phyllis Applegate, a Kane find from Florida, was on the Hughes payroll for three years, living for a while at the Westwood Manor apartments, a Hughes favorite near UCLA. Though she never made a film, she was exposed to the daily sessions in drama and voice, and eventually the time came when Hughes felt confident to make his approach. "It was a matter of rejection with Hughes," Dietrich said. "Unless he felt confident, he never made a move, and that went beyond just sex, right into business." For Phyllis, the approach came several months after her contract, when she felt "that it was right." She described the experience as "very pleasant" with the talk of Hughes purported impotence as exaggerated. "He was just fine," she said.

Zizi Jeanmaire[2] disagreed. The French ballet star was imported by Samuel Goldwyn to this country to perform The Little Mermaid ballet in *Hans Christian Andersen* for Samuel Goldwyn and RKO, choreographed by Roland Petit. Immediately Hughes was captivated by Zizi's lithe form and angular features, a streak of light against a barren canvas. He had been told of her performance as Carmen in Petit's version of Bizet's opera for the Ballets de Paris in London. The press was scandalized by the depiction of sex on stage. In Canada, they called it pornographic and refused to allow the ballet to be performed. This Hughes understood, pushing aside the artistic content to wallow in the controversy. Unfortunately, when Hughes got the opportunity to seduce Zizi, he fell victim to his own anxieties. Hughes' chef, Robert Poussin, revealed in testimony twenty-five years later, that Zizi found Hughes lacking in passion and ardor. "For him, sex was mostly to dance with his head on a

1. Hughes had a similar arrangement with photographer John Engstead in his studio at the corner of Sunset and La Cienega Boulevards in West Hollywood, and with photographer Christy Shepard on Sunset Boulevard in Hollywood.
2. Renee "Zizi" Jeanmaire, a ballet prodigy, was eighteen when Samuel Goldwyn brought her to the U.S. for her first film. She mesmerized New York theater critics when, in 1954, she starred on Broadway as *The Girl in Pink Tights*, a box-office flop that nevertheless confirmed her star power.

shoulder," Poussin said. "He tried to have sex with Zizi Jeanmaire, but she told me he was impotent with her."

Things went somewhat better with Kathryn Grayson. Hughes had developed a possessive crush on the soprano, who at that time was one of M-G-M's biggest stars. A heart-shaped face framed enormous eyes that captivated an entire country of men who did not understand opera but did not need to to fall in love with Kathryn. With Jean Peters away in Rome filming *Three Coins in the Fountain*[3] with Louis Jourdan and Rossano Brazzi, and Terry Moore down in Key West shooting *Beneath the 12-Mile Reef* with Robert Wagner and Richard Boone, the field was open for Hughes to push aside old fears and approach an actress who was very much a woman.

As with all the stars Hughes dated, Kathryn had recently left a failed marriage. In addition to her beauty and incredible voice, what placed her apart in Hughes' view was the fact that she was living with her parents in a refined Tudor mansion in Pacific Palisades, on the edge of the Riviera Country Club with its kikyuyu grass and ocean vistas. As she tells the story, Hughes appeared one night on her front lawn and refused to leave, at which point her father Charles grabbed his shotgun and went to vanquish the intruder. When she next saw her father, the sun had risen, she was heading to work, and the two new best friends were talking aviation.

Hughes needed little more than suggestion to settle into Kathryn's guest room, his impromptu hideaway from the telephone (and thus business), plus an ever-increasing number of process servers who, like bounty hunters of the Old West, would have liked nothing better than to be the first to actually personally slap Hughes with a court summons. Initially, Kathryn was not attracted to this man who had literally roamed into her home like a stray cat that lingers near a back door, hoping to be tossed a scrap of food or be offered a warm leg against which to rub.

Her love built slowly, glimpses stacked upon gestures which when taken alone were meaningless, yet when assembled became like the complex jigsaw puzzle that one feels obliged to show off to neighbors and friends for its difficulty and brilliance. She watched as he crept out in the night to stare at the sky without seeing the stars, and wondered who this man was. A sliver of enigma who would spend hours in the evening patiently playing with her young daughter Patty, and then turn to speak of hating children, his eyes full of anger, or was it misery?

She wanted to peel him like an onion, removing layers that time and stress had placed upon a soul she instinctively felt was decent, humble,

---

3. *Three Coins in the Fountain* was the first film shot in CinemaScope outside of the United States. The post-production on the film delayed its release until late in 1954. It won the Oscar for the title song by Jule Styne and Sammy Cahn.

caring. But to do that required closeness, and Hughes carried his barriers with him, stanchioned behind years of moods and privilege. He was not eager to give anyone a private tour. When he asked her to marry him, she thought that was her invitation, and surprised herself when she said yes without pausing to contemplate what the world of Howard Hughes encompassed. She thought his proposal came from a place of love; she wanted to believe.

It was mid-May, 1954, and Kathryn had yet to hear the news. Louella Parson had only shared it with Greg Bautzer in an effort to get in touch with Hughes for his reaction. "Does Howard know Jean Peters is getting married?" she asked. Bautzer was dumbfounded, and hurried to track down Hughes, who happened, at that moment, to be in California, back at the Beverly Hills Hotel. When Hughes spoke to Louella, he received the news and continued to speak as if unaffected, his heart racing in a scattered cadence that suggested otherwise.

Jean Peters married Stuart W. Cramer III on May 29, 1954, in the Lincoln Chapel of the New York Avenue Presbyterian Church in Washington, D.C., with the Rev. George M. Docherty performing the ceremony. She walked down the aisle on an historic carpet which had last been used for Queen Elizabeth's coronation and then given to the church. Jean had met Cramer only months earlier while on location filming *Three Coins in the Fountain*, and decided to accept the young, handsome and well-to-do Cramer's proposal, despite her continuing affection for Hughes, who seemed content to allow their relationship to linger forever.

When Hughes heard about Stuart Cramer, he pretended indifference. He sent a driver for some flowers, made his way to Kathryn's house, and finding her not at home, talked to her father about California real estate—Charles had been in real estate, first in Winston-Salem, North Carolina, then in St. Louis. Hughes allowed him to ramble, happy for the company. By the time Kathryn had returned from the studio, Hughes had heard about the time Charles sold an empty lot that turned out to be a graveyard full of bones the buyers found when they started to dig their foundation. "It was such a mess. They never did figure out which thigh went with which hip."

Outside along a hedge of roses, he asked Kathryn to marry him, and when she accepted, and smiled through tears, he wanted to be happy. But Howard Hughes was not happy, for he was not in love. Not with Kathryn, not with Jean, and certainly not with Zizi Jeanmaire with her short dark hair and willow-like stance.

That night he wrapped himself in the darkness of his bungalow and tried to sleep. His body, limp with exhaustion and the stress of the day, cursed his mind that refused to stop, even for a second, to give him peace. He thought of happiness, of love, of endless emptiness; he thought of a boy named Sonny, who stood with his mouth opened to catch the light from the French window in the living room as his mother checked his teeth. And only then did he shut his eyes, and allowed himself to dream.

A premonition of disaster kept Kathryn from marrying Hughes as they originally planned, despite the fact that she was dressed and ready for the ceremony. "Whenever I closed my eyes, I saw a little blond head sinking in a whirlpool. Something terrible was happening to a child," Kathryn told writers Peter Brown and Pat Broeske. Hughes was already at his plane preparing to fly the couple to Las Vegas when he received the news, and despite his efforts to change her mind, Kathryn was unwavering. Hughes flew to Las Vegas alone and received word after he had returned to Green House: Kathryn's young nephew Timothy had drowned in her brother's swimming pool at exactly the time their wedding was to take place.

To make time for business amid his growing swirl of romantic entanglements, Hughes started to sleep during the day, refusing to acknowledge the constant ringing of his telephones, and then in the early morning hours of quiet, he would do his best thinking. "Decision time," he called it in his notes, though making an actual decision was no easier for him at three and four a.m. than it had been at noon.

RKO continued to be a concern, despite the fact that Hughes had placed several films in production in the latter part of 1953 with a variety of directors and producers handling the day-to-day labor. Among them were *Underwater*, another vehicle to display Jane Russell's breasts—this time in wet and clinging fabric; and *Son of Sinbad*, a reworked version of *Arabian Nights* featuring forty full-bodied females as the forty thieves. *Sinbad* starred Dale Robertson in the title role, but it was the thieves that caught Hughes' attention as he peppered the cast with starlets he had housed around town. There were names like Claire de Witt, Evelyn Bernard, Marilyn Bonney, Louise Von Kories, and Libby Vernon, making their first—and only—screen appearances. A Hughes-discovered model—Marilyn Novak—who had an uncredited role in *The French Line* turned up again as Kim Novak in *Sinbad* playing one of the forty thieves. Because of her blonde hair, Hughes ignored Kim Novak romantically. She went on to make thirty more films, including the critically-acclaimed *Picnic* and *Vertigo*.

After returning to Green House, Hughes authorized the production of *The Conqueror*, a film that was ostensibly based on the life of Asian warlord Genghis Khan. The fact that Hughes insisted that America's favorite cowboy, John Wayne, be cast in the title role with the glamorous redhead, Susan Hayward, as his Tartar prisoner love interest, moved *The*

Conqueror from epic to the realm of ridiculous. Not even actor-turned-director Dick Powell had enough talent to save the film from being instantly transformed from an adventure into a comedy, though for a year he would try with the hot sand of St. George, Utah, taking the place of the Gobi Desert.[4]

When Terry Moore finished her latest film, Hughes cajoled her into attempting to star in a Las Vegas show for the Flamingo Hotel. That she could neither sing nor dance did not deter the indefatigable actress who went immediately into rehearsals at the Goldwyn studios. Hughes took on the responsibility of designing her costumes, including a black gown on which thirteen women spent twenty-six days hand-appliqueing thousands of bugle beads. Unfortunately for Terry, few of the beads made it to the sheer top. The ones that did were strategically placed and made it appear as if she was naked from the waist up. Despite the fact that she would only wear the dress once ("I was too embarrassed to wear it again," she wrote), he charged her $15,000 for her outfits, a bill that she eventually paid and Hughes accepted.

Just thirty–three days into her marriage, Jean Peters moved out of the Washington, D.C. home she shared with Stuart Cramer, and flew back to California on a Hughes-booked seat on TWA. In her subsequent divorce proceedings, Jean would claim "extreme mental and emotional cruelty." Terry Moore later credited Jean's drinking for the breakup; and at the time Cramer was said to be dumbfounded by the development. In addition to his other mounting responsibilities, Hughes hired an attorney to hasten Jean's divorce and turned to his Washington, D.C.-based tax attorney Seymour Mintz for help in investigating Cramer. Mintz, in turn, placed a call to Robert Maheu, and in doing so would change Hughes' life forever.

Robert Maheu was a one-time FBI agent who, in 1954, established Robert A. Maheu Associates, a private consulting firm specializing in solving sensitive problems. In the nation's capital that translated into a variety of assignments that ran from easing foreign diplomats and businessmen out of embarrassing situations to working as a liaison between the Mafia and the Central Intelligence Agency. The urbane, sophisticated Maheu had a deep voice, a calm demeanor, and excellent connections. He needed only the connections to satisfy Mintz.

---

4. Howard Hughes was aware that St. George, Utah, was near a site of government nuclear testing, yet did nothing to inform the producer, director or cast that the location might be contaminated. After shooting on location was completed, sixty tons of radioactive sand was delivered back to the studio and used during months of additional sound stage filming. More than half of the crew and cast eventually died of various forms of cancer, including John Wayne, Susan Hayward, co-stars Agnes Moorehead and Pedro Armedáriz, as well as director Dick Powell. Many feel that contamination from radioactivity was the cause.

Hughes had heard that Cramer had an association with the CIA, and before tackling that tiger in a cage wanted to know the extent of his involvement. With a single call to former FBI-turned-CIA agent Jim O'Connell, Maheu discovered that Cramer's connection to the CIA was dubious at best, and at no time was he an official operative. "The whole thing probably took me an afternoon, most of which was spent waiting for Jim to call me back," Maheu said. It was time well spent.

A month after delivering his report to Mintz, Maheu received another call from the attorney, who wanted him to take on a second assignment. It was only then that Maheu learned that the man behind Mintz was Howard Hughes. "I have to admit, I was impressed," Maheu said. "At the time, no name carried the same aura of wealth and influence as Howard Hughes."

Mintz wanted Maheu to organize a surveillance team to watch over Ava Gardner. Like Jean Peters, Ava was also planning a divorce. She had been wed to singer Frank Sinatra since 1951, and found his emotional instability and womanizing less than conducive to a happy marriage. Always available to an ex-lover in the throes of marital discord, Hughes moved Ava into the Cal-Neva Lodge at Lake Tahoe to establish residency for a quicky divorce, at the same time he placed Jean in a Nevada home in Glen Cove, a few miles away. Hughes wanted Maheu to keep track of the men who visited Ava, with a special watch posted for Sinatra.

Divorce work was a far cry from the international intrigue of Maheu's typical assignment, but he accepted the job and subcontracted it to a local private detective in Nevada–a very *enthusiastic* private detective, as it happened. When Sinatra appeared at Ava's door and asked her out for a sail on the nearby lake where the two could talk in absolute privacy, the detective rented a boat and followed, at a less-than-discrete distance. The resulting altercation not only found Sinatra intimidating the detective but the detective implicating Hughes, while Ava Gardner found the entire episode amusing, drama being her tornadic drug of choice when alcohol was not readily available.

As Sinatra stomped out of Nevada, Hughes arrived, and Ava found herself back out on the lake yet again, this time in the evening. Against a new moon and a sky washed by the Milky Way, Hughes waxed poetic, looking at the deep blue of the water, comparing it to a sapphire. "It matches your perfection," he told Ava. "I'll try and find a sapphire to match it for you."

Ava knew Hughes well enough to realize that words like *sapphire* and *perfection* were hardly accidental, not from a man who thought nothing of passing an entire evening without saying a single word. Later that night during dinner, his motive became clear. Hughes handed Ava a Kashmiri sapphire ring surrounded by diamonds. And once again he proposed. While it may not have been the most romantic proposal, Hughes, the realist, managed to captivate Ava.

"I know you're not in love with me," he began. "But you've already been married three times, so I wonder if you could now consider me?"

When Ava didn't immediately answer, Hughes began to recite his worth—the companies, the employees, the bank accounts, the real estate. "I used to own a yacht, with a captain and crew and a great chef, and I'll buy another one. We'll travel in style wherever you want to go. If you want to keep working in movies, I'll buy you the best properties available, the greatest directors, the best leading men. You won't have to worry about studios and contracts and all that nonsense. You can have a wonderful life, and you can enjoy every second of it. And you might, eventually, learn to love me," Ava wrote of their conversation in her autobiography.

Ava said she would give it some thought. Years later, she remembered that as she left Hughes that night, he had tears in his eyes. An act? Most likely, she projected. Hughes was certainly capable of performing to achieve his objective. His testimony before the Senate Special Committee proved that. Yet, she somehow felt the sadness was real. Perhaps he knew she could not be bought or possessed. For weeks, she refused to give him an answer, and so he waited, occupying his time by asking Jean Peters out on dates, and spending hours inspecting photos of Hollywood hopefuls supplied by Walter Kane for his approval.

In August, Hughes flew both Jean and Ava to Miami on separate flights, to be close at hand while he negotiated with Fred Odlum over the purchase of RKO. The studio continued to bleed red, and Hughes seriously considered returning the sound stages and film inventory to Odlum, who had owned it during its last profitable period. Stuart Cramer also flew to Miami in a final effort to woo back his wife, encouraged by Hughes, who took demonic pleasure in watching the frustrated Cramer's unsuccessful attempt.

Jean was staying in a rented home on the Intracoastal Waterway while Hughes had checked into a luxury villa with Ava and her maid, Reenie Jordan. Hughes had taken the smallest room, fitted with only a single twin bed, while Ava and her maid both had suites complete with dressing rooms and baths. The Florida sun scorched white hot against a cloudless sky, with temperatures rising above one hundred. While Ava found relief in a cool bath or reading on her balcony, Reenie preferred to bake on a chaise longue at the pool.

After seven days of relaxing, even sunbathing can get tiring. Reenie found herself restless, and began to stroll the grounds. When she passed through a lemon grove, she nodded to a worker she had seen sporadically on the property, and began a conversation. Soon it was maid speaking to groundsman, the shared camaraderie loosening tongues.

"For God's sake," the man begged Reenie. "Can't you get that woman of yours into bed with Mr. Hughes? I've been here day and night for ten days guarding this pearl-and-diamond necklace that once belonged to the Czarina of Russia.[5] It's worth so much I gotta sit with a loaded pistol and not let it out of my sight, even while I'm eating. I can't see a broad, I can't go to a bar, I can't even have a drink. For Christ's sake, if you have any influence with her, get her into bed with him so he can reward her with the necklace and I can rejoin the human race."

When Reenie related the story to Ava, her reaction was predictable and immediate. She began to pack her bags, and made no effort to be quiet about her disgust for a man who thought that money could buy attention. She roiled in contempt, venting as she slammed dresses, coats, shoes, and hose atop one another in a salmagundi of fabrics and colors. When the suitcase refused to shut, she threw it off the bed in frustration, while Reenie began the real work of packing for their exit.

At sunrise the next morning, the two women were on their toes as they silently made their way to the villa's front door. Halfway across the living room, Hughes came out of his room as if on cue (Ava swore the rooms were bugged). He was completely dressed and sociable. His too-sweet smile asked where they were going. Ava answered, "Havana," the first destination that materialized in the filing cabinet of her mind. As she said the word, she pulled at her sapphire ring and threw it across the room at the still-smiling Hughes.

"I wish you wouldn't," he said, the smile painted in place like a mannequin's.

"I don't care what you wish," Ava said. "I've made up my mind and I'm going." And with that, she slammed out of the room, leaving Reenie to wave goodbye and follow.

By the time Ava got to the Miami Airport, she learned the power of the world's richest man. Planes that were supposed to leave hourly were cancelled, one after the other. After waiting at the airport the entire day, the pair finally boarded a plane at 8 p.m. and escaped to Ernest Hemingway's house in Cuba, only to discover that Hughes had flown in ahead of them. It took two weeks of being turned away before Hughes finally gave up and left the island for Los Angeles, and only then because he was negotiating another deal—this one worth half-a-billion dollars.

Venture capitalist Laurence Rockefeller, real estate tycoon William

---

5. Invoices suggest that the necklace was not Russian in origin, but was a standard purchase from Tiffany. Value: $20,000.

Zeckendorf, and Greek shipping magnate Aristotle Onassis had formed a syndicate interested in purchasing Hughes' entire empire, and had offered $400,000,000 cash. While the trio had excluded RKO and the TWA stock from the deal, they were anxious to sign documents transferring ownership of all of Hughes' other companies "within days," according to a statement made by Spyros Skouras, president of 20th Century-Fox studios, who had acted as an intermediary between the parties. If Rockefeller and group expected that Hughes was serious, and later statements suggested they did, they had not allowed for the Hughes mystique. Noah Dietrich testified in deposition that it was "another fishing expedition. Hughes never was serious about selling anything. His whole purchase was merely to gain insight into what he was currently worth. And the easiest way to determine that was by placing the companies in play."

On November 11, 1954, Zeckendorf and Rockefeller flew to Los Angeles from New York, carrying bank documents confirming the solvency of the syndicate, and actually expected to close the deal. They were met at the airport and taken to the Beverly Hills Hotel, where they checked into adjacent suites on the third floor. The following day, the tank-sized real-estate tycoon and the slim investor went by a Hughes-provided limousine to a pre-determined parking lot where they were met by a driver wearing a red shirt, black pants, and penny loafers, who instructed the two men to accompany him to his waiting car, an old Chevrolet that Zeckendorf described as "something the Okies might have used on the trek west twenty years ago."

The driver transported the two men to an area of town Zeckendorf described as "about as far away from humanity as I've ever been." It was in a section of downtown Los Angeles off Central Avenue, surrounded by warehouses and deserted factories. They stopped in front of what appeared to be an abandoned building. It was, in fact, the once-proud Mason Hotel, its glory faded behind termite-eaten windows and padlocked doors, guarded by a squadron of Hughes' drivers, "rather good-looking men with crew cuts."

The entrepreneurs were directed to walk up to the fourth floor, and taken to a door at the end of a deserted hallway. There, after an elaborate "pattern of knocks," the door was opened and Howard Hughes welcomed his guests into a large room, empty except for a sagging sofa and two wooden chairs plus some rusted equipment that resembled boilers or large wash tubs.

Hughes was wearing a soiled white shirt, dirty khaki slacks, stained canvas shoes threadbare at the big toes, and was unshaven for the encounter that the real estate tycoon labeled "the strangest meeting—I guess it was a meeting." There, in the dust, the cobwebs, and the relics from the past, the man who hated germs and refused to shake the men's hands calmly read through detailed contracts which were tailored to satisfy his list of demands. After sitting silent for over an hour, Zeckendorf finally spoke.

"I think you'll find everything is exactly as you wanted," he said.

Hughes looked up slowly from the stack of papers, and nodded his head. "You're right. Except for one thing." Zeckendorf raised his eyebrows, as he felt himself suck in air. "The price. You don't know what you're talking about. Not enough."

"What is enough?" Zeckendorf asked.

"I won't tell you," Hughes said.

"Do you want to sell?"

"Under certain circumstances."

"What circumstances?"

"If the price is right."

"What price?"

"The price you might offer me. If it is enough, I'll sell."

"I'm offering four hundred and fifty million; will you take it?"

"No."

"Howard, five hundred million. Take it or leave it."

"I'll leave it." Without further explanation, Hughes rose and walked toward Zeckendorf, calmly handed him the unsigned contract and left the room. Zeckendorf and Rockefeller were stunned. Zeckendorf moved from his chair, and rushed as fast as his over-weight, swollen legs could to catch up with Hughes, only to see the dust from an old Chevrolet leaving the parking lot as he reached the threshold of the landing. There, in the filth of what Zeckendorf described as a "flophouse," he watched as Hughes' chauffeur opened the rear door of the old car and stood at attention as if this sort of thing happened every day.

The following morning, Zeckendorf[6] gave a news conference in which he labeled the failure of the deal as due to "a completely unpardonable, unilateral and unconscionable reversal on the part of Howard Hughes."

Having thus satisfied himself that his empire continued to grow, Hughes once again retreated into a world without light at the Beverly Hills Hotel. Without the purifying effects of sun and fresh air, Bungalow Nineteen had begun to develop spores and mold, particularly around the air conditioning vents. Hughes blamed the moisture emitted from the air

---

6. William Zeckendorf engaged in a real-life game of Monopoly during his career. Among the properties he bought or sold were the site of the United Nations, the Chrysler Building and the Chase Manhattan Plaza in Manhattan, plus the Mile High Center in Denver. As head of Webb & Knapp, the New York-based real estate company, he built $3 billion worth of commercial properties in twenty years. His credo was, "To do less than the ultimate is to do nothing."

conditioner's fan for the mildew, and promptly ordered it shut off, thereby eliminating the only remaining source of circulation.

Hughes had converted the living room of the bungalow into his new screening room, pushing aside the plush furnishings of the hotel to make room for his Barcalounger and ottoman. His two 35-mm projectors were placed atop two hotel coffee tables, slightly behind and to the left of Hughes' recliner. On the far side of the room, a movie screen and a large speaker covered a wall. The hotel's overstuffed sofa, love seat, and occasional chairs were unused and pushed into another corner, and were stacked with newspapers and magazines that had now accumulated to the point that the piles were multiplying onto the floor into a form of complicated labyrinth dotted with mounds of discarded Kleenex, testament to Hughes' increased use of tissues to insulate his hands and feet from the perception of bacteria.

His concern over germs intensified in early 1955 with the discovery of still another rash on his body, this time around his waist and on the right side of his chest. Dr. Lawrence Chaffin attended to Hughes at the hotel, prescribed penicillin for a "bacterial infection of unknown origin," and charged $300 for his visit. His prescription allowed for six refills of the drug, which Hughes had his favorite driver, Roy Crawford, take to the nearby Roxbury Pharmacy. Crawford returned with 112 penicillin tablets that Hughes subsequently took on an infrequent timetable, thereby decreasing the effectiveness of the drug and allowing the bacteria in his system to mutate and render the prescription potentially useless.

Hughes rented a second bungalow for a staff of attendants who would be on duty around-the-clock. The primary function was to run errands and operate the projectors for Hughes' continuing screening of films. Given the bulkiness of the furniture in the cramped living room, the heat generated from the large projection equipment, and the lack of air conditioning, Hughes began to watch the films wearing little in the way of clothing. When he had his rash, just a soiled white shirt. At other times, he was completely naked with the exception of a single pink linen napkin covering his groin.

Into this haven of squalor stepped a fifteen-year-old girl named Yvonne Shubert, an innocent discovery of Walter Kane's, who had dreams of becoming a famous singer. It was with that hope and a suitcase of clothes that Shubert agreed to move with her mother into a suite at the Beverly Hills Hotel, to be given the Hughes makeover. That Yvonne would prove different from the others was not apparent on first impression, at least not to Kane, who was told to personally handle the new discovery. Yet, after only a few months, it became obvious even to Hughes' aides that Yvonne was being given preferential treatment, including a house on Coldwater Canyon in Beverly Hills and repeated proposals of marriage.

Yvonne was unaware of Jean Peters, who was then living close by in her own rented house in Bel Air. Yvonne the naive teenager, who admitted to being hopelessly in love with a man old enough to be her grandfather, and Jean the naive woman, who trusted Hughes' promises to settle down in a home where she could cook and clean and sew clothes, in a fantasy called "happily ever after." Into this mix of trust and wantonness, actress Susan Hayward fell, rebounding from her failed ten-year-marriage to actor Jess Barker and into the waiting arms of Howard Hughes, who proposed marriage on their second date as he slid a familiar sapphire and diamond ring on her finger. This time, Hughes said that the ring formerly belonged to a Hungarian countess; and this time, he would not get it back.

Between swings of month-long solitary isolation and impulsive sexual assignations, Hughes managed to rid himself of the lingering drama that was RKO Pictures by selling it to Thomas O'Neil, president of the Mutual Radio and Television Networks, a subsidiary of General Tire & Rubber Co., owned by O'Neil's father. The selling price of $25 million included 700 old RKO films, the studio lot and the film distribution system that Hughes had owned outright for just over a year. The deciding factor for Hughes was not the selling price, which was absorbed without celebration into an empire now valued at $700 million. Rather, it was O'Neil's promise not to liquidate the assets of RKO and thus dissolve the famous studio. "Mr. Hughes was opposed to the break-up of RKO Radio Pictures because it would cause widespread distress and unemployment," O'Neil said, without reference to how many people had previously been terminated at RKO due to Hughes' interference. "I think a great deal of credit is due to him for that humanitarian stand."

New Year's Eve, 1955. It was a plan that Hughes felt certain he was capable of mastering. More precisely, he felt that he *alone* was capable of mastering it, when in truth he *alone* was capable of having conceived of it at all. His timing had to be impeccable, his attention span flawless; and his charm, for certain his charm, had to be oozing from every pore, for, after all, it was New Year's Eve and Jean Peters had particularly asked him to put aside his business for a few hours. Unfortunately for Jean, she had not added that he needed to put aside his Lotharian ways.

She sat in the Crystal Room of the Beverly Hills Hotel, an overchilled glass of Moet & Chandon 1947 before her. Jean had arrived precisely at 10 p.m. as planned, and felt the eyes of other patrons follow her to the table as she swept in, elegant in a Jean Louis gown that exposed one shoulder. She was relieved when Hughes joined her at the table, a mood replaced with joy when he handed her a box from Cartier. She opened it to find a diamond and sapphire bracelet, and as he placed in on her wrist, there was noticeable awe from the adjacent tables. Jean had barely been able to thank him when Hughes was called away by the waiter for a phone call.

As Susan Hayward saw Hughes enter the Polo Lounge at the back of the hotel, she waved to him from her corner booth, slid across the red banquette to stand and kiss him eagerly on the lips, thanking him for the beautiful flowers he had sent. The gardenias floated in the center of the table as if carved from white butter, their waxed leaves in contrast to the fragrant blossoms frozen in the moment. Hughes slid in beside her, and complimented Susan on her gown. Designer Edith Head had created it, and the 38-year-old star was radiant against sheer white organdy. She spoke of how she was looking forward to the evening—even more, the new year, and as she looked into Hughes' eyes, he started to respond, when he was interrupted.

"Excuse me, Mr. Hughes. A call for you," the waiter said, waving his hand loosely in the direction of the lobby.

For Yvonne Shubert, the evening was like a dream. Her own bungalow at the Beverly Hills Hotel, dinner with Howard Hughes—the man she loved, and a movie career about to begin. He had filled the suite with roses; she had never seen so many. Yes, the evening was like a dream. She hardly noticed that Hughes was twenty minutes late. She was occupied watching the burning logs, carefully stoked by the attentive waiter, his white gloves protecting his hands. When Hughes arrived, he apologized—something about TWA and a problem with the airport. His work confused her, so she did not question, rather smiled the vague smile that belongs to teenagers in love. He had scarcely arrived when he excused himself. He had forgotten something—a gift for her. And after he left, she hugged herself with delight, she was that happy.

Jean Peters was staring at her empty glass of champagne when Hughes made it back to the Crystal Room. She was not upset; Jean never caused a problem. Hughes ordered his usual: a New York steak, peas, and a salad with freshly made Roquefort dressing. Jean would have the same. The waiter had barely filled her glass, when again a call, and again she was alone. The champagne was good, she thought, as she felt its tartness against her tongue. She signaled the waiter to refill her glass.

Susan Hayward did not rise this time when Hughes came back into the Polo Lounge. Her smile said she felt neglected and hoped his excuse would calm her mood. She was expecting this night to be something special; perhaps even a prelude to a wedding. Her own divorce from actor Jess Barker was final, and she knew how Howard felt about her. He loved her twins; he loved her; and wanted to get married, he told her often. As the waiter brought the menu, Hughes took her hand and together they looked over the choices. He never ordered from the menu, of course, but Susan liked to see it just the same. They had not yet reached the listings of the entrees when Hughes was called away again. He gave her the irritated look of one oppressed, shrugged his shoulders and left again.

Something was wrong, Susan thought. Something dreadful that Hughes had to handle. More out of curiosity than a desire to help, Susan pulled her full-length mink around her shoulders, and went scouting for her erstwhile lover. She found him in the dining room of the hotel, about to cut into his steak, and with a mouthful of peas.

The scene that followed was described by the hotel's maître d' as being "very Hollywood," which in Beverly Hills is not a compliment. It took the two stars less than a minute to compare notes, grab their purses, and exit in high dudgeon. Hughes finished the night with Yvonne Shubert, who was none the wiser, and was thrilled to receive her New Year's Eve gift: a diamond and sapphire bracelet.

Well after 2 a.m., Hughes walked alone back to his bungalow, without hearing the mockingbirds trilling their serenade. His mind was on romance, though not on Yvonne. He thought of ways to assuage Jean. *That will take some work*, he thought to himself.

Upon seeing Hughes walk down the path, the aide standing at the bungalow door began to frantically swat at invisible flies, hoping that no one else could see his performance. Kleenex in hand, he opened the door and Hughes leaped inside to allow for an immediate closing. Hughes walked along the narrow maze of piled newspapers, across discarded tissues, and felt empty pecan shells crush under his shoes. In the bedroom, he removed his clothing, carefully hanging each piece up in the closet, before falling naked in bed.

It was the first day of a new year, but he made no resolutions. Hughes was not superstitious, firmly believing that he was in control of his own destiny. As he shut his eyes, he felt a chill shake his body. It unnerved him slightly, but not enough for him to realize that it warned of stormy months ahead. And he did not see a lady with hornet hair pulling a tired mule that night, but she would come. Oh, yes, she would come.

Til Death Us Do Part

*The man serving HRH first unfolds the tablecloth
and spreads it on the eating table with HRH's help.
He then hands HRH the sterile knife and fork;
warm dinner plate; plate of salad; steak; butter plate
with the pepper, salt, paprika, vegetables, and pours
the V-8 juice if HRH indicates. HRH accepts all of
those items by holding Kleenex, and putting them on
the table himself. When HRH has completed the
steak course, he will gather all the empty plates and
hand them to the server who, in turn, places them
back on the serving table. HRH will then indicate
when he is ready for dessert. The signal is then given
to the waiter outside, and he obtains the ice cream
from the kitchen along with the bakery goods which
are kept in sterile cardboard boxes. These items are
handed to the server inside the room who, in turn,
opens them at the eating table. HRH also accepts the
dessert plates with Kleenex, and sets them on this table.*

Beverly Hills, California
January, 1958
Howard Hughes' written instructions for
serving him dinner. The meal itself, at the
time, never varied.

ON JANUARY 23, 1956, NOAH DIETRICH WROTE A LETTER
to the Wilshire Country Club, where Howard Hughes had
been a member for thirty-two years. He requested that
Hughes' membership be changed from resident to non-res-
ident status, an annual savings in dues of several hundred
dollars. As proof of his claim, Dietrich attested that Hughes

was now a legal resident of Florida, and listed a P.O. box in the Ocean View Branch of the Miami Beach Post Office. "Your records will indicate that he has not availed himself of any of the Club's privileges for a number of years," Dietrich wrote, a dramatic understatement since Hughes' last game of golf was in 1944. The Wilshire Country Club granted the request despite the fact that the membership committee continued to send his bills to his office on Romaine Street, and Hughes remained housed at the Beverly Hills Hotel.

Hughes lay in his bed in Bungalow Nineteen, and wondered what time it was. It was a passing thought, nothing more, for the time of day meant little to a man who lived in total darkness. The single lamp in the room had remained unlit for the past nine days, as Hughes fought through a depression that arrived with the new year, and lingered like a head cold in summer. It could be traced to the November 29, 1955, decision by the Internal Revenue Service denying Howard Hughes Medical Institute tax-exempt status as a charity. The ruling sent Hughes into a deep depression that was only slightly eased by Dietrich's employment of the Washington law firm of Hogan & Hartson, whose senior partner was Seymour Mintz, a one-time special attorney with the IRS, and the man who had hired Robert Maheu.

By the time Mintz filed a protest against the IRS decision in March, 1956, Hughes had risen from his bed, but only on a single occasion had traveled further than the living room of his bungalow—a room increasingly littered with used Kleenex, walkways of paper toweling (yet another form of insulation), and meticulously arranged stacks of newspapers and magazines, organized by date. His only visitor was Dr. Verne Mason, who continued to medicate Hughes for his headaches, back pain, and mental state. Mason gave him multiple prescriptions of Empirin Compound #4 with codeine; Hughes gave Mason the directorship of the Howard Hughes Medical Institute.

In an effort to convince the government that the Institute was in the throes of being established, Hughes had his press agents release a statement that various areas in Florida were being considered for a "major medical research facility." In addition, Hughes said he had long-range plans for the state because of its favorable business tax code. "The developments I desire to carry out in Florida are entirely new and apart from the companies, plants and projects with which I am now associated in Texas, California and Arizona. They will in no way affect these operations."

Governor Leroy Collins lauded Hughes for his foresight and said that he had reached an agreement "which will result in new developments by Mr. Hughes in Florida of special significance to our state."

Hughes had taken Collins to dinner at the Beverly Hills Hotel, given him a private tour of Hughes Aircraft, and flown him in his private jet to see the lights of Los Angeles. The governor was unaware that this was Hughes' first time out of his bungalow in two weeks, and the first time off hotel property in four months.

In early April, Hughes announced that he was purchasing a 30,000-acre parcel of land in Florida to develop an aircraft manufacturing plant that the governor said would "far transcend in importance, payrolls and future development any industrial development now in the state." Fuller Warren called the announcement "strictly a hoax." The former Florida governor, who was involved in a bitter Democratic gubernatorial primary race with Collins at the time, said that Hughes had absolutely no "property, development plan or business" that would be able to support his purported plant, and that the announcement was designed "to deceive and mislead the people of Florida" into voting for Collins.

As if to answer Warren's doubts, Hughes petitioned the Civil Aeronautics Board on behalf of TWA for permission to buy twenty-five jets from Hughes Aircraft.[1] It was a time of metamorphosis for the airline industry as it transformed from propeller planes to jet aviation. By late 1955, Pan American, United and American Airlines all had placed large orders for Boeing 707 and Douglas DC-8 jets. Some $1 billion worth. TWA, which in the past had been the leader in new aircraft orders, had none. In February, 1956, Hughes half-heartedly reserved thirty-three 707s from Boeing, still not believing that he was making the right decision. He paced in the dark of his bungalow, worrying that he had committed $186 million to an inferior plane; and eventually leaked the rumor that he was contemplating cancelling the order, and quickly followed it up with the petition to the CAB for a plane of his own design. The aviation industry was stunned into prophesy. Analysts went on record projecting that Hughes had plans for a "transonic jet airliner capable of speeds and distance far in excess to anything Boeing or Douglas have in development."

The management of Boeing and Douglas had spent millions developing their rival jets. The threat of a Hughes advance that might make their latest equipment obsolete overnight was taken extremely seriously. This was, after all, the man who owned Hughes Aircraft–the company that several years earlier had perfected the Falcon Guided Missile, labeled by the military as the "best symbol of ingenuity and achievement in the Air Force missile program." Boeing attempted to learn details of Hughes'

---

1. Hughes had gradually increased his ownership of TWA, reaching 78.2 percent in 1956. At the time of his original purchase of TWA stock, he had agreed to get permission from the CAB for any transaction between the airline and a Hughes company that would exceed $200.

design from the CAB filing, which cryptically suggested only that "no current design has the range desirable for all-year operations across the Atlantic so as to permit nonstop services in both directions under extreme conditions." They needn't have lost any sleep.

At the time that Boeing and Douglas were worried about being put out of business by Howard Hughes, the multimillionaire was busying himself in the privacy of his bungalow designing an apparatus to keep his toes apart. He had instructed the engineers at Hughes Aircraft to manu-facturer the device—he labeled it on his drawings HTS-1—the purpose of which was "to provide a comfortable means to separate toes to keep their nails from hitting." The drawing Hughes had made on his yellow legal pad resembled a metal foot brace with metal rods separating each toe. The rods were expandable to adjust as the toe nail grew. The drawings were refined five times from April 19 through May 1. No mention was made of the obvious solution of trimming the nails to avoid the problem altogether.

While the executives at TWA were frantically attempting to reach Hughes as the weeks slipped into months and the competition for jet aircraft became essentially unbeatable, Hughes left written instructions with Operations at Romaine Street to deal with the situation:

> Telephone calls from Ralph[2] or another executive from TWA's headquarters should be logged and a message taken with the EXACT words of the message written. Do not volunteer that HRH is in town. Say that you have not heard from me and that you expect to hear from HRH within the week. Please reply with just those words, then let HRH know that someone has called when HRH asks for his messages.

STILL UNWILLING to leave his bungalow, trapped by his own indecision and incapable of asking for help for fear it would appear as a sign of weakness, HRH pondered his fate and vanished into the world of cellu-loid, viewing the film *Summertime* starring Katharine Hepburn six consecutive times, according to company logs. The marathon screening session was followed by a two-hour visit to the bathroom, while Hughes left his aide operating the projection equipment sitting alone in the darkness.

While in the bathroom, Hughes took the opportunity to write a memo dictating instructions for his drivers to follow when they delivered reels of film to his bungalow:

---

2. TWA president Ralph Damon, who was so stressed by Hughes' inaction to acquire jets for the airline that he had a heart attack and died in January 1956.

When delivering films to the bungalow area of the hotel, park one foot from the curb on Crescent near the place where the sidewalk dead-ends into the curb. Get out of the car on the traffic side. Do not at any time be on the side of the car between the car and the curb. When unloading film do so from the traffic side of the car, if the film is in the rear seat. If it is in the trunk, stand as close to the center of the road as possible while unloading. Carry only one can of film at a time.

Step over the gutter opposite the place where the sidewalk dead-ends into the curb from a point as far out into the center of the road as possible. Do not ever walk on the grass at all, also do not step into the gutter at all. Walk to the bungalow keeping as near to the center of the sidewalk as possible.

Do not sit the film cans down on the sidewalk or the street or any-where else, except possibly on the porch of the bungalow area if the third man[3] is not there. While waiting for the third man to arrive, do not lean against any portion of the bungalow or the furniture on the porch, but remain there standing quietly and await his arrival. When the third man clears the door, step inside quickly carrying the can (single) of film, just far enough to the inside.

Do not move and do not say anything and do not sit the film down until you receive instructions where to sit it. If possible, stay two feet away from the TV set, the wire on the floor and the walls. When leaving, kick on the door and step outside quickly as soon as the third man opens the door.

THE BALANCE BETWEEN the adventurer-playboy and entrepreneur had tilted ominously, and like a tomato sliding off a serving plate onto the floor, Hughes had crashed into a muddle of frayed nerves and physical torment. Now skipping meals for days on end, Hughes' already lanky frame was turning skeletal as his body consumed its own muscle and brain tissue for support. The executives running his various divisions unwittingly added to the problem by continually attempting to reach him for answers to pressing business decisions. The more pressure, the less response, in a vicious, never-ending circle of self-persecution.

Stoking the furnace of unyielding pressure, Hughes' own reputation became his worst enemy. The longer he failed to respond, the greater the mystery behind his lack of performance became, yielding projections by the media that a huge announcement was imminent, one that would not only propel aviation into the future, but all of America as well. It was this publicity speculating on his own forthcoming genius that eventually forced Hughes into action, albeit in an unexpected direction.

---

3. The "third man" was Hughes' nickname for the person who swatted flies and opened the bungalow's door.

He opened a telephone dialogue with the Convair Aircraft Company, a San Diego producer of piston-driven planes, to manufacture a custom-made short-range jet, initially for the exclusive use of TWA. So eager was the company to generate business that its vice-president, Jack Zevely, leapt at the opportunity to work with the unpredictable Hughes, and sent him a preliminary design for a jet plane labeled the Convair 880. Hughes made some minor modifications including requesting that the plane be made from gold-toned aluminum and renamed the plane TWA's Golden Arrow.

In June, 1956, Convair announced an order from Hughes for thirty of the jetliners, at a total price of $126.4 million. Coupled with Hughes' previous order from Boeing and an additional order for $90 million in back-up engines from Pratt & Whitney Aircraft Company, Hughes had obligated Hughes Tool to purchase over $400 million dollars in equipment, which the company would then lease back to TWA. It was the largest single order in the history of aviation. It made newspaper headlines around the world and reworked the image of TWA from a laggard to a trailblazer. The aviation world was once again talking about Hughes and his incredible investment in TWA. What no one mentioned, at least in print, was that Hughes had little available cash to pay for the planes.

Noah Dietrich was dumbstruck when he heard the news from a journalist who telephoned him for a comment. Not only had Hughes not told anyone at TWA about his plans, he also neglected to mention them to his own executives. As the resident keeper of the cashbox, Dietrich was placed in a position between his boss's commitment to Boeing and Convair, and Hughes Tool's ability to generate the necessary capital. Hughes Tool had an amazing cash reserve of $100 million that could be tapped for initial deposits. Dietrich recommended floating a bond issue for the remaining money with the bonds guaranteed by Hughes Tool.

Hughes initially refused to even consider issuing bonds, equating it with asking for a loan. "What are people going to think?" he asked Dietrich. "That Howard Hughes doesn't have enough money?"

"You don't have enough money, Howard," Dietrich responded. "*Nobody* has this kind of money."

After some intense discussion and mild arm-twisting on the part of Dietrich, Hughes finally agreed to allow the Manhattan brokerage house of Dillion, Reed & Company to handle the bond issue. The concept was a solid one and Dillion, Reed jumped on the assignment. The stock firm had just finished printing the prospectus for the offering when Hughes telephoned Dillion, Reed president Fred Brandi, and cancelled the deal. When Dietrich heard the news from Brandi, he came very close to resigning. He later said that if he had not been previously slated to take a three-month safari with his two sons, he would have. As it was, he called Hughes and told him that now it was the multimillionaire's personal responsibility to figure out a solution. Dietrich wanted no part of it. Yet, as with everything Hughes, it would not be that simple.

Dietrich was besieged by his boss during the days before his departure. He was repeatedly informed that Hughes could not afford his absence from the organization, despite the fact that Dietrich had not taken a single full week off in thirty-one years with the organization. Hughes called talent agent Pat Di Cicco, who was initially to accompany Dietrich, and bribed him to cancel the trip. Hughes then phoned the TWA terminal at Los Angeles Airport and attempted to keep Dietrich on the telephone long enough so that he would miss his flight. He found him in Rome; then again on the plains of Tanganyika as Dietrich hunted antelope. Still, Hughes' *major-domo* was not intimidated and refused to move from his safari tent.

During Dietrich's absence, Hughes showed little concern for his near half-billion-dollar liability, and concentrated on accomplishing what he labeled "matters of urgency." The first one involved gossip columnist Louella Parsons. Hughes' notes indicate that Louella had contacted Bill Gay at Romaine Street and advised him that she wanted to travel to Europe "on an extended holiday with friends." Then Louella added in her message, "Perhaps, Mr. Hughes would like to accompany us." Hughes had never taken a vacation with anyone since he traveled with Dudley Sharp and his mother to Europe after the death of his father. This could only mean that Louella was trolling for some free travel on TWA, and Hughes was only too happy to oblige.

He alerted his staff at both Operations and at TWA that Louella was to be given her usual VIP treatment, the extent of which is evident in the memo regarding the arrangements from TWA's Special Services division, dated July 18, 1956.

In accordance with instructions from HRH, conveyed to this department through Walter Kane, the following arrangements were made for Miss Louella Parsons' trip to London. Accompanying Miss Parsons were Mr. John Haskell and her nurse.

Miss Parson' tickets were delivered to her home on July 16 as per her wishes. At that time, an offer was made for us to provide the transportation for her to the airport but she had made other arrangements.

At 8 p.m. on the evening of the 17th of July, the Parsons party was met at (Los Angeles) International Airport by Mr. Robert Montgomery, a vice-president of TWA; Mr. Carlo Belliero of the TWA Hollywood office and Mr. Charles Woodcock of Mr. Hughes' staff.

The Parsons party was taken to the Ambassador Club Rooms at the

Airport and refreshments were served until plane time. There were over twenty persons in the party seeing Miss Parsons off.

Flight #90 was on time and departed LAX at 9 p.m. July 17, 1956.

Arriving in New York on July 18, 1956, the Parsons party was met at the airport by Mr. Walter Menke of TWA and taken by limousine to the Waldorf-Astoria Hotel where a three-bedroom suite had been reserved for them.

Mr. Menke stayed with the Parsons party the entire day and took them to the airport in New York where they boarded TWA Flight #860 for London at 4 p.m. This flight was scheduled to arrive in London at 9:40 a.m. the following morning.

TWA official Mr. Larry Langley in London met the Parsons party in London and extended to them all of the Red Carpet courtesies of TWA. Mr. Langley was further instructed to stay with the party during their stay and to see that everything possible was done for their convenience and pleasure.

This office is keeping in touch with the situation and will add such information to this memorandum as may accumulate during the Parsons party visit in Europe and will handle things upon their return.

LOUELLA PARSONS SPENT four weeks in London, during which time Larry Langley arranged for dinner reservations, theater tickets, and a town car for Parsons' use. Walter Menke, rail thin and with a reservoir of extra energy, worked in New York in TWA's accounting department but was called upon by Operations to meet Hughes' guests. "We weren't paid any extra," Menke said, "but every once in a while, Hughes would do something totally unexpected. Once he sent one of his drivers all the way from Los Angeles to New York with instructions to take me to Abercrombie & Fitch and buy me a suit. And he did."

Louella fawned excitedly upon her return, writing, "I hardly know how to put this down on paper," in a letter she sent to Hughes on August 30. "I have never had such a good time in my whole life as I had in Europe. To say, 'Thank you, dear,' seems inadequate. I can only say I think this trip prolonged my life. I feel so much better than I felt when I left."[4]

On September 10, 1956, Hughes' Uncle Rupert died. He had been in ill health for several years after suffering a stroke. Hughes made no effort to assist him during that time, nor made any effort to console his Uncle Felix, Rupert's brother, after Rupert's death. When Dietrich asked Hughes if he cared to send flowers to the funeral, Hughes replied, "I never liked Rupert, and he never liked me. I think it's a little late to care, don't you?"[5]

4. Louella Parsons lived for another sixteen years, and died at age 92 in 1972.
5. Rupert Hughes was cremated and his ashes buried next to his last wife, Patterson Dial, in Forest Lawn Memorial Park, Glendale, California.

Dietrich shook his head and wondered about a man who could give someone like Louella Parsons a red-carpet holiday and yet had so little compassion for his own family. As a rule, Hughes had far more concern for his employees, though even that translated into over-payment in cash as reparation for the emotional abuse he rendered. Dietrich was growing tired of the routine, the hours of broken sleep, and constant disruption. After the discussion of Rupert's death, he took the opportunity to mention his retirement to Hughes. The workaholic could not even conceive of the concept. When Dietrich pressed the issue, Hughes offered him a million dollars, cash, if he would postpone any decision until the following year, when Hughes hoped that the TWA financing situation would be handled. Dietrich reluctantly agreed, although he never pressed Hughes for the money.

Hughes did not vote in the presidential election of 1956, nor any other time in his life for that matter, finding it easier to buy his influence than cast a ballot for it. Nevertheless, he was pleased when Dwight Eisenhower was reelected to his second term in the White House for he brought with him Richard Nixon as his vice-president, and a man Hughes thought of as *his*.

With the IRS still noncommittal on Hogan & Hartson's appeal of Hughes' tax-exempt status of the Howard Hughes Medical Institute, the multimillionaire decided to improve his chances of an IRS turnaround by approving a loan to Nixon's brother Donald for $250,000. Donald Nixon was trying desperately to cash in on his brother's growing political fame through a string of three restaurants that served Nixonburgers, a questionable commodity at best. On December 10, 1956, Hughes had Dietrich transfer funds to Nixon's mother, Hannah, who secured the loan with a piece of property she owned at the corner of Santa Gertrudis and Whittier Boulevards in Whittier, California. It had once been the site of the Nixon family home, and, after several transformations, was then leased to Union Oil and converted into a gas station.

Soon after Dietrich had handled the details of the loan, he received a rather mysterious call from Dr. Verne Mason, who wanted to schedule an imperative and extremely private meeting. Given the urgency in Mason's voice, Dietrich offered to have Mason come to his home. It was an offer that Mason accepted. When Mason arrived at the Dietrich home, he declined a drink, although, according to Dietrich, he was nervous enough to need one. The reason for the secrecy and the spate of nerves became clear as he spoke: "Noah, I think the time has come for you to have Howard declared incompetent."

A single housefly buzzed around a table lamp in the Dietrich living room. Attracted by the light or the heat it dispensed, the fly hit the bulb and instantly fell to the table, spinning on its back in a uncontrolled orbit as if praying to be swatted. Dietrich looked at the fly, heard the buzzing, and perceived a kinship. For years, he had felt like he was going in circles, barely keeping up with Hughes in an effort to shore up weaknesses in a crumbling foundation. It seemed that he stared at the fly for hours (really only about ten seconds) when he looked up at Mason and angrily told him to go to hell.

"I'm not about to play Doctor," he told the head of the Medical Institute, who he thought in a better position to attempt such a maneuver, if indeed it was necessary. Mason mumbled about his salary ($50,000) and his expense account (unlimited), and hurried toward the door.

When Hughes received news about the visit, as his notes indicate he did just after the first of the year, his first thought was of Miss Genia of the hornet hair. He stared around the living room of Bungalow Nineteen with tissues and paper toweling strewn with the abandon of someone tossing crumbs in a public square; unread newspapers accumulating in stacks that were threatening to topple from their height; and a stench that hovered between that of a wet goat and grass decaying in a pond, and he wept. Miss Genia and her mule had nothing on him.

In what can only be described as a catharsis, Hughes pulled himself out of his depressive and obsessive paranoia, and placed a call to Romaine Street. He wanted a barber sent to his bungalow immediately. And then he took a long, hot shower. He thought of little else for the next few hours. Against the threat of being committed, Hughes knew he had to find a wife—and quickly. One that he could control. One that would bar any betrayers who might think that he was going crazy.

Howard Hughes arrived at Kathryn Grayson's home on the afternoon of January 6, 1957. He looked like a suitor and felt like a fiancé. He charmed her with reminiscences about the past and presumed to invent for her a future—as his wife. Yes, again he proposed; but this time Grayson was not so quick to answer. She thought of her dear nephew, her horrible premonition. She sidestepped the issue and talked about her upcoming concert tour; he insisted she cancel and marry him immediately. She said that she was leaving the next day, and would talk upon her return; he said that it had to be *immediately*, and then stalked across the room and slapped her hard across the face.

It was not the first time Hughes had struck a woman. He hit Ava Gardner repeatedly one night, turning her left eye into a casaba melon before pushing her onto the floor. Ava, venting her own anger in response, picked up a large heavy bronze bell and threw it across the room, hitting Hughes in the head, knocking out two teeth and causing a gash that required twenty-two stitches to close. Hughes got the worst end of the fight, Ava's eye only requiring a thick piece of raw steak and a comforting maid.

Kathryn Grayson did not have Ava Gardner's temper or strength. She did, however, have her self-respect. She turned her back on Hughes and left the room, but not before she told him that she never wanted to see him again in her life. Hughes returned to the Beverly Hills Hotel, and plunged back into darkness. Once there, his thoughts drifted to Terry Moore, who by this time had married a mysterious entrepreneur named Eugene McGrath, lived in Panama, and was traveling the world swept up in McGrath's exotic intrigue. He next contemplated Yvonne Shubert, still a minor so of no use now. And then there was Jean.

In January, 1957, Jean Peters was 30 years old, and had not made a film in three years, her last project being *A Man Called Peter*[6] shot in 1954 in Georgia for 20th Century-Fox studios. She had moved into a Hughes-rented house on Strada Vecchia Road in Bel Air, where she spent her time gardening and sewing, seeing no one except Hughes whenever he called for the occasional screening or dinner. "It was a quiet life," she later said, though Peters did not mind. Although Hughes offered to buy her anything she desired, her needs were simple. Hughes liked that.

He also liked the fact that she was unimpressed by his money. She was more inspired by the fact that he wanted to leave his entire estate to medical research than anything his fortune could purchase for her. When Hughes called her on the evening of January 8 and asked her to be his wife, she did not hesitate to accept. She asked for only one commitment on the part of her future husband: that they live in a house together. It seemed like a natural enough request; that she should have to make it all, of course, suggested the strangeness of their relationship.

Hughes called upon his Los Angeles tax attorney James J. Arditto to make the secret arrangements for the ceremony. Arditto was told that the wedding was to take place in Tonopah, Nevada, a site with which neither he nor Peters was familiar. Hughes was well aware of the small town two-hundred miles northwest of Las Vegas. It was not far away from the farm where he had gone into hiding with Billie Dove, and it was to Tonopah he flew on January 12, 1957, to legally marry for the second time.

Hughes and Jean flew into Tonopah in the early morning hours aboard a TWA Constellation, accompanied by aides George Francom and Roy Crawford, attorney D. Martin Cook, plus a TWA pilot and co-pilot. Sworn to secrecy, the aides and Cook were told to dress as if

---

6. *A Man Called Peter* was the filmization of the popular biography of Peter Marshall, the Scottish emigrant clergyman who became chaplain of the U.S. Senate. Jean portrayed Catherine, the preacher's wife, who had written the best-seller. Peter Marshall was portrayed by Richard Todd.

they were going hunting. Arditto, in on the masquerade, was dressed in fishing gear when he picked them up at a private landing strip outside of Tonopah and drove them the short distance into the nearly deserted town. There on the second floor of a dilapidated hotel, G.A. Johnson married Marian Evans in front of county clerk Eudora V. Meyley. Nevada allowed the use of false names in weddings, although other information on the marriage license was sworn to be correct. In Hughes' case, G.A. Johnson was said to be 46, born on June 8, 1910, and a resident of Las Vegas (Hughes was 51, born September 24, 1905, and lived in Beverly Hills); Jean's Marian Evans was 29, born on October 15, 1927, and a resident of Los Angeles (Jean was 30, born on October 15, 1926, and lived in Bel Air).

After the duck hunter and his wife (dressed in a silk suit) were officially married, they kissed chastely, clinging to one another like a pair of praying mantises. And then they left that place where dereliction replaced solemnity and flew back to L.A. as husband and wife. The newest Mr. and Mrs. Hughes were dropped off at her home on Strada Vecchia where they cohabited for exactly five days before Hughes returned with his wife to the Beverly Hills Hotel—separate bungalows please, Hughes in number four, Jean in Hughes' former bungalow, number nineteen. The aides occupied the cluster called Bungalow One—1-A was used strictly for storage of Hughes' stock of bottled water, Kleenex, and paper towels; 1-B housed a rotating group of drivers; and 1-C was for the cooks and waiters, Carl Romm, Charles Moran and Fernand Harvey.

Soon after the marriage, Jean reminded her new husband of his agreement, and shortly thereafter he dutifully took her to a rented house in Palm Springs where they were surrounded by guards as they walked the desert gardens, and watched the grapefruit grow. Hughes tried to cooperate, and do his part as a husband—not sexually, of course. Their relationship was built on shared interests, at least to Jean, since her husband really had no interests that weren't related to business or films or flying.

One day, as they walked hand-in-hand, Jean pointed to the sky and the fat, wondrous clouds that seemed to move across the yonder enveloping everything in their path like an archangel spiriting away a follower.

"Look," Jean said, sweeping her arms upward.

"A DC-4," Hughes said, missing the clouds but finding a pin-prick in the distance that was an ascending plane.

While the Hugheses were in the desert, Dietrich tackled the continuing challenge of Donald Nixon. Even with the infusion of cash, the Nixonburger was not destined for the culinary hall of fame and in February, 1957, Dietrich scheduled a meeting in the Romaine Street offices to see if anything could be done for Donald Nixon that might prevent his defaulting on the loan. While the meeting did not produce cogent results for Donald, it managed to achieve remarkable results for Howard. On March 1, 1957, soon after Vice-President Nixon was notified of Hughes' increasing efforts to assist Nixon's brother, the Howard Hughes Medical Institute was officially reclassified as a tax-exempt charity by the IRS, which mysteriously had reversed its earlier position.

When he heard the news, Hughes was back living in his bungalow, having given up on Palm Springs as being "too far from work," despite the fact that he did not have an office, and used the telephone for all his business transactions. Jean returned to the Beverly Hills Hotel, seeing her husband once a day, typically over dinner. Although he never told Jean about the IRS ruling—or discussed any other facet of his business with her, for that matter—within the shadows of confinement, Hughes' mood reflected his victory and translated into a request for a second scoop of vanilla ice cream that night at dinner: Hughes' version of a party.

On March 15, a small article in the *Los Angeles Herald & Express* revealed that "Howard Hughes and Jean Peters were married several days ago." The following day, larger pieces appeared in the *Hollywood Citizen-News* plus the *Los Angeles Mirror* headlined "Howard Hughes Weds Secretly." Gossip columnist Florabel Muir was credited with the exclusive, though in her article about the wedding, she incorrectly reported, "I happen to know they plighted their troth in an auto in a lovers lane atop the Santa Monica Mountains overlooking the twinkling lights of filmland" and said that the wedding occurred "three days ago" which would have pegged the date as March 12, 1957, three months after it actually had occurred.

Although there was no way that Florabel could have known, that date had an enormous significance to Hughes—far greater, as it happened, than his recent marriage. It was on that date that Hughes called Dietrich for an emergency meeting to discuss the TWA airplane financing debacle. Hughes' ready cash had covered the initial deposits on the jet orders, yet in another thirty days, he would need an additional $80 million to cover the next installment due Convair and Boeing. It was cash he did not have. While still arguably the richest man in America, Hughes' fluid cash was committed and profits at Hughes Tool were falling in a recessionary market.

Dietrich's command performance was aimed at developing an emergency plan to pump needed capital into the Hughes accounts. Despite the fact that Dietrich had not seen Hughes in person in nearly a year, and had functioned through telephone conversations relayed by Operations at Romaine Street, Dietrich expected that he would meet with Hughes in Bungalow Four. The financing problem was that severe, and its solution that important. Calling the bungalow from the hotel lobby, Dietrich was instructed to go to a meeting room next to the hotel's ballroom.

Subsequently, Dietrich was moved to two other meeting rooms, in what he later described as "CIA nonsense."

Hughes' insistence that the phone lines might be tapped or his instructions overheard was not enough to prompt the multimillionaire to see Dietrich face-to-face. As Dietrich sat waiting for the phone to ring in yet another meeting room, his thoughts moved back to Dr. Verne Mason, whose comments lingered in his mind, even as the phone rang.

No, Hughes would not see Dietrich in person; no, he would not discuss the cash crisis. What Hughes wanted for Dietrich was his promise to move once again to Houston to "inflate the Toolco profits." It was not a new scheme. Anytime Hughes found himself cash poor, he automatically placed more pressure on the tool division to supply it. Dietrich, now in his late sixties, was tired of jockeying himself about like an executive assistant, for he thought of himself as far more. To Dietrich, he *was* Hughes, at least to the point that profits were being made. He wanted to be a part of those profits; a partner as it were. He wanted what Hughes had so long promised to him: a capital gains agreement in writing.

When Hughes demanded that Dietrich move yet again to Houston, his executive said, "All right Howard. I'll go to Houston under one condition."

Hughes was frosty silence. He did not expect conditions to be part of any agreement. This was not, after all, a negotiation. This was an instruction. "What's that?" he asked after a moment.

Dietrich told him he wanted a capital gains understanding, "nothing fancy, just a one-page agreement. You can do it in long-hand."

"I don't like this, Noah," Hughes responded. "You're pushing me. Putting a gun to my head. Nobody puts a gun to my head."

And with that Dietrich was finished—with both the conversation and his career with Howard Hughes. After thirty-two years, the last words he would hear from Hughes' mouth were those he had coveted most of all: "Jesus, you can't mean that, Noah. I can't exist without you." Yet, somehow he managed.

Not two minutes after Dietrich had hung up the telephone, Hughes called Romaine Street and told Bill Gay to change the locks. At the time, Dietrich's salary was an incredible $500,000 a year (equivalent in today's market to $1,800,000), plus an *unlimited* expense account. He had come a long way from the young accountant who was making $10,000 a year to handle the books while his boss made movies. Yet, the impact on the two men could not have been more different. Dietrich was now free of the insanity; Hughes, trapped more than ever in the world he had created. It was a universe of shadows, of invisible threats, of imagined enemies, and paranoiac delusion. One in which he existed alone, even when others were in the room. And one from which he would not budge, for to do so would be to face reality.

FOURTEEN

To the Asylum Born

*The speed of the car should not exceed thirty-five
miles per hour at any time and then this speed should
be governed only by perfectly smooth roads. Ample
time should be allowed in order that this speed limit
be adhered to at all times. When crossing any bump,
dip, swale, ditch, railroad track or any uneven part
of any road, the speed should be reduced to such a
minimum speed that the car can move over the
uneven part of the road with no violent motion that
would tend to disturb the position of the party. (Two
miles per hour has been suggested as such a speed
going over rough or uneven roads).*

Beverly Hills, California
February 20, 1958
Hughes' written instructions to his drivers,
to prevent any unnecessary jarring of the
breasts of his starlets.

BUNGALOW FOUR AT THE BEVERLY HILLS HOTEL HAD NO
guard standing watch, no bars on the windows, and no locks.
Well, it actually *had* locks, they were just never used. The
door to the one-bedroom bungalow that housed the richest
man in America was open to anyone who cared to walk in.
No one ever did, of course, except for the select group of
aides, now six in number, who catered to Hughes' every
whim. They consisted of George Francom, a religious man
who spent his off-hours reading the Mormon Bible; Roy E.
Crawford, also a Mormon, who held a degree from the
College of Wooster in Wooster, Ohio, and had been a Navy
flight instructor during World War II; John Holmes, a
Catholic and chain-smoker, who once sold cigarettes for

P. Lorillard Company; plus Charles Woodcock, Norm Love, and Lloyd Hurley, former drivers who had been promoted to Hughes' personal aides.

After Hughes' marriage to Jean Peters, who the aides dubbed "The Major," their duties extended to her care and feeding as well. The same rules that applied to Hughes extended to Mrs. Hughes, with the exception of the use of Kleenex. Jean only used them when she had a head cold, while her husband's usage had now grown to twelve boxes a day, despite the fact that he had not had a cold for sixteen years.

If Howard Hughes qualified as America's most notorious eccentric (and he did), Jean Peters had to rank within the top ten among unique wives. During the remainder of 1957, she did not venture out of the confines of her bungalow at the hotel unless accompanied by an aide, and only then on rare occasions. Her husband had to be contacted before an order for an aide could be issued, and her husband did not return Jean's calls any quicker than he returned anyone else's. She spent most of her days knitting, sewing, or gardening—to the extent that one *could* garden in a hotel that had a staff of eight gardeners full time.

They never once went to a restaurant, a store, a library, or to visit her aunt or sister, or his Uncle Felix. Nor did they ever take a airplane ride or a yacht sail, as they often did in the Forties. She infrequently went with her husband to screen films at the Goldwyn studios. That was the extent of their nights on the town, during their entire first year of marriage. She seldom complained, and when she did, Jean always asked for the same thing: a home to share with her husband.

Hughes used his TWA financing dilemma as a perpetual excuse for his inability to relocate during February, March, and April. To any other businessman, the TWA situation would have been a major crisis. And, in fact, executives at Hughes Tool and TWA were considering it as such. Hughes, however, allowed entire weeks to go by without addressing the issue, let alone responding to the pleas of Carter Burgess, the one-time assistant secretary of defense under Eisenhower, who agreed to take over the presidency of the airline on the condition that Hughes *not* interfere. For once, the multimillionaire kept his promise, and went one step further. He did not even return a telephone call.

With the Boeing 707s about to roll off the assembly line, Carter Burgess left repeated messages at Operations to receive some guarantees from Hughes that the jets that TWA desperately needed would indeed be delivered. To Burgess' torment, not only did Hughes *not* return his calls, he had left the country with TWA's largest plane, a Constellation, and one of its pilots, Ted Moffitt, in addition to a TWA flight engineer. On May 22, 1957, Hughes walked out of his bungalow at the Beverly Hills

Hotel, without his wife, and was driven to the Burbank (California) Airport by John Holmes. There the two men were joined by aide Chuck Woodcock and Hughes' executive assistant Bill Gay.

With Noah Dietrich's departure from the organization, Gay, who only nine years earlier was no more than a temporary worker, was now effectively in charge of Hughes Inc. Since he controlled both the telephone operators and Hughes' aides, he was the conduit through which all other executives had to negotiate in order to reach the "Old Man," as Hughes was now called when out of ear-shot. Tall, thin and soft-spoken to the point of being milquetoast, Gay had not seen his boss in over a year. While he had aspirations of an expanded role in the Hughes empire, Gay was not about to accomplish that goal on this trip. As Hughes stepped on the plane, he announced to Gay that his sole purpose in Montreal was to "handle dictation," to the amusement of both Holmes and Woodcock, whose smiles were quickly snuffed by the withering glance Gay shot their way.

Hughes' alleged purpose for going to Montreal was to test fly two turbo-prop planes, the Vickers Viscount and the Bristol Britannia, presumably to add to the TWA inventory. And while he did fly both planes, it was only to take them on vacation hops across Canada, and with the aircraft companies picking up the bill for the fuel. For the remainder of the three months spent in Canada, Hughes remained sequestered within the hotel's Royal Suite, refusing to allow housekeeping access, as he set about laying Kleenex tissues across the antique Anatolian rugs. With Hughes in seclusion, his aides enjoyed *Le Jardin du Ritz*, the outdoor café with its manicured gardens and duck pond, cruises of the harbor, the villages of Estrie, near the Vermont border, and unlimited use of room service. While indulging in the use of a hotel sun lamp, Woodcock fell asleep and severely burned himself—albeit only on the backside of his body. Though unfortunate for Woodcock, the accident proved uniquely opportune for Holmes, who now was the sole aide on duty, and thus further ingratiated himself into Hughes' favor.

Holmes proved particularly useful in arranging for the clandestine appearance of Yvonne Shubert in Montreal, who, when questioning Hughes about his marriage to Jean Peters, was told that it was an "outrageous lie," "irresponsible journalism," "the penalty paid by the rich," and once again promised to marry Yvonne "when the time is right"— presumably when he was not otherwise occupied with a wife. As it happened, the current one remained in Beverly Hills, apparently none the wiser.

Jean Peters looked out the paned window of her bungalow at a noisy blue jay she had named Mrs. Porter for no apparent reason and laughed—the giddy, melodic laugh of a schoolgirl who has just shared a secret with a close friend. The blue jay, whose nest was in the ficus tree adjoining the walkway across from her window, had taken to attacking a brutish man with a barrel chest and shoulders thick enough to pull a plow. The mother jay, protecting her babies against the lout who dared to walk too close, was frantically dive-bombing the poor unsuspecting guest who had thrown up his arms to shield his face against the assault. When he heard Jean laugh, his face reddened, a crimson head on a too-large body, frightened away by a bird not eight inches long.

Jean was watering a gardenia plant that sat on the window sill. She was dressed in blue jeans, a blue and white checked shirt, and wore no shoes. It was hardly the look of a Hollywood star, but then she never thought of herself that way, in any case. She wore no makeup; never liked the fuss; nor missed that career that made her dress up to look like a person she never was. Jean longed for the simple life, and the farm she left in Canton, Ohio, where she could plaster walls and make furniture, grow corn, and watch the sun grow old.

Being the richest wife in America, as she was labeled in the press, brought with it an entirely unique sense of responsibility. There was the threat of kidnaping, but she really had not given it much thought. The bodyguards that waited outside 24 hours a day took some getting used to, particularly when all you wanted from life was a home, a garden, and a man. What she had achieved with her marriage to Hughes was a bungalow rented by the day, coffee cans with house plants, and a husband she left messages for who sometimes returned her call.

Jean was more tolerant than most—certainly most wives. When Hughes was gone for two days over two months and was neglecting to telephone for days at a time, she knew that tolerance had its place, just like anger. It was time for anger, she told herself, and placed a call to Operations that left little doubt that Mr. Hughes had better call Mrs. Hughes within the hour. Mr. Hughes did.

In response to her call, The Major was flown to Nassau, The Bahamas, where she joined her husband on August 2, 1957. Gay had booked the entire fifth floor of the Emerald Beach Hotel for Mr. and Mrs. Hughes, without ever mentioning their names. Again, housekeeping was not allowed to enter any of the rooms, with Hughes moving from one to another as he dirtied them. As he did, Jean remained cloistered in her own suite at the far end of the hall. She typically met her husband only for dinner, or during several test flights aboard the Constellation. It was more than she had seen of him for the past several months, so she did not complain—except, of course, about the width of the armrests on the Constellation, but then he had asked her what she thought. (She thought it was like riding with your arms in your lap, the seats were too narrow and the armrests as well. Hughes ordered every TWA plane refitted with wider seats and wider armrests that very day. Total cost: $1.8 million.)

Jean flew back to Los Angeles in September without her husband, who still refused to return to face the pressures of business. Los Angeles had become a joyless place. Every conversation centered on money; he could no longer bear to hear the talk. Nassau with its government run by the Bay Street Boys—corrupt of course, but quietly bought off because of it—was far easier to control. No one could get in or out without somebody knowing. *It's an island, for Christsake*, Hughes thought. Which is how it happened that the paranoid multimillionaire called upon Robert Maheu in mid-October to fly to Nassau immediately. The answer seemed so simple. Hughes would buy Nassau; and Maheu could make it happen.

As pretentious and illogical as the concept might seem, all it basically took was money. Maheu was used to greasing palms to expedite arrangements. Buying Nassau, or at least a sizable portion of the eighty square miles, was a challenge he readily accepted. Checking into the Emerald Beach Hotel in a suite on the fourth floor, Maheu began a dialogue with Hughes that began with talk of Nassau and ended with Maheu becoming Hughes' public persona, his alter ego to the world. It was heady stuff to the former FBI agent, who saw dollar signs and smelled the roses. He would later say, "Like good champagne, it can go right to your head. It went to mine."

Fortunately for Maheu, before he had the opportunity to get too drunk on power and appoint himself Crown Prince of an island on which Hughes would be King, he discovered that the timing of such a move could have been catastrophic. Nassau was undergoing major political unrest. There was a move afoot to sever ties with the British by the Black locals who wanted a larger role in leadership. There were rumors of a general strike that, if it took place, would have effectively made Hughes a prisoner on the island. In early December, 1957, at sunrise, Hughes left the fifth floor of the Emerald Beach Hotel, totally alone for the first time in months. He boarded the Constellation, and flew it by himself all the way to Los Angeles, landing later that day.

If Carter Burgess thought that the arrival of his company's airplane back in Los Angeles meant that it could reasonably be expected to return to active service, he was to be disappointed. Though Hughes no longer had a need for the plane, he kept the Connie if only to show Burgess, now eleven months on the job, that just because he was president of TWA did not mean he ran the company. In the course of a telephone conversation about TWA's financing, Burgess mentioned the Constellation and how desperate the airline was to use it during the Christmas travel season.

Desperate and *need* were two words that Hughes failed to apply in any part of his life, and turned the executive down. Burgess promptly quit,[1] leaving TWA again without a rudder as it as it navigated a sea of red ink and entered the most challenging months of its long history.

Hughes retreated back into his two-room asylum in which he controlled every moment of every day through a new outpouring of memos dictating procedure. As each memo was received by his aides, the pages were sent to the Romaine Street offices to be copied and placed into an ever-growing Operations Manual.

One such memo detailed the procedure to be used in the daily purchase of reading material. "The man on duty in Bungalow 1-D purchases the daily papers and magazines in the hotel drug store," the memo instructed, "and places them in a sterile box. When HRH calls for the papers, the man in 1-D will deliver the box with the papers, and holding them at a 45-degree angle, present them to HRH. The purchaser is to buy three copies of all editions of newspapers and magazines. HRH takes only the center copy of each." Upon receiving his paper, Hughes would carefully place it on top of a stack of similar papers from previous days, carefully lining up the edges. When one stack became perilously high, he moved on and began another. He did not, however, read the papers, for he determined that the newsprint that transferred to his hands contained the "germs of unknown handymen."

Jean was no longer allowed to share dinner with her husband. Hughes told his wife that while he "would love nothing better than to spend the entire evening with you, my work precludes such luxury." Exactly *what* work she never knew. Certainly, it was not arranging funding for the TWA jets, which still remained underfinanced.

To celebrate their first wedding anniversary, Jean and her husband traveled to a second floor screening room of the Goldwyn studios, where Hughes' projectionist, a patient and tolerant man named Carl, would dutifully run and rerun certain portions of films as the Old Man desired. It began a ritual which continued for months and involved a pair of aides who would arrive at the studio gates and transfer Hughes' white leather Barcalounger chair and ottoman up the exterior stairs and into the screening room, to be followed by yet another white chair, smaller in size, for Jean Peters. The exact position of the chairs never varied, and was marked on the screening room floor with white paint. Once the chairs were in position, a Chevrolet driven by John Holmes would enter the studio lot, carrying the Old Man and his wife. Not surprisingly, Hughes

1. Carter Burgess went on to become the United States Ambassador to Argentina. In his file was an FBI report in which Hughes, when asked for a recommendation, labeled Burgess, "the most honest man I know."

wore the same white shirt, tan slacks and brown oxfords that comprised his entire wardrobe. By way of contrast, Jean was dressed as if for a cocktail party, from designer dress to mink coat. It was, after all, their anniversary.

The winter of 1958 was one of the coldest on record in California, with overcast days and few glimpses of a sun too discouraged to make an appearance. The gray weather cast its mood on Hughes, who went without speaking for days on end, only to neurotically revert to childish behavior, running halfway down the newly-waxed floors of the hallways at the Goldwyn studio and then sliding to a stop.

As March pushed into April, Hughes sporadically began to screen films alone, leaving Jean mysteriously behind at the hotel. Eventually, all screenings at the Goldwyn studio came to an abrupt halt as suddenly as they had started, when Hughes discovered that during the day, while he was sleeping, producer Otto Preminger was using the room to screen the daily footage from the George Gershwin opera, *Porgy and Bess*, then filming at Goldwyn. When Hughes learned of the practice, he became physically nauseated,[2] upset that Blacks had been allowed in his screening room, "*my* screening room, for Christsake," and never entered the lot again.

Within days, he moved his screening ritual to a rundown private projection room on Sunset Boulevard not far from the Beverly Hills Hotel, and owned by one-time producer Martin Nosseck. It was located in a building that housed offices of producers and performers including Eddie Fisher, who at the time was at the height of his career and just beginning an ill-advised affair with the recently-widowed Elizabeth Taylor. The basement screening room was rather small and dank, yet accommodated Hughes' purpose as well as the two white chairs and one ottoman. It had a bathroom just big enough for a toilet and a sink, a lobby barely comfortable with its sofa and coffee table, and an editing room that was the size of a closet filled with a bay of equipment.

In between marathon movie screenings, and those days when he refused to pull himself out of bed, Hughes reluctantly handled his business dealings during moments of intense mental activity. These flashes of brilliance lasted from between ten minutes to two hours, never longer. Like a lone traveler caught in a blizzard, Hughes would occasionally reach a clearing and diligently utilize those moments of clarity. It was during one such burst of business activity that Hughes made the decision to hire Charles Thomas as the newest president of TWA. At the time, he was Eisenhower's secretary of the navy, and, when Hughes learned that

---

2. Hughes was not the only one to become sick over *Porgy and Bess*. The Gershwin family was so upset by the firing of original director Rouben Mamoulian that, immediately after its release, they withdrew all copies of the film. The only screening copy remaining is at the Library of Congress in Washington, D.C.

the well-seasoned executive was eager to leave government service, he began negotiations aimed at bringing Thomas aboard the struggling airline.

Hughes and Thomas had once played golf together during the period Hughes was married to Ella Rice. True, it was old history, but Hughes remembered, and when prompted, so too did Thomas. After several months of prodding, Thomas agreed to run the airline for a period of two years. "If, within that time, you're not completely satisfied with what I'm doing, all you have to do is say it and I'll get out," Thomas told Hughes. "At the end of the two years, Howard, neither you nor I have any commitment. We'll just see what happens." It was the type of deal both men appreciated, and in July, 1958, TWA had a new president.

Thomas was well aware of Hughes' tendency to interfere, and fully expected his boss to attempt to countermand his authority. He was quite amazed to find that in his first six months with TWA, he did not hear from Hughes at all. He would have been far more amazed to learn why.

In the middle part of July, Hughes was taken to Nosseck's for an evening screening, and at its conclusion announced to his aides that he was going to remain "for quite a spell." The aides, Norm Love, Lloyd Hurley, and head driver Ron Kistler, prepared for what they imagined would be a two or three-day stint, rotating their watches over the Old Man and observing his extraordinary behavior. When he was not otherwise occupied with the screening of a film, Hughes would spend hours arranging and rearranging his back-up boxes of Kleenex,[3] some dozen in number. They would be piled in a single row, then doubled, sometimes tripled, before being returned to single file like soldiers in a barracks standing at attention.

Every three days or so, John Holmes would make an appearance, carrying a brown paper bag containing what Hughes casually called his dinner. The delivery process never varied; nor, for that matter, did the contents of the bag. Two Hershey bars with almonds, a quart of homogenized milk, and one four-ounce cellophane bag of Laura Scudder's unsalted pecans. Holmes would stand directly in front of his employer without saying a word, tilt the bag at a 45 degree angle, and wait while Hughes removed each item from the bag, using a different piece of Kleenex for each item. The process of consuming the two Hershey bars, pecans and milk would take hours, as Hughes portioned off the chocolate into half-inch squares, chewing each square individually and completely, followed by a swallow of milk. Today, doctors would diagnose this eating ritual as a symptom of anorexia.

For the next five months, the process would be repeated just over

---

3. Hughes approved only one type of Kleenex: White, regular size, 400 count per box.

three dozen times, and amounted to the total food intake that Hughes received. The result of such of a diet had a drastic effect on the millionaire's already perilous health, causing his weight to drop dramatically and fainting spells to be recurrent. Constipation was another continuing consequence, causing Hughes to spend hours in the bathroom. According to the aides' notes, on September 18, 1958, he entered the bathroom at 3:30 p.m. and did not emerge until 6:45 the following evening—over 27 hours later.

He washed sporadically in the sink, using paper towels from the bathroom, and developed a stench that rivaled the Ganges on a warm summer night. His shirt and trousers stained, Hughes eventually asked Kistler to attempt to clean them, and when told that they were beyond saving, remarked, "But this is my favorite outfit," with the reverence normally accorded for the Shroud of Turin. When Kistler stood his ground, Hughes shrugged; said, "Very well then, if we can't clean them, we'll have to throw them away," and stripped naked, handing the aide his shirt and pants.

Kistler later wrote: "The man who owned seventy-eight percent of Trans World Airlines, the man who was in dire need of $250 million or so in cash to pay for jet planes, hadn't had a shave or haircut in God knows how many months. His gray-white beard fell six inches down on his chest and the hair on the back of his head was almost to his shoulders. There was only one thing that could be called impressive about Hughes at that moment: sexually, he was very well endowed."

Summer moved into fall into winter, all unseen by a man who kept his physical location a secret even from his wife. To explain his lengthy absence, Hughes created a phony illness and told Jean Peters that he had been hospitalized, giving his aides the nicknames Nurse Sarah (who took blood pressure readings), Nurse Grace (handled intravenous feedings), and Nurse Hannah (supposedly into enemas). He refused to allow her to see him, citing the dramatic change in his appearance. That much, at least, was true.

His normal weight, an already slight 155 pounds, had dropped to just under 100, on a frame that, even stooped, measured 6'3". Naked, his white-on-white skin hung in folds like the neck of an old bulldog. Every day, he grew weaker, thinner, and more delicate. He resembled a specter from a nightmare, unshaven, and reproachful.

As if sensing his own demise, Hughes finally left his self-imposed isolation after five months and twenty-two days, returning not to the world of the living, but rather to one of more shadows. His arrival back at Bungalow Four at the Beverly Hills Hotel went unnoticed, except by his cook, waiters, and aides. The fact that he had exchanged one tomb for another was accepted by his employees, who had grown complacent with his world and learned to question nothing. By doing so, they gave Hughes the ability to operate outside the rules of society, and, by default, the laws of the land.

He refused to see Jean Peters, alluding to his mysterious recent illness and his weight loss. Although she was less than one hundred yards away and walked past his door almost daily on her way to the hotel's restaurant, Jean deferred to her husband's wishes and did not intrude into his world. Instead, she continued to speak of buying a home on a hilltop, of raising vegetables and flowers, and wrote that she wanted to "throw open every window to allow the air and sun to bless us."

Hughes crumbled at the thought. Air and light were now his enemies. They carried germs and allowed a visibility that he could not risk. He was a simulacrum of the husband she thought she had married. The hero aviator, the strutting playboy, the little boy who needed to be mothered. He needed to hide and took to disappearing inside himself, only emerging at infrequent moments when his mind snapped back into the present and attempted to return long over-due messages.

For the remainder of the time, most of the time really, he lay on soiled sheets in a black room that buried his reality behind the cover of darkness. He was so constipated that waste hardened in a twisted colon, causing piercing abdominal cramps. He urinated at will on the walls and floor of the bathroom, unwilling to focus long enough to target the toilet. He refused to wash and refused to dress, while ordering movies screened in marathon sessions that often ran longer than forty-eight hours without a break.

He was a clock that was gaining time, ticking faster than his confused mind could comprehend, wound too tight and moving too slow for organized thought or speech. Fear of contamination was always hanging, forever suspended, levitated before his mind's eye, and forcing him to produce a bumper crop of memoranda to Operations—some 142 sets of instructions produced in long-hand over the course of three months. Among them was this set of instructions for the proper way to open a can of fruit:

> The following procedures and steps are to be followed, in every detail, in the preparation of fruit to be used on any cakes, pies, or desserts of any kind for HRH. This work will be done in Bungalow 1-C.
>
> These procedures will only be carried out in the event that the cans of peaches, apples, figs, etc. are obtained from the Beverly Hills Hotel storeroom, or from any grocery store where the handling of such cans is not or cannot be followed in accordance with HRH's instructions on same, with regard to sterility.

The equipment used in connection with this operation will consist of the following items: 1 unopened newspaper; 1 sterile can opener; 1 large sterile plate; 1 sterile fork; 1 sterile spoon; 2 sterile brushes; 2 bars of soap; sterile paper towels.

STEP #1: Preparation of Table. An unopened newspaper will be opened in the middle of the paper to its full size (double page), and placed on top of the table in Bungalow 1-C. This newspaper may be one of the papers purchased from the hotel drug store that are rejects from HRH's supply. Under no circumstances is this paper to be handled again until the can opening operation has been completed.

STEP #2: Procuring of Fruit Can. The man designated to do this job goes to the hotel storeroom and picks up the can of fruit desired. In so doing, he must be very careful in not touching the bottom of the can, and in not touching any surface within two inches of the bottom of the can, at any time. He should grasp the can in the center, preferably with his hand around the center of the label. He then carries the can of fruit back to 1-C. If this fruit is packed in a jar, instead of a can, the same handling and carrying instructions apply.

STEP #3: Washing of Can. The man in charge then turns the valve in the bathtub on, using his bare hands to do so. He also adjusts the water temperature so that it is not too hot nor too cold. He then takes one of the brushes, and, using one of the bars of soap, creates a good lather, and then scrubs the can from a point two inches below the top of the can. He should first soak and remove the label, and then brush this cylindrical part of the can over and over until all particles of dust, pieces of the paper label, and, in general, all sources of contamination have been removed. Holding the can in the center at all times, he then processes the bottom of the can in the same manner, being very sure that the bristles of the brush have thoroughly cleaned all the small indentations on the perimeter of the bottom of the can. He then rinses the soap from the cylindrical sides and the bottom of the can. Taking the second brush, and still holding the can in the center, he again creates a good lather and scrubs the top of the can, the perimeter along the top, and the cylindrical sides to a point two or three inches below the top of the can. He must be very careful in this part of the operation in not only seeing to it that the crevices along the perimeter are thoroughly cleaned, but he must not press so hard in scrubbing the top that he would "oil can" it, thus causing the can to fracture in any way. He should continue this scrubbing until he literally removes the tin protection from the can itself. After the man is certain that he has completely scrubbed and cleaned the entire surfaces and cracks of the perimeter rim, he should rinse the soap from the can.

STEP #4: Drying the Can. The can should then be dried thoroughly. This is best accomplished by using six thicknesses of paper towels (not five or seven). These are obtained from the sterile towel dispenser located on the wall of the bathroom in 1-C. Please be sure that the entire surfaces of the top and the bottom of the can, as well as the cylindrical sides of the can, and also the crevices and cracks on the perimeter of the top, are carefully handled while drying, so as not to allow the fingers to break through the towels, thereby touching the can. Also, be very careful not to allow any portion of the towels to come into contact with any part of the clothes, body, furniture in the room, table, etc. The can is then placed on the table.

STEP #5: Processing the Hands. The man next processes his hands thoroughly. This action will consist of washing and rinsing the hands four distinct and separate times, being extremely careful to observe the four phases in each washing. That is to say, the man must first brush every minute particle and surface of his hands and fingers. He then puts each finger tip into the palm of the opposite hand and leans each finger by rotating and pressing the fingers against the palm. He then interlocks the fingers and slides them together, and back and forth, scrubbing them all the time. The last phase is grasping the palms together and wringing and rotating the palms together, and also by washing the back of the hand with the palm of the opposite hand. The four phases of this washing operation should be done while the hands are lathered. The hands should then be rinsed thoroughly and then the complete operation should be performed three more times, making a total of four complete washings and rinsings. The hands are then dried by using the sterile paper towels provided for this purpose. After the hands are dry, the man then takes six thicknesses of dry paper towels (not five or seven), and turns the water valve off. He must be extremely careful in not touching anything else whatsoever that would contaminate his hands and force him to begin the process all over again.

STEP #6: Opening the Can. Returning again to the table, the man takes the sterile can opener, and, holding the can in the cylindrical area between the two-inch limitations of the top and the bottom, opens the can of fruit.

STEP #7: Removing Fruit from Can. This step in the operation is extremely important, as under no circumstances does HRH want any contact between the fruit itself and the outside of the metal can. In spearing peaches or whatever fruit is being used, under no circumstances should the fork itself touch any part of the can whatsoever. In removing fruit from the can to the sterile plate, please be sure that the fruit is not pressed or pushed into the side or the bottom of the can while spearing. This part of the job should be done very slowly and gently, so as to keep the fruit from accidentally brushing against the inside of the can. The man may use his sterile spoon to lift the fruit out of the can if this will prevent any further contact between the fruit and the inside of the can.

STEP #8: Fallout Rules While Around Can. While transferring the fruit from the can to the sterile plate, please observe the fallout rules as closely as possible. That is, be very sure that no part of the body, including the hands, be directly over the can or the plate at any time. If possible, keep the hand, upper part of the body, arms, etc. at least one foot away from the can of fruit and the sterile plate at all times.

STEP #9: Conclusion of Operation. The fruit is then carried directly to the bakery shop and given to the baker responsible for baking the cake. There must be absolutely no talking, coughing, clearing of the throat, or any movement whatsoever of the lips en route from 1-C to the bakery. There must also be no discussion with the baker in any way. In other words, the fruit is just handed to the baker without any words being spoken or signs with the hands exchanged at all. Then the man returns and discards the remains of the can of fruit, and also the newspaper underneath the can. This completes the operation.

HRH requests that this operation be carried out in every infinitesimal detail, and would deeply appreciate it if the man be as careful and diligent as he possibly can be, and follow each phase very slowly and thoughtfully, giving his full attention to the importance of the work at hand.

HUGHES WROTE MEMOS dictating the correct procedure to lift a toilet seat, hang a towel, open a door, close a door, enter a room, remove a bug, answer a telephone, take a message, and dozens of other tasks, including a four-page memo dedicated to the art of speaking without moving one's lips. What makes these memos all the more compelling is not the mere fact that they were written, but rather that they were followed—exactly and without question. In this asylum, the patient dictated correct performance to the caregivers, who never once examined the instructions in light of their absurdity, for to do so would have accomplished only one thing—their immediate firing.

Into this obscure world walked Robert Maheu in the spring of 1959, assuming that he would be carrying out the directives of the astute if mysterious businessman who had built an empire second to none in America. In one way, Maheu was lucky. He insisted that he remain an independent contractor, hired by Hughes through his Robert A. Maheu Associates.

He demanded and received a large home in Bel Air, a maid to keep it clean, two Cadillac convertibles (one for him, the other for his wife Yvette), and a $200,000 retainer. For that money, he was not required to scrub fruit cans or even wash his hands if he did not care to. He merely had to perform miracles, and as Maheu would later remember, "He seemed to expect them with increasing frequency."

First among Maheu's assignments was to attempt to contain an overtly feisty Yvonne Shubert, known as "The Party," who was becoming increasingly irate over being held a virtual prisoner in her Hughes-rented home. She had called Operations and demanded to speak to Hughes, threatening to barge into his bungalow if she did not. In the four years that Yvonne had been under Hughes' rule, she had turned from a naive fifteen-year-old into a beautiful, foul-mouthed woman who was used to getting her way.

When Hughes deemed it necessary to call Yvonne, the resulting conversation was overheard on Hughes' amplifying system by Ron Kistler, who later wrote about the tirade as blunt and aggressive:

> YVONNE: "You tell those fucking assholes in Operations that when I call and tell them to do something I want it done that same fucking minute."
> HUGHES: "Well, honey. . . "
> YVONNE: "Don't you honey me, you old bastard. I'm sick and tired of being a fucking prisoner in this fucking house and I'm leaving."

THE CONVERSATION CONTINUED that way for several minutes before The Party slammed down the receiver. While peace was eventually brought to bear that evening, it was not to last, culminating with Yvonne paying a two a.m. visit to Hughes' bungalow, accompanied by a man with a .38, tucked in his belt. She reached the door just as Kistler was arriving, and the resulting standoff ended in a draw. Yvonne and friend went away unhappy; Hughes, thereafter, stationed a guard at his door round-the-clock.

Hughes instructed Maheu to learn the identity of the thug and eliminate the unpleasantness from the picture. Locating the man was not a problem, for he had become Yvonne's live-in lover. Removing him was apt to be more of a problem since the guy was a tough, ex-Marine—long on muscle, short on brains. As it turned out, that feature worked in Maheu's favor when the man went with Yvonne to a firing range in Long Beach, California, to practice using his .38. While doing some target shooting, the gun misfired. Not the brightest of men, the guy turned the pistol around to look into the barrel, at which point the gun went off, with the bullet making a beeline between the man's eyes.

Yvonne was hysterical at the sight of her fatally-wounded boyfriend lying at her feet. It was certainly one way to put her in her place, and Hughes thrilled at the intrigue of it all, refusing to believe that Maheu was not responsible. "I knew you were good, Bob. But I didn't know you were *that* good," Hughes told Maheu when he called with the news. Hughes showed no concern for the shattered Yvonne, but rather wanted Maheu's reassurance that "the hit," as he called it, could not be traced back to him. Since Maheu was not involved, it was safe to say it could not, and the accident served to cement Maheu's place in the Hughes hierarchy at the very top.

June 9, 1959. Hughes placed a call to Bill Gay and reported that The Party "had been terminated." Subsequently, Gay wrote a memo to all staff at Operations that should Yvonne telephone, she was to be treated "as a total stranger."

> This instruction applies to Lieber, Bautzer, Cashman, Vinson, Kay Glenn, Paul Winn, Lloyd Hurley, Chuck Waldron, Bob Taylor, Walter Kane, Ed Marr,[4] plus anyone else who has had any contact with her, either in person or by telephone, or in any way whatsoever. In other words, if she calls Operations, we are not to recognize her voice or her name—not be rude, either—but treat her as we do any of the strangers who call here each day.

HUGHES SUBSEQUENTLY ARRANGED to have Yvonne's apartment burglarized on October 3, 1959, to retrieve jewelry he had given her over the course of their relationship. Among the items taken: a 14-carat gold and diamond bracelet, a 14-carat gold necklace with a gold and diamond clasp, an 18-carat gold necklace with ten diamonds and twenty emeralds, and a Ceylon sapphire gold link bracelet. The total value of the heist was reported to be $31,530, according to FBI file 62-101375-39.

Hughes continued his brief periods of lucidity countered by ever-increasing stretches of obsessive-compulsive behavior, that now had extended to cleaning the cord on the telephone before he would use it to answer calls. The cleaning procedure varied in intensity, depending on the state of Hughes' mind, culminating in a two-hour procedure that used eighty-four Kleenexes and a cup of boiled water.

As Hughes spent his hours cleaning bits from the accumulating filth that surrounded him, Charles Thomas began to accept delivery of the first Boeing 707s for use by TWA. Travelers suddenly flocked to the airline, as much to try out the new equipment as to reach a destination and

---

4. Various aides, lawyers and staff who worked for Hughes.

TWA experienced a period of enormous prosperity as a result. To pay for the planes, a financing plan was conceived by the investment banking house of Dillon, Read that called for a consortium of banks and insurance companies to lend TWA $168.8 million. Their one condition: that the management of the airline remain in place. To the amazement of practically everyone, Hughes telephoned his approval of the deal during a March, 1960, TWA board meeting, and it appeared that the Old Man's biggest problem for the past four years was finally solved. Certainly, Dillon, Read believed it, as did Equitable Life Assurance Society of America and Metropolitan Life Insurance Company, plus the six banks helping to fund the loan. All of them succumbed to business logic without factoring into the equation that unknown quantity called Hughes.

At the beginning of July, just weeks before the loan was to be transferred, Charles Thomas alerted Hughes that his two-year agreement to remain at the helm of TWA was nearly concluded. During his tenure at the company, the airline had been transformed. It was making a profit for the first time in four years, and the investment community was looking upon the transportation giant with renewed interest. Thomas advised Hughes that he would happily stay on in his current position if Hughes would grant him a stock option in the company in order to offset his taxes. As he had done repeatedly in the past, Hughes balked at sharing even the smallest percentage of his profits with anyone. That history extended to Thomas. As with Noah Dietrich before him, Thomas threatened to quit, and Hughes used his "gun to my head" logic. Two days before Hughes' emergency loan was to close, Thomas announced to the world that he had left his position with TWA to join the Irvine Company in Orange County, California. The lenders exercised their "change in management clause option" and stopped the transfer of funds.

Hughes faced this crisis with the aplomb of Sleeping Beauty pricking her finger on a spindle: he fell into a deep trance from which he did not stir for sixty-two hours. When he next picked up a telephone, it was not to deal with the TWA emergency, but to call Operations to alert them that his bungalow was "uncomfortably pungent" and blamed them for allowing it to deteriorate to a level of near condemnation. He moved himself out of Bungalow Four and into room 395 of the Beverly Hills Hotel, to allow for his former rooms to be cleaned and fumigated.

The stench that met the crew from the privately contracted Emil's Cleaning Service was beyond anything the firm had ever encountered in its twenty-eight years of operation. The bathroom alone required two men working for eighteen hours over three days to completely clean and disinfect. The carpeting had to be shampooed a total of four times to

remove years of grime, after forty-nine cartons of "newspapers, magazines, and other flammable material" were removed from the bungalow.

His new asylum resembled the old in that it had been completely
blacked out before Hughes moved his white Barcalounger and ottoman
and took up official residence. The only move Hughes made to contain
his growing financial drama was to place a call to Robert Maheu and
order him to check out other sources of generating cash. It was a last-
ditch effort that would generate a sixty-page report that condensed
Maheu's findings. What Hughes' alter ego determined and conveyed
back to the Old Man was that all other airlines were, in fact, being offered
more favorable terms than TWA. It was apparent that Hughes was being
singled out by the East Coast financial institutions. It was payback time
for years of abusive treatment on the part of Hughes, and the glee the
banks and insurance companies took was increasingly evident as dozens
of Hughes-ordered jets sat idle on the tarmacs of Boeing and Convair.

With no options remaining, his back again at a very hot wall, Hughes
had no choice but to accept the Dillon, Read plan, complete with its
requirement that he place his TWA stock in trust immediately, transferring
his voting rights to the senior lenders until such a time as his debt was
repaid—a period of ten years. In the ultimate game of Benching the Boss,
Howard Hughes lost control of the airline he loved on December 15,
1960. The capitalist wraith had apparently finally run out of luck. The
financial journals were writing him off as insolvent, an opinion shared by
Noah Dietrich, who had filed suit to be paid the million dollars Hughes
had orally promised him in 1956. Having smoldered against convention
for so long that he viewed this latest turn of events with indifference,
Hughes' only concern was not his ability to pay his bills, but rather the
perception of the public regarding his ability to reinvent himself.

That he was still a popular subject of conjecture and opinion could
not be denied. There was a certain hush that fell across the land when the
news of the TWA loss was announced; a perceptible longing for a
Phoenix to rise from the ashes. It was a world stage set for triumph or
defeat on the most spectacular level, and it was a challenge that the amazing
Mr. Hughes was only too ready to accept, in a performance that even he
could not have predicted.

FIFTEEN

Hey! Ba-Ba-Re-Bop

*I have been notorious through the years for
conducting all my business orally, usually by
telephone. I am sure you have heard of this
characteristic. When I started sending you long
hand notes, my people protested long and loud.
They wanted to retype my messages at least, and
correct mistakes in composition, and spelling, etc.
I said no, that there was not time, and that I
would ask you to return the messages so they
would not get out of my hands in that condition.*

> Las Vegas, Nevada
> December 4, 1966
>> Hughes' note to Robert Maheu explaining
>> his need to keep his handwritten
>> documents secured.

RANCHO SANTA FE IS A SUBURB OF SAN DIEGO, CALIFORNIA, a bedroom community of large estates and old money into which Howard Hughes hoped to disappear. There, among the tall eucalyptus trees planted for use as rail ties by the Santa Fe Railroad, was a heavily-wooded compound that Hughes acquired in late 1960. Jean Peters was so excited by the prospect of moving into her own home after years of hotel living that she forgave her husband all the false starts and empty promises of the past.

On December 24, 1960, in celebration of what Hughes said was his fifty-fifth birthday, he got behind the wheel of Jean's limousine and drove for the first time in four years. His personal driver, John Holmes, packed the trunk with luggage and then made himself comfortable in the large back seat for the two-hour ride along the Pacific Coast

Highway. His wife, looking poised and proper in the front passenger seat, was fleetingly uneasy, as her husband jerked the car into motion and down a side street of Beverly Hills before turning onto Sunset Boulevard.

Jean was unaware that she had a cake to thank for the move. A pineapple upside-down cake to be precise. Hughes often had cake with his dinner, and for years followed the same procedure with his order. A call to his waiters a half-hour before he wanted to eat, the coded knock on the front door, the entrance of the tray containing his meal, followed by the delivery of his dessert—usually ice cream, sometimes cake.

On one particularly night several weeks earlier, Hughes felt like a change. He wanted a pineapple upside-down cake with his dinner, and placed his order accordingly. When the meal was delivered, he picked over his steak and peas, allowed his glass of milk to warm, all the while anticipating his first bite of cake, gooey with the thick sweetness of pineapple. When the cake was delivered, sectioned into an ample square occupying a good portion of a dessert plate, Hughes used his sterile fork and cut into the treat with overt glee. He was just beginning to enjoy the taste when he noticed the edge of the bill peeking from underneath the plate. *P. upside-down cake Special order Hughes $3.75.*

Hughes immediately spit out the cake on the pink linen table cloth and took a extended look at the words on the slip. *$3.75 for cake was absurd*, Hughes thought, and a two dollar and twenty-five cent premium over his normal $1.50 price for a piece of cake. Milliseconds later, an outraged Hughes was on the telephone to the front desk, lodging a complaint. There *had* to have a been a mistake, he stressed.

The clerk apologized profusely and offered to track down the source of the problem. Hughes, never one to appreciate excuses, insisted on speaking to Ben L. Silberstein, the hotel's owner. By the time Silberstein was located and a call placed to Hughes, the Old Man was in such a lather that he had telephoned Operations, telephoned Bill Gay, telephoned Robert Maheu, and telephoned his wife. As Silberstein's daughter, Muriel Slatkin, remembers the incident, her father pronounced the charge not only correct, but reasonable. "We had to race around downtown to get all the ingredients," Silberstein informed his disgruntled guest, but said he was only too happy to absorb the cost. It was *not* what America's richest man wanted to hear.

At that point in time, Hughes had been a resident of the Beverly Hills Hotel for thirteen years, and had rented between two and eight bungalows and as many as ten rooms—all charged at a daily rate. He neither asked for nor received a penny discount. His discovery that he had been overcharged two dollars and twenty-five cents gnawed at his patience until it ripped. Hughes told Silberstein to come and pick up his cake, he no longer wanted it—nor any of his rooms and bungalows for that matter. Hughes and company were leaving.

Silberstein tried cajoling, offering Hughes the *entire* cake for free. He tried complimenting, telling Hughes how clever he was to notice the increase. All to no use. Hughes, the ultimate game-player, would have none of it. And notified his staff to find him a house, same state, different city.

After Hughes' departure, Bungalows Four and Nineteen at the Beverly Hills Hotel were locked by his aides, and became time capsules, of sorts. For the next seven years, Hughes continued to pay for five bungalows and four rooms—still at a daily rate, kept his Chevrolets parked in the hotel garage, and maintained his private staff, at full wages. Hotel guests still pointed to his bungalow, believing America's richest man was still in residence, and the hotel did nothing to discourage the rumors, for indeed, not even Ben Silberstein knew for certain.

Meanwhile, in Rancho Sante Fe, Mr. and Mrs. Howard Hughes began what Jean hoped would be their new life of connubial bliss. Although they officially shared a bedroom, Hughes often kept to himself in a smaller room down the hall, furnished with a twin bed, night stand, the torchiere from Muirfield Road, and a bay of three telephones and amplifiers to help compensate for Hughes' still-deteriorating hearing. Hughes had the windows locked, sealed and blacked-out with drapes, in marked contrast to the master suite.

There, Jean had a queen size bed, a dressing room with vanity, a master bath with walled-in shower, a toilet and bidet. A fresh air fanatic, she flung wide the windows, allowing the cool night air to stimulate her sleep. The fact that her husband was horrified by the practice did not deter the single-minded woman, who fully expected to convince Hughes of the foolishness of his ways.

Jean was not alone in her resolve to win over her husband. She had the help of Nefertiti[1] and Foony, Jean's black cat and Weimaraner dog. Despite his choice to never own a pet, Hughes was nevertheless a lover of all animals and worried about Jean's two pets incessantly. Nefer, as the cat was called, had a way of sneaking into Hughes' room and leaping onto the bed as he slept during the day, initially sending the recluse into fits of disinfecting with Kleenex in hand, the most obvious result of which was an entirely new set of written procedures to be added to the growing Operations Manual. For his part, Foony had developed the custom of greeting Hughes with an energetic tongue bath, an equally appalling experience, but one that he eventually grew to tolerate, if not like.

---

1. Nefertiti was named after the queen of Egypt and wife of King Akhenaton (reigned 1353-1336 B.C.).

Jean maintained an open-door policy with her animals, allowing them to run freely across the Hughes estate. After Foony developed a particular fondness for Jean's compost pile in the back yard, Hughes instructed his staff to construct a run for the dog, surrounded by chain-link fencing. Nefer was not about to be so easily contained, and paid the price when she found herself "with child," as Jean politely said. The mother cat commandeered a corner of the garage for her maternity, and gave birth to three healthy kittens of mixed and unknown origin several weeks later.

While Jean busied herself in her newly-planted flower garden, her husband continued to deal with the aftermath of the TWA decision, as well as the results of the recent Presidential election that found a Kennedy in the White House. While history had laid the close election to Richard Nixon's performance in the first televised Presidential debates, Hughes played a major part in his defeat as well. Shortly before the November, 1960, election, Washington columnist Drew Pearson revealed the details of the loan Hughes had made to Nixon's brother Donald, as well as the apparent favors that Hughes' various businesses received as a result. Nixon's major blunder occurred when he denied the loans were Hughes-funded. Caught in a lie thanks to Pearson's dogged reporting, Nixon's bid for the Oval Office suffered critical damage, and his defeat caught Hughes lagging in the game of political palm greasing.

Since Hughes had been certain that *his* candidate Nixon would be rendered victorious, he had failed to ingratiate himself with the Kennedy campaign. Part of his reluctance was a deep-seated dislike for the Kennedy family that dated back to the days when paterfamilias Joseph Kennedy romanced Billie Dove, among other actresses. The fact that Dove was living with Hughes at the time was the genesis of the problem. It did not matter that Hughes ultimately got the girl. The slight stoked in the mind of the romantic ruminant for thirty years, as his fury grew. It was therefore with the kind of two-faced sincerity that only a true entrepreneur could deliver that Hughes decided to make a splash at the Kennedy inaugural, buying four $10,000 box seats at the swearing-in ceremony, and paying for the tickets by supplying a TWA jet to provide round-trip transportation for the entertainers and VIPs.

Bob Maheu, finding great relish in his role as Hughes' new alter ego, coordinated the trip and joined a planeload of celebrities reduced to tears at the humorous antics of a very "on" Milton Berle, who knew a captive audience when he saw one. Ditto the entire thirty pieces of the Nelson Riddle Orchestra that performed in flight.

While Hughes stayed locked inside an airless room in Rancho Santa Fe listening to a cat attempting to invade his sanctum sanctorum, Maheu hosted a pre-gala dinner at Washington's swank La Salle du Bois, and then traveled directly on to Miami to handle an assignment that was not on the Hughes docket. His Robert A. Maheu Associates still had many other clients at the time, among them the United Steel Workers, Westinghouse, and the Central Intelligence Agency. It was the CIA that caused Maheu's appearance in Miami, to act as an internuncio between the CIA (called the Company) and the Mafia (called Sam Giancana). In a five-room suite at the Fontainebleau Hotel, Maheu and Giancana laid the groundwork to carry out a plan conceived by the Company to assassinate Fidel Castro. The operation ultimately became known as the Bay of Pigs and found its own place in history.

With Maheu otherwise preoccupied, Hughes found himself without a front man, and in need to vent new frustration over TWA. The fresh batch of trustees now running the airline had sent Hughes notification that they would not need the Convair 880s he had ordered to be manufactured, and had planned on leasing to TWA. Instead, the trustees had initiated their own negotiations with Boeing for an outright purchase of 707s.

Unable to digest his swallowed pride, Hughes had his attorneys send a letter to the Securities and Exchange Commission declaring that the airline's new trustees were "disregarding the best interests of TWA stockholders." The veiled threat was made all the more laughable by a $115 million antitrust lawsuit TWA filed in its wake, charging Hughes with forcing the airline to lease all its jets from Hughes Tool, thus requiring TWA to effectively boycott all other potential suppliers in restraint of trade. Upon hearing of the suit, steam rose off the Old Man like a bad smell.

Hughes' initial thought was to settle the suit out of court, and with that intent he sought advice from Floyd Odlum, the millionaire financier from Hughes' RKO days, and in whose Atlas Corporation Hughes owned eleven percent of the stock.[2] Odlum, in turn, recommended Chester A. Davis, a heavy-drinking, street-wise senior partner with the Wall Street law firm of Simpson, Thacher & Bartlett. Davis was the legal equivalent of a pit bull, ready to tear at the throat and advised against any thought of settlement, lest it imply some guilt on Hughes' part. While an extended fight frightened Hughes to the point that he thought it might "consume the biggest part of the remainder of my productive life," his reputation was never that of a quitter. When common sense is at the mercy of pride, there is usually no contest. In this case, Hughes' ego refused to permit TWA to dictate policy to him. On August 6, 1961, he relayed instructions to Chester Davis to formally fight the anti-trust, and in so doing began the longest running and most studied antitrust case in legal history.

---

2. Hughes received the stock as part of his sale of RKO.

As the legal volleying began to gain momentum, Hughes unloaded the Convair 880 jets that TWA rejected by selling them to Northeast Airlines, a struggling regional carrier controlled by Floyd Odlum's Atlas Corp. Hughes also entered into negotiations with Odlum in an effort to buy his Northeast stock, a move that brought him into direct conflict once again with the Civil Aeronautics Board (CAB), which, after seeing what Hughes had managed to do to TWA, was not eager to give him control of yet another U.S. carrier.

Throughout the intense activity that surrounded the posturing and allegations connected with both battles, Jean Peters was playing the most demanding role of her career—suburban housewife. Needing the extra room offered by the master suite, Hughes had taken to living full time on his side of their bed. Jean attempted to ignore the aides who kneeled next to the mattress taking dictation as she tried to sleep, and the constant ringing of phones delivering the most urgent of messages from Operations, which continued to act as intermediary, even with Hughes' attorneys.

Unknown to Hughes, Bill Gay had moved his own offices out of the Romaine Street building and into a rented space at 17000 Ventura Boulevard in Encino, California, not far from his home. He had brought with him a band of loyal Mormon followers, originally hired as drivers, and now serving in various administrative positions within the company. It was the first indication that Gay was operating under his own agenda, and a silent prophesy of things to come.

With Hughes concentrating on his legal woes with TWA, and Hughes Tool vice-president and chief financial officer Raymond M. Holliday attempting to keep the Tools Division from sinking under the weight, Hughes Aircraft Corp. was flourishing. Since Hughes Medical Institute took over legal responsibility for the Aircraft Division, the Old Man remained unusually detached from its business. As a result, its president, Laurence A. (Pat) Hyland, was given the kind of autonomy that all other executives within the Hughes empire could only envy. As no small result of the company's ability to control its own destiny, its profits were extraordinary. Contracts with the military totaled $349 million at the start of the decade, with Hughes Aircraft awarded new deals to build the first submarine-launched Polaris missiles as well as to design and build the first stationary communications satellite to be launched for the National Aeronautics and Space Administration (NASA). Ironically, Hughes heard about both contracts, worth over $30 million, on television.

Until his move to Rancho Santa Fe, Hughes thought television screens emitted harmful radiation and refused to allow a set in any room.

Jean Peters, who was addicted to the daytime soap operas, insisted on having a TV in their bedroom. Once exposed to the small screen, Hughes kept it on round-the-clock, even if the volume was muted, and joined his wife in watching *The Guiding Light*, set in the mythical town of Springfield.

It was during an episode of *The Guiding Light* that a local sheriff came to the Rancho Santa Fe property attempting to serve a subpoena, ironically not on Hughes, but on the owner of the property, who was being sued by a former employee. The aide on duty, Alan Stroud, happened to mention the incident later in the day to Hughes' wife, in the course of conversation. It was a move he would come to regret.

Upon hearing the news, Jean turned various shades of red and was approaching plum by the time she burst into the master suite, ordered aide Roy Crawford out of the room, and confronted her husband. He had told her that *he* owned the house. To now find that she was living in a house that was just another rented property in a long string of rented properties infuriated Jean, who felt manipulated and deceived. Jean was not by nature a fighter and her rage startled Hughes, who hated confrontations of any kind. Any other time, he might have tried to make up an excuse. Now, he just asked, "Would you rather be in a hotel?" and, without waiting for an answer, went back to work.

In September, 1961, two events of import dramatically affected Hughes' world. First, the plumbing in the house in Rancho Santa Fe stopped up and required that the subflooring be removed to repair the problem. Then, Robert Maheu agreed to give up his other clients, move permanently to California, and become Hughes' full-time front man. The effect of the former was yet another move to yet another rented house, this one high on a hill in Bel Air. As for Maheu, his arrival as a permanent fixture on the scene gave Hughes a sense of surety he had not felt since he circled the globe in his Lockheed. He liked Maheu's confidence that all jobs could be accomplished; and he did not balk at his demand for half a million dollars in annual compensation for his efforts in addition to the requisite Cadillac convertibles.

Hughes' house at 1001 Bel Air Road was of French Regency design, oversized, beautifully landscaped, with an enormous iron fence that secured the property and tall hedges that obscured it from view. It was into that palace that Hughes relocated into a room pre-prepared for his arrival. In the window was an air-conditioner with removable filter to scour the air for any trace of impurity; the now-customary black-out drapes to prevent even a slip of light from gaining entrance; a double bed, an end table, 19" color television, Hughes' white leather Barcalounger and ottoman, plus two occasional chairs for the aides' use. He was driven onto the property on Thanksgiving Day, 1961, hidden on the floor in the back of an old Chevrolet and covered with a blanket. He went directly to his room, and never left for the next five years.

Moving into new surroundings took a jarring toll on the Old Man. He became disoriented with the smallest movement. Rolling in bed caused him to lose track of his thoughts, and when that happened, as it often did, he would call out as if in pain, a child lost in a black woods of damask draperies and artificial air. Jean was now ensconced in her own room at the opposite end of the Brobdingnagian dwelling, unable to hear his pleas for help, if that is what they were. He did not really know. Finally, unable to settle himself after several weeks, Hughes insisted that an aide remain with him at all times. More Mormons were called in from Romaine and a schedule arranged so that at least one aide was seated at a small desk within earshot of a bell that Hughes could ring if he needed help.

Nearly a year to the day that Hughes lost control of TWA, the CAB approved Hughes' purchase of the Atlas Corp.'s stake in Northeast Airlines, giving the one-time aviator a new toy for his playbox, but no less enthusiasm to retrieve his crown jewel. To that end, on February 13, 1962, Hughes Tool filed a $366 million counter-suit against Trans World Airlines, demanding that the court dismantle the voting trust which ripped control of the company from its 78 percent owner. Further clouding already murky waters, Hughes' suit alleged that the voting trust was itself in violation of the antitrust laws by conspiring to perpetuate its control over TWA.

The docents of antitrust law were quick to point out that legal precedent did not exist in either case, therefore leaving the courts to adjudicate, but not before platoons of lawyers would spend millions of dollars erecting the legal breastworks and gabions on which to defend their cases. It an unusual twist of irony, since Hughes owned over three-quarters of TWA, he was essentially paying for the attorneys who were suing him as well as for the attorneys suing his airline. It was little wonder that Hughes was in constant pain.

Dr. Norman Crane was one of the few people actually welcomed inside the guarded sanctuary of 1001 Bel Air Road. The former partner of Dr. Verne Mason, Crane was placed on staff as Hughes' on-call physician, Mason having now moved on to head the Howard Hughes Medical Institute. He was paid an annual retainer to ensure his availability, and became responsible for supplying Hughes with prescriptions for his Empirin compound.

It was late in 1961 when Crane made the decision to end Hughes' dependency on Empirin, largely due to his concern that the drug might trigger nephritis[3] of the kidneys. To help control the pain Hughes continued to experience in his head and back, Crane substituted one grain codeine tablets that were dissolved in water, placed in a syringe and injected. Hughes watched eagerly as Crane demonstrated the procedure with an enthusiasm normally reserved for a dog observing the ritual of a can of food being placed in an opener, tail wagging in anticipation of the treat to come.

The drug dulled the pain, but never truly removed it completely. It smoothed the edges of a life sharp with contrasts. Given Hughes' compulsive personality, it seemed likely that he would abuse the drug and he did, though not on a level to cause extreme concern on the part of Crane, who was quite content to write prescriptions in the names of Hughes' various aides in order not to attract attention to the Old Man. John Holmes, Roy Crawford, and George Francom were less comfortable with an arrangement that was blatantly against the law. Still, they carried out Hughes' instructions and dutifully filled the prescriptions at one of several pharmacies, feigning innocence or at least ignorance.

They pretended not to notice the track marks left at the multiple injection sites, or Hughes' impromptu singing, "Hey! Ba-Ba-Re-Bop, Hey! Ba-Ba-Re-Bop" as he plunged the needle into his forearm, the Lionel Hampton hit from the Forties preceding the rush of stuporous relief. They actually came to look forward to the refrain, for in its wake their boss became more docile, less vitriolic with his demands. They liked Crane's prescription of Valium even better. The drug helped Hughes to fall asleep, something he found increasingly impossible to do on his own.

As the tangled legal battle for TWA progressed, the airline's trustees made a concerted effort to force Hughes to appear in court to answer their charges in person. TWA's attorney, John Sonnett, of the Wall Street law firm of Cahill, Gordon, Reindel & Ohl, gave a young lawyer named Frederick P. Furth the unenviable job of serving Hughes with a subpoena. Furth, in turn, hired private eye Alfred E. Leckey, who put a team of ten men on the assignment. In what was the ultimate game of hide-and-seek, the private detectives began chasing a shadow that had previously managed to elude the press for over ten years. Maheu added his own devilishness to the scenario by hiring Brucks Randell, an actor and Hughes lookalike, to make appearances all over the world as the ever-elusive multimillionaire. San Diego one day, Mexico the next, with the detectives and process servers always one beat behind. And all the while, the real Howard Hughes was lying naked under a white sheet in a rented house in Bel Air, singing "Hey! Ba-Ba-Re-Bop" whenever the mood struck.

---

3. Nephritis is a chronic disease of the kidneys causing degeneration and loss of function.

Newsweek magazine joined the party with its cover story of May 21, 1962: "The Hunt for Howard Hughes." The news journal said that the search for the man they labeled "the most compelling multimillionaire U.S. business has ever produced," had been spurred on by "rumors 'reliably' reporting (him) observed in a New York elevator, a Los Angeles drugstore, and a Mexican cabaña, and obscured by the camouflage that covers all of Hughes' doings." Amazingly, the article included a photo of his 1001 Bel Air Road home, accurately listed the rent as $50,000 a year, the number of bathrooms as eight, the length of the pool as fifty feet, without guessing he was actually in hiding there. The romantic intrigue of Hughes being such as it was, it was far easier to picture the handsome aviator surrounded by a bevy of starlets sipping tropical drinks on the British-held island of Cay Sal in the Caribbean.

Maheu found joy in relating the various escapades that seemed to twist daily in the wind, with Hughes finding equal enchantment with each retelling. Hughes' alter ego made certain that he was as visible as Hughes was elusive, "purely for business reasons," Maheu later said. Maheu and Yvette merged into the Los Angeles social scene with the ease of a racer at the Daytona 500. They joined the California Yacht Club, the Jonathon Club, the Navy League, the Silver Dollar Club, and the Balboa Bay Club in Newport Beach, where they maintained a penthouse suite for entertaining and moored their thirty-four-foot motor cruiser, the *Alouette*, nearby for the occasional sail. The *Alouette* slept six. It would be replaced several years later by the *Alouette II*, a Sports Fisherman that was twice as big.

While Hughes was existing on one steak dinner every three days, Maheu and company were entertaining the A-list of society, strapping on the feed bag with congressmen, senators, and the grand pooh-bah of show business. "It was work," Maheu said in 1990. "Hard work. But necessary to establish needed contacts."

It was Maheu's contacts that managed to save the *Hercules*, still housed in its hangar in Long Beach and at the mercy of government cut-backs. "Bob, at five p.m. Washington time, my whole deal with the government is going down the drain. Washington is going to pick up the flying boat in Long Beach and have it destroyed. I've had people working on stalling them for two years, but now they won't give me any more extensions." A typical Hughes drop-everything emergency. In this case, Maheu's connections within the General Service Administration allowed Hughes to pay rent for the wooden plane, which by this time had been given its famous nickname, the *Spruce Goose*. The rent amounted to an insignificant $800 per month. Maheu made the deal in time for the deadline by the close of business. Still devoted to the plane he would never see again, Hughes continued to spend a million dollars a year to keep it flight ready.[2]

Hughes existed in a routine that alternated between brief sessions of frenzied activity and long periods of total silence. It was a surreal world lit by the changing patterns of a television set and sustained through the tolerance of aides who accepted demands that were increasingly outrageous. They were not to talk with Hughes or look at him for any reason, unless specifically instructed to do so. No calls were to be put through to the bedroom, not even those from his wife, whose visitation rights had been cut from daily sessions to bi-weekly snippets.

Their intimacy had developed into a touching form of compassion in which Jean served as Hughes' eyes on the living. She talked about the blooming bougainvillaea, the nest of cardinals in the sycamore, her efforts at painting. The thread of courtship now long cut, her ability to even reach out and physically touch her husband now totally restricted, Jean contented herself with attempting to ease what she saw as fear in her husband's eyes that were as cold as holes cut in an ice lake for fishing and just as dark.

She never realized that Hughes had come to dread the visits, for in those brief minutes, he had to command his mind to function when it wanted to drift to a place where memories smeared and pain diminished. It was a friendship sustained by their history and tapped every bit of his energy to brook, its tropism guided by respect. She knew nothing of his injections accompanied by the haunting song, nor the comfort he found in knowing his syringes were hidden inside the Kleenex box on his night stand. If Hughes was caught up in an asylum of his own making, Jean was trapped by the same cage. Constantly guarded, never truly free to express herself to anyone. Still, she pretended she lived in a normal world. After all, she was an actress.

In federal court, Chester Davis was running sprints, attempting to keep Hughes from having to give a deposition in his own defense. He maneuvered through a maze of court orders and affidavits, evading the inevitable with delays and postponements. Finally, however, on October 29, 1962, Judge Charles M. Metzner, in whose New York courtroom the case was being adjudicated, declared that Hughes was to appear in person in the United States Courthouse in Los Angeles at 10 a.m. on February

2. The arrangement continued until 1979, when the plane was sold to the Aero Club of Southern California which, in turn, leased it to the Wrather Corporation that turned the plane into a tourist attraction in Long Beach, California. In 1988, the Wrather Corporation was sold to the Walt Disney Company for $152 million. Four years later, Disney sold the *Hercules* to Del Smith, founder of the Evergreen International Aviation Museum, which dismantled the plane and barged it from Long Beach to its new home in McMinnville, Oregon, just south of Portland, where it has been put on permanent display.

11, 1963, or face a default judgment in the case. On that date, the court-room had been equipped with special amplifying devices to allow Hughes to hear the proceedings, similar to the accommodation supplied for his appearance during the Senate hearings.

News crews had been dispatched to Hughes' rented homes in Rancho Santa Fe, Bel Air, Beverly Hills, Palm Springs, and Las Vegas. Anticipation ran high that the potential of losing $115 million plus court costs might prompt Hughes into an appearance. Outside the courtroom, twenty-eight television, radio, and newspaper reporters were waiting on the street, all to no avail. Through a last-minute maneuver by Davis, one in which he suddenly rested his case, the pre-trial deposition hearing was brought to a sudden halt. Davis theorized that an end to the hearing effectively eliminated Hughes' need to appear.

When the newsmen were asked why they continued to wait outside the courtroom, one cameraman echoed the feelings of the crowd of spec-tators gathered at the scene: "With Hughes, you never know." At 10 a.m. on February 11, as much of the nation turned to rubbernecking rather than miss even a remote possibility of spotting the eccentric who had not been seen in public for over a decade, Hughes was lying naked on his bed watching a TV rerun of Randolph Scott in *Shoot-Out at Medicine Bend.* The attraction wasn't so much Scott or the shoot-out, as it was the acting debut of Angie Dickinson and her ample breasts. It would prove to be an expensive diversion.

Hughes' no-show opened the way for TWA to ask for a default judgment in their case as well as a "dismissal with prejudice" of Hughes' $385 million counter-suit. Judge Metzner called Hughes' failure to appear "a willful and deliberate default." Metzner seemed prepared to award TWA extensive damages when Hughes proved he was not out of wind or out of the fight. His lawyers asked for the CAB's blessing to allow Hughes to prematurely pay back the loan that brought the voting trust to life in the first place.

It was the ultimate twist in a plot that already had more of them than a knotted shoelace. Since the new management had taken over control of TWA, the value of Hughes' stock had more than skyrocketed as the airline went from a loss of $39 million in 1961 to record profits of $37 million in 1964. That gain coupled with a similar gain in the value of Hughes Tool and Hughes Aircraft had catapulted the eccentric recluse into true billionaire status for the first time in his life.

With the recent award of yet another Air Force contract worth $61 million to Hughes Aircraft to supply electronic equipment to upgrade three models of supersonic jet fighter-interceptors, the company had increased in value to $300 million. Hughes Tool maintained its value at

$500 million. The increased value of Hughes' TWA stock tallied $365 million. His real estate in Culver City including the land he had purchased during the production of *Hell's Angels*, was worth $150 million, while land purchased in Tucson for a Hughes Aircraft plant added another $100 million. And his holdings in Northeast Airlines and Atlas Corp. were worth $17 million. Gathered together in one big pot: Hughes was conservatively worth $1,432,000,000,[5] and that did not include his three white shirts, one pair of khaki slacks, four pairs of draw string cotton boxers, two pairs of socks, and a pair of brown Oxford shoes—the sum total of his personal possessions.

Ultimately, the CAB denied Hughes permission to pay off TWA's debt in advance of its maturity thus withholding his chance to regain control of the airline—a logical decision given the current management's success with the company. The news festered like a lanced boil as Hughes pondered his next move. He berated Davis for his courtroom failure, unable to believe that he, himself, was ultimately at its root for his failure to appear to be deposed. He alternately screamed at his aides with increasingly uncontrollable fits of temper, and then would slump into depressed periods of total silence, a do-not-disturb scrim hovering around his bed. When his irritability reached his wife, she refused to speak to him at all, cloistering herself in her own wing of their home. It was there she pondered her fate. Alone, detached, living a lie, Jean searched her soul to give some meaning to the charade and found none.

Unwilling to wait for Judge Metzner to deliver what was projected to be a default judgment to total well over $100 million, Hughes ordered a preemptive strike on his own airline, and instructed his Houston attorney, Raymond Cook, to dispose of his stock in TWA in May, 1966. He placed his entire block on public sale through the Wall Street office of Merrill Lynch, Pierce, Fenner & Smith, and within half-an-hour, every one of the 6.6 million shares was sold for a record total of $566 million. It was the second biggest underwriting in the nation's history (the first being the 1956 sale of Ford Motor Co. shares for $657.6 million) and the largest check ever issued to an individual. At the time of the sale, Hughes' stock had risen 950%, thanks in large part to his being forced to suspend his involvement with the company.

The sudden sale raised speculation that Hughes was terminally ill, with reporters noting that he had failed to renew his pilot's license in years.[6]

Still others described to the move as an astute business decision, since the sale had generated hundreds of millions in profits, and with it, mil-

---

5. Estimates based on the calculations of *Fortune* magazine financial editors.
6. Howard Hughes renewed his pilot's license for the final time on February 11, 1955, in Miami, Florida.

lions in capital gains taxes. Hughes hated paying taxes, and considered the tax law "a legal excuse for government rape," according to a memo he sent to Robert Maheu. The thought of now having to pay a large percentage of his profit on the sale of TWA to the government annoyed him to the point that he was willing to pay "any amount necessary" to escape it, and told his Washington, D.C. tax firm, Hogan & Hartson, to find a solution. Their initial advice was for him to leave California immediately, for to accept the TWA check while in the Golden State would result in state as well as federal taxes on the income. The California tax code managed to do what federal courts, private detectives, and process servers could not—roust Hughes from his bed.

Aide George Francom was standing in Hughes' darkened room when he heard the news from the Old Man. He was moving to Tucson, he said. Francom was told to call Maheu who was to make the arrangements. That Francom did, but not before spreading the news to Operations, who shared it with Hughes' other aides. The thought of leaving California and their families for an open-ended amount of time in Arizona was upsetting, and each contemplated ways of changing Hughes' mind.

Maheu's assignment proved no less taxing, as he sought out and rented a variety of homes not far from Hughes' operation in Arizona. Security was placed around the homes, all billed to Robert A. Maheu Associates and paid for by Hughes. Within the confines of Hughes' blacked-out asylum, however, indecision replaced resolve. As usual, Hughes began to vacillate, uncertain that he was making a wise choice.

When Maheu received Hughes' telephone call that he had decided to move to Montreal, his alter ego was not surprised. "I knew he had visited the city some years before and liked it, so I checked out the availability of the Ritz-Carlton." Maheu also backed up the move by making reservations at the Emerald Beach Hotel in the Bahamas, attempting to second-guess his boss. "My hunch was so strong that I even rented a barge in Miami. That way, if Howard wanted to travel by train to Florida, I could have his Pullman cars barged across the Atlantic." As things turned out, Maheu would have done as well by throwing darts blindly at a map.

"Boston, Bob. I want to move to Boston," Hughes said, after finally making up his mind. And he wanted to travel by train. Maheu found that decision extraordinary, given his love of flying, and suddenly began to wonder if the pundits who had prophesied his illness were correct. Boston was the home of Dr. George Thorn, the physician-in-chief of Peter Bent Brigham Hospital in Boston as well as the director of medical research at Howard Hughes Medical Institute.

The logistics of moving Hughes by train were enormous. He needed two private railroad cars which had to be secured and then arranged to be inconspicuously hooked onto a scheduled train. Hughes' Pullman car had to be blacked out and secured, just as his room in Bel Air had been. There was also the question of housing. An entire floor of the Ritz-Carlton in Boston had to be reserved, private phone lines installed, elevators re-keyed to forbid public access and knobs removed from emergency stairwells—all without alerting the hotel that Howard Hughes would be a guest. It was an incredibly complex undertaking, and one that Maheu eventually accomplished over a period of five weeks.

July 7, 1966. Maheu alerted Hughes that all the elements for the move were in place, each detail having been checked and double-checked. Maheu wanted no hint of a problem. He had cleared the route with the presidents of the Sante Fe, Union Pacific, and Chicago, Burlington and Quincy Railroads. The limousine was gassed and John Holmes was positioned to drive Hughes to the train station in Pasadena to avoid the prying eyes of the passengers at Los Angeles' Union Station.

Maheu's son was in place in Pasadena to coordinate the loading of Hughes' Pullman cars, which were being moved closer to the departing train. And then came the call. Hughes had changed his mind; not about moving, just about moving *then*.

For the next ten days, Hughes confirmed his plans to make the trip and then cancelled at the last possible moment. The railroad lines kept blaming Maheu for the delays, and threatened to cancel all the arrange-ments if he did not utilize the private Pullmans. On July 17, 1966, all was readied one last time, when Hughes attempted to stall plans again. It was the closest that Robert Maheu had ever come to having a nerv-ous breakdown. He screamed, he threatened, then finally he broke down and cried like a baby, blabbering incoherently about train switches and signal guards. It was the crying that finally did it. Hughes agreed to get out of bed. He even decided to put on his one pair of pants, a clean white shirt, and as a last-minute thought, placed his lucky fedora upon his head.

When Hughes walked down the stairs of his home at 1001 Bel Air Road and out the front door, he did not look back. He did not tell his wife he was leaving nor where he was going. In fact, at that point, he had had no conversation with her for over two weeks. Jean had seen the prepa-rations around the house, however. She had known he was contemplating leaving California for tax reasons and was planning a move somewhere. She had actually packed her own bags, in anticipation of the day she would be told that they were leaving the house as husband and wife, together. It was not to happen.

She looked down from a window and saw the limousine. She saw her husband exit the house and move across the driveway to the open car door. He had an ancient quality about him, his body invisible under a blanket he had wrapped around his shoulders, the folds obscuring his form, skeletal in the draped layers of wool. She watched him sitting in the backseat, slumped like a furled umbrella. She heard the crunch of the limousine's wheels on the driveway; the whirr of the motor of the front gate. She sucked in a breath and held it, waiting—waiting for her husband to at least turn and wave goodbye. She watched as the car passed through the gate, turned right and moved slowly down the road, its headlights disappearing into the night. She continued to watch for several more minutes, as if in disbelief. Only then did she turn, only then did she know. Jean Peters was no longer a part of Hughes' life, and she found herself wondering if she ever was.

Because of Hughes' delay in leaving the house, the train's schedule was now seriously behind. An airline machinists' strike had filled the passenger cars to capacity, and disgruntled customers were uncomfortable in the heat of the compartments. Crossing guards had been dropped and cars began to back up at intersections along the line, as Hughes' train blocked traffic for miles in both directions. The chaos only heightened the urgency to get Hughes onboard and into his private Pullman. When the transfer finally took place and the train eventually departed, the delay had created so much attention that newspapers carried stories about the event. "Mystery Train Headed East," the headlines proclaimed.

Midway along the route, Hughes demanded to be served with special food that had not been loaded onto the train. Maheu's security chief, an ex-cop named Jack Hooper, telephoned from a stop, frantic because Hughes was threatening to leave the train if he was not fed. Hughes wanted ten prime steak filets at least one-inch thick, six cans of baby peas, six cans of French-cut string beans, a half-dozen semi-ripe bananas with no black spots, six cans of mixed fruit, a vanilla cake with no frosting, and an assortment of freshly baked pastries, heavy on napoleons.

A frenzied Maheu called upon an old FBI buddy who then lived outside of Cleveland, the train's next stop, and begged a favor. The fact that Cleveland was in the throes of a race riot at the time did not help matters, but fortunately his friend took up the challenge with humor, albeit laced with skepticism regarding Maheu's mental health. The man ultimately accomplished his task and got paid double for his effort without ever knowing he was shopping for the eccentric billionaire.

When Hughes was carried off the train and into a waiting limousine, he had taken a Valium and had fallen asleep. He continued to snore as he was brought into the service elevator, moved down the fifth floor hallway of the Ritz-Carlton, and did not wake up until the next day to find himself once more in the darkness of yet another anonymous room. His first comment was not of thanks or appreciation. He demanded to know the location of the toilet, and then proceeded to urinate on the floor.

The headlines blared, "Train Mystery Solved; Howard Hughes Aboard" as reporters descended on the hotel and attempted to gain entry on to the fifth floor, turning the normally staid Ritz-Carlton into a media circus. Twenty four hour security, hired by Maheu and composed of off-duty policeman, kept even the hotel's manager T. Roger Kane from leaving the elevator on Hughes' floor. The blockade remained in place for the next four months and was only broken a single time, when Jean Peters walked into the hotel and asked to be taken to her husband.

Jean had learned of Hughes' location like everyone else—through the media. She had watched a report on television about the mystery train, and found the reports of Hughes' arrival in Boston as perplexing as the rest of America. Hughes eventually called her in Bel Air, and she insisted on coming to Boston for a talk. She was not about to listen to any excuse why she should not come, although Hughes attempted to talk her out of the trip.

When Jean finally arrived at the hotel, her husband would not allow her to enter his suite. He was worried about germs, he said, and asked her to speak to him by standing in the doorway. Jean made no effort to complain, for truthfully, it no longer mattered. She had made her decision. She was leaving her husband, and told him that day that she had given it a great deal of thought.

Hughes' response was one she had heard before. Promises of a home, away from public view, a place off-limits to even his aides. He begged her to reconsider; to give him another chance to prove his love. Jean did not answer him that day. But she knew that she had made up her mind. Now it was *her* turn to leave without saying goodbye. There was no objection from her husband as she walked down the hall; the only sound she heard coming from the room was the faint chorus of a song. It echoed through the empty hall even after she watched the elevator doors close off that chapter of her life. "Hey! Ba-Ba-Re-Bop, Hey! Ba-Ba-Re-Bop". . . and then there was silence.

The King of Las Vegas

If the gigantic nuclear explosion is detonated, then in the fraction of a second following the pressing of that fateful button, thousands and thousands, and hundreds of thousands of cubic yards of good potentially fertile Nevada soil and underlying water and minerals and other substances are forever poisoned beyond the most ghastly nightmare. A gigantic abyss too horrible to imagine filled with poisonous gases and debris will have been created just beneath the surface in terrain that may one day be the site of a city like Las Vegas. I say Nevada is no longer so desperate for mere existence that it has to accept and swallow with a smile poisonous, contaminated radioactive waste material more horrible than human excrement.

Las Vegas, Nevada
April 14, 1968
Hughes' memo to Robert Maheu projecting
the effect of a proposed nuclear test that
the government had certified as being
"totally safe and without human damage."

THE MARRIAGE OF CONVENIENCE THAT DEFINED THE union of Howard Hughes and Jean Peters was never particularly easy. With Hughes' refusal to touch his wife or even to allow her to visit him across an empty room, it became increasingly combative. It was a development that Hughes neither anticipated nor acknowledged, yet the impact would be far-reaching and undeniable. From that point forward, every person in Howard Hughes' life would be paid to be there. He had no friends, no confidantes, no lovers, no companions. His entire life, his reason for being, had been reduced to his incredible wealth and his reputation, and preserving both became his primary preoccupation.

Hughes had become a modern-day Dorian Gray. Rather than a picture in an attic, there was a real man growing older and decaying in a darkened room where no one could see, while his public image stayed young and virile, the envy of millions who looked upon the billionaire as having everything that they did not. The irony of his situation was not lost on Hughes, who lamented to his aides that if they were able to spend one day in his place, or even a single hour, they would opt for what they already had.

After his wife's hasty departure, Hughes soured on Boston and grew tired of the efforts of the media to invade his privacy. Almost immediately, he announced his decision to leave the city. He went through a check-list of alternative destinations, like a pilot preparing for take-off. Montreal, check; Nassau, check; Lake Tahoe, check. And with each possibility, Robert Maheu arranged for an entire floor of a hotel, phone installations, security provisions, and food availability. Each time Hughes changed his mind, arrangements were cancelled, people were dispatched, and days were wasted. So it came as little surprise to Maheu when, on November 8, 1966, Hughes altered his plans yet again. "Las Vegas, Bob. Make it Las Vegas."

Hughes wanted to stay at the Dunes Hotel, where Cary Grant was the goodwill ambassador. Naturally, he wanted the entire top floor, and total control over access. While the Dunes initially had the space (although not on the top floor, which actually housed a restaurant), the hotel was unable to guarantee the continued availability of all the rooms and suites due to a celebrity function previously booked for the period between Thanksgiving and Christmas, forcing Maheu to search for a back-up location. Maheu eventually settled on the Desert Inn by default. Nine stories high, the hotel had a securable top floor, and, more importantly, the hotel was available.

Hughes decided to travel once again on Thanksgiving Day, a time when families would be preoccupied with traditional celebrations, and, hopefully, so would the press. Hughes neither thought nor cared that his aides would be denied the chance to observe the holiday with their families or considered that the day before Thanksgiving was invariably the busiest travel day of the entire year, thus making arrangements for special Pullman cars more difficult. Compounding matters for Maheu was the near certainty that Hughes would either refuse to leave his bed or change his mind about the destination at the last minute. As Thanksgiving approached, Maheu uneasily set the final pieces in place, essentially replaying the train trip to Boston, though now in reverse, still certain that his time was being wasted. Ordinarily, Maheu would have been right. But this was not an ordinary time.

After months of spending days alone in serious introspection, Hughes had come to the realization that his efforts in California had been futile; his impact had been tempered, despite his successes in aviation and his notoriety in films. The problem, as Hughes saw it, was that California had too many stars—not just movie stars, but stars of industry and technology, education and athletics. So many stars, in fact, that not one of them stood out above the others, he included.

In contrast, Nevada had no stars. Nevada had a lot of sand, some cheap hotels, loud casinos awash with gamblers and transient celebrities, and, most importantly, had no income tax. It was run by one of the smallest governments in the country, had fewer residents at the time than the city of Passaic, New Jersey, and was larger in size than the states of Pennsylvania, Delaware, New York New Jersey and Rhode Island combined. In short, while his aides were busy enjoying the fruits of Beantown, Hughes had uncovered the one state ripe for invasion and takeover.

Hughes not only kept his appointment to board the *Spirit of Los Angeles* to take him to Chicago and on to Las Vegas, he was early. He could barely contain his glee. For years, he had passed through the honky-tonk cabaret of a city, used it for its thrills, availed himself of its liberal laws where marriage and divorce were concerned, and then moved on. He chided himself for having been so blind, if only to congratulate himself on his new vision. Nevada was more than an untapped resource. It was a kingdom in need of a monarch.

Maheu handled the transfer from the Ritz-Carlton to the train with ease, using a decoy limousine and a lookalike, while spiriting the real Hughes down the service elevator and out the back door. The train trip was flawless, each detail precise. Not even an unexpected delay derailed Maheu's success. When he heard that the train had developed brake trouble and was stranded in Ogden, Utah, Maheu ordered up a new engine and caboose and brought Hughes into the gambling Mecca under his own steam, on schedule, and under the cover of darkness. He never got authorization to spend the extra $18,000 on the auxiliary engine. He did not think it necessary, for by then Maheu was too flushed with the smell of glory—his own.

Hughes was transferred by stretcher from the Pullman car to a waiting van, and as a stream of five decoy limousines pulled up to the front of the Desert Inn, the billionaire was loaded like baggage through the service entrance and up to the top floor that had been transformed into a secure *Lebensraum* which could only be reached by using a key to access the elevator control.

Those who managed to gain entry to the ninth floor found themselves in front of a security guard seated at a desk. To the left stretched a long hallway leading to the floor's various suites, only one of which was occupied.

Penthouse One was a three-room suite with its own locked front door that featured a grill through which people hoping to gain entrance were viewed. The aides who formed a human bunker between the world and the Old Man were positioned in the center of the suite, in the living room. On the far side of this room was Hughes' sanctuary—the smallest room on the floor, measuring no larger than fifteen feet by seventeen feet, with its own adjacent bathroom. The windows were sealed and blacked-out, and the room devoid of furniture other than a double bed, a night stand, a dresser, a 19-inch color television, and Hughes' Barcalounger and ottoman, plus his film projector and screen.

Even his aides did not have free access to Hughes' bedroom, and were only allowed to pass over his threshold after being summoned. Although he had been equipped with the same small silver bell that had been so useful in the Bel Air house, Hughes preferred to call for help by thumping the side of the brown paper bag that held his used Kleenex supply, snapping his long fingernails against the sack, a pistol shot that commanded attention.

Outside phones lines were installed at the aides' desk with two extension telephones and sound amplifiers next to Hughes' bed and his easy chair. Barely able to hear, Hughes still refused to wear a hearing aid. Under ordinary circumstances, no one was permitted to speak in Hughes' presence anyway—their purpose was merely to listen and follow instructions. He was neither interested in nor wanted to hear their opinions, took no interest in their personal lives, and formed no bond of any kind with any of the men on his staff.

While he was in daily contact with Maheu, it was only by telephone, never in person. Moreover, despite Maheu's initial requests for personal meetings, Hughes had no desire for a face-to-face conference. "He wanted me to keep the image I had of him, not as he was," Maheu said of Hughes. "He said I would never be able to effectively represent him if I ever laid eyes on him." And Maheu never did.

The fact that Hughes was well aware of his appearance and the effect it would have on his ability to conduct business erases any doubt that the billionaire was delusional and unable to comprehend his situation. The insistence of Hughes to remain invisible was both calculated and deliberate. He was all too aware of his deteriorating mental condition during those times when he was functional and lucid. Rather than choose to get help and risk public exposure of his situation, he selected seclusion and constructed every single element of his business and personal life around that prerequisite.

For the management of the Desert Inn, having Hughes as a guest was a mixed blessing. While they had no worry that he would pay his bill, the hotel depended on its guests to generate income in the casino as the major part of its profit. When Hughes gambled, it was with entire industries, not chips on a blackjack table. His mostly Mormon aides did not gamble, drink or smoke. The Desert Inn was not even able to capitalize on Hughes' residency, since his very presence was a well-publicized secret.

While Hughes was playing hide-and-seek on the top floor, his alter ego had placed himself in a suite on the floor below. The two began their daily sessions of phone calls that would become the basis of their relationship as America's strangest odd couple—Hughes naked on his throne (well, actually his Barcalounger insulated against imaginary germs by layers of paper towels) and Maheu, impeccably attired and carrying out the Old Man's wildest fantasies, regardless of the implausibility of the order. While Maheu was not actually able to leap tall buildings with a single bound, he certainly made it seem like he could to those who watched his performance in person.

Through intricate layers of friendships and connections, Maheu managed to solve the various problems that Hughes created for himself and threw in Maheu's path. If his arrangements weren't always traditional, at least they were not blatantly illegal, which gave Maheu a roguish charm that served him well in organizations that others might find intimidating. The Mafia was one; the Teamsters was another. Maheu had met Jimmy Hoffa during his Washington days while doing work for the United Steel Workers. It was a casual relationship, but it took little more than that for Maheu to ask a favor when necessary. It became necessary two weeks after the Hughes circus came to town.

The management of the Desert Inn wanted their rooms back for previously reserved guests arriving for the Christmas/New Year's holidays and were not particularly polite when telling Maheu to vacate. Las Vegas in the Sixties was notorious for being little more than a front for organized crime, and the Desert Inn was no exception. The majority owner of the hotel was a man named Morris Barney "Moe" Dalitz, who had come to town from Cleveland where he ran the crime syndicate's local branch of Lucky Luciano's operation.

Dalitz had moved to Las Vegas and was now regarded as the Epimenides of gambling. With high rollers arriving, Dalitz did not care how much money Hughes had in the bank if it was not passing through his casino, and he ordered him off the premises. Hughes passed the buck to Maheu, Maheu called Hoffa, Hoffa called Dalitz, and suddenly suites that had been reserved for an entire year became unavailable for Christmas.

Even Jimmy Hoffa could only do so much, and when Hughes was still in his Barcalounger as New Year's Eve approached, Dalitz was through playing games and began to threaten. While Hughes was pretending not to hear, Maheu was very much aware that their housing, if not their lives, were in danger. The answer to the dilemma proved to be a turning point for both Hughes and Las Vegas. Rather than move from his blackened hole, Hughes told Maheu to buy the entire hotel—for cash.

The Desert Inn was not for sale, which, of course, made the purchase that much more exciting for the reclusive billionaire. It was the hunt, not the trophy that thrilled him. Negotiation was his game, and with each serve, Hughes seemed to regenerate. At times, he left his chair and paced, waiting for Maheu to telephone with word of offers and counter-offers.

Dalitz' partner, Ruby Kolod, another Cleveland mobster, did most of the negotiating, and quickly tired of Hughes' style which came directly from the get-them-to-agree-to-your-price-and-then-knock-them-down-another-quarter-million school. Kolod had also learned that Hughes was still paying rent on the entire top floor of the Ritz-Carlton in Boston, which to Kolod meant he was not serious about buying the Desert Inn at all.

Fortunately, Kolod was in a weakened bargaining position, having been convicted in April, 1965, of federal conspiracy charges for attempting to extort repayment of a debt from Denver attorney Robert Sunshine. While appealing his conviction, he remained free on bail, and the Nevada Gaming Licensing Board was looking to strip him of his casino license. A timely sale of the Desert Inn to Hughes would line his pockets with cash and get the Gaming Licensing Board off his back.

Kolod was correct in his assumption that Hughes was playing games, but it had nothing to do with not being serious about his purchase of the Desert Inn. If Kolod had known Hughes better, he would have realized that the game playing was proof positive of his intent to strike a deal, and he finally did. He bought control of the Desert Inn for $13.25 million; $6.3 million in cash, with Hughes assuming just under $7 million in Desert Inn liabilities.

Maheu was naive enough to actually celebrate the sale, taking his wife Yvette to the Monte Carlo Room for dinner on the night before the deal closed. He was midway through his Surf 'n' Turf when he received word that Hughes had objected to a $13,000 item on the disclosure statement and wanted the item dropped off the sale price, or the purchase of the hotel was cancelled. It was a lesson well learned.

Maheu set a Desert Inn record for traveling from the ground floor to the penthouse that night. He stormed past the guard on duty, and into the suite across from the one occupied by Hughes and his aides. He took out a piece of Desert Inn stationery and wrote a "Dear Howard" letter that said:

> I've given my word. And now you're playing games for a matter of peanuts. I just don't want to be involved with you anymore.

AT FIRST when Maheu handed the note to aide George Francom in Penthouse One, Francom refused to pass the note along to Hughes. An infuriated Maheu threatened to push past the aide and "give it to Hughes myself." Only then did Francom acquiesce, and agree to deliver the message. When Maheu left the ninth floor, he felt confident that he had made his position clear. This was a man who moved mountains, not dickered about ant hills, and he was not about to change for Hughes or anyone.

In the darkened room, Hughes received the note in silence. Upon reading the three sentences, he felt his body numb, anesthetized against the news. Maheu was not playing his game; the gun was against his head again. His first thought was to fire Maheu; his next was to imagine life without him. He needed his alter ego in place to live in his paperweight world where everything went according to plan—his plan. Inspired by fear, he quickly telephoned Richard Gray, the Houston attorney who had been hired by Maheu to handle the legalities of the transaction. Hughes instructed Gray to close on the deal immediately. He next phoned Maheu to test the temperature of his rage.

Maheu answered Hughes' pleas to reconsider his resignation by playing a game of his own. He told Hughes that he was packing his bags and leaving Las Vegas that very night. He laced his words with disgust, playing his hand.

"Bob, I'm not going to argue," Hughes said. "I'm too tired to argue. Please promise me that you'll at least be in your suite tomorrow morning at eight. I want to talk to you. Please promise me that."

Maheu agreed and was waiting by the telephone the next day at eight. Exactly on cue, the call from Hughes came, and Maheu listened while Hughes convinced him to stay. "We can't get involved in this world and start playing games at the last minute. You were absolutely right. Please forgive me," Hughes said. "And please don't pack." After a prolonged period of time, calculated to give Hughes just enough insecurity, Maheu relented and agreed to stay, confident that he had won a battle and made an impact on Hughes' method of doing business. He could not have been more incorrect.

What Maheu had managed to do was prove to his boss that Maheu could be manipulated just like the rest. What Maheu learned was that he was important to the Old Man. In fact, that morning Hughes told Maheu that they would be partners "for the rest of our natural lives." And at that moment in time, Hughes meant every word.

The Desert Inn officially became a Howard Hughes property on April 1, 1967. The way the newspaper reports read at the time, Hughes owned the land, the buildings, the pool, and the casino. Not so. The physical building and the land on which it was built were owned by Desert Inn Associates, a division of the Helmsley-Spear Corporation, as in Harry Helmsley, as in Leona Helmsley–the Queen of Mean. What Hughes had paid over $13 million for was the Desert Inn Operating Company,[1] the business that ran the hotel. Helmsley made no noise about the distinction because with the Hughes name attached to the Desert Inn, the hotel suddenly glistened. The citadel of organized crime had gone legit. Now the showroom where Nöel Coward had made his only Las Vegas appearance, the pool where Johnny Weissmuller had done aquacade diving, and the suites where kings, queens, and presidents had felt at home, all took on a rejuvenated air as if a cloud of pure oxygen had dropped on the place like a bomb from heaven.

The casino was packed; so too the restaurants, for one never knew when Howard Hughes might decide to make an appearance, the new King of Las Vegas anointing his subjects with a favorable glance. Word had circulated that the reason Hughes had not as yet appeared was because of his health. Indeed, Dr. Norman Crane was soon summoned to the penthouse suites from Beverly Hills for an emergency, flown in on Hughes' private plane and rushed to the ninth floor. From bellhops to waiters to the manicurists in the hair salon, the news pushed through the hotel like a swarm of mosquitoes on a summer's night. The casino dealers heard that Hughes had cancer of the pancreas; the night auditors were spreading the news that he had a heart condition. None of them knew that Crane had stayed three minutes, never saw his patient, and his entire consultation involved writing two prescriptions for codeine tablets.

The cover of illness made it convenient for Maheu, who had to ride shotgun on Hughes' application for a casino license. State law required an appearance in person by the applicant. Hughes was now owned by his room, at times not leaving his Barcalounger for days. In what could have been a tense stand-off between the determined billionaire and the typi-

---

1. The Desert Inn Operating Company was owned by Moe Dalitz, Jack Donelley, Ruby Kolod, Allard Roen, Morris Kleinman, Samuel A. Tucker, Cornelius J. Jones, Frank Soskin, Sam Solomon, Martin Kutzen, Cecil Simmons and John Joseph Licini.

cally unbending licensing board became, instead, a lovefest, thanks to the intervention of Nevada's new governor, Paul D. Laxalt. The son of an immigrant sheep herder from the French Pyrénées, the 44-year-old Laxalt was elected governor just weeks before Hughes' arrival in the state, and had been in office only two months when Hughes wrote him a letter. In it, Hughes said that he had read an article in the *Las Vegas Review Journal* about the need for funds for a University of Nevada Medical School. He offered to make a gift to the university of between two hundred thousand and three hundred thousand dollars, "every year for twenty years, commencing whenever the university requires the money. I attach no strings or conditions to this proposal," Hughes wrote. The letter arrived two days before his gaming application was due for review.

Laxalt lavished praise on Hughes for his donation and greeted the businessman to Nevada, "where we intend to make him feel very welcome." The first example came by way of the Gaming Licensing Board that took less than five minutes to approve Hughes' application. District Attorney George Franklin said, "This is the best way to improve the image of gambling in Nevada by licensing an industrialist of his stature. It will be an asset and blessing." When asked why he waived the required personal appearance, Chairman of the Board and Sheriff Ralph Lamb said, "Because I feel this is a good thing for the county."

Now firmly committed to Las Vegas, Hughes began an elaborate campaign to convince his wife to forgive him for his behavior in Boston and move with him into a home in the desert. Jean Peters was understandably reluctant to take anything her husband said at face value. She had been fooled twice into believing his intentions were sincere to live together as a family without the accompaniment of aides, drivers, and a plethora of security. This time, Jean demanded proof.

Maheu moved quickly to secure two separate properties, one adjacent to the Las Vegas Strip. The estate of Major A. Riddle, a part-owner of the Dunes Hotel, included a sprawling home in an exclusive section of town popular with entertainers. Hughes demanded Riddle move so quickly that he took temporary lodging in the home of Hughes' chief banker, Parry Thomas.

The second property was a 518-acre ranch owned by Vera Krupp, ex-wife of the German munitions manufacturer, who had been attempting to interest the state in purchasing her land for use as a park. It included a home and stables, and sat well away from the city. Vera was a former German actress, who had divorced her husband and moved permanently to Nevada in 1954. The ranch and its owner made headlines five years later when three men broke into the home, tied up Vera and her ranch foreman, and stole the world-famous Krupp diamond,[2] a 33.19-carat gem worth a quarter of a million dollars at the time. It was later located in Elizabeth, N.J., and seven men were arrested and convicted of the robbery.

Hughes had several photo albums assembled with pictures of each place, hoping to entice his wife to move from the comfort of their rented home in Bel Air. "I had no interest in moving to Las Vegas," Jean said in sealed court depositions. "It is not my kind of town, although he did try to make it sound very attractive and I agreed to go, but I didn't want to. I told him, I wouldn't go unless he moved out of the hotel. I was not going to live in a Las Vegas hotel."

Of the two homes, Jean preferred the Riddle estate, which she described as a "Spanish hacienda look." She never seriously considered moving to the Krupp ranch, which "Howard said was great," Jean recalled. "But he also said it was twenty-five miles out of town and the road was very bumpy, so I had visions of myself being stuck on a ranch twenty-five miles from nowhere." Her move, however, was contingent upon his move, and at the moment, Hughes was finding it difficult enough just shifting from his chair to his bed, let alone across the Las Vegas Strip.

Newsweek magazine ran a story about the billionaire, saying Hughes would leave his suite "only occasionally for clandestine tours of the state by car and private airplane. He is thought to leave and return to the Desert Inn by ruses similar to his original arrival by stretcher. One hotel employee who was asked to remove a freezer from Hughes' suite is said to have remarked afterward, 'I just know he was inside that freezer.'"

Supposition aside, the world according to Howard Hughes was awash in activity (if not clandestine tours of the city). The prospect of control had snapped the Old Man's mind back into gear. He worked incessantly, driven to expand his empire like a conqueror invading foreign soil. His weapon of choice was his wealth, and he wielded it wisely.

His war cry was "buy," anything and everything that became available in the city. The 778-room Sands Hotel, its surrounding 183 acres of land, a championship golf course, five restaurants, two swimming pools and a casino were the first to fall after the Desert Inn. Maheu offered and got the hotel and grounds for $14.6 million of Hughes' money, a bargain rate, plus the assumption of $9 million in hotel debt. For an additional million, Hughes picked up the Alamo Airways Airport from owner George Crockett. Situated adjacent to Las Vegas' McCarran

---

2. In 1968, Richard Burton laid out $305,000 for the fabled diamond, with Burton gloating as he presented it to his mistress, Elizabeth Taylor, "It's even bigger than Mike Todd's engagement ring" (which weighed in at 29.7 carats).

International Airport, the private flying field came complete with its own charter airline.

In quick succession, Hughes paid $3.6 million for KLAS-TV, the CBS television affiliate previously owned by Hank Greenspun, the publisher of the *Las Vegas Sun* newspaper. He bought the land and facilities of the 571-room Frontier Hotel, across the street from the Desert Inn, for $12.5 million; paid another $1.3 million for raw land next to the Frontier, including 750-foot frontage on the Las Vegas Strip; the North Las Vegas Airport for $2 million; and the 229-room Castaways Hotel and Casino and its 31 acres, across the street from the Sands for $3 million.

This Monopoly game Hughes was playing, with real hotels and real houses, was so enjoyable to the billionaire that he stayed up for two and three days at a stretch, unwilling to have it end even for sleep, according to logs kept by his aides. He ordered overlay maps of Las Vegas and marked out his territory, blocking out huge sections of the town with a green marking pen. He envisioned the expansion of the gambling capital to the west and earmarked an entire section in the north for an airport, an enormous supersonic transport "terminus." He projected the day that Las Vegas would be "as large as, say, Houston, Texas, is today. If this growth should take place, the present location of McCarran Airport would be approximately comparable to having the airport in Los Angeles located on Wilshire Boulevard at the Miracle Mile."

While most of Las Vegas was dropping to its assorted knees in the greatest display of homage since Caesar received his "Hails" in Rome, not everyone found Hughes' wholesale purchase of the city advantageous. Frank Sinatra, under contract at the Sands since its opening, and still smarting over the loss of Ava Gardner, took out his anguish on the hotel when he was denied credit on the casino floor. After trying unsuccessfully to set fire to his suite, he ripped all the telephone trunk lines out of the hotel switchboard, promised a casino pit boss he would break both his legs, and turned a table over on casino manager Carl Cohen, a 250-pound powerhouse who answered the aggression by punching Sinatra in the mouth and knocking the crowns off his two front teeth. Rumor had it that when Hughes was told that Frank had quit the Sands to move over to Caesar's Palace, he replied, "Frank who?" He was said to be smiling.

November 29, 1967. Hughes finished out the year by buying the gambling casino of the Frontier Hotel, the one piece of the hotel he did not as yet own, for an even million in cash and the assumption of $8 million in casino debt. It had been a year since he first came into town, under the cloak of darkness to avoid being noticed. In the twelve months that followed, he had attracted more attention than any single individual had in the entire 20-year history of the gambling oasis. He had spent more than $100 million and became the Silver State's biggest landlord.

While Maheu pretended that Hughes had a grand plan for Las Vegas and made several official announcements in support of the fact, Hughes' purchases were actually a crap shoot that were based more on availability than on calculated economics. "He wanted it all," Maheu said. "He wanted so much, in fact, that the Federal government trumped up a notice from the Justice Department's antitrust division in San Francisco. They did not like the fact that I had begun making inquiries about buying the Stardust Hotel and casino." With that threat in mind, further purchases were halted, at least temporarily.

With Hughes firmly mired in Nevada, the Operations offices on Romaine Street had taken on all the signs of faded glory. The phones that at one time rang continuously and were manned with a quartet of male Mormon operators who diligently transcribed every word of each caller's message, were now silent. Gone were the pool of drivers taking starlets to voice lessons; gone were the late night screenings; gone were the runs between bungalows at the Beverly Hills Hotel; gone were the clandestine meetings in flea-bag hotels where the stench of vomit rivaled cheap perfume. Bill Gay, Nadine Henley, and Chester Davis still held their jobs and their titles, but the real action was no longer in California.

Two hundred and seventy miles across the Mojave Desert, Robert Maheu had formed Hughes Nevada Operations and named himself Chief Executive Officer. It was more for appearance than legality, since Hughes was still calling each step with Maheu acting out the motions with bravado. He had moved into the former home of Moe Dalitz on a green at the Desert Inn Country Club and had built a cabin at Mount Charleston, a 13-minute helicopter flight away from his office on the second floor of the Frontier Hotel. Maheu had opened a restaurant, the Charleston Park, with partners producer Frank Sennes and Jack Hooper, who had moved to Las Vegas himself as Hughes' head of security. The place had a cocktail lounge and liquor store, as well as a heliport for Maheu's drop-in visits.

The deep-voiced problem-solver clung to his role like a sheet of Saran wrap on a cold bowl. Nothing broke through his image as Hughes' major-domo, with magazine reports speculating on the daily meetings that took place between Maheu and the Old Man.

No one knew that Maheu had never met Hughes face-to-face, for surely such an arrangement was without precedent. Even Maheu found it difficult to believe that he received all his instructions through lengthy telephone calls and, with increased frequency, memos handwritten on lined, yellow legal paper. The memos were lengthy dialogues that each made a specific point, albeit occasionally in roundabout ways. In March,

1968, however, one memo was delivered to Maheu and stood out from the rest. There was a plaintive wail about the note, and a warning, if only Maheu had noticed.

> Please dont [sic] declare war upon me so early in the day. I am well aware that this is not anything that is important to you, but merely something you were pressured into doing by certain groups here. I am speaking of the Easter Egg Hunt.
>
> I have been told, however, that although there are a number of people in Las Vegas who favor this event, there is a more powerful group who are dedicated to discrediting me and that this second group will stop at nothing.
>
> The substance of this story (and it has already been fed to certain Hollywood columnists, who very fortunately are friends of mine from my motion picture days) the substance is that: I am ashamed for my sinful past (adventures with females, etc.) And I am having a backlash here, manafest [sic] in my extreme isolation from social contact, presumably for the purpose of putting temptation out of reach, and an intensive and very expensive campaign to reform the morals of Las Vegas. I am supposedly waiting to start a real all-out war again the normal customs of Las Vegas—such as: topless show girls, etc. etc., dirty jokes, dirty advertisements, etc.
>
> Now, I am further informed, and this is what really has me worried, that this militant group plans to stage a really viscious [sic] all-out juvenile riot at our Easter party.
>
> I am not eager to have a repetition, in the D.I., of what happened at Juvenile Hall when the ever-lovin little darlings tore the place apart. I am sure your reply to that will be that, with our better-trained security force, such a thing just could not happen. However, my information is to the effect that our opponents hope we do set this riot down, because they feel they can get more publicity if we do.
>
> Quietly explore alternate possibilities such as: Moving it to the Sunrise Hospital and making it a charity event. We could start the ball rolling by donating 25 or even $50,000. I just want to see it moved to a place where, if something goes wrong, it will be a black mark against Las Vegas—not a black mark against us.

HUGHES' PARANOIA about unknown forces crouched and ready to spring had first come to Maheu's attention during the purchase of the Desert Inn. While Hughes wanted the hotel and casino, he did not want its Tournament of Champions golf tournament, a prestigious event on the PGA tour. "It was a gold mine," Maheu said, "but Hughes felt trapped by the fact that the thousands of people who attended would know where he was living, and perhaps even gain entry to his rooms."

Despite Maheu's impassioned pleas to the contrary, the tournament was excluded from the sale even though it was set to begin just thirteen days after Hughes took possession of the hotel. Tickets had been printed, players were set to arrive for practice; and the PGA was dumbfounded.

The official announcement in the press quoted Desert Inn executive Allan Roen as stating, "Hughes is a tough negotiator but the tournament was one asset we wanted to keep." The truth of the situation was never known as the tournament moved to the Stardust golf course, with Hughes paying to cover the cost.[3] As for the Easter Egg Hunt, Maheu moved it as commanded, and the event came off without a hitch.

With Hughes' periods of intense business activity lengthening, his reliance on codeine tapered off. The logs kept by his aides meticulously recorded every moment within his suite, including his consumption of pills. During the period between late-1967 and mid-1968, his codeine use was negligible, in marked contrast to Hughes' stay in Boston and arrival in Las Vegas. It did not, however, mean that he was less concerned about the continuing availability of the drug, or his susceptibility to germs.

Dr. Norman Crane had been engaged as his personal physician for an $80,000 retainer.[4] Crane was given a suite at the Desert Inn and was promised he could return home on the weekends. Hughes reneged on the arrangement starting with the very first weekend, and suddenly Crane found himself living in virtual captivity. He began to drink heavily as a result. The smell of liquor on his breath and his shaking hands did not instill confidence in Hughes, who insisted that a second doctor be placed on retainer.

Dr. Robert Buckley was familiar to Hughes through Jean Peters. Buckley had also saved the life of security chief Jack Hooper. Hooper had checked himself into the Las Vegas hospital complaining of headaches, and after some tests, had been released. In a subsequent conversation with Buckley, Hooper related his symptoms. "Something he said made Buckley suspicious," Maheu recalled, "and he told Hooper to check himself back in the hospital immediately. Buckley flew into Las Vegas on the next plane. That night, Hooper was operated on for a misdiagnosed and life-threatening brain aneurysm."

Hughes was impressed by Buckley's performance and told Maheu to offer the doctor an $80,000 salary to move to Las Vegas with his family. It was a proposition that Buckley was considering when Hughes asked to see his curriculum vitae. Buckley had an excellent background and

---

3. The tournament eventually moved to La Costa Spa in California, another property in which
   Moe Dalitz had an interest.
4. An amount equal to $500,000 today.

proudly presented his resumé, which indicated his background in psychiatry. This knowledge sent Hughes into a panic, and removed Buckley from consideration. "If word ever got out that I was seeing a psychiatrist," Hughes told Maheu, "all hell would break loose. It would have an effect on the government contracts and everything else." Such logic was flawed, of course, since Hughes' government contracts were awarded to his aircraft company that was under the control of the Howard Hughes Medical Institute. Logic notwithstanding, Buckley was out.

The doctor did help Maheu, however, to purchase equipment that was delivered to the suite directly across the hall from Penthouse One. It turned the top floor of the Desert Inn into a mini-hospital in case Hughes ever needed intensive care. Unfortunately, while the equipment would have helped with a physical emergency, it was useless to assist in stopping Hughes' mental condition, which began to deteriorate as the rush to purchase casinos finally cooled.

By 1968, most of Hughes' Las Vegas expansion had ended, though there were brief flurries of suggested activity. In January, Hughes picked up the telephone and placed a personal call to Governor Laxalt, to thank him for his support and spoke of his future plans for the state. "It was the most interesting conversation of my life," Laxalt admitted. The same month, Hughes made the announcement that he intended to build the world's largest hotel, a 4,000-room addition to the Sands Hotel and Casino. Although he never followed through with his plan, it was remarkable for its prediction of Las Vegas' future.

"This hotel will be a complete city within itself," the handwritten statement said. "It would include an entire floor devoted to stores open 24 hours a day, one entire floor devoted to family recreation—including the largest bowling alley and billiard and pool facility in any hotel in the world." Hughes also planned an ice-skating rink, video game rooms (before any video game had been invented), and a theater for first-run motion pictures. He announced an indoor golf course that would be electronically computerized "so carefully designed that the shots will feel just like outdoors, and the spin of the ball in a slice or hook is even measured electronically and indicated to the player."

In March, Hughes purchased the Silver Slipper Casino for $5.4 million, and officially became the largest single employer in the state with 7,000 employees. He also reached out beyond city limits to begin a campaign to buy old mining sites. Romaine Street computer expert John Meier was put in charge of the project that included the purchase of 260 acres and four mining claims,[5] and announced that he had calculated

---

5. The claims were for the Delaware, Red Jacket, Pacific Lode and Southeast Lode silver and gold mines.

there remained over $12 million in untapped gold within the Sierra Nevada mountains.

Hughes had created the perfect world, his plans unfolding with such timing and effect that it seemed almost too good to be true. It was. The Camelot of Las Vegas for all its strengths had a major flaw. The very wide-open space and sparse population that had attracted Hughes was also a lure to the Atomic Energy Commission that used the desert surrounding the city for occasional nuclear tests. Several small tests had been detonated since Hughes' arrival at the Desert Inn, causing his room to vibrate and sway. He hated the proximity of the tests, and feared their effects. Still, they were infrequent, and were temporarily forgotten in the rush for acquisitions.

April 16, 1968. In his darkened room, Hughes had just settled back in his Barcalounger after spending two hours on his toilet in a losing battle with constipation. He adjusted his reading lamp, and picked up his copy of the *Las Vegas Sun*. He opened the paper on his lap and then held up his "peepstone," his name for a lighted magnifier that he had begun to use in place of much-needed glasses for his failing eyesight. He would not need the peepstone to read the headlines that day, however. They were in typeface an inch high.

HISTORY'S MIGHTIEST A-BLAST NEAR VEGAS.

Hughes' naked body went cold. His skin drank in the darkness and he found himself shivering as he attempted to control his racing mind. The threat of nuclear poison was so obvious to him that he wondered how others could possibly be so blind. Hughes read the remainder of the story, allowing each word to torture his conscience like nails driven through flesh. The blast was to be one megaton, equivalent to one million tons of TNT. It would be fired at the base of a 3,800-foot shaft at Pahute Mesa in the Nevada Test Range, 120 miles northeast of the city.

"This is the last straw," he quickly wrote Maheu. "I just this minute read that they are going to shoot off the largest nuclear explosion ever detonated in the U.S. And right here at the Vegas Test Site. I want you to call the Gov. at once and the Senators and Congressmen. If they do not cancel this one extra large explosion, I am going direct to the President in a personal appeal and demand that the entire test program be moved."

"Oh, he was scared all right," Maheu said in 1990. "It was Hughes' worst nightmare coming true. He wanted it stopped and was willing to spend his last dime to achieve it."

Hughes began a memo-writing campaign to Maheu that produced

sixteen separate sets of instructions that night. The memos would continue for days, each increasing in fear, the handwriting shaky at times. He offered to fund an independent study on the effects of underground testing. He pledged campaign financing to Congressmen who might agree with his stance. He offered to personally pay all "overtime and all other expense required to achieve a completion of any weapons program based on this test at the original target date for completion, should the Defense Department decide they need those weapons."

He instructed Maheu to "burn up all of your blue chip stamps, all the favors you have coming, and every other last little bit of pressure you can bring together in one intense, extreme, final drive." And so he did. Maheu made calls, he promised funds, he sent a trio of lobbyists[6] to Washington in an effort to be heard. Ultimately, nothing was effective in even slowing the countdown. Frustrated beyond endurance, Hughes finally handwrote a letter to the President in which he said in part:

> Based on my personal promise that independent scientists and technicians have definite evidence, and can obtain more, demonstrating the risk and uncertainty to the health of the citizens of southern Nevada, if the megaton-plus nuclear explosion is detonated tomorrow morning, will you grant even a brief postponement of this explosion to permit my representatives to come to Washington and lay before whomever you designate the urgent, impelling reasons why we feel a 90-day postponement is needed?

After expressing that he was not a "peacenik," Hughes asserted that his position would ultimately help the defense department by allowing the nuclear test program to proceed more rapidly than it was currently progressing. He mentioned an agreement he had with the AEC to move large explosions to Central Nevada.[7]

> It just does not seem to me that the citizens of southern Nevada should be forced to swallow something that the citizens of central Nevada would not tolerate and something that was removed from the Aleutian Islands because the Russians objected. I think Nevada has become a fully accredited state now and should no longer be treated like a barren wasteland that is only useful as a dumping place for poisonous, contaminated nuclear waste material, such as normally is carefully sealed up and dumped in the deepest part of the ocean.

---

6. Maheu sent Gillis Long, one-time Louisiana congressman to the AEC; Grant Sawyer, former Nevada governor met with Vice-President Hubert Humphrey; and Lloyd Hand, former White House chief of protocol attempted to see Lyndon Johnson.
7. Hughes never had any agreement with the Atomic Energy Commission.

Hughes went on to ask, "The AEC technicians assure that there will be no harmful consequences, but I wonder where those technicians will be ten or twenty years from now?"

Johnson received the rambling letter on the evening before the test and promptly ignored it, noting that the letter and its contents should not be exhibited at any future Johnson Library. He later confided to Robert Maheu that the letter was an embarrassment to Hughes. Yet, despite the hysteria of its contents, much of what Hughes wrote was prophetic.

Even as the test was detonated at 7 a.m. on April 26, 1968, the government was assuring its citizens that there was absolutely no danger from any nuclear fallout. The force of the explosion vibrated the Desert Inn and every other building in Las Vegas and was felt in three surrounding states. It created a hole 700 feet across, and left Hughes so distraught that he increased his drug consumption six-fold. When he woke from his stupor two days after the blast, he wrote Maheu yet another memo in which he said, "I was physically very ill and emotionally reduced to a nervous wreck by the end of the week and life is too short for that."

The day following the test, Hubert Humphrey declared his candidacy for the Democratic presidential nomination. When he did, Howard Hughes saw an opportunity to regain control of the White House, and began a concerted campaign to influence Washington. Its impact would ultimately change the course of U.S. politics forever.

SEVENTEEN

The Richest Man in America

I hate to disturb you this late, but I just saw
something on TV that litterally [sic] and actually
physically made me nauseated and I still am!
I saw a show on NBC in which the biggest
ugliest negro you ever saw in your life
was covered—litterally [sic] covered
from head to foot with vaseline
almost ¹/₂ of an inch thick.
It made you sick just to look at this man.

> Las Vegas, Nevada
> April 20, 1969
>> Hughes' memo to Robert Maheu after
>> watching a scene from *The Great White*
>> *Hope* starring James Earl Jones on the 23rd
>> Annual Tony Awards.

HOWARD HUGHES SANK INTO HIS BARCALOUNGER AND collapsed under the weight of his own fear. He reached for a pad of yellow legal paper and began to write. *Darkness to shadows. Darkness to shadows. Darkness to shadows.* He repeated the phrase running down the left side of the page twenty-six times and then boxed in his writing with a neatly drawn double line. He then flipped the page to a fresh sheet and began the exercise all over again. He was haunted by angry demons, raging with warnings about nuclear waste. He feared the water supply, he feared the air, he feared the soil, he feared his food—all potentially contaminated by the blast that had shaken the very floor on which he walked and had made him throw up all over himself, after which he wiped the vomit off his chest and legs and watched it splatter onto the carpet.

Hughes knew he had to be very careful not to appear

fanatical as he pushed forward with his plan. Nevada *had* to be freed from further testing at all costs. No amount was too great; it was *that* important. Hughes was proud of America's military and was committed to continuing as its largest defense contractor. He even approved of nuclear bombs. No problem there. He did not even care about nuclear testing. "I don't give an anthill if they want to blow each other up," he wrote Maheu. "Just don't let them do it *here*." This was not a case of national security. This was a personal issue. The care and preservation of Howard Robard Hughes.

In the April 1968 issue of *Fortune* magazine, Howard Hughes was declared the richest man in America. He shared the honor with oilman J. Paul Getty who, at 75, was thirteen years older than Hughes and accustomed to the title. Since the last time *Fortune* had conducted its survey of American millionaires, eleven years earlier, Hughes' fortune had more than tripled while Getty's estate had only doubled in value. According to *Fortune*, Hughes was worth $1.3 billion; Getty, $1.25 billion; and both figures set records for wealth. Until that point, *Fortune* had never placed any American in billionaire status at all.

With an ever-growing wallet, Hughes proposed to spend "every last penny if necessary" to buy his way into controlling the White House and thus stop nuclear testing in Nevada. In an effort to interest Vice President Hubert Humphrey in Hughes' determination to short-circuit the AEC, Maheu went to Humphrey's son Robert who happened to work for Radiarc, Inc., an electronics firm that Maheu owned. It was an open conduit that served Maheu well.

On May 9, 1968, he met with the Vice President in the Hilton Hotel in Denver, Colorado, and received Humphrey's guarantee to work on stopping nuclear tests in Nevada in exchange for a campaign contribution of $100,000—$50,000 in cash and $50,000 via a number of small checks. For his part, Humphrey (whom Hughes repeatedly referred to as *Humphries* in his memos) suggested that a panel of experts be assembled and a study financed to determine the safety of underground tests. While Hughes went along with the plan and authorized a $300,000 expenditure to pay for the study, he was ultimately interested in results, not independent panels of experts.

As an afterthought, Hughes promised $25,000 to Robert Kennedy, Humphrey's main competitor in the Democratic presidential primary

---

1. *Fortune* ranked six Americans in the $500 million to $1 billion class: oilman H. L. Hunt, Polaroid founder Dr. Edwin H. Land, shipping magnate Daniel K. Ludwig, plus bankers Paul Mellon, Richard King Mellon and Alisa Mellon Bruce. Kennedy patriarch Joseph P. Kennedy as well as all of the Rockefellers were among a group of 27 Americans with estates valued in the $200 million to $300 million class.

race. Hughes' opinion of the Kennedy family had not improved since JFK was in the White House, but after a personal plea from Pierre Salinger, fed through Maheu and onto Hughes, the billionaire opted for a token contribution. Salinger had arranged to pick up the money in cash from Maheu following the California primary, then several weeks away.

June 4, 1968. Hughes looked at his bowl of chicken soup and decided it needed to be reheated. Snapping his fingernails against the brown paper sack next to his bed, he roused George Francom from his chair outside the closed bedroom door and pointed to his soup bowl. Francom knew what Hughes intended by the gesture. He had already reheated the bowl of soup eight previous times that evening, only to watch his boss take a single spoonful and then leave the remaining soup to cool.

Hughes could not help it. His evening was not going well. Robert Kennedy was winning a lopsided victory in the California primary. As Kennedy raised his hand in triumph, forming the V-sign with his fingers, Hughes jeered loudly at the TV screen, cursing the candidate and shuddering at the thought of yet another Kennedy in the White House. Hughes continued to jeer as Kennedy left the stage of the ballroom at Los Angeles' Ambassador Hotel and walked through the hotel's kitchen to his waiting limousine.

Hughes knew the route well. He had used it himself on several occasions, and was originally shown it by his father as a teenager. This particular exit would be different, however. In an instant, another Kennedy lay shot and dying, his blood pooling on the tile floor. Hughes watched the replays on his own station, KLAS, ironically the only station still on the air, thanks solely to Hughes' erratic sleep habits. He callously and cruelly cheered the violent end that had come to the candidate, disappointed only that he was not pronounced dead at the scene.

Alternating between rambling outbursts and fits of laughter, Hughes waited eagerly for the announcement that would stun the country. He did not leave his television set for over twenty-four hours, not wanting to chance missing the moment. When Frank Mankiewicz walked before waiting TV cameras at L.A.'s Good Samaritan Hospital and announced to the world that Robert Kennedy had died, Hughes leaped off his chair and did a dance around his room, his frail, thin legs finding the life to celebrate. His impromptu display left him winded but pleased as he reached for a legal pad. Where the rest of America saw horror, Hughes saw opportunity.

> Bob—
>   I hate to be quick on the draw, but I see here an opportunity that may not happen again in a lifetime. I dont [sic] aspire to be President, but I do want political strength.

I mean the kind of an organization so that we would never have to worry about a jerky little thing like this anti-trust problem—not in 100 years.

And I mean the kind of a set up that, if we wanted to, could put Gov. Laxalt in the White House in 1972 or 76.

Anyway, it seems to me that the very people we need have just fallen smack into our hands.

MAHEU WAS APPALLED BY Hughes' candor, the blatancy of his request: hire Kennedy's people, *all* of them. "I am sure my impression must be wrong," Maheu wrote back, unable to believe the insensitivity of Hughes' memo. "Obviously Sen. Ted Kennedy will be their heir apparent. I expect to see some very strange alliances. In any event, Howard, will you please clarify my impression?"

Hughes' return memo was a klieg light wildly sweeping. "I want us to hire Bob Kennedy's entire organization. They are used to having the Kennedy money behind them and we can equal that. I dont [sic] want an alliance with the Kennedy group, I want to put them on the payroll."

Robert Kennedy's campaign chairman was Larry O'Brien, a man who had run several previous campaigns, including John Kennedy's run for the White House. He would soon would be picked up by Humphrey to manage his campaign as well. That Hughes wanted to place O'Brien on his payroll had to be handled discreetly. Neither O'Brien nor Hughes would be helped if the fact became publicly known.

Although Maheu was working sixteen-hour days managing five casinos and four hotels, he still arranged time to meet with O'Brien to explain Hughes' expectations. Basically, Hughes needed O'Brien to open doors in Washington—a town where no door stays closed for long in any case. Maheu met with O'Brien over the Fourth of July weekend, and the two men not only came to terms, they became good friends.[2] When Maheu made the appointment, his calendar was open. Hughes made certain that it would not stay that way.

Three days before O'Brien flew to Las Vegas, Howard Hughes announced his intention to acquire another company. It was a major acquisition, even for a man known for thinking big. Hughes offered to purchase forty-three percent of the American Broadcasting Company at $74.25 a share. It was a purchase worth $148.5 million plus change, and Hughes presented the deal in take-it-or-leave-it fashion, giving shareholders two weeks to sell him their stock at a price well in excess of the current market value of $58.87.

---

2. Ultimately, it was decided that O'Brien would receive $15,000 a month, paid through Joseph Napolitan Associates, a public relations firm in Washington, D.C.

At the time, ABC was a third-place also-ran that had yet to develop the sterling reputation its news and sports divisions would achieve in the decade ahead. "I have no desire to produce a long line of 'Batmen,'" Hughes wrote attorney Greg Bautzer. "I have no desire to be associated with a lot of artistic crap. I have no desire to remake the entertainment policy of TV, as many people want to do. My only real interest is in the very areas in which I understand ABC is really hopeless, News and Public Events and the technical side of the business in which field I am equipped to do a really outstanding job." Hughes' memos to Maheu were even more candid. He wanted the network to toss the weight of its news division behind the presidential candidate of his choice, and at the moment that choice was Hubert Humphrey.

When ABC President Leonard Goldenson met with Bautzer on July 3, he made his position very clear. The network was filing suit to derail Hughes' bid, and on July 9, he made good on his promise in the United States District Court in New York, charging that the takeover violated FCC rules and federal antitrust laws. Goldenson pleaded with his stockholders not to attempt to capitalize on Hughes' offer, stating, "The offer is substantially below the intrinsic per share value of ABC and overlooks future growth prospects of the company."

The FCC leaped into the fight by announcing that it would hold its own public hearings on the deal, and warned Hughes not to use any stock he might purchase in the meantime "to influence the policies or operations of ABC." It also hinted that it would expect Hughes to attend a licensing hearing, the thought of which sent the billionaire into alternating fits of sweat and temper. His memos to Maheu reflect his concern.

> I don't see how I dare launch into our campaign unless I have some assurance of the FCC's support, without my personal appearance. Now, I see only one way such support might be assumed, and that is in case one of the candidates or the white house on behalf of its favorite candidate wants the support of ABC. If such a trade could be made, it seems to me that we have the tools with which to make it. In other words, our present position plus white house or Humphries' [sic] full support would spell certain FCC approval in my book, and with that assurance, I would go full blast ahead. Now, you really have to be careful how you approach this bag of hot potatoes.

THE ONE-POINT-THREE-BILLION-DOLLAR MAN needed reassurance. And, as it happened, an enema. He had not had a successful bowel movement in eight days, and slowly lifted himself out of his lounge chair, pieces of damp paper towel insulation sticking momentarily to his back before falling in a death glide to the floor. According to the activity logs meticulously maintained by Hughes' aides, while ABC frantically pushed its case for an injunction against his takeover, the Old Man conducted his business while sitting on the toilet for most of July 9 and into July 10. In an attempt to cleanse himself of the bacteria and spores he was convinced were released in the underground nuclear tests, Hughes began to wash his arms and his face with rubbing alcohol, using paper towels to wipe the liquid repeatedly up and down over the same spots on his body—those he felt were particularly contaminated.

Unaware of Hughes' incapacity, Maheu continued to relay messages and memos to the ninth floor suite, updating Hughes on the progress of the stock tender. "We still have time to condition the individual members of the board and at all levels below," Maheu wrote to Hughes, promising to have his team of Washington attorneys "condition" the FCC to the fact that Hughes would not make a personal appearance.

His back now breaking out in bedsores, and a tumor beginning to grow on his temple, Hughes absorbed the pressure of the moment by swallowing four 10-mg Valium tablets and turning out his bedside lamp. When he awoke a day and a half later, he began writing memos at a feverish pace, making up for lost time and relaying his thoughts at machine-gun speed as if he feared they would be otherwise lost forever.

In addition to his other challenges, Hughes received word that the Justice Department was making noises about anti-trust conflicts with Hughes Tool owning a CBS TV affiliate, and Hughes Aircraft manufacturing communications satellites plus electronic equipment. "It is beginning to look as if the name of the game is "Justice Dept. Anti-Trust Pressure,'" Hughes wrote to Maheu. "Bob, I think it is imperative that we make an alliance with Humphries, the White House, Nixon, or McCarthy and agree to supply all-out unlimited support in return for taking this Justice Dept. off my back but *now!*"

Hughes' panic translated itself into a series of extraordinary plans that the billionaire formulated and then discarded in rapid succession until finally arriving at one he labeled "fool-proof." Hughes suggested to Maheu that he wanted him to leak word that he intended to sell his newly tendered ABC stock to Texas millionaire James J. Ling,[3] the Carl Icahn of his day, in

---

3. James J. Ling founded a small electrical company in Dallas in 1947 that he took public in 1955 by selling his stock from a booth at the Texas State Fair. Through acquisitions and mergers, he acquired speaker manufacturer Altec Electronics, missile maker Temco Aircraft, defense contractor Chance Vought and renamed his company Ling-Temco-Vought (LTV Corp.) in 1961, and became the first financier to issue junk bonds. Later acquisitions included Braniff Airways, National Car Rental, Jones and Laughlin Steel, plus resorts in Acapulco, Guerrero, Mexico, and Steamboat Springs, Colorado. His estate in Dallas was modeled after Versailles. His motto: "Don't tell me how hard you work. Tell me how much you get done."

the hope that the network would prefer Hughes over Ling, "The Acquisition King." "It seems to me the only hope lies in the remote possibility of persuading Goldenson that he really won't gain anything if he forces me, through threats of personal appearances, etc., to sell out to a Ling or somebody equally tough."

With time running out, and his options with them, Maheu volleyed back to Hughes, "I know that you don't like to hear anything you don't want to hear. As you know, I was selling positive thinking before [Dr. Norman Vincent] Peale ever thought of writing a book. But even affirmative thinking must have some foundation in the realm of realism. If you are prepared to tell me that, at a given point, you will make an appearance, I'll guarantee you that we'll deliver ABC to you on a silver platter."

Federal Judge Dudley B. Bonsal refused ABC's motion for a temporary restraining order against Hughes, who suddenly began to sniff victory. Bonsal ruled based on the possibility that stockholders "might suffer real injury" if not allowed to take advantage of Hughes offer of $74.25 a share purchase price.

ABC's Goldenson reacted to the setback by taking out full-page ads in the *New York Times* and *Wall Street Journal* reiterating the inadequacy of Hughes' offer, while ABC's attorneys returned to court in an effort to serve Hughes with a subpoena, a fruitless task if past experience were any indication. Despite Judge Bonsal's attempts to keep a cap on the media exploitation of the proceedings, the specter of Hughes reached across the continent when an overeager newsman pointed to a man seated at the back of Bonsal's courtroom and identified the lanky man in a gray suit as Hughes himself.

The embarrassed man, who had been sitting quietly in the rear of the courtroom, raced for the door followed closely by a gaggle of reporters and anxious ABC attorneys, leaving Bonsal hammering his gavel to a nearly empty gallery. Cornered in the hallway, surrounded by newsmen and subpoena-wielding lawyers, the tall, thin, moustached man identified himself as someone named William Donovan, an insurance salesman from Manhattan, who blanched at the attention and excused himself to return to work.

Now facing the very real prospect that the FCC would insist on a face-to-face meeting with the real thing, Hughes was having second thoughts about his eagerness to buy a television network. The more ABC fought his stock tender offer, the more relieved Hughes became, despite his seeming anger in the press. Maheu was placed in the uncomfortable position of having to defend Hughes' offer while at the same moment attempting to give the Old Man an emergency escape route if he wanted out.

The seesaw that was Hughes' mind continued to teeter up and down, alternating between extreme enthusiasm at the prospect of owning a network and the power of its news organization, and profound terror at the prospect that he would be sued when he failed to appear before the FCC. On July 14, just one day before Hughes' self-imposed two-week deadline would expire, less than 100,000 shares had been tendered.

"It seems to me, Bob," Hughes memoed Maheu, "there is a comparatively easy way to get an immediate answer to the network decision. I think such an answer should be obtainable by Mr. O'Brien or Mr. Finney[4] marching in and collaring Johnson or Humphries and saying: 'Look, my friend, my client Mr. Hughes has initiated the machinery to acquire control of ABC. He has ridden out the first very controversial weeks and is in pretty good shape. He had no idea that there would be as much resistance from Mr. Goldenson." Hughes thought that O'Brien or Finney had only to stroll into the office of the President of the United States and "work the conversation around to where he (our man) can gracefully say: 'What do you think Mr. Hughes should do? I think he would like your counsel.'"

While Maheu attempted to discourage Hughes from attempting to inject Lyndon B. Johnson into the mix, Judge Bonsal opened the floodgates by ruling on Friday, July 12, 1968 that Hughes was not compelled to appear in court to answer the network's objections to his tender offer, and in a special Saturday ruling, sided with Hughes by denying ABC's last-ditch injection plea. As Hughes and Maheu helplessly watched, one and a half million shares came pouring into Hughes' brokers during the final day of his offer. It was obvious to even the most casual observer that Hughes had won. By merely extending his offer for as little as an extra day, he could easily have had the necessary votes to take control of the American Broadcasting Company.

On Tuesday, July 16, the New York Stock Exchange halted all trading on ABC stock while it waited for Hughes to announce his decision. For three hours, Goldenson huddled with his attorneys to develop the network's strategy for what he was certain would be a Hughes victory. In the penthouse of the Desert Inn, the billionaire fretted, his thirst for the power of ABC News balanced against his fear of appearing in public. In the end, fear won out. At noon, Hughes had his brokers announce that he was canceling his offer.

"This decision results from the inordinate opposition to our offer interposed by ABC's management through Leonard Goldenson, its president," Hughes' statement read in part. "While Hughes Tool Company

---

4. Washington attorney Thomas Finney who represented Hughes.

has prevailed in the litigation precipitated by the ABC management, it has no desire to continue its offering if, as Mr. Goldenson contends, it is not in the best interest of ABC or its stockholders." He did not add, "and make me come out of hiding."

Twenty years earlier, Howard Hughes would have relished the fight. Now, at 63, he was unable to conceive of ever leaving the darkness of his solitude again. It had been nearly eleven months since he had even walked to the door of his bedroom, let alone go outside. It had taken every ounce of his strength that day to just look around the corner when he heard voices. John Holmes was on duty at the aides' desk, speaking to a man unfamiliar to Hughes. As the billionaire stood frozen in the doorway to his bedroom, a muscular blond man looked directly at him. Hughes pulled instinctively at his long, unwashed hair, then stroked his gray beard with his curling fingernails, and without saying a word, retraced his steps, a stooped figure backing into his bedroom, shutting the door behind him.

For Gordon Margulis, the sighting of Howard Hughes would dramatically alter his world. The waiter at the Desert Inn was a British import, a one-time middleweight boxer who had arrived in Nevada hoping to make a life for himself in America. He did that, and more. Soon after beginning to work at the hotel, he was given the assignment to deliver room service meals to the ninth floor. For over eight months, he wheeled trays of food onto the elevator, rose to the top floor, logged in with the guard, walked down the long hallway, and into Penthouse One. It was only then, in April 1967, that the Old Man appeared in the doorway and looked him straight in the face.

"Who was that man?" Hughes later asked Holmes, grilling the aide about the unwelcome outsider. It was not easy for Holmes to calm Hughes' fears. He imagined newspaper headlines painting the image of an ancient, bearded hippie, naked in hanging flesh and visible bedsores. It was an invasion of his privacy in the most intimate way. He wanted an explanation, and barely stopped obsessing long enough for Holmes to attempt to allay his apprehension. Margulis had been cleared, even recommended by hotel security, Hughes was told, then tested by his Mormon aides for months, and found to be both totally discreet and reliable.

"We'll keep him then," Hughes said in an aboutface, and went back to worrying about nuclear testing. Just that easily, Margulis was in, added to that rarest of men—the ones who had recently seen Hughes. The number was currently down to less than ten. His aides, a pair of doctors, and now Margulis. He also had the distinction of being the only one not on the Hughes Tool payroll, and not under the direct control of Bill Gay.

Aide Mell Stewart formed a kinship with Margulis, since Stewart was also something of an odd-man-out among Gay's team of the Palace Guard. Stewart was a barber, and a good one, who ran his own shop in Huntington Park, California. He had been recruited by a friend of his wife's to cut the hair of "a very important man." The year was 1961 and when Stewart traveled the distance to the Beverly Hills Hotel, he did not realize that he was about to enter a whole new world.

John Holmes was on duty at Bungalow Four that day, and gave Stewart the crash course in paper towel insulation and no-talking rules. Hughes was naked, "as usual," when he received the stranger, who did his best not to look amazed at the appearance of the then-multimillionaire. At the time, Hughes' hair hung a foot down his back and had not been trimmed in over four years. Hughes' former barber, a man named Eddie Alexander, had been on call the previous seventeen years, before giving a revealing interview to Thomas Thompson writing in *Life* magazine, in which he likened Hughes' appearance to that of Moses. Out went Alexander, in came Stewart who had no desire to repeat the error, especially after being paid $1,000 for his work that day.

Eventually Stewart closed up his barber shop and headed to Utah in semi-retirement. Even though Hughes was getting less than one haircut a year, the thought of losing his personal barber festered in the Old Man's mind until he asked for Stewart and his family to be brought to Las Vegas and put on the permanent payroll. Stewart was given an assortment of outside assignments to keep him busy, since a trim every other year or so was hardly justification for his $75-a-day salary.[5] In addition to picking up the mail from Hughes' private post office box, it was Stewart's assignment to purchase Hughes' rubbing alcohol at various shops around Las Vegas. And Hughes was going through as many as a four pint bottles a day, particularly after he lost ABC.

It was at this same time that Hughes began to urinate into Mason jars that he capped and stored "for protection" in various closets on the ninth floor. Although not based on any specific medical urgency, Hughes increased his use of codeine and Valium as well. Drugged to excess, Hughes wallowed in his own filth, refusing once again to leave his recliner and insisting on allowing no one in his suite. With no active acquisition in progress to distract him, he began to obsess again about the threat of further underground nuclear tests. He was enduring a paranoiac depression that skirted the limits of sanity, writing pages of notes to himself that featured the word *OUT* printed in bold letters repeated four times per page without explanation. This episode of behavior was only

5. Stewart's annual salary was originally $27,375, equal to $170,000 today.

broken by his sudden decision to buy—this time back in familiar territory, aviation.

His target was a company called Air West, formed several years earlier when three struggling airlines, Bonanza Air Lines based in Phoenix, West Coast Airlines out of Seattle, and Pacific Air Lines headquartered in San Francisco, joined together and, thus banded, attempted to fly. The result was a hodgepodge effort at best, beginning with a reservation system that frequently misplaced passengers as well as entire flights, that soon gained it the nickname "Air Worst." It was the kind of quagmire that seemed to fit Hughes best. A scenario in which he could wait until the airline was breathing fumes instead of air, and arrive in a dramatic fashion to save the company.

"The plan necessitates that the stock edge downward with the existing continuous bad news, and then that we come along with a spectacular offer to pay the stockholders in liquidation a price substantially above the market," Hughes wrote to Maheu. "Any rise in the market before our offer will adversely affect the plan."

July 29, 1968. Maheu flew from Las Vegas to Los Angeles (not on Air West) and checked into the Century Plaza Hotel. He had an appointment to meet with the airline's chairman, Nick Bez, the following day. Also in the hotel that night: Vice President Hubert Humphrey. It was not a coincidence.

Maheu originally planned his visit to L.A. to attend a $5,000 a plate political fund-raiser for the Democratic candidate, and had arranged to host a VIP cocktail party for Humphrey before the event. During the dinner, Lloyd Hand, who was traveling with the vice president, invited Maheu to join the candidate and his wife in their limousine after dinner, a setting that afforded the privacy needed to handle another Hughes assignment: the transfer of $50,000 in cash to Humphrey's campaign for the White House.

When Maheu entered the vice-president's limousine outside the Century Plaza Hotel, he was carrying a brown attaché case; when he got out of the car one block down the street, he left the case behind. Later, when quizzed about the campaign contribution, Humphrey denied ever receiving the money. "I don't want to call him a liar," Maheu said at the time. "Let's just say that he has a conveniently poor memory." Apparently, Humphrey also forgot that he sent Maheu a note thanking Hughes for the money.[6]

---

6. Humphrey received a second $50,000 in contributions from Hughes via checks drawn on the account of Robert A. Maheu & Associates on October 17, 1968, and later reimbursed by Hughes. The checks were in various amounts, none over the $3,000 legal limit, and made out to various Humphrey reelection committees.

The day following the Humphrey money drop, Maheu turned to the issue of Nick Bez. He described the large, 73-year-old Yugoslavian as a "diamond in the rough, who doesn't have very good command of the English language." Good English or not, Bez was a multimillionaire in his own right, and known as the "Sultan of Salmon" for his fishing fleet and canning empire. Convincing Bez to sell was simple. He was anxious to unload the fast-disintegrating airline, though at an inflated price. Since Hughes loved negotiating, he played with the numbers in a back-and-forth volley that found Maheu growing increasingly restless after weeks with no signed deal. The delay, as usual, could be laid to Hughes, who refused to respond to Bez's latest offer to sell Air West at $22 a share.

Maheu never did learn the cause for Hughes' procrastination. At the time, the billionaire was in a quandary over turkey breast, and in typical fashion, he gave it his full attention. The situation originated when Hughes saw an advertisement on television for Swanson's Turkey TV Dinners. He watched as the black-and-white commercial showed the metal tray with its various compartments filled with sliced turkey, gravy and stuffing, mashed potatoes, and apple-cranberry cobbler. Suddenly, the man who had to have all his food prepared with special equipment, his meat from special butchers, his utensils sterilized, his soup a specific temperature, wanted frozen dinners. Night after night, the richest man in America was served nothing but Swanson's turkey in a three-part aluminum tray. He was eating like never before. Then, just as Bez was arriving at his sale price for Air West, Hughes discovered that certain other Swanson's TV Dinners came with peach cobbler—the billionaire's favorite.

While Bez fretted and Maheu waited for a response to the $22-a-share offer, Hughes sent word to his aides that he wanted his turkey dinner with peach cobbler, not "this soggy cherry stuff," as he called Swanson's apple-cranberry dessert. "Also, suggest that they start using all white meat turkey rather than the white and dark slices they now use. That is to say, do not include any dark meat in the turkey that is placed in the turkey TV dinner," Hughes wrote. "While they are at it, it would be better if the dressing was placed in a separate compartment instead of under the turkey. This will keep the meat and the dressing from sticking together." He demanded that the aides contact C.A. Swanson & Sons, then owned by the Campbell Soup Company. "Please ask them to supply the correctly made meals to R.M. Johnson in care of the Desert Inn." It hardly seemed like much to ask. He even offered to buy "up to three dozen turkey dinners per month."

For a moment, Hughes' aides thought they might one day hear that their boss had bought Campbell Soup, just to get peach cobbler in a frozen meal. Fortunately for all concerned, before Campbell could be contacted, Hughes saw another advertisement—this time for a roast beef sandwich from a fast-food chain called Arby's. Hughes thought the sandwich looked pretty good and decided to order one (to go). What was basically a simple request became a major challenge when Hughes informed aide Gordon Margulis that he wanted the local Las Vegas Arby's to purchase a special stainless steel slicer to be used only on his order, at their own expense, of course. For his part, Hughes authorized Margulis to inform the fast-food franchisee that if he liked the sandwich, it could look forward to repeat business. While Margulis paced the Desert Inn formulating a plan to explain such a unique request, Maheu was busy in California doing some pacing of his own.

On August 11, 1968, Hughes officially announced that he would pay $90 million to buy Air West Inc., in a deal confirmed by Bez, who said that "he and others representing a substantial amount of the stock of Air West have agreed to use their best efforts to effect the sale of the assets and transfer of the business" to Hughes.

What should have been a simple stock buyout turned into a screaming match when Bez' partners in the airline were informed of the deal, after the fact. "It's an out-and-out giveaway in terms of the potential of the company," the airline's president G. Robert Henry said. "It's not in the best interests of the stockholders," he added, while pouting that he was not consulted during the negotiations. Edmund Converse, the airline's vice-chairman and David R. Grace, chairman of the airline's executive committee, joined him in his protest. "We don't need a merger to produce a future," Henry insisted. "What we need is to be left alone so we can get along with realizing the company's tremendous potential." The airline's thirteen thousand stockholders, who watched as the value of the airline slipped on the open market thanks to its poor service and declining passenger load, entered the fray shouting.

While Maheu left the Air West principals to fight among themselves like alley cats over rotting garbage, he returned to Las Vegas in time to initiate damage control over the seemingly endless TWA litigation. On September 21, 1968, Hughes learned that he had been hit with the largest judgment ever made against an individual defendant when special master Herbert Brownell, a one-time Unites States attorney general, recommended that TWA be awarded $137 million from the Hughes Tool Company. Brownell's report, which ran 323 pages, agreed with most of TWA's claims and found that Hughes' failure to appear in court was a flagrant attempt to subvert the country's legal system. Davis, who had originally projected that Hughes' maximum liability would not top $5 million, promised to continue to fight the opinion, which was then forwarded to Federal Judge Charles Metzner for final judgment.

Hughes' frustration did not lessen when he watched the political polls on television showing Richard Nixon with a decided lead over Hughes' candidate, Hubert Humphrey. In an effort to equal his odds, Hughes authorized Maheu to send $100,000 to Nixon as well. It was a donation that Maheu did not anticipate would be a problem. Former FBI agent Richard A. Danner, who was then working for the Nixon campaign, had approached Hughes' Washington attorney Edward Morgan about arranging for the donation after Hughes' gift to Humphrey became known.

The $50,000 in small checks posed no problem, but the cash transfer was a bit more difficult. Originally, Hughes was to get the money to Maheu, with Maheu giving the money to Morgan. Morgan was to hand off the cash to Danner who in turn would give it to his friend, millionaire banker Bebe Rebozo, whom he had introduced to Richard Nixon. Rebozo would then hold the cash for the presidential candidate. It was a convoluted path that was designed to make the money trail difficult to follow. Too difficult, as things unfolded. Rebozo did not want to deal with Morgan, who was a lifelong Democrat, and soon Danner wanted Maheu to handle the entire transaction.

In November 1968, Nixon beat Humphrey in the Presidential election, making Maheu's job more difficult since candidate Nixon was now president-elect. Anxious to rid himself of the $50,000 still in his safe, Maheu decided to take the money and give it to Nixon himself at the Republican Governors Conference in Palm Springs, California, a function at which Nixon was to speak. With the cash hidden under the carpet in the trunk of his car, Maheu drove to Palm Springs, but an opportunity never presented itself for the exchange. The well-traveled $50,000 was returned to the safe, while Maheu went to San Francisco to wrap up Hughes' purchase of Air West.

In late December the stockholders had voted to sell their shares to Hughes, happy to receive his $22 per share. The Air West board was not going to acquiesce without a fight and found an angel of mercy in the form of Northwest Airlines, which made a pitch to buy Air West in an end run. With the help of Chester Davis, the stockholders slapped their own board with a lawsuit two days later in Delaware superior court, in what looked like a standoff, with the clock ticking down to a Hughes deadline set for New Year's Eve.

Taking no chances, Hughes persuaded several of Air West's larger stockholders, including Las Vegas Sun publisher Hank Greenspun, to unload 86,000 shares on the market, promising to make up any loss they might incur. The move had the predictable effect, with the stock dropping even further in price. When Northwest heard about the collapse of the stock, the airline backed out of the deal, leaving the board little choice but to settle with Hughes, and place Air West under his control. It was a triumphant end to a chaotic year. Though Hughes never did get his peach cobbler and turkey breast, or an Arby's roast beef sandwich carved with his own stainless steel slicer, he managed to successfully skirt process servers, judgments, and illness without ever once seeing the light of the sun.

With Richard Nixon taking his oath of office, it became more important than ever for Hughes to feel secure with his White House connection, for his affairs were now interwoven like braided hair with the federal government. His move to buy Las Vegas had been stalled by the threat of an anti-trust action. The TWA judgment seemed headed to the Supreme Court. His takeover of Air West still needed the approval of the Civil Aeronautics Board. And he remained the nation's top defense contractor at the mercy of the Pentagon and NASA for business.

Hughes' insistence on placing Larry O'Brien on the payroll gave him political connections, but not White House clout. For that, Hughes was relying on his long-standing relationship with the president-elect, helped along by Maheu, who hired Richard Danner as managing director of the Frontier Hotel. Hughes was impressed, of course, that Danner was ex-FBI, and even more impressed that he had a direct pipeline to Nixon. Still it was not enough. "I want to see just how much water we really draw with this Administration after so many years of all-out effort to achieve it," Hughes wrote Maheu in January 1969.

Yet only weeks into the administration he began to see the first signs of failure. "Not one of the Nixon appointees was given to me for consideration and none such nominee was made in my behalf with my approval," he complained after Nixon selected his cabinet. The billionaire not only wanted to be viewed favorably by the administration, he also wanted to have a say in its personnel.

Maheu reminded Hughes of John Mitchell, Nixon's choice for attorney general. "Mitchell is thoroughly acceptable and we have excellent entrees to him," Maheu memoed, and two weeks later noted, "I am most happy with the new head of the anti-trust division. He was our #1 choice from among several very highly qualified candidates whose names were submitted to me well in advance of the appointment."

Hughes remained unconvinced, raging at Maheu with increased intensity, as the administration began making decisions and awarding contracts, all without a word of advice from Hughes. "When Nixon ran for President, I told you I wanted to go just as far as necessary to have some voice in the new administration, but I just have no assurance at all as to what the future holds."

That Nixon did not plan to cater to Hughes was obvious from his first day in office. The president was only too pleased to accept Hughes' contributions, but never seriously considered approaching him for advice. If anything, Nixon *feared* a direct association with Hughes. The man was too unpredictable and under too much scrutiny to prove helpful to the administration, and could easily have generated damaging press, given the extent to which the government was involved with Hughes Aircraft.

In his efforts to isolate himself from a curious world, Hughes had managed to provide it with the fodder of speculation. The less that was actually known, the more that was made up, until no one, not even the President of the United States, knew what to believe about the recluse.

With the dawn of the Nixon administration, subterfuge became the order of business, intimidation the key to success. Unwilling to accept anything short of a pivotal role, Hughes continued to push Maheu to make his power felt, and in doing so sent his alter ego down an irreversible path. The line between where Hughes ended and Maheu began became blurred to the point that not even Maheu was able to tell the difference between himself and Hughes anymore. He was a caricature of his boss's creation, ripe for disaster with nowhere to hide.

EIGHTEEN

The Great Divide

Bob, I want you to remember one thing.
I can buy any man in the world, or I can
destroy him. If that wasnt [sic] true,
people like me wouldnt [sic] exist.

Las Vegas, Nevada
May 12, 1969
Hughes' memo to Robert Maheu.

IN THE TWO YEARS THAT HOWARD HUGHES HAD BEEN IN Las Vegas, his bed sheets had only been changed five times. The shag carpet in his bedroom had never been vacuumed; the end table had never been dusted; and the bathroom never cleaned. His closets were beginning to fill with Mason jars filled with urine, and the odor of rubbing alcohol barely camouflaged the stench from his rotting teeth and fungus-contorted nails.

But that was not what was causing him to obsess in frustration as he lay tormented on his recliner, livid at the situation in which he found himself. The problem, as Hughes saw it, was that his alter ego was *thinking*. Robert Maheu, his consummate problem-solver, seemed to be operating on his own agenda; having *opinions*; even *arguing*, for crying out loud. It was a situation that Hughes could no more understand than he could tolerate.

After all, Hughes thought, he had given Maheu everything he had requested—the yacht in the marina in California, the penthouse in Newport Beach, two Cadillacs, and just recently, permission to spend half a million dollars on a brand new mansion in Las Vegas. There was his $10,000-a-week salary and his unlimited expense account into which he lavishly dipped. All in the name of representing Hughes to the world.

Yet Maheu had failed to stop the nuclear testing in Nevada; he had failed to settle the TWA lawsuit; he had failed to get the anti-trust clearance to buy more casinos; and he had failed to acquire the ABC network for him. There were any number of excuses, of course. Maheu always had an excuse. The change of administration in Washington, the failure of Chester Davis in court, the refusal of Hughes to appear in Washington. Hughes was not paying for excuses. He was paying for results—results that he failed to see.

Perhaps the biggest failure of all, however, was Maheu's handling of Kirk Kerkorian. Now *there* was a problem, Hughes reasoned. A thorn in his abscessed side that Maheu had not only tolerated but also seemingly encouraged. Kerkorian was an eighth-grade dropout who built a multimillion-dollar fortune through hard work and good luck. When he arrived in Las Vegas at the end of 1967 flush with $100 million in cash from the sale of Trans International Airlines, a charter service, and bought the Flamingo Hotel on the Las Vegas strip, neither Hughes nor Maheu paid much attention. That was before, of course. Before Kerkorian put Las Vegas on notice that he intended to build the largest hotel in the world—the International, with fifteen hundred rooms, a casino the size of two football fields, and a swimming pool that was big enough to qualify as the largest man-made body of water in Nevada, if you did not include Lake Mead.

It was an entrance that rivaled Hughes' own, and Kerkorian needed to be stopped at all costs. Upon Hughes' first instruction, Maheu attempted to buy out Kerkorian, stop construction, and, hopefully, leave the skeleton of a partially finished building to weather and age. When that ploy fell on deaf ears, Hughes offered to join forces with Kerkorian, perhaps even meet with him. Maheu knew as well as Hughes that such a meeting would never take place, but to sidetrack the International, Hughes was willing to make any offer, suggest any scheme.

Kerkorian was not interested in doing business with anyone. With his financing in place, his plans drawn, his land purchased, and his construction underway, he was amused by Hughes' continuing overtures, and played his own game of up-the-ante. Not only was he not interested in selling the International, Kerkorian was eager to publicize the fact, and gave an interview in which he mocked Hughes' vain efforts to stop its construction. Not content with simply embarrassing the billionaire, he took the challenge to a new level and invited Hughes to attend his opening gala, set for July 4, 1969.

Hughes countered Kerkorian's playful attitude by buying the tallest building in Las Vegas—the thirty-one story Landmark Hotel. Originally constructed in 1961, the hotel had sat dormant and unfinished due to financial problems and litigation. Maheu strongly objected to the purchase because its unusual design limited its profit potential. But Hughes did not care about profits; he cared about beating Kerkorian. Despite its ugly facade, a circular space needle with a flattened saucer on top, the Landmark had two major assets—it was directly across the street from the International, and, symbolically, looked down on the hotel.

Hughes was able to circumvent the justice department's determination to prevent additional Hughes investments in Las Vegas hotels and casinos under its failing-business concept that allowed for emergency takeovers of bankruptcies. In addition to overruling Maheu on the purchase, he refused to allow his alter ego to negotiate the price, publicizing the fact that he was paying one hundred percent on the dollar as well as assuming all the Landmark's long-overdue debt. The building cost Hughes $17,300,000.

Once resigned to the purchase, Maheu immediately began planning a grand opening for the hotel and casino, aimed at robbing the excitement from the International. It was not an easy assignment. Kerkorian was not only opening the largest hotel, he had signed Barbra Streisand to perform in the hotel's showroom. Celebrities and journalists from around the world were being flown in for the occasion, and Maheu had determined to counter Kerkorian's event with one that was bigger, brighter, and more exciting. He anticipated the event would seal his place in Hughes' hierarchy, a celebration of the magic of the Hughes-Maheu marriage.

Initially, Maheu had every reason to think that his plans would go expeditiously forward. He had, after all, planned many private parties, entertaining as Hughes' head man in Las Vegas, reinforcing his position in the magic kingdom. Those functions, however, were Maheu events. The grand opening of the Landmark was going to belong to Hughes, his first party since claiming Las Vegas as his own personal property. He would not attend, of course, but that was not the point.

Initially, Hughes entered into the excitement of staging the event, suggesting a headliner to open the small 400-seat showroom that topped the hotel. Hughes wanted Dean Martin for the job, even though he was part-owner of the Riviera Hotel and under contract there. Hughes suggested that perhaps Martin would jump at the opportunity if it were sweetened by the offer to finance a future film. "Bob, there is not an actor alive who does not have some pet idea he would like to make into a movie," Hughes wrote Maheu. "If Dean Martin does not have such a pet idea, he will be the first movie star I have ever heard of in my entire life who does not."

Maheu upped the bar. Why not get Martin, Frank Sinatra, and

Sammy Davis, a Rat Pack reunion that Maheu suggested be called "Hughes Parade of Stars." He pitched the concept with unbridled enthusiasm, suggesting that the Landmark could outshine the International by opening on July 1, ahead of the competition. It was the kind of coup that recalled previous Hughes triumphs—the *Hell's Angels* premiere and the flight of the *Hercules*.

Despite their lengthy association, Maheu's suggestion revealed his lack of complete comprehension of the man for whom he worked. Hughes was appalled at the suggestion that his name be attached to a Las Vegas production, fearing that "critics will consider that (he had) moved into the theatrical realm and (had) thereby placed (himself) in their target range." Classic Hughes. Fear of criticism. Memories of *The Outlaw*. He was sweating as he wrote the memo, leaving a phantom stain on the legal pad.

"Now, regarding the opening date," he added. "I humbly beg you not to permit anything to leak out in confirmation of any July 1st date. Just as determined as you are to beat K to the punch with an earlier opening than the International, I am equally convinced it is a mistake.

"In two nearly simultaneous dates such as this, the later one is always the climax, and the one remembered. Also, the entity opening second is always the newest, and the first one is as old as yesterday's newspaper."

Maheu was used to Hughes' early objections to many of his ideas, and initially thought little of the memo's issues. Placing the opening date on hold temporarily, Maheu began to assemble a guest list of four hundred invitees based on names he had cultivated in the course of business. It was only after getting Hughes' response that Maheu began to realize how difficult this assignment was to be. Hughes rejected every name on the list.

> I understand your anxiety to get started on the list of invites. However, the only lasting damage will come from failure to invite certain important people while inviting others, about whom said important people will no doubt learn. Now, Bob, I simply dont [sic] have the man-hours, and you dont [sic] want to wait for me to go thru this list name by name. You will just have to appoint somebody to make a new list using this concept:
>
> Categorize the people you want, and where you invite one such person, invite likewise the others in the same category who have equal merit, who are equal friends, etc., unless they have done something to be disqualified, or unless they should be disqualified because of simple lack of stature, or disloyalty, or such-like.
>
> For example, if you intend to invite actors and actresses, as you evidently do, I think somebody should go thru the Central Casting

Directory, or the Academy lists and pick out all the actors or actresses above a certain level of importance, unless they are ruled out for some reason such as I have suggested above.

I only ask that it be based upon some consistency. For example, in view of some of the people included, such as the head of Reynolds Electric, I certainly think you should include all the very top people at Lockheed, and this may make it necessary to include the heads of other aircraft companies, and this immediately brings up the question of the heads of the airlines whom I know well.

This is one most important question, Bob. If you ask too many people who are good friends of mine, then you must consider how many of these may be disappointed if I do not see them. Also, you must consider how many others may unavoidably be forgotten and who will be deeply hurt for this reason. When you boil it down, Bob, I think, for a number of reasons, it would be a mistake to invite anybody just because he is a friend of mine.

I think you should divide the list into categories and try to be *consistant* (sic) in inviting all people in each category who are *equally qualified*.

MAHEU HAD A SINKING FEELING when he read Hughes' memo. He looked at his list of names, looked again at Hughes' memo, walked across his office, opened a hidden panel in the wall, and poured himself a drink. It was going to be a long month. Had he realized just how long, he would have made the drink a double.

Assuming that the easiest way around the invitation list was to let Hughes invite the guests, Maheu made that request and once again asked for some direction as to the opening date. "I sincerely hope that you understand the truly unbelievable position in which I am placed when I still cannot commit a day of opening," he lamented. "Howard, we are not the least bit stubborn on July 1 *per se*. If you prefer that we do it a few days after the International, please give us a fixed date and we will proceed accordingly. But darn it, Howard, if you care about what happens to the Landmark, you simply cannot hold this decision in abeyance any longer."

When Hughes received Maheu's note, he wrote across the page *How much you bet*, followed the sentence with two big question marks dug into the paper and placed the memo on top of his neatly stacked boxes of Kleenex. He then took a legal pad and a Parker pen, and wrote two lines:

Bob, I dont [sic] have the facilities to compile a list. You will have to make the list.

IT WAS with great control that Maheu read the returned memo and sat back in his chair. Planning the opening party for the Landmark should have been the easy part. The hotel itself was causing enough of a challenge. After having sat vacant for eight years, the physical property was in need of extensive work. The air conditioning was malfunctioning, seeming to run out of energy as it rose toward the top floors. It was a quality it shared with the outside elevator, its glass walls designed to provide a dramatic panoramic view of the city. It did—when it worked.

The hotel itself was a strange mix of dated space-age murals, fake Inca woodcarvings, and Italian statues, which seemed remarkably at home in Las Vegas. It needed to be repainted, cleaned and polished, with extensive work required on its exterior paving as well as neglected landscaping. And all finished in time for an opening that might or might not be less than a month away.

"Here I am on the front line talking to Dean Martin, Danny Thomas, the Astronauts, the public, the Governor, and I don't know what in the hell I am talking about because you still have not given us a date," Maheu wrote in desperation. "I am getting to the point where I frankly don't know what in the hell to tell them when they ask the very simple question—when are you going to open? Honest to God, Howard, if this question is not resolved forthwith, I am simply going to have to get the hell out of town because I just simply cannot continue facing all these people any further." It was the kind of ultimatum that Maheu hoped would generate action. It did, but not the kind of action he anticipated.

Hughes read Maheu's memo and released a scream that reverberated through Penthouse One and brought aide Roy Crawford running into Hughes' bedroom. Seeing the aide enter his room, Hughes gestured with his thin, long arm toward the door and promptly dispatched Crawford back to his desk. Only then did Hughes reread the memo and angrily write a response that would bring into question the future of the Hughes-Maheu relationship.

Bob, there are some things in life becide [sic] money and success. I am afraid I have reached the point where I have a great reserve allowable tolerance in my money-success column, than I have in my health-and-remaining-years column.

If, under these circumstances, you think my failure to give you a specific date has placed you in a position of embarrassment under which you dont [sic] want to be in Las Vegas, I think maybe the time has come when, for my health's sake, a somewhat less efficient and less successful man, but one who would not find it so difficult to put up with my, admittedly less-than-perfect operation, should perhaps be the resident managing executive here in Las Vegas.

Re: the Landmark opening, I have told you repeatedly that I dont [sic] want the Landmark to open until after the International. Bob, I say this only in the interest of harmony.

If I were indifferent to your barbs and inferences, it would be no problem, but I am not indifferent, and some of your implications get under my skin and my blood pressure goes higher than Landmark Tower, which is not good.

MAHEU HAD BEEN GIVEN an out. Years later, he would reflect on the opportunity and say that he wished he had taken it. But Robert Maheu had grown into his life as crown consort to the Royal Court of Hughes. It was an addiction that was no less severe than the one Hughes had for his codeine. Maheu craved the life that Hughes afforded him. The private jet, the mansion on the golf course, the respect of politicians, the power. He was seduced and willingly sold his soul in a way Hughes, himself, never had.

Rather than simply cancel the event and wait for Hughes to come around, Maheu dug in, pressing for answers, forcing the issue. Unable to stop, unwilling to capitulate, Maheu rewrote his suggested list of guests, broken down by category, listed in importance, and supported by facts. With less than a week to the projected opening of the hotel, not a single invitation had been extended, nor a single hors d'oeuvre ordered.

When Hughes returned the list to Maheu, he had approved three names out of the four hundred on it.

"Howard, I really don't know what you are trying to do to me, but if your desire is to place me in a state of complete depression you are succeeding," Maheu wrote back. "Now, Howard, this may come to you as a shock, but we are soon entering the realm of not being believable. All I know is that we have an opening taking place in a few days. Everyone seems prepared for it, except you. There have been many hours of sweat and blood poured into this project, and all we need is evidence of confidence from you. After all, Howard, in the last analysis, only you have something to gain or lose. In my present state of mind, I couldn't care less if it takes place or not."

Hughes read the note with annoyance. He had not hired Maheu to be insubordinate. This was another gun to his head, and once again, Hughes was not about to be rushed. "I am sorry but I cannot give a go-ahead on the Landmark until the situation of discord that has developed between us is put in better condition," Hughes wrote, the defiant, unbendable dictator. "I assure you that, if you feel even half of what you said in your message, it has to be straightened out to the point where you look at the situation entirely differently."

Hughes toyed with his alter ego, annoyed at his defiance, and intolerant of his problems. In the process, Hughes had forgotten about the comeuppance of Kerkorian, for he had found a greater threat of defiance in his own camp. "I am asking you, for the record, not to give a go-ahead on the basis of any specific date, and not to make any preparations for the opening. . . Bob, the above is really important if we are to have any chance at all of healing this breach between us."

Hughes recognized the signs. The freedom that he had awarded Maheu, the encouragement to represent him to the world, had turned his problem-solver into the problem itself. Maheu, however, was far too involved in *being* Hughes to allow the billionaire to exercise the eccentricities that consumed him.

"Even a person who professes to be as rough and strong as I do will eventually hit the canvas when he is consistently clobbered on all parts of his body and head," Maheu wrote back, no hint of retreat. "As to the Landmark, Howard, I am sure you realize that the logistics involved in an opening are many. If we are not going to open on July 1, we would very much appreciate your giving us a fixed date."

Hughes had expected an apology. In its place, he got a continuation of the war of words. He had tired of the game; he had tired of Maheu's growing ego; and he had tired of having to make excuses for his behavior. "Sixty-four years of my life have been devoted to hard work. What I have to show for this consists of assets, liabilities, and a small amount of cash. If the above items will not purchase a certain amount of freedom for me, then my 64 years have been wasted." It was Hughes, the martyr at his best. Camille on his recliner, hand-to-forehead, lamenting his existence. If Maheu had any inkling that Hughes was being serious, his reply did not suggest it.

"Any decision is better than none from this point on. Howard, the impression is being gained in certain quarters that we are not very well organized."

It was the type of note that Hughes was not used to receiving, and one that he was not about to tolerate. He grabbed a legal pad and began to write, his words flooding the page, his writing pinched, his pen digging into the paper. "Bob, I have just received your note, which I consider to be inaccurate and inconsiderate. Perhaps it is time that we. . . " Hughes stopped writing and reconsidered his options. He wanted to maim; he did not want to kill. He needed Maheu, but only on his terms. They were an alloy of greed and illusion that hung together by necessity, nothing more. And with that in mind, Hughes ripped off the top sheet of paper and began to write again. This time slower. This time with enough acid to melt but not destroy.

Bob—

I am very grateful to you for the many contributions you have made toward the success of the various activities I have assigned to you.

However, Bob, there comes a time when the success of a man's business endeavors are not as important as his peace of mind and the condition of his health.

Bob, I have worked as hard and devoted myself as completely to my work as anybody I know.

So, I now wind up a supposedly successful business man who has wrecked his health and consumed the best part of his life in the process.

Bob, I have tried to be scrupulously honest, and I have tried to give, for charitable purposes, a sum in relationship to my earnings in excess of what is considered fair.

When the newspapers print stories of the unbelievable increase in business revenues in this area and the incredible increase in population, I can't help but feel I must have given something to this community.

Yet, somehow, this supposed success story does not seem to be enough for you, Bob.

Your messages, every so often, disclose a resentment lying beneath the surface. Sometimes it is only a few words, sometimes it is more.

I got the impression from you that the purchase of the Landmark constituted an important contribution to the community.

But now, you tell me that I dont [sic] have enough reserve of good will on deposit with the Governor and our other friends to permit a moderate delay in the announcement of the opening date of the Landmark.

Bob, I think the most disturbing feature of your message is the statement that I should reconcile myself to the fact that the appearance is being gained in 'certain quarters' that we are not very well organized.

The shocking part of this whole thing, in my opinion, Bob, lies in the fact that you and I dont [sic] have enough good will stored up to bridge over a delay of a few days in an announcement of this kind as if it were nothing.

So, Bob, my point is that, if, after all the contributions to the community, which have led to unprecedented income and growth, if, after all this, I cannot tell you that I will give you this opening date in a few days without being warned that the Governor, etc. are going to lose faith and think the entire operation is 'not very well organized,' then I say my life is drawing too short for this kind of pressure.

Bob, you are one of the most high powered units of manpower I have ever come across. But, like most extremely competant [sic] people, you have enough pride in your work to resent any interference at all.

I am convinced that you will not ever be happy in an organizational set-up such as we have. I think you will only be truly content when you are in a position comparable to working for yourself.

I am sure you can see that, so long as you are in the position of administering all of the details and loose ends that go to make up my every-day life, complete independence free of any interference is just not possible.

So, I am going to make a suggestion, Bob.

I suggest, Bob, that you assign this Las Vegas job to any of your men you select.

On this basis, Bob, I would be happy for you to spend the entire summer in Newport, and on your boat as much of the time as you wish.

I think you subconsciously blame me for every week-end you are not on your boat, and it would be my hope that this plan would end that.

WHAT HUGHES WAS SUGGESTING was pasture to the race horse. Maheu had pushed too hard, too fast. It was Hughes' game; Hughes' rules, and Maheu was not playing according to them. For the master manipulator, the answer was simple. Correct the situation by finding another player, for this game was making him weary.

Maheu's response was one of caution, though not of wisdom. He was secure in his position, deceived by an ego that had grown with his income and prestige. It was the foolishness of the glutton, unable to stop eating from the endless buffet. Rather than merely allow the Landmark to sit empty and permit Hughes to discover the folly of his ways, Maheu chose to continue the fight, but from a rather different perspective—the sidelines. "I would not want to deprive you of being right once more as to the opening of the Landmark. After all, Howard, it is one thing to argue and for me to make known all of my thinking, but there can be only one Captain," he wrote.

Hughes was appeased, if not pleased. He was in pain, mentally dulled by drugs, in need of sleep and nourishment and wanted nothing more than to be free from aggravation. The concept of freedom was never far from his mind, as he obsessed over a plan to achieve it. He felt trapped by the government, trapped by his isolation, and now trapped by his alter ego. He thought about flying, the freedom of the skies, and wondered if he would ever see it again.

On June 29, Hughes finally approved July 1 as an opening date for the Landmark. It did not make him happy. In fact, he thought the entire event was sure to be a fiasco, both from an entertainment standpoint and a political maneuver. He wanted his name disassociated with the event and sent Maheu a note confirming the date, then adding, "I only want to ask that the record show I want the opening delayed."

But Maheu would not allow a delay. He had won, but it was a Pyrrhic victory and had come at a high price, and for very little pay-off. With one day remaining before the official opening of the Landmark Hotel and Casino, Maheu now had a date, but no guest list and no food. It was exactly the way Hughes had orchestrated it, expecting his alter ego to succeed, and holding him responsible for the failure. On June 30, Hughes sent Maheu a list of forty approved names, to which Maheu had secretly added four hundred more of his own choosing. He had staffed the hotel, hired the entertainment, and placed calls to invite his guests.

Given the hectic activity that surrounded him on June 30, he did not welcome receiving another memo from Hughes. After reading its contents, he welcomed it even less.

> Bob I want to lay it on the line with you. I simply am not happy under present circumstances. And I dont [sic] have such an abundance of years remaining that I can afford to continue on with a pattern of life which seems to fall such a long way short of what I really want.
>
> I have a number of very important new projects and investments that I want to commence at once. If it is to be in Nevada, fine.
>
> On the other hand, if a program to sell the hotels is going to be attempted, then naturally I want to commence the new projects at a new location to be selected either in Baja or in the Bahamas.
>
> Bob, I have been in this frustrated position for a number of months. This has left me in an uncertain, faltering frame of mind which, combined with a tendency to be overcautious anyway, has resulted in sort of throwing me off balance.
>
> Well, all these months I have been fuming and boiling here in a state of intense frustration. I want either to go ahead in a big way, or I want out—and *now!*
>
> Please reply, Bob, on a most urgent basis.

IN THE PRECEDING THREE WEEKS, Hughes and Maheu had exchanged forty-seven memos, and spoken on-average four times a day. The relationship had gone from unconventional to barely tolerable, with neither man able to move beyond his inability to dominate the other. Control was as fundamental as it was unattainable.

It was on the afternoon of July 1 that Hughes reluctantly authorized the ordering of food for the event, now only hours away. Even then, it was not a carte blanche allowance. "I will be very grateful if you will keep such procurement to the bare minimum, until I am able to discuss with you, in considerable length, some of my views relative to the procurement of food."

Maheu was literally on the verge of a nervous collapse. The depth of the argument over the Landmark opening had dug into raw nerves and past scar tissue still healing from past disagreements. As Maheu rode the glass elevator on the outside of the Landmark, he was confident that the evening would be a success. Dean Martin would perform; Danny Thomas as well. The guest list was a strong assortment of powerful shakers and political advocates that would be helpful to Maheu and thus to Hughes in the future. Yet Maheu could not shake an ominous feeling of pending doom that played on his mind like a tocsin. Even as the party started and the invited guests made their way up the glass elevator to the bubble lounge, Hughes was not finished. He had one last thought for the evening; the last word on the event. "Bob, You and your people have my wishes for good luck tonight, in every way. Is there anything further I can do to be helpful?" he asked.

The day following the opening of the Landmark, there was silence from Penthouse One. Hughes did not call to inquire how the party went, or receive a dramatic re-enactment from Maheu. It was unusual behavior for the billionaire who lived vicariously through his alter ego. It should have given Maheu an indication of the extent to which their relationship had deteriorated because of the event. Instead, Maheu allowed the incident to slide by unnoticed, happy that the Landmark was open and pleased with the press coverage of the event.

Hughes read the reports printed in the *Las Vegas Sun*, including the mention that Kirk Kerkorian attended the party. Ordinarily his outrage would have been channeled into an immediate phone call. This was not an ordinary time, however, and Hughes moved with methodical purpose. He had decided to leave Las Vegas, but he had yet to decide if Maheu would be joining him as he did.

Hughes' alter ego continued to operate as if there were no change in the basis of his relationship with the billionaire. Calls were placed to Penthouse One, memos were sent, memos read, and orders received. There was a subtle variation in tone in Hughes' memos, however. Less tolerant, more perplexed, as if patience had dissipated along with trust.

America was in a mood of celebration on July 20, 1969, with the landing on the moon of Neil Armstrong and Buzz Aldrin. Hughes watched the Apollo 11 mission from the darkness of his room, reflecting back on the progress of flight in the thirty-one years and one week since he was the hero of the world. He was pleased with the role he had played, and took special pride in Hughes Aircraft's contribution to the moon mission. Surveyor 1, the first spacecraft to soft-land on the moon, was designed and built by Hughes Aircraft. The pictures relayed back to the television sets around the world were beamed by the Hughes-built Early Bird satellite. Surveyors 2 through 7 had made this moment possible, and when Armstrong uttered, "That's one small step for man, one giant leap for mankind," Hughes found himself crying.

When the astronauts returned to Earth, President Nixon decided to honor the two men as well as the command module captain Michael Collins with the largest state dinner in the history of Washington, D.C. The guests would number 1,500, and in addition to the three Apollo 11 astronauts, the honored guests were slated to be aviation pioneers Charles Lindbergh, Wernher von Braun,[1] and Howard Hughes.

When Hughes received his invitation, he reacted with his usual skepticism. Nixon wanted something. "Re the President's party, what is it you actually need from me?" Hughes asked Maheu. Paranoia pushed against mistrust, and a simple invitation became a cause for crisis.

Maheu was only too happy to attend the President's party in Hughes' place, and, at his insistence, threw a party for the astronauts and their wives aboard a 150-foot yacht, with Vice President Agnew and CBS news anchor Walter Cronkite in attendance. The triumph of the moon landing was cause for celebration, but was soon overshadowed by news that linked Nixon and Hughes in a very unorthodox way.

John Meier was by this time introducing himself as Dr. Meier, with an alleged degree in mining engineering. As the man whom Hughes had placed in charge of his mine leases, he had developed a business relationship with the President's brother, Donald, who had taken a job with the food division of Ogden Corporation after his restaurants failed. Both men were in Washington, Meier bragging about his close relationship with Hughes and Nixon boasting of his pull with the President. While the FBI was keeping a close watch on Donald Nixon, by orders of the White House, Maheu attempted to rein in Meier, but with little success.

Unknown to Hughes, and even to Maheu, the bespectacled, bragging Meier had built his own cottage industry trading on the Hughes name. On the basis of his initial purchases of mining claims in Tonopah, Meier began to negotiate the sale of leases through a variety of intermediary parties, and received a finder's fee in addition to his Hughes salary, essentially operating on both sides of the negotiating table.

Donald Nixon cultivated Meier's friendship secure in the belief that Meier spoke with Hughes daily, and would be useful in securing the food concessions at the various manufacturing plants of Hughes Aircraft. While Hughes was aware of Meier and his mining purchases, he made no effort to verify the validity of Meier's assessment of their value. With each successive purchase, Meier became more daring, combining bravado with greed. Leases in Nevada's Ney and Esmeralda counties for mines that

---

1. Wernher von Braun was instrumental in developing the Explorer satellites; the Jupiter and Jupiter-C rockets; as well as the Saturn rockets, used to launch Columbia; and Skylab, the world's first space station. He immigrated to the U.S. from his native Germany where he had been involved with Adolph Hitler's V-2 rocket program.

Meier said contained millions of dollars in untapped gold and silver were added to Hughes' holdings. And the President's brother, while not participating, dallied attentively on the sidelines.

Donald Nixon joined Meier and Salt Lake City businessman Anthony G. Hatsis for trips to Europe and the Dominican Republic—trips funded by Hughes without his knowledge or endorsement. Hatsis had met Meier at Hughes' Sands Hotel where he was a guest, and after discovering that Hatsis was the president of the Toledo Mining Company, Meier suggested that Toledo provide Hughes with a prospectus of its various claims. Over the next several months, Meier made deals for over $4 million in mines owned by the Toledo Mining group, despite a report issued by the United States Security and Exchange Commission that there were "no known commercially mineable ore bodies on any of the claims." That Donald Nixon should find himself in their company was not surprising, since all three men were determined to capitalize on the name of Howard Hughes.

The first Meier/Hatsis/Nixon trip took place in August 1969, with Meier/Hatsis forging a partnership and opening several European bank accounts, and Nixon allegedly along to meet with investors. He later testified during the Senate Watergate hearings that he spent his time "relaxing by myself." He continued his free-wheeling the following month in the Dominican Republic, where Meier and Hatsis were looking for mining opportunities and the trio met with Dominican president Joaquin Balaguer. It was an amazing bit of propaganda that spoke to the lack of reins placed on Meier's activities within the Hughes organization.

While Donald Nixon was spending Hughes' money in South America courtesy of John Meier, his brother, the President, was accepting Hughes' money via the long-promised $50,000 campaign contribution. Robert Maheu's son Peter hand-carried the funds and handed the case containing the cash to Bebe Rebozo at his Miami estate. Rebozo later said that he placed the cash in his safe-deposit box. Maheu reported to Hughes that the contribution had been successful, and, for the moment, the billionaire felt that his control of the White House was secure.

He was unaware, however, that his executive in charge of mining acquisitions was running an independent operation, one that not only threatened to expose Hughes to a government investigation, but placed the President in a vulnerable position as well. Meier had been placed on the Hughes payroll through the insistence of Bill Gay, who continued to approve his purchases. It was through the grace of Gay that Meier stayed on the payroll until the irregularities of his deals for mining rights reached the attention of Robert Maheu and could no longer be ignored. By November 1969, Meier had become so flagrant in his abuse of power that he was openly buying mining leases with Hughes' money, and having the money paid through an associate, Everd B. Van Walsum who was headquartered in the Netherlands. By funneling the money through Walsum, and arranging for kickbacks into his own accounts, Meier was able to skim funds from many of the nearly $20 million in mining leases he arranged.

On November 2, 1969, Maheu called Meier into his office at the Frontier Hotel and demanded his resignation. Though Maheu kept control of Meier's files, and assigned ex-FBI agent Dean Elson to untangle the monies spent and ownership rights, the labyrinth left by Meier in his wake was such a complicated maze of sub-leases and assignments that Elson finally bent under the strain. Maheu received the following memo from Elson, five months later.

> When [John Meier] left the organization in November, 1969, I again demanded from him that he produce his records regarding the acquisition of claims, and at that time I was astounded to find that he had no records whatsoever regarding any of the properties we had purchased, even as to legal documents. He informed me that he did not know who had possession of the Deed, Titles, and other records that pertained to our purchase of mining properties. To say the least, I stepped into a chaotic condition, with absolutely nothing to refer to or work with.
>
> Due to John Meier's reluctance to produce his records regarding the acquisitions of mining claims, I began to have some strong suspicions that something was wrong, and from that point I began endeavoring to reconstruct files as best I could. It has not been until the last several days, and through tedious effort, that I have finally assembled a group of records—though no means a complete group as yet.
>
> In reviewing what transpired while John Meier was in change of the mining operations it appears to me that there have been many irregularities in the purchasing of various mining claims. Although the situation looks very serious, at this point I am not in a position to give you a final reading as to the extent of the situation.

BY THE TIME that Maheu received Elson's warning, more than just Meier's name had been sullied. Hughes had begun receiving memos from the Gay/Henley/Davis camp strongly implying financial improprieties

---

2. Meier was subsequently hired by the Toledo Mining Company as a consultant. Three years later, the IRS indicted Meier for income-tax evasion. Meier fled the U.S. to escape the charge, moving to British Columbia where he still remains. In 1978, the Hughes organization filed its own charges against Meier for fraud in connection with the various worthless mining acquisitions he made using Hughes' money. The Hughes organization received a $7.9 million judgment against Meier, but was unable to collect. Meier never received the doctorate degrees in mining that he claimed, and, in fact, never attended college at all.

on the part of Maheu. The reality of the situation in Las Vegas was that Hughes' casinos and hotels were, in fact, losing a great deal of money. The operation lost over $3 million in 1968, and nearly three times that in 1969.

Maheu had left many of the previous casino bosses in place, and there was every indication that money was being skimmed from the casino banks. The situation was allowed to exist for a number of reasons, including Hughes' repeated statements that profits were not his primary purpose for his Las Vegas investments. Control was paramount, and the simplest way to establish control, at least initially, was to allow major management to remain in place and answer to Maheu (and thus to Hughes). Had Maheu stayed in power for a longer period of time, his organization would have matured. As it was, however, forces were at work to under-mine his authority, a situation that Maheu was ill-prepared to prevent.

The disenchantment with Maheu that had begun with the opening of the Landmark Hotel moved toward overt dislike in January, 1970, when Hughes decided to purchase yet another hotel and casino in Las Vegas. The Dunes Hotel and Country Club had periodically surfaced as a potential candidate for acquisition, despite Maheu's continuing objection to the resort as a source of profit. On January 8, 1970, Hughes formally overruled his alter ego, instructing him to test the "mood in Washington for another hotel purchase."

Hughes had been informed repeatedly that any move to purchase more of the Las Vegas Strip would subject him to intense anti-trust scrutiny. With a new administration in the White House, however, Hughes felt confident that his position would be viewed "with eyes, bought and paid for." In accordance with Hughes' instructions, Maheu sent Richard Danner to speak with Attorney General John Mitchell, a personal friend from his days working on the Nixon campaign.

The meeting produced no substantive answers. It was not an accept-able result for Hughes, who demanded answers. Immediate answers. It had nothing to do with the Dunes, or even the anti-trust mood of the administration. It had everything to do with Jean Peters, whom Hughes had managed to virtually ignore in his push to take over Las Vegas.

For over three months, his aides had been relaying messages from his wife, who was pressing Hughes to make a decision. Jean Peters had nearly given up all hope of ever seeing her husband again. At first he refused her attempts to visit, continuing to promise that he was still searching for the perfect house. In frustration, Jean began to mention divorce. Rather than receiving the response she expected, pleas for time and reassurances, Jean found herself cut off completely. Suddenly, her husband was no longer taking her calls, nor responding to her messages. She saw no future in waiting, and on January 15, 1970, alerted Robert Maheu that she was seeking a divorce from her husband of thirteen years.

That the confirmation of the divorce occurred through Maheu infuriated Hughes, even though he had refused to speak to his wife directly. The announcement made headlines across the world, as much to confirm that Hughes was still alive as to verify the dissolution of his marriage. The official announcement began: "Jean Peters Hughes, wife of industrialist Howard Hughes, stated today that she and her husband have discussed a possible divorce and that she will seek to obtain one."

Jean refused to comment on the announcement other than to say, "This is not a decision reached in haste and it is done only with the greatest regret. Our marriage has endured for thirteen years which is long by present standards. Any property settlement will be resolved privately between us." Hughes had not seen his wife during his entire stay in Las Vegas, and had not touched his wife in nine years. Yet, his loss was dramatic, and in some ways terminal. He still had his life, at least what remained of it, but he no longer had hope. He blamed Maheu, for he needed to blame someone—anyone—other than himself.

Vulnerability was as much a strain for Hughes as accountability, particularly in areas of romance. He did not even attempt to stop Jean, for there would be no stopping Jean, through he stationed a private investigator across the street to record who she admitted into the house. He maintained the surveillance even after their divorce became final in June, 1971.[3] With the irreversible loss of his wife, and a severely damaged relationship with Maheu, Hughes retreated into a world in which business played a part far smaller than paranoia.

While the billionaire was consuming an ever-increasing amount of codeine, self-dissolved and injected, he never approached his previous periods of lucidity. His writing became scrawled into elongated sentences, their message garbled by his inability to concentrate. Major decisions were left hanging as minor activities tallied hours of his time. At the very moment that Maheu was reporting success with John Mitchell relating to anti-trust issues with the proposed purchase of the Dunes Hotel, Hughes occupied his time in rewriting instructions for the correct handling of the envelope containing the cord for his hearing aid.

The door to the cabinet is to be opened using a minimum of fifteen Kleenexes. (Great care is to be exercised in opening and closing the doors. They are not to be slammed or swung hastily so as to raise any dust, and yet exceeding care is to be exercised against letting insects in.)

---

3. Jean Peters married writer-producer Stanley Hough, and lived happily with him in Beverly Hills until his death in 1990.

Nothing inside the cabinet is to be touched—the inside of the doors, the top of the cabinet, the sides—no other objects inside the cabinet are to be touched in any way with the exception of the envelope to be removed. The envelope or packages to be removed using a minimum of fifteen Kleenexes. If it is necessary to use both hands, then fifteen Kleenexes are to be used for each hand. (It is to be understood that these fifteen Kleenexes are to be sterile on both sides of each tissue with the exception of the very outermost edge of the tissue. The center of the tissue only should come in contract with the object being picked up.) If something is on top of the package to be removed, a sterile instrument is to be used to lift it off.

THE CONTENT OF the memo on the handling of the hearing-aid cord did not differ substantially from one that Hughes had dictated eleven years earlier. The major distinction lay in the fact that when Hughes was devoting days to the rewrite in 1970, he had not worn his hearing aid in over six years, and never asked for the wires.

While Hughes' memo-writing to his Romaine staff was increasing, the number of memos he was sending to Maheu was on the wane. From Maheu's perspective, this was Hughes simply being Hughes, moving through yet another phase of disenchantment with Las Vegas, and had even accepted Kerkorian's presence, if only because it took some of the anti-trust pressure off Hughes Nevada Operations.

Maheu had moved into his sprawling new mansion on the Desert Inn Golf course, a house dubbed Little Caesar's Palace by the locals for its grandeur. He entertained lavishly and often, content in his role as Hughes' front man, now more so than ever. And he remained naively unaware that Hughes was continuing to receive negative reports on Maheu's honesty from Hughes' Romaine Street team who had begun to make disparaging remarks to Hughes' aides about his alter ego.

He might have had more opportunity to heed the wake-up call if another crisis had not surfaced in Penthouse One in March 1970. At the time, Robert Maheu had traveled to New York to finalize Hughes' purchase of Air West, when the White House announced plans for another underground nuclear test in Las Vegas. Suddenly, nothing was more important to Hughes than stopping the test. As with the previous blast, he was determined to mount a counterattack, and pressure the White House to see the long-term harm such tests were having on the environment—Hughes' environment.

Hughes ordered Maheu to fly to Key Biscayne immediately and offer Nixon, through Rebozo, a million dollars cash to halt the test. Hughes coined the phrase, The Big Caper, to refer to the bribe—a bribe which

Maheu was too embarrassed to actually offer to Rebozo. He did, however, make the trip to Key Biscayne, along with Richard Danner, and came away with an offer from Nixon to meet personally with Hughes at Camp David to explain the importance as well as the safety of the underground tests.

Hughes viewed Maheu's report as a total failure. Meeting Nixon was hardly an option for Hughes, although Maheu did not fully appreciate how impossible the suggestion actually was. He foolishly told Hughes that Nixon really did not care that the blast was taking place in Hughes' backyard; did not care about the extent of Hughes' investments in the area; did not care about his threats to leave Las Vegas if the test continued. In effect, Nixon was not under Hughes' control after all. It was a situation that Hughes could not tolerate, and once again saw Maheu's failure to perform as the sole cause of his problems.

When the blast took place as scheduled on March 2, 1970, Hughes was scared into hiding in his bathroom, and was coaxed out of the room only after hours of effort by his aides. When he reemerged, his first item of business was another memo to Maheu. This time, however, the threats that were made were no longer idle, something Maheu still did not realize.

Bob, I dont [sic] know where to begin.

You said the president couldnt [sic] care less whether I remain in Nevada.

This may well be true in the literal sense.

However, bear in mind that, if I pull up stakes here, I am not going to some neighboring state.

I am going to move the largest part of all of my activities to some location which will not be in the U.S.

The president already has the young, the black, and the poor against him. Maybe he will be indifferent if the richest man in the country also finds the situation in the U.S. un-livable, and because of the country's intense preoccupation with the military.

I know one thing:

There is at present a violent feeling in this country against all the experimental activities of the military.

So, I just don't know how the public would react to a frank statement by the wealthiest man in the U.S. that he, also, considered he was being elbowed aside by the military.

I know one thing: It would, or, at least, it *could* be a hell of a newspaper story.

MAHEU DISMISSED Hughes' intention to liquidate his Las Vegas holdings as sheer delusion, for he knew that Hughes was incapable of making such a move without his knowledge and assistance. He likewise filed away in the same basket the threat of a physical move for the billionaire knowing full well the elaborate preparations that would precede such an effort would certainly need his input.

Maheu was hopelessly out of touch with what was actually taking place in Penthouse One. He did not know about Hughes' declining physical and mental condition. He did not know about Hughes' own determination to escape Maheu's control. And he certainly was unaware that there was a widening circle of evidence against his ability to handle his duties to Hughes' satisfaction.

Ironically, the most damaging input did not come from the Gay/Henley/Davis camp, but rather from Hughes Tool, where executive vice president Raymond Holliday was watching with increased alarm the hemorrhaging of cash from the company's bank accounts. Holliday projected Maheu's losses for the year 1970 at $13-14 million, including losses at every one of Hughes' hotels and casinos.

Holliday also notified Hughes that his current cash reserve was $111 million. Of that amount, $75 million was kept on perpetual hold for an anticipated payout in the still-ongoing TWA case, with an additional $17 million held as collateral in a series of bank loans. According to Holliday's computations, Hughes needed more than $10 million in cash to keep his businesses running over and above what was in the bank. Worse still, the figure did not include any money for Hughes' own expenses, which at that point were running over $30,000 a day. Holliday did, however, take the time to take a swipe at Maheu, personally.

> However, provision is made for payment to Maheu of his $10,000 per week basic compensation, but without provision for expenses that will be considerable. In other words, no provision is made for the purchase or use and the personnel that might be required of a right hand or left hand ass wiping machine that he may require.

WHILE HUGHES did not respond to Holliday's memo, he began to keep a list. It was an accounting of Maheu's failings. And while it did not accurately reflect either Maheu's actual shortcomings, nor attempt to present a balanced view of his accomplishments, the list was constantly in view and actively added to during May, June and July, 1970.

Maheu continued to be blissfully unaware of having fallen into terminal disfavor, continuing to perform in gregarious fashion and, in doing so, providing ample fodder for his enemies. If anything, Maheu was reaching for more control over the Hughes empire, posturing with increased disregard for his own position. Among the deals Maheu concluded during mid-1970 was the purchase of a commuter helicopter service known as Los Angeles Airways. Although there was mention of the proposed purchase in early 1969 memos from Maheu to Hughes, there was no further written discussion of the deal until an announcement was released by LAW in May, 1970. According to the press release, Hughes was paying $3,116,640 for the struggling operation in a deal which ultimately was unauthorized by Hughes.

Maheu insisted at the time that Hughes had, in fact, verbally given him the authority to conclude the acquisition. For whatever reason, Hughes denied that such conversations had ever taken place, and refused to sign any paperwork concluding the purchase. It was a public abrogation that blind-sided Maheu and his reputation. It was so blatant, in fact, that mere common sense suggested he had at least some form of initial authorization from Hughes.

Attempting to pick up the pieces of the deal after-the-fact, Maheu scheduled a hasty meeting with Gay and Davis in Los Angeles, and asked their help in reviving the dead carcass of the helicopter negotiations. Neither Gay nor David were in a rush to commit themselves, and would have been of little help to Maheu even if they would, for no one, Gay and Davis included, could move Hughes to action in the summer of 1970. As facts became known, however, Los Angeles Airways was the least of Maheu's immediate problems.

In the course of his effort to secure the Dunes Hotel and Country Club for Hughes, Maheu entered into an agreement to make a business loan to part-owner Sidney Wyman. Wyman needed $4 million in quick cash, and Maheu offered to lend him the money in exchange for a speedy closing on the Dunes. The money Maheu was offering was not his own, of course. It belonged to Howard Hughes, who did not know of Sidney Wyman, and would not have loaned him money even if he did.

With his entire reputation now hanging in the balance, Maheu called another meeting with Gay and Davis, and this time literally begged them to assist him over this "precarious position." Davis testified in a resulting court action in 1975 that Maheu pledged his "solemn word not to commit (himself) to anybody any more without written authorization." It was a rather complete admission of culpability in the dealings, and placed Maheu's future in the hands of two men who were quite anxious to see him fired.

While feigning understanding and compassion for Maheu's position, Gay and Davis played their roles well, convincing Maheu that they would work on his behalf within Penthouse One. It was the kind of evidence that Gay would not have been able to generate on his own, detailing Maheu's irresponsibility as Hughes' front man, and that very afternoon Gay dictated a memo to be taken into the Old Man verifying the pledge of Hughes' funds. "The commitment of an unauthorized loan in the amount of $4 million by Maheu has been confirmed."

Hughes' response to Maheu was deepening silence. Where there were once incessant calls, now there was ominous restraint. It did not, however, reflect on Hughes' mental capacity, which fed off of the campaign to discredit Maheu and panicked at the thought of a loose cannon in his midst. For the secluded billionaire, options were few. His dislike for Gay equaled his distrust of Maheu. In desperation, he turned to a surprise source for rescue—his longtime aide John Holmes.

In a banter of memos, Hughes pressured Holmes to coordinate his rescue from the clutches of Maheu and imagined freedom. He ordered Holmes to contact Jack Real, who had offered to supply a private Lockheed jet. He insisted that he wanted to leave immediately for the Bahamas, despite the fact that nothing had been prepared for his arrival on foreign soil. The jockeying between worry and frustration took its toll on Holmes, who was not used to having a position of authority, let alone decisionmaking. Despite Hughes' insistence on the need for an immediate move, his fear of leaving his room repeatedly stymied each plan, until Holmes neared the same breaking point that Maheu had encountered over the Landmark opening a year earlier.

> I have so much pressure on me since we talked about this trip 2 months ago that I don't know how much more I can stand. You keep asking *me* if we can go and I have told you repeatedly, "let's go." . . . I have other problems such as schedules here, health, trying to keep my family happy, etc. For instance, I don't tell you about such things as my wife calling me and waking me to tell me that we were robbed and for a change she was frightened to be alone with my little girl. These are all sources of worry to me and I am about to toss in the sponge.

HUGHES' CONCERN did not extend to the personal life of his aides. He had no interest in their pressure from home, and refused to even acknowledge any statement that referred to issues other than business. From his perspective, he had his own problems consuming his life, and did not need to become involved in what he referred to as "the pettiness of life aside [sic] these four walls."

As autumn approached and Maheu found himself in a vacuum, his own memos began to take on a frantic tone of impending disaster. "Howard, things are truly falling apart. We have now been formally advised by the three banks holding the Nigro guarantee[4] that they want

---

4. One-time air force general Edward H. Nigro, who Maheu had hired as deputy chief-executive for Hughes Nevada Operations, had guaranteed two loans to Los Angeles Airways to keep the helicopter service flying.

immediate payment from us. The attorneys for Belinn[5] now have completed their complaint in order to file a lawsuit. Howard, I don't know what else I can tell you about this entire situation except to repeat that it is going to be one hell of a mess."

Maheu's memo deepened Hughes' determination to expel his alter ego, and he ordered Gay to begin an internal investigation of Maheu's activities. With Holmes now totally involved with the logistics of moving Hughes, the billionaire turned to his aide Levar Myler, who was dispatched to Los Angeles to personally inform Gay that Hughes wanted Gay and Davis to prepare a proxy for his signature that would give Gay, David and Raymond Holliday complete control of Hughes' Nevada business.

Gay's satisfaction was immediate. His quiet campaign of subterfuge had yielded success beyond his initial hopes. With a crippled Maheu now locked in his sights, he moved forward for the kill with calculated efficiency. Gay dispatched his assistant Kay Glenn to Washington to formally hire Intertel (International Intelligence Inc.), run by former Justice Department attorneys Robert D. Peloquin and William G. Hundley, to audit Maheu and uncover proof of theft or embezzlement.

Holmes had completed arrangements for the entire top floor of the Britannia Beach Hotel in the Bahamas to be leased, and private telephones installed. Jack Real had been contacted and a Lockheed Jet Star had yet again been made available for Hughes' use. Each element had been doubled-checked and re-verified all without the knowledge or input of Maheu, who was now clearly labeled as the enemy in Hughes' memos to his staff. "John, I am accutely [sic] aware of the throttle-hold Maheu has gained on my entire organization, and this is one of the principle reasons for this trip," he wrote. Only the proxy remained to be signed before Hughes' named "Big Caper" could begin.

Hughes received a draft of the proxy via fax on the morning of November 14, 1970, handed to him by aide Howard Eckersley. Shortly before noon, Hughes signed the piece of paper, witnessed by Eckersley and Levar Myler and notarized by Myler. Myler then notified Gay and Davis that the proxy was received and signed. He then folded the piece of paper, put it in his jacket pocket, and there it would remain for the next month, unseen by anyone.

On Thanksgiving Eve, Operation Big Caper commenced. Holmes notified the aides on duty—Eckersley, Myler and George Francom—that the move was happening. As the city of Las Vegas busied itself with holiday preparations, Hughes was placed on the same narrow stretcher on which he had arrived in Las Vegas and carried by Margulis, Eckersley,

---

5. Clarence M. Belinn was the president of Los Angeles Airways Inc.

and Myler down nine floors, using the emergency exit at the far end of the penthouse hallway.

Outside in the parking lot, Hughes was hit by the cold air, his frail body wrapped only in a bathrobe and covered by a blanket. His long gray hair formed a mat under his head, his long nails hidden from view. On his head lay a new brown Stetson, a replacement of Hughes' signature lucky fedora bought by Mell Stewart. The stretcher was placed into a waiting unmarked van and moved unobserved out of the Desert Inn parking lot, heading to Nellis Air Force Base, northeast of Las Vegas.

A half-hour later, Dr. Norman Crane joined the aides aboard the Jet Star. Only then were the pilot and co-pilot allowed to board the plane, given instructions to file a flight plan for the Bahamas, and instructed not to enter the passenger compartment of the plane during the trip. At just after midnight, November 26, 1970, the plane left Nellis carrying the richest man in America. The pilot banked right, and proceeded to chart a course across the Grand Canyon, the Hualapai Indian Reservation disappearing below them.

The escape from Las Vegas went flawlessly. Without the intrigue of a major Maheu enterprise, with its off-duty policemen and ex-FBI agents placed at strategic points along the route, with not even a hint to the security guard still on duty at the far end of the hallway at the Desert Inn, the man who had transformed the face of Las Vegas was no longer its most famous resident.

Secure in the luxury of his cabin at Mt. Charleston, Robert Maheu and his family had placed the finishing touches on the preparation of their Thanksgiving feast and were preparing for bed. For Maheu, it had been a busy day. Only later would he realize how calm it was in contrast to what was to come, for his life as he knew it was about to change forever, as closest friend became bitterest foe.

Isolation

I never had a manicure. I don't know. Maybe it is an
outgrowth of my childhood when they used to teach
people about males and about having manicures.
Anyway, I never have had them. But, I have always
kept my fingernails a reasonable length. I cut them
with clippers, not with scissors, and a nail file the
way some people do. I use clippers because they don't
leave a rough edge afterwards. Anyway, I take care
of them the same way I always have—the same way
I did when I went around the world and times when
you have seen me and at the time of the flight of the
flying boat, and every other occasion I have come in
contact with the press. I care for my fingernails in the
same precise manner I always have in my life.

Paradise Island, Bahamas
January 7, 1972
> Hughes speaking on the phone to the press
> while looking at his two-inch long finger-
> nails that had not been trimmed in over
> three years.

THERE WAS A SMELL ABOUT THE PLACE THAT HOWARD
Hughes did not like. Not really an odor. It was more a clammy
humidity that permeated his room on the ninth floor of the
Britannia Beach Hotel. A dampness that seemed to hang
thick in the air, like fog in a forest. It was a humectant that
made his sheets cold and moist, and sent shivers down his
long, thin legs.

Hughes looked out into the darkness of his room and
thought about the blackness that wrapped him in seclusion.
It was different from the pitch of Las Vegas, where not a

shred of light entered day or night. Here, there was a haze, like dots of black scattered among layers of dark gray. No sun of course, but different nonetheless. Hughes did not like it as well, but sighed in resigned tolerance.

He missed sleeping on his Barcalounger. While the chair had made the trip to the Bahamas and the Britannia, his aides had installed a hospital bed in its place, operated by electricity and motorized to lift and move at the touch of a button. Not like the hospital bed he had designed in the Forties. This one moved as if powered by diesel, with a mattress that groaned even under his light weight. The control was difficult to operate, the buttons hard to push, as Hughes felt them with his fingertips, struggling to depress the control to elevate his feet.

Over his head, he heard footsteps. His aides had posted an armed sentry on the roof of the hotel, with his own German shepherd for added protection. There were two more guards on the ninth floor—the first immediately opposite the elevator similar to the set-up in Las Vegas, and another inside a partition that had been built to section Hughes' portion of the ninth floor from the public rooms. He did not trust the set-up. Too many people. But there was not much he could do in a foreign country like the Bahamas. Not like the old days, he remembered. The Bay Street Boys were long gone, replaced by Lynden O. Pindling, the first Black premier of the Bahamas. *Negroes*, Hughes thought. *More trouble.* Then he felt the sores on his back and returned to struggling with the control to raise the foot of the bed.

He was thousands of miles away from the panic that had become Hughes Nevada Operations. Hughes had been gone nearly a day before security chief Jack Hooper had called Robert Maheu at his cabin and interrupted his Thanksgiving dinner with the news. At the Desert Inn, Hughes' aides had methodically cleaned out his rooms, carted away his empty pill bottles and jars filled with urine, shredded documents, removed the blackout drapes, and cleaned and then cleaned again to eradicate any trace of Hughes' lifestyle.

Maheu returned that night from his cabin and cloistered himself in his office at the Frontier Hotel, where he kept a tight lid on any publicity about the disappearance of his billionaire boss while he attempted to determine what had taken place. Though Hughes had openly discussed leaving Las Vegas for over a year, and had received feasibility reports on the Bahamas from both Maheu and Hooper, neither man initially thought of the island. Tahoe, Phoenix, Boston and Montreal—cities in which Hughes had considered living in the past—were at the top of Maheu's short list of possibilities. The news that an unscheduled flight had left Nellis Air Force base for the Bahamas immediately altered his list, but not his impression that Hughes had been kidnapped, somehow forced to leave his suite by parties unknown. He sent his son Peter, along with Dean Elson, to Miami to establish a base of operations to rescue the billionaire from his unknown captors.

Maheu was still basing his assumptions on the logic that *he* was firmly in control. If Hughes had meant to leave, surely he would have known, Maheu rationalized. Yet, as night slipped into day back into night, and no ransom note was received, no word of any kind for that matter, Maheu realized that perhaps he had made a serious miscalculation. In retrospect, the knowledge that the aides had disappeared with their employer should have been Maheu's single biggest clue that this was an inside job done with Hughes' full consent.

But at the moment, he still thought a crime had been committed. The kidnapping of the King of Las Vegas.

As newspapers across the country began to leak the word that Howard Hughes had mysteriously vanished from Nevada, Maheu went on the offensive as a guest on CBS' *60 Minutes*, and in a dramatic appeal to Hughes pleaded, "Howard, please call me." When Hughes learned of Maheu's appearance, the call he placed was not to his former alter ego, but rather to Bill Gay, to delivered an edict. "Get rid of Maheu—now."

Gay, known neither for his courage nor his tact, met with Chester Davis and together they presumed to conceive a plan to rid themselves of Maheu without confronting him in person. On December 4, 1970, they telephoned Maheu's friend and sometime employee, Washington attorney Ed Morgan, and summoned him to a meeting in Los Angeles, California, at the Century Plaza Hotel. Morgan had been selected to do what Gay and Davis would not—confront Maheu directly and give him the news. He was fired, immediately. The meeting lasted all of three minutes.

When Morgan flew back to Las Vegas and relayed the news to Maheu, the power broker's reaction was as fast as it was predictable. "Tell Davis he can go fuck himself, and Gay too. I'm not going anywhere. I'll be right here. And in case he can't reach me, because my personal telephone lines are now unlisted, you let him know they'll be listed by tomorrow."

Bill Gay and Chester Davis received Maheu's ultimatum and responded by flying to Las Vegas. They took over the top floor of the Sands Hotel, ejecting twenty-two guests in the process. With Maheu ensconced in the Frontier and the Gay/Davis camp at the Sands, Las Vegas was a city under siege, and poised for the most public corporate war in modern history. At the center of the feud, of course, was Howard Hughes; and Hughes, at that moment, was sleeping. He had taken his usual four Valium pills, the Blue Bombers as his aides called them, and was snoring in the fits and starts of apnea.

When he finally was cognizant enough on the afternoon of December 5, 1970, to be informed about the events that had unfolded in Nevada, he learned that Gay had attempted to send auditors from the firm of Haskins-Sells as well as guards from Intertel into the casino cages of Hughes' hotels. Maheu had countered by having the accountants branded as trespassers and thrown off the properties. He had also gone to court to have a restraining order filed against Gay and Davis to keep them from "interfering with the orderly operation of Hughes Nevada properties."

Hughes riled with furor—not at Maheu, but at Gay. He had fully expected Maheu to put up a fight. He had, after all, hand-picked his alter ego for his ability to hold his ground. But Gay, who never commanded respect from Hughes, was once again showing his inability to take control. So it was to Davis that Hughes complained, hoping that his attorney might be able to proceed legally.

"You can tell Maheu for me that I had not fully determined to my mind to withdraw all support from his position until he started playing this cat and mouse game for his own selfish benefit. In other words, Maheu does not believe for one second that I am dead, disabled, or any of the other wild accusations he has been making," Hughes wrote to Davis, insisting that he force Maheu to stop all activities on his behalf.

On the evening of December 6, the accusations were so intense that Nevada's Governor Paul Laxalt flew to Las Vegas and joined Clark County District Attorney George E. Franklin Jr. to first speak with Maheu and then with Gay, to "somehow avoid a public blood-letting." At one in the morning on December 7, Howard Hughes placed a call to Gay's suite and spoke to Laxalt as well as Franklin. "He just wanted to clear up the misunderstandings that have arisen in the press," Laxalt later told reporters, discussing his conversation with Hughes. "He was very disturbed about the speculation that he had been kidnapped and that he was not going to return. He assured us that he was just on a vacation that he had planned a year ago."

"He said he was going to return soon to Las Vegas and spend the rest of his life here," Franklin added. "He's still the boss, period. He's merely firing a couple of people that were working for him," he said, referring to Maheu and Hopper.

The news represented a direct defeat for Maheu, who continued to maintain that Howard Hughes had hired him and only Hughes could fire him. "That's all I want," Maheu said. "I want to hear it from Howard. I don't think it is much to ask."

Hughes received the news in the dark solitary confinement of the Britannia Beach Hotel with confusion. Panicking impulses beat in the obscurity of his room, as the walls closed in and his frustration rose. What he had hoped would be an easy transition was turning into another trying debacle, and Hughes' tolerance for such things no longer extended into days, let alone weeks. He reacted by reaching again for his yellow legal pad.

> Dear Chester and Bill,
>
> I do not understand why the problem of Maheu is not yet fully settled and why this bad publicity seems to continue. It could hurt our company's valuable properties in Nevada and also the entire state [sic].
>
> You told me that if I called Governor Laxalt and District Attorney George Franklin, it would put an end to the problem.
>
> I made these calls, and I do not understand why this very damaging publicity should continue merely because the properly constituted board of directors of Hughes Tool Company decided, for reasons they considered just, to terminate all relationship with Maheu and Hooper.
>
> I ask you to take whatever actions are necessary to accomplish the objectives briefly outlined above.
>
> I ask you now please to inform the members of the board of Hughes Tool Co. of my desires and feelings in respect to this matter.
>
> It is not my wish to try to tell the board what action should be taken. That is their job. But it seems there has been some uncertainty as to where I stand, and I want this cleared up at once.
>
> I do not support Maheu or Hooper in their defiance of the Hughes Tool Co. board of directors and I deeply desire all concerned to be fully aware of this immediately.
>
> I ask you to do everything in your power to put an end to these problems, and further I ask you to obtain immediately a full accounting of any and all funds and/or property to which Mr. Maheu may have had access.
>
> As I have said, this matter has caused me the very gravest concern, and is damaging my company and all the loyal men and women associated with me in the very deepest and far-reaching way.

DESPITE MAHEU'S INSISTENCE to Hughes that he wanted to be released from his job prior to the billionaire's departure from Las Vegas, he now seemed more determined than ever to keep it, and continued to fight through the court system. On December 9, 1970, District Judge Howard Babcock heard testimony from handwriting expert Ralph Bradford that the signature was genuine on Hughes' proxy giving unlimited power to Gay, Davis, and Holliday. Maheu countered with his own handwriting expert, Charles A. Appel Jr., who testified the signature was a fake.

It was a tug of war that saw no movement on either side, despite the repeated assertion from the Gay-Davis camp that they had Hughes' fullest cooperation. In any other corporate melodrama, the CEO would have handled the firing of a division head with precision and speed—two words that did not exist within the Hughes domain. The Board of County Commissioners' chairman James Ryan made several direct appeals for Hughes to appear in person to settle the dispute, and lamented that in the old days of Las Vegas, the gangsters ran a tighter ship. "It kind of looks like the racketeers ran a better business than Mr. Hughes does. At least when they were here, people played by the rules—and when there was a problem with the rules, they went outside the county line," Ryan said.

Hughes lived in a state of constant agitation during the next few weeks. Logs kept by his aides indicate the he spent hours in his bathroom, muttering to himself in fury. During one two-day period in mid-December, he fell asleep on the toilet and stayed there for six hours, only to later awaken and continue to ramble.

He was particularly incensed to read a newspaper report that a grading and paving contractor named LeVane Malvison Forsythe testified that he was paid five one hundred dollar bills by Roy Crawford to stand guard in the Desert Inn parking lot after midnight on Thanksgiving. Forsythe claimed to have seen a man dressed in a "topcoat or a raincoat or a bathrobe" being helped by two other men to walk to a car. Upon further questioning, Forsythe said that he had "no idea" why he was paid to stand in the parking lot, but happily accepted the money.

It took another week of legal dancing before Judge Babcock ruled in favor of Gay and Davis, with the men moving to oust Maheu not only from his office at the Frontier Hotel but from his mansion on the golf course of the Desert Inn. The expulsion found Maheu plunging into a serious depression, not unlike what his former boss was experiencing.

For Hughes, it had less to do with losing his alter ego than it did with losing control of his businesses, his money, his life. Since leaving Las Vegas, Hughes had become increasingly dependent on his aides. No longer willing to walk more than a few steps, Hughes insisted on being lifted from his bed to his Barcalounger, lifted into the bathroom, and lifted back to bed.

Although his kidneys continued to malfunction due to his limited intake of fluids, his physical condition was remarkably good for a man who refused to exercise or even walk. His mind, however, was being con-sumed by his increasing dependence on codeine. In constant pain from the open and festering wounds on his back, Hughes refused to be treated, despite the fact that the bone of his shoulder blade on his right side was now exposed. His rotting teeth had begun to abscess, causing his upper jaw to swell and drain, and further limiting his ability to chew.

As his body absorbed increasingly large doses of codeine, Hughes' constipation, already severe, became impacted and required Mell Stewart to administer repeated enemas to free the blockage.

Despite the fact that Hughes' suite had six televisions, the poor television reception made viewing difficult, and while Hughes' eyesight was no worse than any other sixty-five-year-old, his refusal to wear glasses made reading newspapers impossible. He, therefore, had become totally dependent on his aides as a source of information. That single factor, more than any other, made Hughes' a virtual prisoner of the six men providing his care. Those men, in turn, were totally under the control of Bill Gay, who now found himself in complete charge of Hughes' growing empire.

Though the TWA lawsuit remained unsettled, and Maheu filed a suit for breach of contract, the legal atmosphere for Hughes Tool and its various subsidiaries was rather stable. With Hughes no longer able to interfere in the direction of his businesses, his profits were growing in all areas other than his Nevada operations, and Gay moved to immediately remove those employees loyal to Maheu and replace them with employees from Intertel, instructing them to get a firm grip on the bottom line. In addition, he found a new source of unexpected revenue, courtesy of the CIA.

CIA director William Colby had contacted Hughes Tool executive VP William Holliday in the fall of 1970 about a top-secret project to salvage a Russian submarine that lay sunken in the Pacific Ocean, midway between the Hawaiian and Midway Islands. Colby wanted Hughes Tool to design an enormous mining ship capable of lifting the submerged submarine from its grave three miles below the surface. Since Hughes was already involved in mining operations, albeit through John Meier's worthless mining claims, and had already supplied top-secret equipment through its aircraft division, the CIA looked upon the organization as the perfect fit and cover for its covert operation that it called Project Jennifer. Although Hughes had a vague concept of the plan, he was only marginally involved in its acceptance, and had no knowledge that the giant mining ship, named the *Glomar*, went into production at the Sun Shipbuilding yards in Chester, Pa., utilizing a design conceived by Hughes Tool's partner, Global Marine Corp.

Hughes' own time was monopolized by a round-the-clock screening of films that the aides continued to provide in endless supply. When he was not watching films, he was sleeping in a drug-induced stupor, allowing his aides ample free time to enjoy the hospitality of the Britannia Beach

Hotel. For aide Howard Eckersley, it meant something else—the opportunity to go into business for himself.

In the early months of 1971, Eckersley conceived a plan to open Pan American Mines Ltd. and name himself president. According to Pan American Mines' prospectus, its investing shareholders were Hughes' aides Levar Myler and George Francom, as well as Gay's assistant, Kay Glenn. The firm's stock was listed on the Canadian Stock Exchange, and initial press releases freely mentioned the name of Howard Hughes. While not directly labeling the company as a Hughes property, releases on the firm referred to Eckersley as "Chief Personal Staff Executive to Howard Hughes" with Myler and Francom listed as "Hughes Tool Co. staff executives."

As word began to spread throughout Canada of a Hughes investment in the area, the stock price rose from an initial offering at one dollar to ten times that amount. It was only after Canadian officials learned that Pan American Mining Ltd. had no active mines that an investigation was begun into the company, culminating in a Canadian warrant for Eckersley's arrest. Word of the fiasco was reported in the *New York Times*, *Wall Street Journal*, *Los Angeles Times*, and every Canadian paper, yet Hughes himself remained blissfully ignorant of the situation until Eckersley was forced to reveal the existence of the company to his boss. While the charges against Eckersley were eventually dismissed, several others involved in the company were convicted of stock fraud.

Fraud was something that Hughes disliked. He liked it even less than losing money, which he did not like at all. And when he was told about a writer claiming to have worked with him on an autobiography, the word fraud came quickly to mind. He initially heard about the project from aide John Holmes, who delivered the news and then stood back expecting an explosion of expletives from the Old Man.

None was forthcoming, for despite his love of privacy, at that moment Hughes was less concerned about a fraudulent book than he was about his stockpile of codeine—a supply that had run dangerously short on the ninth floor of the Britannia Beach Hotel.

While Hughes repeatedly asked when he could expect delivery of his next "message," Hughes' code name for drugs, the aides found themselves in the center of a growing melodrama unfolding in New York City at the office of book publisher McGraw-Hill. There, in the otherwise quiet hallowed halls of *literae scriptae*, a manuscript from writer Clifford Irving and co-writer Richard Suskind was being set in type and rushed into production. *The Autobiography of Howard Hughes (with a commentary by Clifford Irving)* was predicted to be a blockbuster best-seller by the publisher. McGraw-Hill had paid $750,000 to "any account of H.R.

Hughes" and given the checks to Irving, who claimed to have written the manuscript based on meetings with Hughes over a period of months.

While Hughes found Irving's claims of only passing interest, saying, "He didn't get any of *my* money," according to aide Gordon Margulis, for Gay and Davis it posed a far bigger problem. With a new governor in place in Nevada,[1] the political tolerance for Hughes' continuing failure to follow Las Vegas' gaming laws was waning. If Hughes indeed had found the time and strength to meet with Irving, while declining to meet in person with Nevada gaming officials, it appeared that the billionaire was flaunting his power in the face of the politicians. To prove that Irving and Hughes never met, however, required more than just Davis' insistence in court. It required positive proof that the entire book was a hoax.

For Gay and Davis, the solution came in the form of an elaborately staged press conference, Hughes' first in over twenty years. On January 7, 1972, seven seasoned journalists, who had previously met or written about Hughes, were assembled at the Universal Sheraton in Universal City, California. The collected journalists[2] spoke over a speakerphone system with the billionaire, who admitted that he was living on Paradise Island in the Caribbean and then proceeded to answer questions lobbed from the newsmen for the next two and a half hours.

Under intense heat from the glaring spotlights, the journalists wiped sweat from their foreheads, and quickly emptied their water glasses that beaded humidity next to the place cards inscribed with their names. Hughes was comfortable speaking with the men, helped along by a recent injection of codeine. Thus sedated and anxious to clear up any misimpressions, Hughes sat naked on his Barcalounger and calmly gave the performance of his life.

While Hughes truthfully stated that he had never spoken to Irving ("I don't know him; I never saw him; I have never even heard of him until a matter of days ago when this thing first came to my attention"), he openly lied about his appearance, laughing away the reporters who dared to claim that he had unclipped fingernails and hair down to his shoulders. And while the press conference was called to discredit Irving, Hughes saved his most vitriolic comments for his portrayal of Maheu. "He's a no-good dishonest son-of-a-bitch, (who) stole me blind."

For Maheu, the comment hurt far more than his dismissal. The fol-

1. Governor Mike O'Callaghan took office in January, 1971, several months after Hughes' departure from the state.
2. The seven journalists included James Bacon (Hearst Syndicate), Marvin Miles (*Los Angeles Times*), Vernon Scott (UPI), moderator Roy Neal (NBC News), Gene Handsaker (AP), Wayne Thomis (*Chicago Tribune*), and Gladwin Hill (*New York Times*).

lowing month, he filed a $17.5 million lawsuit for libel and slander against Hughes, which joined Maheu's then ongoing lawsuit for $50 million for wrongful dismissal. While Maheu would be later vindicated through a court judgment, it would take years of litigation.[3]

Hughes' press conference did more than place his name in the front pages of newspapers across the country and eventually send Clifford Irving and Richard Suskind to jail. The exposure drew the attention of the Bahamian government—specifically the political foes of Prime Minister Lynden Pindling and members of the Free National Movement, who started a campaign of intimidation. They began to publicly question Hughes' immigration status. He was a foreigner who had managed to remain on Bahamian soil without immigration papers, a valid passport, work permits or investments in the region. The Free National Movement suggested Pindling had granted Hughes special privileges, which, of course, he had.

When Hughes' aides began being questioned themselves by the immigration authorities, who attempted to gain access to Hughes' private quarters, there was a decided panic among the ranks. At one point, the aides moved Hughes from his own suite to one on the sixth floor of the hotel in an effort to keep him isolated from the invading officials, who found nothing but an empty room with a hospital bed covered in soiled sheets when they finally forced their way into the Hughes wing of the hotel. That evening, Hughes was returned to the ninth floor, but only for an overnight. The uncertainty of their political status demanded a hasty getaway—a maneuver unto itself that was not so simple.

The island of Paradise was separated from the capital of Nassau by a long bridge, which allowed police and immigration to easily track all those coming and going from the Britannia Beach Hotel. The very arrangement that aided in Hughes' seclusion made his escape by that route just as problematical. The decision was made to leave the island by the only other possible means—boat. Despite the fact that Chester Davis maintained a yacht in Nassau for his own pleasure, Hughes' aides leased a yacht named the *Cygnus*, and hired its captain, Robert Rehak, and Rehak's first mate to sail them to Florida's Key Biscayne.

Gone was any pretense of secrecy. In the rush of their emergency exit, the aides took Rehak into their confidence and pledged him to silence. It was not a simple oath to keep. The sight of the billionaire, long toenails curling around old sandals and gray hair stringing to his shoulders, wearing only a bathrobe to protect him from the winter sea air, was

---

3. Maheu was ultimately victorious in court, when a jury awarded him $2,823,333.30. The judgment was successfully appealed on a technicality, although a settlement in Maheu's favor was eventually reached out of court.

as unexpected as it was shocking. Rehak later told a Miami newspaper that the look of Hughes was the "craziest thing I ever saw."

With Jack Hooper no longer handling security, Bill Gay had hired an Intertel employee named James Golden to take over the responsibility. Like Hooper before him, Golden never met Howard Hughes face-to-face, but rather functioned in an executive capacity to make certain that no one else saw him face-to-face either. It fell to Golden to locate a suitable refuge for the billionaire, who had quite literally become a man without a country.

The continuing threat of subpoenas from ever-widening lawsuits made it unwise for Hughes to settle back in the United States without fear of exposure. Foreign travel was difficult since Hughes refused to be photographed for a passport. Yet, through his connections with Turner Shelton, the Ambassador to Nicaragua under Richard Nixon, Golden gained assurances from Nicaraguan President Anastasio Somoza that Hughes would be both welcome and undisturbed. That decision made, and arrangements quickly handled with the InterContinental Hotel in Managua, Hughes had only to tolerate a rough crossing to Key Biscayne and be carried aboard a chartered Eastern Airlines jet before he was on his way to yet another blacked-out suite in yet another invisible city.

Managua in 1972 was more than the largest city in Nicaragua. It was its cultural and economic center. Against the tin-roof shanties of a population struggling amidst poverty, modern skyscrapers stood in stark defiance, proclaiming the strength of the Somoza dictatorship. The Intercontinental Hotel, nine stories high and shaped like a pyramid, was the finest hotel in the entire country. And Hughes occupied the finest suite in the Intercontinental.

According to logs kept by his aides, Hughes' days and nights were no longer consumed by business. With the absence of a Maheu in his life, Hughes had no one off whom to bounce ideas. No one to argue against his excesses. No one to tell him *no*. Surrounded now by yes-men whose major goal was to maintain the status quo, there would be no more high-powered acquisitions, no more interference in operations. Those were replaced by a repetitive round of sleep, films, drugs, and more films.

Hughes' stay in Nicaragua was brief. Three and a half weeks after he arrived in the Central American country, Hughes was on the move again, this time to Vancouver, Canada. The purpose for the Canadian trip was said to provide Hughes better communication facilities and American television reception. By no small coincidence, it also brought his aides closer to their families. Before departing from Nicaragua, however, Hughes cemented his relationship with the country's president by agreeing to meet with General Somoza to thank him for his hospitality. It was the first time Hughes had met with a total stranger since he invited the governor of Florida to join him for dinner in 1955.

The meeting took place aboard Hughes' private jet, a Grumman Gulfstream II flown in specifically for the trip. Hughes was moved from the hotel to a waiting Mercedes via wheelchair, a decided improvement over the previously used stretcher. He had been freshly barbered by Mell Stewart, who also trimmed his finger and toe nails, leaving a half-inch extension on Hughes' left thumb nail for what Margulis called Hughes' "screwdriver."

Somoza was escorted aboard the Gulfstream by Ambassador Shelton, and was greeted by Hughes in his pajama bottoms, bathrobe, and sandals, with a firm handshake. For the next hour, Hughes resorted to familiar banter about pursuing future investment opportunities in Nicaragua, the prospect of which had its president eager to hear non-existent details, and Shelton promising the cooperation of Richard Nixon, who had utilized Somoza's anti-communist stance for overt propaganda operations.

Perhaps the most startling development from the meeting, other than the fact that it happened at all, was the press conference given after Hughes' plane departed the airport by the Ambassador to Nicaragua. Shelton told the *New York Times* that Hughes "looks extremely well. He was wearing a short beard that covers his face and builds into a Vandyke on his chin. His hair is cut short and so are his nails."

Hughes' arrival at Vancouver's Bayshore Inn was extraordinary for a number of reasons. First, Hughes arrived in daylight and elected to walk into the hotel through the main lobby, eschewing the preparations made for his backdoor arrival by Gay's administrative assistant Kay Glenn, who was at the hotel to view his boss for the first time in over thirty years. Still dressed in his soiled bathrobe, pajama bottoms and sandals, Hughes made no effort to rush through the lobby, preferring instead to look around at the sumptuous furnishings and yacht-filled marina.

When coupled with Hughes' meeting with Somoza, the billionaire's behavior was bordering normal. It was a frightening display to his personal aides, who saw in Hughes' increasing comfort beyond the seclusion of his private suite as a threat to their importance within the organization, if not their continued employment. Their nervousness was only compounded when they finally got Hughes into his suite on the hotel's twentieth floor. It was there that Hughes walked into the suite's living room and dared to stare out the windows at Vancouver's marina and the one-thousand-acre Stanley Park. He thought of leaving the windows unblocked and turning the living room into a sitting area for contemplation.

Horrified that their boss was usurping their office space, the aides maneuvered Hughes into the corner bedroom, once again darkened against any intrusion. As quickly as it had appeared, Hughes' ease with the outside dissipated as he relented to the wishes of his aides, and moved silently toward his Barcalounger. It was there that he would stay for the next thirty-six hours, sleeping and watching films, before finally moving to the bathroom.

Hughes was still in Vancouver when, on June 17, 1972, the Democratic National Committee Headquarters in the Watergate Building in Washington, D.C., was burgled. It was 2:30 a.m. in the morning when the burglars were captured by District police, and began the investigation that would bring down a Presidency. Hughes was unaware of the break-in, of course, happily watching *The Brain That Wouldn't Die* for the seventh time. To critics, the American International Picture was the worst horror film ever made. To Hughes, it ranked as one of his favorites, never tiring of seeing Virginia Leith play a woman whose decapitated head was kept alive in the laboratory of her fiancé, played by Jason Evers.

Despite his best efforts to remain drugged, entertained, and completely secluded, Hughes was nevertheless unable to escape his tormented life completely. The lingering TWA litigation still played heavily into his obsessions, for he knew that sooner rather than later, a court would levy unimaginable penalties on his bank accounts. In an effort to prevent Hughes Tool from being seized by the courts to provide collateral for his project debt, Hughes allowed himself to be convinced to dispose of the company through a stock issue. Tool company executive VP Raymond Holliday was solidly behind the plan that would place him outside of Hughes' control and still keep him as head of the publicly traded company. Bill Gay, as well, approved of the sale since it would bring needed fluid cash into the accounts, and place him completely in charge of a restructured Hughes organization. It remained only for them to convince their boss to do something that he swore his entire life he would never even consider.

It was Chester Davis who first broached the subject of a sale of Hughes Tool, relayed, of course, through Hughes' aides. At first, Hughes reacted predictably, refusing even to consider a decision he labeled "asinine. . . no, not asinine, *idiotic.* That's the word." At this point in their respective relationships, Hughes' opinion was important, but hardly sacrosanct. Lacking the ability to closely follow most of the progress of his assorted businesses, Hughes was now an outsider. While he had the ultimate say in everything, he said very little. So little, in fact, that Gay and Holliday continued to move forward with the proposed sale, hiring Merrill Lynch, Pierce, Fenner & Smith to offer the public stock for sale.

Sleeping in long stretches, followed by even longer periods of intense discomfort caused by his chronic constipation, Hughes increasingly lived an existence of dulled pain and mindless entertainment designed to fill time. No thoughts of flying, no memories of faded glory, Hughes existed in the moment, handing each day's decisions in isolated ignorance. He knew only what he was told, and what he was told was that Hughes Tool had to be sold.

Before Merrill Lynch had finished preparing its offering, Hughes began to feel pressure from the Canadian immigration officials who began questioning his intentions, and pointed to the fast-approaching end to his tax-free status in the country. The law was clear. After six months, any visitor was considered a resident, Howard Hughes included. The threat of taxes, actually even the mention of the word, was enough to cause Hughes to alert his aides to prepare to depart. He needed to escape, and he remembered the invite that General Somoza had extended. Four days later, Hughes left Canada, routed back to Managua and the eighth floor of the Intercontinental.

Returning to his room was something of a homecoming for the billionaire. In the six months since he had been gone, his suite had been recarpeted and painted. Hughes took it as a personal compliment, never realizing that the stench of urine had necessitated the overhaul. It did nothing to remove the constant dampness in the air, however, and as he fell back on his hospital bed, he shivered against the cold, wet air coming from the air-conditioning vent near the ceiling.

On September 25, 1972, less than a month after arriving in Managua, Hughes agreed to see representatives from Merrill Lynch to confirm his approval of the Hughes Tool sale. Julius H. Sedlmayr, Merrill Lynch VP, was dubious. For Howard Hughes to sell the company that created his fortune, and his father's legacy, was a decision so counter to everything the billionaire had previously expressed that Sedlmayr would accept nothing less than a face-to-face acknowledgment in the presence of Merrill Lynch attorney J. Courtney Ivey. His apprehensions were well-founded. Indeed, Hughes himself was questioning the need for the sale, repeatedly asking his aides to clarify the position of Holliday, Gay, and Davis.

Had Sedlmayr been aware of Hughes' original will, he would have been even more suspicious of Hughes' real intentions. In Article V of that document, Hughes wrote, "It is my will and desire that my Trustees shall continue the operation of Hughes Tool Company as far as practicable as now carried on."

> This institution was founded by my father and promoted through his genius and ability, to the success which it now enjoys, and it is my purpose and intention, so long as I shall live, to continue its development and progress, by following out the policies practised [sic] by my

father; and it is my will and desire that my Trustees, so far as practicable, shall continue the same course after my death, thus building to my father a permanent monument marking his initiative, judgment, and foresight in the founding and upbuilding of a great business. My Executors and Trustees shall never pledge the stock of said company. They shall never sell the same as long as said company may be profitably operated; and it is my will and desire that they shall exhaust every means to see that its profitable operation is continued.

HOLLIDAY, GAY, AND DAVIS had no binding loyalty to the firm, or vested interest in its continuing success. A younger Hughes, a more diligent executive, would have fought the sale until his last breath. But Howard Hughes at 67 was in no condition to fight. The billionaire who could barely walk had no place to run. He did as he was told, up to a point. While Sedlmayr and Ivey waited in their rooms at the Intercontinental, Hughes drugged himself with Blue Bombers, seventy milligrams worth, and slept. Under strict orders never to wake him, his aides let him sleep, postponing the meeting with Sedlmayr and Ivey repeatedly through the day. Finally, near midnight, Sedlmayr had his fill and made it known to aide John Holmes that if Hughes did not see him before he needed to leave the hotel to catch his 6:45 a.m. flight back to Manhattan, Merrill Lynch was no longer interested in continuing with the stock issue.

Ultimatums never sat well with Hughes. This was another "gun to his head." So he waited until 5:30 a.m. to see the two men, never rising from his Barcalounger, nor offering to shake hands. He did, however, give them what they wanted. A signed paper attesting to his desire to sell Hughes Tool. His only requirement: "I want the employees to be treated well."

The sale of Hughes Tool was a hit on Wall Street. At $30 a share, it was also judged a bargain. The company that had made Hughes three-quarters of a billion dollars since he inherited it in 1924 was sold for $150 million. In less than a year, the stock would rise to nearly $100 a share, generating a profit of three hundred percent for its shareholders. Among them: Raymond Holliday, then chairman of the company and no longer a Hughes employee.

Hughes seemed content to live out his days in the Managua Intercontinental, repeating his ritual of watching films and drugging himself to sleep, and might well have, if it were not for the catastrophe that struck the city just after midnight on December 23, 1972. Hughes had just finished viewing *A Face in the Rain*, the 1963 Embassy Picture release starring Rory Calhoun as a U.S. spy in Italy, when he called Jim Rickard into his room. Rickard had been added to the aide pool in Vancouver, and was a one-time drive-in theater operator who had first joined the Hughes organization in 1953. As Rickard crossed the room to face his boss lying naked in his recliner, the largest earthquake to ever hit Nicaragua began to roll its way through Managua.

The shock waves sent furniture, plaster, and Hughes' movie projectors crashing to the floor, with Rickard catching Hughes' large speaker as it fell, deflecting it away from the billionaire who remained unscathed in his chair. Hughes, who had been through several earthquakes in California, was calm during the ordeal, as much from his drugs as his previous experience. Outside, the wail of car alarms and fire sirens competed with the screams of terrified people as thousands poured into the streets, dazed and injured.

As aftershocks continued to shake the hotel, Rickard ran to the telephone to report the situation to Hughes' Romaine office and request an evacuation plane. Hughes, however, was in no hurry to leave, preferring to stay in his chair, hidden as he had been. As Howard Eckersley, Mell Stewart and George Francom rushed into the suite, the aides immediately countermanded any thought of remaining in the damaged hotel, and promptly dressed Hughes into a pair of slacks and a white shirt, covered him with his robe and carried him down the nine flights of stairs to the lobby level.

For the remainder of that night and early morning, Hughes remained in the back seat of a Mercedes sedan used by his aides as he was driven through the broken city. Hughes never saw the bloodied corpses lying by the roadside or the injured and helpless, pleading for aid. His head was covered by a dark blanket, protected from the cold reality of the tragedy. When he finally emerged, he had been taken to the summer palace of President Somoza, where he remained until that evening. Aftershocks continued to plague the futile rescue efforts of a country in ruin. Nicaragua was in desperate need of fresh drinking water, since its own treatment plants had been severely damaged by the quake. Yet, when one of the first emergency landing clearances was given at the Managua airport, it was for a Lear jet flown in empty from Miami to transport Hughes and his aides out of the country.

Hughes flew into Fort Lauderdale International Airport, arriving in the pre-dawn hours in an effort to escape any interrogation by immigration officials. The normally invisible billionaire actually drew increased attention to himself by the timing of his flight. The lone immigration official on duty insisted on being allowed on board to verify Hughes' identity and, despite the best efforts of his aides to prevent it, actually succeeded. Huddled in the back of the plane, hidden beneath dark blankets, his eyes barely visible in the beam of the agent's flashlight, Hughes refused to speak other than to acknowledge his identity to the befuddled worker.

His curiosity apparently satisfied, the customs agent departed as quickly as he arrived, leaving Hughes and his aides free to travel to a rented home on nearby Sunset Island for what was to be Hughes' final night in America.

The following day, Jack Real provided a leased Lockheed Jetstar to transport Hughes to his third home in 1972, a luxury suite on the top floor of London's Inn on the Park. The hotel was the property of the Rothschild banking family, and as a courtesy to Hughes, the entire top floor was emptied with the exception of one long-term guest, a man named Barry Cowan.

The Rothschild office became an unofficial clearinghouse for the curious seeking to have an audience with Hughes. Among them was the man who shared the honor as the richest man in America—John Paul Getty. On New Year's Day, 1973, Hughes received an internal memo that read, "The private secretary of Mr. J. Paul Getty called Mr. Rothschild's office today extending an invitation to you to renew aquaintanceship [sic] with Mr. Getty while you are in London." Since Getty and Hughes had never met, except on the pages of *Forbes* magazine, Hughes ignored the memo and returned to watching a movie, his fourth repeat of *The Deserter*, an Italian western starring Richard Crenna and Chuck Connors as cavalrymen hunting for Indian chief Ricardo Montalban. It was the repeated viewing of *The Deserter*, called *La Spina Dorsale del Diavolo* in its original release, that caused Hughes to issue an edict to his aides outlawing spaghetti westerns from his screening list.

Life at the Inn on the Park quickly settled into Hughes' now familiar routine of drugs, films, sleep and bathroom, though with a decided change in tone. For the first time in recent memory, Hughes felt content. His aides were comfortable being in an English speaking country, Hughes' television reception was excellent, he could once again read the daily papers (albeit with the aid of his peephole), and even his supply of drugs had improved, courtesy of Dr. Wilbur Thain, who had been added to his medical staff.

Thain, who had worked in the Romaine office for a short while during medical school, was the brother of Bill Gay's wife, Mary. Despite having a successful family medical practice in Logan, Utah, Thain decided to join Hughes' staff when he received assurances from the billionaire that he would be placed in charge of the Howard Hughes Medical Institute in the future. Like most things promised Hughes' employees, this was not in writing. To Thain, however, it was as binding an agreement as if it had been written in a contract, and he approached his work with the optimism of a prizewinner. To Hughes, the addition of Thain brought the promise of an uninterrupted drug supply, now ordered directly from the pharmaceutical houses.

The only thing missing to make Hughes' life of virtual retirement complete was the news that the continuing TWA case had been settled.

On January 10, 1973, the Supreme Court of the United States granted him something even better. By a vote of six to two, the justices ruled that the Federal courts that had been ruling against Hughes for a decade had no jurisdiction in the case. The Supreme Court agreed with what Chester Davis had been saying all along: the Civil Aeronautics Board had approved of Hughes' handling of TWA, therefore effectively eliminating Hughes' antitrust liability.

Despite the fact that he had sold his father's company to finance anticipated court damages that never materialized, Hughes was elated by the news. Eckersley told reporters, "Hughes didn't stomp his feet or say, 'Hell, it's about time.' But he was happy. He was absolutely ecstatic." TWA, which had spent 55,000 man-hours and $7.5 million on its legal expenses, was dumbfounded.

Hughes allowed the breath to escape slowly from his lungs as he finished laughing. His back pushed roughly against the paper towel insulation on the Barcalounger, as the raw flesh from his shoulder blade stuck to the Naugahyde cover. Jack Real had rarely seen his old friend so excited as he watched Hughes relate his version of how the TWA lawyers took the news. "Crapped in their pants," he had said, before breaking out in his nasally snorts of glee.

Real had been brought to London for precisely this kind of moment. Shared memories, storytelling, a willing listening, a friend. As he listened to Hughes' laughter, Real knew he had been wise to come when Hughes called. Through the haze of drug-induced nirvana, he saw the smallest hint of his old friend. The old spark, the adventurer reborn. He nursed the souvenirs of the past until they were bright, clear memories, and as he watched the billionaire dig past his addiction to something even more powerful, his love for the sky, he was amazed at what he uncovered.

Hughes wanted to fly again. No, more than merely fly, he wanted to pilot a plane and experience the release that only flying brings. When Hughes asked Real to make it happen, he did not have to explain why. Real knew the feeling, he had had it himself, and promised his old friend that it would happen. Looking now at the man he first met as a test pilot of the XF11, it was difficult to believe the toll life had taken. The wasting of muscle, the thinning of bone had left Hughes so weak that Real wondered if he could physically handle the controls.

Time was Hughes' enemy; and now it was Real's. Yet, as he moved to set in motion the various elements that would bring together plane, runway, pilot and friend, he had no clue that he faced a far bigger challenge than Hughes' deteriorating health. He had to face the remonstration of Hughes' aides who were determined to keep the billionaire from ever again seeing the light of day.

TWENTY

Being of Sound Mind and Body

If you knew how much it disturbs me, and how unhappy it makes me when you are completely cold and unfriendly as you were tonight, I really don't think you would turn on the punishment outlet quite all the way. So, all I ask is that the next time you get ready to give me a really harsh expression of your views, you merely take into account the fact that my life is not quite the total 'bed of roses' that I sometimes get the impression you think it is.

Freeport, Bahamas
July, 1975
Hughes' note to his aides.

"HE WANTS TO *WHAT?*" BILL GAY'S VOICE RAISED AN octave as if he were rehearsing for an Italian operetta.

"Fly. . . he wants to fly," John Holmes repeated. The men were incredulous at the development.

"Talk it over with Levar and handle it," Gay instructed, aware that there was little even the aides could do if Jack Real successfully found a plane. "Remind him again of the governor. That might help."

As the senior aides, John Holmes and Levar Myler had been made directors of the newly formed Summa Corporation[1] and were therefore in a position of elevated importance among Hughes' caregivers. The ringleaders of the most elite guard in the world, they found themselves under attack by an outsider, a man whose history with

---

1. The other directors of the board of Summa were William Gay, Nadine Henley, and Chester Davis.

Hughes far preceded their own. He was a danger not only to their autonomy, but their jobs themselves. Jack Real was someone who needed to be handled.

As Howard Hughes turned restlessly in his bed, he knew nothing of the internal intrigue within the Inn on the Park. His dreams were of the sky, and he was more determined than ever to fight his way past the cloud banks in his mind to achieve his goal. He knew what he had to do; he knew he had to stop craving that nirvana—the one that codeine provided. Yet, as good as it was, the floating high of dulled pain, it was nothing, *nothing*, compared with the thrill of flying. That, he knew, was *really* his drug of choice.

When John Holmes wrote Hughes a note reminding him yet again of the urgency of a meeting with the Republican governor of Nevada to assure that his gaming licenses would be renewed, he expected the same response he had received the last five or six times he handed his boss the same note. Holmes was prepared to be brushed aside, to look into the dull brown eyes that barely blinked life and watch as a withered hand rose and pointed toward the door.

John Holmes was not disappointed. Hughes went through his normal display of distress, indicating his demand for solitude, but this time when he found himself again alone, he wrote his chief aide a note that acknowledged his acceptance of a meeting. He would, in fact, he happy to see Governor Mike O'Callaghan if the Irishman would accommodate him on St. Patrick's Day. As Hughes wrote the note, he felt his lips turn into a smile, and suddenly remembered what it was like to be happy.

When the meeting took place as scheduled on March 17, 1973, it lasted one hour and ten minutes. Hughes was drugged with 250 milligrams of codeine, which while more than a normal dose for a terminally ill cancer patient, represented only half of what Hughes was used to tolerating. The governor arrived with Philip Hannifin, chairman of the Nevada Gaming Board, and was exuberant after his conversation, admitting to the *New York Times*, "Hughes has a commanding personality," and one which convinced the governor that Hughes would soon return to Nevada. The billionaire, freshly washed and coiffed, had not lost his ability to manipulate. O'Callaghan returned to Nevada a convert, with Hannifin assuring everyone in forthright tones that Hughes' casino licenses were legal and binding.

Hughes took little notice of Chester Davis and Bill Gay, who sat in on the meeting. Davis, who had never met Hughes in person, sat off to the side in the darkened room along with Gay, who had not seen his boss in over twenty-five years. Any attempt by Gay or Davis to interject a comment in the conversation was ignored by Hughes, who never addressed his employees or even acknowledged their presence.

After his visitors from Nevada left the hotel, Gay made every effort to impress upon Hughes' aides the need to speak to the Old Man about Gay's plans to rebuild the Desert Inn in Las Vegas. Gay had brought an elaborate scale model of a shopping complex that he had envisioned to stretch along the Las Vegas Strip, and proudly told the aides of the impact the mall would have on the gambling Mecca. Hughes, however, would not be pressured into hearing about "a damn shopping mall" nor even convinced to look at the scale model, which was eventually covered with a sheet and left untouched as well as unbuilt.

Having thus satisfied his aides' demands and passed another outside scrutiny, Hughes was ready for his reward. In the past that would have meant more drugs. Now, it was his promise to fly. Since Hughes' only existing wardrobe consisted of his old bathrobe, one pair of pajama bottoms, and a few worn pairs of drawstring underpants, Real decided to treat his friend to some new clothes to commemorate the occasion and turned to Gordon Margulis, the Brit among the aides, for help. Together they shopped for shirts, pants, a new Fedora, and a leather flight jacket similar to the one Hughes wore when he conquered the skies four decades before.

Predictably, the aides attempted to convince Hughes that he was too ill to leave the hotel, realizing the very real danger of such folly. Still, Hughes was determined. He even ordered sliced chicken sandwiches to be boxed for the flight, a throwback to the memories of youth.[2] He was excited to the point that he had daily conversations with Real about the plans for the initial flight, the first of what he hoped would be many more to come. He wanted to hear the elements of the arrangements repeated over and over in exacting detail, and glowed with anticipation with each retelling.

On the guise that Hughes was interested in purchasing a turboprop Hawker Siddeley 748, Real was able to convince test pilot Tony Blackman to accompany Hughes on a flight, which departed London's Hatfield Airport on June 10, 1973. Hughes was accompanied on the flight by Real and aide Chuck Waldron, and promptly took off all his clothes as soon as he sat in the pilot's seat. Blackman remained nonplussed throughout the experience, which he later recalled with apprehension as being one of the most challenging of his career.

As Hughes attempted repeated take-offs and landings, Blackman was forced to take control of the plane to prevent a crash and potential loss of life. While he could see that Hughes was tall, thin, and his flying style prone to pushing the limit of safety, he was unaware that the man in the

---

2. No one reminded Hughes that he used to carry roast beef sandwiches on his flights, since sliced roast beef was now impossible for the billionaire to chew.

pilot's seat was extremely hard of hearing, had failing eyesight, faulty equilibrium, and lacked coordination. "It was a thrill ride," Blackman remembered, in understatement.

In the next month, Hughes left the Inn on the Park three additional times, and flew with Blackman, Real, and Waldron, in another Hawker Siddeley 748 as well as a de Havilland 125 Twinjet aircraft. Those hours spent flying were the happiest moments in the last decade of the billionaire's life. His mood was elevated, his humor intact, his mind sharp, and his outlook refreshed. Unfortunately, it was not to last.

On August 9, 1973, in the early morning hours, Howard Hughes got out of bed and walked to the bathroom. At his side was aide Levar Myler. Leaning heavily on Myler, Hughes' slight frame suddenly slipped from Myler's grip, and the billionaire slumped to the floor, a limp skeleton collapsing on itself. Hughes groaned in pain as the disturbing crunch of bone against bone pierced the darkness. Afraid to move his employer, Myler raced to telephone for help. Later, his report would shed little news on what caused the fall, but one thing was certain. Howard Hughes had a multiple fracture of his left hip, an injury verified by Dr. William Young, a radiologist called to the Inn on the Park and asked to x-ray the hip of a patient identified only as Hugh Winston.

There, in the darkness, being moved and turned by strange hands forced to use paper towels as insulation, Howard Hughes' life ended. Not his physical life, of course. He continued to breathe and talk and watch films. But his spirit was gone. He felt it as surely as if it had tipped his fedora and left the room. His life was finished.

Dr. Walter Robinson, London's top orthopedic surgeon, was brought in to set the hip and implant a steel pin to help support the weakened joint. Despite the aides' insistence that the billionaire could not leave his darkened suite, Robinson was adamant that his patient had to be moved to a hospital for surgery. Robinson refused to consider doing the operation in a hotel room, no matter how well equipped. As a result and over his loudly-voiced objections, Hughes was taken by stretcher from the Inn on the Park and transported to the London Clinic, a private hospital used to handling the health concerns of the country's richest patrons.

In depositions given by Drs. Young and Robinson, both physicians were astounded by Hughes' poor physical condition, remarking on his dehydration and malnutrition. Dr. Robinson, in fact, made a point of speaking at length to Dr. Wilbur Thain, who checked into a room at the hospital to watch over Hughes. Robinson recommended and completed extensive testing of Hughes' blood and organs in what was to be the most complete physical the billionaire had in the last fifty years of his life. The results of those tests indicated that Hughes' muscles and organs were

Being of Sound Mind and Body

atrophied and barely functioning, suggesting a biological age at least twenty years in advance of his actual sixty-eight years.

Despite Hughes' fragile health, under Robinson's experienced hands, the surgery went well and within days, Hughes demanded to be released from the hospital and returned to the Inn on the Park. Robinson was unable to overrule Hughes' insistence, notwithstanding the fact that he wanted his patient to begin physical therapy on his hip, and recommended a course of exercises to stimulate muscle growth and reconditioning. Hughes, of course, was not only not interested in therapy, he was not interested in walking. Once Hughes returned to his bed at the hotel, he never walked a single step on his own again.

"WHAT THE HELL IS WATERGATE?" Hughes asked aide George Francom several months after his return to the hotel. Hughes could not escape the news reports running daily on London television broadcasts as well as in the headlines of the British newspapers. Nor could he escape the reports that he was somehow involved. That Hughes should be confused was understandable, since it had been years since he had ordered Robert Maheu to give cash contributions to Richard Nixon via Bebe Rebozo. He had no way of knowing that the contributions had been unreported and undiscovered until just days before.

The Hughes connection to Watergate became a topic of much debate within the Senate committee investigating the burglary of the Democratic National Headquarters. As the facts became known, and various pieces fell into place, Howard Hughes' name remained one of the few constants, along with that of Nixon and Rebozo. By late October, 1973, the relationship between Hughes' money, Richard Nixon, the Justice Department's Antitrust Division and Las Vegas was making the headlines and it was only a matter of time before the Old Man himself would bring up the topic. When it happened, Francom sidestepped the question, and waited for it to fade into Hughes' slipping memory. The fact that it did reflected the extent to which his mind was clouded with the excesses of drugs, and the toll they took was as much physical as mental.

In late November, Chester Davis was alerted by his contacts within the Securities and Exchange Commission that an indictment was being prepared against Hughes for illegal activities in the Air West acquisition. Despite Hughes' contentment with the hotel accommodations and security arrangements in London, Davis advised the billionaire to prepare to be moved immediately. The extradition agreements between the United States and Great Britain gave the local authorities permission to return Hughes to America to answer federal charges. It was an alarm that not even the strongest drugs could muffle.

With the suite in turmoil, once again preparing for a major move, a letter arrived at the Inn on the Park, addressed to Mr. Howard R. Hughes (whom the front desk still refused to acknowledge was a guest), and sent up to the penthouse. The envelope bore the return address of London Broadcasting, a new radio station headquartered on Fleet Street, and contained a letter from an eager reporter typical of the hundreds of requests Hughes received each year.

> Dear Mr. Hughes,
>
> I know I am trying for what hundred of others have tried for and failed, but you never get anything unless you try.
>
> What I would like is an interview with you. Just a minute or two of your time would be enough.
>
> I work for the new independent radio station, London Broadcasting, and an interview with you would really make our name. And it would certainly make mine.
>
> I promise that I am friendly and charming, and have no evil intentions towards you.
>
> Please, please, please will you see me?
>
> Yours very hopefully,
> Angela Storer

HUGHES READ ANGELA'S LETTER, and marked it "What is London Broadcasting?" He then placed it on a file that was packed for shipping out of the country.

On December 20, 1973, just a week after Hughes was inducted into the Aviation Hall of Fame in Dayton, Ohio, the billionaire left England on a private DC-9 bound for the Bahamas. The aides were stunned at the decision to return to a country that previously had been so hostile. To Mell Stewart, it was like going back "into a bear trap." Davis and Gay had made the arrangements for Hughes to take over the top two floors of the Xanadu Princess Hotel in Freeport on Grand Bahama Island, and were aware of what Stewart and the other aides were not. The country had abolished its extradition treaty with the U.S. to accommodate financier Robert Vesco, himself in hiding in the country. What worked for Vesco would be equally as effective for Hughes, particularly since Gay had arranged for the Old Man to acquire the Xanadu Princess Hotel and therefore handsomely exceed Bahamian investment requirements for permanent foreign-resident status.

Barely one week after Hughes' arrival in the Caribbean, the SEC handed down its indictment naming Hughes, Davis, Maheu, producer David Charnay and a Hughes employee named James Nall as co-defendants in the suit. The thrust of the SEC charges was that Hughes and company knowingly manipulated the stock price of Air West to force the company's sale. Hughes had essentially done just that, and all the defendants were aware of it. Maheu had even warned him of the potential conflict these actions might cause.

From his haze on the top floor of the Xanadu Princess, the specter of a criminal conviction on security charges weighed heavily on Hughes' mind. No longer writing extensive memos, Hughes relied instead on dictated messages that were passed to his aides and then relayed to the proper individuals. Responses into his suite were now in written form, since Hughes' conscious mind had precious few minutes of perceptive thought. Even his screening of films was affected by his limited attention span, as scenes were repeated continuously for hours until the plot penetrated Hughes' awareness.

Living in a state of perpetual confusion and irritation, Hughes demanded and received increasingly large doses of codeine. By February 1974, Hughes was medicating himself to such abundance that Drs. Crane and Chaffin were concerned about his body's ability to tolerate the constant abuse. Both doctors were adamant about refusing to prescribe additional codeine for Hughes, and were joined in their concern by Dr. Wilbur Thain. Thain, however, continued to supply Hughes with codeine and other drugs, talked into it by his patient, who faithfully promised to reduce his drug intake until he was weaned entirely off them by the end of the year. While Thain may have been serious, Hughes, of course, was not, and, like most addicts, was willing to promise anything in the short term to maintain the supply of his drug of choice.

While Gay was aware of Hughes' growing drug dependency, his own plate was overflowing with the sheer volume of decisions that needed to be made to keep the Hughes empire productive. Officially, he was now the executive VP of the Summa Corporation, the renamed Hughes Tool Company with the tool division removed. He had charge of every division, including the Las Vegas business, the aircraft division, Hughes Air West, and the landholding companies.

The Hughes Air West lawsuit concerned him. If Hughes were found guilty on all counts of alleged stock manipulation, he could be sentenced to twelve years in prison. Fortunately for Hughes and for Gay, the U.S. District Court judge hearing the case labeled the government's case "the worse criminal pleading I've ever encountered," and dismissed the charges in February 1974. While the Security and Exchange Commission threatened to refile its suit, the immediate challenge to Hughes' legal culpability was lifted.

The Summa Corporation found no such relief, however. After years of neglect within the Hughes organization, primarily due to the billionaire's own failure to make prompt decisions, the infrastructure of the business was out of control. Employees who had long since been fired were still being paid to keep them from talking to the press. Systems were dangerously outdated, to the point that the only means of linking the various business divisions was via physical meetings with a myriad of executives.

The biggest problems, however, continued to exist in Las Vegas, where the physical buildings were simply wearing out, having not been remodeled since Hughes' purchase of them years earlier. The building housing Hughes' television station was in danger of being condemned, its septic tank malfunctioning and illegal. The Desert Inn had closed entire wings due to leaking plumbing, crumbling walls, and soiled carpet. The runways at the North Las Vegas airport were in need of repair and expansion. The showroom at the Sands was in need of new lighting and sound equipment. All were waiting for the approval of a man more determined than ever not to interrupt his nonstop movies with anything as aggravating as a decision. During one month in 1974, Hughes watched *Westworld*, *Trader Horn*, *Deaf Smith and Johnny Ears*, *Pat Garrett and Billy the Kid*, *Kid Blue*, *Emperor of the North*, *Story of a Woman*, *Grand Prix*, *Paper Moon*, *Patton*, *Love Story*, *Poseidon Adventure*, *The Godfather*, and *The French Connection* repeatedly.

His aides, still reduced to communicating with their boss solely through typewritten memos, handed him files of paperwork marked "URGENT," only to see them slide off the arm of the Barcalounger and drop to the floor unread. Requests for money transfers, purchases of planes, even approvals for his aides' vacations met a similar fate. Only memos from Jack Real managed to break through the indifference; Jack Real, who had been elevated in importance to trusted confidante, master of focused advice, and the connection to the past. It was to Real that the task of running the Xanadu Princess Hotel was given, as well as the assignment to evaluate the proposed purchase of the Lucayan Beach Hotel, the Lucayan Harbor Inn and the Daylight Apartments on Grand Bahama Island. It was capped by Hughes' decision to appoint Real as the head of Hughes East Coast, a new position that would rival Gay's own, if indeed it ever happened.

There was dissatisfaction among the staff; the need for some security. With Real making inroads into the aides' inner sanctum and Gay's executive status, the wagons were circled in a concerted effort to keep Hughes and Real apart. Suddenly, the Old Man was too sick, or too sleepy to see his old friend. And when Hughes asked to speak with Real, he was conveniently unavailable or out of town.

On the West Coast, the Internal Revenue Service had begun an extensive audit of the Summa Corporation, demanding to have a break-down of deductions and an explanation of Hughes' earnings, which seldom ever topped $50,000 in a single year, despite the fact that his wholly-owned companies were generating in excess of $175,000 per day. The IRS demanded to see records from the Maheu years just as the SEC had reinstated its Air West case and demanded to see memos relating to the takeover of the airline.

June 5, 1974. Mike Davis, the security guard at Hughes' Romaine Street headquarters, had just finished making his rounds outside the building. It was a little after midnight. He opened a side door to the concrete and steel fortress and felt the barrel of a gun stuck in his back.

He was pushed forward inside the building, his hands taped behind him, a blindfold placed across his eyes and gag put in his mouth. He was tossed on a ground floor sofa and told not to move.

Davis later told police that he thought he heard the footsteps of four men enter the building. For four hours the men went about their business, looking into safes, desk drawers, and filing cabinets. In a second-floor conference room, Chester Davis had filled the table with Hughes' written memos, neatly piled for indexing. All the memos were taken, as was a stack of cash, Nadine Henley's butterfly collection, and a ceramic samovar. Offices were ransacked, drawers were emptied onto the floor with seeming indiscretion, and then the burglars disappeared into the warmth of a still Hollywood night.

On the heels of the Watergate break-in, there was some indication that perhaps the White House was behind the theft; or the CIA; or the FBI. Yet the ease with which the burglars entered the building, the way they went about selecting their destinations, and how casually they proceeded with their business suggested something far more likely to the detectives investigating the crime. The Los Angeles Police Department had no proof, but was of the common opinion that it was an inside job: Hughes, or a member of his staff, arranged the burglary. The documents that were taken had been subpoenaed only days before the crime by the SEC, by Maheu, and by the Senate committee investigating the Watergate break-in.

The timing of the burglary was convenient for Hughes, and a little too convenient for the Los Angeles Police Department to believe that it was arbitrary timing. The initial suspect was Mike Davis, who, when questioned by the detectives, repeatedly proclaimed his innocence.

Hughes himself was told of the burglary in a memo from the aides, and was concerned primarily about the aftermath of an investigation, rather than by the burglary itself. "He does not want some insurance investigator to take it upon himself to start opening boxes and crates," the aides wrote to Nadine Henley, accountant Lee Murrin, and Kay Glenn. Hughes wanted no meddling, particularly not from the LAPD.

The Hughes staff balked at cooperating with the police with typical silence, even after a telephone call came into Romaine from a man identifying himself as Chester Brooks, demanding $1 million for the return of the Hughes papers. That the Hughes organization had made copies of the majority of the missing documents did not seem common knowledge among the thieves. Neither did Hughes' lack of interest in recovering his missing memos.

The entire incident might have died for lack of interest had it not been for a discovery made several weeks after the break-in. Apparently, among the items taken by the burglars was paperwork detailing Hughes' involvement in Project Jennifer, the CIA recovery of the sunken Soviet sub. When that word reached the CIA from Romaine Street that interdepartmental memos concerning the *Glomar* mining ship had been stolen, the CIA arrived in Hollywood determined to take over the responsibility for the case.

Cooperating with the CIA in a covert operation was one thing; being investigated by the agency was an entirely different matter. And the prospect of CIA intervention in his business caused Hughes to plunge deeper into the quagmire of his addiction. Had Hughes been more able to play an active part in the investigation, the unraveling of the case might actually have amused him. As it was, Hughes never learned the details of the evidence as it began to trip upon itself.

Hughes would have certainly found it fascinating to discover that an actor who once appeared as a Tartar captain in his 1956 film *The Conqueror* had received a call from an ex-con-turned-car-salesman concerning the Romaine street break-in. The actor, a big hulk of a man named Leo Gordon, and the car salesman, a con man named Donald Woolbright, had done business with each other in the past. Gordon had purchased a car at the automobile dealership employing Woolbright. According to the story Woolbright spun, he had come in contact with "an acquaintance from the St. Louis area" who wanted him to act as a "middle man in disposal of the [Hughes] papers." He contacted Gordon because at the time the actor was writing scripts for the TV series *Adam-12* and presumed he might have some publishing contacts that would be interested in acquiring the stolen memos.

Gordon, who also had criminal record,[3] reported Woolbright's effort to dispose of the papers to a friend, Frank Hronek, who worked for the Los Angeles County district attorney. Hronek, in turn, contacted the

---

3. Gordon had been sentenced to San Quentin for 11 years after having been found guilty of robbery and assault with intent to commit murder in 1947.

CIA who met with Gordon, allegedly asking him to attempt to obtain the stolen documents from Woolbright. In the course of re-establishing himself with Woolbright, Gordon fronted the ex-con $3,500 to travel to St. Louis to acquire the files. Soon afterward, the CIA mysteriously lost interest in the case, and Woolbright disappeared, leaving Gordon minus $3,500.

"My reasons for becoming involved, aside from my friendship for Frank Hronek, were, to be candid, to do Howard Hughes a favor and trust that he would in some way help me, either as an actor or writer," Gordon later wrote in a letter to the Los Angeles Police Department. "Right now, I feel I have been a patsy, my money gone, in possible danger."[4]

The Summa Corporation ordered eighteen of its employees to take lie detector tests in connection with the burglary. Sixteen of the employees passed the tests. One, the security guard, Mike Davis, refused to take the test and was fired. It was later learned that he had previously worked at a car dealership across the street from where Woolbright was employed. The other, Summa's West Coast head of security and Davis' boss, Vincent Kelley, took the test and failed. Inexplicably, he was neither fired nor charged with a crime despite the fact that in the report filed by the Los Angeles Police Department it noted that Kelley "displayed guilty knowledge to all four examiners who reviewed the tape.[5]

By early 1975, any hope of keeping the content of the CIA memo secret were destroyed when the *Los Angeles Times* published details of Hughes' involvement with the Project Jennifer. The CIA, in an effort to control the extent of the press coverage, actually began holding press conferences on the story, hoping to spin it into the most positive light.

What details did emerge included the information that Project Jennifer cost $350 million, employed more than 4,000 people, and that the Hughes *Glamor* had been successful in retrieving a portion of the Russian submarine sunken 16,000 feet below the surface—the forward third of the Soviet vessel. While the CIA looked like fools for allowing the secret mission to leak to the press, Howard Hughes was painted as a patriot, having taken on the project "for no profit to aid his country's defense."

When Hughes heard about the praise, he was lying on his Barcalounger on the top floor of the Xanadu Princess watching the torture sequence from *The Ipcress File* and could not have been less interested. He had seen the third reel of *The Ipcress File* four times that day, and would watch it another time before he grew tired of the experience,

---

4. Gordon died on December 26, 2000, after a brief illness.
5. Kelley subsequently took a second polygraph test, administered by a private eye, and is said to
    have passed. The private eye, Robert Duke Hall, was found murdered on July 22, 1976.

injected himself in the groin with codeine, and switched to watching *Two Rode Together* starring Jimmy Stewart as a frontier marshal dealing with the Comanche nation.

Hughes no longer felt. Not hatred, not love, not pain. He had been consumed by his desire to escape a world in which he could no longer participate, guided by a group of men whose singular reason for tolerating his excesses was the hope that soon he would die and leave them exceedingly wealthy through the terms of his will.

The will. Now *there* was the rub. Hughes continuously swore to each and every one of his aides that they would be cared for upon his death by a will he handwrote several years earlier. The exact location of the will was unknown, and when asked about it, Hughes gamely dismissed the question with, "You don't actually expect me to tell you, do you?"

The fact was that his aides would have liked nothing better. So too, Bill Gay, Nadine Henley, and Kay Glenn. Only Jack Real, Mell Stewart, and Gordon Margulis seemed immune from the will patrol which during the last year of Hughes' life became a near daily subject of debate. Whenever the aides broached the subject of a will, Hughes' answer remained the same. He advised his staff that he not only had a will, but it was a handwritten, holographic one. He had prepared it while living in the house on Sarbonne Road, the "Gray House" he called it, presumably during the period he was dating Faith Domergue, and under the supervision of attorney Neil McCarthy.

He had repeatedly informed each of his aides that they were included in his will via codicils added after the original draft was signed and witnessed. In late summer 1975, Jim Rickard, the newest aide on the team, and the one least likely to be included in any will, was also the one told by Hughes that he was considering updating it. It was the timing of the update that concerned the Summa executives. If, as his employees thought, Hughes had left his estate to the Howard Hughes Medical Institute, Bill Gay and Chester Davis felt reassured that all the Hughes' businesses would remain intact after his death, since they comprised the Institute's entire executive committee. While this was a likely assumption, given Hughes' multiple statements of his intentions, it was by no means guaranteed.

It was therefore with a great deal of relief that the occupants of the Summa executive suite received word from aide Jim Rickard that Hughes was at last ready to update his last will and testament. Nadine Henley took it as a personal duty to assist the billionaire since she had worked on the early 1947 version of his will, still unsigned. In response to Rickard's version of his conversion, she wrote Hughes a note on September 16, 1975.

Two pages
Dear Mr. Hughes—
I was told by Jim Rickard that you had inquired about your Will.
I am so glad you did because I have been worrying about it, as it needs updating very much indeed. Noah Dietrich is named as one of your executors, as well as Ralph Damon, and others you may want to re-evaluate.
You may want to change the Will substantially (after 28 years) rather than just adding a codicil.
The Will was typed and printed on blue-line and I can send you (or carry to you) the blue-line, or a copy of it to correct. Then I can retype it, or the person of your choice can do it for you.
You realize, of course, that no one else has ever seen your Will so you must instruct me as to exactly how you want me to handle it.
Awaiting your instructions.

Sincerely,
Nadine

When Hughes received Henley's letter, he was infuriated by its presumptions—first, that he should want her involved in any preparation, and, second, that they should have been contacted by Rickard. Hughes not only considered it a breach in confidentiality, but also totally inaccurate. He was, in fact, in no particular rush to rewrite his will. He individually told his aides this, and dismissed it outright for the immediate future with, "We've got time." Such was not the case.

With his mind wandering further from reality with each passing day, and his intake of codeine escalating beyond human tolerance, it became apparent to Hughes' aides as well as his doctors that their employer's excesses had to be curbed. The larger questioned remained, how?

Dr. Wilbur Thain was the physician responsible for supplying Hughes his medication, and therefore the only one able to cut off its flow. It was a delicate business for Thain to address, given his own immediate goals.

For months, Thain had been pressing Hughes to provide him with an employment contract signed and approved by the board of directors of the Summa Corporation. Hughes had repeatedly stalled Thain's requests, and as weeks pushed into months, the doctor was becoming more adamant about the need for an immediate decision.

"I have discussed this at length with my attorney and the offer of having a guarantee by any bank is totally unacceptable to both of us," Thain wrote to Hughes in early September. "The *only* thing acceptable is that the contract I now have be ratified by the Board, that it be similar to the other executive contracts and that the Board be notified that you *approve* of this contract."

Hughes was well aware that any false step on his part could quite easily incite Thain to stop providing the drugs he craved. He even discussed this possibility with his aides who continuously asked to be relieved of any association with his deepening drug use. The paranoia that the aides felt was compounded by Thain's own anxiety when he heard from them that Hughes was openly discussing his supply.

"For hell's sake," Thain wrote Hughes, "stop talking to your staff about our 'subscription' problems. *They could* be forced to testify about what you have told them in court or in front of a grand jury. They have absolutely no immunity."

By the end of January 1976, Hughes had not signed his approval for Thain's employment contract. He had not written a new will. The status quo was draining the patience of every staff member who watched helplessly as their benefactor ignored them, their needs, their greed, and his own health. It was a situation that was desperate for leadership at a time when no one was willing to assume it. Even when a decision was made, no one within the Summa organization was willing to accept responsibility.

On February 10, 1976, Howard Hughes was taken from his suite at the Xanadu Princess Hotel on a stretcher and flown to Acapulco, Mexico, where the top-floor of the Acapulco Princess Hotel had been reserved for his party. Mexico. Land of incredible poverty, home to a language that none of the aides spoke, where the electricity and water were unreliable, and the food was routinely tainted. It is little wonder that no one admitted at the time, or later under oath, responsibility for the selection of Acapulco as Hughes' next home. Certainly it was not Hughes himself, who was in no condition to even know that he had changed countries, for in the dark all rooms appear essentially the same.

The aides later testified that the move was made to keep a constant supply of drugs available to the billionaire. Thain denied that he had ordered the switch, and knew full well that the drugs he was supplying to Howard Hughes were coming directly from the American manufacturers.

Less than two mouths after arriving in Acapulco, Howard Hughes had dropped sixteen pounds from his already slight frame, had been increasingly unresponsive to food, which he failed to recognize, found the mood of his aides to be abrupt, and neglected to ask about any phase of his businesses. Calls in and out of his suite were mainly centered on his last will and testament and employee contracts.

His physical condition finally deteriorated to such an extent that Dr. Lawrence Chaffin ordered blood drawn for a profile. In his notes, Chaffin wrote: "Today he seemed more confused at times and when I tried to persuade him to eat, his reply was, 'For the record, I want to be left alone.'"

Less than twelve hours later, Howard Hughes was boarded on a charter flight for his final plane ride. Despite a bumpy take-off, it was a perfect day for flying, with cloudless skies stretching to the horizon and the freedom that Hughes cherished with his very soul. His breathing was shallow, but his eyes were wide open, staring into space to a place where neither money nor power meant anything at all. Dr. Chaffin watched as Hughes took his last breath, and heard only a muffled sound. If he had leaned his ear to Hughes' lips, he might have heard the voice whisper, "Hey! Ba-Ba-Re-Bop," and known of his peace.

And the Winner Is...

*My Will is deposited in Houston. The probation of
my Will and the fulfillment of all its terms will
take place in Houston. The terms of my Will have
remained unchanged for a little more than twenty
years. Under those terms, there will be founded
a large, permanent, charitable, medical
institution as an endowment.*

> Los Angeles, California
> August 11, 1944
>> The only existing formal letter written by
>> Hughes concerning his will. It was
>> addressed to the California State Income
>> Tax Board.

HOWARD HUGHES HAD BEEN DEAD FOR LESS THAN TWENTY
hours when the speculation about the existence of a will, or
lack of one, began to surface in the press. At the Summa
Corporation offices in Encino, California, Bill Gay, Nadine
Henley, and Chester Davis were caucused in meetings in an
effort to address the immediate issue of maintaining their
authority over the Hughes companies while exploring their
options in getting control of the Hughes finances.

At the time of his death, Hughes' entire estate consisted
of an eclectic assortment of businesses and a handful of col-
lected mementoes. Among his assets, of course, were the
Desert Inn Hotel and Casino; the Frontier Hotel and
Casino; the Sands Hotel; the Silver Slipper Casino; plus the
Castaways and Landmark Hotels and Casinos, all in Las
Vegas. His Nevada holdings also included KLAS-TV; the
Paradise Valley Country Club; the Desert Star Laundry
Company; the Desert Inn Improvement Company (which
ran the sewer and water services for the Desert Inn Hotel);

Hughes Aviation Services (operating the charter terminal at McCarran International Airport); Harold's Club Casino in Reno; 209 acres in Paradise, Nevada; plus another 151 acres on the Las Vegas Strip; some 25,000 acres of desert and grazing land, including Warm Springs, a working cattle ranch; as well as the grazing rights to large tracts of federal land; plus more than 3,000 claims to gold and silver mines in and around Tonopah, Nevada, a legacy of the John Meier buying sprees.

In addition, Hughes owned the Xanadu Princess Hotel in Freeport, Bahamas; Hughes Air West; Hughes Helicopters (a portion of the former aircraft division that was never transferred to Howard Hughes Medical Institute); 1,317 acres around Marina del Rey, California; a 1964 Chrysler with a $15,000 air-filtration system in the trunk; 13,232 acres of land in Tucson, Arizona; 1,060,179 shares of Atlas Corporation (received for the sale of RKO Pictures); Hughes Television Network (responsible for closed-circuit feeds inside Madison Square Garden); H-Tex Inc. (the holding company for oil and gas leases); non-transferable memberships in the Wilshire Country Club (Los Angeles), the Lakeside Golf Club (Los Angeles), the Westchester Country Club (Rye, New York), and the Los Angeles Country Club; plus the *Hercules* flying boat in storage in mint condition in Long Beach; California, in addition to three new Hawker Siddeley airplanes valued at $2.26 million.

Hughes owned master prints and all rights to his films, including several edited versions of *Hell's Angels*, two uncensored prints of *The Outlaw*, plus *Scarface, The Conqueror, Jet Pilot, Cock of the Air, Two Arabian Knights, Gambling House, Angel Face, The French Line,* and *Underwater.*

Also included in the Hughes estate and no doubt long forgotten by the Old Man himself: a house in Riverside, California (completely furnished and unused); $671,068 in the Texas Commerce Bank; $1,799 in cash; three Bank of America cashier's checks to be paid to the order of M. Gerber, each in the amount of $1002.60 and dated December 2, 1952; a lapel pin proclaiming "Team Championship SCGA, 1927"; a twenty-balboa gold coin from Panama; sixty-four $5 casino chips from the Desert Inn Hotel, a wedding ring with thirty-six square-cut diamonds; and a gold money clip inscribed "Happy Days, Cary."

In an effort to uncover the will that Hughes insisted he had written, executives of the Summa Corporation placed an advertisement in newspapers in forty cities across the country.

HOWARD ROBARD HUGHES Jr., son of Howard Robard Hughes Sr. and Allene Gano, born December 24, 1905, died April 5, 1976. Anyone having any information regarding this death, please phone (213) 986-7047.

His executives broke into filing cabinets that had remained locked and untouched since Hughes was a film producer. The contents of safes were itemized; the search for a safe deposit box was initiated; and a list was assembled of individuals that might have been a logical depository for Hughes' legal papers.

Simultaneously in courts in Texas, Nevada, and California, executors were assigned to handle Hughes' affairs coordinated by his closest living relative, his maternal aunt, Annette Gano Lummis, and her son William Rice Lummis, an attorney at Hughes' Houston law firm, then known as Andrews, Kurth, Campbell & Jones. Lummis was married to the daughter of senior partner Palmer Bradley—the same man who had written years earlier to Noah Dietrich for Annette Lummis. Texas probate judge Kenneth Pat Gregory appointed the mother-son team as administrators of the Texas portion of the estate, with Keith C. Hayes, probate judge in Nevada, appointing the First National Bank of Nevada as the administrator in that state. In California, Richard C. Gano, Jr., Bill Lummis' cousin and the son of his late Uncle Chilton, was appointed to administrate the California portion of the probate and spearhead the search for Hughes' last will and testament.

These appointments were hardly arbitrary, but rather reflected inheritance laws and family trees overseen by the Chancery Court in Delaware. If Hughes were found to have a valid will, the terms and conditions of its dictates would apply. In the absence of a will, however, the heirs would be determined by the laws of the state determined to be Hughes' legal residence at the time of his death. If that residence was deemed to be Texas, both maternal and paternal heirs would be included. The laws of California and Nevada recognized only the closest living relative. In that case, Annette Gano Lummis would be designated as Howard Hughes' sole heir.

It mattered little to the various courts that Hughes consistently voiced his intention to leave his estate to medical research. In the absence of a will, the estate laws were clear. So, too, was the probability that the federal government would claim a major percentage of Hughes' billions in estate taxes. And with it, the tax man that Hughes spent his entire life successfully avoiding would be declared the winner. If Howard Hughes were not already dead, that bit of news alone would have killed him.

Since his mother was in no condition to undertake the responsibility, Hughes' cousin, Bill Lummis, became the titular head of Summa Corporation. Officially, he was elected the chairman of the board by an agreement with Bill Gay, Chester Davis, and Nadine Henley, who welcomed Lummis into their ranks as a conciliatory gesture aimed at continuing the status quo. What they did not expect was for Lummis to find the time while in the throes of the probate hearings to dissect the inner workings of the various Hughes industries.

In the first three weeks following Hughes' death, alleged heirs on both sides of the family began to reveal themselves, many totally unknown to the others in the case. On the Gano side of the Hughes grabfest, the family tree was fairly straightforward. Hughes had no brothers or sisters. His Aunt Annette had four children, though only one, William, had actually met Hughes as a child. Annette's other children were Allene (named after Hughes' mother), Annette, and Frederick.

Annette's late sister, Martha Houstoun, had three living children—all of whom were still in Houston—Janet, Sara and James, plus a fourth, the deceased William, whose own children, John, Margot, James, and Richard now stood in line to inherit their portion of the estate. Annette's late brother Richard had four children in addition to Richard C. Gano who was the California administrator of the estate—William, Doris, Annette, and attorney Howard Hughes Gano, all still living in Houston as well.

The picture clouded substantially when the paternal side of the family was examined. Hughes' late Uncle Rupert, from whom he was estranged, had married three times, and had one daughter by his first wife, Agnes. The girl's paternity was thrown into question by the highly publicized divorce proceedings in 1904, in which multiple extramarital affairs were claimed by both Agnes and Rupert. After the divorce, Rupert failed to provide for the girl named Elspeth, who lived with her mother. Elspeth, who died in 1945, had three daughters named Agnes, Elspeth and Barbara. In addition, Rupert Hughes' second wife, Adelaide, had two children by a previous marriage that Rupert unsuccessfully attempted to adopt. Those children, Avis and Rush Bissell, took the name Hughes despite their legal status.

As the cousins and second cousins met with their attorneys and attempted to come to an agreement on what, if any, inheritance might be due them, Richard Gano launched into an extensive and far-reaching search for a will that could possibly make their entire effort moot. Gano was helped along by officials of the Mormon Church, who announced the discovery of a three-page will purported to have been handwritten by Hughes in 1969, and just filed with Loretta Bowman, the clerk of the courthouse in Clark County, Nevada.

Addressing to the discovery, the Summa Corporation issued a response stating that it could not give a "firm statement denying the authenticity of the will," although it indicated that the will "contained many errors that make it look suspicious." Former aide Noah Dietrich, named as its executor and driven by the potential for millions in fees, filed a petition with Judge Keith Hayes to admit the document to probate, despite the rather startling gaffes it contained. Chief among them was the naming of Dietrich, whom Hughes disliked and distrusted after their acrimonious break-up. Further, the so-called Mormon will left money to the Boy Scouts of America and the Mormon Church of Jesus Christ of Latter-day Saints, two organizations in which Hughes had absolutely no interest. It gave one-quarter of his estate to the Howard Hughes Medical Institute rather than the entire estate, as Hughes repeatedly had suggested was his intention. Additionally, the will called the foundation the Hughes Medical Institute, a phrasing Hughes himself never used.

In addition, the Mormon will averred that Hughes left an eighth of his estate to Rice Institute of Technology, the University of Nevada, and the University of California—three institutions to which he showed no previous alliance; one-sixteenth to "establish a home for Orphan Cildren" [sic], when Hughes passionately disliked children and refused to provide for those in his immediate family; one-sixteenth to Jean Peters of Los Angeles and Ella Rice of Houston, when both of his previous wives had alimony arrangements that specifically disallowed further claims on Hughes' estate; one-sixteenth to William R. Lommis [sic], misspelling his cousin's name and not mentioning William's mother, Hughes' Aunt Annette; one-sixteenth to be "devided [sic] amoung [sic] my personal aids [sic] at the time of my death," misspelling words he repeatedly did not in any number of memos; and one-sixteenth to be used as a "school scholarship fund for the entire Country," when Hughes had absolutely no interested in education. And in what was perhaps the most telling blunder of the purported will: the bequeathing of the "spruce goose" to the city of Long Beach. Hughes not only never used the nickname for his beloved *Hercules* (and, in fact, detested its use by others), but also did not even own the plane in 1968. He continued to lease the *Hercules* from the General Services Administration until 1972, when it was donated to the Smithsonian Institute by the government and sold back to Hughes.

The paragraph of the will that received the most public attention, however, was the one marked "eighth." In it, a man named Melvin Dumar of Gabbs, Nevada, was given one-sixteenth of Hughes' estate. The Melvin Dumar of the will turned out to be Melvin Dummar, the owner of a gas station in the town of Willard, Utah, a town of just over 1,000 where the major attraction was the local state park with its walleye and wiper fishing. Dummar, who originally claimed no knowledge of the will and recited a story about picking Howard Hughes out of the gutter in the desert in January 1968, had difficulty explaining how his thumb print ended up on the envelope containing the document. He later changed his story to suggest that a stranger dropped off the envelope at his filling station. After steaming open the letter and seeing his name included in the will, Dummar told the court that he resealed the letter and took it to the headquarters of the Mormon Church.

What for Dietrich and his attorney, Harold Rhoden, should have been the final clue to drop their probate of the document instead only energized them to locate the unknown messenger of the will. As the publicity on the Mormon will increased and made daily headlines in newspapers across the country, additional "wills" began to surface, through the mail, in garage sales, through clairvoyants, and even several that used pre-printed forms from stationery stores. Among the more bizarre was one filed by a woman in Columbus, Ohio, that named Judge William Bear as its executor. It was dated in 1961, ignoring the fact that Bear did not become a judge until 1967. Another, dated in 1969, named the Summa Corporation as executor despite the fact that Summa was not incorporated until December 1972.

A claimant named Joseph Michael Brown, who asserted that he was the son of Hughes and began using the name Richard Robard Hughes, was the beneficiary of a will filed in Clark County by a man named Grover Albert Walker, who maintained that he had been a Hughes aide. Brown claimed to communicate with Hughes through a radio transmitter surgically implanted in his brain which he turned on and off by touching his tongue to the roof of his mouth.

Another will, also filed for probate in Clark County, Nevada, left $400 million to a man identified as Hughes' son and named Dwayne Clyde Byron Hughes. Dwayne Clyde was said to have been born in a flying saucer over Oklahoma in 1946. There was no mention whether Hughes was present for the birth.

Familiar names resurfaced in a nonprobated will that was received at the offices of the *New York Times* addressed to its managing editor using his name clipped from the newspaper's masthead. It gave "To Clifford Irving, for his troubles—the sum of ten million dollars. To Edith Irving, the same—the sum of five million dollars. To Richard Susskind [sic], the same—the sum of two million dollars." Irving, his wife and Suskind, having served their sentences and been released from jail, all disavowed any knowledge of the forgery.

For Philip Hamersmith, a former newspaper reporter, the search for a Hughes will spawned a cottage industry. As the number of official fake wills topped seventeen, Hamersmith placed an advertisement in the *Miami Herald* offering to sell a Hughes will naming anyone who would send him $2 as the sole Hughes beneficiary. "Impress your friends, your bank and your attorney," Hamersmith's ad read. In the same edition, a man named Kenneth Salzman offered the same service for half the price.

In Hollywood, actress Terry Moore, still blonde, perky, and basking in the attention, revealed that she had been Hughes' legal wife. In deposition, she related her tale of the shipboard "marriage," a revelation that she swore would have gone with her to the grave had it not been for the need to share her story with the estate. Still playing the star, Terry touched up her makeup and checked her hair during her testimony, while continuing to flawlessly recite her well-rehearsed tale. Although at that moment she made no claim on Hughes' money, she asked to be included in all updates on filings and developments in court.

On the Dummar front, while Dietrich continued to press forward with two concurrent trials to validate the Mormon will—one in Nevada, another in Texas—the mysterious stranger who alleged to have delivered the document to Dummar's gas station surfaced in the person of LeVane Malvison Forsythe, the construction worker who testified for Robert Maheu as having been paid $500 to guard the parking lot of the Desert Inn the Thanksgiving eve that Hughes left Las Vegas. Forsythe now contended that he had worked as a messenger for Hughes sporadically since 1947.

It was also revealed that Bonnie Dummar, who was married for a period of time to Melvin's uncle Richard, had access to Hughes' memos and signature through her job as a writer for an Orange, California, publication called *Millionaire*, distributed free to 30,000 wealthy readers. Bonnie Dummar, who was then living in Bellflower, California, and running a twenty-four-hour answering service, denied forging the will and then dropped from sight.

By September 1976 the collection of Hughes' first and second cousins on both sides of the family had reached agreement among themselves concerning the fairest way to carve up the billionaire's estate. In that agreement, Annette Lummis would receive slightly less than twenty-four percent of the total, with the sixteen maternal first cousins receiving 47.6 percent. The remaining estate was to be split among the paternal heirs, with the granddaughters of Rupert Hughes each receiving six and a half percent, the two children of Adelaine Bissell Hughes each receiving four and three-quarters percent. In addition, the heirs authorized spending $400,000 for the stockbrokerage house of Merrill Lynch, Pierce, Fenner & Smith to prepare an appraisal of the estate, then rumored to be worth nearly $2 billion.

While the various Hughes descendants were presenting a united front, the power structure within the Summa Corporation was anything but stable. Lummis, who had moved his family to Las Vegas and was being paid over $100,000 a year as chairman of Summa, had quietly observed the way business was handled within the organization. With Chester Davis in New York, and Bill Gay and Nadine Henley in Encino,

California, Lummis was thought to be a non-threat by the ruling triumvirate. Davis, in particular, was comfortable with fellow lawyer Lummis, and felt little hesitation in instructing him on matters of ongoing Summa policy. It was a serious misjudgment of both Lummis' skill and intentions.

In early 1977 Lummis moved to have Davis removed from the board of Summa after repeated disagreements with the attorney who insisted on intervening in the probate process. By this point, the Nevada court had added Lummis' name as co-administrator in Nevada as well as Texas, and the soft-spoken Southerner was intent on taking the reins of control. When Lummis was named chairman of Summa, long-time Hughes attorney Mickey West and Hughes financial officer William Rankin joined him on the board. Predictably, when votes were taken, Davis, Gay, and Henley voted as a team along with Holmes and Myler, with Lummis, West, and Rankin on the opposite side of the vote.

In late May 1977, Lummis successfully removed Davis, Holmes, and Myler from the board, and fired Davis' law firm as the corporation's legal representative. Able for the first time to freely search through the financial records of the corporation, what Lummis found was a company in total disarray, with losses in the first nine months of 1976 at over $22 million. Compounding the situation at Summa was the appraisal filed by Merrill Lynch, Pierce, Fenner & Smith that found that Hughes' estate was valued at only $168,834,615. The value was presented to the Internal Revenue Service for the purpose of establishing taxes on the estate, a value which the IRS initially accepted, despite the fact that a decade earlier, Merrill Lynch had paid Hughes $546,549,771 when he sold his TWA stock, and collected an additional $130 million with the sale of Hughes Tool.

By that time, Richard C. Gano had submitted his report on his exhaustive five-nation search for a legal, signed will. He was paid $25,000 for working 750 hours on the fruitless search. In addition to letters, memos, and notes referencing the will, he found unsigned copies and codicils of wills, but nothing that could be considered valid and legally binding.

Courts in both Nevada and Texas found that the long-litigated Mormon will was a forgery to be discounted. Amazingly, no criminal fraud charges were brought against any of the perpetrators. Therefore, in the absence of a legal will, the attention of the administrators turned back to probate court in an effort to determine Hughes' legal residency at the time of his death.

As the attorneys generals of Texas and California began battling each other for the right to litigate residency, Mickey West filed suit in

Chancery Court in Wilmington, Delaware. He cited Chester Davis, Bill Gay, and Nadine Henley for losses by Summa of $131,799,000 in the previous six years, mainly on its casinos and hotels, at a time when all of its competitors in Las Vegas were making banner profits. "The administrators of the Hughes estate are confronted with the task of raising large sums to defray claims against the estate, including private claims, including those of government of both income and death taxes with an ailing business and non-related, non-liquid assets as the only source thereof," West said in his filing. The suit also revealed that while Summa lost $29.7 million in 1975 alone, Gay's salary equaled $400,680, plus a bonus of $188,583. In an effort to stem the losses, in addition to the termination of Davis, Lummis hired Philip P. Hannifin, Nevada's former chief gambling law enforcement officer, to run the hotels and casinos.

Meanwhile, Lummis began to unravel the details of Hughes' last days. In a letter written to Federal District Court Judge Alfonso Zirpoli, then handling the remaining lawsuits covering Hughes' purchase of Air West, Lummis referred to information gained during the deposing of Hughes' aides. ". . .testimony has come forth which may well raise serious questions as to the emotional and physical condition of Mr. Hughes at the time or times his testimony was requested in the Air West litigation and the extent to which Mr. Hughes was kept informed by those surrounding him of the nature of the Air West proceedings and the possible consequence of his failure to give testimony." Two months later, Zirpoli ruled that Hughes' estate must pay the Air West stockholders $71 million in damages due completely to Hughes' failure to appear as ordered.

While the state of California called upon the United States Supreme Court to involve itself in deciding the residency issue, a grand jury in Las Vegas was considering evidence based on depositions taken by the Drug Enforcement Administration concerning the source of Hughes' continuing drug flow. On March 1, 1978, the grand jury returned indictments against both Dr. Norman F. Crane and Hughes' senior aide John Holmes for illegally supplying the billionaire with drugs for over two decades. Word began to leak out that Dr. Wilbur S. Thain's activities were also under investigation.

In an effort to avoid jail sentences, both Crane and Holmes entered pleas of *nolo contendere*, no contest, which, though not a guilty plea, carried the same penalties. Both Holmes and Crane agreed to testify against Thain when in June 1978, an indictment was filed against the Utah doctor in his home state. Thain was charged with the dispensing of codeine phosphate "without legitimate medical purpose."

In the trial that began the following September, Thain's attorneys argued that he had worked for months in an effort to reduce Hughes' use of the drug, and had finally accomplished remarkable progress, despite Hughes' claim of being in constant pain. Among the many facts that came to light during the trial was the fact that no medical records were being kept in an attempt to chart Hughes' level of abuse. Despite the testimony of Holmes and Crane, Thain was found innocent of the charges in late September, 1978.

By that time his brother-in-law Bill Gay had resigned his position with Summa Corporation under pressure from Lummis, who was making other sweeping changes within the organization. In addition to selling the Landmark Hotel for $13 million, $5 million less than Hughes had paid for the famous Las Vegas destination, Lummis began paying the Internal Revenue Service based on the Merrill Lynch assessment of the value of the billionaire's estate. The IRS, in accepting the $16.7 million, reserved the right to question the appraisal. Several months earlier, the courts in both Nevada and Texas rejected the Mormon will as being an authentic document, opening the potential for as much as seventy-five percent of the estate to be awarded to the federal government.[1]

Throughout the war of litigation, suits, and countersuits, there was one constant. Eighty-eight year old Annette Gano Lummis lived just as she had for all of her life, as a dignified Southern lady who resented the intrusion of the outside world into her refined and charmed existence. Although she gladly gave her deposition to the Texas attorney general, she often moved beyond his personal questions, responding instead through reflective glory at the love she continued to harbor for the only son of her favorite sister. "He was perfectly beautiful," she said. "And he was a charming boy. He always was a charming young boy to me."

On July 24, 1979, Annette Lummis died at the Diagnostic Center Hospital in Houston. The only money she received from the estate of her late nephew was $626,800 for her services as an administrator to his estate. That money, as well as her share of any eventual Hughes estate, was in turn left to her children.

As he continued on his slow and steady course to return Summa to profitability, Lummis elevated a familiar name, former Lockheed executive Jack Real, to head Hughes Helicopter, Summa's aircraft construction division. Lummis personally watched over the real estate division with its remaining 29,000 acres in Nevada (second only to the United States government in land ownership in the state). He attempted to liquidate the 12,500 acres in Tucson, donated the *Hercules* to the Aero Club of

---

1. In 1980, director Jonathan Demme brought the film *Melvin and Howard* to the screen. It was a delicious slice-of-life comedy recounting the events of the alleged Dummar-Hughes meeting. Mary Steenburgen won a Best Supporting Actress Oscar as Melvin's wife. Bo Goldman also won an Oscar for his script.

Southern California, negotiated with Republic Airlines to purchase Hughes Air West for $38.5 million, sold Hughes' fleet of 34 aging airplanes as well as KLAS-TV, the Xanadu Beach Hotel, and the 3,000 inactive mining claims. In the first year without Gay, Davis, and Henley in charge, Summa earned $30.9 million on sales of $762.3 million.

Gay, Davis, and Henley, still in charge of the Howard Hughes Medical Institute by virtue of their own appointments after Hughes' death, continued to doggedly pursue the issue of a will, despite the formal declaration by Texas Judge Pat Gregory that Hughes died intestate. Their chief hope laid with a comment made by a reporter for the *Las Vegas Sun*, Dan Newburn, who stated that he had seen an executed will while interviewing Terry Moore about her alleged marriage. According to Newburn, Moore had a document some fifteen pages long that was signed by Howard Hughes and three witnesses. Many of the pages concerned a detailed breakdown of the responsibilities of the Howard Hughes Medical Institute. "It seemed to be a very meticulous kind of breakdown," Newburn said.

When Gay's attorneys questioned Moore about the document, she did not remember a thing. She could not remember ever having a will, could not produce the document, and was not even certain of her interview with Newburn. There were, after all, so many interviews when she announced her claim of marriage to Howard Hughes. When Newburn was questioned about Moore's convenient memory, he attributed her statements to the fact that she regarded Gay as a driver. That was, after all, how they met, and that was how Gay would always remain. "I think in her mind she sees him still as a chauffeur, and as a go-fer, and that kind of thing, and there's some resentment there."

When Gay's attorneys attempted to get Newburn to give a sworn deposition to the existence of the Hughes will he saw in Terry Moore's possession, Newburn claimed his information was protected by media privilege. He also had no love lost for Gay or Davis, and went to court in an effort to protect his right not to sign an affidavit. Newburn repeatedly refused and was eventually declared in contempt of court and sentenced to be incarcerated. It took a stay from the Supreme Court of Nevada to keep him out of jail. Newburn's silence continues to this day.

By March 1981, the Internal Revenue Service had completed its own evaluation of the Hughes estate, and came up with a figure more than double that reached by Merrill Lynch. A comprehensive audit by the IRS valued Hughes' estate at $460 million, and announced estate taxes due the federal government were $274,714,977, computed at a rate of 77 percent. The fact that the government wanted more from the Hughes estate than Merrill Lynch computed it was worth sent Lummis back into meetings and sent him scrambling to maximize assets.

In Houston, Texas, Pat Gregory opened the estate hearings on July 13, 1981, in an effort to piece together an official record of Hughes' next-of-kin, with twenty lawyers, over 600 claimants, and a jury of six waiting to participate. While Gregory had ruled the previous month that Terry Moore's shipboard marriage was not legal and therefore not binding, he had two other women in his courtroom who claimed to have married Hughes.

Gregory quickly dismissed the claim of Alma Hughes of Houston, who said that she had first met Hughes in Shreveport, Louisiana, in 1931, at a concession stand he was operating offering airplane rides for a dollar each. Alma said that she continued to rendezvous with Hughes through the years, eventually agreeing to marry him in 1973, after which she was artificially inseminated at age sixty-four during a hemorrhoid operation, and gave birth to a baby girl.

Alyce Hovsepian Hughes, a glamorous redhead, told Gregory that she met Hughes in 1946 at Philadelphia General Hospital. She stated that on June 6, 1946, she performed in what she presumed was a screen test, but it was actually a legally binding wedding ceremony in which she promised to "love, honor and obey" her new husband, Howard Hughes. Asking Alyce to assume the name Jean Peters, Hughes saw her only once after the ceremony, when she was a patient at the Trenton State Psychiatric Hospital, where she was raped by Hughes in an act observed by a man she called Sam the Jew. Gregory was not impressed, denying her claim as well.

While Claire Benedict Hudenberg did not claim to have married Hughes, she did attempt to convince Gregory that she was the billion-aire's daughter. Although the self-described cult leader and ordained minister had no birth certificate to support her claim, she said that she has deduced her heritage through an odd set of coincidences, including the fact that she walked like Hughes, worked in the Bahamas at the same time Hughes was in residence, was told by a man she called Claude Haag that she looked like Howard Hughes, and she had once been followed around Las Vegas by twenty-five men with "great big necks." This com-pelling evidence aside, Gregory once again dismissed the claim, as well as that of Joseph Brown, who filed his claim under the name Donald McDonald yet insisted on being addressed as Richard Robard Hughes. Richard continued to insist he communicated with the billionaire through his brain-implanted radio transmitter.

By Labor Day 1981, the jury in Judge Gregory's courtroom needed to deliberate only an hour and 45 minutes before they accepted the claims of heirdom lodged by Barbara Cameron, Agnes Roberts and Elspeth DePould, the daughters of Rupert Hughes' alleged daughter Elspeth Hughes Lapp. In establishing the trio's legal claim, the court removed over 300 additional heirs, who were deemed to be in a secondary position and thus not eligible for a portion of the estate under Texas law. "I'm delighted," Elspeth DePould said after the verdict. "I was beginning to doubt who I was from the accusations."[2]

Less than two weeks later, Judge Gregory ruled that Avis Hughes McIntyre and the late Rush Hughes were adopted children of Rupert Hughes. Gregory based his ruling on the process of estoppel, adoption based on intent rather than legal proceedings. With the signing of those documents, Gregory had reached a plateau where the names of Hughes' heirs with right to inherit were legally established. In doing so, of course, he opened up the floodgates for those who had been denied access to the money to appeal his rulings.

February 15, 1982. Noah Dietrich passed away in his bed at Desert Hospital in Palm Springs at the age of 92, with his third wife Mary at his side. Dietrich had suffered from myasthenia gravis, a neurological disorder, for years. The passing was not noticed in Summa headquarters in Las Vegas, where William Lummis was busy negotiating the sale of Hughes' 12,500 acres of land in Arizona to the Pima Services Corporation for $75 million.

Alyce Hovsepian Hughes, still going by the name Jean Peters, had pressed her claim to the Hughes estate all the way to the Texas Supreme Court, where, on December 18, 1982, the justices determined that Hughes' promise to have her crowned Miss Atlantic City and their screen-test marriage were not adequate grounds to inherit his wealth. Nor, it seemed, was her additional claim that Hughes forced her to shoplift from Black's Department Store in Philadelphia.

The following May, Terry Moore had better luck. Though she never took her claim of marriage in international waters to the Texas Supreme Court, the legally established heirs of the Hughes estate found that she did have a legitimate, long-term relationship at one time with the billionaire, and agreed to give her a token sum. The 54-year-old Moore said her settlement was "not more than eight figures." Attorneys found the statement amusing and countered, "substantially less than eight figures." The figure widely circulated was $350,000.

---

2. The 300 Hughes cousins, mostly from the Midwest, contended that Rupert Hughes could not have been the father of Elsbeth Hughes Lapp because childhood bouts with German measles had left him sterile. Another group of 200 cousins contended that Elsbeth replaced Rupert Hughes' actual daughter, whom they claimed was named Leila and drowned in her father's swimming pool in 1921.

Moore began to call press conferences and started signing auto-
graphs as Terry Moore Hughes, while her live-in manager, a 34-year-old
named Jerry Rivers, pronounced her "the celebrity of 1984." She freely
talked about her four public marriages—the first to Glenn Davis and the
next to Gene McGrath. It was her third marriage, to Jean Peters' ex-hus-
band Stuart Cramer in 1959, that lasted the longest—thirteen years—and
produced two sons. Her last husband, Richard Carey, whom she married
in 1972, had been indicted on sixty-eight criminal counts including grand
theft and forgery when Moore received her settlement. "It turned out he
wasn't divorced at the time of our wedding," Moore told *People* magazine,
"so I guess we weren't really married."

By the end of 1983, Lummis had sold Hughes Helicopters to
McDonnell Douglas Corporation for $470 million, based on a contract
the helicopter division had been awarded by the Army to build 515 AH-
64 Apache helicopters over a six-year period, thereby ensuring that the
Hughes estate would have adequate cash reserves to pay the federal government its final tax assessment. A year later, in a brokered deal,
California and Texas finally signed a compromise inheritance tax agreement, placing the subject of Hughes' residency to rest. Texas' share of the
estate was set at $50 million, with California receiving $44 million, plus
trust control of 73 acres in Marina Del Rey near the Los Angeles
International Airport.

The residency settlement cleared the way for the distribution of
estate funds to the twenty-one court-designated heirs. Yet in 1985, nearly
ten years after Hughes' death, the first and second cousins he had never
met had received only a small portion of the total due. Small, when discussing the Hughes estate, was relative, of course. By 1985, the heirs had
shared $90 million of Hughes' money. Agnes Roberts had quit her job at
a skating rink snack bar in Ohio and moved to the warmth of Arizona.
The others merely went about their businesses, having been relatively
well-off before the scrutiny that the estate actions created.

"All of these Houstouns, Ganos and Lummises are really pretty well-
established families. The people who live in River Oaks didn't move
there because of the inheritances. They were already pillars of society. It
probably cost them some tax problems," said one attorney involved in the
litigation.

At the Howard Hughes Medical Institute, Donald S. Frederickson,
the president of the foundation, had managed to do what Howard
Hughes had always dreamed. He turned the non-profit institute into a
first-class medical research organization. In December 1985,
Frederickson sold the Hughes Aircraft corporation to General Motors
Corporation for $5 billion. With the sale, the Howard Hughes Medical

Institute became the richest independent research institute in the world. Frederickson initially estimated that the institute would allot $1 billion a year in funding for research on genetics, the immune system, cell metabolism, and the nervous system. "It's what Howard Hughes would have wanted," he said.

In 1986, Dr. Raymond Fowler, the one-time chairman of the University of Alabama's psychology department, released a psychological autopsy he prepared on Howard Hughes in which he stated, "His mother's overprotectiveness and preoccupation with his real or imagined illnesses and his social difficulties may well have heightened his anxieties and reinforced his avoidant tendencies. In absence of healthier role models, it is not surprising that Hughes accepted and internalized his mother's excessive fears for his health."

That same year, Trans World Airlines was award $17.2 million in what remained of the 24-year-long lawsuit, having gone back to the United States Supreme Court to reinstate the case. Later in 1986, Melvin Dummar bought a café in Gabbs, Nevada, from his brother Ray "for nothing down, nothing a month," where he said that people "either think I'm rich or a crook."

In November 1988, Edward Lund, Hughes' co-pilot on his round-the-world flight, died at the age of 82 in Newport Beach, California, of complications from a stroke. In his eulogy, his daughter Delores Tippo said that her father bore a striking resemblance to Hughes and often impersonated the billionaire at his request.

March 31, 1990. William Rice Lummis, who had proven to be the tonic that saved the Summa Corporation from self-destruction announced his retirement, and appointed John L. Goolsby, the 47-year-old president and chief executive officer to replace him as Summa's chairman. "I've not had one boring moment in 14 years," Lummis said as he departed. "When Howard Hughes died, none of us who have since dealt with the estate anticipated—or could have been prepared for—the extremely complex, difficult and bizarre experience which lay ahead." As he left Summa, the company had plans for its undeveloped land in Marina Del Rey, California, where it anticipated building 12,000 housing units on the site of what once was Hughes Airport. Summa was also developing plans to turn 23,000 acres of land northwest of Las Vegas into homes for 200,000 people. Named Summerlin after Hughes' grandmother, the development eventually featured a $25-million PGA golf course.

Goolsby continued to build on Summa's real estate base, opening the Hughes Center in Las Vegas on 120 acres. Monthly rents in the office tower are the highest in Nevada. Hughes Airport Center was opened as an industrial park. In Los Angeles, Howard Hughes Center was opened on 70 acres adjacent to Los Angeles International Airport.

In 1993, Judge Pat Gregory, who oversaw the entire Texas portion of the estate probate, was indicted for third degree felony theft in the misappropriation of funds from the Ewing Halsell Foundation of San Antonio. Gregory was alleged to have accepted funds to set up a probate school in Texas, and instead used the money for his own personal use. Several months later, Gregory was also charged with filing false income taxes, and pleaded guilty to the latter charge in exchange for the dropping of the money laundering allegations. He was sentenced to one year in prison for his tax violation, and was ordered to never hold public office or preside as a judge for the remainder of his life.

In 1995, the Smithsonian Institute's National Air and Space Museum placed on public display Hughes' H-1 aircraft in which he established the 1935 land-speed record. In its literature, the Smithsonian described the H-1 as "the most beautiful airplane ever built." It had been flown only 40 hours, less than half of that by Howard Hughes.

February 23, 1996. The Rouse Company paid over $520 million for the remnants of the Summa Corporation, with Hughes' shareholders receiving $150 million in dividends as a result of the sale. With the Rouse purchase, the estate that Howard Hughes created from his $650,000 inheritance was ended. Well, almost. A careful study of the Rouse Company transaction indicated that William Lummis reserved a contingent interest in undeveloped Summerlin property, amounting to 16,000 acres. As Summerlin continues to grow into the new millennium, Lummis and the other Hughes heirs are expected to continue to reap profits in the multimillions. When asked to estimate exactly how much, Lummis' former law partner David Elkins said, "Family secrets are family secrets. It's just their style. They don't want attention." That statement would have gotten no argument from the Old Man himself.

In 1925, Howard Hughes set out his goals: "Things I want to be: 1. The best golfer in the world. 2. The best pilot. 3. The most famous producer of motion pictures." In the end, he would not be best remembered for having accomplished any of those dreams. Instead, the richest man in America would be forever thought of as an eccentric original who never disappointed those who expected the unexpected.

"My father never *suggested* that I do something," Hughes told writer Dwight Whitney in the 1940s. "He just *told* me. He shoved things down my throat and I had to like it. But he had a hail-fellow-well-met quality that I never had. He was a terrifically loved man. I am not. I don't have the ability to win people the way he did. I suppose I'm not like other men. Most of them like to study people. I'm not nearly as interested in people

as I should be, I guess. What I am tremendously interested in. . . "
Hughes said, pausing then to think. "What I am tremendously interested
in is science." And with that he closed his eyes and dreamed.

Acknowledgments

EVERY WRITER thinks of a finished book as a newborn, the freshest of life, conceived with passion and delivered in pain. It is really a collective project that is the result of many minds, hearts and souls working together to construct a lasting monument with a specific theme. In this case, the eccentricity, manipulation and power of Howard Robard Hughes.

My publisher, Michael Viner, has long been a Hughes afficionado, and is the real reason you are now holding this book. His determination and belief in this project has never wavered, and I am forever in his debt for giving it life. To editors Julie McCarron and Jim Pinkston and designer Kurt Wahlner, your excellent work is showcased here, and I am honored to have shared the experience.

Thanks and appreciation to the many, many librarians and archivists across the country who gave of their time and expertise. You made my work and this project what it is. Deserving special mention: the Port Orange Branch of the Volusia County Library, Port Orange, Florida, and its dedicated staff; Rebecca Sherman, Nadine Burroughs and Nancy Bonsall at the University of Delaware Research Library; Brad Gernand in the Manuscript Division of the Library of Congress, Washington, DC; Sondee Weiss at the Jesse H. Jones Central Library of the Houston Public Library System; and especially Eddie Williams and Nancy Webb at the Texas State Archives, Austin.

My extended gratitude to the librarians at the Margaret Herrick Library, the Academy of Motion Picture Arts and Sciences; the Louis B. Mayer Library of the American Film Institute (Los Angeles); the Biomedical Library at the University of California at San Diego; and the Los Angeles City Hall Archives.

To Robert Deaton, my thanks for your encouragement and typically enthusiastic proofreading. To attorney Lou Petrich, my continuing appreciation for your vetting of this document. Applause to billionaire Marvin Davis, for your always fascinating stories about Hollywood and Howard Hughes. And to Carole White and Ronald Saleh, who opened their homes out of love, my special thanks just for you.

There is a special place in my heart for my family members who overextended themselves as always to provide housing, encouragement and emotional therapy during the months of pressure that any writer approaching a deadline faces. Especially my sister Joan Henn, for her unique contribution to my life; Patty, Harry, Timmy, Matthew, and Joey Barker, who gave up their own space to make room for my research—and me; and Michael, Richard and Traci Henn, who supplied continuing amusement to preserve my sanity.

To Jon Eryk Handersen Hanut who guided me from afar and continues still; and Sebastian Toulouse-Eisenmann, whose creativity is always an inspiration. Plus, Daniel Eastman, Evan Harlow, Anne Jordan, Tony Melluzzo, and Laine Quinn. . . because.

And finally, to my mother, Anne, who provided me with the kind of motivation only a mother could. There are no appropriate words for your contribution to this book and my world.

—*Richard Hack*
Maui, Hawaii

Source Notes

Interviews and Depositions

HOWARD HUGHES spent the majority of his adult life in hiding. Shy, withdrawn, hard-of-hearing and uninterested in having any interaction with people, he hid in self-imposed isolation. His decision to exclude himself from public view only served to heighten curiosity about this most private of men. His life, therefore, has been the subject of much speculation, and multiple books on his achievements, romances and businesses. Unfortunately, along with them came much misinformation.

In *Hughes*, every effort has been made to separate invention from reality, rumor from truth, and conjecture from fact. To that end, I am extremely indebted to a number of people who chose to share their experiences with this remarkable and eccentric man. Among them, Noah Dietrich, Jean Peters, and Robert Maheu deserve special mention. Dietrich, in the final stages of his fight against the debilitating neurological disease, myasthenia gravis, was kind enough to speak to me at length during the late Seventies about his experiences as Hughes' chief executive for over thirty years. Jean Peters, Hughes' second wife, maintained a policy of never discussing her reclusive husband, and broke her vow only once, and then only briefly, many years after her divorce from Hughes. In 1988, we spoke on the set of the Universal TV series *Murder, She Wrote*, in which Jean had a guest-starring role. Her comments were as insightful as they were appreciated. Maheu, Hughes' alter ego during his seclusion in Las Vegas, graciously donated hours of his time and provided memos and other business documents to support his description of a period in his life that was cloaked in intrigue and immersed in the highest-level manipulation of government and business.

An extensive list of books and periodicals was used as source material to verify stories and events uncovered through independent research. In the event the story was unable to be corroborated through additional sources, the author is quoted or the book referenced. In addition, FBI files, detailing the forty-year surveillance of Hughes, were declassified through the Freedom of Information Act, and referenced using the FBI's own file numbering system.

The bulk of this book was researched and written using interviews of Hughes' colleagues, lovers, and employees, whose own collections of documents, letters and memorabilia were culled. In addition, over 110,000 pages of since-sealed court documents were read, indexed, and excerpted. These documents were the result of the discovery process produced during the decades-long trials that followed Hughes' death, trials that attempted to determine his legal heirs in the absence of a licit last will and testament. Chief among them were subpoenaed documents from Hughes' Houston law firm—Andrews, Kurth, Campbell and Jones. Among the documents were powers of attorney, as well as hundreds of client files detailing the legal maneuvering of Hughes Tool Company, the Summa Corporation, and Hughes' Las Vegas acquisitions. In addition, the documents included multiple affidavits, letters and memos from Hughes' associates Bill Gay, Chester Davis, John Holmes, Levar Myler, Raymond Cook, Nadine Henley, and Pat Hyland.

Also among the subpoenaed items were contracts from many of the Hughes-produced films, including those of Jane Russell, Jean Harlow, Ben Lyons, John Wayne, Katharine Hepburn, and Cary Grant. Hughes' pilot logs, notes receivable, minutes of board meetings, and documents relating to dozens of lawsuits were inspected and indexed.

In the course of research, sworn depositions from the following Hughes associates were uncovered: Dr. Lawrence Chaffin, Dr. Norman Crane, Roy Crawford, Chester Davis, Noah Dietrich, Howard Eckersley, Raymond Fowler Ph.D., George Francom, Frank William "Bill" Gay, Kay Glenn, Nadine Henley, Raymond M. Holliday, John Holmes, William R. Lummis, Dr. Donald T. Lunde, Robert A. Maheu, Seymour Mintz, Levar Myler, Glenn Edward Odekirk, Vernon C. Olson, Dr. John T. Pettit, William E. Rankin, Jack Real, James

H. Rickard, Dr. Wilbur S. Thain, Bill Utley, Clarence A. "Chuck" Waldron, Milton J. "Mickey" West, and Lloyd Wright.

Long-sealed depositions, documents, and/or interviews with the following people were also utilized in the preparation of this book. Listed alphabetically, these include Lillian Adams, Buddy Adler, Lillian Albertson, Mitzi Albertson, Harris Albright, Don M. Alder, Eddie Alexander, Alex Alexander, J.B. Alexander, Bill Allen, Robert Altman, A.E. Anderson, Richmond Anderson, H. Frank Angell, Army Archerd, Lucia Archibald, James J. Arditto, Clarence Argyle, Jim Armstrong, Reginald B. Armstrong, Delmar J. Asbury, Dr. Franklyn Ashley, Lee Atwood, Alfred E. Augustini, Richard Ault, Charles Ausley, Fred W. Ayers, James Bacon, Joseph A. Ball, Lyman Bannister, George Barnes, Eddie Barry, George Barsumian, Joe Bartles, Greg Bautzer, Wellwood Beall, Chief Dan Beard, Colleen Truax Beban, S. Clark Beise, Ed Bell, Harold Bell, Jeanne Viner Bell, Tom Bell, William Holden Bell, Gordon Bench, Al Benedict, Tom Bernard, John Bernhard, William L. Berry, Elizabeth Best, Bill Bew, Joseph P. Binns, Tony Blackman, John Blaffer, Carl Blake, Helene Blankenhorne, Leila Bliss, Albert J. Bodine, Al Bond, Hal Borne, J. Boudwin, Glenn J. Bourland, J.M. Boyd, J.M. Boyd, Grace Ebdon Boyer, Tom Bradshaw, Harry Brand, Judson Brandreth, Shirley Peters Brandreth, Walter Branson, Frank Breuning, Raymond Glenn Brewer, Bill Brimley, Dr. Reed Broadbent, Albert Broccoli, John Brody, Cliff P. Broughton, Dr. Robert Buckley, Eric Bundy, Bruce Burk, Jules Burnstein Ph.D., David Butler, Loren J. Butler, Zelma Butte, and Carl Byoir.

Also, Robert Campbell, W.H. Cann, Howard Cannon, Ben Carlisle, George Carnicero, Richard Carrington, Harrison Carroll, Laurie Carroll, Keath L. Carver, Norman Chandler, Dr. John Nelson Chappel, Cyril Chappellet, Dr. Homer A. Clark, Douglas Clarke, Christopher Clarkson, Patrick C. Clary, James Clavell, Brenda Clements, Geraldine H. Cleveland, Clark Clifford, Jacqueline Cochran, E. O. "Oz" Cocke, Carl Cohn, Beatrice Cole, Calvin J. Collier, John Collings, Bill Comeau, Ted Conant, Paul Conley, Robert Conley, Mike Conrad (aka Gerald C. Chouinard), Bob Considine, D. Martin Cook, Raymond Cook, Stephen Cook, Kenneth Cory, George Tyler Coulson, Hiram H. Coulter, Maxwell E. Cox, Stuart Cramer, Charles H. Creel, George Crockett, Margaret Nickerson Crockett, Jack Cromar, Clyde Crow, Arthur Crowley, Daryl B. Crown, Robert Martin Cummins, Florence Cunningham, Dr. Merrill C. Daines, Moe Dalitz, Dick Dallas, Richard Danner, Eleanor Boardman D'Arrast, Justin Dart, Dick Davis, Frank Davis, Marvin Davis, Oran Deal, Shirley DeBurgh, Patte McKee Dee, Cecil B. DeMille, Donald A. Dewar, Bernard J. "Ben" Di Cicco, Pat Di Cicco, Dick Dickerman, W.G. Dickman Jr., James C. Dickson, Carol Hoyt Dietrich, Dudley Digges, Katherine Dillon, James Dilworth, Salvatore V. DiMarco, Hank Diroma, Joan Dixon, Bob Dodson, Faith Domergue, Rodgers Donalson, Hedley Donovan, Al Done, Donald Douglas Jr., Norma Douglas, Billie Dove, Harbert J. Doyle, Richard Dreher, Terrell C. Drinkwater, Kathryn Driscoll, Jim Drury, Larry DuBois, Dr. Stanley Dubrin, Vickie Dugan, Ernie Dunlevie, J.C. Dunlop, and William L. Durkin.

In addition, Ira C. Eaker, Thirza Kate Ebdon, Sir George Edwards, John F. Egger, Dwight D. Eisenhower, Ralph Ellinger, Gary Eugene Elliot, Jim Ellsworth, Dr. John Emmett, Marla English, Jack Entratter, Louis Enz, Richard Epley, Dr. LaVerne Erickson, George Etter IV, Charles E. Evans, Roy Evans, Sherman Fairchild, Milton Falkoff, Dr. Harold Feikes, Vernon N. Ferguson, Paul Finkelman, Lester Finkelstein, Eddie Fisher, G.A. Fitzpatrick, Robert Fleming, Captain C.B. Flynn, William Forrester, Bill Fox, Francis Fox, Matty Fox, Cis Francombe, George Franklin, Garth Frazier, Al Freeman, Jack Frye, Elsa Fuchs, George Funival, Jules Furthman, Rodney Fye, Mary Fyfe, Don Gales, Chilton Gano, Richard C. Gano Jr., Genevieve Bickmore Gardner, George Gardner, Michael Garner, Mary E. Gay, Mitzi Gaynor, Eunice Gayson, Larry Germaine, Percy R. Giblin Jr., George Gile, Gordon Gilmore, Fred Glass, Harry Gold, Paul J. Goldberg, Jim Golden, Dick Goldwater, Samuel Goldwyn, John Goolsby, Mack Gordon, Gerre Goss, Don Goul, Harold Graham, Cary Grant, Dave Grant, Ralph Graves, Martha Jo Graves, Richard Gray, Kathryn Grayson, Lawrence Green, Herman M. "Hank" Greenspun, Dr. Frank Griffith, Arthur Groman, Robert Gross, Joe Grothgut, Carl Grover, Alfred Grunther, Angelo Gualtieri, Charlie Guest, Bill Gunston, and Edyth Gynne.

Also, Hector Haight, George Haldeman, Howard Hall, Dr. Nate Hall, Joy M. Hamann, William R. Hannah, Phillip P. Hannifin, Robert Harris, Ferdinand Harvey, Ross Hastings,

Dan Haughton, Dr. Leland Hawkins, Howard W. Hawks, W.E. Haynes, David Hearst, William Randolph Hearst Jr., Marion Henderson, Bruce Henstell, Katharine Hepburn, Barbara Hilgenberg, Dr. William T. Hill, William Hinckle, Oscar Holcombe, Lou Holland, Dr. George M Hollenback, Linda Gray Hollings, C.T. Homan, Jack Hooper, Hedda Hopper, Rea Hopper, Herbert E. Horn, Jean Peters Hough, Henry Huff, Martin Huff, Howard R. Hughes Sr., Jacob Rutherhouse Hughes Jr., Rupert Hughes, Rush Hughes, Peter Hurkos, Lloyd Hurley, Lawrence A. "Pat" Hyland, Bill Irvine, Dr. Rodman Irvine, Clifford Irving, Woodrow N. Irwin, J. Courtney Ivey, Dr. Joseph Jachimczyk, Howard Jaffe, William A. James, Murray Jarvis, Sheila Quinlan Jay, Fred Jayka, John Jeffries, Jack Jerman, Dr. Harmon Heyre, Earl Johnson, Lyndon B. Johnson, Mary D. Johnson, Jesse Jones, Jona Jones, and William Jones.

In addition, Henry J. Kaiser, Walter Kane, Alan Kaplan, Dallas Keller, Charles Kennedy, S.R. Kent, Mickey Kilgore, Linda Kinnear, Ron Kistler, Patricia Knox, Harold Koontz, Mary Lou Kopp, Joe Kowalski, R.C. Kuldell, Lucille P. Lacy, Abbe Lane, George Larson, Paul Laxalt, James R. Lesch, A.V. "Vic" Leslie, Ed Lewis, Fred Lewis, Lewis Lieber Jr., Perry Lieber, Dr. Allen Linn, Janice Ann Littleton, Don Litty, Robert C. Loomis, Norman Love, Martha Lovett, Henry Luce, Annette Gano Lummis, Edward Lund, Gage Lund, Dr. Donald T. Lunde, Howard Lundeen, Ben Lyon, Homer Mabry, John Machio, Sally Macon, Johanna Madsen, Dr. Oscar Maldonado, Harold W. Mallet, Eddie Mannix, Gordon J. Margulis, Sherwin J. Markman, Abraham J. Markowitz, Marion Marsh, Bob Martin, Jack Martin, Trudi Martin, Trudy Marshall, Elsa Martinelli, Earl Martyn, Peter Masefield, Patricia Ann Mason, Dr. Verne Mason, Charlotte Mays, Mary McAllister, Jerome F. McBreaty, Neil S. McCarthy, Frank McCullough, Donald McDonald, Avis Hughes McIntyre, A.Y. McLain, Charlie McVarnish, John H. Meier, Dr. John Merrill, Dr. Frederick H. Meyers, Marie Denise Miller, William T. Miller, Ronald Minkin, Harold Minniear, Seymour Mintz, Robert Mitchum, Chris Moller, Queenie Mollthstrom, Bert Monesmith, Ralph Monroe, Dr. Victor Manuel Montemayor, M.E. "Monty" Montrose, Taylor Moore, Terry [Helen Koford] Moore, Jean Moorehead, Charles E. Moran, Edward P. Morgan, Robert L. Morgan, Clinton Morse, Jim Morton, Aline Mosby, Jake Moxmess, Florabelle Muir, Johnson Murray, Robert Murphy, Lee Murin, and Jerome L. Murtaugh.

Plus, J.V. Naish, James Herbert Nall, Charles Navaro, Edward Nechling, Don Neuhaus, Rev. Dan Robert Newburn, Jean Negulesco, Edward H. Nigro, Donald Nixon, Sally Norton, Anthony Norwell, Mike O'Callaghan, Glenn Edward Odekirk, Floyd Odlum, Vernon C. Olson, Eugene Oncken, Tom O'Neil, Dan O'Shea, Gerald Owens Jr., Frank Oxarart Sr., William Padon, Arthur J. Palmer, Richard W. Palmer, Dr. Robert Palmer, Jack Parkinson, Louella Parsons, Nat Paschall, Dr. Everitt Payne, Drew Pearson, Gerry Pearson, Warren Pearson, Westbrook Pegler, Fred Perry, Arthur Peterson, Dwight Peterson, Jimmy Pettey, Dr. John Tanner Pettit, James Pfeiffer, James R. Phelan, Larry B. Philips, Marvin Pickholtz, Mel Pierovich, Warren Lee Pierson, Virgil Pinkley, Tom Plumb, Ruth Polansky, Jack Poor, Ennie Potts, Mary Norris Poulson, Robert Andre Poussin, Dick Powell, John Robert Powers, Charles E. Price, John R. Price, Perry Price, Dr. Mulloy Prince, Allen Puckett, Joe Purtell and John Quinn.

Also, Brucks Randell, William Rankin, Gary Louis Ray, Jimmy Read, Gil Reed, Jerry Reed, Bernard Reich, D.W. Rentzel, Debbie Reynolds, Lee E. Reynolds, Walt Reynolds, Daniel D. Rhodes, Ella Rice, John H. Richardson, Natalie Richardson, Paul Riddle, Ruth Robinson, Sir Walter Robinson, Mrs. Verna Rockefeller, Roy Rodde, Ginger Rogers, Eleanor Rohrbeck, Carl Romm, Elliott Roosevelt, Ned Root, Russell Rourke, Dick Rouzie, John C. Rowe, Joe Rowen, Bob Rowley, Bob Rummel, Jane Russell, Cornelius Ryan, Ray Ryan, Dr. Michael Saleh, Gordon E. Sawyer, Jack Scarbrough, Charles E. Schaaf, Lew Schreiber, Chuck Schutz, Herb Schwab, Leonard Schwartz, Sol Schwartz, Vernon Scott, Herb Seagram, Arelo C. Sederberg, Julius Sedlmayr, Gus Seidel, Jean Sewall, Agnes Sexton, John Seymour, Jack Shalitt, Dudley Sharp, Pat Sheehan, Miles Sheridan, Tom Sheridan, Yvonne Shubert, Ben L. Silberstein, Bill Simons, James F. Simons, Frank Sinatra, Norman Sklarewitz, Spyros Skouras, Tom Slack, Muriel Slatkin, Robert F. Slatzer, Malcolm Smith, Tommy Smith, Walter Smith, Dr. William Smith, Winthrop H. Smith, Fred Smye, Jimmie "The Greek" Snyder, Sidney Paul Solow, Robert Spenseley, Mike St. Angel, Jimmy Starr, Bruce Stedman, Jim Steele, Karl Stemmler, Jolene Stettler, Art Stewart, Mell Stewart, Dick

Stoddard, Paul Stoddard, Ed Stokes, Jeanne Stone, Buddy Floyd Stonecipher, David Storm, Frederick Strickland, Paul Strohm, Allan Stroud, Shell Stuart, Lea Sullivan, Lee Sullivan, Anne Arnold Suman, Roger Sutton, Ronald D. Swanson, and Larry Sykes.

And finally, Harold Talbott, Dr. Charles M. Taylor, Elizabeth Taylor, Joyce Taylor, Raymond E. Tedick, Forest Searls Tennant Jr., David Thayer, Charles Thomas, Duane Thomas, Tex Thornton, Lt. Colonel Thurlow, Charlotte Tillbrook, David B. Tinnin, Dr. Jack L. Titus, Macy E. Todd, Gordon Treharne, Virginia Tremaine, Colonel Jerome M. Triolo, Mary Tucker, Edward W. Turley, Bill Turner, Wally Turner, Bob Uline Jr., Bill Utley, Thomas J. Van Boart, Angela Van Clot, Vinton Bruce Vernon, Al Veta, George Vetters, Elliston A. Vinson, James K. Voelkel, William Voker, Gustaf Von Reis, Cedric Von Rolleston, Charles W. Von Rosenberg, James L. Wadsworth, Jerry Wald, Jack Warner, W.F. Warren, Frank Waters, Walt Wayman, John Wayne, Del Webb, Toni Webb, Cliff Weisman, Bert Wells, John Wells, Edward West, Harry West, Bill White, Lillian Dixie White, Steve White, Billy Wilkerson, Tichi Wilkerson, Jim Wilkerson, Joseph B. Williams, Carolyn Williamson, C.E. Wilson, Dwight E. Wilson, Fred Wilson, Prudence Wilson, Paul Wimbish, Walter Winchell, Paul Winn, Ralph Winte, Dr. Ray Wixom, Donald Woodard, Chuck Woodcock, George Woods, Warden Woolard, Michael Woulfe, Kenneth E. Wright, Margaret Ann Wright, Captain Brien Wygle, Dana Wynter, Alfred R. Wypler, Dr. Victor Yanchick, Leo Yoder, Kirk Yost, Gordon Youngman, Darryl Zanuck, and John G. Zevely.

Books

Adler, Bill. *Sinatra: The Man and the Myth.* New York: Signet 1987.

Allen, Oliver E. *The Airline Builders.* Alexandria, Va.: Time Life Books, 1987.

Allgood, Jill. *Bebe and Ben.* London: Robert Hale, 1975.

Ambrose, Stephen E. Nixon: *The Education of a Politician, 1913-1962.* New York: Simon & Schuster, 1988.

Ambrose, Stephen E. *Nixon: Triumph of a Politician, 1962-1970.* New York: Simon & Schuster, 1990.

Anderson, Christopher P. *A Star, Is a Star, Is a Star!* Garden City, New York: Doubleday, 1980.

Anderson, Christopher P. *Young Kate.* New York: Henry Holt, 1988.

Anderson, Jack with James Boyd. *Confessions of a Muckraker.* New York; Random House, Inc., 1979.

Arce, Hector. *The Secret Life of Tyrone Power.* New York: William Morrow, 1979.

Ardmore, Jane. *The Self-Enchanted: Mae Murray, Image of an Era.* New York: McGraw-Hill, 1959.

Astor, Mary. *My Story: An Autobiography.* Garden City, New York: Doubleday, 1959.

Bacon, James. *Hollywood Is a Four-Letter Town.* New York: Avon, 1977.

Bacon, James. *Made in Hollywood.* New York: Warner Books, 1977.

Barlett, Donald L., and James B. Steele. *Empire: The Life, Legend and Madness of Howard Hughes.* New York: W.W. Norton, 1979.

Barton, Charles. *Howard Hughes and His Flying Boat.* Fallbrook, Ca.: Aero Publishers, 1982.

Bell, Jerry. *Howard Hughes: His Silence, Secrets and Success!* New York: Hawkes, 1976.

Berg, A. Scott. *Goldwyn: A Biography.* New York: Knopf, 1989.

Bergman, Ingrid, and Alan Burgess. *Ingrid Bergman: My Story.* New York: Dell, 1981.

Boller, Paul F., Jr. *Hollywood Anecdotes.* New York: Ballantine Books, 1987.

Brooks, Louise. *Lulu in Hollywood.* New York: Knopf, 1982.

Brownlow, Kevin. *Behind the Mask of Innocence.* New York: Knopf, 1990.

Burk, Margaret Tante. *Are the Stars Out Tonight?* Los Angeles: Round Table West, 1980.

Burlson, Clyde W. *The Jennifer Project.* Englewood Cliffs, N.J.: Prentice-Hall, 1977.

Burnham, David. *A Law Unto Itself: Power, Politics and the IRS.* New York: Random House, 1989.

Calvet, Corinne. *Has Corinne Been a Good Girl?* New York: St. Martin's, 1983.

Canales, Luis. *Imperial Gina: The Strictly Unauthorized Biography of Gina Lollobrigida*. Boston: Branden, 1990.

Carey, Gary. *Katharine Hepburn: A Hollywood Yankee*. New York: St. Martin's, 1983.

Carpozi, George, Jr. *The John Wayne Story*. New York: Arlington, 1972.

Cassini, Igor. *I'll Do It All Over Again*. New York: G.P. Putnam's Sons, 1977.

Cassini, Oleg. *In My Own Fashion: An Autobiography*. New York: Simon & Schuster, 1987.

Ceplar, Larry, and Steve Englund. *The Inquisition in Hollywood: Politics in the Film Community, 1930-1960*. Garden City, New York: Doubleday, 1980.

Chaplin, Charles. *My Autobiography*. New York: Pocket Books, 1966.

Clark, James A. and Michael Thomas Halbouty. *Spindletop*. Houston, Texas: Gulf Publishing Company, 1952.

Clarke, Gerald. *Capote: A Biography*. New York: Simon & Schuster, 1988.

Clifford, Clark, with Richard Holbrooke. *Counsel to the President: A Memoir.* Garden City, New York: Doubleday, 1992.

Cochran, Jacqueline, with Maryann Bucknum Brinley. *Jackie Cochran*. New York: Bantam Books, 1987.

Colby, William, with Peter Forbath. *Honorable Mention: My Life in the CIA*. New York: Simon & Schuster, 1978.

Colman, Juanita Benita. *Ronald Colman: A Very Private Person*. New York: William Morrow, 1975.

Considine, Shaun. *Bette & Joan: The Divine Feud*. New York: Dutton, 1989.

Conway, Michael, and Mark Ricci. *The Films of Jean Harlow*. New York: Cadillac, 1965.

Croce, Arlene. *The Fred Astaire & Ginger Rogers Book*. New York: Outerbridge & Lazard, 1972.

Crow III, Jefferson Brim. *Randolph Scott: The Gentleman from Virginia*. Carrollton, Texas: WindRiver Publishing Co. 1987.

Curcio, Vincent. *Suicide Blonde: The Life of Gloria Grahame*. New York: William Morrow, 1989.

Dallek, Robert. *Lone Star Rising: Lyndon Johnson and His Times, 1908-1960*. New York: St. Martin's, 1982.

Dardis, Tom. *Keaton: The Man Who Wouldn't Lie Down*. New York: Scribner's, 1979.

Davenport, Elaine, Paul Eddy, and Mark Hurwitz. *Howard Hughes' Final Years.* London: Andre Deutsch, 1977.

Davenport, Elaine, and Paul Eddy, with Mark Hurwitz. *The Hughes Papers*. New York: Ballantine Books, 1976.

Davenport, Joe, and Todd S.J. Lawson. *The Empire of Howard Hughes*. San Francisco: Peace and Pieces Foundation, 1975.

Davidson, Bill. *Spencer Tracy: Tragic Idol*. New York: Dutton, 1987.

Davidson, Bill. *The Real and the Unreal*. New York: Dutton, 1987.

Davies, Marion. *The Times We Had: Life with William Randolph Hearst*. Indianapolis: Bobbs-Merrill, 1975.

Davis, Bette, with Michael Herskowitz. *This 'N That: Bette Davis*. New York: Berkley, 1988.

Davis, Bette. *The Lonely Life*. New York: G.P. Putnam's Sons, 1962.

Davis, Donald L. *Hollywood Beauty: Linda Darnell and the American Dream*. Norman, Okla.: University of Oklahoma, 1991.

Davis, Ellis A., and Edwin G. Grobe. *The New Encyclopedia of Texas*. Dallas, Tex.: Texas Development Bureau, 1926.

Dean, John. *Blind Ambition: The White House Years*. New York: Simon & Schuster, 1976.

DeCarlo, Yvonne, with Doug Warren. *Yvonne*. New York: St. Martin's, 1971.

Demaris, Ovid. *The Director: An Oral Biography of J. Edgar Hoover.* New York: Harper's Magazine Press, 1975.

Dickens, Homer. *The Films of Katharine Hepburn*. New York: Citadel Press, 1971.

Dietrich, Noah, with Bob Thomas. *Howard: The Amazing Mr. Hughes*. New York: Fawcett, 1972.

Diliberto, Gioia. *Debutante*. New York: Pocket Books, 1987.

Dmytryk, Edward. *It's a Hell of a Life but Not a Bad Living*. New York: Times Books, 1978.

Drosnin, Michael. *Citizen Hughes*. New York: Holt, Rinehart and Winston, 1985.

Dunne, Philip. *Take Two: A Life in Movies and Politics*. New York: McGraw-Hill, 1980.

Dwiggins, Don. *Famous Flyers and the Ships They Flew*. New York: Grosset & Dunlap, 1980.

Dwiggins, Don. *Howard Hughes: The True Story*. Santa Monica, Calif.: Werner, 1972.

Edmonds, Andy. *Hot Toddy: The True Story of Hollywood's Most Shocking Crime—The*

Murder of Thelma Todd. New York: Avon, 1989.

Edwards, Anne. *A Remarkable Woman: A Biography of Katharine Hepburn.* New York: William Morrow, 1985.

Eels, George. *Ginger, Loretta, Irene Who?* New York: G.P. Putnam's Sons, 1976.

Evans, Peter. Ari: *The Life and Times of Aristotle Onassis.* New York: Summit, 1986.

Fay, Stephen, Chester Lewis and Magnus Linklater. *Hoax: The Inside Story of the Howard Hughes-Clifford Irving Affair.* New York: Viking, 1972.

Finstad, Suzanne. *Heir Not Apparent.* Austin, Texas: Texas Monthly Press, 1984.

Flamini, Roland. *Ava: A Biography.* New York: Coward, McCann & Geoghegan, 1983.

Fleischer, Richard. *Just Tell Me When to Cry: A Memoir.* New York: Carroll & Graf, 1993.

Foxworth, Erna B. *The Romance of Old Sylvan Beach.* Austin, Tex.: Waterway, 1986.

French, Philip. *The Movie Moguls: An Informal History of the Hollywood Tycoons.* Chicago: Henry Regnery, 1971.

Friedman, B.H. *Gertrude Vanderbilt Whitney.* Garden City, New York: Doubleday, 1978.

Gardner, Ava. *Ava: My Story.* Thorndike, Me.: Thorndike Press, 1991.

Gardner, Gerald. *The Censorship Papers: Movie Censorship Letters from the Hays Office.* New York: Dodd-Mead, 1987.

Garnett, Tay with Fredda Dudley Balling. *Light Your Torches and Pull Up Your Tights.* New York: Arlington House, 1973.

Garrison, Omar V. *Howard Hughes in Las Vegas.* New York: Lyle Stuart, 1970.

Geist, Kenneth L. *Pictures Will Talk: The Life and Films of Joseph L. Mankiewicz.* New York: Scribner's, 1978.

Genevoix, Sylvie. *HRH.* Paris: Plon, 1972.

Gerber, Albert B. *Bashful Billionaire.* New York: Lyle Stuart, 1967.

Golden, Eve. *Platinum Girl: The Life and Legends of Jean Harlow.* New York: Abbeville, 1991.

Goldsmith, Barbara. *Little Gloria. . . Happy at Last.* New York: Knopf, 1980.

Graham, Don. *No Name on the Bullet: A Biography of Audie Murphy.* New York: Viking, 1989.

Graham, Sheilah. *Garden of Allah.* New York: Crown, 1970.

Graham, Sheilah. *The Rest of the Story.* New York: Coward-McCann, 1964.

Granger, Stewart. *Sparks Fly Upward* New York: G.P. Putnam's Sons, 1981.

Griffin, Merv, and Peter Barsocchini. *Merv: An Autobiography.* New York: Pocket Books, 1980.

Gubernick, Lisa Rebecca. *Squandered Fortune: The Life and Times of Huntington Hartford.* New York: G.P. Putnam's Sons, 1991.

Guiles, Fred Lawrence. *Marion Davies: A Biography.* New York: McGraw-Hill, 1972.

Gussow, Mel. *Don't Say Yes Until I Finish Talking: A Biography of Darryl F. Zanuck.* Garden City, New York: Doubleday, 1971.

Guthrie, Lee. *The Life and Loves of Cary Grant.* New York: Drake, 1977.

Haldeman, H.R. *The Haldeman Diaries: Inside the Nixon White House.* New York: G.P. Putnam's Sons, 1994.

Haldeman, H.R., with Joseph DiMona. *The Ends of Power.* New York: Times Books, 1978.

Hanna, David. *Ava: A Portrait of a Star.* New York: G.P. Putnam's Sons, 1980.

Harris, Marlys J. *The Zanucks of Hollywood: The Dark Legacy of an American Dynasty.* New York: Crown, 1989.

Harris, Radie. *Radie's World: The Memoirs of Radie Harris.* New York: G.P. Putnam's Sons, 1975.

Harris, Warren G. *Cary Grant: A Touch of Elegance.* Garden City, New York: Doubleday, 1987.

Hatfield, D.D. *Howard Hughes H-4 Hercules Airplane.* Los Angeles: Historical Airplanes, 1972.

Hays, Will H. *The Memoirs of Will H. Hays.* Garden City, New York: Doubleday, 1955.

Hearst, William Randolph, Jr. with Jack Casserly. *The Hearsts: Father and Son.* Niwot, Colo.: Roberts Rinehart, 1991.

Hecht, Ben. *A Child of the Century.* New York: Donald I. Fine, 1954.

Helenthal, Francis J. *Howard Hughes: The Keokuk Connection.* Texas: Francis J. Helenthal, 1976.

Hepburn, Katharine. *Me: Stories of My Life.* New York: Knopf, 1991.

Hess, Alan. *Viva Las Vegas: After-Hours Architecture.* San Francisco: Chronicle Books, 1993.

Heymann, C. David. *Poor Little Rich Girl:*

The Life and Legend of Barbara Hutton. New York: Random House, 1983.

Hobart, Rose. *A Steady Digression to a Fixed Point: The Autobiography of Rose Hobart.* Metuchen, New Jersey: Scarecrow, 1994.

Hougan, Jim. *Spooks: The Haunting of America—the Use of Secret Agents.* New York: William Morrow, 1978.

Hyman, B.D. *My Mother's Keeper.* New York: Berkley, 1985.

Investigations of the National Defense Program. Washington, D.C.: Government Printing Office, 1948.

Irving, Clifford. *The Hoax.* New York: Permanent Press, 1981.

Irving, Clifford, with Richard Suskind. *What Really Happened: His Untold Story of the Hughes Affair.* New York: Grove Press, 1972.

Jennings, Dean. *Barbara Hutton: A Candid Biography.* New York: Frederick Fell, 1968.

Jewell, Richard B. and Vernon Harbin. *The RKO Story.* New York: Arlington House, 1982.

Johnston, Marguerite. *Houston, the Unknown City.* College Station, Texas: Texas A & M University Press, 1972.

Kaminsky, Stuart M. *The Howard Hughes Affair.* New York: St. Martin's, 1979.

Kanin, Garson. *Hollywood.* New York: Limelight, 1967.

Kanin, Garson. *Tracy and Hepburn: An Intimate Memoir.* New York: Viking, 1971.

Katz, Ephraim. *The Film Encyclopedia.* New York: Thomas Y. Crowell, 1979.

Keats, John. *Howard Hughes.* New York: Random House, 1966.

Kelley, Kitty. *Elizabeth Taylor: The Last Star.* New York: Simon & Schuster, 1981.

Kistler, Ron. *I Caught Flies for Howard Hughes.* Chicago: Playboy Press, 1979.

Klein, Herbert G. *Making It Perfectly Clear.* Garden City, New York: Doubleday, 1980.

Klurfield, Herman. *Winchell: His Life and Times.* New York: Praeger, 1976.

Konolige, Kit. *The Richest Women in the World.* New York: Macmillan, 1985.

LaGuardia, Robert, and Gene Arceri. *Red: The Tempestuous Life of Susan Hayward.* New York: Macmillan, 1985.

Lacey, Robert. *Little Man: Meyer Lansky and the Gangster Life.* New York: Little, Brown, 1991.

Lamarr, Hedy. *Ecstasy and Me: My Life as a Woman.* New York: Fawcett, 1966.

Lambert, Gavin. *Norma Shearer.* New York: Knopf, 1990.

Lambert, Gavin. *On Cukor.* New York: G.P. Putnam's Sons, 1972.

Lamour, Dorothy, as told to Dick McInnes. *My Side of the Road.* Englewood Cliffs, N.J.: Prentice-Hall, 1980.

Lamparski, Richard. *Lamparski's Hidden Hollywood: Where the Stars Lived, Loved and Died.* New York: Fireside, 1981.

Lane, Abbe. *But Where Is Love?* New York: Warner Books, 1993.

Lasky, Betty. *RKO: The Biggest Little Major of Them All.* Santa Monica, Calif.: Roundtable, 1989.

Lasky, Victor. *It Didn't Start with Watergate.* New York: Dial Press, 1977.

Lawford, Lady, with Buddy Galon. *Bitch: The Autobiography of Lady Lawford.* Brookline Village, Me: Branden, 1986.

Lawrence, Jerome. *Actor: The Life and Times of Paul Muni.* London: W.H. Allen, 1975.

Laytner, Ron. *Up Against Hughes: The Maheu Story.* New York: Quadrangle, 1972.

Leamer, Laurence. *King of the Night: The Life of Johnny Carson.* New York: William Morrow, 1989.

Leamer, Laurence. *The Life of Ingrid Bergman.* New York: New American Library, 1986.

Leaming, Barbara. *Bette Davis: A Biography.* New York: Simon & Schuster, 1992.

Leaming, Barbara. *If This Was Happiness: A Biography of Rita Hayworth.* New York: Viking, 1989.

Leigh, Janet. *There Really Was a Hollywood.* Garden City, New York: Doubleday, 1984.

Lenzner, Robert. *The Great Getty: The Life and Loves of J. Paul Getty—Richest Man in the World.* New York: Crown, 1985.

LeRoy, Mervyn, as told to Dick Kleiner. *Mervyn LeRoy: Take One.* New York: Hawthorn, 1974.

Liddy, G. Gordon. *Will: The Autobiography.* New York: St. Martin's, 1980.

Linet, Beverly. *Susan Hayward: Portrait of a Survivor.* New York: Atheneum, 1980.

Lovell, Mary S. *Straight on Till Morning: The Biography of Beryl Markham.* New York: St. Martin's, 1987.

Lovell, Mary S. *The Sound of Wings: The Life of Amelia Earhart.* New York: St. Martin's, 1989.

Lukas, J. Anthony. *Nightmare: The*

Underside of the Nixon Years. New York: Viking, 1976.

MacAdams, William. *Ben Hecht: The Man Behind the Legend.* New York: Scribner's, 1990

Maddox, Brenda. *Who's Afraid of Elizabeth Taylor?* New York: Jove/HBJ, 1976.

Magruder, Jeb Stuart. *An American Life: One Man's Road to Watergate.* New York: Atheneum, 1974.

Maheu, Robert, and Richard Hack. *Next to Hughes: Behind the Power and Tragic Downfall of Howard Hughes.* New York: HarperCollins, 1992.

Mailer, Norman. *Harlot's Ghost: A Novel.* New York: Random House, 1991.

Mankiewicz, Frank. *Perfectly Clear: Nixon from Whittier to Watergate.* New York: Quadrangle, 1973.

Mankiewicz, Frank. *U.S. vs. Richard M. Nixon: The Final Crisis.* New York: Quadrangle, 1975.

Mann, William J. *Wisecracker: The Life and Times of William Haines.* New York: Viking, 1999.

Mansfield, Stephanie. *The Richest Girl in the World: The Extraordinary Life and Fast Times of Doris Duke.* New York: G.P. Putnam's Sons, 1992.

March, Joseph Moncure. *The Wild Party.* New York: Citadel Press, 1979.

Marchetti, Victor, and John D. Marks. *The CIA and the Cult of Intelligence.* New York: Knopf, 1974.

Martin, Tony, and Cyd Charisse, as told to Dick Kleiner. *The Two of Us.* New York: Mason/Charter, 1976.

Marx, Arthur. *The Nine Lives of Mickey Rooney.* New York: Stein and Day, 1986.

Marx, Samuel, and Joyce Vanderveen. *Deadly Illusions: Jean Harlow and the Murder of Paul Bern.* New York: Random House, 1990.

Mathison, Richard R. *His Weird and Wanton Ways.* New York: William Morrow, 1977.

McBride, Joseph. *Hawks on Hawks.* Berkeley: University of California Press, 1982.

McClelland, Doug. *Susan Hayward: The Divine Bitch.* New York: Pinnacle, 1973.

McComb, David G. *Houston: A History.* Austin: University of Texas Press, 1981.

McCracken, Robert D. *Tonopah: The Greatest, the Richest, and the Best Mining Camp in the World.* Tonopah, Nev.: Nye County Press, 1960.

McDonald, John J. *Howard Hughes and the*

Spruce Goose. Blue Ridge Summit, Pa.: Tab, 1981.

McGilligan, Patrick. *Backstory: Interviews with Screenwriters of Hollywood's Golden Age.* Berkeley: University of California Press, 1986.

McIntosh, William Currie. *The Private Cary Grant.* London: Sidgwick & Jackson, 1983.

Messick, Hank. *The Beauties and the Beasts: The Mob in Show Business.* New York: David McKay, 1973.

Miller, Patsy Ruth. *The Memories of Patsy Ruth Miller.* London: O'Raghailligh, 1988.

Moore, Terry. *The Beauty and the Billionaire.* New York: Pocket Books, 1984.

Morella, Joe, and Edward Z. Epstein. *Lana: The Public and Private Lives of Miss Turner.* New York: Dell, 1974.

Morella, Joe. *Paulette: The Adventurous Life of Paulette Goddard.* New York: St. Martin's, 1985.

Moseley, Roy. *Bette Davis: An Intimate Memoir.* New York: Donald I. Fine, 1989.

Mosley, Leonard. *Lindbergh.* New York: Dell, 1976.

Nass, Herbert E., Esq. *Wills of the Rich & Famous: A Fascinating Look at the Rich, Often Surprising Legacies of Yesterday's Celebrities.* New York: Warner Books, 1991.

Navasky, Victor S. *Naming Names.* New York: Viking, 1980.

Nelson, Nancy. *Evenings with Cary Grant: Recollections in His Own Words and by Those Who Knew Him Best.* New York: William Morrow, 1991.

Nicholson, Patrick J. *William Ward Watkin and the Rice Institute.* Houston: Gulf Books, 1991.

Niven, David. *The Moon's a Balloon.* Great Britain: Hamish Hamilton, 1971.

O'Brien, Larry. *No Final Victories.* Garden City, New York: Doubleday, 1974.

Odekirk, Glenn E. *Spruce Goose: HK-1 Hercules: A Pictorial History of the Fantastic Hughes Flying Boat.* Long Beach, Ca.: Frank Alcanter, Inc. 1982.

Parrish, James Robert, and Michael R. Pitts. *The Great Gangster Pictures.* Metuchen, N.J.: Scarecrow, 1976.

Parrish, James Robert. *The RKO Gals.* London: Ian Allen, 1974.

Parsons, Louella. *Tell It to Louella.* New York: G.P. Putnam's Sons, 1961.

Pastos, Spero. *Pin-Up: The Tragedy of Betty*

Grable. New York: G.P. Putnam's Sons, 1986.

Payton, Barbara. *I Am Not Ashamed*. Los Angeles: Holloway House, 1963.

Pero, Taylor, and Jeff Rovin. *Always, Lana*. New York: Bantam Books, 1982.

Pfeiffer, Lee. *The John Wayne Scrapbook*. New York: Citadel Press, 1991.

Phelan, James. *Howard Hughes, the Hidden Years*. New York: Random House, 1976.

Phelan, James. *Scandals, Scamps and Scoundrels*. New York: Random House, 1982.

Pilat, Oliver. *Drew Pearson: An Unauthorized Biography*. New York: Harper's Magazine Press, 1973.

Preminger, Otto. *An Autobiography*. Garden City, New York: Doubleday, 1977.

Presley, James. *A Saga of Wealth: The Rise of the Texas Oilmen*. New York: G.P. Putnam & Sons, 1978.

Quirk, Lawrence J. *Fasten Your Seat Belts: The Passionate Life of Bette Davis*. New York: Signet, 1990.

Rappleye, Charles and Ed Becker. *All American Mafioso: The Johnny Rosselli Story*. Garden City, New York: Doubleday, 1991.

Rashke, Richard. *Stormy Genius: The Life of Aviation's Maverick, Bill Lear*. Boston: Houghton Mifflin, 1985.

Reynolds, Debbie, and David Patrick Columbia. *Debbie: My Life*. New York: William Morrow, 1988.

Rhoden, Harold. *High Stakes: The Gamble for the Howard Hughes Will*. New York: Crown, 1980.

Rickenbacker, Edward V. *Rickenbacker*. Englewood Cliffs, N.J.: Prentice-Hall, 1967.

Russell, Jane. *An Autobiography: My Path and Detours*. New York: Franklin Watts, 1985

Schary, Dore. *Heyday: An Autobiography*. New York: Little, Brown, 1979.

Schell, Jonathan. *The Time of Illusion*. New York: Knopf, 1976.

Scott, Peter Dale. *Crime and Cover-up: The CIA, the Mafia, and the Dallas-Watergate Connection*. Berkeley, California: Westworks, 1977.

Serling, Robert. *Howard Hughes' Airline: An Informal History of TWA*. New York: St. Martin's/Marek, 1983.

Sheppard, Dick. *Elizabeth: The Life and Career of Elizabeth Taylor*. New York: Warner Books, 1974.

Shevey, Sandra. *The Marilyn Scandal*. New York: Jove Books, 1990.

Shulman, Irving. *Harlow: An Intimate Biography*. New York: Dell Books, 1964.

Signoret, Simone. *Nostalgia Isn't What It Used to Be*. New York: Harper & Row, 1978.

Smith, Elinor. *Aviatrix*. New York: Harcourt Brace Jovanovich, 1981.

Somoza, Anastasio, as told to Jack Cox. *Nicaragua Betrayed*. Belmont, Massachusetts: Western Islands, 1980.

Spada, James. *More Than a Woman: An Intimate Biography of Bette Davis*. New York: Bantam Books, 1993.

Spoto, Donald. *Madcap: The Life of Preston Sturges*. Boston: Little, Brown, 1990.

Stack, Robert, with Mark Evans. *Straight Shooting*. New York: Berkley, 1980.

Stauffer, Teddy. *Forever Is a Hell of a Long Time: An Autobiography*. Chicago: Henry Regnery, 1976.

Stenn, David. *Bombshell: The Life and Death of Jean Harlow*. Garden City, New York: Doubleday, 1993.

Stine, Whitney, with Bette Davis. *Mother Goddam: The Story of the Career of Bette Davis*. New York: Berkley Medallion, 1974.

Stine, Whitney. *I'd Love to Kiss You. . . Conversations with Bette Davis*. New York: Pocket Books, 1990.

Strait, Raymond. *Mrs. Howard Hughes*. Los Angeles: Holloway House, 1970.

Stuart, Sandra Lee. *The Pink Palace*. New York: Pocket Books, 1978.

Sturges, Preston, adapted and edited by Sandy Sturges. *Preston Sturges*. New York: Simon & Schuster, 1990.

Summers, Anthony. *Goddess: The Secret Lives of Marilyn Monroe*. New York: Onyx, 1986.

Thomas, Bob. *Selznick*. Garden City, New York: Doubleday, 1970.

Thomas, Tony. *Howard Hughes in Hollywood*. Secaucus, N.J.: Citadel Press, 1985.

Thomason, David. *Showman: The Life of David O. Selznick*. New York: Knopf, 1992.

Tierney, Gene with Mickey Herskowitz. *Self-Portrait*. New York: Wyden Books, 1978.

Tinnin, David B. *Just About Everybody vs. Howard Hughes*. Garden City, New York: Doubleday, 1973.

Todd, Michael, Jr., and Susan McCarthy

Todd. *A Valuable Property: The Life Story of Mike Todd*. New York: Arbor House, 1983.

Tomkies, Mike. *The Robert Mitchum Story: 'It Sure Beats Working.'* New York: Ballantine Books, 1972.

Torme, Mel. *It Wasn't All Velvet*. New York: Viking, 1988.

Tosches, Nick. *Dino: Living High in the Dirty Business of Dreams*. Garden City, New York: Doubleday, 1992.

Turner, Lana. *Lana: The Lady, The Legend, The Truth*. New York: Pocket Books, 1982.

Van Doren, Mamie, with Art Aveilhe. *Playing the Field: My Story*. New York: G.P. Putnam's Sons, 1987.

Vanderbilt, Gloria. *Black Knight, White Knight*. New York: Knopf, 1987.

Varner, Roy, and Wayne Collier. *A Matter of Risk: The Incredible Inside Story of the CIA's Hughes* Glomar Explorer *Mission to Raise a Russian Submarine*. New York: Random House, 1978.

Wansell, Geoffrey. *Haunted Idol: The Story of the Real Cary Grant*. New York: William Morrow, 1984.

Warrick, Ruth, with Don Preston. *The Confessions of Phoebe Tyler*. Englewood Cliffs, N.J.: Prentice-Hall, 1980.

Waterbury, Ruth. *Elizabeth Taylor*. New York: Popular Library, 1964.

Wayne, Aissa, with Steve Delsohn. *John Wayne: My Father*. New York: Random House, 1991.

Wayne, Jane Ellen. *Ava's Men: The Private Life of Ava Gardner*. New York: St. Martin's, 1990.

Wayne, Jane Ellen. *Crawford's Men: The Private Life of Joan Crawford*. New York: Prentice-Hall, 1988.

Wayne, Jane Ellen. *Lana: The Life and Loves of Lana Turner*. New York: St. Martin's, 1995.

Wayne, Pilar, with Alex Thorleifson. *John Wayne: My Life with the Duke*. New York: McGraw-Hill, 1987.

Whalen, Grover A. *Mr. New York*. New York: G.P. Putnam's Sons, 1955.

Whitehouse, Arch. *The Sky's the Limit: A History of the U.S. Airlines*. New York: Macmillan, 1971.

Whiting, Charles. *Hero: The Life and Death of Audie Murphy*. Chelsea, Michigan: Scarborough House, 1990.

Whyte, Edna Gardner, with Ann L. Cooper. *Rising Above It: An Autobiography*. New York: Orion, 1991.

Wilkerson, Tichi, and Marcia Borie. *The Hollywood Reporter: The Golden Years*. New York: Coward-McCann, 1984.

Wilkie, Jane. *Confessions of an Ex-Fan Magazine Writer*. Garden City, New York: Doubleday, 1981.

Wilson, Earl. *Hot Times: True Tales of Hollywood and Broadway*. Chicago: Contemporary Books, 1984.

Wilson, Earl. *Sinatra: An Unauthorized Biography*. New York: Macmillan, 1976.

Wilson, Earl. *The Show Business Nobody Knows*. New York: Bantam Books, 1973.

Winchell, Walter. *Winchell Exclusive: "Things That Happened to Me—and Me to Them."* Englewood Cliffs, N.J.: Prentice-Hall, 1975.

Winters, Shelley. *Shelley: Also Known as Shirley*. New York: William Morrow, 1980.

Woodward, Bob, and Carl Bernstein. *The Final Days*. New York: Simon & Schuster, 1976.

Woody Jack. *Lost Hollywood*. Altadena, Calif.: Twin Palms, 1987.

Wray, Fay. *On the Other Hand*. New York: St. Martin's, 1988.

Wynne, H. Hugh. *The Motion Picture Stunt Pilots and Hollywood's Classic Aviation Movies*. Missoula, Mont.: Pictorial Histories, 1987.

Yablonsky, Lewis. *George Raft*. New York: McGraw-Hill, 1974.

Zeckendorf, William with Edward McCreary. *Zeckendorf*. New York: Holt, Rinehart and Winston, 1970.

Zierold, Norman. *The Moguls*. New York: Coward-McCann, 1969.

Zimmer, Jill Schary. *With a Cast of Thousands: A Hollywood Childhood*. New York: Stein and Day, 1963.

Periodicals

"$137 Million Judgment Against Hughes." *Los Angeles Herald Examiner*, September 22, 1968, p. 1.

"$8,000,000 Buy-Back by Hughes." *Hollywood Reporter*, January 6, 1956, p. 1.

"'Fantastic' Airplane Pact Told to Senate Probers." *Hollywood Citizen-News*, July 28, 1947, p. 1.

"'Hell Heat' Pressure Told in Kaiser-Hughes Deal." *Los Angeles Herald Examiner*, July 24, 1947, p. 1.

"'Hell's Angels' Completed." *American Cinematographer*, January, 1930, p. 16.

"'Mr. Hughes Had a Lot of Things Cooking.'" *Fortune*, August, 1954, p. 35.

"'Premature Publicity' Nicked Skouras $5,000,000 in Deal for Hughes' Empire." *Daily Variety*, August 4, 1954, p. 1.

"'Spy' in Mothballs." *New York Times*, October 30, 1983, sec A, p. 49.

"'Will' Includes Man Who Says He Rescued Hughes in Desert." *New York Times*, April 30, 1976, p. 17.

"'Will' Letter Tied to Hughes Hotel." *New York Times*, May 29, 1976, p. 21.

"999 Hughes' Friends Will Get Medallions." *New York Times*, May 21, 1977, sec. A, p. 10.

"A Deadline for Howard Hughes?" *Fortune*, July , 1959, p. 112.

"A Howard Hughes Debt Flies Home to Roost." *New York Times*, September 11, 1977, sec. 3, p. 15.

"A Star Is Born." *Time*, October 1, 1945, p. 81.

"AAF Blames Hughes." *Aviation Week*, August 11, 1947, p. 12.

"ABC Asks Court Injunction to Nip Hughes' Tender." *Variety*, July 10, 1968, p. 1.

"ABC Calls Hughes Offer Violation." Hollywood Citizen-News, July 9, 1968, p. 1.

"ABC Loses Bid to Block Offer by Hughes Tool." *Wall Street Journal*, July 11, 1968, p. 4.

"ABC Loses Second Court Fight to Halt Hughes Bid." *Los Angeles Times*, July 16, 1968, p. 4.

"ABC Seeks Injunction Against Tender Offer Made by Hughes Tool." *Wall Street Journal*, July 10, 1968, p. 1.

"ABC Setback in Hughes Bid; Net Continues Fight Today." *Hollywood Reporter*, July 15, 1968, p. 1.

"ABC to Appeal Refusal by Court to Stay Bid from Hughes Tool Co." Wall Street Journal, July 15, 1968, p. 6.

"ABC to Fight Hughes' Effort to Gain Control of Company." *Variety*, July 3, 1968, p. 1.

"ABC Urges Agency to Declare Tender by Hughes Illegal." *Los Angeles Times*, July 9, 1968, p. 1.

"ABC's Dark Angel." *Newsweek*, July 15, 1948, p. 69.

"Action in Las Vegas." *Time*, September 22, 1967, p. 101.

"Administrator Holds Tax Claims Exceed Value of Hughes's Estate." *New York Times*, July 12, 1979, p. 17.

"Advertising Cancellation." *New York Times*, June 10, 1980, sec. D, p. 5.

"After Long, Tedious Journey, Spruce Goose Has New Home." *New York Times*, March 1, 1993, sec A, p. 13.

"Aide Says Hughes Paid Politicians." *New York Times*, December 3, 1977, p. 10.

"Aides' Log Shows How Howard Hughes Spent Day." *New York Times*, November 20, 1976, p. 10.

"Air Prize to Hughes; Jean Batten Honored." *New York Times*, March 1, 1937, p. 9.

"Air West Director Opposes Hughes Bid." *Aviation Week & Space Technology*, December 9, 1968, p. 51.

"Air West Set for Hughes Proxy Fight." *Aviation Week & Space Technology*, September 30, 1968, p. 30.

"Airline Shares Go to Howard Hughes." *New York Times*, March 22, 1940, p. 31.

"Aleman Lead Grows in Mexican Returns." *New York Times*, July 14, 1946, p. 3.

"An Angel to 'Angels.'" *New York Times*, May 11, 1930, sec. 9, p. 6.

An Ex-Wife Says Hughes Planned to Leave Fortune to Aid Medical Research." *New York Times*, April 23, 1978, p. 39.

"An Old Flame Returns." *Time*, February 23, 1953, p. 93.

"Annette Lummis, Co-Executor of Hughes Estate, Dead at 88." *Houston Chronicle*, July 24, 1979, sec. 4, p. 8.

"Annette Lummis, Aunt of Howard Hughes, 88." *New York Times*, July 25,

1979, sec. B, p. 6.

"Another Hughes 'Will' Arrives Here." *Houston Post*, August 6, 1977, sec. A, p. 4.

"Arguments Begin Today in 'Mormon Will' Case." *New York Times*, November 28, 1977, p. 18.

"Arrival of Hughes' Aides Fires New Sale Reports." *Variety*, August 18, 1954, p. 1.

"At the Controls Once Again." *New York Times*, September 11, 1946, p. 9.

"Atlas in RKO Stock Offer." *Los Angeles Times*, June 30, 1954, p. 34.

"Attempt to Move Lawsuit on Hughes Estate Rejected." *New York Times*, November 28, 1978, p. 16.

"Attorney Reich Wins First Round in New 751G Suit Against Hughes." *Daily Variety*, November 22, 1955, p. 1.

"Attorneys for Hughes's Relatives Argue 'Mormon Will' Is Bogus." *New York Times*, September 15, 1977, sec B, p. 15.

"Aunt and Cousin Will Get Fees from Hughes Estate." *New York Times*, May 23, 1978, p. 16.

"Ava, Hughes Hit Miami Spots." *Los Angeles Mirror*, August 14, 1954, p. 14.

"Battle for Hughes Estate Delayed Pending Will Ruling." *New York Times*, August 17, 1976, p. 53.

"Battle for T.W.A." *Time*, January 6, 1947, p. 76.

"Battle for the Shrinking Millions." *Time*, July 4, 1977, p. 64.

"Beatty Will Play Hughes for Warner." *New York Times*, April 16, 1976, p. 10.

"Being of Sound Mind, He May Try Snake Oil Next." *New York Times*, June 6, 1976, sec. 3, p. 17.

"Benching the Boss." *Newsweek*, October 17, 1960, p. 86.

"Billie Dove Asks Divorce." *New York Times*, June 13, 1930, p. 26.

"Billie Dove Gets Divorce." *New York Times*, July 2, 1930, p. 26.

"Billie Dove Quits Husband." *New York Times*, January 3, 1930, p. 20.

"Billionaire Howard Hughes' Book Tells Why He Hated Blacks." *Jet*, April 15, 1985, p. 12.

"Biography of Hughes." *New York Times*, June 19, 1979, sec. C, p. 6.

"Break Off Miami Negotiations for Odlum to Buy Hughes' RKO Picts. Corp. Holdings." *Daily Variety*, September 9, 1954, p. 1.

"Brewster Defends Course on Hughes." *New York Times*, August 12, 1947, p. 15.

"Brewster Hints of New Inquiries." *New York Times*, August 10, 1947, p. 3.

"C.A.B. Permits Hughes Tool to Acquire Northeast Airlines." *New York Times*, July 20, 1962, p. 1.

"CAB Finding Favors Hughes in TWA Case." *Aviation Week*, July 24, 1950, p. 51.

"CAB Starts Another Investigation of Hughes' Airline Operations." *Business Week*, October 6, 1956, p. 78.

"California Asks Supreme Court to Help Resolve Hughes Dispute." *New York Times*, November 12, 1977, p. 18.

"Can AEC Defuse Hughes?" *Business Week*, April 5, 1969, p. 19.

"Cash In on Hughes." *Business Week*, July 23, 1938, p. 23.

"Celebrated Hermit." *Time*, May 10, 1963, p. 91.

"Check, Please!" *Time*, August 4, 1947, p. 10.

"Chest Expansion of an Airline." *Fortune*, April, 1945, p. 132.

"City Mourns as Death Comes to Mrs. H.R. Hughes." *Houston Post*, March 31, 1922, p. 5.

"Clears Howard Hughes." *New York Times*, July 16, 1936, p. 20.

"Come In, Come In, Wherever You Are!" *Time*, April 27, 1962, p. 84.

"Comeback." *Time*, September 23, 1946, p. 58.

"Comet-Like Flyer." *Literary Digest*, January 25, 1936, p. 33.

"Conflicting Testimony as to Hughes Signature Authenticity." *Daily Variety*, December 15, 1970, p. 20.

"Contact." *New York Times*, November 19, 1936, sec. 10, p. 7.

"Contact." *New York Times*, April 13, 1987, sec. 12, p. 9.

"Court Denies ABC Injunction Versus Hughes." *Variety*, July 11, 1968, p. 4.

"Court Refuses ABC Injunction; Goldenson Urges Reject Hughes." *Hollywood Reporter*, July 11, 1968, p. 1.

"Court Rules Against Claim for Fortune Left by Hughes." *New York Times*, December 30, 1980, sec. A, p. 6.

"Court Subpoenas Howard Hughes on ABC Stock Deal." *Hollywood Reporter*, July 12, 1968, p. 1.

"Court to Select Trustee for Hughes Interest." *New York Times*, July 14, 1983, sec. D, p. 15.

"Court Won't Call Hughes on ABC Offer." *Los Angeles Herald Examiner*, July 13,

1968, p. 8.

"Cousins of Howard Hughes to File Motion for New Trial." *New York Times*, December 13, 1981, p. 39.

"Credit Hughes' Presence for Nevada Casinos' $387 Mil Record Year's Profits." *Daily Variety*, July 15, 1968, p. 4.

"Deal on Hughes Casino Purchase Is Linked to 1970 Plea by Laxalt." *New York Times*, December 4, 1986, sec B, p. 25.

"Death 'Saddens' Vegas Publisher." *Houston Post*, April 6, 1976, Sec. C, p. 22.

"Did Hughes Leave Vegas on a Stretcher?" *Los Angeles Herald Examiner*, December 19, 1970, sec. A, p. 1.

"Dietrich, Summa Settle." *Houston Post*, December 16, 1976, sec. C, p. 7.

"Doctor Denies Hughes Got Hospital Care." *Los Angeles Times*, July 30, 1966, sec. 3, p. 3.

"Doctor Recounts Hughes's Last Day." *New York Times*, April 14, 1976, p. 17.

"Documentary on a Ghost." *Newsweek*, May 30, 1966, p. 95.

"Draw Papers for Hughes to Sell Entire Empire—Except RKO—for $400,000,000." *Daily Variety*, November 11, 1954, p. 1.

"Duel of Aces in Las Vegas." *Business Week*, July 12, 1969, p. 49.

"Duel Under the Klieg Lights." *Time*, August 18, 1947, p. 4.

"Electronic Blow-Off." *Time*, October 5, 1963, p. 91.

"Electronic Chicks." *Time*, October 17, 1955, p. 100.

"Elliot Tells of Loan; Claims 'Smear' Attempt." *Los Angeles Times*, August 5, 1947, p. 1.

"End of Air Fatalities by 1939 Is Forecast." *New York Times*, March 5, 1937, p. 23.

"Ennis Links Poulson with Hughes Aides." *Los Angeles Examiner*, March 28, 1957, sec. 1, p. 9.

"Enter Howard Hughes." *Life*, August 18, 1947, p. 38.

"Estate Will Auction Hughes Movie Rights." *New York Times*, September 29, 1976, p. 27.

"Ex-Howard Hughes Adviser Gets Prison Term in Obstruction Case." *New York Times*, August 25, 1979, p. 7.

"Ex-Hughes Aide Admits Role Against Oil Shipments." *Houston Post*, August 3, 1977, sec. B, p. 1.

"Ex-Hughes Aides Accused of Plot." *New York Times*, January 25, 1979, P. 16.

"Ex-Salesman Guilty in '74 Coast Theft of Hughes Papers." *New York Times*, April 23, 1977, p. 33.

"Exit Hughes." *Newsweek*, October 6, 1952, p. 83.

"Fabulous Team." *Time*, August 31, 1942, p. 19.

"Family Cook Held Spot Close to Hughes' Heart." *Houston Post*, April 10, 1976, sec A, p. 19.

"FCC Brakes Hughes ABC Bid." *Hollywood Reporter*, July 5, 1968, p. 1.

"FCC to Hold Hearings If Hughes Tool Closes Plan to buy 42% of ABC." *Wall Street Journal*, July 5, 1968, p. 1.

"FCC Will 'Examine' Hughes 'Qualifications' to Hold Control of ABC." *Variety*, July 5, 1968, p. 1.

"FDR's Son Challenges Meyer on Girl Issue." *Hollywood Citizen-News*, August 5, 1947, p. 1.

"FDR's Son Terms His Role 'Unimportant.'" *Hollywood Citizen-News*, August 4, 1947, p. 1.

"Federal Judge Told, in Tax Case, to Rule on Hughes's Residence." *New York Times*, October 28, 1980, p. 28.

"Fiction Apparently by Hughes Is Found." *New York Times*, May 2, 1976, p. 2.

"Figure in Hughes Case Arrested for Shoplifting." *New York Times*, August 1, 1977, p. 10.

"Files Shows Summa Chief Balked at Discussing Hughes's Medication." *New York Times*, July 13, 1977, p. 32.

"Film Director Cuts Air Time from Coast." *New York Times*, January 14, 1936, p. 3.

"Final Arguments Are Set on Reported Hughes Will." *New York Times*, May 9, 1978, p. 27.

"Finder of Hughes 'Will' Allowed to Leave Nevada." *New York Times*, January 24, 1977, p. 9.

"Finder of Hughes 'Will.'" *New York Times*, January 29, 1977, p. 9.

"Fine in Bogus Hughes Will." *New York Times*, February 11, 1984, sec A, p. 32.

"First Round Is Hughes's." *Newsweek*, February 22, 1954, p. 81.

"Flamboyant Privacy Hughes' Style." *Houston Post*, April 7, 1976, sec. A, p. 4.

"Flight: Hughes Makes Newark a 9-Hour Step from the Coast." *Newsweek*, January 25, 1936, p. 31.

"Flyer Rallies to Dictate Report on Crash Cause." *Los Angeles Times*, July 12, 1946, p. 1.

"Flying Award to Hughes." *New York Times*, May 27, 1940, p. 16.

"Flying Boat of Movie Man Under Quiz." *Los Angeles Herald-Examiner*, July 20, 1947, p. 1.

"Food Dropped by Plane to Five on Hughes Boat." *Los Angeles Times*, July 9, 1954, p. 1.

"Former Aide Says Hughes Wrote Will and Put It in Bank." *New York Times*, April 16, 1976, p. 25.

"Former Aide to Hughes Fails to Answer Subpoena at a Hearing on Estate." *New York Times*, October 7, 1976, p. 17.

"Former Cinema Plant Acquired for Brewery." *Los Angeles Times*, November 23, 1923, p. 14.

"Funeral for Hughes Will Be Wednesday." *Houston Chronicle*, January 15, 1924, p. 1.

"Gay Hughes Parties Told by Actress." *Los Angeles Herald-Examiner*, July 25, 1947, p. 1.

"General Tire Goes Hollywood." *Business Week*, July 23, 1955, p. 32.

"Glenn Odekirk Dead; Builder of Flying Boat." *New York Times*, January 15, 1987, p. 41.

"Good Fortune: Hughes Heir Keeping Candy Business Going until Millions Arrive." *Houston Post*, September 14, 1981, sec. A, p. 7.

"Governor Seeks Peace in Hughes Showdown." *Los Angeles Herald-Examiner*, December 8, 1970, p. 1.

"Grabbing Again for TWA Controls." *Business Week*, May 16, 1964, p. 168.

"H. Hughes $1 Mil LV Cultural Fund." *Hollywood Reporter;* January 6, 1969, p. 8.

"Handsome Hughes Was Ladies' Man." *Houston Post*, April 6, 1976, sec. A, p. 3.

"Handwriting Expert Calls a Hughes Will Authentic." *New York Times*, December 16, 1977, p. 18.

"Hanging Together." *Time*, August 16, 1976, p. 52.

"Having Hoped in Vain for a Chunk of Howard Hughes's Cash, Melvin Dummar Is Now Slinging Hash." *People*, September 29, 1986, p. 93.

"Head Injuries Transformed Hughes into 'Shattered Relic,' Doctor Says." *Houston Post*, April 22, 1986, sec. F, p. 12.

"Hear Skouras Renews Howard Hughes Deal." *Los Angeles Herald-Examiner*, September 30, 1954, p. 1.

"Hearing Friday in Hughes-ABC." *Los Angeles Herald-Examiner*, July 11, 1968,

sec. C, p. 4.

"Hearings to Begin on Hughes Estate." *New York Times*, July 12, 1981, p. 38.

"Heirs Will Divide the Hughes Estate, Newspaper Says." *New York Times*, August 16, 1976, p. 34.

"Help for the Line That Jack Built." *Time*, January 20, 1947, p. 66.

"Heron International." *New York Times*, July 14, 1982, sec D, p. 5.

"Hi-Yo, Silver." *Newsweek*, March 31, 1969, p. 64.

"High Court Bars a Suit Over Hughes Estate." *New York Times*, June 23, 1978, p. 10.

"Hold Last Rites for H.R. Hughes." *Houston Post*, January 17, 1924, p. 12.

"Howard (Robard) Hughes." *Current Biography*, 1941, p. 421.

"Howard al-Rashid." *The Nation*, May 15, 1976, p. 580.

"Howard Hughes (1905-1976)." *Las Vegas Business Press*, April 24, 2000, p. 19.

"Howard Hughes Able to Walk." *New York Times*, September 5, 1946, p. 22.

"Howard Hughes and Las Vegas." *Variety*, January 8, 1969, p. 2.

"Howard Hughes Biggest 20th-Fox Stockholder." *Hollywood Reporter*, November 27, 1956, p. 1.

"Howard Hughes Critical." *Los Angeles Times*, July 8, 1946, p. 1.

"Howard Hughes Flies Here." *New York Times*, September 12, 1946, p. 9.

"Howard Hughes Fails to Appear in Court On Antitrust Charges." *Wall Street Journal*, February 12, 1963, p. 4.

"Howard Hughes Gravely Injured in Crash on Test of New Plane." *New York Times*, July 8, 1946, p. 1.

"Howard Hughes Held in Motor-Car Death." *New York Times*, July 13, 1936, p. 11.

"Howard Hughes in Las Vegas." *Film & TV Daily*, March 9, 1970, p. 5.

"Howard Hughes in Plane Crash." *New York Times*, November 16, 1936, p. 15.

"Howard Hughes Improves." *New York Times*, July 20, 1946, p. 12.

"Howard Hughes Meets Tight Money." *Business Week*, December 12, 1970, p. 26.

"Howard Hughes Moves on Reno; Buys Harolds." *Hollywood Reporter*, May 18, 1970, p. 15.

"Howard Hughes Named in Suit for $1 Million." *Los Angeles Times*, January 19,

1962, sec. 3, p. 2.
"Howard Hughes Puzzle." Newsweek, January 15, 1968, p. 20.
"Howard Hughes Said in Bahamas." Los Angeles Herald-Examiner, December 3, 1970, p. 3.
"Howard Hughes to Build Plane Plant in Florida." Los Angeles Times, April 10, 1956, sec. 1, p. 8.
"Howard Hughes Testifies: 'Our Flight Doesn't Compare with Wiley Post's.'" Newsweek, July 25, 1938, p. 37.
"Howard Hughes To Sell His 75.18% Interest in TWA." Wall Street Journal, April 11, 1966, p. 18.
"Howard Hughes Vanishes at Vegas." Los Angeles Herald-Examiner, December 2, 1970, sec. A, p. 1.
"Howard Hughes Vs. Howard Hughes." Newsweek, January 24, 1972, p. 12.
"Howard Hughes Weds Jean Peters, Says N.Y." Hollywood Citizen-News, March 16, 1957, p. 1.
"Howard Hughes Weds Secretly." Los Angeles Mirror, March 16, 1957, p. 1.
"Howard Hughes' Wife at Hideaway." Los Angeles Herald-Examiner, October 29, 1966, p. 1.
"Howard Hughes' Firm Called Insolvent in Suit." Los Angeles Times, July 11, 1959, p. 6.
"Howard Hughes' Lucrative 'Beating.'" Newsweek, April 18, 1966, p. 75.
"Howard Hughes' Exit." Newsweek, July 25, 1955, p. 70.
"Howard Hughes' Messy Legacy." Time, October 3, 1977, p. 78.
"Howard Hughes—1937." New York Times, January 24, 1937, sec. 11, p. 9.
"Howard R. Hughes, Noted Business Leader, Dies While at Work in Office." Houston Post, January 15, 1924, p. 1.
"Hub Press Foiled By Gumshoe V.I.P." Variety, July 27, 1966, p. 1.
"Hughes Abandons Hotel Purchase; Justice Role Cited." New York Times, August 16, 1968, sec. 3, p. 1.
"Hughes Acquires Kattleman's 67-Acre Vegas Strip Property in $11-Mil Deal." Variety, January 1, 1969, p. 1.
"Hughes Agrees to Give Up TWA Control in New Pact." Los Angeles Times, October 8, 1960, p. 1.
"Hughes Aide Testifies to Removal of Maheu Boxes." Los Angeles Herald-Examiner, December 11, 1970, p. 1.
"Hughes Aides to Give Away a Grounded

Heirloom.'" New York Times, March 7, 1980, sec. A, p. 16.
"Hughes Air West Gets 'Shutdown Warning' from City." Los Angeles Herald-Examiner, October 28, 1970, sec. A, p. 7.
"Hughes and Brewster Exchange Charges." Los Angeles Times, August 7, 1947, p. 1.
"Hughes and Grant Fly On." New York Times, January 12, 1947, p. 2.
"Hughes Appeared 'Wasted.'" Houston Post, April 6, 1976, sec. A, p. 3.
"Hughes Asks 12 Million for Flying Boat Damage." Los Angeles Times, March 18, 1954, p. 1.
"Hughes Asks Dismissal, Resists Appearance." Aviation Week and Space Technology, August 14, 1961, p. 42.
"Hughes Asks Flight License." New York Times, August 14, 1936, p. 6.
"Hughes Bids 23 Million to Buy RKO." Los Angeles Times, February 8, 1954, p. 1.
"Hughes Breaks a Date in Fight for TWA." Business Week, February 16, 1963, p. 26.
"Hughes Buying Vegas Landmark for $17,300,000." Variety, October 25, 1968, p. 6.
"Hughes Buys 518-Acre Nevada Ranch From Ex-Wife of Krupp." Los Angeles Times, June 22, 1967, p. 3.
"Hughes Buys Into Teleprompter." Hollywood Reporter, May 8, 1967, p. 1.
"Hughes Called 'Man of Steel' by Physician." Los Angeles Herald-Examiner, July 11, 1946, p. 1.
"Hughes Charges PAA-TWA Rivalry Stirred Senate Probe." Aviation Week, August 4, 1947, p. 11.
"Hughes Charity." Aviation Week, January 18, 1954, p. 14.
"Hughes Companies Settle S.E.C. Suit." New York Times, January 20, 1979, p. 28.
"Hughes Consummates RKO Deal." Hollywood Reporter, April 1, 1954, p. 1.
"Hughes Continues to Improve." New York Times, July 15, 1946, p. 13.
"Hughes Corp. Empire Savior to Retire." Houston Post, January 18, 1990, sec. C, p. 4.
"Hughes Coup." Business Week, February 13, 1954, p. 33.
"Hughes Deal for Home Reported." New York Times, December 5, 1976, sec 1, p. 16.
"Hughes Death Believed Caused by Drug Excess." Houston Post, April 21, 1976, sec. A, p. 15.
"Hughes Defies Film Writers." Los Angeles

Times, March 28, 1952, p. 1.

"Hughes Denies $100,000 Offer to Lift Movie Ban." *Hollywood Citizen-News*, November 11, 1947, p. 1.

"Hughes Drops ABC Stock Bid." *Hollywood Reporter*, July 17, 1968, p. 1.

"Hughes Drops His Plan to Acquire Stardust, Vegas." *Daily Variety*, August 16, 1968, P. 8.

"Hughes Drops Plan to Buy Stardust after Federal Query." *Hollywood Reporter*, August 16, 1968, p. 3.

"Hughes Establishes Caltech Fellowship." *Los Angeles Herald-Examiner*, December 28, 1948, p. 1.

"Hughes Estate Is Valued at $460 Million by I.R.S." *New York Times*, March 8, 1981, sec. A, p. 22.

"Hughes Extravaganza." *Newsweek*, August 11, 1947, p. 22.

"Hughes Falcon Missile Hailed as U.S. 'Best.'" *Hollywood Citizen-News*, January 24, 1956, p. 1.

"Hughes Favored." *Los Angeles Herald-Examiner*, July 14, 1968, p. 17.

"Hughes Finally Acquires Site of Rancho Vegas." *Daily Variety*, June 8, 1970, p. 5.

"Hughes Flies 200_Ton Airplane at 95 M.P.H." *Los Angeles Times*, November 3, 1947, p. 1.

"Hughes Flying Boat Damaged." *New York Times*, March 1, 1949, p. 1.

"Hughes Fondly Recalled." *Houston Post*, April 6, 1976, Sec. C, p. 22.

"Hughes Forms Medical Research Foundation." *Los Angeles Times*, January 11, 1954, p. 1.

"Hughes Fought for Plane." *New York Times*, July 10, 1946, p. 25.

"Hughes Gambles on Las Vegas." *Business Week*, September 30, 1967, p. 80.

"Hughes Gives Ambulance." *New York Times*, March 23, 1940, p. 4.

"Hughes Gives Aviation a New Jolt." *Business Week*, May 19, 1956, p. 29.

"Hughes Halts Tool Firm Sale." *Los Angeles Herald-Examiner*, January 3, 1949, p. 1.

"Hughes Has Transfusion." *New York Times*, July 17, 1946, p. 25.

"Hughes Historian, Novelist, Soldier." *Los Angeles Herald-Examiner*, September 10, 1956, p. 1.

"Hughes Hopes to Fly at a 400-Mile Rate." *New York Times*, April 26, 1936, sec. 2, p. 1.

"Hughes in Air Record, Cracks Up." *Los Angeles Herald-Examiner*, September 19, 1936, p. 1.

"Hughes in Conference." *New York Times*, July 26, 1946, p. 19.

"Hughes Institute Will Use Sale's Proceeds on Research." *Wall Street Journal*, February 14, 1986, p. 2.

"Hughes Is Back." *Newsweek*, December 11, 1961, p. 84.

"Hughes Is Gaining." *New York Times*, July 16, 1946, p. 25.

"Hughes Is Reported at Acapulco Hotel." *New York Times*, February 13, 1976, p. 65.

"Hughes Kidney Ailment a Mystery to His Doctor." *New York Times*, December 24, 1977, p. 12.

"Hughes Kin Asks Jury to Act." *New York Times*, September 9, 1976, p. 15.

"Hughes Kin Reportedly Okay Split." *Houston Post*, June 19, 1977, sec. D, p. 3.

"Hughes Land in Arizona Sold." *New York Times*, May 16, 1982, sec A, p. 58.

"Hughes Lands in Ohio, Non-Stop from Coast." *New York Times*, August 11, 1936, p. 17.

"Hughes Leases on Tahoe." *Los Angeles Herald-Examiner*, July 8, 1970, p. 4.

"Hughes Leaves Hospital." *New York Times*, August 13, 1946, p. 31.

"Hughes Leaves More Mystery." *New York Times*, April 11, 1976, sec. D, p. 2.

"Hughes Levels New Charges in Pan American-TWA Feud." *Aviation Week*, August 11, 1947, p. 11.

"Hughes Loan Bid Denied by Meyers." *New York Times*, November 12, 1947, p. 1.

"Hughes Loans $8,000,000 to RKO." *Daily Variety*, September 24, 1952, p. 1.

"Hughes May Fly Again." *Business Week*, January 11, 1968, p. 32.

"Hughes May Testify at ABC Stock Hearing." *Hollywood Citizen-News*, July 5, 1968, p. 1.

"Hughes Mine Claims to be Sold or Leased." *New York Times*, January 8, 1977, p. 44.

"Hughes Near Death; Plan X-Ray Study." *Los Angeles Herald-Examiner*, July 13, 1946, p. 1.

"Hughes off the Hook." *Time*, February 11, 1974, p. 26.

"Hughes Often Talked About His Home." *Houston Post*, April 6, 1976, sec. A, p. 3.

"Hughes OK's Film, Ignores Triangle." *Los Angeles Mirror*, May 4, 1949, p. 1.

"Hughes Ordered to Appear Oct. 29." *Aviation Week and Space Technology*,

October 1, 1962, p. 32.
"Hughes Party-Tosser Hunted." *Los Angeles Daily News*, July 26, 1947, p. 1.
"Hughes Picked to Build 'Stationary' Satellite." *Los Angeles Times*, August 14, 1961, p. 1.
"Hughes Plane Set for Test Tomorrow." *Hollywood Citizen-News*, November 1, 1947, p. 1.
"Hughes Plane to British." *New York Times*, August 10, 1940, p. 6.
"Hughes Plant Slipshod, Claim; Meyer Flies Home." *Los Angeles Daily News*, July 31, 1947, p. 1.
"Hughes Probate Judge, a Mormon, Disqualified." *New York Times*, August 10, 1977, sec. D, p. 17.
"Hughes Pulls Out of ABC Contest." *Los Angeles Herald-Examiner*, July 17, 1968, p. 1.
"Hughes Quits 'Temporarily.'" *New York Times*, January 12, 1948, p. 16.
"Hughes Rebels." *Business Week*, May 4, 1946, p. 20.
"Hughes Regains Control Of RKO; Apparently Didn't Put Up a Cent." *Wall Street Journal*, December 15, 1952, p. 1.
"Hughes Report Snagged." *Houston Post*, July 27, 1976, sec. A, p. 1.
"Hughes Says Empire Sale Rumor Untrue." *Los Angeles Daily News*, November 12, 1954, p. 1.
"Hughes Says Plane Too Big for One Man." *Hollywood Citizen-News*, August 9, 1947, p. 1.
"Hughes Seen by Two Pilots as Worn Out." *New York Times*, April 6, 1976, p. 58.
"Hughes Seen Challenging TWA Award." *Aviation Week & Space Technology*, September 30, 1968, p. 30.
"Hughes Sets 347 M.P.H. Air Record, Foils Crash Death." *Los Angeles Times*, September 12, 1935, p. 1.
"Hughes Sets Mark Chicago to Coast." *New York Times*, May 15, 1936, p. 27.
"Hughes Sets Mark in Flight from Miami; Time Is Four Hours, 21 Minutes, 32 Seconds." *New York Times*, April 22, 1936, p. 1.
"Hughes Sez He's Alive and Kicking; Maheu Out of His Nev. Operations." *Variety*, December 9, 1970, p. 1.
"Hughes Shows 'Noticeable' Gain." *New York Times*, July 22, 1946, p. 23.
"Hughes Still Gaining." *New York Times*, July 24, 1946, p. 27.

"Hughes Still the Invisible Man." *Los Angeles Herald-Examiner*, October 28, 1962, p. 1.
"Hughes Story Goes into Act Two." *Life*, August 11, 1947, p. 34.
"Hughes Surviving Air Crash Injuries." *New York Times*, July 9, 1946, p. 15.
"Hughes Takeover Sports Net Inc. Spurs Step-Up." *Hollywood Reporter*, September 11, 1968, p. 8.
"Hughes Takes a Trick." *Business Week*, July 18, 1964, p. 27.
"Hughes Takes Off; Controversial Flying Boat." *Life*, November 17, 1947, p. 51.
"Hughes Testifies on Firing Jarrico." *Los Angeles Times*, November 21, 1952, p. 1.
"Hughes Tests Photo Plane; Sen. Cain 'Ground Observer.'" *Los Angeles Herald Examiner*, August 16, 1947, p. 1.
"Hughes to File for CAB Approval of Proposed Air West Purchase." *Aviation Week & Space Technology*, January 13, 1968, p. 26.
"Hughes to Fly Plane Like One That Crashed." *Los Angeles Times*, February 27, 1947, p. 1.
"Hughes to Get $25,000,000 Cash for RKO." *Los Angeles Mirror News*, July 19, 1955, p. 1.
"Hughes to Sell Helicopter Unit." *New York Times*, July 16, 1983, p. 30.
"Hughes to Show Solon Huge Flying Boat Today." *Los Angeles Daily News*, August 13, 1947, p. 1.
"Hughes Told to Show Why His Firm's Buying of ABC Can't Be Barred." *Wall Street Journal*, July 12, 1968, p. 9.
"Hughes Turns Down RKO Stock Offer." *Los Angeles Times*, December 16, 1954, p. 16.
"Hughes Upsets the Market." *Time*, February 15, 1954, p. 91.
"Hughes Views for Site of SST Airport." *Hollywood Citizen-News*, October 5, 1968, p. 18.
"Hughes Vs. Brewster: Last Chapter." *Aviation Week*, April 26, 1948, p. 14.
"Hughes Vs. Wright Field." *Aviation Week*, August 18, 1947, p. 12.
"Hughes Watched World on Film, Doctor Says." *Houston Post*, April 18, 1976, sec A, p. 15.
"Hughes Who." *Newsweek*, August 18, 1947, p. 15.
"Hughes Will." *New York Times*, December 14, 1982, sec. B, p. 18.
"Hughes Wins Second Court Round in

Fight for Control of ABC." *Wall Street Journal,* July 16, 1968, p. 4.

"Hughes Worse, Tells How Plane Crashed." *New York Times,* July 12, 1946, p. 38.

"Hughes Wouldn't Kick Drug Habit, Doctor Says." *Houston Post,* September 14, 1978, sec. C, p. 28.

"Hughes' $58 Million Flying Boat Still in Hangar." *Los Angeles Herald-Examiner,* January 19, 1963, sec. A, p. 5.

"Hughes' Death Pictured as Caused By Neglect." *Houston Post,* April 15, 1976, sec. A, p. 3.

"Hughes' Ex-Aide Fails to Show." *Houston Post,* October 7, 1976, sec. A, p. 8.

"Hughes' Fatal Condition Described." *Houston Post,* April 14, 1976, sec. A, p. 12.

"Hughes' Ghost V. the Wolves." *Time,* November 22, 1976, p. 78.

"Hughes' Jet Financing Hindrance Charged." *Aviation Week & Space Technology,* August 14, 1961, p. 42.

"Hughes' Jet Plan Rekindles Old Debate." *Aviation Week,* May 21, 1956, p. 41.

"Hughes' RKO Cleanup Reported Under Way." *Los Angeles Times,* July 10, 1948, p. 1.

"Hughes' Silence Is Major Issue in Merger." *Aviation Week & Space Technology,* February 4, 1963, p. 47.

"Hughes' TWA." *Business Week,* October 28, 1944, p. 60.

"Hughes' Views." *Business Week,* February 22, 1947, p. 31.

"Hughes' Wife to Ask for Divorce." *Los Angeles Herald-Examiner,* January 16, 1970, sec. A, p. 1.

"Hughes's 'Spruce Goose' Becomes Historic Site." *New York Times,* November 29, 1980, p. 10.

"Hughes's Air Record Accepted." *New York Times,* March 13, 1937, p. 3.

"Hughes's Death Laid to Massive Drug Use." *New York Times,* June 26, 1977, sec. A, p. 22.

"Hughes's Kin Challenge Claim to Inheritance." *New York Times,* December 1, 1976, sec. 1, page 18.

"Hughes's Mental State Put Under Study in Texas." *New York Times,* October 9, 1976, p. 6.

"Hughes's Plane Guarded." *New York Times,* January 24, 1937, sec. 2, p. 7.

"Hughes's Western." *Time,* February 22, 1943, p. 85.

"Hughes, Atlas Extend Northeast Discussions." *Aviation Week & Space Technology,* October 14, 1961, p. 50.

"Hughes, Bennett Meyers Testify on $200,000 Loan Proposal." *Aviation Week,* November 17, 1947, p. 14.

"Hughes, Here, Silent on His Flight Plans." *New York Times,* August 12, 1936, p. 12.

"Hughes, Riding Gale, Sets Record of 7-Hours in Flight from Coast." *New York Times,* January 20, 1937, p. 1.

"Hughes: Expert Quizzed on Signature." *Los Angeles Herald-Examiner,* December 15, 1970, sec. A, p. 1.

"Illnesses' Effect on Writing of Hughes Will Is Questioned." *New York Times,* September 23, 1976, p. 28.

"In with the Fuel Bill." *Time,* December 1, 1961, p. 87.

"In Xanadu Did Howard Hughes." *Newsweek,* January 7, 1974, p. 26.

"Injured Hughes Inventive." *New York Times,* August 14, 1946, p. 22.

"It Flies!" *Time,* November 10, 1947, p. 27.

"It's Never Say Die for Hughes." *Business Week,* January 12, 1963, p. 34.

"Jet Helicopter Wrecked." *New York Times,* June 23, 1950, p. 28.

"Jubilant Hughes Hops Off for Home; Ready to Resume Fight in November." *Los Angeles Daily News,* August 12, 1947, p. 14.

"Judge Backs Tax Pact on the Hughes Estate." *New York Times,* December 21, 1977, sec. B, p. 11.

"Judge Denies Attempt to Get Hughes in Court on ABC Bid." *Los Angeles Times,* July 13, 1968, p. 14.

"Judge Dismisses Suit by Woman Claiming to be Hughes' Kin." *Houston Chronicle,* February 17, 1993, sec. A, p. 18.

"Judge Dismisses Claims of Four to Hughes Estate." *New York Times,* July 14, 1981, sec A, p. 12.

"Judge Frees Hughes Aide in Mexico on Bail of $200." *New York Times,* April 13, 1976, p. 13.

"Judge in Nevada Orders Texas Not to Take Hughes Estate Funds." *New York Times,* October 30, 1977, p. 40.

"Judge to Enter Default Order Against Hughes." *Wall Street Journal,* Mary 3, 1963, p. 1.

"Jury Finds So-Called Mormon Will of Hughes a Fake." *New York Times,* June 9, 1978, p. 10.

"Jury in Las Vegas Begins Deliberation on

'Mormon Will.'" *New York Times*, June 8, 1978, sec. A, p. 18.

"Jury's Verdict on Heirs to Hughes Wipes Out 500 Relatives Claims." *New York Times*, September 5, 1981, p. 6.

"Krug's Woe Is a Tabloid Wow." *Life*, August 4, 1947, p. 26.

"Las Vegas Loses an Icon as Strip's Desert Inn Closes." *Los Angeles Times*, August 29, 2000, p. 1.

"Law Firm Sues Howard Hughes." *Los Angeles Times*, June 4, 1957, sec. 1, p. 5.

"Law Firm to Be Qualified in Hughes Case." *Houston Post*, July 19, 1978, sec. A, p. 23.

"Lawyer Asserts Ink on Hughes Will Matches That on Known Documents." *New York Times*, September 11, 1977, p. 24.

"Lawyer in Hughes Case Subpoenas Foes' Experts." *New York Times*, December 20, 1977, p. 20.

"Lawyer Suggests Dummar Had Role in Hughes 'Will.'" *New York Times*, December 1, 1977, p. 18.

"Lawyers Quiz Two Doctors Involved in Hughes Autopsy." *Houston Post*, October 28, 1976, sec. A, p. 28.

"Legal Dispute over Howard Hughes's Newly Profitable Empire Is Approaching Climax." *New York Times*, June 3, 1979, p. 14.

"Legal Heirs Win Round in Hughes Estate Case." *New York Times*, November 14, 1981, p. 16.

"Life Without Hughes." *Newsweek*, November 8, 1971, p. 88.

"Longtime Hughes Adviser to Leave Post at Summa." *New York Times*, February 18, 1978, p. 26.

"Lummis Is Upheld as Hughes Estate Administrator." *New York Times*, July 29, 1978, p. 7.

"Maheu Disputes Backers of Howard Hughes 'Will.'" *New York Times*, April 6, 1978, p. 18.

"Maheu Says He'll Depart on Direct Order By Hughes." *Daily Variety*, December 17, 1970, p. 1.

"Maheu Settles Defamation Suit Against Hughes; Details Secret." *New York Times*, May 31, 1979, sec. B, p. 14.

"Matters of Concern." *Time*, July 22, 1946, p. 46.

"McDonnell to Purchase Hughes Helicopter Unit." *New York Times*, December 17, 1983, sec A, p. 29.

"Medical Facility Is Beneficiary in New Purported Hughes Will," *New York Times*, June 13, 1976, p. 32.

"Memo Suggests Hughes Sought Watergate Role." *New York Times*, December 1, 1976, sec. 1, p. 18.

"Mergers: ABC's Dark Angel." *Newsweek*, July 12, 1968, p. 64.

"Merrill, Jean Batten Win Harmon Awards." *New York Times*, February 18, 1938, p. 21.

"Mexican Official Appeals Clearing of Hughes Aide." *New York Times*, April 20, 1976, p. 12.

"Midnight Sale." *Time*, October 6, 1952, p. 100.

"Minority Report Backs Hughes." *Aviation Week*, May 24, 1948, p. 10.

"Modern Ocean Flight." *Newsweek*, July 18, 1938, p. 17.

"Money at Work." *Time*, July 12, 1968, p. 64.

"Money Isn't Everything." *Time*, January 20, 1947, p. 86.

"Mouth Smashed, Sinatra to Perform at Caesars." *Hollywood Citizen-News*, September 12, 1967, p. 1.

"Mrs. Hughes Passes Suddenly Wednesday." *Houston Post*, March 30, 1922, p. 1.

"Nevada Bank to Act for Hughes Estate." *New York Times*, April 23, 1976, p. 70.

"Nevada Court Told Hughes Is Author of 'Mormon Will.'" *New York Times*, November 29, 1977, p. 19.

"Nevada Trial Set on Hughes 'Will.'" *New York Times*, August 28, 1976, p. 22.

"Never Met Hughes Face-to-Face— Maheu." *Los Angeles Herald-Examiner*, December 13, 1970, Sec. A, p. 1.

"New Crew for TWA." *Time*, October 17, 1960, p. 104.

"New Official Urged for Hughes Estate." *New York Times*, April 17, 1976, p. 24.

"New Purported Will Is Found in the Howard Hughes Case." *New York Times*, August 9, 1981, p. 24.

"New Stock Battle Seen over RKO." *Los Angeles Times*, May 14, 1955, p. 1.

"Newsmen See Hughes' Sanctuary of Research." *Los Angeles Times*, September 29, 1961, sec. 3, p. 8.

"Nine Hundred and Ninety-Nine Friends Will Get Medallions." *New York Times*, May 21, 1977, sec. A, p. 10.

"Nine Museums to Get Parts of Hughes's Flying Boat." *New York Times*, May 25,

1980, sec. A, p. 22.

"Nixon Data Show a Watergate Hint." *New York Times*, May 29, 1987, sec. A, p. 19.

"Nixon Lauds Hughes for Jarrico Case." *Los Angeles Times*, April 4, 1952, p. 1.

"Nothing Sensational." *Time*, January 27, 1936, p. 31.

"Odlum Asks Hughes to Settle RKO Management." *Los Angeles Times*, December 1, 1954, p. 1.

"Officials Raise Questions on Hughes's Alleged Drug Use." *New York Times*, June 29, 1977, p. 15.

"On Howard Hughes' Account." *Time*, September 27, 1968, p. 87.

"Pact Reported to Make Hughes Plane a Museum." *New York Times*, July 27, 1980, sec. A, p. 20.

"Pay Dirt." *Time*, August 11, 1947, p. 18.

"Personality: Howard Hughes, Man of Mystery and Wealth." *New York Times*, June 24, 1962, sec. 7, p. 1.

"Physician Who Treated Hughes Barred as Witness Without Patient's Consent." *Daily Variety*, December 18, 1970, p. 1.

"Plan to Name Administrator of Howard Hughes Estate." *New York Times*, April; 14. 1976, p. 16.

"Plane Expert Dodges Query on Elliott's Aid to Hughes in Contract." *Los Angeles Herald-Examiner*, July 29, 1947, p. 1.

"Pneumonia Hughes Peril." *Los Angeles Herald-Examiner*, July 10, 1946, p. 1.

"Potshot." *Newsweek*, June 12, 1961, p. 78.

"Power Struggle

"Pressure to Head Off Hughes Inquiry Charged." *Los Angeles Times*, July 26, 1947, p. 1.

"Print Tied to Man in Hughes 'Will.'" *New York Times*, December 29, 1976, p. 10.

"Project Jennifer." *Nation*, April 5, 1975, p. 389.

"Queries on Hughes 'Will' Continue." *New York Times*, January 28, 1977, p. 11.

"Record into Beet Patch." *Time*, September 23, 1935, p. 66.

"Record: Rebuilt Hughes Ship Lowers Transcontinental Time." *Newsweek*, January 30, 1937, p. 21.

"Red Hot Lollobrigida Strictly a Deep-Freeze Item to Howard Hughes." *Daily Variety*, September 15, 1954, p. 5.

"Refund of $455,972 Goes to Hughes on '45-46 Tax." *New York Times*, November 14, 1947, p. 3.

"Refusal Could Cost Licenses." *Los Angeles Herald-Examiner*, December 12, 1970, p. 1.

"Relative of Hughes Sues to Bar 'Will.'" *New York Times*, May 21, 1976, sec. B, p. 6.

"Render Unto Caesars." *Newsweek*, September 25, 1967, p. 32.

"Report Howard Hughes Wed." *Los Angels Herald & Express*, March 15, 1967, sec. A, p. 17.

"Report Howard Hughes on Verge of Buying Sports Network for $18-Mil and Taking Aim on Bigtime Events." *Variety*, August 28, 1968, p. 46.

"Report Hughes Wants Maheu Accounting of Operations." *Daily Variety*, December 11, 1970, p. 30.

"Republic Airlines Signs Airwest Pact." *New York Times*, June 10, 1980, sec. D, p. 5.

"Researcher Says 1946 Plane Crash Gave Hughes 30-Year Drug Habit." *New York Times*, August 30, 1979, p. 8.

"Rich Youth, Caddo Head, Bares Plans." *Film News*, November 12, 1927, p. 1.

"Richard Danner, Vegas Hotel Manager Who Gave Hughes' Cash to Nixon, Dies." *Los Angeles Times*, August 7, 1987, sec. 1, p. 38.

"Richest of American Men." *Time*, May 3, 1968, p. 72.

"Rise in Air Travel on U.S. Lines Near." *New York Times*, February 14, 1946, p. 27.

"RKO Approves a Deal." *Time*, February 22, 1954, p. 96.

"RKO Control Sought by Hughes." *New York Times*, January 15, 1948, p. 35.

"RKO Ownership Back to Hughes." *Daily Variety*, February 9, 1953, p. 1.

"RKO Takes Hughes $23,489,487 Offer." *Hollywood Citizen-News*, February 13, 1954, p. 1.

"RKO: It's Only Money." Fortune, May, 1953, p. 123.

"Roosevelt Presents Trophy to Hughes. New York Times, March 3, 1937, p. 18.

"Saddle Soar." *Time*, February 1, 1937, p. 62.

"Saga of the Spruce Goose." *Newsweek*, February 18, 1967, p. 39.

"Saving Face." *Newsweek*, January 22, 1973, p. 62.

"See Proxy Fight Ahead on Hughes' Air West Bid." *Variety*, August 14, 1968, p. 3.

"Senate Group Will Probe Hughes' Deals." *Aviation Week*, July 28, 1947, p. 12.

"Senate Probe of Hughes Ends Abruptly with Meyer Missing." *Aviation Week*, August 18, 1947, p. 11.

"Senator Charges FDR's Son 'Power' in Hughes Contract." Los Angeles Herald-Examiner, July 28, 1947, p. 1.

"Senators Row at Probe; Meyer War Record Hit." Hollywood Citizen-News, August 2, 1947, p. 1.

"Settlement in Hughes Estate." New York Times, May 26, 1983, sec. A, p. 14.

"Sharing the Stick." Time, February 24, 1947, p. 92.

"Shock Hinders Hughes in His Fight for Life." Los Angeles Herald-Examiner, July 9, 1946, p. 1.

"Shootout at the Hughes Corral." Time, December 21, 1970, p. 62.

"Silent on Plane Sabotage." New York Times, May 17, 1949, p. 8.

"Sixteen Cousins Declared Heirs to Hughes Estate." New York Times, August 11, 1981, sec. A, p. 18.

"Society." Houston Chronicle, June 2, 1925, p. 12.

"Society: Rice-Hughes Wedding." Houston Post-Dispatch, June 2, 1925, p. 16.

"Spruce Goose Gets Its Wings—to Star in Exhibit." Los Angeles Times, November 19, 2000, p. 16.

"Spruce Goose to Go on View." New York Times, November 21, 1983, sec 10, p. 3.

"Spyros Skouras in Vegas; Report Syndicate Offers Hughes $400,000,000 for His Empire." Daily Variety, September 30, 1954, p. 1.

"State Announces Replacement for Suspended Judge Gregory." Houston Post, March 13, 1993, sec. A, p. 26.

"Status of Hughes Estate a Mystery." Houston Post, April 6, 1976, Sec. C, p. 22.

"Stockholders Fight Hughes Sale of RKO." Hollywood Citizen-News, April 5, 1955, p. 4.

"Strike at T.W.A." Time, December 1, 1958, p. 72.

"Study of Mice Ties Chemical in the Brain to Overeating." New York Times, December 6, 1996, sec. A, p. 34.

"Stunt." Time, July 25, 1938, p. 37.

"Sturges and Hughes Disagree on Policy, End Partnership in California Pictures." New York Times, October 31, 1946, p. 22.

"Success Stories Plentiful." Houston Post, August 21, 1980, sec. A, p. 2.

"Summa Wins Reversal in Maheu's Libel Suit." Houston Post, December 19, 1977, sec. A, p. 9.

"Supreme Court Hears Two States in Hughes Case." New York Times, March 31, 1978, p. 14.

"Sure Thing." Time, July 25, 1938, p. 36.

"T.W.A. Creditors Sued by Hughes." New York Times, February 4, 1962, p. 45.

"Tailor-Made Bed." Scholastic, September 30, 1946, p. 29.

"Takeover Will Straitjacket Web, FCC Told." Variety, July 9, 1968, p. 1.

"Ten Hour Travel from Coast Seen by Hughes After Record Flight." New York Times, January 15, 1936, p. 21.

"Texas Courts Rebuffs Actress on Claim to Hughes's Estate." New York Times, December 19, 1982, sec. A, p. 56.

"Texas Judge Calls Recess in Howard Hughes Case." New York Times, November 22, 1977, p. 22.

"The $100,000 Coincidence." Newsweek, December 10, 1973, p. 37.

"The $23.5 Million Check." Time, April 12, 1954, p. 102.

"The Case of the Invisible Billionaire." Newsweek, December 21, 1970, p. 75.

"The Deal over RKO." Newsweek, May 17, 1948, p. 80.

"The Drug That May Have Killed Howard R. Hughes." New York Times, July 11, 1979, sec. B, p. 4.

"The Fabulous 'Falcon' that Can't Miss—Howard Hughes Hits the Mark." U.S. News & World Report, March 25, 1955, p. 16.

"The Great Submarine Snatch." Time, March 31, 1975, p. 20.

"The Heat on Mr. Las Vegas." Business Week, January 20, 1973, p. 42.

"The Heritage of a Silent Billionaire." Business Week, April 19, 1976, p. 38.

"The Hughes Caper." Newsweek, December 28, 1970, p. 56.

"The Hughes Connection." Newsweek, October 22, 1973, p. 52.

"The Hughes Connection." Time, October 22, 1973, p. 25.

"The Hunt for Howard Hughes." Newsweek, Mary 21, 1962, p. 71.

"The Invisible Hand of Howard Hughes." Fortune, November, 1968, p. 56.

"The King Is Dead, Long Live ESOP!" Forbes, November 1, 1976, p. 48.

"The Law." Time, June 27, 1977, p. 42.

"The Mechanical Man." Time, July 19, 1948, p. 38.

"The Missing Will." Time, June 27, 1977, p. 42.

"The Spruce Goose Will Take Off." New York Times, August 2, 1992, sec. 6, p. 3.

"There's Gold in Them Thar Losses!" *Saturday Evening Post*, April 17, 1954, p. 12.

"Third Aide to Hughes, a Doctor, Indicted on Drug Charges." *New York Times*, June 7, 1978, p. 16.

"Top County Aide Prefers Era of Hoods to Cloak of Hughes." *Daily Variety*, December 14, 1970, p. 1.

"Trippe's Big Bid." *Time*, December 28, 1962, p. 18.

"Trouble at RKO." *Time*, April 21, 1952, p. 104.

"Truman Cheers Hughes." *New York Times*, July 13, 1946, p. 17.

"Turbulence at TWA." *Time*, August 18, 1961, p. 66.

"Turnabout at TWA." *Newsweek*, August 21, 1961, p. 68.

"Turner Aims at Hughes Mark." *New York Times*, May 20, 1936, p. 2.

"Turner Plans New Speed Dash." *New York Times*, May 24, 1936, p. 2.

"TWA Completing Finance Plan; Hughes Passing Control to Trust." *Aviation Week*, October 17, 1960, p. 41.

"TWA Is Awarded Damages in Hughes Estate Lawsuit." *Wall Street Journal*, May 21, 1986, p. 55.

"TWA Loan Deal." *Business Week*, October 15, 1960, p. 68.

"TWA Names Hughes in $115-Million Suit." *Business Week*, August 12, 1961, p. 29.

"TWA's Financing Is Up in the Air Again." *Business Week*, August 13, 1960, p. 30.

"TWA: New Hands at the Helm." *Forbes*, July 1, 1961, p. 11.

"Twenty-Seven Claims to Estate of Hughes Are Rejected." *New York Times*, March 3, 1981, p. 5.

"Two Hughes Aides Change Pleas." *Houston Post*, September 12, 1978, sec. A, p. 2.

"Two More Heirs Named." *Houston Post*, September 17, 1981, sec. A, p. 25.

"Two More Hughes 'Wills' Filed." *New York Times*, June 3, 1976, p. 75.

"Two Seek Share of Hughes Estate." *New York Times*, November 7, 1976, sec. 1, p. 32.

"Two-Front ABC War on Hughes." *Variety*, July 9, 1968, p. 1.

"U.S. Judge Dismisses Suit on Taxes of Hughes Estate." *New York Times*, July 28, 1979, p. 6.

"U.S. Judge Doubts Forgery in Hughes's Affidavits." *New York Times*, October 13, 1977, p. 18.

"Unsigned 1944 Will Alleged." *New York Times*, March 31, 1978, p. 16.

"Up in the Air." *Time*, November 8, 1943, p. 83.

"Victory for Hughes." *Time*, January 22, 1973, p. 69.

"Waiting for Hughes." *Newsweek*, September 13, 1971, p. 92.

"We Like Mr. Hughes." *The New Republic*, July 20, 1938, p. 289.

"What's Behind the Big TWA Sale." *Business Week*, April 16, 1966, p. 145.

"When Will It Fly?" *Time*, January 21, 1946, p. 90.

"Where to Tax Hughes Estate." *New York Times*, June 15, 1982, p. 27.

"Where's Hughes?" *Newsweek*, April 23, 1962, p. 76.

"Who'll Get Hughes' Stock?" *Business Week*, February 17, 1951, p. 121.

"Whodunit: Tracing the Hughes Manuscript." *Business Week*, February 5, 1972, p. 24.

"Why Break In? Magruder Offers Answers." *New York Times*, November 23, 1987, sec. A, p. 14.

"With 'Mormon Will' Rejected, Taxes May Consume Hughes Estate." *New York Times*, June 10, 1978, p. 7.

"With Sincere Regards, Howard Hughes." *Life*, January 22, 1971, p. 24.

"World Flight for Hughes." *New York Times*, August 18, 1936, p. 15.

"Yes, Virginia City, There Is a Hughes; One Exec Saw Him!" *Variety*, December 16, 1970, p. 1.

"Zeckendorf Blasts Hughes' 'Unconscionable' Nixon Deal." *Daily Variety*, November 12, 1954, p. 1.

Alpern, David M. with Every Clark, Anthony Marro and Lloyd H. Norman. "CIA's Mission Impossible." *Newsweek*, March 31, 1975, p. 24.

Altman, Lawrence K. "'Forum' Urged to Clarify Cause of Hughes's Death." *New York Times*, April 26, 1976, p. 10.

Altman, Lawrence K. "Hughes Institute to Grow Bigger If Courts Back Purported Will." *New York Times*, May 1, 1976, p. 20.

Ashlock, James R. "Hughes Battles to Avoid Court Appearance." *Aviation Week & Space Technology*, February 11, 1963, p. 39.

Ashlock, James R. "TWA Will Seek Hughes Default Order." *Aviation Week &*

Space Technology, February 18, 1963, p. 49.

Asker, Jim. "Hughes Grave Visited." *Houston Post*, April 12, 1976, sec. A, p. 1.

Bacon, James. "Howard Hughes Makes News with an Eight-Year Eyesore." *Los Angeles Herald-Examiner*, July 3, 1969, p. 18.

Bacon, James. "Recalling Howard Hughes." *Los Angeles Herald Examiner*, December 16, 1970, sec. C, p. 1.

Bacon, James. "Story of Howard Hughes, Fabulous Figure in Life of U.S." *Los Angeles Herald & Express*, January 18, 1954, sec. A, p. 3.

Bangs, Scholer. "Hughes Answers Senate Probe with First Flying Boat Flight." *Aviation Week*, November 10, 1947, p. 11.

Banoff, Sheldon I. and Richard M. Lipton. "IRS Challenges, Law Firm's Mega Partnership with Howard Hughes's Heirs." *Journal of Taxation*, April, 1998, p. 250.

Barron, James. "Prime Seating." *New York Times*, April 17, 1998, sec. B, p. 2.

Barrs, Rick. "Annette Lummis, Hughes' Aunt, Dies." *Houston Post*, July 25, 1979, sec. A, p. 9.

Bates, William. "A Handful of Dust." *Harper's*, February, 1978, p. 30.

Beatty, Jerome. "A Boy Who Began at the Top." *American Magazine*, April, 1932, p. 34.

Beck, Paul. "Train Journey Violates Hughes' Cardinal Rule." *Los Angeles Times*, July 24, 1966, p. 1.

Beck, Paul. "Train Mystery Solved; Howard Hughes Aboard." *Los Angeles Times*, July 23, 1966, p. 1.

Beissert, Wayne. "Howard Hughes' 'Heirs' Defeated." *USA Today*, June 21, 1988, sec. A, p. 8.

Bird, David. "Notes on People." *New York Times*, April 14, 1977, sec. C, p. 2.

Bishop, Jerry E. "Hughes Medical Institute Is Expected to Use Funding from Sale of Its Aerospace Company to Double Spending." *Wall Street Journal*, June 6, 1985, p. 15.

Blackburn, Cliff. "'Bug' System at Hughes Hotels, Casinos Bared." *Los Angeles Herald Examiner*, December 16, 1970, sec A, p. 1.

Blackburn, Cliff. "Bare Story of Trip to Bahamas." *Los Angeles Herald Examiner*, December 17, 1970, sec. A, p. 1.

Blackburn, Cliff. "Battle Over Signature in Hughes Case." *Los Angeles Herald Examiner*, December 9, 1970, p. 1.

Blackburn, Cliff and Jack Brown. "Billionaire Declares He Fired Pair." *Los Angeles Herald Examiner*, December 8, 1970, sec. A, p. 1.

Blackburn, Cliff. "Hughes Sends Evidence; Bitter at Long Fight." *Los Angeles Herald Examiner*, December 10, 1970, p. 1.

Blackburn, Cliff. "Judge to Rule Saturday in Hughes Case." *Los Angeles Herald Examiner*, December 18, 1970, p. 1.

Blackburn, Cliff. "Residence Would Be Near Holdings." *Los Angeles Herald Examiner*, December 14, 1970, sec. A, p. 1.

Borders, Myram. "Hughes Buys 4th Las Vegas Casino." *Los Angeles Herald Examiner*, November 28, 1967, p. 1.

Botto, Louis. "Billionaire Howard Hughes Has a High Price on His Head." *Look*, October 29, 1968,

Boynoff, Sara. "Hughes Hides While U.S. Marshal Seeks." *Los Angeles Daily News*, August 1, 1947, p. 1.

Breo, Dennis. "Howard Hughes' Doctor Gives a Chilling Description of His Strange Patient's Final Hours." *People*, July 39, 1979, p. 64.

Broad, William J. "Institute Loses A Bid for Hughes's Billions." *Science*, February 20, 1981, p. 800.

Broad, William J. "The Tradition of Hughes Medical: Support of Superior Research." *Science*, February 20, 1981, p. 800.

Brooke, James. "Book Links Nixon to '72 Watergate Break-In." *New York Times*, September 24, 1984, sec B, p. 14.

Bush, Thomas W. "Hughes Bids $90 Million for Air West; Dispute Develops." *Los Angeles Times*, August 13, 1968, sec. 3, p. 9.

Bylinsky, Gene. "Hughes Aircraft: The High-Flying Might-Have-Been." *Fortune*, April, 1968, p. 101.

Byrnes, Nanette. "The Last Bequest of Howard Hughes." *Business Week*, July 24, 1995, p. 78.

Carlson, Peter. "A Startling Book Throws Light on Howard Hughes' Murky Politics." *People*, January 28, 1985, p. 57.

Carr, Stanley. "Judge Orders Lawyers to Report in 60 Days on Hughes Will Search." *New York Times*, January 18, 1977, p. 12.

Carr, Stanley. "Nevada Refuses Immunity to Hughes Will Claimant." *New York*

Times, January 22, 1977, p. 9.

Carr, Stanley. "Notes: Jet-Set Pets, a Growing Breed." *New York Times*, January 16, 1977, sec. 10, p. 5.

Carroll, Doug. "TWA Vs. Hughes $17.2M." *USA Today*, May 28, 1986, sec. B, p. 5.

Chapman, Betty T. "Hughes Tool: New Industry Was Forged in a Saga of Father and Son." *Houston Business Journal*, July 3, 1998, p. 22.

Chriss, Nicholas C. "Hughes Pact with Jean Peters Filed." *Los Angeles Times*, June 10, 1976, sec. 1, p. 20.

Christiansen, Richard. "Hughes' Life Is Perfect Foil for Shepard the Mythmaker." *Chicago Tribune*, September 24, 1967, sec. 2, p. 8.

Churchill, Douglas W. "Hollywood Legend." *New York Times*, December 15, 1940, p. 1.

Churchill, Douglas W. "The Gilded Lillian." *New York Times*, February 3, 1940, sec. 9, p. 5.

Clawson, Ken W. "Hughes Retained Firm to Keep Out the Mob." *Washington Post*, December 6, 1970, p. 15.

Cohen, Jerry and David Shaw. "Stretcher Story Adds to Hughes Mystery." *Los Angeles Times*, December 19, 1970, sec. 1, p. 1.

Cohen, Jerry. "Deputies Raid Howard Hughes Hotel Penthouse." *Los Angeles Times*, December 7, 1970, p. 1.

Cohen, Jerry. "Howard Hughes Mysteriously Disappears from Las Vegas." *Los Angeles Times*, December 3, 1970, p. 1.

Cohen, Jerry. "Howard Hughes Takes Over Hotel Suite on Bahamas Island." *Los Angeles Times*, December 5, 1970, p. 1.

Cohen, Jerry. "Hughes Firing Policy Blamed for Confusion." *Los Angeles Times*, December 12, 1970, p. 1.

Cohen, Jerry. "Story Behind the Hughes Mystery." *Los Angeles Times*, December 12, 1970, p. 1.

Considine, Bob. "More Hughes News." *Los Angeles Herald Examiner*, April 24, 1969, p. 3.

Cook, Robert H. "CAB to Demand Appearance by Hughes." *Aviation Week & Space Technology*, June 15, 1964, p. 39.

Cooke, Richard P. "Howard Hughes Seeks Merged Airline System, Risks Being Grounded." *Wall Street Journal*, April 23, 1962, p. 1.

Coulter, Bill. "Blood Tests Ruled Out in Hughes Heirs Case." *Houston Post*, August 15, 1981, sec. C, p. 11.

Coulter, Bill. "Bulk of Fortune Remains Tied Up." *Houston Post*, December 15, 1985, sec. A, p. 1.

Coulter, Bill. "Judge Determines Howard Hughes' Maternal Heirs." *Houston Post*, August 11, 1981, sec. A, p. 8.

Coulter, Bill. "Jury Finds Trio Heirs of Hughes." *Houston Post*, September 5, 1981, sec. A, p. 1.

Crewdson, John M. with Lawrence K. Altman and Nicholas M. Horrock. "Search for a Hughes Will Is Extended to 40 Cities." *New York Times*, April 22, 1976, p. 1.

Culliton, Barbara J. "Chopping Takes Reins at Howard Hughes." *Science*, September, 1987, p. 1406.

Culliton, Barbara J. "Fredrickson's Bitter End at Hughes." *Science*, June, 1987, p. 1417.

Culliton, Barbara J. "Hughes Settles with IRS." *Science*, March 13, 1987, p. 1318.

Dalton, Joseph. "The Legend of Hank Greenspun." *Harper's*, June, 1982, p. 32.

Davis, Al. "Hughes' Round-the-World Flight Captured Attention of Houston." *Houston Business Journal*, July 24, 1998, sec. A, p. 27.

Demaris, Ovid. "You and I Are Very Different from Howard Hughes." *Esquire*, March, 1969, p. 73.

Didion, Joan, and John Gregory Dunne. "The Howard Hughes Underground." *Saturday Evening Post*, September 23, 1967, p. 18.

Dietz, Lawrence. "Accused by Judge of Lying on Will, Alleged Hughes Heir Stands Firm." *New York Times*, January 26, 1977, p. 10.

Dietz, Lawrence. "Howard Hughes: The Hidden Years." *New York Times*, January 23, 1977, sec. 7, p. 2.

Dighton, Ralph. "Howard Hughes? Loves Privacy—Steals Spotlight." *Hollywood Citizen-News*, August 17, 1968, sec. 5, p. 1.

Dowling, A.V. "Hughes Using Air West to Test Government." *Los Angeles Herald Examiner*, August 13, 1968, p. 1.

Dullea, Georgia. "Students in Bronxville Give Howard Hughes a Will (81, in Fact) of Their Own." *New York Times*, June 6, 1976, p. 29.

Durslag, Melvin. "What Do You Do with

an $18,000,000 Check." *TV Guide*, October 25, 1969, p. 18.

Egger, Gerald. "Summa Corp. to Survive, Officials Say." *Houston Post*, April 7, 1976, sec. B, p. 1.

Fetridge, Robert H. "Sky Merger." *New York Times*, July 25, 1948, sec. 3, p. 3.

Fetridge, Robert H. "That Man Again." *New York Times*, November 12, 1948, sec. 3, p. 3.

Finston, Charles. "Probers Quiz Krug on Hughes' Lavish Wartime Parties." *Los Angeles Herald Examiner*, July 24, 1947, p. 1.

Flint, Ralph. "Here and There in Hollywood." *New York Times*, June 8, 1930, sec. 9, p. 6.

Flynn, George. "'We Expected Something Bigger.'" *Houston Post*, April 6, 1977, sec. A, p. 7.

Folkart, Burt A. "Edward Lund, Hughes' Co-Pilot, Dies." *Los Angeles Times*, November 22, 1988, sec. 1, p. 22.

Foote, Timothy. "The Object at Hand." *Smithsonian*, February, 1995, p. 20.

Footlick, Jerrold K. with Martin Kasindorf. "The Hughes Legacy." *Newsweek*, December 27, 1976, p. 63.

Fowler, Raymond D. "Howard Hughes: A Psychological Autopsy." *Psychology Today*, May, 1986, p. 22.

Fox, Fred W. "Out of the Past." *Los Angeles Mirror-News*, September 17, 1957, p. 14.

Fraker, Susan with Martin Kasindorf and John Barnes. "A Wealth of Wills." *Newsweek*, May 24, 1976, p. 30.

Fraker, Susan with Martin Kasindorf. "Heirs Apparent?" *Newsweek*, May 17, 1976, p. 40.

Francis, Warren B. "Advice to Halt Hughes Contract Said Ignored." *Los Angeles Times*, July 27, 1947, p. 1.

Francis, Warren B. "Meyers Attacks Hughes' Story of Job and Loan." *Los Angeles Times*, November 12, 1947, p. 1.

Francis, Warren B. "Senators Issue Hughes Subpoena." *Los Angeles Times*, August 1, 1947, p. 1.

Francis, Warren B. "Hughes' Offer of Refund Told Senate Probers." *Los Angeles Times*, November 7, 1947, p. 1.

Francis, Warren B. "Hughes' Concerns Face Tax Claim of $5,591,921." *Los Angeles Times*, November 6, 1941, p. 1.

Francis, Warren B. "Meyers Said 'Furious' at Rejection." *Los Angeles Times*, November 10, 1947, p. 1.

Freeman, William M. "Dick Hannah, a Publicity Man for Howard Hughes, 60, Dies." *New York Times*, January 17, 1976, p. 28.

Gambardello, Joseph A. "Now an Oil-Drilling Ship, *Glomar Explorer* Was Built to Recover Lost Subs." *The Philadelphia Inquirer*, August 16, 2000, p. 16.

Garrison, Glenn. "Counsel for Hughes, CAB Spar Over His Appearance at Hearing." *Aviation Week*, July 29, 1957, p. 98.

Gerber, Albert B. "Howard Hughes: The Story Behind His Las Vegas Empire." *Family Weekly*, July 28, 1968, p. 6.

Gordon, John Steele. "Businessmen's Autobiographies." *American Heritage*, May/June, 1995, p. 20.

Grady, Denise. "Engineered Mice Mimic Drug Use and Mental Ills." *New York Times*, February 20, 1996, sec. C, p. 1.

Graham, Marty. "Former Probate Judge Receives Year in Prison for Tax Evasion." *Houston Post*, November 10, 1993, sec. A, p. 1.

Green, Abel. "Hughes Woos Mayer as Indie." *Daily Variety*, May 7, 1952, p. 1.

Green, Michelle. "Hoping to Make a Comeback, Terry Moore Cashes in on Her New Role as Mrs. Howard Hughes." *People*, September 5, 1983, p. 34.

Greene, Andrea D. "Accused Judge Faces Disbarment If He's Convicted, Law Experts Say." *Houston Chronicle*, July 10, 1993, sec. A, p. 30.

Greene, Andrea D. "Commissioners Recite Lawyer Litany of Volunteers for Vacant Probate Bench." *Houston Chronicle*, July 13, 1993, sec A, p. 6.

Gregory, William H. "Battle Goes on Over Hughes' TWA Control." *Aviation Week and Space Technology*, May 7, 1962, p. 123.

Gregory, William H. "Hughes Faces Crisis on TWA Financing." *Aviation Week*, October 31, 1960, p. 35.

Haberman, Clyde and Albin Krebs. "Notes on People." *New York Times*, June 19, 1979, sec. C, p. 6.

Haberman, Clyde and Albin Krebs. "Notes on People." *New York Times*, July 11, 1979, sec. B, p. 4.

Haden-Guest, Anthony. "The Billionaire's Lover." *Harper's Bazaar*, August, 1984, p. 199.

Haitch, Richard. "Spruce Goose." *New York Times*, September 27, 1981, p. 49.

Hall, Mordaunt. "Exciting Air Battles."

New York Times, August 24, 1930, sec. 8, p. 5.

Hall, Mordaunt. "Sky Battles." *New York Times*, August 16, 1930, p. 8.

Hanson, Eric. "Protesters Cheer Suspension of Probate Judge." *Houston Chronicle*, March 12, 1993, sec. A, p. 22.

Harmetz, Aljean. "Suit Over a Hughes Will to Be Film." *New York Times*, December 11, 1978, sec. C, p. 17.

Hartt, Julian. "Hughes Gets Missile Site Pact." *Los Angeles Examiner*, February 17, 1961, p. 4.

Hensel Jr., Bill. "Court Enables Resumption of Wyatt-Sakowitz Battle." *Houston Post*, May 1, 1992, sec. A, p. 18.

Hensel Jr., Bill. "Judge in Wyatt-Sakowitz Court Battle Steps Down." *Houston Post*, May 12, 1992, sec. A, p. 1.

Hensel Jr., Bill. "Motion Seeks Reopening of Howard Hughes Case." *Houston Post*, January 19, 1992, sec. A, p. 20.

Hensel Jr., Bill. "New Turn in High Society Case." *Houston Post*, March 12, 1992, sec. A, p. 1.

Hensel Jr., Bill. "Sakowitz's Attorney Asks Appeals Court to Intervene in Lawsuit." *Houston Post*, March 25, 1992, sec. A, p. 16.

Herring, Hubert B. "Billable Decades: Howard Hughes, Untangled." *New York Times*, February 25, 1996, sec. 3, p. 2.

Hevener, Phil. "Autopsy Findings in Death of Hughes Normal." *Houston Post*, September 17, 1976, sec. A, p. 1.

Hevener, Phil. "Hospital Queried on Hughes Death." *Houston Post*, July 20, 1976, sec. A, p. 1.

Hevener, Phil. "Howard Hughes—Making Headlines from the Grave." *Houston Post*, April 3, 1977, sec. D, p. 2.

Hevener, Phil. "Hughes Cousin Met Billionaire Only Two Times." *Houston Post*, December 16, 1976, sec. C, p. 7.

Hevener, Phil. "Hughes Tax Report Fails to Satisfy Texas Comptroller." *Houston Post*, July 9, 1977, sec. A, p. 3.

Hevener, Phil. "Judge Plans to Review Hughes Autopsy Data." *Houston Post*, July 28, 1976, sec. A, p. 1.

Hevener, Phil. "Mexican Officials Considered Charges in Hughes Death." *Houston Post*, May 20, 1977, sec. A, p. 1.

Hevener, Phil. "Mishandling of Hughes Funds Alleged." *Houston Post*, June 20, 1977, sec. A, p. 1.

Hevener, Phil. "Polygraph Backs Hughes

Will Tale." *Houston Post*, August 10, 1977, sec. A, p. 1.

Hevener, Phil. "Psychic Used in Hughes Will Search." *Houston Post*, July 4, 1977, sec. A, p. 1.

Hevener, Phil. "Specialist Gets Call for Hughes Report." *Houston Post*, October 8, 1976, sec. A, p. 14.

Hevener, Phil. "Test Results Back Hughes Competency." *Houston Post*, April 15, 1977, sec. A, p. 5.

Hevener, Phil. "Texans to Examine Last Days of Hughes." *Houston Post*, June 23, 1976, sec. A, p. 1.

Hilchey, Tim. "Two Genes Identified in Heart Malfunction." *New York Times*, March 14, 1995., sec. C, p. 12.

Hill, Gladwin. "About 355 of 'Those Things' Have Exploded in Nevada." *New York Times*, July 27, 1969, sec. 6, p. 6.

Hill, Gladwin. "No-Man in the Land of Yes-Men." *New York Times*, August 17, 1947, sec. 7, p. 14.

Hodge, Shelby. "'Special' Case Stirs Hospital." *Houston Post*, April 6, 1976, sec. A, p. 3.

Holson, Laura M. "Hughes Electronics Recasts Itself as a Media Company." *New York Times*, October 23, 2000, sec. C, p. 16.

Hooper, Carl. "Hughes Tool Woodlands-Bound." *Houston Post*, July 18, 1991, sec. B, p. 1.

Hopper, Hedda. "Love Stirs Vitality in Quiet Jean." *Los Angeles Times*, July 11, 1954, sec. 4, p. 2.

Horrock, Nicholas M. with Lawrence K. Altman and John M. Crewdson. "Howard Hughes at the End: The Recollections Conflict." *New York Times*, April 21, 1976, p. 1.

Hughes, Howard. "Hughes Bares Rival Airline Row; Plane Builder Subpoenaed." *Los Angeles Herald Examiner*, August 1, 1947, p. 1.

Hughes, Rupert. "Howard Hughes: The Story of an Exciting Life." *Liberty*, February 6, 1937, p. 24.

Johnson, Stephen. "Judge Pleads Guilty to Tax Fraud." *Houston Chronicle*, July 9, 1993, sec. A, p. 1.

Johnston, Laurie. "Notes on People." *New York Times*, May 20, 1976, p. 33.

Kaiser, Jocelyn. "Med Schools Receive Hughes Windfall." *Science*, January 12, 1996, p. 138.

Kaufman, Ben. "Hughes Wins Third Court

Round." *Hollywood Reporter*, July 16, 1968, p. 1.

Keats, John "Howard Hughes: A Lifetime On the Lam." *True: The Man's Magazine*, May, 1966, p. 60.

Keerdoja, Eileen with Martin Kasindorf and Stephen H. Gayle. "The Hughes Estate." *Newsweek*, November 6, 1978, p. 22.

Kennedy, Bill. "The Hughes Caper." *Los Angeles Herald Examiner*, September 18, 1968, p. 34.

Kennedy, Tom. "1961 'Hughes Will' Names Judge Who Wasn't." *Houston Post*, May 8, 1976, sec. A, p. 4.

Kennedy, Tom. "Supervision Okayed for Hughes Estate." *Houston Post*, April 15, 1976, sec. A, p. 3.

Kihss, Peter. "Hughes Attendants Say the Billionaire Was Used by Aides." *New York Times*, January 11, 1977, p. 20.

Kirk, Christina. "Howard Hughes: What's He Up To?" *Los Angeles Herald Examiner*, October 25, 1970, sec. A, p. 6.

Kirk, Christina. "Setting Sights on TV and Satellites." *Los Angeles Herald Examiner*, October 26, 1970, sec. A, p. 6.

Klass, Philip. "Hughes Takes Wraps Off Avionics Giant." *Aviation Week*, May 25, 1953, p. 14.

Kleiner, Dick. "Would He End Gambling?" *Hollywood Citizen-News*, March 16, 1968, p. 7.

Klemin, Alexander. "The World's Fastest Landplane." *Scientific American*, December, 1935, p. 321.

Kliewer, Terry. "Hughes Recalled by Pilot's Widow." *Houston Post*, April 7, 1976, sec. A, p. 4.

Kliewer, Terry. "Mystery Figure Howard Hughes, 70, Dies." *Houston Post*, April 6, 1976, sec. A, p. 1.

Knickerbocker, Cholly. "Call Beauties in Hughes Quiz." *Los Angeles Herald Examiner*, July 22, 1947, p. 1.

Kotkin, Joel. "Interesting, But It Doesn't Explain His 7" Toenails." *New Times*, August 7, 1978, p. 15.

Koziol, Ronald. "Hughes, Vegas Still Together." *Chicago Tribune*, February 8, 1988, sec. 4, p. 1.

Krebs, Albin. "Jean Peters." *New York Times*, February 2, 1978, sec C, p. 2.

Lawrence, John F. and Arelo Sederberg. "Hughes Ends Buying Phase, Maps Development Plans." *Los Angeles Times*, November 11, 1968, p. 12.

Ledgard, Laurie. "Government Expands Gregory Case." *Houston Post*, March 16, 1993, sec. A, p. 1.

Ledgard, Laurie. "Gregory Pleads Innocent in U.S. Court." *Houston Post*, March 25, 1993, sec. A, p. 25.

Lee, John M. "Pan American and T.W.A. Approve Plan for Merger." *New York Times*, December 21, 1962, p. 1.

Lehmann-Haupt, Christopher. "You Can't Buy Happiness." *New York Times*, January 10, 1977, p. 19.

Lenzner, Robert. "Thanks, Cousin Howard." *Forbes*, November 4, 1996, p. 88.

Lewis, Craig. "CAB Investigates Hughes-Northeast Link." *Aviation Week*, October 8, 1956, p. 45.

Lindsey, Robert. "'Spruce Goose' Is Donated to Business Group for a Museum." *New York Times*, July 15, 1977, sec. B, p. 1.

Lindsey, Robert. "Cousin Says Hughes Sent a Will to Bank in '38, but It's Missing." *New York Times*, April 27, 1976, p. 42.

Lindsey, Robert. "Ex-Aide Files Suit on Hughes Book." *New York Times*, April 24, 1985, sec. B, p. 32.

Lindsey, Robert. "Small Staff Runs Hughes's Summa Corp." *New York Times*, April 7, 1976, p. 61.

Lindsey, Robert. "Three Relatives of Hughes Join Will Dispute." *New York Times*, April 28, 1976, p. 31.

Linkin, Barbara. "Judge Previously Accused of Wrongdoing." *Houston Post*, March 11, 1993, sec. A, p. 27.

Linkin, Barbara. "Judge Removes Self from Bench after Indictment." *Houston Post*, March 12, 1993, sec. A, p. 23.

Loddeke, Leslie. "Hughes Auction 'Quite a Cool Deal.'" *Houston Post*, February 20, 1989, sec. A, p. 4.

Loddeke, Leslie. "R.I.P., Howard Hughes." *Houston Post*, May 19, 1985, sec. A, p. 13.

Long, Ari. "Nevada Atty.-Gen. Asks Ceiling On Number of Casinos One Man Can Own." *Daily Variety*, February 2, 1968, p. 14.

Loving, Jr., Rush. "The View from Inside Hughes Tool." *Fortune*, December, 1973, p. 106.

Lubove, Seth. "Living Long Is the Best Revenge." *Forbes*, April 22, 1996, p. 147.

Lukas, J. Anthony. "The Hughes Connection." *New York Times*, January 4,

1976, p. 8.

Luque, Sulipsa. "Convicted Judge Bids Staff Goodbye." *Houston Post*, July 10, 1993, sec. A, p. 1.

Luque, Sulipsa. "Judge Pleads Guilty to Tax Charge." *Houston Post*, July 9, 1993, sec. A, p. 1.

Lyman, Rick. "Jean Peters, Actress of the 50's, Dies at 73." *New York Times*, October 21, 2000, sec. B, p. 8.

Lyons, D.L. "America's Richest Wife." *Ladies' Home Journal*, November, 1968, p. 100.

Lyons, D.L. "The Liberation of Mrs. Howard Hughes." *Ladies' Home Journal*, March, 1971, p. 112.

Main, Dick. "Robert Maheu Able Opponent in Hughes Row." *Los Angeles Times*, December 10, 1970, Sec. A, p. 3.

Makeig, John and Earnest L. Perry. "Probate Judge Gregory Charged with Felony Theft." *Houston Chronicle*, March 10, 1993, sec. A, p. 1.

Manners, Dorothy. "New Hughes Book." *Los Angeles Herald Examiner*, June 29, 1970, p. 35.

March, Joseph Moncure. "About 'Hell's Angels.'" *Look*, March 23, 1954, p. 14.

Mayer, Allan J. with Martin Kasindorf. "The Hughes Legacy." *Newsweek*, August 16, 1976, p. 60.

McCormick, Robert. "Wing Talk." *Collier's*, October 18, 1942, p. 8.

McDonald, John. "Howard Hughes's Biggest Surprise." *Fortune*, July 1, 1966, p. 119.

McDonald, John. "T.W.A.: The Struggle for the Corporate Cockpit." *Fortune*, May, 1965., p. 107.

McGrath, Anne. "Collectors." *Forbes*, October 1, 1984, p. 228.

McKinlay, Colin. "Howard Hughes Reportedly Ill at Las Vegas Hotel." *Los Angeles Times*, December 1, 1966, p. 1.

McKinlay, Colin. "Hughes Vegas Empire Expands in Airport Area." *Los Angeles Times*, September 2, 1968, p. 11.

Miles, Marvin. "Automatic Jet Pilot Developed." *Los Angeles Times*, October 6, 1955, sec. 1, p. 1.

Morgan, Ted. "Poor Big Rich Man." *New York Times*, May 6, 1979, sec. 7, p. 3.

Morganthau, Tom with Margaret Garrard Warner. "Biography of a Billionaire." *Newsweek*, January 28, 1985, p. 33.

Moskal, Jerry. "IRS Tags Hughes' Heirs for $35.5 Million." *Las Vegas Business Press*,

July 5, 1999, p. 6.

Muir, Florabel. "Hughes Secretly Signs Jean Peters as Bride." *New York Daily News*, March 16, 1957, p. 3.

Murphy, Charles J.V. "The Blowup at Hughes Aircraft." *Fortune*, February, 1954, p. 116.

Murphy, Charles J.V., and T.A. Wise. "The Problem of Howard Hughes." *Fortune*, January, 1959, p. 79.

Newman, Barry. "Behind the *Glomar* Sub Hunt." *The Nation*, October 11, 1975, p. 329.

Nichols, Robert E. "Battle of the Billionaires: Howard Hughes Plays 'David' in Fight for Control of TWA." *Los Angeles Times*, February 18, 1962, sec. 4, p. 1.

Nichols, Robert E. "Feeder Lines Vital Pawns in TWA Battle." *Los Angeles Times*, February 22, 1962, sec. 4, p. 1.

Nichols, Robert E. "Hughes' Future with TWA Up to Judge." *Los Angeles Times*, February 25, 1962, p. 1.

Nichols, Robert E. "Howard Hughes Flies High in Films, Finance." *Los Angeles Times*, February 19, 1962, sec. 4, p. 1.

Nichols, Robert E. "Hughes: From Little Bits, a Mighty Fortune." *Los Angeles Times*, February 20, 1962, sec. 4, p. 1.

Nichols, Robert E. "Hughes: Oil and Air an Explosive Mixture." *Los Angeles Times*, February 21, 1962, sec. 4, p. 1.

Nichols, Robert E. "Upheaval at General Dynamics, Battle to Control TWA Linked." *Los Angeles Times*, February 23, 1962, sec. 4, p. 10.

O'Connor, John J. "TV: Howard Hughes Saga." *New York Times*, April 13, 1977, sec. C, p. 26.

O'Hanlon, Thomas. "The High Rollers Shoot for Power in Las Vegas." *Fortune*, January, 1971, p. 36.

O'Lone, Richard G. "Hughes Faces Battle in Bid for Air West." *Aviation Week & Space Technology*, August 19, 1968, p. 26.

O'Neil, Thomas F. "Why I Bought RKO." *Film Bulletin*, August 8, 1955, p. 7.

Olafson, Steve. "Hughes' Office Items on the Block Today." *Houston Post*, April 17, 1993, sec. B, p. 1.

Ornstein, Bill. "ABC Fights Hughes Stock Bid." *Hollywood Reporter*, July 3, 1968, p. 1.

Ornstein, Bill. "Howard Hughes Bids for ABC." *Hollywood Reporter*, July 2, 1968, p. 1.

Othman, Frederick. "The 21 Million Dollar Question." *Hollywood Citizen-News*, August 2, 1947, p. 1.

Overton, Tom. "Howard Hughes' Mysterious S-43." *Houston Post*, October 19, 1980, sec. BB, p. 1.

Parsons, Louella O. "In Hollywood with Louella O. Parsons" *Los Angeles Examiner*, April 8, 1951, p. 16.

Parsons, Louella O. "Jean Peters, Who Leaped to Stardom, Plans Divorce." *Los Angeles Herald Examiner*, September 13, 1955, sec. 4. p. 1.

Parsons, Louella O. "Hughes Deal Confirmed by Skouras." *Los Angeles Examiner*, May 18, 1958, p. 32.

Phelan, James R. "Howard Hughes, Beyond the Law." *New York Times*, September 14, 1975, sec. 6, p. 14.

Phelan, James R. "Howard Hughes: He Is Battling for Control of a Billion-Dollar Empire." *Saturday Evening Post*, February 6, 1963, p. 19.

Piersol, James V. "Air Currents." *New York Times*, November 28, 1937, sec. 12, p. 6.

Pillar, Ruth. "Panel on Ethics Suspends Judge from His Post." *Houston Chronicle*, March 12, 1993, sec. A, p. 21.

Piller, Ruth and John Makeig. "Gregory Suspends Himself." *Houston Chronicle*, March 11, 1993, sec. A, p. 1.

Pitman, Jack. "Hughes Fails to Obtain Control of ABC; Drops Effort; To Return Shares." *Daily Variety*, July 17, 1968, p. 1.

Quigley Jr., Martin. "Hughes Reconsiders." *Motion Picture Herald*, April 23, 1955, p. 4.

Reese, Michael with Ronald Henkoff. "The Hughes Treasure Hunt." *Newsweek*, September 14, 1981, p. 34.

Reeves, Monica. "Hughes Buried Near His Parents in Brief, Simple Ceremony." *Houston Post*, April 8, 1976, sec. A, p. 1.

Reeves, Monica. "Hughes' Life Began, Ended in Greenbacks." *Houston Post*, April 6, 1976, sec. A, p. 3.

Reeves, Monica. "Hughes' Youth Recalled." *Houston Post*, April 7, 1976, sec. A, p. 1.

Reeves, Monica. "Kidney Failure Killed Hughes." *Houston Post*, April 7, 1976, sec. A, p. 1.

Regan, Mary Beth. "A Research Behemoth Gets Even Bigger." *Business Week*, February 21, 1994, p. 56.

Rich, Allen. "If Howard Hughes Should Buy ABC-TV." *Hollywood Citizen-News*, July 10, 1968, sec. D, p. 12.

Riding, Alan "Mexico Accuses Aide to Hughes of Falsifying His Tourist Card." *New York Times*, April 11, 1976, p. 31.

Riding, Alan. "At Hughes Hotel, a Sense of Disbelief." *New York Times*, April 7, 1976, p. 18

Riding, Alan. "Mexican Police Say Aide Forged Hughes's Name." *New York Times*, April 10, 1976, p. 25.

Rill, Derrick. "'Flying Penthouse' May Return to City, This Time Via the Sea." *Houston Post*, March 11, 1991, sec. A, p. 13.

Rogers, Bogart. "4 Million Dollars and 4 Men's Lives." *Photoplay*, April, 1930, p. 30.

Rogers, Frank. "Angry Elliott Hurls Challenge to Senators." *Los Angeles Daily News*, August 4, 1947, p. 1.

Rogers, Frank. "Hughes Lines Up Parade of Witnesses." *Los Angeles Daily News*, November 9, 1947, p. 1.

Rogers, Frank. "Kaiser Angrily Charges 'Brush-Off' at Plane Quiz." *Los Angeles Daily News*, July 29, 1947, p. 1.

Rogers, Frank. "Solons Told Gen. Arnold Gave Hughes Plane Order." *Los Angeles Daily News*, August 1, 1947, p. 1.

Saxon, Wolfgang. "Hughes Relatives Reported Agreed on Dividing Estate." *New York Times*, June 20, 1977, p. 16.

Schallert, Edwin. "Howard Hughes' Interest in RKO Studios Sold." *Los Angeles Times*, September 23, 1952, p. 1.

Scharff, Edward E., and Michael Moritz. "Summa Comes Back from Debacle." *Time*, October 6, 1960, p. 82.

Schary, Dore. "I Remember Hughes." *New York Times*, May 2, 1976, sec. 6, p. 42.

Schieb, Mary Jane. "Renal Deaths Common." *Houston Post*, April 7, 1976, sec. A, p. 4.

Scibilia, Leon F. "Hughes Buying Hint Spurs Columbia Stock." *Los Angeles Herald Examiner*, May 4, 1967, p. 8.

Sederberg, Arelo. "Howard Hughes Empire Rising with Purchases in Las Vegas." *Los Angeles Times*, September 17, 1967, p. 1.

Sederberg, Arelo. "Hughes Sinks Another $55 Million in Vegas." *Los Angeles Times*, August 27, 1969, p. 9.

Sederberg, Arelo. "Hughes' ABC Quest Raised Question of Public Appearance." *Los Angeles Times*, July 8, 1968, p. 1.

Shearer, Lloyd. "Howard Hughes: Hollywood Outlaw." *Pageant*, August, 1946, p. 14.

Sherrill, Robert. "A Will, But No Way." *New York Times*, September 7, 1980, sec. G, p. 7.

Shirley, Bill. "$13 Million Buys Desert Inn but Not Tourney." *Los Angeles Times*, March 20, 1967, sec. 3, p. 5.

Smith, Liz. "If Women Didn't Exist." *Newsday*, November 24, 2000, p. 4.

Smith, Robert M. "G.S.A. Says It Held Title to Plane in Hughes 'Will.'" *New York Times*, May 4, 1976, p. 1.

Smith, Robert M. "Three Hughes Aides Quizzed about Customs Matters." *New York Times*, April 9, 1976, p. 42.

Sorel, Nancy Caldwell. "Ingrid Bergman and Howard Hughes." *Atlantic Monthly*, September, 1993, p. 87.

St. Johns, Adela Rogers. "Unmarried Millionaires: Howard Hughes" *American Weekly*, April 6, 1947, p. 24.

Star, Jack. "Why Is Howard Hughes Buying Up Las Vegas?" *Look*, January 24, 1968, p. 69.

Sterba, James P. "Caretakers Named for Hughes Affairs." *New York Times*, April 15, 1976, p. 1.

Sterba, James P. "Cause of Hughes's Death Is Given as Kidney Failure." *New York Times*, April 7, 1976, p. 18.

Sterba, James P. "Howard Hughes Dies at 70 on Flight to Texas Hospital." *New York Times*, April 6. 1976, p. 1

Sterba, James P. "Hughes Is Buried in Brief Ceremony." *New York Times*, April 8, 1976, p. 48.

Sterba, James P. "Life of Howard Hughes Was Marked by a Series of Bizarre and Dramatic Events." *New York Times*, April 6, 1976, p. 53.

Sterngold, James. "Twenty Years after Howard Hughes Died, His Empire Ends." *New York Times*, February 23, 1996, sec. D, p. 4.

Sterngold, James. "Vast New DreamWorks Film Lot." *New York Times*, December 14, 1995, sec C, p. 11.

Stingley, Jim. "Attempt to 'Bug' Hughes' Hotel Fails." *Los Angeles Times*, December 19, 1970, p. 1.

Stingley, Jim. "Hughes Is a Mystery in the Bahamas, Too." *Los Angeles Times*, December 14, 1970, p. 33.

Stump, Al. "The Rich Man's Game." *Golf*, December, 1991, p. 62.

Sutherland, Henry. "Howard Hughes' Wife Says She Will File Suit for Divorce." *Los Angeles Times*, January 16, 1970, sec. A, p. 1.

Taylor, Gary. "Lawyer Still Clings to Part of Mystery of 'Mormon Will.'" *Houston Post*, September 23, 1979, sec. A, p. 19.

Theis, William. "Air Force General Admits $4,000,000 Deal in War Bonds." *Los Angeles Examiner*, November 13, 1947, p. 1.

Theis, William. "Hughes Asks Rival Aviation Firm Be Probed by Senate." *Los Angeles Examiner*, November 11, 1947, p. 1.

Thompson, Thomas. "Riddle of an Embattled Phantom." *Life*, September 7, 1962, p. 20.

Tinnin, David B. "Hughes Aircraft Up for Grabs." *Fortune*, December 12, 1983, p. 158.

Torgerson, Dial and Jerry Cohen. "Hughes in Control, Gov. Laxalt Says." *Los Angeles Times*, December 8, 1970, sec. A, p. 1.

Torgerson, Dial. "Howard Hughes' Old Guard Stages Coup in Power Fight." *Los Angeles Times*, December 6, 1970, p. 1.

Torgerson, Dial. "Hughes Assistant Gives First Details of Recluse's Life." *Los Angeles Times*, December 15, 1970, p. 1.

Torgerson, Dial. "Hughes Letter Backing Tool Co. Verified by Handwriting Expert." *Los Angeles Times*, December 11, 1970, p. 1.

Torgerson, Dial. "Hughes Reported Seen Leaving Desert Inn." *Los Angeles Times*, December 14, 1970, sec. A, p. 1.

Torgerson, Dial. "Letter Doesn't Match Hughes Handwriting, Expert Testifies." *Los Angeles Times*, December 13, 1970, p. 1.

Torgerson, Dial. "Maheu Charges Show Scope of Battle for Hughes Empire." *Los Angeles Times*, December 9, 1970, Sec. A, p. 1.

Torgerson, Dial. "Man Paid as Guard Describes Possible Hughes Departure." *Los Angeles Times*, December 16, 1970, p. 1.

Torgerson, Dial. "Promised a Lifetime Job, Maheu Testifies." *Los Angeles Times*, December 17, 1970, sec. A, p. 3.

Torgerson, Dial. "Ruling on Hughes' Empire Awaited as Testimony Ends." *Los Angeles Times*, December 18, 1970, p. 1.

Torgerson, Dial. "Settlement Reported Near in Struggle for Hughes Empire." *Los Angeles Times*, December 10, 1970, p. 1.

Townsend, Dorothy. "Hughes Aide Maheu Files Suit over Best-Seller." *Los Angeles*

Times, April 28, 1985, sec. 2, p. 3.

Tucker, Ray. "News Behind the News." *Hollywood Citizen-News*, August 4, 1947, p. 1.

Turner, Wallace. "'Billionaire' Hughes's Wealth Put at Only $168,824,615." *New York Times*, March 16, 1977, p. 1.

Turner, Wallace. "A Hughes Unit Plans a Biography after Long Efforts at Suppression." *New York Times*, February 11, 1977, sec. D, p. 13.

Turner, Wallace. "Accused by Judge of Lying on Will, Alleged Hughes Heir Stands Firm." *New York Times*, January 26, 1977, p. 10.

Turner, Wallace. "Aide Who Resided with Hughes to Be Questioned in Suit on Will." *New York Times*, October 6, 1976, p. 20.

Turner, Wallace. "Aides Blocked Hughes Plan to Reorganize Empire." *New York Times*, August 21, 1977, p. 1.

Turner, Wallace. "All the Hughes That's Fit to Print." *Esquire*, July, 1971, p. 64.

Turner, Wallace. "Appeals Court Reinstates Hughes Case Indictments." *New York Times*, May 12, 1976, p. 68.

Turner, Wallace. "Aunt and Cousin Will Get Fees from Hughes Estate." *New York Times*, May 23, 1978, p. 16.

Turner, Wallace. "Bank of America Had Hughes Stock." *New York Times*, May 6, 1976, p. 1.

Turner, Wallace. "Battle Over Hughes Estate Opens in a Courtroom in Las Vegas." *New York Times*, May 12, 1976, p. 17.

Turner, Wallace. "California Assembly Delays Deal on Hughes Estate Tax." *New York Times*, July 7, 1984, p. 6.

Turner, Wallace. "Casino Sale Seen as Step to Liquidation of Hughes Gaming Interests." *New York Times*, January 16, 1978, p. 19.

Turner, Wallace. "Consent Decree Ends S.E.C.'s Air West Case." *New York Times*, May 13, 1980, sec. D, p. 13.

Turner, Wallace. "Court Proceedings Focus Attention on Howard Hughes's 'Lost' Will of 1938." *New York Times*, January 9, 1977, p. 26.

Turner, Wallace. "Court Report on Hughes Shows He Toyed with Staff on Will Revision." *New York Times*, March 19, 1977, p. 8.

Turner, Wallace. "Courts Are Told about Appraisal in Hughes Case." *New York*

Times, May 12, 1977, sec. A, p. 18.

Turner, Wallace. "Details of the Private Life of Howard Hughes Will Be Disclosed in a Book." *New York Times*, July 15, 1976, p. 14.

Turner, Wallace. "Dismissed Summa Board Member Asks Court to Oust Hughes Cousin." *New York Times*, June 10, 1977, sec. A, p. 16.

Turner, Wallace. "Elusive Howard Hughes Leaves a Heavy Impact on Las Vegas." *New York Times*, December 6, 1970, sec. 6, p. ?.

Turner, Wallace. "Evidence of Possible Forgery In a Hughes Will to Be Produced." *New York Times*, December 15, 1978, sec. 2, p. 18.

Turner, Wallace. "Ex-Aide to Hughes Is Seeking Probate of Purported Will." *New York Times*, May 1, 1976, p. 1.

Turner, Wallace. "Ex-Chief of Gambling Board to Run Hughes Casinos." *New York Times*, September 1, 1977, sec. C, p. 14.

Turner, Wallace. "Ex-Companion Is Silent on Source of Hughes's Drugs." *New York Times*, December 11, 1976, p. 10.

Turner, Wallace. "Ex-Hughes Aide Appears in a Court in Los Angels after Warrant Is Issued." *New York Times*, October 29, 1976, sec. 1, p. 17.

Turner, Wallace. "Ex-Salesman Guilty in '74 Coast Theft of Hughes Papers." *New York Times*, April 23, 1977, p. 33.

Turner, Wallace. "Existence of Hughes Will Suggested in Court Data Filed by Three Cousins." *New York Times*, June 8, 1977, sec. D, p. 20.

Turner, Wallace. "Expert Calls Hughes 'Will' a 'Textbook' Forgery Case." *New York Times*, May 7, 1976, sec. A, p. 10.

Turner, Wallace. "Fear and Raving in Las Vegas." *New York Times*, February 17, 1985, sec. 7, p. 14.

Turner, Wallace. "Former Hughes Aide May Drop 'Mormon Will.'" *New York Times*, June 2, 1976, p. 18.

Turner, Wallace. "Greenspun Is Awarded $1 Million in Suit Against Hughes Company." *New York Times*, June 4, 1977, p. 9.

Turner, Wallace. "Houston Jury Says Hughes Estate Must Pay Texas Inheritance Tax." *New York Times*, February 16, 1978, p. 18.

Turner, Wallace. "Howard Hughes's Multimillion-Dollar Borrowings Reported to Have Been Plan to Cut

Income Taxes." *New York Times*, October 24, 1976, sec. 1, p. 25.

Turner, Wallace. "Howard Hunt Questioned in a Hughes Case." *New York Times*, April 29, 1977, p. 29.

Turner, Wallace. "Hughes Aides Seek to Halt Subpoenas in Inquiry on Drugs." *New York Times*, November 16, 1977, sec A, p. 17.

Turner, Wallace. "Hughes Cousins Say Utah Man Forged Mormon Will; Service Station Operator Would Share in the Estate." *New York Times*, December 14, 1976, p. 20.

Turner, Wallace. "Hughes Depicted as Prisoner of Own System." *New York Times*, December 5, 1976, p. 1.

Turner, Wallace. "Hughes Estate Fight Seen as Doubts Rise about Will." *New York Times*, April 8, 1976, p. 1.

Turner, Wallace. "Hughes Estate Said to Owe $71 Million to Air West Group." *New York Times*, September 7, 1977, sec. D, p. 1.

Turner, Wallace. "Hughes Estate: New Questions." *New York Times*, March 17, 1977, p. 19.

Turner, Wallace. "Hughes Inheritance Cut Up By Cousins, Aides, Courts." *New York Times*, September 5, 1976, sec. 1, p. 32.

Turner, Wallace. "Hughes Organization Ends Secrecy." *New York Times*, September 29, 1977, p. 36.

Turner, Wallace. "Hughes Properties Being Reorganized." *New York Times*, February 19, 1978, p. 22.

Turner, Wallace. "Hughes Will Forged, Nevada Official Says." *New York Times*, April 16, 1977, p. 12.

Turner, Wallace. "Hughes's Cousin Makes Changes to Keep Assets." *New York Times*, April 24, 1977, sec. A, p. 22.

Turner, Wallace. "Hughes's Former Key Aide Loses His Post as Summa's Chief Counsel." *New York Times*, August 27, 1977, p. 16.

Turner, Wallace. "Hughes's Stewards Move to Prevent Breakup of Estate." *New York Times*, May 14, 1976, p. 6.

Turner, Wallace. "Investigators in Hughes Case Seek Grand Jury Aid on Drug Sources." *New York Times*, October 10, 1977, p. 77.

Turner, Wallace. "Investigators in Hughes Case Seek Grand Jury Aid on Drug Sources." *New York Times*, October 13, 1977, p. 18.

Turner, Wallace. "Judge Backs Control by Hughes Relative." *New York Times*, July 23, 1977, p. 7.

Turner, Wallace. "Judge Orders Lawyers to Report in 60 Days on Hughes Will Search." *New York Times*, January 18, 1977, p. 12.

Turner, Wallace. "Legal Dispute Over Howard Hughes's Newly Profitable Empire Is Approaching Climax." *New York Times*, June 3, 1979, p. 14.

Turner, Wallace. "Legal Fees at Issue in Hughes Probate." *New York Times*, February 15, 1977, p. 13.

Turner, Wallace. "Log Shows that Hughes Disposed of Major Company in a Half-Hour." *New York Times*, November 20, 1977, sec A, p. 26.

Turner, Wallace. "Los Angeles Judge in Hughes Case Refuses Bids for Lawyer Fees in Hunt for Industrialist's Will." *New York Times*, August 19, 1977, p. 12.

Turner, Wallace. "Lummis Says Hughes Was Not Given Data." *New York Times*, August 8, 1977, p. 26.

Turner, Wallace. "Major Losses Cited in Hughes Operations." *New York Times*, June 28, 1977, p. 16.

Turner, Wallace. "Medical Discharge Is Cited for Figure in Hughes 'Will.'" *New York Times*, January 27, 1977, p. 22.

Turner, Wallace. "Medical Foundation Expected to Receive $1.5 Billion Hughes Estate if a Will Exists." *New York Times*, April 7, 1976, p. 18.

Turner, Wallace. "Millions in Hughes Cash Assets Were Dissipated, Tax Aide Says." *New York Times*, July 8, 1977, sec A, p. 6.

Turner, Wallace. "Nevada Refuses Immunity to Hughes Will Claimant." *New York Times*, January 22, 1977, p. 9.

Turner, Wallace. "New Moves Hinted on Hughes Estate." *New York Times*, July 17, 1976, p. 20.

Turner, Wallace. "New Report Says Search Fails to Show that Hughes Left Will." *New York Times*, July 15, 1877, sec. B, p. 2.

Turner, Wallace. "Petition Could Validate a 'Lost' 1938 Hughes Will." *New York Times*, January 13, 1977, p. 20.

Turner, Wallace. "Probate Court Told that Hughes's Mental Faculties Were Unimpaired." *New York Times*, April 15, 1977, p. 15.

Turner, Wallace. "Probate Judge Defers Decision in Struggle Over Hughes

Estate." *New York Times,* July 9, 1976, p. 11.

Turner, Wallace. "Probate Judge in Texas Rules That No Will Was Left by Howard Hughes." *New York Times,* February 19, 1981, sec A, p. 71.

Turner, Wallace. "Publishers Offered Hughes Documents." *New York Times,* April 21, 1977, sec A, p. 18.

Turner, Wallace. "Purported Will of Hughes Found at Mormon Office." *New York Times,* April 30, 1976, p. 1.

Turner, Wallace. "Second Hughes 'Will,' Sent to Texas, Termed Fraudulent on Its Face." *New York Times,* May 8, 1976, p. 48.

Turner, Wallace. "Secrecy Shrouds Hughes Empire's Fate." *New York Times,* April 6, 1976, p. 59.

Turner, Wallace. "Six Hughes 'Wills' Disclosed So Far." *New York Times,* May 13, 1976, p. 17.

Turner, Wallace. "Some of Hughes Secret Life Bared by Struggle." *Los Angeles Herald Examiner,* December 10, 1970, p. 1.

Turner, Wallace. "Students of Hughes's Life Doubt Will's Authenticity." *New York Times,* May 3, 1976, p. 1.

Turner, Wallace. "Suits Disclose Fight for Access to Hughes." *New York Times,* September 12, 1977, p. 25.

Turner, Wallace. "Summa Corp.: Rebuilding the House of Howard Hughes." *New York Times,* June 17, 1979, sec. C, p. 3.

Turner, Wallace. "Three Hughes Associate Deny Guilt in Air West Case." *New York Times,* January 15, 1977, p. 14.

Turner, Wallace. "TV: Howard Hughes Saga." *New York Times,* April 13, 1977, sec. C, p. 26.

Turner, Wallace. "Two Ex-Hughes Aides Cited in Drugs Case." *New York Times,* March 17, 1978, p. 13.

Turner, Wallace. "Two Hughes Officials at Odds over Estate." *New York Times,* January 23, 1977, sec. 1, p. 10.

Turner, Wallace. "Two States Resolve Hughes's Tax Bill." New York Times, August 30, 1984, sec A, p. 18.

Turner, Wallace. "Two Suits by Nevada Publisher Show Tangle of Hughes Deals." *New York Times,* February 9, 1977, sec. A, p. 14.

Turner, Wallace. "U.S. Judge Doubts Forgery in Hughes's Affidavits." *New York*

Times, October 12, 1977, p. 18.

Turner, Wallace. "Utah Man Plans to Press for Hughes 'Inheritance.'" *New York Times,* May 5, 1976, p. 34.

Turner, Wallace. "Would-Be Hughes Beneficiary Is Said to Have Lied." *New York Times,* January 14, 1977, p. 12.

Urban, Jerry. "Ex-Judge Gets One-Year Prison Term." *Houston Chronicle,* November 10, 1993, sec. A, p. 1.

Urban, Jerry. "Judge Also Faces U.S. Indictment." *Houston Chronicle,* March 16, 1993, sec. A, p. 1.

Urban, Jerry. "Probate Judge Indicted on New Charges Alleging Tax Violation." *Houston Chronicle,* May 12, 1993, sec. A, p. 22.

Volkers, Nancy. "Hughes' Unexpected Legacy: A Thriving Research Enterprise." *Journal of the National Cancer Institute,* February 17, 1999, p. 306.

Wade, Nicholas. "A New Criterion for Howard Hughes Medical Institute: Adventure." *New York Times,* December 20, 1999, sec. F, p. 3.

Waggoner, Walter H. "Noah Dietrich, the Chief Aide to Howard Hughes, Is Dead." *New York Times,* February 16, 1982, sec. B, p. 7.

Welling, Jr., Brenton. "The $115-Million Battle that Hughes Won." *Business Week,* December 8, 1973, p. 12.

Westlake, Donald E. "A Prison of His Own Making." *New York Times,* June 16, 1996, sec. 7, p. 2.

White, Stephen "The Howard Hughes Story." *Look,* February 9, 1954, p. 21.

White, Stephen. "A Star and a Plane." *Look,* March 9, 1954, p. 96.

White, Stephen. "The Seven Fat Years." *Look,* February 23, 1954, p. 74.

White, William S. "$5,919,921 Tax Debt Is Laid to Hughes; Charge Is Denied." *New York Times,* November 6, 1947, p. 1.

White, William S. "Ex-Officer Sought $50,000 of Hughes Soon after Inquiry." *New York Times,* November 8, 1947, p. 1.

White, William S. "Hughes Accuses Brewster, Senator Counter-Attacks on War Plane Contracts." *New York Times,* August 7, 1947, p. 1.

White, William S. "Hughes Promises to Exile Himself if Big Plane Fails." *New York Times,* August 10, 1947, p. 1.

White, William S. "Hughes Refuses to Produce Agent; Hits 'Detractos.'" *New York Times,* August 9, 1947, p. 1.

White, William S. "Opposition Is Told to Hughes Plane." *New York Times,* November 7, 1947, p. 1.

White, William S. "Senators Suspend Inquiry on Hughes; Cowardly, He Says." *New York Times,* August 12, 1947, p. 1.

Wickware, Francis Sill. "Howard Hughes." *Cosmopolitan,* December, 1946, p. 59.

Williams, Nigel. "Hughes Grants Brighten Outlook for Elite Researchers." *Science,* August 9, 1996, p. 732.

Wilson, Earl. "U.S. Calls Two Hollywood Beauties in Hughes Quiz." *Los Angeles Daily News,* July 22, 1947, p. 1.

Winship, Frederick M. "Hughes Rivals Getty For 'Richest' Tag." *Los Angeles Herald Examiner,* April 29, 1968, sec. A, p. 4.

Wise, T.A. "The Bankers and the Spook."

Fortune, March, 1961, p. 142

Wittenberg, Pete. "State Judge Surrenders on Felony Theft Charge." *Houston Post,* March 10, 1993, sec. A, p. 1.

Woo, Elaine. "Jean Peters; Actress in Film, TV Married Howard Hughes." *Los Angeles Times,* October 21, 2000, p. 4.

Wood, Charles D. "ABC Files Suit Against Hughes Offer for Stock." *Los Angeles Times,* July 10, 1968, p. 1.

Wood, Charles D. "Is Hughes Selling Out for Health Reasons?" *Los Angeles Times,* April 13, 1966, p. 1.

Wood, Robert H. "Politics Again." *Aviation Week,* July 28, 47, p. 50.

Yuen, Mike. "Memorabilia of Howard Hughes to Go on Auction Block Here." *Houston Post,* February 13, 1989, sec. A, p. 3.

Index

Note: In this index, the initials HRH stand for the subject
of this biography, Howard Robard Hughes Jr.

HRH inheritance, 50–51, 390
Hughes Aircraft Corporation
Air Corps XF-11 (D-2) aircraft $48 million appropriation, 148
Hughes Tool Company
1940, 121; 1948, 186–187; 1949, 190; 1956, 238; 1964, 276–277
Nevada expenditures, 294
The Outlaw advertising campaign, 155
personal worth
billionaire status: achieving, xi, 277; approaching, 167; self-reflection about, 284; 1925, 93; 1946, 167; 1964, 277; 1968, 302
RKO
HRH $23.5 million check, 216; 186; selling price, 229;
ruin, 91–93
TWA, 122, 144, 168, 169
War Department contract for *Hercules* (HK-1) flying cargo ship, 137
World War II Hughes Aircraft Corporation expansion spending, 128
Flanagan, Francis D., Senate committee chief assistant counsel confiscation
Hughes Aircraft
Corporation records, 171
subpoenas for Hughes Aircraft Corporation audit, 167
Flying. *See also* Racing
as American Airlines co-pilot, 92
automatic pilot testing, 102
Aviation Hall of Fame induction, HRH, 364
Bristol Britannia testing, 249
crashes
HRH piloting Sikorsky in 1944, 152; Lake Mead, Nevada, 144–145; XF-11 (D-2) aircraft, 158–161
in deteriorating health, 358–359, 361–362
first HRH airplane, 69
first ride, HRH, 42
as goal, 55, 56
lessons, 64
lessons refused by father, 48
license HRH, 69
Lindbergh inspiration/preoccupation, 63, 66
Lockheed Constellation Los Angeles-New York flight, HRH piloting, 156
natural ability, HRH, 64
racing, HRH, 95
Vickers Viscount testing, 249
Flying Bullet (H-1) speed plane
completion, 96
retooling, 99
test flight, 96–97
transcontinental record flight, 103–104
world speed record, 97
Flying Laboratory (Douglas DC-1), 102

Flying Penthouse Douglas DC-3 false missing reports, 169–170
Francom, George, HRH aide, 3, 6, 247, 273, 278
and Maheu resignation attempt, 289
transports HRH, 327
Frankenstein, 75
Franklin, Harold B., 86
Frazier, Brenda Diana Duff, 120–121
The French Line, RKO, 209, 221
The Front Page, HRH production, 65
Frye, Jack, TWA president, 122, 168–169
The Fugitive, 182
Furthman, Jules and motion picture production, HRH, 126

G

Gambling House, RKO, 199
Gano, Allene (see Hughes, Allene Gano HRH mother)
Gano, Chilton (HRH uncle), 21, 377
in 1925 HRH will, 21
Gano, Richard C. Jr., California probate administrator, 376
Gardner, Ava, 139–141, 142, 145, 151, 161, 165, 172, 223–224, 224–225
divorce from Frank Sinatra, 223
engagements rejected, 140, 224
The Loves of Carmen, 172
violent fight, 242–243
Gay, Bill, HRH aide, 7, 9, 15, 202, 217, 255, 261, 294
assuming control, 249
total, 347
The Autobiography of Howard Hughes media conference, 349–350
characterized, 227
decontamination instructions, HRH, 191
Desert Inn rebuilding plans, 361
deteriorating HRH desire to pilot, 359
drug dependency, HRH, 365
first assignment, 181
hiring by HRH, 180
and Howard Hughes Medical Institute after HRH death, 385
after HRH death, 375, 377
Hughes Tool Company sale, 353, 355
informed to prepare proxy of control, 327
and John Meier, 318
Las Vegas departure, HRH, 343–345
Mormon connection, 181, 270
Noah Dietrich firing, 246
personal agenda, 270
resignation from Summa Corporation, 384
restraining order against, 344, 346
Robert Maheu, firing, 343, 344–346, 325. 327
George, Harold L., Hughes Aircraft Corporation, 180

move of *Hercules* (HK-1) flying cargo
ship, 155
"mystery train," 281
Nicaragua departure, HRH, 352
Pan American Mines Ltd. fiasco, 348
post-death speculation about will, 375
Project Jennifer/Russian submarine
salvage, 347, 368
publicity love by HRH, 161
Robert Mitchum marijuana conviction,
186
and Special Senate Committee
Investigating the National Defense
Program, 172, 175–177
Supreme Court and TWA suit, 358
TWA $115 million antitrust suit, 276
whereabouts speculations, HRH, 274
XF-11 (D-2) aircraft test flight/crash,
160, 161–162, 165
Meier, John, HRH computer expert
and Anthony G. Hatsis, 316
and Bill Gay, 318
and Donald Nixon, 317–318
and Everd B. Van Walsum, 319
Dean Elson memo, 319
in vacuum, 326
fired, 319
mining claims holdings, 297–298, 347, 376
sued, 319n
travels to Dominican Republic, 318
Meighan, Thomas, 70
Melvin and Howard, 384n
Memos, HRH
and ABC takeover bid, 305
and Blacks, 16
dinner, service of, 233
dissatisfaction with Nixon, 323
driver instructions for starlet passengers,
247
"Easter Egg Hunt," 294
entry instructions, bungalow, 215
FCC and ABC takeover bid, 305
film reel delivery instructions, 237
fruit, can opening instructions, 256–259
about *The Great White Hope*, 301
handling of, 191
hearing-aid cord, 321–322
Landmark Hotel opening, 320–321,
322–323, 325– 339
and legal pads, 143, 163, 184, 189, 294
millionaire/billionaire status, xi
new projects, 327
on nuclear testing in Nevada, 283,
298–299
and Operations, 256–259
into Operations Manual, 252
pets, 267
political power desire, 303–304
on reading material daily purchase, 252
Robert Maheu firing, 345

subject range, 259
and TWA executive telephone queries,
237
for will, typing of, 143
Menjou, Adolphe, 86
Mental decline, HRH. *See also*
Contamination fear, HRH; Memos;
Nervous breakdown, HRH; Obsessive-
compulsive behavior, HRH; Paranoia
1956, 237
air and light, closed off, 234, 256, 342
brief frenzy/long silences, 275
and codeine, 346–347
competency concerns, Dr. Verne Mason,
241–242
and flashes of brilliance, 253–254, 261
in Las Vegas, 286–287
motion picture screening marathon,
253–255. *See also* Memos, HRH
and move to Bel Air Road, 272
Merrill Lynch, Pierce, Fenner & Smith
estate appraisal, 381, 382, 383, 385–386
and Hughes Tool Company sale, 353,
354–355
and TWA stock, 277
Methodist Hospital, Houston, Texas, 22n
death accommodations, 10
Metropolitan Studios, 67
Meyer, Johnny, HRH press aide, 146, 147,
154, 157, 165, 171
chased federal marshal, 173
Federal Bureau of Investigation
surveillance, 156
Special Senate Committee Investigating
the National Defense Program, 175
Meyers, Bennett E., seeking HRH interest-
free loan, 149–150, 181
Milestone, Lewis and motion picture
production, HRH, 63, 70, 86
Mining claims, HRH, 297–298, 347, 376
Mitchell, Thomas, 138
Mitchum, Robert, 209
marijuana conviction, 186
Montemayor, Dr. Victor Manuel
death theory, 16–17
final treatment, HRH, 5, 7–8
Moore, Terry, 199–200, 202, 243
courtship, 191
HRH, 188
dinner with family, HRH, 187–188
and estate, HRH, 380–381, 385, 386
Flamingo Hotel, Las Vegas, act, 222
invalid shipboard marriage to HRH,
192–194, 385, 386
meeting HRH, 187
pregnancy, 205
Stuart Cramer, husband, 388
Morgan, Marilyn, a.k.a. Marian Marsh, 93
Mormons, aides, 181, 188, 247, 272, 287,
309